Management and Society

An Institutional Framework

DALTON E. MCFARLAND
University Professor
and Professor of Business Administration
University of Alabama in Birmingham

PRENTICE-HALL, INC., *Englewood Cliffs, New Jersey 07632*

Library of Congress Cataloging in Publication Data

McFarland, Dalton E.
    Management and society.

    Includes bibliographical references and indexes.
    1. Industry — Social aspects.   2. Management.   I. Title.
HD60.M38   658.4'08   81-17772
ISBN 0-13-549147-9   AACR2

Editorial/production supervision and interior design by Margaret Rizzi
Manufacturing buyer: Ed O'Dougherty
Cover design by Robin Breite

Printed in the United States of America

10   9   8   7   6   5   4   3   2   1

ISBN 0-13-549147-9

Prentice-Hall International, Inc., *London*
Prentice-Hall of Australia Pty. Limited, *Sydney*
Prentice-Hall of Canada, Ltd., *Toronto*
Prentice-Hall of India Private Limited, *New Delhi*
Prentice-Hall of Japan, Inc., *Tokyo*
Prentice-Hall of Southeast Asia Pte. Ltd., *Singapore*
Whitehall Books Limited, *Wellington, New Zealand*

Dedicated to students and teachers

in all walks of life

Contents

Part II

MANAGEMENT, EXPECTATIONS
AND
SOCIAL CHANGE

Part III

MANAGERIAL VALUES, ETHICS, AND MORALS

Part IV

SOCIAL ISSUES
AND
MANAGERIAL STRATEGIES

COMPREHENSIVE CASES

Preface

This book explains the societal context of managerial and organizational behavior. It develops a macromanagement framework for analyzing the interacting elements that influence how managers and organizations meet their social responsibilities. Managers need an understanding of this intricate web of interacting elements if they are to cope effectively with the complex issues the social system presents to them.

Business is inextricably linked with government, education, health care, and other social institutions. Because business plays a key role throughout society, it is treated in this book as the focal institution. Since management issues are inherent in all social problems, it is necessary to develop a macromanagement level of analysis which provides an integrated, systems view of the interrelationships among our major social institutions.

This book is written as a college-level textbook for junior, senior, and graduate level courses in Schools of Business, Public Administration, Education, Public Health, Social Science, and others. It will also be useful to managers, the general reader, and those in the helping and service occupations who use administrative processes to accomplish their aims. The text is managerial in its orientation, in the sense that it focuses not only on the linkages among social institutions and their constituent organizations, but also on the roles of those in positions of power and influence. In a spirit of cautious optimism, it portrays the capabilities and limitations of managers who grapple with complex issues in the postindustrial society.

The argument of the book is presented in four parts. Part One describes the relationships of management to the societal framework of the postindustrial society and its social institutions, together with an analysis of knowledge and influence centers. Part Two discusses the basic structural elements of society as they bear on the manager's task. Part Three explains how managers function with respect to their social responsibilities, and analyzes the values, ethics, morals and beliefs that underlie managerial decisions. Part Four discusses leading issues and problems to which managers and their organizations must address themselves in meeting their responsibilities to society. The macromanagement approach treats specific problems such as pollution, energy shortages, consumerism and the like in the context of interacting social institutions. By recognizing that decisions on specific issues cut across the institutional framework, the macromanagement approach helps managers translate theory into practical actions.

The arguments, examples, and issues presented here are confined primarily to the societal context of the United States. This in itself is complexity enough. Although many vital concerns relate to other nations and cultures, these relationships are not explicitly treated. We shall, however, note the impact of the futurists, who are attempting to view the world as a single social system.

Clearly the objectives of this text require an interdisciplinary view. I do not wish to register, as is often the case, a kind of spurious interdisciplinary gloss. Nevertheless, no single academic discipline can claim sole proprietorship of the ideas presented here. In such a setting, macromanagement theory drawing on the behavioral and social sciences holds much promise for achieving new levels of integration and coordination. The resulting eclecticism will be apparent to the reader, as I hope my personal biases will also be. I write both from the perspectives of the behavioral sciences, and from a long and stimulating association with the fields of management and business administration.

This work seeks the elusive goals of synthesis, integration, and perspective. Since empirical research is not abundant, I have drawn heavily upon qualitative sources in management, political science, sociology, anthropology, philosophy and the humanities. Through the use of discussion questions, class projects, incident cases, and comprehensive cases, students can practice and test their application of necessarily abstract ideas to the realities of management action. The book attempts to be definitive and clear about what can and should be done by those at the centers of power to strengthen and improve our society.

Acknowledgments

Many persons have assisted me in writing this book, and I wish to express my appreciation for their interest, energy, and special capabilities. While I gladly accept the ultimate responsibility for the book's contents. I herewith record my special thanks to all who have worked with me on this project.

Ms. Barbara Piercecchi of Prentice-Hall, Inc., provided expert editorial guidance in the planning and final stages of the manuscript. Perceptive critiques of materials in process came from several reviewers who provided specific suggestions and queries. My colleague, Dr. Louis Dow, provided many valuable comments on economic issues, and Ms. Mary Elizabeth Wilson, my research assistant, read and criticized most of the manuscript, and devoted many hours to checking references and searching out source materials. Mr. Stanley Gwynn incisively reviewed the chapters on ethics and values.

Ms. Robbie Armstrong skillfully and rapidly typed several drafts of the manuscript while resourcefully managing my office. My colleagues, Dean M. Gene Newport and W. Jack Duncan provided both tangible support and continuous encouragement for my efforts. To my wife Jean A. McFarland, I express my thanks for her many helpful ideas, and for help in proofreading.

Dalton E. McFarland

Part I

MANAGEMENT, SOCIETY, AND THE INSTITUTIONAL FRAMEWORK

I

Management in the Postindustrial Society

We live in an era of unbelievable and perhaps unbearable change. Institutions and practices that have withstood the test of centuries are being challenged on every hand. No adjective has become more commonplace in the twentieth century than "obsolete." Among the institutions said to be out of date are the free market economy, the sovereign nation state, the family, and the self-reliant individual. And when we protest that time has not destroyed the timelessness of, say, sovereignty or individualism, we know this is only partially true. Time does "make ancient good uncouth."

KENNETH W. THOMPSON, *The Moral Issues in Statecraft: Twentieth Century Approaches & Problems* (Baton Rouge: Louisiana State University Press, 1966), p. 85.

CONCEPTS DISCUSSED IN THIS CHAPTER

1. THE IMPACT OF SOCIAL CHANGE ON MANAGEMENT
2. THE EMERGENT POSTINDUSTRIAL SOCIETY
3. THE MACROMANAGEMENT PERSPECTIVE
4. SOCIAL INSTITUTIONS AS A FRAMEWORK FOR MANAGERIAL DECISION

Management today faces new problems and new demands based on the changing expectations of society. It is no longer possible to manage with precepts derived primarily from the internal needs of organizations; managers increasingly must act and decide within the social framework of the organization's external environment.

Passive responses to society's new expectations are inadequate.

Citizens, government officials, opinion leaders, and managers must not only cope individually with social issues, but also work together to influence society for the better. Although the issues are so complex that they seem impossible to manage, there is reason for optimism and hope as well as frustration and despair. By viewing the problems as challenges and opportunities, managers in all sectors of society can play a significant role in our survival and progress.

This book depicts these challenges and opportunities, and analyzes how managerial action can help to meet them. It explains the interrelations and interdependencies among organizations and describes the role of management in improving the functioning of our social institutions.[1]

Although all social institutions are important, we will focus primarily on the interactions among three of the most important: business, education, and government. Business will be the focal institution from which the interrelationships of these and other major social institutions, such as science and technology, religion, or private property, will be explored. This chapter presents three elements of the conceptual framework of this book: (1) the individual, organizational, and institutional levels of analysis, (2) the concept of the postindustrial society, and (3) the concept of macromanagement.

THREE LEVELS OF ANALYSIS

Throughout this book, three interacting levels of analysis will be examined. Figure 1.1 shows the relationships of the individual, the organizational, and the institutional levels of analysis. Managers are involved in social issues because they administer resources and pursue objectives that create or solve society's problems. They are entrusted with the resources, skills, and power through which society maintains order, achieves coherence, and meets its other needs. The behavior of managers is conditioned by expectations, role prescriptions, values, norms, and beliefs which they draw from society as a whole. In their interactions and interrelationships, organizations form the institutional fabric of society. Macromanagement focuses on the array of societal influences and problems that cut across the three levels of analysis.

THE INDIVIDUAL AND SOCIAL ISSUES

Although our primary focus concerns individuals who are managers, we will refer to other roles of individuals, such as that of citizen or politician. But humans are social animals, and every individual is shaped by

---

[1] The word *institutions* is sometimes used to refer to specific, well-established, large organizations. In this book the word *institution*, unless otherwise noted, refers to collectivities or organizations having significant interrelationships that form the structures and processes of society. Social institutions will be analyzed in greater detail in Chapter 6.

FIGURE 1.1

Levels of Analysis in the Social System

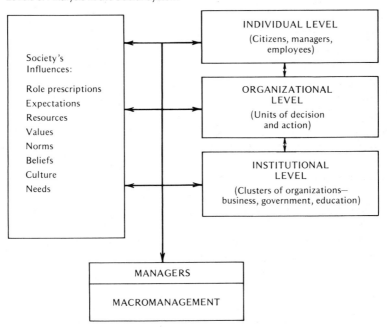

the social and cultural environment. Individuals by necessity are learners, and the social institutions of family, school, church, and state condition them for adult life in their society. Society's expectations for appropriate behavior are not only extremely varied, but also change over time. So there are few clear, unalterable rules. Individuals also vary in intelligence, perception, temperament, emotional and mental balance, knowledge, skills, the assumptions they make in everyday life, physical capabilities, and many other factors. We use the word *personality* to describe all the traits and elements that make each individual unique.

That the individual's personality is unique means that we can never completely understand others. We can observe what a person says and does, and from this data draw inferences and make assumptions. The resulting generalizations allow for reasonable interaction and discourse, but their accuracy is often uncertain. Among the riskier assumptions, for example, is that individuals always act in their own self-interest, and the accompanying one that self-interest is measured by the desire for money. We know now that the economic man has been joined by social man, group man, organization man. Individuals are both rational and emotional, predictable and unpredictable, selfish and unselfish.

Managers are a special category of individuals who devote a significant portion of their lives to running organizations. They live in two

5

interrelated spheres—as citizens of a national culture and as wielders of influence and power within organizations. The manager is a special kind of social creation. The idea of a person who does not work with his or her hands but rather acts on the environment at a distance and indirectly through others is historically a monumental social invention. It is therefore logical that society expects managers to be concerned with social needs.[2]

To some it appears that the fast pace, long hours, precarious tenure, and transient influence of managers reflect a dedication to money, status, and power. Walton rightly suggests an alternative explanation—that a work-oriented, wealth-pursuing society creates a milieu in which individuals are expected to earn their keep by making a social contribution. Organizations themselves recognize the importance of making achievement the focus of satisfaction and fulfillment for their managers. But this is not to deny that managers also play a symbolic role in which they perform according to rituals and ceremonies largely directed to preserving the organization's interests.[3] But the decisions of managers have many consequences for society itself, and it is important for them to consider both the welfare of the organization and its impact on society.

THE ORGANIZATIONAL LEVEL

Just as the manager represents a socially created idea, so too does the organization. Like individuals, organizations take a bewildering variety of forms—public and private, temporary and permanent, large and small, profit and nonprofit, production-oriented and service-centered. Our main concern is with work organizations, although we will take note of voluntary associations, trade associations, and special interest groups such as labor unions, consumer advocates, and the like.

The organizational categories are not always clear-cut; a given organization may belong to more than one category. For example, a trade association generally has a staff of paid employees and so is much like organizations in other categories. A hospital uses large numbers of volunteers as well as regular employees. All organizations have a business aspect in that they must obtain and use scarce resources.

An organization is by definition composed of collectivities formed as structural units, as well as informal groupings. As a collectivity in its own right, an organization acquires an identity, a legal and social status, and an image in the community. By directing the collective efforts of managerial, technical, and nonmanagerial employees toward its goals,

---

[2] Clarence C. Walton, *Ethos and the Executive: Values in Managerial Decision Making* (Englewood Cliffs, N.J.: Prentice-Hall, 1969), p. 9.

[3] Ibid., pp. 73–74. See also Jeffrey Pfeffer and Gerald R. Salancik, *The External Control of Organizations: A Resource Dependence Perspective* (New York: Harper & Row, 1978), pp. 9–19.

the organization is able to accomplish things that individuals acting alone or in informal groupings cannot do.

Through increased research on organizations, a change in the way we view them has occurred. The history of management thought to date has produced three major models that seek to explain how organizations work. The first is the concept of the bureaucracy, the second is the human relations model, and the third is the organic, adaptive, open-system model.

No actual organization fully fits one particular model; most fall between the polar models of bureaucracy and the open system. A given organization may be bureaucratic in some respects, and human-relations-oriented or adaptive in others. What the three models basically describe is the focus of managerial attitudes and leadership styles.

Bureaucracies: The model for bureaucracies originated from studies of governmental bureaus or offices. The elements of this model, based on the work of Weber, a German sociologist, include formal positions patterned in a hierarchy of levels of authority and responsibility and division into functional units such as departments; planned succession to office; a disciplinary system of rules, rewards, and sanctions against deviant behavior; and various protections for the security and well-being of position occupants.[4]

Bureaucracies have been attacked as mechanistic, unfeeling, autocratic empires that foster impersonality and the subservience of employees. Weber's notion of bureaucracy as the "ideal type" has been misunderstood. He did not regard it as perfect, but rather as the best model for achieving efficiency. There are real flaws in bureaucracies because they are human enterprises, but they also make it possible to design extremely large-scale systems of enormous complexity and remarkable achievement. Perrow runs counter to much current organizational literature when he suggests that many of the defects of bureaucracy are the result of mismanagement rather than inherent in the nature of bureaucracy itself.[5] The bureaucracy remains a notable and viable mode of organization for industrialized society.

The Human Relations Movement: The human relations movement began in the mid-1930s. By the mid-fifties it had begun to go out of fashion, and it has now become the field called organizational behavior. Along the way its advocates and their research made many lasting contributions to our understanding of the human problems in bureaucracies. The substance of this work includes interpersonal relations, the theory and

---

[4] Max Weber, *The Theory of Social and Economic Organization*, trans. and ed. A. M. Henderson and Talcott Parsons (New York: Oxford University Press, 1947).

[5] Charles Perrow, *Complex Organizations: A Critical Essay*, 2nd ed. (Glenview, Ill.: Scott, Foresman, 1979), p. 55.

practice of groups, and extended concepts of job satisfaction, conflict resolution, attitudes, communication, motivation, and leadership. These
bodies of knowledge are still of key importance in understanding the
behavior of people in work settings.

The decline of the movement was spurred by demands for more rigorous research, the growth of new concepts, the mistakes of consultants
and other practitioners, and the natural tendency to change in human affairs. Human relations was in the nature of a work reform movement, but
it was not fully embraced by managers and organizations.[6] Its emphasis
on social groups ran counter to philosophies of individualism, as did the
untenable posture that all conflict is bad and cooperation and equilibrium
always good. The movement became identified more with the happiness
of workers than with productivity; but assumptions that satisfied
workers would be more productive have not held up under later research.
Its attention to subjective, emotional forms of behavior collided with
views of Weberian bureaucracy as a purely rational system.[7]

The Open, Adaptive Organization: Whereas the bureaucracy and its
modifications for human relations provide a relatively closed system,
there are conditions under which organizations may choose a more open
system. Systems are open or closed according to their need to interact
with their perceived environments, either to adapt to change or to influence events outside the organization.

No organization can be completely closed; every organization is an
input-output mechanism that processes inputs into outputs of goods or
services. Highly open systems take greater notice of the environment to
detect the need for change, to avoid undesirable intrusions, or to shape it
for better impact on internal activities, goals, and security. Open organizations systematically provide for exchanges at their boundaries by training and developing the boundary-spanning functions of managers. The
open organization is proactive, taking initiatives to more fully exploit
available and emerging opportunities.

Open organizations employ more than the cosmetic touch of human
relations approaches. They view the individual's needs and rights
as significant to their performance, and take a broad view of people as
motivated by challenge, opportunity, and self-fulfillment. Whereas a
bureaucracy operates as a direct control system with channeled communications and emphatic power structures, open systems put less stress on
position and formal authority and more on the authority of knowledge
and expertise, with evaluation by results rather than vague or general appraisal. The open system makes operational the concepts of participa-

---

[6] An important book on this subject is Ivar Berg, Marcia Freedman, and Michael Freeman, *Managers and Work Reform: A Limited Engagement* (New York: Free Press, 1978).

[7] Perrow, *Complex Organizations*, pp. 90–138.

tion, involvement, and democracy that originated in the earlier human relations movement.

Relatively open systems thus attempt to create a different organizational climate for their members than a bureaucracy might tend to provide. This requires new insights about leadership style and managerial supervision. Managers with deeply ingrained habits of authoritarian, call-the-shots, hard-nosed management often find it difficult to apply the newer thinking without undergoing extensive retraining.

The idea of the open system was first broached in a major way by two British researchers, Burns and Stalker. They called it the "organic" organization to reflect a dynamic view by analogy to a living organism.[8] In the United States, the critics of bureaucracy were led by Argyris, Bennis, and other theorists known as revisionists. They were dissatisfied with existing mechanistic theory and with features of the bureaucracy they considered outmoded. They sought to bring the individual back as the focus of organizational action.[9]

The open system idea came at a time when circumstances favored it. Behavioral science research expanded beyond the human relations movement, opening up new frontiers. Society's expectations for greater freedom, justice, equality, and human rights received new emphasis. The field of computers and operations research added a quantitative dimension of greater theoretical and practical rigor. Decision making thus became a powerful concept with possibilities for greater integration of viewpoints in approaching organizational problems. This combination of operations research, computers, and behavioral science in management thought holds much promise for better theory and practice in the world of organizations.

It is now generally agreed that open system approaches are not universally or automatically correct and that bureaucracies in some form will remain, though with modifications. The choice of which model of organization to follow depends on technological, environmental, and human factors and upon the particular goals being sought. Large, complex organizations typically use mixed models drawn from all three patterns to find the best fit for existing and potential conditions. Bureaucracy's strength lies in efficiency. But if a bureaucratic organization wishes also to achieve more innovation, adaptation to change, better communications, higher morale, and increased self-fulfillment for its members, and to act on society's growing expectations for social responsibility, it will need to introduce some of the modifications open system approaches suggest.

We turn now to a brief description of the institutional framework,

---

[8] Tom Burns and G. M. Stalker, *The Management of Innovation* (New York: Barnes and Noble, 1961).

[9] Chris Argyris, *Interpersonal Competence and Organizational Effectiveness* (Homewood, Ill.: Dorsey, 1962); Warren Bennis, *Changing Organizations* (New York: McGraw-Hill, 1966).

and following that, to an analysis of the postindustrial society and of the concept of macromanagement.

THE INSTITUTIONAL FRAMEWORK

The purpose of our social institutions is to organize society by expressing its needs and authenticating its norms and values, while at the same time providing mechanisms for change and the mediation of social conflict. Education, business, government, and other social institutions are complex in themselves, but even more so in their mutual and overlapping interactions.

Although social institutions greatly influence the values, beliefs, and actions of individuals, their structure basically consists of organizations or clusters of organizations. Within each social institution is a great diversity of structures and functions. Each institution develops an array of characteristic organizations that provide a structural basis for fulfilling social needs. For example, business is comprised of corporations and other business firms. Education is organized into schools and colleges; government operates bureaus, offices, and branches. Through its organizations, each institution vies with others for resources, for dominance, for control. Each serves the public in accordance with its technology, its values, and its perceptions of human needs.

A social institution is not an organization per se, but rather a pattern of relationships, social roles, belief systems, norms, and values that unites individuals and organizations according to common aims and interests with respect to the ongoing life of a society. Society creates business and other social institutions, such as the family, religion, marriage, or the criminal justice system, to serve the needs of people and to provide stability, cohesion, role structures, and normative standards for the social order. Structural elements are thus the means by which institutions attempt to achieve and preserve their fundamental ideals and aims. Institutional motivations and constraints guide the organizations and the transactional processes that link them together. Managers in turn influence people and organizations as they work to meet the needs of the system of social institutions and of society as a whole.

Social institutions do not die, but their form and content change as they react to the human condition. The scale of activity and change is so vast that on the one hand we accept change as inevitable, while on the other, paradoxically, we fear and distrust it. To understand the forces of change, managers need to be aware of the role social institutions play in the daily pressures for decision and action within their organizations.

The institutional framework requires us to view organizations as wholes, in recognition of their organic character, their uniqueness, and their interrelationships. Perrow cites three main contributions of the institutional school of thought on organizations. First, the emphasis on the

TABLE 1.1

Organization and Institution in Flexible and Nonflexible Organizations

	Organization	Institution
Nonflexible, internal source of values	The tool view; a rational, engineered instrument, with technicians directing it	The committed polity, with clear identity and purpose, serving the selfish strivings of its participants
Flexible, external source of values	The drift view; opportunism without goal-directed leadership	Adaptability, responsiveness, impregnated with community values

SOURCE: Charles Perrow, Complex Organizations: A Critical Essay, *2nd ed. (Glenview, Ill.: Scott, Foresman, 1979), p. 187. Used by permission.*

organization as a whole leads to a conception of variations as to type, purpose, structure, and modes of operating. Second, it shows how at least some organizations take on a life of their own. Third, and perhaps most important, is its emphasis on the organization in relation to its environment.[10]

This relationship is reflected in a continuous process called institutionalization. The process helps to clarify the distinction between open and closed systems because it identifies an important shift in values from those that support only the organization itself to those that incorporate social values into organizational behavior. Perrow, following Selznick, presents the matrix shown in Table 1.1. As organizations achieve greater flexibility, institutionalization processes help them avoid drifting aimlessly and opportunistically as pawns of the environment; instead, they achieve the kind of adaptability that tends to recognize and fulfill communitarian values. For example, a relatively closed organization such as a college fraternity could find itself transformed by environmental pressures to become more open to members from other social groups. Such openness would require the institutionalization of changes in membership policy, in effect setting new goals.[11]

THE POSTINDUSTRIAL SOCIETY

Our concern for the future, necessitated by constant change, is expressed in the concept of the postindustrial society. Ours is an emergent society whose realities point to sweeping changes in the social values that affect

---

[10] Perrow, *Complex Organizations*, pp. 183–186.

[11] Ibid., pp. 186–189; Philip Selznick, *Law, Society, and Industrial Justice* (New York: Russell Sage Foundation, 1969). Philip Selznick, *Leadership and Administration* (Evanston, Ill.: Row, Peterson, 1957), pp. 5–22.

organizations and how they are managed. The concept does not define a goal, nor consist of mere predictions. Rather, it is a shorthand way of describing the nature and direction of change.

Although the history of an idea is difficult to trace, Bell was the first to describe the postindustrial society in detail. He used the term in a 1959 lecture, but later discovered that David Riesman had used it narrowly in 1958 to analyze leisure in contrast to work. Bell presents the main ideas of the postindustrial concept as follows: (1) Society has passed from a goods-producing stage to a service-based, knowledge-oriented society, and (2) therefore the dominant social institution of the future will be the university.[12]

Bell holds that as economic growth reaches its limits, the economic, social, and political values of industrialization are changing. Whereas economic values spurred mass production, mass finance, mass marketing, and assumptions of universal continuous growth, the postindustrial society envisions the slowing the unbridled, unplanned economic expansion, the stabilization of populations, the open-system, adaptive organization equipped by management style and task structure to deal with changing, turbulent, uncertain environments, and new views of competition and hierarchy.

The postindustrial society implies a gradual but dynamic transformation rather than the sudden end of industry as we know it. Bell depicts changes already under way, describes new institutional and organizational frameworks, and expresses a faith in technology that runs counter to the pessimism of many social critics. He portrays a humanistic outlook through new growth horizons in the creative arts, improvement of the quality of life, leisure-time pursuits, and greater equality and justice throughout society. The postindustrial society will provide universal education for living rather than making a living, and increased opportunities for citizen participation in public and private pursuits of enduring value to humankind.

He presents an almost utopian, speculative dream. He sees a transition from the power of the old ruling classes based on real property to a new class with power based on the earned authority of knowledge. All humans would be released from burdensome labor. They would be free to achieve according to their ability and to enjoy education and self-development to the extent of their capabilities. Differences among people would be based on intellectual capacity and attainments, and in all respects except intelligence equality could reach a new high in society.

The history of humankind is the history of the ebb and flow of institutional power structures. No one social institution has remained powerful or dominant without yielding to some extent to the struggle of some

---

[12] Daniel Bell, *The Coming of the Post-Industrial Society* (New York: Basic Books, 1973).

other institution for dominance. Religion was the supreme institution for centuries as humans crawled out of their caves and threw off the shackles of bondage to animal instincts and superstition. Business and economic institutions came to power as industrialization and large-scale corporate enterprise superseded feudal, cottage-industry, and handcraft societies and mercantilism. With the intensification of war, poverty, alienation, crime, and other social problems, government has become the dominant institution.

Bell thinks that in the postindustrial society education, primarily the universities, will become the dominant social institution. They are already producing a new, powerful class—a professional-technical elite of specialists who control the use of knowledge. But Drucker doubts that one social institution can be superior to another. He sees them as an interrelated network in which each has an evolving, changing part.[13] Drucker's view is more persuasive in the absence of definitive evidence for Bell's speculations on higher education. However, Drucker and others agree with Bell that we live in a knowledge-oriented society, that there is an increasingly influential educated elite, and that managing "knowledge workers" in today's organizations differs from managing workers in the traditional occupations.

The new class of knowledge workers will create problems, but it will also help to solve them. Kristol notes that the new educated elite consists of college-trained persons whose skills and vocations proliferate in a postindustrial society: scientists, teachers, administrators, journalists and others in communications industries, social workers, lawyers and doctors who make their careers in the public sector, city planners, staffs of large foundations, the upper levels of government bureaucracies, and the like. He writes: "It is now quite a numerous class; it is an indispensable class for our kind of society; it is a disproportionately powerful class; it is also an ambitious and frustrated class."[14]

The frustrations of the new class are reflected in its hostility to the business community. Only a few managers in profit-seeking enterprises are members of this class; most of its members work in government, private associations, and various interest or pressure groups. They are highly mobile, and they favor more power in government, where they will have a say over how it is exercised. Its members are idealistic, more interested in reshaping society than in money.[15]

The influence of the new class depends largely on the effectiveness of universities in educating and training its members. Thus the interests of three major social institutions—business, government, and education—

[13] Peter F. Drucker, *The Age of Discontinuity* (New York: Harper & Row, 1969), chap. 8.

[14] Irving Kristol, *The Wall Street Journal*, May 19, 1975, p. 7.

[15] Ibid. See also "Our New Elite: For Better or for Worse," *U.S. News and World Report*, February 25, 1980, pp. 65–68.

TABLE 1.2

National Social Structure in Transition

Social Characteristic	Preindustrial Society	Industrial Society	Postindustrial Society
1. People	Low life expectancy at birth	Higher life expectancy	Life expectancy above 70–75 years
	Low education	Much more education	Highly educated, more mobile population
			Greater specialization and professionalization
2. Nonhuman resources	Little development of natural resources	Large-scale use (and waste) of natural resources	Large-scale conservation of natural resources
	Handcraft production	Mass production	Cybernetic systems linking computers with power-driven machinery
3. Subsystems:	Little differentiation	Considerable differentiation The organizational society	Further differentiation
Agriculture	More than 60 percent of labor force	Below 30 percent of work force	Below 10 percent of labor force
Government	Small	Large government and mixed sector	Services (public and private) above 60 percent of labor force
Manufacturing	Small	15–20 percent of labor force	Below 10–15 percent of labor force
4. External relations	From colonialism to independence	From empire to bloc or commonwealth	Extensive transnational, intersecting and interpenetrating relations
5. Internal relations:	Centrifugal tendencies	More integration with growth of nationalism	Less integration with growth of transnationalism
Communications and transportation	Weak networks	Highly developed networks	Still more highly developed networks
6. Values	Localism Individualism	Nationalism Cosmopolitanism Activism	Transnationalism Megalopolitanism Humanism
7. Guidance	Restricted elites	Multiple elites National planning systems	Dispersed elites Transnational planning systems

Adapted from: Bertram M. Gross, "The State of the Nation: Social Systems Accounting," in Raymond A. Bauer (ed.), Social Indicators *(Cambridge: MIT Press, 1966), pp. 214–215.*

are intertwined. Business needs the stable society that government can provide; business and government need highly trained, well-educated people; education needs public support and good business management. How such interrelationships work out in practice is a macromanagement problem for society as a whole.

Many doubt the validity of the postindustrial concept, and are suspicious of the implications drawn from it. Many countries are still making heroic efforts to industrialize. Furthermore, some degree of productive economic-industrial effort will remain an important base for achieving truly humanitarian ends. There is no need to yield to future shock. However, the trends pictured by Bell and others generate a host of new perspectives for managerial leadership throughout society, but especially in business and government.

Table 1.2 shows how seven key social characteristics have undergone major transitions from preindustrial to industrial to postindustrial social structures. Though the pace of change may vary for each of the characteristics, the summary descriptions of the postindustrial society in column 3 indicate new roles for managers in the decades ahead.[16] The trouble now is that our concepts of organization and management are still based largely on past habits and traditions. Until now management theory has been preoccupied with the internal operations of organizations — the micromanagement level. A macromanagement level of analysis will help organizations and managers meet the new demands of the postindustrial society.

MACROMANAGEMENT

The term *macromanagement* denotes the use of systems theory to analyze the relationships of organizations to each other and to society as a whole. A system is composed of interrelated parts called subsystems, which interact with each other and exist in a state of mutual interdependence. Interdependence in subsystems is manifested by the fact that a change introduced into one results in changes in one or more of the others.[17] For example, the human body may be viewed as a system, with subsystems called the nervous system, the reproductive system, the circulatory system, and the like. A brain tumor can cause changes in other parts of the system, affecting speech, locomotion, balance, or other functions.

The definition of a particular system is arbitrary, depending on the purposes of the observer. Both the system and its subsystems have boundaries that confer their identity and make it possible to analyze their interactions. The system may be studied in relation to its environment; the environment of the subsystems is the total system itself.

Preston and Post identify several models that describe macrolevel

---

[16] See also Magorah Maruyama, "Post-Industrial Logic," *Futurology*, Summer 1976, pp. 28–30.

[17] Systems theory, widely used in the physical, biological, and social sciences, now has a substantial body of literature. A major work is Ludwig von Bertalanffy, *General Systems Theory* (New York: Braziller, 1968).

FIGURE 1.2

Basic Social Systems Models

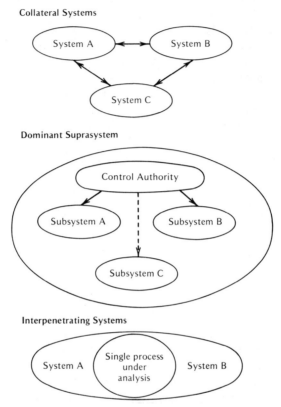

Collateral Systems

System A ⟷ System B

System C

Dominant Suprasystem

Control Authority

Subsystem A   Subsystem B

Subsystem C

Interpenetrating Systems

System A   Single process under analysis   System B

SOURCE: *Lee E. Preston and James E. Post,* Private Management and Public Policy: The Principle of Public Responsibility, *(© 1975), p. 17. Reprinted by permission of Prentice-Hall, Inc., Englewood Cliffs, N.J.*

systems.[18] There are, first, *collateral systems* in which, for example, systems A, B, and C have independent identities but interact with one another. An automobile manufacturer buying steel from one firm and paint from another would be an example. Exchange activities are the main characteristic of collateral systems.

A second model is called the *dominant suprasystem*. Dominant suprasystems acquire an independent existence as entities in which a system-wide authority exerts control over the internal components. A totalitarian government, for example, uses central planning to control its economy and other features of its society. Our own federal government can

---

[18] Lee E. Preston and James E. Post, *Private Management and Public Policy* (Englewood Cliffs, N.J.: Prentice-Hall, 1975), pp. 14–27.

also be considered a dominant suprasystem, although many countervailing forces affect the degree of control that results. The controlling authority of a suprasystem attempts to relate the behavior of its subsystems more to itself than to one another.

A third model is called an *interpenetrating system*. Interpenetration exists when systems interact, but none is totally contained by nor contains the others with respect to a particular event or process. One may examine a business transaction, for example, in terms of its financial, human, moral, ethical, and other related dimensions — which is to say, in terms of interpenetrating systems. In this view, the transaction is more than an exchange or the result of collateral relationships. When an event in a micro unit generates new flows of activity or structural changes in other units, not simply altering the volume or character of inputs and outputs, we need an interpenetrating systems model to understand the complexities involved.

Figure 1.2 is a schematic diagram of the three basic models. While we will at various later points refer to the collateral and suprasystem models, the interpenetrating systems model is the most useful for explaining macromanagement issues.

Macromanagement theory is still in the early stages of development. One reason is that social issues have traditionally been the province of single disciplines rigidly separated from one another by academic, philosophical, or scientific doctrines that defy conceptual integration. Some disciplines, however, such as philosophy, sociology, or management, have provided a macromanagement level, interdisciplinary view such as that provided in this book.[19]

SOCIAL PROBLEMS AND RESPONSIBILITIES

More than ever before, the issues we face are global in nature, and solutions are at best tenuous and elusive. We are baffled by fast change and events that threaten our stability and progress. Goals and issues are unclear, so that we are, in effect, at sea without a compass. The resulting frustrations impede our ability to act with confidence.

To force some kind of action, we overwork the word *crisis*. The word seldom appears without modifiers — energy, population, economic, health care, urban. Surrounded by so many alleged crises, it is no wonder that we seek scapegoats, or turn to anyone who appears to understand this complexity well enough to lead us out of despair. The crisis orientation may help to mobilize resources for coping with social problems.

---

[19] See, for example, Asterios G. Kefalas, "The New International Economic Order (NIEO): Approaching the Limits to Organizationability," *Proceedings of the 1980 Southeast Regional Meeting*, Southeast Region, Society for General Systems Research, 1980, pp. 88–91.

However, our problems display an ambiguity, inconsistency, and uncertainty that call for integrative solutions. Macromanagement analysis, however inadequate at the moment, holds much promise for these integrative efforts.

It is too presumptuous to assert that managerial knowledge and skills can provide automatic or easy answers to social problems. Some even allege that society suffers from too much management, and that we should revert to simpler, less complicated structures. Although our problems are at least partly of managerial origins and should be approached essentially by managerial methods and theories, we must nevertheless remain skeptical of easy claims that better management will solve or prevent our deeper, more complex problems. For example, it is doubtful whether more or better management techniques can solve urban decay or even the fiscal problems of our cities; while mismanagement is rife in cities and should be corrected, the cities' problems are complicated by political elements.[20]

But although it is wrong to saddle management with the entire responsibility for solving social problems, it is likely that gradual changes in social values and expectations will throw an increasingly heavy burden on managers. For changes of all kinds will be forged from reciprocity and interaction among groups wielding power. The macromanagement perspective implies an ever greater need for managers and organizations to discover and meet their social responsibilities. An important feature of the postindustrial society is the way in which social responsibility has come to play a major role in the decisions and actions of managers, especially in the business sector.

In the turmoil of recent years, crusaders for an improved society have virtually ignored the potentials of management theory and practice for achieving that goal. Managers and administrators, when they are not the subjects of direct attack, are tolerated as a necessary evil or ignored. Without absolving them from blame for this predicament, it should be noted that the low esteem in which managers are held is part of a larger phenomenon in which people are coming to hold increasingly critical views of major social institutions. The attacks of social critics and the low esteem for important action centers of society have given rise to some defensiveness and smugness. Fortunately, these attitudes have not kept managers from reassessing their roles and capacities for helping to solve or prevent social problems.

But neither managers nor any other social sector alone can improve, destroy, or control society: the elements of society sink or swim together. Managers in all our social institutions (not merely in business) can no longer plow furrows entirely of their own choosing, and their key decisions are increasingly subject to review not only for internal effi-

---

[20] David Rogers, *Can Business Management Save Our Cities?* (New York: Free Press, 1978).

ciency, but also for their impact on society. The costs of pollution, environmental damage and depletion, waste disposal, dangerous products and by-products, and the various forms of damage to human beings have in the past been ignored, unrecognized, and borne primarily by society. In the postindustrial society, business firms must accept more of the responsibility for minimizing and paying these costs. The economic success reflected as profits can no longer be justified unless those profits meet or exceed the social costs insofar as these can be measured.

The increasing burden of government regulation has arisen to establish at least minimum guidelines for society's expectations. This burden will be eased as expectations are absorbed into managerial thought so that we need not rely on law alone for socially responsible management. This line of reasoning implies the possibility of a major role for managers in coping with society's central concerns. For this to happen would require, at the very least, a determined rejection of the narrow, insular, and selfish views often ascribed to managers.

What is missing in the current travails of society is a sense of mission, purpose and direction — all functions of leadership. Society has as yet produced no central strategy to replace the one of unlimited industrial expansion. Without coherent and vigorous leadership, we can only pick at individual problems in isolation, without recognizing the deeper issues that underlie them. The macromanagement view points out the ways in which managers, in recognition of newly emerging social responsibilities, can contribute at least in part the necessary leadership.

In the criticism and reform of social institutions we have assigned important roles to prophets, leaders or managers of dominant organizations, editors, journalists, politicians, experts, professionals, academicians, speechmakers, celebrities, philosophers — in brief, to the creative, educated, intellectual classes. They help to define our problems, inform our judgments, interpret our past, and design our future. The difficulty lies in knowing whom to believe, in judging their ideas, and in deciding on appropriate strategies for action.

We will elaborate on the nature of social responsibility and other macromanagement issues in the chapters to follow. We turn next to a consideration of the problems managers face as they grapple with the problems of knowledge and expertise.

Incident Case

Mr. William Whitely, the chairman of the board of the Foster Manufacturing Company, received a letter from a group of dissident stockholders saying that they intended to introduce a resolution at the next board meeting that would abolish the company's expenditures of funds for philanthropic purposes.

What should Mr. Whitely do about this situation, and why?

Issues for Discussion and Analysis

1. Develop arguments pro and con for the statement that "The idea of the postindustrial society has little or no significance for the managers or owners of a small business."

2. Analyze the kinds of problems business managers face because of major changes occurring in these social institutions: (1) education, and (2) government.

3. Argue for or against the proposition that managers will benefit from the efforts of the rising new class of specialists, professionals, and other highly educated members of society.

Class Project

Purpose: To develop a comparative analysis of how managers in different types of organizations are affected by the changes pointing to the postindustrial society.

Procedures:

1. Divide the class into investigative teams to interview a manager or administrator in each of the following: (a) a business firm, (b) a school, (c) a hospital, and (d) a government bureau.
2. After preparing for and conducting the interviews, each team will report its findings to the rest of the class, for the purpose of comparing similarities and differences among the managers interviewed.

For Further Reading

BELL, DANIEL. *The Coming of the Post-Industrial Society* (New York: Basic Books, 1973).

CHEIT, EARL F. (ed.). *The Business Establishment* (New York: Wiley, 1964).

ELLUL, JACQUES. *The Technological Society* (New York: Knopf, 1964).

ETZIONI, AMITAI. *The Active Society* (New York: Free Press, 1968).

GABOR, DENNIS. *The Mature Society* (New York: Praeger, 1972).

KUHNS, WILLIAM. *The Post-Industrial Prophets: Interpretations of Technology* (New York: Harper & Row, Colophon edition, 1973).

LIPSET, SEYMOUR MARTIN (ed.).   *The Third Century: America as a Post-Industrial Society* (Stanford, Calif: Hoover Institution Press, Stanford University, 1980).

PHILLIPS, KEVIN P.   *Mediacracy: American Parties and Politics in the Communications Age* (Garden City, N.Y.: Doubleday, 1975).

ROSE, MICHAEL.   *Servants of Post-Industrial Power.* (New York: M. E. Sharpe, 1979).

TOURAINE, ALAIN.   *The Post-Industrial Society* (New York: Random House, 1971).

2

Knowledge and Managerial Action

The first law of expert advice: don't ask a barber if you need a haircut.

DANIEL GREENBERG, quoted by ALAN L. OTTEN
in *The Wall Street Journal*,
September 18, 1977.

Professing themselves to be wise, they became fools.

ROMANS 1:22.

CONCEPTS DISCUSSED IN THIS CHAPTER

1. KNOWLEDGE AND ITS SOURCES AND FORMS
2. OBJECTIVE AND SUBJECTIVE KNOWLEDGE
3. SCIENCE AND SCIENTISTS
4. ROLES AND FUNCTIONS OF EXPERTS
5. MANAGERS AND THE USE OF EXPERTISE
6. MANAGERS AS EXPERTS

The purpose of this chapter is to show how the various forms and sources of knowledge affect the performance of managers and organizations. Knowledge plays an important role in the emerging postindustrial society. To understand their function in relation to society and its problems, managers need to be aware of how knowledge shapes decision making in society and in organizations.

Much of the knowledge in society and in organizations is in the hands and minds of experts. We will first discuss the significance of knowledge in human affairs, and then take up the problems of experts and their role in management decisions.

THE ROLE AND FUNCTIONS OF KNOWLEDGE

Knowledge about knowledge is uncertain. What we know about knowledge is that (1) philosophers have grappled with this idea for centuries; (2) there are many different kinds of knowledge; (3) what is "known" depends on who knows it; (4) knowledge, even the most scientific, is tentative, uncertain, and accompanied by skepticism and conflict; and (5) to possess knowledge is not necessarily to act on it. Knowledge is thus elusive and ever-changing. The human brain is a unique instrument for thinking about thinking, and it enables humans to review and evaluate knowledge, to learn continuously, to engage in invention and discovery, and to manipulate and cope with ideas.

Knowledge is not fixed. It must be continuously discovered, disseminated, and applied. What we think we know keeps changing. New knowledge, however, does not always readily replace the old, since managers may have founded long-lasting if not permanent decisions on the old knowledge.

Figure 2.1 is a schematic diagram showing the major elements in the use of knowledge, which takes many forms ranging from objective to subjective. Prophetic wisdom, intellectual and historical ideals, opinions, beliefs, and attitudes are relatively subjective influences that shape our awareness and perceptions and govern the discovery and use of knowledge. The knowledge and skills of experts, and factual data are more objective. The forms of knowledge and their uses are conditioned by social and organizational attributes, such as policies, traditions, values, habits, needs, communication patterns, and the like.

Although the dividing line between objective and subjective knowledge is not always clear-cut, it is important to note the distinctions between them. Objective knowledge more readily authenticates

FIGURE 2.1

Elements in the Development and Use of Knowledge in Social Action by Managers

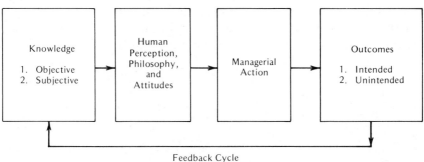

Feedback Cycle

managerial decision; subjective knowledge lies deeply within the self of the knower and is harder to observe in the manager's actions, yet the manager uses it to interpret the meaning of objective knowledge. Objective knowledge is based on evidence, with known systems of measurement or verification. Subjective knowledge springs from emotions, intellect, attitudes, reason, and philosophy.

The most reliable knowledge is that which is verified by research evidence, both pure and applied. Pure research seeks truth and builds theories of the natural and social world. Applied research facilitates action in the pursuit of human purposes. The Western world has always valued pure research—truth for its own sake. We live in a time of pressure for practical action; doers are coming into their own, joining with the thinkers in society to serve humanity.

The desire to learn arises from several different motives. As Bacon aptly stated:

> For men have entered into a desire of learning and knowledge sometimes applying natural curiosity and inquisitive appetite: sometimes to entertain their minds with variety and delite; sometimes for ornament and reputation; and sometimes to enable them to victory of wit and contradictions; and most times to lucre and profession.[1]

Systems of education and training do better in discovering and disseminating objective knowledge than in comprehensively educating men and women in critical understandings, values, and other subjective forms of knowledge important to public policy and the duties of citizens.[2] Beyond scientific knowledge lies the subjective knowledge unique to individuals and particular to time, place, and personal experience. It is this knowledge that is the basis for advocating the participation of individuals in the political and economic decisions affecting them.[3]

Knowledge today is highly specialized. Universities are organized into departments, schools, or divisions built around academic disciplines. They train specialists occupationally fitted for corresponding positions in organizations. Once on the job, however, the specialist finds an organizational context that not only requires factual knowledge or special skills, but also imposes a need for moral and ethical judgments. But to be specialized in one or two areas of knowledge is to be less knowledgeable in others. And degrees of ignorance are often unbalanced and

---

[1] Francis Bacon, *The Advancement of Learning*, Everyman edition (London: Oxford University Press, 1930), pp. 34–35.

[2] Carl H. Madden, *Clash of Culture: Management in an Age of Changing Values* (Washington, D.C.: National Planning Association, 1976), p. 31. For a philosophical view of knowing and awareness, see Alvin W. Gouldner, *Enter Plato: Classical Greece and the Origins of Social Theory* (New York: Basic Books, 1965), pp.267–273.

[3] F. A. Hayek, *The Use of Knowledge in Society* (Menlo Park, Calif.: Institute of Human Studies, 1977), pp. 5–9.

unrecognized. Specialization creates the need for coordinating the understandings of the separate disciplines. This is difficult because some fields of knowledge are insulated from use by nonspecialists. Natural scientists, for example, are more likely to comment on social issues than social scientists are to discuss quantum mechanics.[4] Awed by technical expertise, we are tempted not to examine carefully the nontechnical opinions the specialist declares. There are also subtle differences between knowledge, information, and data. Knowledge is the end product of interpreting information, which may or may not be data-based. Our best knowledge comes when information is accurate and complete, and when supporting data are properly collected and verified by research or testing by experience.

Managers and citizens alike seek more and better knowledge. Despite advances in the kinds and amounts of knowledge, many limitations remain. Knowledge tends to be partial, incomplete, or tentative. Managers also may first decide, and then marshal the information that supports their decision. Technical and scientific knowledge outpaces our knowledge of people and societies, making it hard to apply what we do know. We do not have an exact understanding of human behavior, of how societies function, or how to connect knowledge to change, so that in the practical sphere we still have difficulty in designing a new town or an effective urban transport system.[5]

There are two primary functions of knowledge: (1) It provides information that can be used by managers and other actors in society with a means for testing reality; and (2) in conjunction with values from religion, ideology, and other sources it provides the evaluative interpretations we call *meaning*. Like scientists who revise their theories on the basis of research data, managers test reality by revising their ideas according to experience. The manager's testing is, of course, less rigorous and more informal than that of scientists.

Managers, like other social actors, tend to draw a sharp distinction between facts and values. Facts compel practical action; values introduce a degree of uncertainty or confusion. Nevertheless, managers commonly mix factual information with such factors as common sense, evaluational interpretation, science and folklore, empirical observation, and insight. The impulse to pragmatic action tends to cause them to set value judgments aside, or at least to recognize that values are not the same as facts. But facts without normative (value) interpretations are of limited use.

The testing of reality occurs in the context of those with whom the manager interacts. Knowledge takes on a social character to the extent it

---

[4] Robert M. Young, in *New Scientist* (London), March 29, 1979, pp. 1026–1028.

[5] Stuart Hampshire, "The Future of Knowledge," *The New York Review of Books*, March 31, 1977, pp. 14–18. See also Erwin Chargaff, "Knowledge without Wisdom," *Harper's*, May 1980, pp. 41–48.

is shared with others. Knowledge sharing is commonly low, but not so low as to prevent groups from acting in unison. Shared knowledge may permit specific acts even though there is little agreement on policies or values.[6]

We will now examine the realm of scientific knowledge to see how, despite its limitations, science contributes to the knowledge base of managers.

> . . . a confused societal actor, in whom different images of the world and himself are in conflict, can still function quite effectively. Hence, the term "societal" knowledge should not conjure up simply images of science, information, or openmindedness — although these are included — as it may be more likely to resemble thick, foggy, and multilayered filters through which societal actors relate to one another and to themselves.
>
> AMITAI ETZIONI, The Active Society (New York: Free Press, 1968), p. 141.

SCIENCE AND SCIENTISTS

Though the humanities and other areas of knowledge are important for human action, scientific knowledge is our most reliable source. The accuracy, reliability, and verifiability of knowledge are the hallmarks of science, though subjective factors may also be present. Scientists, like other experts, often find that their advice is not followed. Moreover, "science" does not hold monolithic, homogenized views: scientists in the various disciplines present contradictory or only tentative findings. Finally, the abstractions and the jargon of science make findings difficult to understand and apply.

Today there are over 500,000 American scientists, and 1.5 million additional persons in related scientific and technical fields.[7] There are also over 900,000 social scientists. This enormous pool of expertise attests to the importance we attach to science. Science is revered by a society with a voracious appetite for material benefits; science is also admired for its excitement and daring at the frontiers of discovery. In recent times, however, science and scientists, along with other professionals, have lost respect and esteem. Morison suggests that in part our unease about science follows from a general decline in public esteem for authority figures of all kinds. Scientists are suspect because they have become identified with the power structure of society, which to many seems

---

[6] Amitai Etzioni, The Active Society (New York: Free Press, 1968), pp. 135–143.

[7] Nathan Reingold, "O Pioneers," The Wilson Quarterly, 2 (Summer 1978), p. 56.

overbearing and untrustworthy. The growth of science and technology has forced us to think about questions of ethics and philosophy, and greater attention to ethics supports those who would limit or redirect science.[8]

Many of the deeper ethical questions for scientists are found in their relationships to government and industry. In a study of science and politics, Primack and von Hippel state:

> . . . the way in which technical experts make their services available to society can significantly affect the distribution of political power. If scientists give government and industry the exclusive benefit of their expertise, they may inadvertently be contributing to the creation of a technological dictatorship in which the uninformed citizen must accept whatever these organizations tell him is in his interest. If, on the other hand, scientists make available to the citizen the information and analyses he needs for the defense of his health and welfare, they can help bring about more open and democratic control of the uses of technology.[9]

Because so much of their advice goes to the federal executive branch, scientists have an almost unchallenged influence on decisions. Yet it is difficult for scientists effectively to inform the democratic decision process. Furthermore, government officials may ignore or distort advice not compatible with political or bureaucratic interests.[10] Bureaucracies cloak officials with an authority that protects them from issues affecting their agencies, permitting them to avoid debate by invoking expertise. What is often missing is a hearing for "public interest" scientists in universities, professional societies, or public interest groups.[11]

Clearly the expert's organizational base influences the manager's use of knowledge and advice. Experts who are independent or act as individuals are taken less seriously than those connected to arenas of power and action such as the federal government. It is probable also that we have misconstrued the purposes of science by insisting on material benefits. As Sir Bernard Lovell observes:

> Society was persuaded to give material support to scientific activities in the belief that the discoveries would, inevitably, in some way, be of practical benefit to humanity. Already we see that this is not the case. The more science has progressed, so the divisions between the good and evil and its applications have vanished. The belief in automatic material progress by

---

[8] Robert S. Morison, in the introduction to "Limits of Scientific Inquiry," *Daedulus*, (Spring 1978), pp. vii–viii, x.

[9] Joel Primack and Frank von Hippel, *Advice and Dissent: Scientists in the Political Arena* (New York: Basic Books, 1974), p. ix. Copyright © 1974 by Joel Primack and Frank von Hippel. Reprinted by permission of the publisher.

[10] Ibid., p. 4. See also Philip Boffey, *The Brain Bank of America* (New York: McGraw-Hill, 1975).

[11] Ibid., pp. 286–287. See also J. D. Bernal, *The Social Function of Science* (Cambridge, Mass.: MIT Press, 1967).

means of scientific discovery and application has become a tragic myth of our age.[12]

Science has in effect deluged society with information overload. The result is not only the difficulty of choosing what to believe, but also the providing of spurious support for those willing to distort or suppress knowledge in the service of wrong or selfish interests, or to be careless or indifferent with respect to facts. Barzun believes that all too often we assume we are working with accurate facts because they appear as statistics. Scholarship and opinion become mixed and colored by emotion. In the past there were fewer facts to be mastered; now knowledge is spread so wide it is wearing thin. People too often profess to speak from facts without really ascertaining them.[13]

SOCIAL SCIENCE

In the world of science, the social scientists focus primarily on human behavior in all its aspects and contexts. They study individuals, groups, organizations, societies, and their interrelationships, thus providing guidance for understanding managerial, organizational, and public policy issues. Both micro- and macromanagement theories and practices have developed around the disciplines of psychology, sociology, economics, social psychology, anthropology, and political science.

Social science differs from other kinds of science. Methodological, theoretical, and philosophical assumptions and precepts are different, leading to status differences that give an edge to the older sciences. Social science is newer and less mature in its development. It relies more on statistical inferences and probabilities than on controlled experiments. Its failures are spectacular, its successes less obvious. Hayek notes that scientific knowledge is so prominent in the public imagination that we forget it is not the only relevant kind.[14]

Social scientists at first tried to emulate the basic sciences by insisting on rigorous methodologies, experiment, mathematics, and statistics. The concept of "value-free social science" emerged, about which a storm of controversy still rages.[15] Today many social scientists reject this notion and are developing such concepts as "action research," "social policy research," or "muckraking sociology" to connect their disciplines with actual problems and concrete situations. Freeman and Sherwood assert, for example, that "the social scientist should direct his work toward the solution of contemporary problems and that the amelioration of the ills of our society should be a guiding force in the work of social

---

[12] Sir Bernard Lovell, *In the Center of Immensities* (New York: Harper & Row, 1978), p. 150.

[13] Jacques Barzun, in *U.S. News and World Report*, August 6, 1979, p. 49.

[14] Hayek, *The Use of Knowledge*, p. 7.

[15] Herbert C. Kelman, *A Time to Speak: On Human Values and Social Research* (San Francisco: Jossey-Bass, 1968).

researchers."[16] Berger believes that sociology should face up to its moral and political consequences.[17] Glazer writes that social scientists are not rejecting their traditional uninvolvement in society and are becoming participants.[18] MacRae argues the impossibility and undesirability of a value-free social science.[19]

Putting social scientists in the doghouse has become almost a national sport. Social scientists are insecure about their role in society, and they are often their own severest critics. Andreski charges them with obsessive triviality, self-serving and arrogant ways, verbal gimcrackery, jargon, and faulty methods. He alleges a connection between patronage and the products of their research. Although these charges are partially valid but also unfair, he sums up all the worst traits of social science.[20]

Despite the abundant criticism, social science research is, contrary to general opinion, widely if not wisely used. Social psychologist Nathan Caplan found a high receptivity to the use of social science research among top-level government policy makers, particularly where they intuitively feel that the work is correct. Use is affected, clearly, by political feasibility and other factors not directly related to objective validity.[21] Although social scientists are often judged harshly, they increasingly recognize that a new role in social problem solving is possible. Our failures to solve problems of enormous difficulty are not their fault alone. Though as experts they are at times prophets without honor and guilty of errors, they remain a national resource of great value for both social and organizational problem solving.[22]

---

16 Howard E. Freeman and Clarence C. Sherwood, *Social Research and Social Policy* (Englewood Cliffs, N.J.: Prentice-Hall, 1970). See also Leonard Goodwin, *Can Social Sciences Help Resolve National Problems?* (New York: Free Press, 1975), and Burton R. Clark, *Educating the Expert Society* (San Francisco: Chandler, 1962).

17 Peter L. Berger, *Facing Up to Modernity, Excursions in Society, Politics, and Religion* (New York: Basic Books, 1977).

18 Nathan Glazer, "Theory and Practice in the Social Sciences," *The Chronicle of Higher Education*, July 31, 1978, p. 28.

19 Duncan MacRae, Jr., *The Social Function of Social Science* (New Haven: Yale University Press, 1976). See also Thomas L. Haskell, *The Emergence of Professional Social Science* (Champaign: University of Illinois Press, 1977).

20 Stanislav Andreski, *Social Sciences as Sorcery* (New York: Sr. Martin's Press, 1972). For another critique, see Chris Argyris, *The Applicability of Organizational Sociology* (New York: Cambridge University Press, 1972). For a more balanced set of critiques, see a symposium of varying opinions by leading social scientists, "Social Science: The Public Disenchantment," *The American Scholar* 45 (Summer 1976), pp. 335–359. See also Robert Lekachman, *Economists at Bay: Why the Experts Will Never Solve Your Problems* (New York: McGraw-Hill, 1976).

21 *Behavior Today*, August 18, 1975, p. 539. See also Laurence E. Lynn, Jr. (ed.), *Knowledge and Policy: The Uncertain Connection* (Washington, D.C.: National Academy of Sciences, 1978); and Charles E. Lindblom and David K. Cohen, *Useable Knowledge: Social Sciences and Social Problem Solving* (New Haven, Conn.: Yale University Press, 1978).

22 Jean Jacques Salomon, in "The Contribution of the Social Sciences," *Omega* 5 (1977), pp. 635–647, presents a positive view; Goodwin, *Can Social Sciences Help?* provides a critical view, along with suggestions for how the batting average of the social sciences can be improved. No doubt there has been, as Dr. Peter Bourne suggests (*Behavior Today*, January 22, 1979, p. 4), an overreaction to the imperfections of our social programs, which have not solved problems of enormous difficulty while with technological expertise and enormous cost we put men on the moon. Senator Proxmire's Golden Fleece Awards are often amusing and occasionally justified, but on the whole they have detracted from the laurels of social science as well as other fields of inquiry.

Proposals for social action depend on research generally based on statistical probabilities. This means that a margin of error exists even for competent statistical work. Both sides of a controversial issue, such as national health insurance, have studies which support their views. What appears at first to be firm knowledge requires interpretation and judgment if social actions are to be based on it.

Our failure to solve many of our social problems may be because we do not know how to do it. The problems are genuinely hard. They involve not only conflicts among people or groups, but also among objectives. These conflicts create technical or design difficulties that conflict with political ones. For example, we want a medical care system that simultaneously ensures quality care to all who need it, plus efficient, non-wasteful use of medical resources. No one knows how to do it. Instead, politicians find villains or exhort people to accept new values, to work together, or to restore individualism. We complain about powerlessness and exhort each other to try harder, instead of facing the conflicting objectives and designing solutions that might work. Bendix adds that knowledge cuts two ways:

> . . . we are not sure that the constructive use of knowledge will prevail over its destructive potential. This uncertainty is long overdue. The opinion is gaining ground that human benefit may not be the only or automatic end product of advancing knowledge.[23]

In sum, scientific and technical knowledge plays a strong part in determining our social goals and priorities, and in measuring the social responsibilities of managers, corporations, the government, and other groups. The following sections of this chapter discuss the problems of knowledge and the role of the expert.

THE ROLES AND FUNCTIONS OF EXPERTS

The knowledge explosion of the postindustrial society has generated the "new class" of knowledge workers described by Kristol and Bell. Its members are experts in the sciences, professions, and other fields of knowledge who have become influential and active in government, schools, and businesses. But the concept also includes vast numbers of true and professed experts in thousands of technical and service occupations.

People become experts through practical experience and training as specialists. Some fields require formal credentials such as college degrees, state board examinations and licenses, or the certification proc-

---

[23] Reinhard Bendix, *Embattled Reason* (New York: Oxford University Press, 1970), p. 1. Copyright © 1970 by Oxford University Press, Inc. Reprinted by permission.

esses of trade associations and other groups. The possession of such credentials does not, of course, guarantee expertise or quality of performance. It does indicate that someone's minimum standards have been met. However, building a track record of successful experience and acquiring appropriate values and attitudes are the main routes to becoming known as an expert.

Some experts have to be sought and persuaded to help, but most who make their livings as experts are generally more aggressive. Competition is stiff, and they need contacts with centers of action. All this makes the selection process difficult and expensive, for mistakes are costly. In addition, the selection of an expert may be influenced as much by expediency and politics as by the objective assessment of qualifications.

THE FUNCTIONS OF THE EXPERT

The primary functions of experts are (1) discovery, (2) invention, (3) the interpretation of knowledge and techniques, (4) application of the knowledge and skills needed by society and its organizations, and (5) assisting in the assimilation of knowledge into theory, practice, and social discourse. These functions are reflected in a variety of roles for experts which include professional spokesperson, analyst, diagnostician, intervenor or project director in organizational systems, advisor or counselor, forecaster, and many others.

Some experts, such as scientists, specialize in discovery. Others focus on invention, interpretation, application, or assimilation. There are only a few whose statesmanlike qualities, humanistic vision, and social values impel them to communicate more widely than to other scientists. Some risk losing credibility by stepping outside their ascribed roles; storms of controversy have raged around scientists who warn us of the potential dangers of their discoveries. For example, many physicists who helped develop nuclear energy capabilities expressed strong social concerns over what they were doing.

To apply knowledge and skills, experts may concentrate on one or more of their major roles, or enact them at different times or stages of their careers. The substantive context of their work ranges from the specific and technical to the highly abstract — from the expertise of the actuary to the scholarly work of the philosopher in the interpretation of wisdom. Universities and schools employ research and teaching experts who play a major role training and educating a growing number of experts in a variety of fields.[24]

The separateness of the functions of discovery and application

---

[24] The university participates with a number of other social institutions, such as the family, the church, and the state, in the evolution and preservation of culture, values, knowledge, and wisdom, as well as of technical and other skills.

results in differential social statuses and a disproportionate sharing of rewards among the types of providers. Society accords a high social standing to scientists, but they are relatively low in the reward scale. Conversely, experts in the practice sector are lower on the status scale, but they frequently rank higher in the reward system. There are other potentials for conflict. Discoverers tend to look down on the experts of application, who in turn may not pay homage to them. Specialists within organizations are often at war with one another, making coordination of expertise a problem. Managers with limited knowledge have difficulty resolving such conflicts.[25]

Much of our knowledge is masked in a semantic jungle and specialists are often better at talking to each other than to those unfamiliar with their subjects or their jargon. Furthermore, the pronouncements of experts often go beyond their expertise. Once cloaked with the aura of expert, an individual seems believable even beyond his or her special field. It is easier for a mathematician to seem more expert in mathematics if he or she also appears knowledgeable in philosophy or sociology.

Assimilation is a largely unheralded, slow, unconscious, and cumulative process. It is also an inexorable process in a society with enormous problems and mass communications. To assist in the interpretation and dissemination of knowledge, many journalists specialize in fields such as business, science, or medicine, translating their discoveries into ordinary language in the media. Dissemination is also dependent on the success of the educational system in developing experts for cultural maturity and social responsibility. Clark writes:

> As a society veers toward expertise, the cultural strains highlighted by the old distinctions between the cultivated man and the expert, the pure and the applied, are made severe. The efforts to bring liberal education to the expert constitute a social response to the strain, an attempt to avoid a barbarism of men acute in technical judgment but myopic in social affairs, politics, and cultural understanding. The future of the expert society challenges education to close a gap that in the natural course of affairs will ever widen.[26]

The functions of experts are facilitated by special groups such as professional associations, academies, or societies. These groups work to advance their fields of expertise, to recruit clients and practitioners, and to fulfill an array of other member needs. They impose member controls, such as codes of ethics or certification requirements. But in many cases, their influences on members are informal rather than formal.

---

[25] Talcott Parsons, "The Institutional Function in Organization Theory," *Organization and Administrative Sciences* 5 (Spring 1974), p. 9.

[26] Clark, *Educating the Expert Society*, pp. 290–291.

People are ambivalent in their attitudes toward experts. We need them and trust them, yet are rightly skeptical of their claims. They are handsomely rewarded, but also condemned by critics. They enjoy high social status, but they are subject to a still higher order of generalists, administrators, and other powerholders who use their services. It is a paradox of our time that despite their widespread use, or even overuse, experts generate much criticism and distrust.

Some of the antagonism is toward "the system" or "the establishment" rather than toward specific experts. In both cases, Fairlie notes, hostility has been less against their power and more against the knowledge on which that power is based. We fear what is unknown or unknowable, so power seems like a conspiracy.[27] The specialist's jargon, meant to impress and exclude nonexperts, reinforces suspicion and distrust. Distrust arises also from the expert's narrow specialization and from the fact that even experts can make mistakes. A single error may outweigh several successes. The cost of mistakes is amplified by the computer which, along with many benefits, also adds to the expert's mystique. Computer hardware and tons of paper-borne data transfer the responsibilities of experts from persons to the machine that symbolizes the mysteries of expertise.

Reliable knowledge is hard to come by, and it is often not permanent. Even science reverses its findings, with consequent effects on technologies, social customs, and beliefs. Voice prints—pictures of sound waves of the human voice—were once considered reliable evidence, as were the results of lie detector tests. Now, however, courts are more cautious in accepting both devices.[28] After years of acceptance, reversals are difficult to impose. For example, saccharin, once thought safe, has again been called into question, but the Food and Drug Administration encountered vehement opposition to banning it.

The public tends to interpret such confusions as faulty expertise. Why do not experts find the difficulties at an earlier stage? Time and ongoing research change the views of experts. In addition, risks once acceptable may no longer be so. Moreover, ordinary people tend to take tentative or preliminary research findings as established truth. What often happens is this: (1) A theory projects the probabilities of harm to humans; (2) the government tries to ban the dangerous agents; (3) scientists do research to test the theory; (4) doubts are raised about the extent or

---

[27] Henry Fairlie, *The Seven Deadly Sins* (Notre Dame, Ind.: University of Notre Dame Press, 1979), pp. 102–103.

[28] *Newsweek* (February 26, 1979), p. 93. Research, however, tends to support the accuracy of lie detector tests at the 90 percent level, and courts have begun to accept them over strong protests from attorneys. See *Behavior Today*, June 9, 1975, pp. 501–502.

imminence of the possible harm; (5) a controversy evolves among scientists, politicians, and interest groups; (6) experiments involving millions of dollars and years of effort are made; and (7) politicians resolve the issue according to political criteria. This is exactly what happened in the case of the ozone layer problem. Theorists suggested that fluorocarbons might destroy the ozone and increase the risk of cancer. The government banned fluocarbons in spray cans. Now some scientists say that the ozone layer is a durable, stable, rugged system little affected by human habits. We can blame no one and everyone for panic and premature social decisions. People want to be safe; politicians want to protect people; scientists want to advance their science. However, such events tend to erode confidence in politicians and scientists alike; when real dangers do arise, they may be perceived as "crying wolf."

We have other surrogate models of expertise. In industry the staff personnel manager, presumably chosen as an expert, calls the line manager the true expert. The corporate executive pays homage to the stockholder, the government, or the consumer. The preacher is a surrogate for God or the teachings of the Bible. The function of these surrogate models is to foist responsibility onto other levels of expertise, with the result that the sources of expert guidance are clouded.

Experts, especially professionals, have lost credibility. But this too is a paradox, for we know that we need their expertise. Skepticism and doubt are healthy forces in motivating better performance through self-review.[29] But when skepticism and demands for evidence turn to attack and disillusionment, we risk throwing out the good with the bad. Those who allude to the "tyranny of experts" may be overlooking the limits we place on them. Such tyranny occurs, but only when, out of fear or indifference, we allow it to hold sway.[30]

MANAGERS AND THE USE OF EXPERTS

All managers face critical problems for which their personal knowledge and skills are limited. Recognizing these limits is therefore an important first step in the use of knowledge and experts. The wide use of inside and outside expertise also requires the recognition of a host of political and psychological problems that surround other problems. Managers sometimes retain outside experts for dubious and not altogether explicit reasons, such as using them as "fronts" or window dressing, to authenti-

---

[29] See, for example, *Behavior Today*, January 29, 1979, pp. 1–2; Jacques Barzun, "The Professions under Siege," *Harper's*, October 1978, pp. 61–68; Reynolds Price, "The Heroes of Our Times," *Saturday Review*, December 1978, pp. 16–17.

[30] For a treatise on these and similar concerns, see Stanley Manfred, *The Technological Conscience: Survival in an Age of Expertise* (New York: Free Press, 1978); and Jethro K Lieberman, *The Tyranny of Experts* (New York: Walker, 1970).

cate preconceived decisions, or as sounding boards or handholders. Going through the motions is a common ritual, and experts are often uncertain as to the motivations of those who hire them.

One major problem for the manager lies in selecting competent outside experts; another is to make more effective use of the expertise of internal staff units such as personnel, legal, or public relations departments. A third problem is to know what knowledge is needed and what effect it will have on the organization utilizing it. For all three problems, the answer is to check up on the experts' reputations, track records, and experiences elsewhere, and to exercise close supervision of the projects to which they are assigned. The expert's advice can be tested only through trial, which entails some risk, but careful planning and administration can help to minimize that risk.

The very notion of experts is founded on the idea that others need them, will consult them, and will follow their advice. Although experts work for organizations in increasing numbers, their ties to organizations are often loose, flexible, and temporary. Many are employees, but many others prefer to serve as consultants or independent practitioners. Consultants are intervenors — outsiders whose externally tested experiences are valuable to organizations. They are sought for their independence and objectivity as well as their expertise. They are also useful as change agents. Though the need for an intervenor implies the absence of internal capabilities or the malperformance of organization members, it may also arise out of growth or developmental change.

The presence of inside or outside experts in an organization complicates the process of decision making. One view holds that the manager, not the expert, makes the decisions, and that experts are mainly advisors. This may be true in simple cases, but it is not so for the highly technical judgments for which many experts are sought. Where managers do not have the knowledge to evaluate and implement actions and alternatives, the expert must often take at least partial responsibility. Managers usually have veto power over the expert's recommendations, but experts may resign or withdraw if they disagree with decisions or their implementation. Traditional linkages between "line" and "staff" units do not provide an answer to this dilemma, especially for the outside intervenor.[31]

Contrary to Parsons' view, Wilensky cites two reasons why scientists and facts-and-figures people cannot achieve an excessive domination over managerial judgment. First, experts and deciders interact so that bosses acquire some sophistication in technical matters, and experts acquire leadership and administrative competencies. Second, the immoderate claims of experts are subject to corrective influences; experts are checked by the training of executives, the use of administrative safeguards,

---

[31] Talcott Parsons, *Structure and Process in Modern Societies* (New York: Free Press, 1960), pp. 66–67.

and appeal to public opinion. Furthermore, executives are sensitive to uncertainties, so they shun exclusive reliance on experts and augment their advice with precedent, experimentation, delay, planning, and group decision. Where problems are narrowly technical, the expert's influence is more likely to hold. Where problems are broad and ambiguous, countervailing strategies come into play.[32]

OVERRELIANCE ON EXPERTS

Overreliance on experts is being more and more questioned today. The number and variety of experts is enormous, and needing clients, they are persuasive in finding outlets for their energies. But despite our urgent needs, too much reliance on experts can be counterproductive. Lasch argues, for example, that the family as a social institution has been a victim rather than a beneficiary of the "helping professions," with a proliferating flock of teachers, doctors, counselors, social workers, and juvenile court officers usurping the child-rearing function formerly belonging to families.[33] And according to Reynolds, the father's image in society has been damaged by the marketing approach to mental health, the "child-business," "the parenting enterprise," the "relationship industry," and the "self-help business" — in short, the meddling of self-appointed experts.[34]

Psychologists and psychiatrists have emerged as a new group of experts with enormous influence on how we see ourselves and others. Pop psychology has come to replace traditional authorities. Gross writes: "By offering us the *hidden truth* behind virtually every act of our waking hours, they have effectively seized the role society once divided among the clergy, philosophers, and statesmen — and in earlier times among oracles, prophets, even magicians."[35]

Overdependence on experts has intensified the tendency toward specialization. For example, corporations use their own staffs of economists, and the National Association of Business Economists has doubled its membership to 2775 in a decade. In 1978, the directory of "personal image consultants" listed 37 individuals specializing in "wardrobe selection" and "personal public relations." The 1979 directory listed 100 such specialists.[36] In all walks of life, people feel it is necessary to turn to a host of experts — legal, medical, educational, social. "How to" books

[32] Harold L. Wilensky, *Organizational Intelligence: Knowledge and Policy in Government and Industry* (New York: Basic Books, 1967), pp. 79–81.

[33] Christopher Lasch, *Haven in a Heartless World: The Family Besieged* (New York: Basic Books, 1977).

[34] William Reynolds, *The American Father: A New Approach to Understanding Himself, His Woman, His Child* (New York: Paddington Press, 1979).

[35] Martin L. Gross, *The Psychological Society* (New York: Random House, 1978), p. 55. See also Jonal Robitscher, *The Powers of Psychiatry* (Boston: Houghton Mifflin, 1980).

[36] *The Wall Street Journal*, February 27, 1979, p. 1.

become best sellers as the common person's expert guide. Personal lives are greatly affected by the abundance of expertise directed at their problems. A person contemplating a divorce, for example, becomes involved with attorneys, social workers, priests or ministers, counselors, and accountants. For even a very simple problem a manager may have to call on attorneys, accountants, social scientists, economists, and many others. Although it is a good thing that our society can make such a variety of expertise available, it is clear that overdependence on them robs the individual of autonomy and independence, and perhaps even of self-respect.

There are broader social issues in the overreliance on experts, illustrated by Brzezinski's "technotronic society" and Bell's "new intellectual technology."[37] If the ordinary person or citizen lacks the necessary knowledge for participating in social issues, the danger is that technocratic experts could shape our society to their own interests. The new technology implies a human subservience to the machine. However, the dangers of overreliance on experts are subject to countervailing forces in people themselves: people create machines; people have purposes to be served; people decide how technology may best serve them.[38]

Overspecialization leads to dealing with problems in a piecemeal fashion, though complexity often makes this approach necessary. It also leads to doing what is expedient. In the military, governmental, and industrial power structures, for example, experts need relationships with that small group of political and business leaders capable of connecting them to problems, resources, and action centers.

Overspecialization also poses questions of conscience and morals. Coordination and control processes at the top of the social structure do not work as well as they once did in helping specialists to see their role in relation to the whole. Overdependence on expertise deprives managers of the benefits of intuition, and collides with the need to grapple with moral issues. Undue reliance on experts also makes them less vulnerable to criticism.[39] As a matter of conscience, however, specialists need to consider the moral consequences of their work, and what they owe to society as citizens and human beings.[40] In the realm of morals, few can claim expertise. Maguire writes: "Morality is certainly too important to be left to the professional moralists, and since everyone is a moralist in his fashion, this abandonment of morals to the experts has never really happened."[41]

---

[37] Zbigniew Brzezinski, *Between Two Ages: America's Role in the Technotronic Era* (New York: Viking Press, 1971); Daniel Bell, *The Coming of the Post-Industrial Society: A Venture in Social Forecasting* (New York: Basic Books, 1973), pp. 27–33.

[38] Henry Fairlie, *The Spoiled Child of the Western World* (Garden City, N.Y.: Doubleday, 1976), pp. 292–295.

[39] Daniel C. Maguire, *The Moral Choice* (Garden City, N.Y.: Doubleday, 1978), p. 272.

[40] Charles Frankel, *The Democratic Prospect* (New York: Harper & Row, 1962), p. 148.

[41] Maguire, *The Moral Choice*, p. xv.

In our highly technological society, it is natural to think in a mechanistic way. Doing the world's work seems more real than abstract philosophies or art. One observer notes that the stress on mechanisms has given rise to "one of the curses of our time: the expert," and that it has made body mechanics out of physicians, cell mechanics out of biologists, and "if the philosopher cannot yet be called a brain mechanic, this is only a sign of his backwardness."[42] Management too is often thought of mechanistically. Most managers are expert in some speciality — marketing, finance, production. The higher managers rise in the organization, however, the more they must become generalists — that is, transcend traditional domains and the provincialism of special interests.

It is small comfort to suggest that generalists offset their loss of technical skills by acquiring expertise of another sort: that of management or administration. For some this may be true, but experience suggests that technical expertise is not necessarily a good preparation for general management, and that the mismanagement so rife in our society largely comes from those who attempt what they are philosophically, temperamentally, and even technically unprepared to do. The administrative disposition leads managers to comfort themselves with the notion, objectively false, that management skills can be applied to activities of which they are largely ignorant. Such managers often appear as meddlers, ignoring vital complexities. This may explain the Taoist assertion that the attempt to do good often results in evil, and "the absence of any distrust in man's ability to do good encourages a misleading optimism and brashness."[43]

Today's managerial experts, almost by definition, are organization people in the sense that they work in and through organizational structures, and in groups such as teams, committees, seminars, and other forms of collaboration. They carry administrative and operational responsibilities for groups with divergent interests — owners, stockholders, employees, customers, regulators, suppliers. In such situations, interpersonal skills overshadow technical ones.

WHAT MANAGERS CAN DO

Managers first of all can consider new techniques for opening up their organizations to relevant inputs on social issues in the same way they are open to economic and technological inputs. This enlargement of the managerial task requires a developmental point of view for the organ-

---

[42] Erwin Chargoff, *Heraclitean Fire: Sketches from a Life before Nature* (New York: The Rockefeller Press, 1979), p. 121.

[43] Herbert Goldhammer, *The Advisers* (New York: Elsevier-North Holland, 1978), pp. 152–155.

ization and all its members. The adaptive organization design and its corresponding participative leadership styles require the development of new expertise on the part of managers. Experts are in large part the creation of their work environments, in which nothing is fixed. Staying expert as a manager requires continuous attention to changing conditions within the enterprise and outside it. Clearly the new expertise requires learning new ways of gathering and applying quantitative and qualitative information. The information on which managers make decisions will grow in quantity, but what is more important is that its nature will be different, posing enormous problems of integration and analysis.

Managers as a whole are generally not viewed as experts on society and its problems. They are more likely to be regarded as part of the problem. Corporations are widely criticized, but their responses are often unconvincing. Mismanagement, to say nothing of fraud, bribery, and other corruption, is so rampant in business and government that it is no wonder doubts arise as to where the experts are. Therefore one of the most socially responsible efforts that needs to be made is to carry out management practices that are both economically and socially sound. The expertise of managers shows up at its best within organizations where traditional roles are clearer. Yet the newer responsibilities entailed by social concerns reflect new kinds of expertise that are gradually developing among managers who probably deserve more credit than they get.

The knowledge and skills of business management are needed in all our social institutions — government, schools, hospitals, and service organizations. Businesspersons have been generous in serving, helping, and supporting all types of organizations not only with philanthropy, but with managerial skills. They occupy a special vantage point for marshaling resources, appraising current problems, and analyzing change. They collaborate with representatives of other institutions in determining priorities, developing policies, and planning programs. These activities reflect genuine concern for social issues.

A second major problem for managers is to develop new philosophies and techniques for the management of knowledge workers. They cannot be managed with traditional managerial styles. They are more mobile; they have different aims, aspirations, and needs; they value autonomy and independence. They are expensive, since they are in demand and the supply is often limited, and since they spend a large share of the organization's resources.[44]

A third contribution of managerial expertise is found in the new specialties springing up in response to needs in the external environment. Social responsibility positions, for example, are increasing in number at

[44] Peter F. Drucker, "Managing the Knowledge Worker," *The Wall Street Journal*, November 7, 1975, p. 16.

the top echelons of organizations. Related specialties, such as forecaster, economist, ombudsman, manager of government or consumer relations, and the like reveal how managers adapt to changing needs and relate to society as a whole. While the cynic finds this self-serving, one may also applaud the process as a logical result of complex forces in society becoming more clearly recognized.[45]

Complexities in the external environment account for a fourth example of the growth of managerial expertise. Management consultants are more numerous than ever. In 1978 their revenues were over $2.5 billion, and they continue to grow at the rate of about 20 percent annually. Furthermore, the proportion focusing on internal problems is declining, while that focusing on the impacts of external pressures, such as government regulation or consumerism, is increasing.[46]

Niels Bohr has said that "an expert is someone who knows some of the worst mistakes that can be made in his field and how to avoid them." This aphorism is a wry reminder that we can only lurch forward haltingly in our search for solutions to organizational and social problems, for the world of experts provides us with few heroes. The expert may sometimes be an honored prophet, but this glory may often be quite temporary.

Incident Case

Company A retained a local minister to sit ex officio on the board of directors to advise on the moral and ethical aspects of major decisions. Company B hired a local minister to be available to all key managers to help them on the moral and ethical aspects of their decisions.

Evaluate the merits and demerits of each approach.

Issues for Discussion and Analysis

1. Argue the case pro and con for believing that managers make decisions, but experts only advise or recommend.

2. Develop a rationale for resolving the conflict between technical and managerial skills that arises when managers advance in a hierarchical organization.

3. Analyze how the growing importance of social responsibility affects the organization's information system and its use of expertise.

---

[45] "The New Corporate Environmentalists," *Business Week*, May 28, 1979, pp. 154–162.
[46] "The New Shape of Management Consulting: A Splintering into Specialties," *Business Week*, May 21, 1979, pp. 98–104.

Class Project

1. Develop a list of criteria to be used in selecting the services of an outside consultant to be hired as an advisor on environmental problems.

2. Evaluate the relative priorities of the various criteria.

For Further Reading

BOOK FORUM. Special issue entitled "Knowledge: How It Gets Around, What Happens to It in the Process." Vol. 5, no. 1, 1971.

CHURCHMAN, C. WEST. *The Systems Approach and Its Enemies* (New York: Basic Books, 1979).

DE GRE, GERARD L. *Science as a Social Institution* (New York: Random House, 1965).

ETZIONI, AMITAI. *Social Problems* (Englewood Cliffs, N.J.: Prentice-Hall, 1976), chap. 3.

ETZIONI, AMITAI. *The Active Society* (New York: Free Press, 1968), part II.

GOLDHAMMER, HERBERT. *The Advisers* (New York: Elsevier-North Holland, 1978).

GROSS, MARTIN L. *The Psychological Society* (New York: Random House, 1978), chap. III.

GRUNFELD, FREDERIC, V. *Prophets without Honor* (New York: Holt, Rinehart and Winston, 1979).

LYNN, LAURENCE E. (ed.). *Knowledge and Policy: The Uncertain Connection. Study Project on Social Research and Development* (Washington, D.C.: National Research Council, 1978).

MANFRED, STANLEY. *The Technological Conscience: Survival and Dignity in an Age of Expertise* (New York: Free Press, 1978).

ROMAN, DANIEL D. *Science, Technology, and Innovation* (Columbus, Ohio: Grid Publishing, 1980).

SCHON, DONALD A. *Beyond the Stable State* (New York: Norton, 1973).

SHAPERO, ALBERT, D. MITLAND HUFFMAN, and ALBERT M. CHAMMAK. *The Effective Use of Scientific and Technical Information in Industrial and Non-Profit Settings: A Study of Managerial Interventions* (Austin: University of Texas at Austin, 1978).

SPENCE, LARRY D. *The Politics of Social Knowledge* (University Park: Pennsylvania State University Press, 1975).

3

Centers of Influence on Managers

. . . in my own studies I passed from the false question "Is this occupation a profession?" to the more fundamental one, "What are the circumstances in which people in an occupation attempt to turn it into a profession, and themselves into professional people?"

EVERETT C. HUGHES
Men and Their Work, 1958

Where is wisdom to be found, and where is the place of understanding?

JOB, 28:20

CONCEPTS DISCUSSED IN THIS CHAPTER

1. THE ROLE OF INTELLECTUALS
2. MANAGERS AND INTELLECTUALS
3. THE FUNCTIONS OF PROPHETS
4. PROFESSIONALISM AND THE MANAGER
5. PROFESSIONAL ATTITUDES AND THE SOCIAL RESPONSIBILITIES OF MANAGERS

In addition to coping with problems of knowledge, managers must also be aware of the ideas and values that shape their judgments and decisions. The internal and external environments daily provide thousands of signals contending for the manager's attention; the potential for information overload would be extremely high without mechanisms for selecting and organizing perceptions of reality so as to produce the ability to act intelligently — that is, as wisely, rationally, and consistently as possible.

What managers do in the realm of practice or problem solving depends on the fundamental ideas they hold about the relationships of the many bits and pieces of reality that make up their world. These ideas are essentially a philosophy of management, or sets of guiding principles which, though they may not be explicitly recognized, help to make sense out of reality. The influences and ideas that affect the manager's philosophy, knowledge, and thought patterns are numerous, but two of the most relevant to understanding issues of social responsibility will be discussed in this chapter: (1) the intellectual bases of social issues, and (2) the concept of the professions.

INTELLECTUALS: WHO ARE THEY?

An *intellectual* is a type of modern prophet who specializes in the rational, critical, and creative use of the powers of the mind we call intelligence. Simply stated, intellectuals are a social class with an occupational focus on serious mental work. The Russians use the word *intelligentsia* to denote this social class; in the United States the term *intellectual* has been applied more widely to include a variety of persons whose work is primarily mental rather than physical. The word *intellectual* is often used disparagingly to describe the coldness and abstraction of thinkers; it is also often used as the butt of humor.

Reprinted by permission of the Chicago Tribune–New York News Syndicate, Inc.

The number of intellectuals in society is not precisely known, for the count depends on how the term is defined. One study included a sample of 200 "leading" intellectuals.[1] Others place the number at about 600.

---

[1] Charles Kadushin, *The American Intellectual Elite* (Boston: Little, Brown, 1974).

This range covers what may be called "true" or "career" intellectuals. The number of self-proclaimed intellectuals is much larger. Of the nation's 400,000 professors in colleges and universities surveyed by the Carnegie Commission, half agreed with the statement "I am an intellectual." Of the 8,100 professors in the humanities and social sciences who have achieved productive scholarship in major universities, 90 percent said they are intellectuals.[2] These may be called fringe or would-be intellectuals. The majority of professors do not qualify as true intellectuals, since their primary careers are as specialists, professionals, scholars, educators, or scientists, or combinations thereof.[3]

Career intellectuals earn their livelihoods from writing, editing, publishing, public speaking, and occasionally teaching.[4] With the exception of the few professors who might qualify, most are freelance rather than employees of organizations. This was not so in the eighteenth century, when it was rare for a person of knowledge to be unconnected with some major institution, predominantly the church or state, but also universities or monasteries. At that time intellectuals, like craftsmen, were organized into guilds.[5]

Intellectuals are united not by agreement on issues or political views, but by their shared concern with public affairs. The relatively small group of highly influential intellectuals is a self-maintaining elite that controls entry to the group through informal acceptance. Aspirants must be well educated, literate, and eloquent in argument and persuasion. Since intellectuals not only write for a small group of periodicals but also serve as their editors, advisors, or even their owners and publishers, they can control admission to the circle. Aspiring intellectuals with serious intent must ultimately participate in the discourse contained in such journals as *Commentary*, *The New York Review of Books*, *The Public Interest*, *The National Review*, or the *Partisan Review*.

FUNCTIONS OF INTELLECTUALS

Intellectuals fulfill a number of social functions having vital though not always recognized effects on management, especially at the macro level. They serve primarily as guardians of the tradition of creative and

---

[2] Ibid., pp. 15–16.

[3] Christopher Lasch, *The New Radicalism in America, 1889–1963: The Intellectual as a Social Type* (New York: Knopf, 1965), p. 317. For a manual of instructions on how to become an intellectual, see Ignace Lepp, *The Art of Being an Intellectual* (New York: Macmillan, 1968).

[4] Raymond Cuvillier has challenged the assumption that since intellectual workers are a rapidly increasing proportion of the salaried work force, they will sooner or later become assimilated into the work force, and hence will conform to existing patterns of social theory and practice. See his "Intellectual Workers and Their Work in Social Theory and Practice," *International Labour Review* 109 (April 1974), pp. 291–317.

[5] Robert Nisbet, *Sociology as an Art Form* (New York: Oxford University Press, 1976), pp. 86–87.

critical thinking about the problems of society, its purposes, and the roles of citizens. Within this broad purpose are several collateral and inter-related functions, among which the following are the most important:

1. Maintenance of the common cultural heritage and its beliefs, values, manners, norms, and other traits.
2. Prophecy: social analysis highlighting problems, goals, and issues calling for change.
3. Criticism and evaluation of social institutions, practices, ideas, theories, policies, and other key areas of society.
4. Synthesis of ideas and information relating to humanistic, literary, esthetic, political, economic, governmental, and human welfare concerns.
5. Maintenance of a continuing discourse on public affairs in furtherance of the above functions.

Although other groups may also contribute to these five functions, they are the wide spectrum of ideas with which intellectuals are primarily concerned. Particular individuals may find their niche in one or two of the areas, in effect building a reputation as an expert observer or specialist in certain sets of ideas. However, most intellectuals comment widely on the human condition and on society. They are free of attachments to traditional scholarly disciplines and are thereby better able to focus on the interconnectedness of seemingly different aspects of the world, and to provide integrative, holistic, macro perspectives. They may also become identified with ideological positions on the political continuum of Left and Right, though they resist such categories. Also, their position can change and may vary according to the problems at hand and the societal conditions they are observing. They remain attached to ideals such as liberty, justice, democracy, and freedom, though differing among themselves as to the meaning of these terms and the means by which humans might achieve the conditions they describe.

ANTI-INTELLECTUALISM

It is a paradox of our time that in a nation so beset with problems, we harbor a mistrust of ideas and thinkers, and especially of intellectuals. *Anti-intellectualism* is chronic hostility, resentment, or suspicion toward the life of the mind and of those who represent it. To Hofstadter, anti-intellectualism is pervasive, and in the modern era, instigated by business with its emphasis on knowhow, self-help, and wariness of the abstract and the unknown.[6] Such a view is too extreme, but it reflects the hostility some intellectuals direct against our major social institutions.

The involvement of intellectuals in political controversy is one of

---

[6] Richard Hofstadter, *Anti-Intellectualism in American Life* (New York: Knopf, 1963).

the generators of this hostility. Another is that intellectuals are often quarrelsome and pedantic, and sometimes follow rules and conventions that reflect their own distrust of reason and are incompatible with a disciplined and responsible conduct of intellectual life. Intellectuals themselves thus do much to foster anti-intellectualism.[7]

Anti-intellectualism is often passive or latent, implicit in its rejection of learning. Certain companies, for example, decline to hire graduates with MBA degrees, on the grounds that they stir up trouble, contribute little of practical value, and hence are unnecessary. However, there is a more aggressive form of anti-intellectualism. White notes three aggressive strategies: total destruction of the enemy, containment of the enemy, and invading the enemy's terrain. Total destruction is the least popular aim, though we see it in the form of efforts to curb science, universities, schools, and the arts. Containment is the most popular strategy, demanding that intellectuals be controlled, limited in influence, and allowed to express only idle curiosity. Invaders aim to force intellectuals to meet standards approved by the invaders.[8]

The anti-intellectualism evident in politics also exists in the rest of society, particularly among managers who stress practical action. The decline in respect for intellectuals parallels a similar fading of favorable attitudes toward the professions and other social institutions. The social upheavals of the 1960s and 1970s threw intellectuals into disorder by intensifying the divisions among them and reducing the level of public confidence in them.

The critical function of intellectuals includes self-criticism. They are critical of each other. There is a difference between valid criticism and anti-intellectualism, however, and not all criticism reflects anti-intellectualism. Rogow and Lasswell, for example, assert that the intellectual community has failed to anticipate the major problems of society, thereby allowing an unnecessary sense of chaos to interfere with the determination of social policies.[9]

Shils has criticized intellectuals for political attitudes that advocate massive government intervention directed toward unrealizable ends. He believes that the restoration of civility requires us to counter the belief of intellectuals that all things are possible and all demands can be met by a government that responds to clamorous spokespersons for the people.[10] But he notes also that there will always be tension between intellectuals

---

[7] Charles Frankel, *The Love of Anxiety and Other Essays* (New York: Harper & Row, 1965), chap. II, "The Anti-Intellectualism of the Intellectuals," pp. 12–39.

[8] Morton White, *Pragmatism and the American Mind* (New York: Oxford University Press, 1973), pp. 78–92.

[9] Arnold A. Rogow and Harold D. Lasswell, *Power, Corruption and Rectitude* (Englewood Cliffs, N.J.: Prentice-Hall, 1963), p. 100.

[10] Edward Shils, "Intellectuals and Their Discontents," *The American Scholar*, Spring 1976, pp. 202–203.

and the laity, and that the discovery and achievement of an optimum balance between civility and intellectual creativity are the tasks of the statesman and the responsible intellectual.[11]

Despite resistance, hostility, and criticism, intellectuals remain an influential force in society. Macdonald writes that intellectuals are one of the constants, and hence necessities, of history.[12]

> *The intellectual appears a gadfly in every age and his contribution to politics in diverse forms is impressive, although it has often been manipulated by politicians in manners not consistent with his aims. His greatest temptation has been to succumb to arrogance and cynicism; his saving grace has been humility and patience. The basis of his strength lies in his capacity to come to terms with himself and, by introspection, to reason through to an understanding of his nature and destiny. Only when he understands himself and has grasped truth as he conceives it, can he turn, confidently and effectively, to the task of influencing his environment.*
>
> H. MALCOLM MACDONALD, "Some Reflections on Intellectuals," in H. Malcolm Macdonald (ed.), *The Intellectual in Politics* (Austin: University of Texas Press, 1966), p. 13.

MANAGERS AND INTELLECTUALS

Managers are outwardly anti-intellectual, though many have a tacit respect for learning and reason. They call intellectuals "eggheads," "liberals," or "leftists." To managers, intellectuals seem out of touch with the practical. Their focus on politics and government and their frequent hostility toward business understandably arouse antagonism.

The tension between managers and intellectuals has serious consequences. They perceive little need for each other and have little mutual respect. Their contacts are limited or occur in arenas of debate, thus deepening their misunderstandings. Their ideological differences over the problems of capitalism and the free enterprise market economy are both real and imagined. Yet, as Wallis asserts, some intellectuals provide promising countercurrents to the "socialism" and government intervention that managers and businesspeople deplore. Because intellectuals are not makers and doers, but rather instruments for disseminating ideas and influencing change, intellectuals are in effect journalistic middlemen — not creators of original ideas, but capable of interpreting knowledge and

---

[11] Edward Shils, "The Intellectuals and the Powers: Some Perspectives for Comparative Analysis," *Comparative Studies in Society and History* 1 (October 1958), pp. 21–22.

[12] H. Malcolm Macdonald, "Some Reflections on Intellectuals," in H. Malcolm Macdonald (ed.), *The Intellectual in Politics* (Austin: University of Texas Press, 1966).

opinion. They get their data secondhand and their experience vicariously.[13]

The middleman function is valuable, but it requires interpretive and integrating skills. Academics who take their intellectual work seriously could fulfill a linkage role between practical problems and the abstractions of intellectuals and philosophers. Thoughtful managers too can effectively mediate the conflicts between the two worlds. For example, they could help to inform computer specialists of the intellectual implications of their problem-solving techniques.

Managers unfortunately have paid little attention to the shift of many leading intellectuals to a neoconservative stance. Neoconservatives are a cohesive group—almost a social class, or at least a definitive type.[14] They are for the market system and against the undue intrusion of government into the private sector. Their views are supportive, though not always uncritical, of capitalism and the business system.[15] But despite this neoconservative trend among intellectuals, continuing hostility between managers and intellectuals deprives managers of valuable insights. Managers, of course, are often good targets for critics, intellectual and otherwise. On the other hand, the ideology of liberalism and the abstract nature of their concerns make intellectuals appear innately hostile. Hoover suggests that managers should and can curtail the antisocial behavior that discredits capitalism.[16]

Intellectuals too can improve their side of the case. Fairlie suggests that the intellectual needs to recover a sense of the imaginative life of human reason. Surprise, wonder, and understanding are the special luxury of the person of intellectual talents. Ortega's phrase "the perpetual ecstasy of the visionary" highlights the intellectuals' prophetic role which, when coupled with reason and imagination, places them strategically at the center of social discourse.[17] Managers are necessarily caught up in the same issues as intellectuals. The emerging class of "technical intellectuals" has joined other intellectuals at the centers of action. The postindustrial society has spawned new occupations in which people live by their expertise and derive power from controlling technical knowledge that is beyond the understanding of most managers as well as ordinary people. This new class has produced controversy among intellectuals. Conservatives such as Kristol believe that its members oppose business and favor the welfare state. Intellectuals on the Left believe that advocates of corporate interests predominate in the new

---

[13] W. Allen Wallis, *An Overgoverned Society* (New York: Free Press, 1976), pp. 28–29.

[14] Richard Gillam, "Intellectuals and Power," *The Center Magazine* 10 (May–June 1977), pp. 15–30.

[15] Peter Steinfels, *The Neoconservatives* (New York: Simon and Schuster, 1979).

[16] Calvin B. Hoover, "Can Capitalism Win the Intellectuals?" *Harvard Business Review* 37 (September–October 1959), pp. 47–54.

[17] Henry Fairlie, *The Spoiled Child of the Western World* (Garden City, N.Y.: Doubleday, 1976), pp. 303–306.

class. The question remains whether the new class will be a force for good or whether it has been coopted by the institutions and organizations it seeks to reform.[18]

Alongside the critical functions of intellectuals, we must place the function of prophecy. Both the critics and the prophets of our time do much to help the manager evaluate options, set goals, and participate actively in the governance of society.

SECULAR PROPHETS

Prophetic voices seek to guide our understanding of current conditions in society and to indicate their implications for social improvement. Prophecy arises in many contexts, with different origins, intensities, guises, and purposes. Prophets rely more on wisdom and conscience than on knowledge, and there are few criteria for judging them. We are, therefore, often skeptical of prophetic claims. Although we prefer evidence as a guide to action, some prophets nevertheless acquire a following that reflects a general influence on public opinion as well as on managers.

In popular usage, prophecy has been wrongly associated with divination, soothsaying, or predicting the future. Christian theology rejects this meaning, treating the biblical prophets as conveyors of the timeless message of God. Although the biblical prophets were primarily preachers or teachers rather than forecasters, there was an element of the future in their declarations about the consequences of moral situations.[19]

Like the early prophets, modern secular prophets portray the present in the light of its apparent consequences for the future. They speak of idealistic social change, thereby threatening the established order. This explains why prophets are often without honor in their own country. R. Buckminster Fuller's faith in technology as a divine answer to problems of the environment, and McLuhan's belief that the medium is the message, generated strong rejection before gaining a measure of acceptance.[20] Another example is Alexander Solzhenitsyn, whose 1978 Harvard University commencement address caused a furor because it contained hard truths as well as possible misconceptions, though little he had not said before.[21] In declaring that America's well-being has corroded the fiber of its people, Solzhenitsyn probed deeply into the minds and hearts of

---

[18] See Alvin W. Gouldner, *The Future of Intellectuals and the Rise of the New Class* (New York: Seabury Press, 1979); and Daniel Bell, *The Coming of Post-Industrial Society*. For a refutation of "myths about the new class," see B. Bruce Briggs, *The New Class?* (New Brusnwick, N.J.: Transaction Books, 1979).

[19] Robert B. Y. Scott, *The Relevance of the Prophets*, rev. ed. (New York: Macmillan, 1968), pp. 1–14.

[20] For a comparison of these two prophets, see Peter F. Drucker, *Adventures of a Bystander* (New York: Harper & Row, 1979), pp. 244–255.

[21] Edmund Fuller, *The Wall Street Journal*, July 13, 1978, p. 14.

Americans. His uncompromising, self-righteous posture aroused both admiration and hatred, the usual lot of the modern prophet.

The tensions that prophets cause are healthy ones, for they call humans to account for their actions. The authority of prophecy is rooted in the past, from which we derive our ties with humanity. Prophets also provide a link with the future by interpreting social experience in ways that give meaning and direction to change. By warning of impending crisis and doom, prophets build a following of true believers dedicated to avoiding disaster or to founding a social movement for the attainment of some ideal. But most prophets are notably detached from the scenes of action we call organizations. They cannot lead as managers lead, in possession of resources and the mechanisms of change. They lead by persuasion, charisma, or personal mystique, and the power of ideas. They also do not provide homogeneous, unified interpretations. But their influence, though general and dispersed over wide areas of behavior, is nevertheless significant in shaping social attitudes and values that have a major impact on the public, and hence on macromanagerial decisions.

To illustrate the role of prophecy and its meaning for the managers of both public and private organizations, consider the growing number of futurologists who assert the need for abolishing nation-states in favor of a unitary world government. Unrealistic and impossible as the idea may seem now, a movement in this direction is in progress, and it has profound implications for management and society as we know it. It is true that the prophets of futurism have not yet proved their case, though they use economic, demographic, and other statistical data to convince us that only a world government can overcome poverty, hunger, and human misery.[22] But for managers to ignore such prophets, even though they may be wrong, could be a mistake.

Some of our most astute prophets come from the world of arts and letters, but many focus also on matters closer to managers, such as the current issue of whether technology will provide the ruin or the rescue of society. Lewis Mumford, Buckminster Fuller, Jacques Ellul, and Norbert Wiener are prophets who have put the impact of technology high on the list of problems in which managers are involved.[23]

There are important distinctions between prophets and intellectuals; neither necessarily claims to be the other. Whereas prophets focus on spiritual and moral values and appeal to the emotions, intellectuals rely on reasoning. Prophets seek to alter the conscience and moral behavior of people; intellectuals focus more on political and government processes as forces of change for social betterment. It is important to note, however,

---

[22] See, for example, Ervin Laszlo, *A Strategy for the Future: The Systems Approach to World Order* (New York: Braziller, 1974).

[23] For a concise review of these and other prophets, and an extensive bibliography, see William Kuhns, *The Post-Industrial Prophets* (New York: Harper & Row, 1971).

that intellectuals may engage in prophecy, and prophets may use intellectual tools. Becker argues that "it is fraud for the intellectual to want to be taken as a prophet," because no single mind can be an authority on the future, and unfolding events are so complex. William James held that when all is said and done, there is no advice to be given. Sigmund Freud deliberately avoided prophecy.[24] But prophecy is not prediction, and the functions of intellectuals are like those of prophets — to interpret how to change from the present to a more desirable future.

PROFESSIONS AND THE MANAGER

One of the vigorous forces in American society that influences managerial decisions is that of professionalism. Much of the organized knowledge managers use is obtained, synthesized, and applied by professionals who, in effect, are a major category of experts. As with other experts, managers face the need to examine and use the services of professionals, and to integrate their work into the organizational system without undue sacrifice of managerial autonomy and responsibility. The problems this poses are more difficult in the area of social responsibility than in quantitatively based decisions of a technological, procedural, or operational character.

A *profession* is an occupation or vocation in which individuals use specialized skills or knowledge in assisting others, or practice an art or service based on their knowledge and skills. Professionals enjoy a special status as one of society's elites. An occupation is recognized as a profession to the extent that it meets standards of public recognition and approval, and often of state certification.

The occupational structure of society is highly segmented. The U.S. Bureau of the Census compiles statistical data under a white-collar category which is subdivided into (1) professional, technical, and kindred workers (further subdivided into medical and other health workers, and teachers, except in colleges); (2) managers and administrators (subdivided into salaried and self-employed workers); (3) salesworkers; and (4) clerical workers. The professional-technical category is broken down into 15 major categories such as engineers, lawyers, or teachers. Census categories provide conveniently organized data, but they do not always fit the needs of behavioral science research. For example, they omit managers from the professional category, though many managers see themselves as professionals.

Another useful system of classifying occupations is by their relative status or prestige rankings. Sociologists periodically make such rankings by opinion surveys. Over the past 50 years, the relative standings of

---

[24] Ernest Becker, *Escape from Evil* (New York: Free Press, 1975), p. 169.

major occupations have remained substantially the same. Lawyers, teachers, engineers, and physicians consistently rank at the top; occupations such as truck driver or coal miner rank at the low end of the scale. Although there has been stability of rank for those at the higher and lower ends of the scale, the middle ranks show changes. Carpenters, electricians, insurance agents, and plumbers have shown gains in prestige; bankers, farmers, foreign missionaries, grocers, and traveling salesmen have lost ground.[25]

The application or use of special knowledge is not a sufficient criterion for identifying a profession, since all occupations do this to some degree. Additional requirements include an ideological foundation of beliefs and values governing the behavior of professionals, enhancing their image and guiding their performance, and an image or identity reflecting society's acceptance.[26] A profession is thus an aggregate of recognized individuals sharing mutual values, aims, and skills developed during intensive training and subsequent practice.

The essential characteristics associated with the professions include (1) a body of special and systematic knowledge provided by formal as well as experiential education; (2) placing community or client interests ahead of self-interest; (3) member discipline through codes of ethical conduct internalized by work socialization and reinforced by professional associations; and (4) attitudes that stress service, nonmonetary rewards, and work achievement over financial gain. Established professions, such as medicine and law, and some semiprofessional occupations, have successfully controlled entry to their fields through examining boards and state licensing requirements.[27]

These elements provide a scale against which to measure the degree of professionalization of occupations. Although such scaling involves subjective appraisals, it provides comparisons of emerging professions with the traditional ones. Specific professions and would-be professions differ in their ability to adopt the characteristic elements. It is doubtful, for example, that management can become fully a profession if the examining and licensing of practitioners is not required.

Professional associations regulate the fulfillment of appropriate professional requirements. They maintain a professional identity, develop

---

25 Maximino Plata, "Stability and Change in the Prestige Rankings over 49 Years," *Journal of Vocational Behavior* 6 (1975), pp. 95–99.

26 Howard M. Vollmer and Donald L. Mills, *Professionalization* (Englewood Cliffs, N.J.: Prentice-Hall, 1966), p. viii.

27 Bernard Barber, "Some Problems in the Sociology of the Professions," in the *Professions of America*, eds. Kenneth S. Lynn and the editors of *Daedalus* (Boston: Beacon Press, 1968), p. 18. It should be noted that this taxonomic approach has produced a variety of lists of components, and that the role of occupational knowledge has not yet been definitively established. See Douglas Klegon, "The Sociology of Professions: An Emerging Perspective," *Sociology of Work and Occupations* 5 (August 1978), pp. 259–283. For a skeptical view of the validity of taxonomic precepts, see Julius A. Roth, "Professionalism: The Sociologist's Decoy," *Sociology of Work and Occupations* 1 (February 1974), pp. 6–23.

standards of training and experience, and reaffirm significant values and codes of ethical conduct. They also protect individual members from attack and criticism, and carry out public relations programs. They lobby for the group's welfare. The self-protectiveness of the associations is defined as necessary to the welfare of clients or the public. Professionals tend to be more concerned with the opinions of peers than with the opinions of ordinary people. They stress autonomy and the right to name and judge one another, and to influence or specify the training and licensing standards of practitioners.[28]

Professionalization is a relatively new social phenomenon, an attribute of a complex industrialized society in which many variables are at work. Increases in professionalization are greater than can be explained by the knowledge explosion. It is plausible that increased professionalization results from sociocultural factors such as the desire for status, privileges, and economic benefits, and the desirability of forming cohesive groups with power and visibility.[29]

The rise of professionalism can also be attributed to the parallel growth of institutions of higher education, and to the reorganization of society that accompanied industrialization and rapid economic growth.[30] The transition to corporate capitalism included a redistribution of power that gave professionalism fertile ground for growth. Industrialism and its emphasis on efficiency spawned the scientific management movement, which advocated rationally designed organizations with special needs for managers, engineers, and other experts. Bureaucracy thus encouraged the professional role model for groups beyond the traditional ones. Data processors, personnel managers, secretaries, public relations workers and many other occupations, including managers, are trying to climb on this bandwagon.

Whereas market control was an important objective of the earlier professions, and relatively easy to attain, the spread of general education and the rise of corporate capitalism made market control more difficult, so that it is now one of the weaker functions of professionalization. Consequently, the assertion of social status became more important and resulted in the rise of the emerging professions along the prestige ranking scale. The professions affirm their collective worth by stressing individual dignity, conscience, and service careers, so that the struggles of emerging professions are not class conflicts but rather a power struggle within the same class against rival occupations splintering off from maturer groups.[31]

---

[28] Christopher Jencks and David Riesman, *The Academic Revolution* (Garden City, N.J.: Doubleday, 1968), pp. 201–207.

[29] Ibid.

[30] Magili S. Larson, *The Rise of Professionalism* (Berkeley: University of California Press, 1977), pp. 136–158.

[31] Ibid.

Most professionals today work for organizations as employees, consultants, or partners. Many are loosely connected to organizations that provide the clients; for others, the organization itself is the client. The old idea of a one-to-one relationship to an individual client has faded in the face of society's vast network of organizational arrangements. Some professionals, such as scientists or other researchers, do not have clients at all in the traditional sense.

The lawyer's client may be an individual, but often it is an organization. The teacher's client is the pupil, though in a sense the pupil's parents and the school's organization enter into the relationship. The physician's client is the patient, but the hospital's client is not the patient but the physician. Though there is sometimes confusion over who the true client is, the common factor among all clients is that they do not have the knowledge base to judge the quality of the professional's services. Indeed, the professions do not want clients to make individual judgments; all professionals make mistakes; many tackle cases with little hope of success; clients may be hard to please. So serious judgments are restricted to peers, a system that is reinforced by the mechanisms of associations and state licensing systems.[32]

Ambiguity in the relationship of professionals to clients raises the important question of loyalties. Professionals face multiple expectations with regard to loyalty: those of the professional association and its codes of behavior, and those of the general public, related professions, and clients. When these loyalties are not in conflict, the professional can readily fulfill them. But when demands for loyalty are in conflict, the professional must adopt priorities based on the situation. Such choices are rife with ethical and moral conflicts. Freidson has noted that the professions' desire for secrecy and for control through state licensing is in effect a form of defense against the judgment of their lay clientele. Thus professional authority is a mixed or impure case, containing some authority of technical competence and some elements of legal or bureaucratic authority.[33]

Professional jargon adds to the difficulties of client understanding, and clients often project socially conditioned or emotional needs rather than explicit factual ones. On the whole, the professional emphasis on pride of service and selflessness, where present, has a beneficial effect on client relationships. However, Frankel has suggested that, although the professions are already strongly represented in public issues, they could do much more to enhance vital, democratic public discussion. He sug-

---

[32] Everett Hughes, *Men and Their Work* (New York: Free Press, 1958), pp. 139–144.

[33] Eliot Freidson, "The Impurity of Professional Authority," in Howard S. Becker et al. (eds.), *Institutions and the Person* (Chicago: Aldine, 1968), pp. 25–34.

gests that they could initiate more dialogue to clarify issues, describe alternatives, and help to educate ordinary citizens through mass communication, adult education programs, and publications geared to the lay reader.[34]

PROFESSIONALS IN ORGANIZATIONS

The earliest professions emphasized face-to-face relationships with clients. If organizations were needed, they were simple, small, and loosely structured. The physician, the lawyer, and the clergyman worked mainly as individuals, with small offices and a few assistants.[35] Most professionals now work for or through complex, bureaucratic organizations. They organize relatively large professional partnerships and incorporated firms, or work for corporations, school systems, or church and government offices. Solo practice has become uncommon even among physicians.

There are tensions and conflicts in the relationship of professionals to bureaucratic organizations. Professionals value autonomy and self-control, believing that only other members of their profession can evaluate their work. Peer review is honored and collegial authority preferred. In bureaucracies, superordinate authority — control by superiors according to rules and policies — is the mode. Professionals resent "red tape" and other hindrances to autonomy. Accommodations to these pressures can occur, but they imply disloyalty to professional ideals. Managers who are unaware of these problems cause professionals to feel frustrated, exploited, or stifled. Bureaucrats see them as privileged, even undisciplined mavericks

Tension between organizations and professionals also occurs in the form of competition for loyalty. Both wish to control the hiring process. Professionals demand a voice in selecting their colleagues, but this dilutes the organization's control of professionals once they are hired and directs the professionals' loyalties more toward themselves than to the organization. The result is resistance to bureaucratic rules, standards, and supervision.[36]

Managers can reduce the problems of professionals in organizations by clearly differentiating the structures of roles, authority, and reward.

---

[34] Charles Frankel, *The Democratic Prospect* (New York: Harper & Row, 1962), pp. 87–92.

[35] Daniel H. Calhoun, *Professional Lives in America: Structure and Aspiration 1750*–1850 (Cambridge, Mass.: Harvard University Press, 1965); and Larson, *The Rise of Professionalism.*

[36] Clifford Elliott and David Kuhn, "Professionals in Bureaucracies: Some Emerging Areas of Conflict," *University of Michigan Business Review* 30 (January 1978), pp. 12–16. See also E. Frank Harrison and James E. Rosenzweig, "Professional Norms and Organizational Goals: An Illusory Dichotomy," *California Management Review* 14 (Spring 1972), pp. 38–48; Richard H. Hall, "Some Organizational Considerations in the Professional-Organizational Relationship," *Administrative Science Quarterly* 12 (December 1967), pp. 461–478; Richard H. Hall, "Professionalization and Bureaucratization," *American Sociological Review* 33 (February 1968), pp. 92–104.

For example, staff authority is used to fit specialists logically into the organization while limiting their authority. A more difficult problem has been to improve morale, motivation, and communication. The dissatisfaction of professionals with their work and careers has increased over the past five decades, as has the variety of professions involved.[37] Standard personnel practices designed for factory workers, clerks, the skilled trades, or even line managers do not suffice for working with professionals. Green suggests strengthening the various forms of professional identity within organizations. He found that identification with a profession instead of the organization was associated with stronger feelings of role conflict and alienation. Indifference to both was associated with role ambiguity and alienation.[38]

The dual track of managerial and professional work in organizations presents difficult career choices for professionals. Success as a professional invites a promotion, but usually also a transfer to the management hierarchy. Professionals who become administrators risk technical obsolescence. Former colleagues are no longer peers; they become subordinates who see the administrator as a defector from the profession; camaraderie lessens. Further, the stresses of conflict, adjudication, and compromise require a hardy, secure personality. Since the training of professionals seldom affords much work in administration or management, they must learn by experience and rely heavily on common sense and personal insight.

Professionals and organizations need each other, and both need to pay attention to the sources of strain and to the accommodation strategies that make possible the attainment of goals and satisfactions for both.

CRITICISM OF PROFESSIONS

Professions are experiencing not only internal turmoil and disaffection, but also the growing disillusionment of society. These trends foreshadow changes in the nature and structure of professions. Respect for the professions and professionals can no longer be taken for granted.

Internal disaffections reflect changing external attitudes, producing conflicting strategies and the questioning of traditional values, precepts, and assumptions. Professional associations have become large and bureaucratic, with management problems of their own.[39] A greater source of dissatisfaction is the discrepancy between the ideals advocated

---

[37] Seymour B. Sarason, *Work, Aging, and Social Change* (New York: Free Press, 1977).

[38] Charles N. Green, "Identification Modes of Professionals: Relationship with Formalization, Role, Strain, and Alienation," *Academy of Management Journal* 21 (September 1978), pp. 486–492.

[39] Edward J. Giblin, "Professional Organizations Need Professional Management," *Organizational Dynamics* 6 (Winter 1978), pp. 41–57.

by professional training and the realities of professional practice. When professionals see the ideals as implausible, factions emerge to challenge the profession itself.[40]

External criticism is increasingly abundant. The professions are grappling with pressures aimed at reshaping them to meet changing social expectations. These pressures highlight deficiencies and point toward improvement. The traditional professions — law, medicine, teaching, and the ministry — are no longer the role models they once were. As new occupations become professional, they introduce new views that conflict with earlier ones. Their numbers alone tend to reduce the importance of the traditional professions, and high status is no longer only for the few.

Even more fundamental are new societal expectations that stress egalitarianism over elitism, and advocate consumer and citizen protections. Society resists the elitist and control tendencies of groups, so it casts a critical eye upon the deficiencies of the professions. In an age of doubt, uncertainty, distrust, and consequently of change, the professions are being tested to evaluate principles formerly taken for granted. A new realism favors results over status; privileges once unquestioned are now challenged. It is therefore a time of conflict and struggle for those whose values come from earlier versions of professionalism.

The rising tide of antiprofessionalism has evoked concerns about the competence of professionals and about the degree of social protection that peer evaluation and other self-administered controls provide.[41] Peer evaluation seems inadequate; it is inhibited by the secrecy necessary to shield both clients and professionals from defamation and unjust attack.[42]

Some of the criticism of the professions takes the form of radical diatribes by an obsessed minority of social reformers. For example, Illich has attacked the medical and educational professions for taking away functions formerly left to families or to individuals themselves, and for creating unrealistic needs for which only they can provide.[43] Citing the arrogance of professionalism, Dumont, a psychiatrist, deplores the professionalization of social control itself. He sees an implacable tyranny of the highly specialized members of Gouldner's "new class" achieved by

---

[40] R. Richard Ritti, Thomas P. Ference, and Fred H. Goldner, "Professions and Their Plausibility: Priests, Work, and Belief Systems," *Sociology of Work and Occupations* 1 (February 1974), pp. 24–51.

[41] Gene W. Dalton, Paul H. Thompson, and Raymond L. Price, "The Four Stages of Professional Careers—A New Look at Performance by Professionals," *Organizational Dynamics* 6 (Summer 1977), pp. 19–42.

[42] Hughes, *Men and Their Work*, pp. 141–142. For an analysis of sanctions used in controlling the work performance of physicians, see Eliot Freidson, *Doctoring Together: A Study of Professional Social Control* (New York: Elsevier-North Holland, 1975), chap. 13; and Vollmer and Mills, *Professionalization*, pp. 110–152.

[43] Ivan Illich, *Medical Nemesis* (New York: Pantheon, 1976); *De-Schooling Society* (New York: Harper & Row, 1971).

their consolidation into the political bureaucracy.[44] But the main thread of criticism of the professions concerns problems of control and responsibility. Knowledge confers power on the professionals, along with client and public demands that it be used wisely and responsibly. This power makes any defects in performance more harmful to the public, intensifying a widespread "revolt of the client." Mistakes or malfeasance evoke latent anger and suspicion. The misdeeds of professionals — exploitation, mistakes, carelessness, indifference, and the like — generate popular reactions directed at change or reform.[45]

The control of professionals over markets for their services has been widely attacked. Larson traces the history of the transition of professions from performing predominantly economic functions to an ideological function which justifies inequality of status and market control of access to favored groups. The power of expertise coupled with the power of market control has been enhanced by the links between the professions and their bases in universities.[46] Forces are at work, however, to reduce market controls. For example, advertising restrictions for physicians, lawyers, dentists, and others are being lifted. [47] Professionals have also been warned by the Antitrust Division of the Justice Department not to form price-fixing guilds to reduce or eliminate competition.[48] Current deregulation movements, in the form of licensing and certification reforms, are under way in several states.[49] Virtually every profession is deeply troubled, and most are in the process of renewal and reform.

The need for professional reform extends to the universities where professionals are trained. Professional schools in universities, in response to the knowledge explosion, have squeezed the liberal arts and humanities out of both the professors' own educations and the students' curricula. According to White, "given the increasingly narrow education of professionals, the subculture of the school that fosters isolation, and professional practice that deemphasizes social accountability, it is not surprising that the professional-school curriculum is deficient in humanistic concerns."[50]

---

[44] *Behavior Today*, May 27, 1974, p. 150. See also Corinne Lathrop Gilb, *Hidden Hierarchies: The Professions and Government* (New York: Harper & Row, 1966).

[45] Bernard Barber, "Control and Responsibility in the Powerful Professions," *Political Science Quarterly* 93 (Winter 1978), pp. 599–615. See also Jacques Barzun, "The Professions under Siege," *Harper's*, October 1978, pp. 61–68.

[46] Larson, *The Rise of Professionalism*. See also Barton Bledstein, *The Culture of Professionalism* (New York: Norton, 1977).

[47] "Ads Start to Take Hold in the Professions," *Business Week*, July 24, 1978, pp. 122–124.

[48] *Behavior Today*, October 29, 1979, p. 2.

[49] *The Wall Street Journal*, January 8, 1975, p. 1; *The Wall Street Journal*, June 14, 1977, p. 48; *Behavior Today*, November 12, 1979, pp. 1–2; Jeffrey Pfeffer and Gerald R. Salancik, *The External Control of Organizations* (New York: Harper & Row, 1975), pp. 208–210.

[50] David E. White, "Minds in a Groove," *The Chronicle of Higher Education*, May 28, 1979, p. 4. See also Chris Argyris and Donald A. Schon, *Theory in Practice: Increasing Professional Effectiveness* (San Francisco: Jossey-Bass, 1974), pp. 139–196.

THE MANAGER AS A PROFESSIONAL

Professionalism is more than education, more than experience, more than training. It is a state of mind.[51] This noble sentiment is striking, but it contains an important question for the manager: How can the benefits of professional attitudes be applied to the management of the socially responsible enterprise?

The collapse of the professions has been largely the result of the insinuation of the spirit of Envy into them. The professions were the true leaders of a middle-class society, when that society still had confidence in its own values. The doctors and the teachers and the ministers were the leaders of opinion in villages, in small towns, in neighborhoods in the large cities, not very well paid and not even with much worldly prestige, but enjoying a deserved respect in their communities, which in turn earned them a deserved authority. Now they are well paid, in comparison with the past, and they enjoy no respect and have ceased to be leaders. They no longer stand inside their societies, but at the same time as the exemplars of the values that society is most likely to let slide; they have become mere mercenaries of their societies, like others, the exemplars of everything in them that corrupts and, if not challenged, is bound to corrupt even the best that they can produce.

HENRY FAIRLIE, *The Seven Deadly Sins Today* (Washington, D.C.: New Republic Books, 1978), pp. 76–77.

There have been minor efforts to turn management into a formally recognized, full-fledged profession. That such efforts have failed indicates that the manager's pursuit of professionalization in its traditional mode is a delusion. This aim lacks the support of history and tradition — which is to say, a chance for public acceptance. Examinations, licensing, and training requirements would be difficult to formalize and administer. Moreover, management is not a homogeneous occupation; it is instead an assortment of many occupational interests.

Another difficulty lies in organizing management as a profession. True professionals have strong associations that provide codes of ethical conduct, rules of entry and exit, standards of evaluation, and a strong sense of identity and unity of purpose for members. There is no overarching association for managers, although some of the subdivisions of the management field have them. There are no uniform codes of behavior, no licensing by state or peer group bodies, and no prescribed

---

[51] Michael Novak, "One Species, Many Cultures," *American Scholar* 43 (Winter 1973–1974), p. 116.

educational requirements. Furthermore, the manager in a typical organization is evaluated primarily by superiors rather than peers and colleagues. Thus autonomy in the selection of clients and in the practice of a specialty is not practical.

The social and economic desirability of regarding management as a profession is also in question. Drucker writes:

> Management . . . is a practice, rather than a science or a profession, though containing elements of both. No greater damage could be done to our economy or to our society than to attempt to "professionalize" management by "licensing" managers, for instance, or by limiting access to management to people with a special academic degree. . . .
>
> Any serious attempt to make management "scientific" or a "profession" is bound to lead to the attempt to eliminate those "disturbing nuisances," the unpredictabilities of business life—its risks, its ups and downs, its "wasteful competition," the "irrational choices" of the consumer—and, in the process, the economy's freedom and its ability to grow.[52]

Even if it were possible to become a profession, managers would still confront the forces of disillusionment with the existing professions.

Although it is futile for managers to chase the rainbow of full professionalization, at least two strategies can help managers reap some of its benefits. First, as Sayles suggests, they can adopt a direct strategy consisting of dropping nonstatus activities, claiming jurisdiction over high-status activities, and restricting management jobs to persons with specific professional training.[53] Limited informal certification programs through continuing education courses and association-administered examinations are increasingly accepted by managers.[54] Such efforts are more successful among the subfields of management than among general managers. Personnel directors, purchasing agents, and public relations directors, for example, have association-sponsored certification procedures and ethical codes. Only a few occupations in management, such as accounting and engineering, have achieved legally based certification through state licensing laws.

A more viable strategy for managers is to internalize in their attitudes and behavior the basic values of professions. This indirect approach is slower and unlikely to ensure high social status. But it will encourage better performance, leading to ultimate improvement in public respect. As organizations shift to more open, adaptive modes, professional attitudes and values will be in greater harmony with prevailing leadership styles.[55]

---

[52] Peter F. Drucker, *The Practice of Management* (New York: Harper & Row, 1954), pp. 9, 10.

[53] Leonard Sayles, *Managerial Behavior* (New York: McGraw-Hill, 1964), pp. 116–117.

[54] Herbert J. David and Harvey W. Rubin, "Professional Certification in Management," *Atlanta Economic Review* 28 (March–April 1978), pp. 48–51.

[55] For an excellent but pessimistic discussion of the conflict between professionals and the needs of organizations, see William G. Scott and David K. Hart, *Organizational America* (Boston: Houghton Mifflin, 1979), chap. 6.

The professional attitudes of greatest benefit to managers include the following:

1. *Autonomy and independence* — rejection of the submissive "organization man" concept.
2. *Objectivity* — a sense of detachment from emotional involvement and a factual, logical approach to problems.
3. *Expertise* — the cultivation of managerial and administrative skill and the ability to think in terms of policy.
4. *Service to others* — commitment to work not only with and through others, but for them as well.
5. *Mobility* — in search of greater challenge and opportunity for the use of expertise, greater movement among as well as within organizations.
6. *Ethical behavior* — responsiveness to ethical and moral aspects of decision making.
7. *A sense of calling* — a feeling that the manager's mission and performance are part of a larger framework that gives meaning to managerial responsibilities.

The social responsibility aspects of the manager's task are clearly reflected in these attitudes. In the next section of the book, we turn to a study of the societal framework within which these attitudes are achieving increasing prominence.

Incident Case

Al Wilson wrote up his résumé for use in applying for a position as instructor of business management in a two-year junior college. He awarded himself a non-existent Ph.D. from a university of high reputation. This was not discovered by the institution that hired him until he was well into his second year. His work performance during this time was excellent. When his dean discovered the false entry in his résumé, Wilson was discharged without a hearing.

Discuss the implications of this case.

Issues for Discussion and Analysis

1. Should managers try to reduce the gaps in understanding between themselves and leading intellectuals? If so, how? If not, why not?

2. Should managers pay greater attention to the prophetic voices of our time? Why or why not?

3. Argue the case pro and con as to whether managers should be examined and licensed for the practice of their profession.

4. How can professionals best meet the criticisms and new expectations prevalent in society?

5. What factors work against the manager who wishes to cultivate professional attitudes in his or her work life?

Class Project

Form class members into an appropriate number of task force groups, each of which is to investigate the problems of specific occupations that are attempting to achieve greater professionalization. Each group will then report orally to the class as a whole.

For Further Reading

BLANKENSHIP, RALPH L. (ed.). *Colleagues in Organizations: The Social Construction of Professional Work* (New York: Wiley, 1977).

BLEDSTEIN, BURTON. *The Culture of Professionalism* (New York: Norton, 1977).

BUCHER, RUE, and JOAN G. STELLING. *Becoming Professional* (Beverly Hills, Calif.: Sage Publications, 1977).

CULLEN, JOHN B. *The Structure of Professionalism* (Princeton, N.J.: Petrocelli Books, 1978).

FREIDSON, ELIOT. *The Professions and Their Prospects* (Beverly Hills, Calif.: Sage Publications, 1974).

GOULDNER, ALVIN W. *The Future of Intellectuals and the Rise of the New Class* (New York: Seabury Press, 1979).

GROSS, RONALD, and PAUL OSTERMAN (eds.). *The New Professionals* (New York: Simon and Schuster, 1972).

JACKSON, JOHN A. (ed.). *Professions and Professionalization* (New York: Cambridge University Press, 1971).

JOFFE, CAROLE E. *Friendly Intruders: Professionals and Family Life* (Berkeley: University of California Press, 1977).

KADUSHIN, CHARLES. *The American Intellectual Elite* (Boston: Little, Brown, 1974).

LANSBURG, RUSSELL D. *Professionals and Management* (Lawrence, Mass.: Queensland University Press, 1978).

LYNN, KENNETH S., and THE EDITORS OF *Daedalus*. *Professions in America* (Boston: Beacon Press, 1967).

MAY, JUDITH V. *Professionals and Clients: A Constitutional Struggle* (Beverly Hills, Calif.: Sage Publications, 1976).

MOORE, WILBERT E. *The Professions: Roles and Rules* (New York: Basic Books, 1970).

NASH, GEORGE H. *The Conservative Intellectual Movement in America since 1945* (New York: Basic Books, 1976).

SLAYTON, PHILIP, and MICHAEL J. TREVILCOCK (eds.). *The Professions and Public Policy* (Toronto: University of Toronto Press, 1978).

STEINFELS, PETER. *The Neoconservatives* (New York: Simon and Schuster, 1979).

STRAUSS, ANSELM L. *Professions, Work, and Careers* (New Brunswick, N.J.: Transaction Books, 1975).

WALLIS, W. ALLEN. *An Overgoverned Society* (New York: Free Press, 1976).

PART II

MANAGEMENT, EXPECTATIONS,
AND
SOCIAL CHANGE

4

Capitalism: The Political and Economic System

Freedom is a system based on courage.

Charles Péguy

I have no respect for the passion for equality, which seems to me merely idealizing envy.

Oliver Wendell Holmes, Jr.

A conservative is a socialist who has become an administrator.

Charles Péguy

Concepts Discussed in This Chapter

1. THE ECONOMIC SYSTEM: CAPITALISM AND FREE ENTERPRISE
2. DEMOCRACY AND THE POLITICAL SYSTEM IN RELATION TO CAPITALISM
3. VALUES OF EGALITARIANISM, FREEDOM, AND JUSTICE IN THE POLITICAL AND ECONOMIC SYSTEM
4. MORAL AND ETHICAL ASPECTS OF THE MANAGER'S POLITICAL AND ECONOMIC BEHAVIOR

More than two centuries after its founding, the United States remains an exemplar of capitalism. The concept of capitalism includes not only relationships among our interacting social institutions, but also certain aspects of democracy and its ideals of liberty, freedom, justice, and equality.

These terms are ideological and abstract, and they are therefore hard to understand. None has definite, unchanging referents, or universal definitions. Usages are subjective and their meaning is therefore related to specific contexts. However, they are key concepts that go to the heart of the structure and functions of our society. And they are vital elements of the manager's approach to social responsibility issues.

THE NATURE OF CAPITALISM

Capitalism is a particular kind of socioeconomic system founded on the idea of private property and consisting of the way society organizes the use and generation of productive resources. Capitalism includes values, attitudes, beliefs, habits, traditions, and an ideology that sets it apart from opposing systems.

Beyond the recognition of its tripartite nature—economic, political, and cultural—there is little agreement as to the basic characteristics of capitalism. Capitalism has an organic, dynamic quality, with the result that it changes as the ideas and needs of people change.

Capitalism is often described by comparison with the feudal system that preceded it in Europe, or with Marxian or other socialist systems. This reflects different conceptions about property rights, private versus public interests, and the relative amounts and kinds of freedom, liberty, justice, and other rights that *ought* to prevail in a society.[1]

The significant elements of capitalism include (1) property: the private ownership of the means of production, including labor, capital, and natural resources; (2) the profit motive as an incentive for the creation and use of productive assets; and (3) the regulation of economic and business activity by the competitive market process, with a minimum of government regulation and planning to maintain the social order. By contrast, the tenets of socialism focus on state ownership of resources and the means of production, the minimal use of profit as an incentive, and on comprehensive if not total regulation and planning by government.

THE EMERGENCE OF CAPITALISM

Pure capitalism in its classic sense does not exist. The classic view, first propounded by Adam Smith in 1776, held that self-interest, rather than government, should be the economy's regulator in a free market, competitive system. Seeking their own self-interest in exchange transactions, individuals would be led by "an invisible hand" to serve an unin-

---

[1] Gordon C. Bjork, *Private Enterprise and Public Interest: The Development of American Capitalism* (Englewood Cliffs, N.J.: Prentice-Hall, 1969), pp. 1–19.

tended ultimate end: the coordination and control of economic life, with benefits to all. The hand was invisible because the rules of the market economy— the laws of supply and demand— were not clearly known and because of the absence of a central planning authority. Competition in the market system would guide and direct the self-interest of the individual.[2]

> *Marx argued that the condition of "the working class" must inevitably grow progressively worse until the time came for a cataclysmic upheaval to destroy "the capitalistic system"; and that might indeed have been the case if the institutional patterns of Western society had proved obdurately unamenable to change. But such has not proved to be the case. The institutional flexibility which had already made it possible for the institution of property to supplant that of feudal fief continued to manifest itself, with the result that the condition of the common people has steadily improved.*
>
> C. E. AYRES, *Toward a Reasonable Society: The Values of Industrial Civilization* (Austin: University of Texas Press, 1961), pp. 292–293.

Adam Smith was, in effect, the founding father of the political economy that was about to emerge. He was not defending an existing social order, and in opposing it he laid the foundations of a liberal system that guided the economic and industrial growth of the next two centuries. This growth brought inevitable changes in interpreting the basic ideas Smith espoused; but despite these modifications, Smith's tenets still have significance for today's capitalism.[3]

The capitalism that began to emerge in the 1840s was thus founded on Adam Smith's philosophy. Business prior to 1840 was essentially mercantile. Merchants carried out commercial transactions, such as exporting, importing, retailing, shipping, banking, and the like. But by 1840 the number of enterprises vastly increased, and different types of specialized firms appeared. Banks, insurance companies, and common carriers were established, with merchants specializing in one or two lines of goods, and concentrating on a single function such as retailing or wholesaling.[4] One of the most profound changes after 1840 was the emergence of the factory system. Capital, only a modest requirement of the earlier modes of production by handcraft or family units, came to be more important. The development of steam power, at first in textiles, spurred the evolution of

---

[2] Adam Smith, *An Inquiry into the Nature and Causes of the Wealth of Nations,* Edwin Cannon edition (New York: Modern Library, 1937), part V.

[3] John E. Elliott, "The Political Economy of Adam Smith: Then and Now," *National Forum, Phi Kappa Phi Journal* 58 (Summer 1978), pp. 41–45. See also William J. Baumol, "The Adam Smith That Nobody Knows," *MBA,* April 1978, pp. 34–35.

[4] Alfred D. Chandler, Jr., *The Visible Hand: The Managerial Revolution in American Business* (Cambridge, Mass.: Harvard University Press, 1977), pp. 15–49.

factories and ushered in the era of industrial capitalism that exists today.[5] This emerging capitalism had a major impact on management. By 1900, the single-unit, owner-managed firm came to be outnumbered by the multi-unit enterprise administered by salaried managers. A wave of mergers in the late nineteenth century eventually led in the United States to the passage of the Sherman Antitrust Act. Large, bureaucratic organizational structures required a new managerial class and spawned a new management movement. A significant result was the separation of ownership from management and the evolution of the corporate form of enterprise. Management itself became a highly specialized form of labor.

THE IDEOLOGICAL BASIS OF CAPITALISM AND SOCIALISM

Neither capitalism nor socialism exists in a pure state. A pure capitalistic system would distribute the basic goods of society entirely by the market system. A pure socialist system would distribute goods entirely by political allocation. The words *capitalism* and *socialism* instead stand for clusters of ideas about opposing political, cultural, and social contexts of economic activity. The two systems are therefore ideologically oriented, and the continuum of ideas makes it difficult to arrive at clear-cut distinctions between them. Some would deny that such distinctions are important. An old joke holds that capitalism is the exploitation of man by man; socialism is the other way around. But contention between the two systems is real, as evidenced in relations between Americans and Soviets, and therefore managers as well as politicians must deal with them. These ideological differences are indicated by phrases modifying the word *capitalism*, such as *democratic capitalism* or *welfare capitalism*.

This warfare of ideas with respect to capitalism, its modifications, and its alternatives divides the political arena into conservatives, liberals, and radicals. Conservatives advocate basic capitalist instruments of the marketplace, finance, and investment; they advocate individualism, and allow only a modest role for government as the provider of order, stability, and occasional economic stimuli. Liberals affirm the free market system and individual political freedoms, but allow for more government regulation against monopoly, unequal bargaining power, business cycles, and environmental problems such as pollution. Radicals reject piecemeal approaches and work for reorganizing the structure of society. They berate capitalism, which they call monopoly capitalism, for poverty amid plenty, sexism, racism, economic idealism, alienation, irrationality, and other evils.[6]

---

[5] Herbert J. Muller, *The Children of Frankenstein: A Primer on Modern Technology and Human Values* (Bloomington: Indiana University Press, 1970), pp. 49–50.

[6] Benjamin Ward, *The Ideal Worlds of Economics* (New York: Basic Books, 1979).

INTELLECTUALS AND IDEOLOGY

Capitalism has much to its credit, as well as many failings and inadequacies. There is ample ground for criticism and change, but the arguments center not only on the means and ends of improvement, but also on ideological attacks and defenses of the system itself. It falls to the intellectuals to carry on the ideological debates, though many are also active in changing the present system.

President Eisenhower once remarked that an intellectual is a fellow who uses more words than necessary to say more than he knows. This bit of anti-intellectualism overlooks the important function of intellectuals as critics. The abundance of capitalism's benefits has not prevented the paradox that strident, often hostile attacks come from intellectuals, who enjoy more freedom to think and speak under democratic capitalism than under any other system.

The majority of intellectuals have been liberal but not revolutionary, dissenters but not radicals. Although some hold leftist views, the majority provide a "loyal opposition" which sharpens debate, helps to define issues, and analyzes political issues along with economic ones. Brademas, a well-known congressman, has argued that politics needs intellectuals as well as intelligent people. Their function, he believes, is to evaluate evaluations, to raise questions about policies and programs and the assumptions underlying them.[7] Intellectuals resist ideological labels as unfair or inaccurate because they view various issues differently, or change their views from time to time. Nevertheless, their function as critics of traditional values, though in the name of reason and progress, accounts for tendencies to associate all intellectuals with the Left, though many are on the Right.

The liberalism of the 1950s and the 1960s, with its elitism and ethics of success, power, and style, was rooted in the rise of intellectuals to the status of a privileged class fully integrated into the social fabric.[8] The number of intellectuals critical of capitalist society has never been greater, but they seldom agree either on what is wrong or what the remedies should be. They have been experiencing an ideological crisis of their own, torn between the defense of liberal capitalism and the advocacy of radical thought. Neither socialists nor capitalists are doing well at analyzing the times or predicting what is to come.

In countries where state-owned enterprise is more prevalent than in the United States, such as Britain, France, Germany, Italy, India, and

---

[7] John Brademas, "The Role of Intellectuals in Politics: An American View," in H. Malcolm Macdonald (ed.), *The Intellectual in Politics* (Austin: University of Texas Press, 1965), p. 105.

[8] Christopher Lasch, *The New Radicalism in America, 1889–1963: The Intellectual as a Social Type* (New York: Knopf, 1965), p. 316.

Japan, problems akin to those of capitalism still exist. Products lack quality, workers go on strike, profits are low or absent, price and profit controls hinder entrepreneurship, and politics is rife.[9] Clearly the alternatives to capitalism offer no sure cure for economic and social ills. Moreover, the American radical Left has been a weak influence in society. It has been unable to instill class consciousness in the working class, and Marx's prediction that capitalists would create their own gravediggers in the working class has not materialized.[10] Yet radicals and other leftist critics have usefully underscored some perennial problems associated with capitalism.[11]

Schumpeter noted that the difficulties of defending capitalism are compounded by an intellectual class whose members, however articulate, are unconnected with direct responsibility for practical affairs. He thought that the demise of capitalism would more likely come from the erosion of institutions such as the family and social class than from a revolt of the workers. He also thought that the alienation of the intellectuals would result in ever-increasing assaults on the capitalist system.[12] There is, however, a group of intellectuals of growing importance who, in the interests of freedom and democracy, support the emerging capitalist system but strongly criticize it. They are known as the neoconservatives.

In the 1970s there was a resurgence of conservatism among a number of leading intellectuals. Many had moved to the Left in protesting Vietnam and Watergate, but for humanistic rather than radical reasons. Later many of them moved back toward the Right, becoming known as neoconservatives who now emphasize the need for stability in our social life. They accept the market economy, along with certain aspects of the welfare state that support liberal values, and a foreign policy aimed at preserving freedom in the modern world. They support a liberal democracy and a liberal capitalism, though with different characteristics than traditional liberalism, and a market system with minimum government controls.[13]

These neoconservative intellectuals are deeply involved in the controversies surrounding capitalism and its related concepts of equality, justice, and democracy. Neoconservatism approves of social and economic reforms that entail a minimum of bureaucratic intrusion into the

---

[9] "Socialism vs. Free Enterprise," *U.S. News and World Report,* May 5, 1975, pp. 55–56.

[10] Harold Wohl, "Requiem for a Dream: The Irony of American Radicalism," *Book Forum* 4 (1979), pp. 703–707.

[11] Campbell R. McConnell, "The Economics of Dissent," *MSU Business Topics,* Autumn 1975, pp. 27–29.

[12] Joseph Schumpeter, *Capitalism, Socialism, and Democracy* (New York: Harper & Row, 1942), pp. 134–155; see also Paul Johnson, *The Enemies of Society* (New York: Atheneum, 1977).

[13] Alexander Bloom, "Neoconservatives: Sounding a Liberal Retreat," *MBA* 11 (January 1977), pp. 22–24. For a critical analysis, see Peter Steinfels, *The Neoconservatives* (New York: Simon and Schuster, 1979). See also George S. Nash, *The Conservative Intellectual Movement in America since 1945* (New York: Basic Books, 1976).

individual's affairs, but not those that spawn paternalism or vast bureaucracies to solve social problems. It respects the market system for its power to respond efficiently to economic realities while preserving individual freedom. Though willing to interfere with the market for overriding social purposes, it prefers to "engineer" the market or create new markets rather than use direct bureaucratic controls. Neoconservatives affirm equality of natural rights but reject egalitarianism—the equality of condition or results. The equality they favor includes the right to become unequal in wealth, esteem, or influence, as a consequence of liberty or merit.[14]

Neoconservatives are acutely aware of the problems of capitalism. Kristol, for example, vigorously defends capitalism, but faults its lack of an overarching commitment to the transcendental or spiritual values in human life, so that society seems shortsightedly materialistic.[15] Ethical critiques of business often compare capitalism with socialism to show the latter's ethical superiority, but the neoconservatives have shown that socialism too is oppressive, paternalistic, and dangerous to freedom, liberty, and justice. Neoconservatism is a current of intellectual thought born of disillusion with contemporary liberalism and certain aspects of capitalism. Its relation to the business community Kristol describes as loose and uneasy, but not unfriendly. However, the neoconservatives do not entirely agree; they deny it is really a movement, and they are not enamored of their label.[16]

In the following two sections we will examine the major criticisms of capitalism and the ways its defenders meet that criticism. The ideological structure of both criticism and defense will be apparent, as will the contributions of intellectuals to both sides of the case.

THE CRITIQUES OF CAPITALISM

In essence, the radical updating of Marxian thought holds that (1) monopolistic corporations dominate the economy; (2) the corporate giants dominate the state, so that the state cannot control corporate power in socially desirable ways; (3) a symbiotic relationship exists between corporations and government so that the public sector is the servant of the corporations; (4) regulatory bodies and other social controls are ineffective and inadequate; and (5) the corporation's expansionist tendencies lead to the exploitation and alienation of workers, an

---

[14] Irving Kristol, "What Is a Neo-Conservative?" *Newsweek*, January 19, 1976, p. 17.

[15] Irving Kristol, *Two Cheers for Capitalism* (New York: Basic Books, 1978).

[16] Kristol has refuted the criticisms of Peter Steinfels. See, for example, "Confessions of a True, Self-Confessed—Perhaps the Only—'Neoconservative,'" *Public Opinion* 2 (October–November 1979), pp. 50–52.

irrational, wasteful society, and a lack of equality and justice.[17] Thus, the denigration of capitalism is on moral and ethical grounds as well as on technical, economic, and ideological arguments.[18]

Radical thought about capitalism is a mixture of economic and cultural elements. For a better perspective, we will analyze these elements separately.

ECONOMIC CRITIQUES

Economists hold views that range politically from Left to Right. Both types are critical of aspects of the capitalistic system. An example of a critic on the Right is Milton Friedman. He believes that capitalism has drifted from fundamental precepts such as those of Adam Smith.[19] An example of a critic on the Left is John Kenneth Galbraith, who has advocated wage and price controls, the restraint of large corporations, and government outlays to provide jobs and other social benefits.[20]

Until the 1940s, managed capitalism grew primarily as an economic phenomenon, with little political support among the American electorate. Indeed, the growing concentrations of power in large-scale enterprise appeared to many as contrary to democratic values, discouraging entrepreneurial activity. Also, managers were largely not required to explain or be accountable for their uses of power.[21] Since the 1940s, however, the public has sought to correct, largely through government, the flaws associated with capitalism.

There are many today who are pessimistic about the future of the economy and of the nation, though they remain optimistic about their personal lives, and express faith in our basic social institutions.[22] Economists are trying to find a way out of a condition that has come to be known as *stagflation* — a combination of unemployment and high inflation. Conservatives believe their lack of success is due not only to the technical difficulties of the stagflation problem, but also to the fact that

---

[17] Ibid., pp. 29–35.

[18] See, for example, Michael Novak (ed.), *The Denigration of Capitalism* (Washington, D.C.: American Enterprise Institute, 1979); and Michael Novak (ed.), *Capitalism and Socialism: A Theological Inquiry* (Washingon, D.C.: American Enterprise Institute, 1979). For a socialist view, see Michael Harrington, *The Twilight of Capitalism* (New York: Simon and Schuster, 1976).

[19] Milton Friedman, *Capitalism and Freedom* (Chicago: University of Chicago Press, 1962); Milton Friedman and Rose Friedman, *Free to Choose* (New York: Harcourt Brace Jovanovich, 1980).

[20] John Kenneth Galbraith, *The New Industrial State* (Boston: Houghton Mifflin, 1967); and John Kenneth Galbraith, *The Age of Uncertainty* (Boston: Houghton Mifflin, 1975). See also Sumner M. Rosen (ed.), *Economic Power Failure: The Current American Crisis* (New York: McGraw-Hill, 1975); and Lester Thurow, *The Zero-Sum Society* (New York: Basic Books, 1980).

[21] Chandler, *The Visible Hand*, p. 497.

[22] "A Report from the Editors on the 'Crisis of Confidence,' " *Public Opinion*, August–September 1979, pp. 2–4, 54. See also George W. Ball, "We Are Not Falling Apart," *Across the Board*, September 1979, pp. 42–47.

the economy is managed not by the traditional market forces of supply and demand, but by a mixture of economic, political, and social forces. Political considerations, for example, enter in when the government manipulates the money supply.

Another economic criticism holds that capitalism intensifies poverty. It is uncontested that capitalism produces enormous wealth; maldistribution is the alleged problem. Poverty is intrinsically bad, a form of inequality. Critics allege that inequalities of many kinds arise from the way capitalism separates the haves from the have nots.

Growth is another target of attack. Opponents of growth contend that an expanding economy is destroying the quality of life, depleting natural resources, and polluting the air and water. They forecast the doom of the human race. Those who are pessimistic about economic growth allege that we must learn to accept a different, less materialistic standard of living. The only alternative to "more" is "less." Today many Americans agree that more is not necessarily better for people. They believe that a qualitatively better life can be achieved with less energy and waste — and more stability — than with the linear pursuit of quantitative growth. Most economists are unwilling to give up growth as a motivator of economic performance. Nevertheless it is increasingly clear that even if ecological issues are overstated and even if social problems can be solved with the existing system, the consensus is moving away from reliance on the market as decision maker and from the business-dominated society. The "cowboy economy" — reckless, exploitative, romantic, aggressive — is at an end.[23] A new growth ethic is emerging as people change their minds about the very purposes of life and work.

Imperfections in the marketplace constitute one of the strongest criticisms of capitalism. In theory, the marketplace functions depend on the perfect knowledge of buyers and sellers. In practice, information is subject to many imperfections: distortions, inaccuracy, incompleteness, unavailability, or manipulation. Monopoly forces impinge on the market system, and these have proved difficult to control. The market system is also accused of fostering such things as materialism, conspicuous consumption, and product obsolescence.

CULTURAL CRITIQUES

Qualitative, value-oriented criticisms of the capitalistic system are intermingled with the economic ones; there is no exact demarcation among them. Poverty, for example, can be viewed as a problem of faulty income distribution, and also as a devastatingly inhumane condition that

---

[23] 'Adam Smith,' "The Last Days of Cowboy Capitalism," *The Atlantic*, September 1972, pp. 43–56.

contradicts professed values. Growth can be viewed as an economic motivator, but also as a generator of greed, materialism, envy, and other character defects.

Bell sees the conflicts over capitalism as arising from a separation of two realms that were formerly joined together: the Puritan work ethic and the Puritan sense of calling. The organizational norms of the economic realm run counter to the norms of self-realization now widespread in our culture. These "cultural contradictions of capitalism" reflect a disjunction between the traditional Puritan ethic and the newer materialistic hedonism. New values did not immediately emerge to replace the old, causing a gap between earlier capitalism and the changing shape of culture and politics.[24]

Imperfections in the market system generate many of the cultural as well as economic criticisms of capitalism. The seeds of self-destruction seemingly inherent in capitalism include its inability to restrain excesses, such as the encouragement of materialism by advertising, and putting competition and profit above the public interest or the common good. Capitalism tolerates faults which the free market system alone cannot correct. Centering on the preferences and appetites of people, capitalism arouses the countervailing idealism of the "new class," which stands for quality of life as opposed to acquisitive, self-centered, win-at-all-costs behavior. It is easier to mobilize activist public opinion behind such issues as environmentalism, ecology, consumer protection, and economic planning, and to couple these with government intrusion and coercion, than to wait for the market system to improve things for ordinary people or the deprived. This encourages a state capitalism, with its limitations on liberty.[25]

Businesspeople themselves abet the "politicizing" of economic decisions by demanding government rescue from their mistakes, and by otherwise escaping the disciplines of the market. Henry Ford II has stated that the market, which has rendered capitalism the most humane and effective of systems, is the one thing capitalists themselves distrust the most. Businesspeople believe in the market and in competition, but they also accept subsidies, resist deregulation, and control market forces. This is self-interest, but it is not immoral; it reflects the difficulties of managers in grappling with ideological issues. It is not their forte; by training and experience, their task is to run their companies in the best interests of the stockholders. It is unrealistic to expect businesspeople voluntarily to forego market rewards or profits to foster social justice, though government coercion has moved them in this direction.[26]

---

[24] Daniel Bell, *The Cultural Contradictions of Capitalism* (New York: Basic Books, 1976).

[25] Irving Kristol, "Business and the 'New Class,'" *The Wall Street Journal*, May 19, 1975, p. 12.

[26] George Melloan, "Mr. Kristol on Liberal Capitalism," *The Wall Street Journal*, April 25, 1978, p. 16.

Wolfe notes that the history of politics in capitalist society is one of tension between liberal and democratic conceptions of the state, and that efforts to reduce these tensions have been unsuccessful. Economic power is accompanied by intractable social problems, leading to an increased drive for authoritarian solutions.[27] Van den Haag believes that the free market idea is resented because it functions independently of moral justice. Traditional morality and the Church defended the status quo and promised to balance accounts in the next world, but the efficiency and rational temperament of the market tended to destroy such supportive mythologies. There is no way, he suggests, for the market to satisfy moral expectations, because for all practical purposes they cannot be quantified. In a planned society, the function of both justice and production is in the hands of the planners. The invisible law of supply and demand is seen as morally capricious, and the unfulfilled promise of capitalism is always resented. When a planned society fails to deliver, it claims to be in a transitional stage to a better one.[28]

Critics also allege personality distortions. People paradoxically yearn to make choices, but they also fear choice as a form of responsibility. They are reluctant to assume the full risk of self-determination and being human. It is an example of what Erich Fromm called "escape from freedom." Capitalism channels aggressive impulses into constructive action, but it does not satisfy the emotional part of the human personality. With all our material needs satisfied by an affluent capitalism, the modern human has become a problem-seeker in need of challenges. This new personality of our time is characterized by a compulsive spirit of contrariness.

The free market society is a fragile institution. It has existed for only a very short time and over a limited portion of the globe. But for most of recorded history, most human beings have led a marginally subsistent life, plagued by famine, disease, ignorance, and tyranny. Capitalism is important not because it is a preordained natural order, but rather because it is linked with the Protestant ethic and the evolution of Western democratic values. Therefore it is a delicate, artificial institution which, though it has alleviated many of the material ills of the human race, has also generated rising expectations. The free market abets its own crisis and spurs its own critics, especially at a time when the traditional props of church, family, and local community are eroding.

The relationship between capitalism and democracy is another major issue. In a devastating critique, Lindblom portrays capitalism as inconsistent with democracy principally because of the immense political power

---

[27] Alan Wolfe, *The Limits of Legitimacy: Political Contradictions of Contemporary Capitalism* (New York: Free Press, 1977).

[28] Ernest van den Haag (ed.), *Capitalism: Sources of Hostility* (New Brunswick, N.J.: Transaction Books, 1979).

of the business community. Business leaders are seen as a privileged class, with privileged access to government and the press, and with a base of financial power by which they overpower other groups. Lindblom objects to the inequalities associated with democracies and generated by property and the inheritance of wealth. His quarrel is not with the democratic process or with the market system, but with the role of business itself.[29]

Another set of criticisms of capitalism centers on its lack of flexibility, innovation, and adaptiveness. One economist, for example, echoing Schumpeter, asserts that capitalism's loss of flexibility is seen in the difficulties of converting from oil to other forms of energy such as coal.[30] Gilder notes that we have come to reject risk and to demand that government shield business from uncertainty. The result is gigantic machinery designed to maintain the status quo, to fight crises one at a time, and to seek short-run benefits at long-run costs.[31]

Another set of critics, among them the futurists and the environmentalists, charge capitalism with the depletion of resources, damage to the earth, the excessive use of energy, materialism, and unrestrained growth. Energy and growth problems lead them to deplore traditional economic theories and to support government constraints and public interest legislation against corporations. They see the present world condition as a race against disaster, and worry about population growth and the unequal distribution of global resources.[32] They advocate drastic changes in the nature of the capitalistic system, such as worker participation in management decisions akin to that in Yugoslavia.

Capitalism is criticized for its social as well as its economic inequalities. For example, certain segments of society, such as blacks, Mexican-Americans, or American Indians, have not achieved parity with the rest of society. We are told that our society is racist, that it suppresses minorities and forces them into the ghettoes. One can scarcely deny that racial prejudice exists in this country or most of the rest of the world. This anti-capitalist charge goes largely unanswered, for many believe that the accusations are at least partly true.

Although people reject specific attacks on the free enterprise system, they also believe that somehow our system is not functioning properly. Citing higher expectations, Alan Greenspan says: "There is no better way to undermine any institution than to set a standard for it which by its

---

[29] Charles Lindblom, *Politics and Markets* (New York: Basic Books, 1978).

[30] *Business Week*, January 14, 1980, p. 24.

[31] George Gilder, "Prometheus Bound," *Harper's*, September 1978, pp. 35–42. See also George Gilder, *Wealth and Poverty* (New York: Basic Books, 1980).

[32] Hazel Henderson, "Redefining the Rights and Responsibilities of Capital," *Management Review* 66 (October 1977), pp. 9–19.

nature or the current state of the art is unachievable."[33] The list of complaints about capitalism can be briefly summarized. It creates social injustice; it is unconcerned with public welfare; it depletes and pollutes the environment; it is permissive about corruption; it has no respect for tradition; it has no vision beyond profit; it tempts us to materialism and subjects us to moral decay. Sennett portrays the most pessimistic view — that capitalist, urban, secular culture has led to unbalanced personal and public life. He sees both public and private life as better in precapitalist days, with public and private lives in better balance than they are now.[34]

THE CASE FOR CAPITALISM

The allegations against capitalism reveal serious problems, but they must be weighed against its attainments: the creation of an enormous productive enterprise yielding a high standard of living, a high level of economic and social mobility for millions, and resources for building great museums, churches, hospitals, and universities. With all its flaws, free enterprise capitalism has done more for people than any other system.

Even the most ardent advocates of capitalism acknowledge its deficiencies, but critics have not shown that alternative systems do better. Beyond its tangible benefits, capitalism provides for the psychic, emotional, esthetic, and spiritual needs of people: freedom, democracy, liberty, and justice are among capitalism's precepts.

Defenders of capitalism may be judged best by what they seek to defend. Those who defend classical, laissez-faire free enterprise capitalism unrestrained by regulation or control are hopelessly foundering on a utopian ideal, though one that contrasts sharply with radical utopian dreams. Defenders of this type seem out of touch with the times, wishing for bygone days. The apologetics of hard-line defenders ignore current realities, changing values, and the serious flaws in capitalism which people are no longer willing to accept. Friedman's desire to return to the precepts of Adam Smith leads him to espouse strategies that could be realized only with great difficulty. For example, he advocates tying the expansion of the money supply to the rate of the economy's growth, simplification and reduction of taxes, the end of central bank manipulations of the money supply and interest rates, a "negative income tax" to replace welfare programs, the end of import restrictions, abolishing big government such as the Department of Energy and other agencies, and

---

[33] Alan Greenspan, "Challenge to Our System" (Washington, D.C.: American Enterprise Institute), reprint no. 13 (April 1973).

[34] Richard Sennett, *The Fall of Public Man* (New York: Knopf, 1977).

the winding down of the social security program.[35] Let us look instead at some more moderate defenses and proposals.

THE MARKET SYSTEM

We now have a system of modified capitalism which has many benefits on the credit side of the ledger. The market system is the prime supplier of information that guides the decisions of millions. Price-cost signals are the most rapid socioeconomic communication device for planning and development as well as for consumers. They transmit information more quickly, more efficiently, and more pervasively than does any other system. The market is a rational way to allocate resources in a developed economy; it is necessarily a key economic institution in modern societies, even under socialism. The freedom of free enterprise includes the freedom to be wrong, to make mistakes. Without this kind of freedom, only the state could specify what is right.[36]

The market is a means of organizing and coordinating the most precious thing any person can offer society—namely, skill and ability. This means that capitalism is supported by its accompanying wage and price system, which regulates the flow of goods and services. Someone must take the risk of bringing labor, materials, and capital together before anything can be produced. This is the entrepreneur's function. The entrepreneur gains from judging the market properly, in the form of profit. Those who are wrong will suffer loss.

McGuire raises the question, is our choice to perfect the capitalistic reality by bringing it into conformance with capitalistic theory, or should we go at it the other way around. In search of the perfect system, he argues, we may have created a quite different system. Since self-interest in a competitive environment failed to fulfill its original promise for regulating the system, controls over self-interest emerged. Capitalism is a vigorous system that can survive an increasingly cumbersome network of laws, rules, and regulations. However, continued governmental tinkering with business control mechanisms could have grave consequences. Too much control, even with good intentions, could stifle the capitalist spirit. The control system has already become too complex, too intricate, too rigid, and too easily misinterpreted, diverting entrepreneurs from their desire to focus on economic self-interest.[37]

---

[35] Friedman, *Capitalism and Freedom*.

[36] Martin Mayer, *Today and Tomorrow in America* (New York: Harper & Row, 1975), pp. 35–37.

[37] Joseph W. McGuire, "Perfecting Capitalism—An Economic Dilemma," *Business Horizons* 19 (February 1976), pp. 5–12.

> *Business needs to demonstrate its dissent, and not just by writing letters to governmental officials or even by putting ads in the newspapers. Businessmen need to demonstrate in Washington as the civil rights activists demonstrated, and as the anti-Vietnam activists, the environmental activists, and the higher-farm-price activists did. We need a businessmen's liberation movement, and a businessmen's liberation day, and a businessmen's liberation rally on the monument grounds in Washington attended by thousands of businessmen shouting and carrying signs. We need a few businessmen to chain themselves to the White House fence—and do it themselves, not have it done by their Washington reps.*
>
> HERBERT STEIN, *The Wall Street Journal*, June 12, 1978, p. 14.

INFLATION

Inflation is not inevitable under capitalism. Though it has existed prior to big government, Stein holds that it is caused by government, not by capitalism. He reasons that if the inflationary policy of government were necessary in the economic system, if it met the demands of people for high real incomes, high employment and security, one might consider inflation a normal part of the system. But these results have not emerged. Inflation has not reduced unemployment, speeded up the growth of real incomes, or moderated insecurity. In fact, its result has been negative on all these scores.[38]

POVERTY

The allegation of creating or not alleviating poverty should be examined in the framework of relative economic well-being. Capitalism has improved the conditions of life for most individuals. Capitalism's wealth is not merely that of cathedrals or pyramids, kings or church, but also of products and services for satisfying the needs and wishes of ordinary people. Although some people are deprived, their numbers are small compared to those who are freed from the misery in which their forebears lived for centuries. Both capitalism and socialism have poverty, but it is not as severe as in many noncapitalistic societies. Capitalism alone cannot provide even a minimum for the unemployables. But capitalism makes possible a large amount of charitable giving, and most economists

---

[38] Herbert Stein, "Economics at the New Yorker," *The Wall Street Journal*, November 12, 1979, p. 12.

agree that some form of income transfer program operating through the tax structure is needed.

ETHICAL AND MORAL ISSUES

According to Pichler, capitalism yields at least three benefits. First, the system encourages creativity by providing an incentive for firms to develop and supply goods and services of the type, quality, price, and esthetic values desired by consumers. Second, capitalism enforces personal responsibility and efficiency in economic activity because it rewards individuals on the basis of their productivity. Those who squander resources or misjudge consumer desires bear the burden of their mistakes by an economic loss. Third, the system operates by purely voluntary transactions.[39]

Pichler also states that ethical standards can be expressed and preserved under capitalism and that competition does not inevitably drive morality to its lowest level. In most cases, these effects occur because the normative system cannot be fully implemented in an imperfect world. Most of the defects of capitalism come from departures from it rather than adherences to it. There is nothing in the classical model of capitalism that inevitably produces immorality; the system reflects the moral standards of consumers in their purchases. The market allows people to act morally or immorally, provided they are willing to pay the consequences.

Competition is a strong force that protects as well as erodes morality. Two conditions are necessary for capitalism to protect ethical standards. First, each individual must possess a set of moral values and be willing to express them in the marketplace. Second, individuals can make moral choices in the marketplace only if they have information on product characteristics, production processes, and managerial practices. The market itself produces substantial information by reflecting the direct experience of purchases, advertising, and reports of independent firms specializing in product testing. It is also important to the information process that we have a free press to provide reliable reports on the policies of firms; investigative reporting is a big help.[40]

One of the attractive features of capitalism has been its view that humans are propelled by self-interest. But since self-interest sometimes collides with the public interest, it has to be controlled through legislation. The propensity of businesspeople to embrace the gospel of social re-

---

[39] Joseph A. Pichler, "Is Profit without Honor? The Case for Capitalism," *National Forum, Phi Kappa Phi Journal* 58 (Summer 1978), pp. 3–6.

[40] Ibid.

sponsibility threatens the concept of self-interest and hence could move society away from capitalism and toward some vaguely defined alternative system.

ECONOMIC GROWTH

The United States has not completed its economic development, but it has the slack to continue its growth, and also to correct some of its pressing social problems. The availability of underused human resources allows for expansion without significant lost opportunities. It should be possible to restore growth, but it would be wrong to feed the fire to let the system take off on its own, duplicating the errors of the past. Greater attention needs to be given to the social dimensions involved in economic change.[41]

> *I myself think that capitalism will survive, because of its enormous intrinsic virtues as a system for generating wealth, and promoting freedom. But those who man and control it must stop apologizing and go onto the ideological offensive. They must show to ordinary people that both the Communist world, and the Third World, are parasitical upon industrial capitalism for their growth technology. That without capitalism, the 200 years of unprecedented growth which have created the modern world, would gradually come to an end. We would have slow growth, then nil growth, then minus growth; and then the Malthusian catastrophe.*
>
> PAUL JOHNSON, "Has Capitalism a Future?" *The Wall Street Journal*, September 29, 1978, p. 14. Reprinted by permission, © Dow Jones & Company, Inc. All rights reserved.

Growth itself is not the cause of capitalism's defects. Beckerman calls the antigrowth theorists blatantly selfish, since zero economic growth would preserve the riches of majorities while condemning millions to poverty and disease. He alleges that they are misinformed about pollution (there is less, not more pollution now and the remainder can be reduced while the economy expands), and they are flatly wrong in their facts.[42]

FREEDOM, EQUALITY, AND JUSTICE

An important defense of capitalism is that it is the most efficient system of production yet devised. In a world of shortages, this is a critical

---

[41] Peter S. Albin, *Progress without Poverty: Socially Responsible Economic Growth* (New York: Basic Books, 1979).

[42] Wilfred Beckerman, *Two Cheers for the Affluent Society* (New York: St. Martin's Press, 1975).

factor. Yet the case for capitalism rests on higher grounds. In providing for material needs, it also yields two things all humans have craved— namely, freedom and order. In noncapitalist systems, the government owns the means of production, and bureaucrats decide what is to be produced and where and how people should work. Planned economies deprive people themselves of important choices.

Another appealing feature of capitalism is its concept of justice, wherein individuals are rewarded according to their contributions. The elite achieve status because of meritorious performance. Ignorant and inefficient people are penalized. Unfortunately, the record of American society in perfecting justice to bring it closer to the theory of capitalism is somewhat mixed. Society needs better ways of rescuing those who are deprived through no fault of their own.

Capitalism is inextricably linked to the pursuit of broad social values associated with democratic principles of government. Freedom, equality, and justice are prime values in democratic capitalism. They provide a system of checks and balances that counteracts the tendency to give way to the pressures of the moment. Democracy's freedom outweighs the totalitarian state's promise of security. Freedom of thought generates opportunities, knowledge, questions, and ultimately wealth, which are the engines of capitalism.

Democracy is both a political philosophy and a system for organizing society. A democratic society is a dynamic system, with freedom, based on reason, the engine of change. Faith in reason insists that the poverty of democracy offers a greater hope for humankind than the prosperity of aristocracy or despotism. Democracy assumes a constant making and remaking of laws and institutions. People always have something to say, and the freedom to say it. Lapham asserts that democratic government constitutes the only morality currently operative in the world. It is the attempt to organize the freedom of the mind against the tyranny of money or superstition.[43]

Except for the neoconservatives, intellectuals have been antagonistic toward capitalism, and they tend to discount the connection between capitalism and liberty. The rise of the new class in the concern of intellectuals for human rights is born of the reassertion of fundamental values. Thus there is hope that the correlation between capitalism and democracy will become clearer. Intellectuals see the oppression of dictatorial regimes and the greedy, exploitative capitalist brought together by the thirst for power and profit. However, empirical data do not support this connection.

Democracy stands at the opposite extreme from totalitarian regimes.

---

[43] Lewis H. Lapham, "The Accounts of Democracy," *Harper's*, February 1980, pp. 8–14.

In between there are socialist countries like England or the Scandinavian countries, which consider themselves democratic but accept a high degree of governmental control. Democratic nations have capitalistic economies with social systems that support them. In socialist and totalitarian nations the government owns most of the capital, and there is less democracy. Democratic regimes throughout the world have capitalist economies. There is no major noncapitalist democracy in the world today, nor is there a single socialist country with a democratic form of government. And it is difficult to find a socialist country with a passable record on human rights, including economic rights.[44]

Businesses can benefit from a renewed appreciation of the correlation between democracy and capitalism. But capitalism will not become attractive to its antagonists by the propagation of economic theory or by educational campaigns showing that capitalism produces more and superior goods. However, they might be persuaded by a better understanding of the correlation between capitalism and moral decency. Conversely, businesspersons might also realize that every linkage of profit and torture, whether in rightwing dictatorships or socialist countries, undermines the moral argument by which capitalism will in the end have to defend itself. Those who grasp the connection between capitalism and democracy could possibly go on the moral offensive.[45]

The enemy of democracy is monopoly of power, whether by a political or an economic class. The health of democracy therefore requires a mixed economy and a pluralist society. It requires a public sector strong enough to check the abuses of private economic power and a private sector strong enough to check the abuses of state political power. Though it is hard for democracy to deal with long-term problems such as energy or ecology, the advantage of democratic pluralism is its capacity to correct its own errors. The political process is, in effect, a feedback system through which mistaken policy generates popular reactions that then alter the policy. Business reflects the adaptation of institutions and values to changing material and moral circumstance. Therefore democracy is bound to survive, and its response to human needs is not an illusion. Its ultimate power lies not just in its economic basis, a relatively superficial matter, but in the mixed character of humans. Reinhold Niehbur summed it all up in one sentence: "Man's capacity for justice makes democracy possible; but man's inclination to injustice makes democracy necessary."[46]

---

[44] Peter Burger, "The Link between Capitalism and Democracy," *The Wall Street Journal*, August 3, 1977, p. 16.

[45] Ibid.

[46] Arthur Schlesinger, Jr., "The Future of Democracy," *The Wall Street Journal*, October 31, 1977, p. 14.

EGALITARIANISM

One of the major criticisms of capitalism is that it has generated a vast social and economic inequality which is unjust and therefore should be eliminated. The implication is that since the ideals of equality and justice are codified in the Constitution as inalienable rights, the government should be the prime mover in maintaining those rights. Critics direct their attention to both inequality of income and of status. Business, with its profits and wealth, is a visible target for those who demand a system of literal equality. Equality of result, not merely equality of opportunity, is demanded as the only way of measuring justice.

These critics attack not only business, but the educational system as well, and they oppose competition, merit differentials, and the rewards of vocational success. They want people to be equal in terms of income, education, quality of jobs, and political power. Gans[47] and Jencks,[48] for example, advocate governmental regulation of income distribution, and Rawls[49] asserts that only through such control can a society minimize individual differences and thereby achieve justice.

Equality and justice are worthy goals, but egalitarianism envisions major changes in capitalism and democracy. Achieving literal equality to some means moving to a more socialistic or government-directed state. Such equality is a threat to the free-enterprise, market system of capitalism.[50] We have already entered a new stage of capitalism that reflects new relationships among business, government, and society. While preserving the profit motive and the market system, these new relationships are an effort to make capitalism more responsive to society by fostering equal employment opportunity, income redistribution, consumer protection, and job safety regulations.[51]

Inequalities in capitalistic systems that would hardly attract attention elsewhere are singled out for powerful social criticism. Tradition, the medieval belief in magical escapes from life's struggles, and the assurance of ultimate equality in heaven once legitimized even the grossest inequalities. But the market economy weakened religious sanctions, destroyed traditional beliefs, and replaced them with economic rationality. Furthermore, inequalities were constantly being redistributed, along with everything else, in such a way that tradition no longer had an opportunity to operate and ideological support was undermined.[52]

---

[47] Herbert J. Gans, *More Equality* (New York: Pantheon, 1973).

[48] Christopher Jencks, *Inequality: A Reassessment of the Effect of Family and Schooling in America* (New York: Basic Books, 1972).

[49] John Rawls, *A Theory of Justice* (Cambridge, Mass.: Belknap Press, 1971).

[50] John Cobbs, "Egalitarianism: Threat to a Free Market," *Business Week*, December 1, 1975, pp. 86–88.

[51] Fred L. Fry, "A New Stage of Capitalism," *Business Horizons* 21 (April 1978), pp. 23–25.

[52] Edwin M. Epstein and Dow Votaw (eds.), *Rationality, Legitimacy, and Responsibility: Search for New Directions in Business and Society* (Santa Monica, Calif.: Goodyear, 1978), p. 15.

The tensions between the egalitarian ideals of democracy and the tenets of capitalism are producing many of the strains of modern society. Democracy is egalitarian, while capitalism is organized on dominance, leadership, and unequal distribution for savings and growth.[53] This conflict is not necessarily fatal to either, but it is one to which earnest attention needs to be given by managers and citizens alike.[54]

Literal equality would be devastating for society and ruinous to capitalistic enterprise. Equality of results has a broad, misleading appeal because conditions of inequality are widely felt, reflecting disappointment in our system and the failure to live up to traditional values of fairness and equal opportunity. Improvement is to be sought in fairness, justice, and equal opportunity, and not in the coercive state.[55]

The distortion of the idea of equality has enabled the enemies of genuine equality to move to the offensive. Fairlie observes that it pits equals against unequals as if they were equals and yields a breeding ground for envy. The idea that we are equal has been perverted into the idea that we are identical; when we find that we cannot all do and experience and enjoy the things that others do and experience and enjoy, we take our revenge and deny that these things were worth doing in the first place. What requires talent, training, and hard work, we will show can be accomplished without them.[56]

Paglin has found the distortion and overstatement of inequality to be of statistical origin. By shifting from a standard of equal annual income to one of equal lifetime family income within age groups, he eliminates the effects of age structure and evolves a standard that is more meaningful and consistent with varying consumption needs at various stages of the life cycle. The effect of this standard would be to narrow the limits for income redistribution. But inequalities would still exist due to the age mix of families and the average age-income profile.[57] Whether correct or not, these ideas reflect a concern for the data upon which assertions of inequality are often based.

THE FUTURE OF CAPITALISM

After more than two centuries of astounding success as a wealth-producing economic and political system, capitalism has come to face

---

[53] Albert T. Sommers, "A Collision of Ethics and Economics," *Across the Board*, July 1978, pp. 14–19.

[54] Joseph W. McGuire, "The New Egalitarianism and Managerial Practice," *California Management Review* 19 (Spring 1977), pp. 12–20.

[55] Norman C. Hill and Gene W. Dalton, "Business and the New Egalitarianism," *Business Horizons* 20 (June 1977), pp. 5–11.

[56] Henry Fairlie, *The Seven Deadly Sins Today* (Notre Dame, Ind.: University of Notre Dame Press, 1979), pp. 63–64.

[57] Morton Paglin, "The Measurement and Trend of Inequality: A Basic Revision," *American Economic Review*, September 1975, pp. 598–610.

serious challenges. What at first was wide acceptance of capitalism as the answer to poverty and the misery of humans has been replaced by hostility and distrust that now threaten the system as never before.

One of the earliest threats was Marxism, a number of variants of which now govern about one-third of the world's population. Marxists and non-Marxists agree generally on ultimate ends, but disagree on means. While Marxists have not overthrown the major strongholds of capitalism, they have raised fundamental questions about the nature and structure of society. They have fostered revolutionary totalitarianism in much of the world. As Boulding notes, Marx did much harm by the answers he gave to social problems, which were both wrong and plausible and helped to set back the understanding of social dynamics for a hundred years or more, as well as creating an enormous amount of human misery.[58]

Other changes have also brought pressures on capitalism. The increased intervention of government into business activity, recurring business cycles, continuing poverty, and unemployment reflect adversely on the system. But capitalism's overriding difficulties are in the moral and social spheres: materialism, energy shortages, ecological and environmental issues, the women's liberation and equal opportunity movements, the egalitarian mood, the problems of large unions and large corporations, and cries for justice feeding the hostility and distrust.

The word *capital* goes back to the Latin *caput*, meaning head, but some spell it *kapeut*, a German word for something that does not work any more. Capitalism is definitely not *kapeut*, but its survival depends on its ability to adapt to changing demands and public philosophy. Heilbroner argues that capitalism is a static social system, unvarying in its privileges won by the few. Those who own property and those in command in the business world, he argues, have always been rewarded disproportionately. Changes do occur, but in a fixed social setting where social relationships, especially the several classes, do not change. The next stage of capitalism, barring revolution, will be a planned state capitalism with increased government regulation and control protecting but redirecting the profit capabilities of large corporations.[59]

Capitalism is not as static as Heilbroner implies. Schumpeter noted that capitalism is a form or method of economic change that can never be stationary. Its evolutionary character is due not merely to the changing social and natural environment, nor to increases in population and capital, nor to the vagaries of monetary systems. For Schumpeter, the fundamental motivating impulse of capitalism comes from new con-

---

[58] Kenneth E. Boulding, "Marxism and the Future of Capitalism," *National Forum, Phi Kappa Phi Journal* 69 (Winter 1979), pp. 18–22.

[59] Robert L. Heilbroner, *Business Civilization in Decline* (New York: Norton, 1976), pp. 22–50.

sumer goods, new methods of production or transportation, and new forms of industrial organization.[60]

Schumpeter eventually came to the same conclusion as Marx— namely, that capitalism would be replaced by socialism. But Marx attributed the coming of socialism to capitalism's failure, whereas Schumpeter attributed it to capitalism's success. Burns writes, however, that experience is not bearing out the predictions of either. He regards the expansion of government and the control of inflation as the most serious threats to the free enterprise system. As the battle of inflation is won, government intervention could decline, thus restoring the impulse to innovation that Schumpeter saw as the driving force of capitalism, and paving the way for a renaissance of economic growth.[61]

There are signs that conditions working for the survival of capitalism are evolving. Problems such as inflation, tax reform, regulation, governmental organization and efficiency, and business-government relations are being recognized and attacked. The emerging public philosophy reflects a will to meet the challenges to capitalism while retaining or even reemphasizing its values of liberty, freedom, and justice. If capitalism fails, it will not be because it failed to produce prosperity and abundance, but because it could not meet its moral ideals and defend these basic values. Only the shortsighted will dismiss the achievements of capitalism lightly, but it would be naive to believe that they will suffice to legitimize the socioeconomic system. If capitalism ignores matters of the soul, heart, and spirit of people, it can easily overlook the fact that people can despise a system even while enjoying its benefits.[62] Capitalism's survival depends on the correction of its defects, not on improving the rhetoric by which the system is defended.

Incident Case

In May of 1978, a large corporation announced a price increase and explained that it had cleared its action with Robert Straus, head of the price and wage board, for conformity with the president's program to "decelerate" inflation. Since that time, several other corporations have made similar announcements. Others have announced that they will keep salary increases of their executives from exceeding 5 percent, as requested by the administration.

---

[60] Schumpeter, *Capitalism, Socialism, and Democracy.*

[61] Arthur F. Burns, "The Future of Free Enterprise," *Across the Board,* January 1979, pp. 18–24. See also Arthur M. Okun, "Our Blend of Democracy and Capitalism: It Works But It Is in Danger," *Across the Board,* March 1979, pp. 69–76.

[62] Kristol, *Two Cheers for Capitalism,* pp. 3–24.

Why do business executives conform to governmental wage and price guidelines? Analyze this with respect to the basic tenets of capitalism.

Issues for Discussion and Analysis

1. In what ways can capitalism be said to be its own gravedigger? What are the arguments pro and con?

2. How can the element of social justice be appraised under capitalism and its alternatives? Is it "just" that Mohammed Ali should earn more than Jonas Salk, for example?

3. Argue pro and con whether it is realistic to expect businesspeople voluntarily to forego profits to help solve society's problems.

4. James Reston of *The New York Times*, reviewing *The Brethren* by Bob Woodward and Scott Armstrong, stated that "freedom could be too much of a good thing," and that "sometimes you can carry the truth too far." Evaluate these statements.

5. What considerations point to the downfall of capitalism? What factors point to its survival?

Class Project

Set up several task forces among class members to make a comparative assessment of how basic values, such as freedom, justice, or equality, exist in democratic vs. socialistic capitalism. Have each group report its analyses to the class.

For Further Reading

BELL, DANIEL. *The Cultural Contradictions of Capitalism* (New York: Basic Books, 1976).

BRAUDEL, FERNAND. *Afterthoughts on Material Civilization and Capitalism* (Baltimore: Johns Hopkins University Press, 1977).

COMMONS, JOHN R. *Legal Foundations of Capitalism* (Madison: University of Wisconsin Press, 1968).

DAHL, ROBERT A. *After the Revolution: Authority in a Good Society* (New Haven, Conn.: Yale University Press, 1970).

DAHRENDORF, RALF. *The New Liberty: Survival and Justice in a Changing World* (Stanford, Calif.: Stanford University Press, 1975).

EELLS, RICHARD. *The Political Crisis of the Free Enterprise System* (New York: Macmillan, 1980).

ELLUL, JACQUES. *The Ethics of Freedom* (Grand Rapids, Mich.: Eerdmans Publishers, 1976).

ETZIONI, AMITAI. *The Active Society: A Theory of Societal and Political Processes* (New York: Free Press, 1968).

FELLNER, WILLIAM. *Contemporary Economic Problems* (Washington, D.C.: American Enterprise Institute, 1979).

GILDER, GEORGE. *Wealth and Poverty* (New York: Basic Books, 1980).

HEILBRONER, ROBERT L. *Business Civilization in Decline* (New York: Norton, 1976).

HILL, IVAN (ed.). *The Ethical Basis of Economic Freedom* (New York: Praeger, 1980).

HORWITZ, ROBERT H. (ed.). *The Moral Foundations of the American Republic* (Charlottesville: University Press of Virginia, 1977).

JOHNSON, PAUL. *The Enemies of Society* (New York: Atheneum, 1977).

KRISTOL, IRVING. *Two Cheers for Capitalism* (New York: Basic Books, 1978).

LIJPHART, AREND. *Democracy in Plural Societies: A Comparative Exploration* (New Haven, Conn.: Yale University Press, 1980).

MACHAN, TIBOR R. *Human Rights and Human Liberties* (Chicago: Nelson Hall, 1975).

MAYER, MARTIN. *Today and Tomorrow in America* (New York: Harper & Row, 1975).

NELSON, WILLIAM. *On Justifying Democracy* (Boston: Routledge and Kegan Paul, 1980).

NOBLE, DAVID F. *America by Design: Science, Technology, and the Rise of Corporate Capitalism* (New York: Knopf, 1977).

NOVAK, MICHAEL (ed.). *Capitalism and Socialism: A Theological Inquiry* (Washington, D.C.: American Enterprise Institute, 1979).

ROUSSEAU, STEPHEN. *Capitalism and Catastrophe: A Critical Appraisal of the Limits of Capitalism* (New York: Cambridge University Press, 1979).

SILVERT, KALMAN H. *The Reason for Democracy* (New York: Viking Press, 1977).

VAN DEN HAAG, ERNEST (ed.). *Capitalism: Sources of Hostility* (New Brunswick, N.J.: Transaction Books, 1979).

5

The Pluralist Society:
Centers of Power

Pluralist society is free society exactly in proportion to its ability to protect as large a domain as possible that is governed by the informal, spontaneous, custom-derived, and tradition-sanctioned habits of the mind rather than by the dictates, however rationalized, of government and judiciary.

ROBERT NISBET, *Twilight of Authority*, p. 240.
Copyright ©1975 by Robert Nisbet.
Reprinted by permission of Oxford University Press, Inc.

Honk if you're an elitist.

Bumper sticker

CONCEPTS DISCUSSED IN THIS CHAPTER

1. THE PLURALISTIC STRUCTURE OF SOCIETY
2. THE ELITE STRUCTURE OF SOCIETY
3. HIERARCHY AND SOCIAL CLASS
4. POWER RELATIONS AMONG GROUPS IN SOCIETY
5. MANAGEMENT AND PLURALISM

The effective functioning of society depends on its ability to maintain coherence and stability amid an enormous diversity of interacting forces and structures. The management process at this level is obscure and mysterious; it is a result rather than a consciously directed process. There is no definitive, single theory that explains how society is managed. Current theorists see the social structure from three points of view: (1) Society is pluralistic — a segmentation of diverse groupings and interests that overlap and interact. (2) A dominant elite controls the functioning of society. (3) Both pluralism and elitism are at work in society, but neither is dominant. In the absence of conclusive evidence, the third position is the only tenable one.

This chapter describes and analyzes the issues of pluralism and elitism. It also discusses the management problems that follow from the analysis and shows how they influence the manager's tasks and responsibilities.[1]

PLURALISM: DEFINITIONS AND ANALYSIS

Pluralism is a broad term that refers to the existence of multiple centers of power and influence in society. This view of pluralism covers two main contexts: the complex system of governance, and the existence of a diversity of groups and associations.

The use of the term *pluralism* is more narrowly defined by adjectives that explicitly or implicitly reveal specific contexts of concern. Questions of governance fall in the realm of *political pluralism*, which holds that instead of a single center of power and influence there are multiple centers, none of which is or can be wholly sovereign. The only legitimate sovereign is the people, but even their power is not absolute.[2] *Social pluralism* describes the existence of many associations and interest groups to which people belong either formally or informally. The freedom of people and organizations to form and join any associations they desire is an important value in our society. *Cultural pluralism* refers to the varied cultural patterns and traits that characterize the nations and the peoples of the world. Cultural pluralism also exists within a society. In the United States, for example, the patterns of thought and behavior vary greatly from region to region and within regions. People also fall into religious, ethnic, or racial groupings that are forms of cultural pluralism. The various types of pluralism are not mutually exclusive. That is, individuals may belong to more than one of the categories, which serve as classification systems for statistical and research purposes.

A central question in society is that of who has the power and is therefore most influential in running the country. Pluralism is one explanation: Power in a democracy rests with the people, who align themselves with interest groups that consolidate their opinions and assert them in political action. But another explanation holds that powerful elites dominate less powerful groups, thereby controlling the masses. Let us examine how pluralism and elitism function in our society.

---

[1] Parts of this chapter are adapted and revised, with permission, from Dalton E. McFarland, "Management and Its Critics: A Look at Social Pluralism," *Journal of Business Research* 2 (October 1974), pp. 395–408, and "From the Corporate State to Managed Pluralism," *The Record* 12 (July 1975), pp. 14–20.

[2] Robert A. Dahl, *Pluralist Democracy in the United States* (Chicago: Rand McNally, 1967), p. 24.

The controversial issues of pluralism are largely political, for the concept describes the interacting participation of groups in society's governance. Historically there are three types of political pluralism: (1) English political pluralism, (2) political pluralism in the United States, and (3) theories of social and cultural pluralism developed by social anthropologists and sociologists. The English pluralists of the early 1900s used the term to describe the dispersal of power among many groups, but without paying much attention to interrelationships among the groups. American pluralists believe that groups exert political pressure in their own interest, but that they are held together in a sort of web by the balance functions of the federal government. Social and cultural pluralists view groups as separated by cultural and social factors, and hold that the state is kept together by power. All three types are concerned with the forces for unity and diversity within a state.[3]

American society is pluralistic by design. The creators of the Constitution purposely tried to prevent undue centralization of power by decentralization of government and law. Industrialization too favored pluralism by the dispersal of economic activity throughout the society. The pluralist system in the United States is a complex one as measured by (1) the number and variety of components, (2) the extent and incidence of relational interdependence among the components, and (3) the variability of the components and their relationships through time. By contrast, an elitist power structure is a simple one.[4]

There are four major tenets of pluralist theory: (1) Political resources are not distributed equally, but the inequalities are not cumulative, so that a group lacking in one (such as money) can make it up with something else (such as political skills); (2) the number and diversity of groups are so large that any given issue will attract the interest of a range of them who will fight the issue out; (3) organizations form coalitions that divide and re-form according to the situation; and (4) the diversity and number of interest groups represent a similar plurality of interests and issues.[5] These tenets, while plausible, have not been definitively confirmed by research. A British researcher found little support for them at the local community level.[6] Yet at the national level there is strong support for the existence of social and cultural pluralism along the lines of the four tenets.

The tension between centralization and homogeneity on the one

---

[3] David Nichols, *Three Varieties of Pluralism* (New York: St. Martin's Press, 1974), pp. 1–4.

[4] Andrew S. McFarland, *Power and Leadership in Pluralist Systems* (Stanford, Calif.: Stanford University Press, 1969), pp. 15–29.

[5] Ibid.

[6] K. Newton, "Voluntary Organizations in Community Politics: The Hidden 90% of the Iceberg," *Social Science Council Newsletter* (Britain), July 1974, pp. 5–7.

hand and pluralistic diversity on the other raises questions of power distribution in society, and of how an effective balancing of the two sets of forces can be achieved. Dahl, a noted pluralist, states that since even legal and constitutional arrangements can be subverted if some citizens or groups acquire disproportionate power, the potential power of some must be balanced by the countervailing power of others.[7]

The forces for centralization and homogeneity have been increasing in recent decades. These include the scientific-technological revolution, centralization of production and marketing, and increased planning in government and business at the national level. Excessive reverence for science and technology in business, government, education, and many other segments of society can undermine our pluralist-democratic ideals. The danger is that the ideology of pluralism might blind us to the growth of opposing tendencies.[8]

THE DYNAMICS OF PLURALISM

Pluralism is not a rigid, fixed social characteristic; rather it changes as new groups come to be significant and older groups fade in relative influence. We are a heterogeneous society in which new forms of pluralism are emerging alongside the old. Both homogeneity and differentiation exist, but in changing patterns. Douglas notes that new forms of pluralism derive from new forms of freedom, and new forms of freedom are generated by pluralism.[9] For example, the growth of professional identities and groups constitutes a new form of pluralism that could become extremely important. Professionals represent a focal point of social identity that facilitates action. Their stress on autonomy and independence confers power by removing them from traditional controls and influences. The growth of the professions has nurtured a new pluralism in which the professions exert power at highest levels of society.

The increased influence of groups such as advocates of the Equal Rights Amendment, the various consumer interest groups, student activist groups, and the like illustrate how people in a pluralist society can make their concerns widely known. A society rich in autonomous or semi-autonomous groups, communities, and institutions is better able to preserve individual freedom of thought and action. The resulting decentralization distributes governmental powers into many hands, so that workers, families, professionals, neighborhoods, and the like flourish in the spirit of voluntary association.[10]

Membership in formal or informal interest groups affords special

---

[7] Dahl, *Pluralist Democracy*, p. 40.

[8] Jack D. Douglas, *The American Social Order: Social Rules in a Pluralistic Society* (New York: Free Press, 1971), pp. 259–276.

[9] Ibid.

[10] Robert Nisbet, *Twilight of Authority* (New York: Oxford University Press, 1975), p. 237.

benefits to individuals. They provide avenues of access to the community and the general stream of social life, and a means of pursuing individual interests and concerns. They provide a means for expressing and carrying out ideas and attaining objectives, both group and individual. Members can spread their efforts around so that the setback of one or a few groups will have a less important effect. The individual is not totally dependent on a single group, and is also protected from manipulation by a single center of opinion or authority. Voluntary organizations are training grounds for the skills of democracy, and forums for testing ideas and opinions.[11] Nobody knows the exact number of associations, because new ones are constantly appearing. There are approximately 6,300 national trade and professional associations,[12] and the 1980 *Encyclopedia of Associations* lists over 14,000 associations of all kinds. There are even associations that specialize in managing groups of other associations.[13]

POWER AND INTERGROUP RELATIONS

Pluralism is closely linked to theories of collective behavior, since groups are its main components. Groups engage in bargaining to achieve goals, and in exchange forms of interaction — tradeoffs in which one group gives something to get something else. The processes of bargaining, lobbying, logrolling, coalition formation, negotiation, conciliation, and compromise are the methods of pluralistic behavior. The success of such endeavors depends, however, on how well groups organize to bring power and influence to bear. There is nothing natural or automatic about the ability to organize, to acquire resources, or to wield power, but associations are free to pursue their aims by such means. Many groups gain strength through participating in social movements.[14]

Pluralism has a moral basis founded upon freedom and democracy. Since science and morality imply the need for uniformity of policy and decision, what is right could be determined and enforced by government. Yet individuals, societies, and moral problems are diverse, complex, and pose many issues for which imposed answers are futile. Only a pluralism of options, loyalties, and obligations can provide a heterogeneous and diversified society with the needed flexibility for change.[15] Pluralism cannot be defended by asserting that it has always existed and therefore should continue, nor by esthetic or moral confidence in the mere need for

---

[11] Charles Frankel, *The Democratic Prospect* (New York: Harper & Row, 1962), pp. 171–172.

[12] *National Trade & Professional Associations, 1979* (Washington, D.C.: Columbia Books, 1979).

[13] *The Wall Street Journal*, January 11, 1980, p. 1.

[14] William A. Gamson, *The Strategy of Social Protest* (Homewood, Ill.: Dorsey Press, 1975), pp. 130–144.

[15] Stephen David Ross, *Moral Decision: An Introduction to Ethics* (San Francisco: Freeman, Cooper, 1972), pp. 259–277.

variety and excitement in public affairs, nor by the belief that society is completely open, nor by the belief that plural societies are automatically self-correcting. Change under pluralism is often slow. American society, for example, has confronted major issues of intergroup relations only with great difficulty. To endure, pluralism must cope more successfully with such problems as race relations, ethnic differences, and regional conflict.

Pluralism is a game of power that goes by rules once more certain than now and that are changing in the light of changing values. In such a game some win and some lose, though in different respects according to the issue involved. With respect to minority groups, such as blacks and ethnic populations, pluralism contends with assimilation for interpreting social conflict and other social processes. Newman holds that both concepts are appropriate and useful if viewed not as absolutes but as reciprocal aspects of group relationships. Like social change and the social order, group conflict and group consensus, pluralism and assimilation are twin aspects of the same structure. By their distinctiveness, groups have their place in the social order, with processes of conflict forming a dynamic tension that tends to hold society together. Every public issue stimulates a rearrangement of group relationships, and multiple allegiances and conflicts among groups result in a creative tension.[16]

Blacks in particular have doubts about the benefits of pluralism. They have struggled hard to win even a minimal entry into good schools, high government and business positions, and a place of greater equality in society. Clark writes: "Calls for pluralism just at the time when the Negro is demanding full freedom of entrance into previously white-monopolized government employment must be viewed with the suspicion that equal interaction is not the intent of white society."[17] And pluralism with respect to racial and ethnic mixtures has spilled over into problems of education at all levels. Admission, busing, and curricular change reflect changes in power relations among groups. These efforts are controversial and have met with mixed success. For example, black studies, women's studies, and ethnic studies widely introduced into school curricula in the sixties and seventies remain only with great difficulty and at great cost. Vermilye expresses the nature of the dilemma for educators when he asks: "Assuming the creation of a pluralistic society, how can our educational institutions handle distinctions based on talent in a truly equalitarian setting?" And "How do we as educators honor excellence within a pluralistic institution without creating new elites?" "To

---

[16] William M. Newman, *American Pluralism: A Study of Minority Groups and Social Theory* (New York: Harper & Row, 1973), pp. 182–183.

[17] Kenneth B. Clark, *The Pathos of Power* (New York: Harper & Row, 1974), p. 109. See also a symposium on blacks in society in *Change*, October 1979, pp. 24–54, and *The Antioch Review*, special issue on "The Rediscovery of Cultural Pluralism" 31 (Fall 1971).

be a pluralist," he writes, "is to see and know that the melting pot did not melt. . . ."[18]

The fading of the melting pot dream shows the persistence of pluralism, a thoroughly American idea. While some critics contend that the melting pot never worked and others that it worked too well, most agree that public policy should encourage cultural diversity. Ethnic pluralism separates language, literature, and cultural traditions from national interests; the state cannot compel people to "melt" either culturally or racially. Citizenship and nationality thus stand as separate issues.[19]

The federal government generally takes a strong role in resolving interest group conflicts. The formation of public policy requires the reaching of some degree of consensus among the groups most affected, and the role of government is to set and follow the norms of permissible behavior among contending groups. This process often results in a "leveling effect" in which the necessary compromises and tradeoffs cause policies to reflect the lowest common denominator of opinion. Offsetting this problem is the fact that the democratic state is not all-powerful; it must seriously consider the demands and needs of society and its citizens.

Today social movements such as consumerism or women's liberation wield great influence in a society where quality and human rights are watchwords. Groups with power and voice, while they may not get everything they want, do get something, and even when they do not they can try to veto what they dislike. Thus pluralism reflects policy by consensus, but only within the context of social norms and values in a state of continuous change.

CRITIQUES OF PLURALISM

Critics of pluralism allege that interest groups are selfish, that they inhibit progress, that they interfere with economic growth, and that pluralism stems from unchallenged values of the marketplace, so that profits motivate the selfish behavior of organizations. In addition to explicit conflict and pressures for change, groups and organizations may also repress change. In a democracy any group is entitled to express opinions, to preserve itself, and to act in its own interests. Yet on balance there is no evidence that groups can stop or prevent social change. Ultimately what society does is to allow all voices to be heard, resolving issues by legitimate political processes.

---

[18] Dyckman W. Vermilye (ed.), *The Future in the Making: Current Issues in Higher Education* (Washington, D.C.: American Council for Higher Education, 1973), p. 141. See also Melvin M. Tumin and Walter Plotsch (eds.), *Pluralism in a Democratic Society* (New York: Praeger, 1977); and Nathan Glazer and Daniel Moynihan, *Beyond the Melting Pot* (Cambridge, Mass.: MIT Press, 1964).

[19] Diane Ravitch, "Integration, Segregation, Pluralism," *The American Scholar* 45 (Spring 1976), p. 214. See also Howard F. Stein and Robert F. Hill, "The Limits of Ethnicity," *The American Scholar* 46 (Spring 1977), pp. 181–189.

Critics allege, however, that government cannot be the balancing institution, for it too is rife with irresponsible power and too willing to collude with the worst in business institutions. Perrow comments that such pluralistic mechanisms as judicial suits and regulatory agencies are ineffective because they have been coopted by the elites they seek to regulate. He also argues that pluralism, closely scrutinized, is an illusion, and that "pluralistic groups are powerless, competition is trivial, independent enterprise is precarious, and autonomy is an illusion."[20]

That pluralism provides a natural, automatic balancing or self-correcting process is a myth. Pluralism holds that the blending of power among groups occurs only temporarily and by coincidence, and that natural and inevitable differences among them result in continuous regrouping and shifting power leading to a balancing effect. However, automatic balancing is not necessary to pluralist theory, although there are mechanisms and influences in organizations and society that are conducive to balancing effects. Revolutions and disruptions can have power-balancing effects, but so also can the administrative initiatives of organizational bureaucracies.[21]

Another objection to pluralism holds that it protects elites, who create rather than solve problems. It is true that pluralism makes room for activists and protest groups which some might view as a type of elite. But elites too are part of the power system comprehended by pluralism. In a major critique, Kariel wrote that "the organizations which the early theorists of pluralism relied upon to sustain the individual against a unified government have themselves become oligarchically governed hierarchies, and now place unjustifiable limits on constitutional democracy." Kariel's scholarly but unconvincing treatise is one of the early attempts by a political scientist to blame organizational giants for thwarting democracy. Although his evidence is thin, he tries to show how technology and large-scale industrialism have aborted the regulating effects claimed for pluralism. He attacks social researchers as well for giving theoretical respectability to the concept of pluralism, and for applying models of small-group behavior to the task of studying essentially large-group problems.[22]

PLURALISM AND BUREAUCRACY

Gawthrop tests pluralism by its ability to meet the demands of social change. Pluralism, he argues, goes by rules of the game known as political bargaining. The decentralized, fragmented, and subnational

---

[20] Charles Perrow (ed.), *The Radical Attack on Business* (New York: Harcourt Brace Jovanovich, 1972), p. 266.

[21] Paul G. Swingle, *The Management of Power* (Hillsdale, N.J.: Lawrence Erlbaum Associates, 1976), pp. 131–132.

[22] Henry S. Kariel, *The Decline of American Pluralism* (Stanford, Calif.: Stanford University Press, 1961).

orientation of those who advocate an incremental approach to change leads to piecemeal, inflexible attacks on social problems, and to relying on programs that become rigid parts of the bureaucracy. Such a system considers only those alternatives that square with the bureaucratic and bargaining rules of the game.

Depicted as a strategy of games, the pluralist system binds the administrator to its rules, the foremost of which demands the maintenance of system stability. Bureaucratic structures and precepts are needed to control the intense dedication and normative commitments that motivate interest groups to express and act upon their needs, thus upsetting system stability. Since conflict is an essential element of any game, the pluralist system must resolve or restrain conflict through negotiation and compromise. Administrators then place the sanctity of the game ahead of other values, and use tactics that limit the scope and intensity of conflict. This inversion of ends and means works well in a relatively stable environment where administrators have successfully internalized the rules of the game. However, instability, uncertainty, and rapid change are the current reality. Therefore, argues Gawthrop, the pluralistic-bargaining-incremental system is becoming vestigial, and we need a new system more capable of coping with turbulent environments.

Gawthrop favors a "rationalist" alternative to pluralism. Whereas pluralists rely mainly on quantitative-economic measures, deal separately with different parts of the system, and focus on inputs, rationalists combine quantitative methods with subjective and qualitative factors, take a total systems approach, and emphasize outputs. Pluralists respond only to defined, tangible, material needs, whereas rationalists assert that sociopolitical needs, symbolic as well as material, should be expected and met through planning, programming, budgeting (PPB techniques), and other management science methods. Whereas pluralists reduce political problems to economic terms and emphasize efficiency, rationalists include qualitative criteria such as social equity, public welfare, intuition, common sense, and educated guesses.[23] Gawthrop's arguments are worth considering, although it is doubtful that rationalism will replace pluralism.

IDEOLOGICAL CHALLENGES

The literature of social discontent contains many criticisms of pluralism. Futurists, for example, portray managers with doubt, if not contempt. In a popular vein, both Reich[24] and Toffler[25] capitalize on gnawing

---

[23] Louis C. Gawthrop, *Administrative Politics and Social Change* (New York: St. Martin's Press, 1971).

[24] Charles A. Reich, *The Greening of America* (New York: Random House, 1970).

[25] Alvin Toffler, *Future Shock* (New York: Random House, 1970).

public anxieties and frustrations, as do writers of the New Left. They depict a futuristic vision of a decaying society being altered by nonviolent but nevertheless relentless and revolutionary change, wresting from managers their pluralist and individualistic initiatives. Growth, materialism, market enterprise, and competition are the villains, targets for radical reform.

The "gloom and doom" apocalyptic writers are of one mind in their failure to see pluralism as anything but a conspiracy against the public welfare. They view the processes of management and administration as subservient to powerful special interests, devoid of integrity, and intent on enriching elites at the expense of the common person. The crepehangers' alternative that we must accept either the "new culture" or fascism are refuted by Beichman,[26] who deplores the falsifications, distortions, and doom-saying born of ideological passions in the counterculture, and Maddox,[27] who turns to facts and science to refute the claims of the more rabid pessimists that the destruction of society is inevitable.

Gamson argues that pluralism is contradicted at several points. First, he sees no connection between the success of challengers and the means of influence prescribed for members of a group. Challengers have to be aggressive, unruly, perhaps violent (as in the case of some protest movements). Challengers want to gain membership and benefits, not necessarily the group's substantive aims. Second, he asserts that groups use social control strategies against challengers to restrain their coming to power. Even if a society maintains rules that are just, their violation by challengers may evoke control techniques. Third, he notes that groups often have difficulty organizing and staying organized.[28] Most critics of pluralism believe that pluralism has a strongly upper-class tone, and that groups exclude many people from participating in the pressure system.[29] They allege that pluralism is a "partial truth" that misses or blurs certain problems and is overly optimistic about the role of power in society.

Hacker sees pluralism as promoting a declining, increasingly superficial society. Of being Lutherans or Methodists, from Ohio or Oregon, or of being from Swedish or German origins, he writes: "These plural features may add color to the national landscape, but their influence on attitudes and behavior is more apparent than real at a time when much of America is becoming a single homogeneous nation." Differences among people and groups are superficial and overwhelmed by the encroachment of concentrated corporate power, causing a fading of the autonomy

---

[26] Arnold Beichman, *Nine Lies about America* (New York: The Library Press, 1972).

[27] John Maddox, *The Doomsday Syndrome* (New York: McGraw-Hill, 1972).

[28] Gamson, *The Strategy of Social Protest*, pp. 141–142.

[29] E. E. Schattschneider, *The Semi-Sovereign People* (New York: Holt, Rinehart and Winston, 1960).

necessary to pluralism.[30] Such views, however, are in the minority, a cavil with respect to the meaning of ethnic, cultural, and group differences.

THE LIMITATIONS OF PLURALISM

It is difficult to develop and maintain a pluralistic system free of concentrations of power. Concentration arises from the passing of power, wealth, and opportunity through inheritance, and from the advantages of size that accrue to large organizations. It also ensues from luck or skill in winning control over resources, as when a nation discovers rich deposits of oil. Pluralism also is better at coping with short-run rather than long-run public interests. Competitiveness in the system encourages efficiency, but also waste. Pluralism reflects an amoral if not an immoral cast by accepting people and their motivations for what they are, rewarding selfish, competitive behavior rather than cooperation or altruism.[31]

While recommending that pluralism should be an important concept of the political order, Drucker acknowledges that it has difficulty providing principles and institutions of political integration. Its success has not been so great as to prove it valid, nor has it failed so completely as to disprove it. He writes further that there is still no cure for the old flaw in pluralism: the danger that the commonwealth will disappear under the efficiency of pluralist institutions and partial power centers. He writes: "No pluralist has ever escaped this disease. In most pluralist systems it has been fatal."[32]

The pluralist model is under constant criticism and refinement, but it remains an important conceptual framework for understanding society. Pluralism is not an accident of history, and alternative systems, such as a hierarchical, state-organized society, endanger freedom of association, freedom of speech, and freedom to pursue self-interest, which are the hallmarks of democracy.

The concept of pluralism is intertwined with theories of elitism and democracy; it is the antithesis of elite domination. At the heart of the issue of pluralism versus elitism is the conflict between the idealistic and the practical aspects of democracy, and ambiguity as to the countervailing forces at work. Dahl sees the issue as a conflict between idealism and accomplishment. Pluralism has defects when compared with unrealized ideals, but it looks much better compared to the alternatives. Dahl writes

---

[30] Andrew Hacker, *The End of the American Era* (New York: Atheneum, 1970), pp. 33–34.

[31] Harold J. Leavitt, William R. Dill, and Henry B. Ewing, *The Organizational World* (New York: Harcourt Brace Jovanovich, 1973), pp. 272–277.

[32] Peter F. Drucker, *Landmarks of Tomorrow* (New York: Harper & Row, 1959), p. 226. In *Men, Politics, and Ideas* (New York: Harper & Row, 1971), Drucker cites two main difficulties of pluralism: the ability to deal with foreign policy and the political organization of an industrial society; see pp. 117–125.

that pluralism "looks to be not only incomparably closer to genuine rule by the people but much more humane, decent, tolerant, benign, and responsive in dealing with its own citizens."[33]

THE INFLUENCE OF ELITES

In addition to the structural elements embodied in the concept of pluralism, society consists of hierarchical strata in the form of classes — upper, middle, and lower. These are general rather than precise categories, and they are important concepts for the analysis of social behavior, especially in political and economic matters but also in studying culture, life styles, and so on.

An *elite* is a relatively small, loosely organized but identifiable group which has leadership, authority, or dominant influence over other groups with which it has a political or cultural relationship.[34] It is a type of social class whose members view one another as equals but see outsiders as social inferiors. Thus the elite structure relates primarily to the upper classes, with the rest of society called the *masses*. As in the case of pluralism, adjectives denote the various types of elites — political, intellectual, military, and so forth.[35] Individuals belong to a given class depending on various combinations of attributes, such as possessing values around which particular class systems are organized, occupational status, family background, educational attainment, or wealth. Our society is a mobile one in which individuals may climb upward in the class structure through educational and occupational efforts. Elites exist in all societies and are found in all ages. Social theory views them as essential, functional components of social organization. This is due to the need for order and centers of influence within the operating mechanisms of society. Nevertheless, the term *elitism* is often used as an epithet because it implies a degree of superiority that some dislike.

Two important issues exist with respect to elites: (1) whether there is a dominant political elite directing other elites and the nonelite mass of the people, and (2) the problem of justifying the inequality implied by the existence of elites. We turn now to a brief overview of the theory of

---

[33] Robert A. Dahl, *After the Revolution: Authority in the Good Society* (New Haven, Conn.: Yale University Press, 1970), p. 141.

[34] Piet Thoenies, *The Elite in the Welfare State* (London: Faber and Faber, 1966), p. 25.

[35] See, for example, C. Barnett, "The Education of Military Elites," *Journal of Contemporary History* 2 (July 1967), pp. 15–36; Mark Kaplan, "The Elite Schools," *The Wilson Quarterly*, Autumn 1978, pp. 72–80; Harriet Zuckerman, *The Scientific Elite: Nobel Laureates in the United States* (New York: Free Press, 1977); Jeanne Kirkpatrick, *The New Presidential Elite: Men and Women in National Politics* (New York: Russell Sage Foundation, 1976); T. B. Bottomore, *Elites and Society* (New York: Basic Books, 1964); and Edward O. Laumann, Peter V. Marsden, and Joseph Galaskiewicz, "Community-Elite Influence Structures: Extension of a Network Approach," *American Journal of Sociology* 83 (November 1977), pp. 594–631.

elites, and then to a discussion of the two major issues of domination and inequality.

THE THEORY OF ELITES

The existence of multiple elites is consistent with pluralism, which can be viewed as consisting not only of organized groups, but also of the elites as leaders of groups with special influence or power. The concept of a single dominant elite, however, is inconsistent with the concept of pluralism.

The modern theory of elites began with Mosca, whose theories emerged in 1878–1881. He observed that in any country, power is never wielded by any one person, nor even a community of citizens, but actually by a particular group always fairly small in numbers compared to the total population.[36] Mosca's work greatly influenced the work of Pareto and other later theorists. Pareto divided society into two subclasses, the nongoverning elite—those who are successful in key occupations—and the governing elite. Power relations between nonelites and governing elites are affected by a "circulation of the elites" in which power shifts between the existing and emerging governing elites and between the governors and the governed. He noted two kinds of governing elites: the foxes, who use stealth and cunning, and the lions, who use brute force. In his view elites do not retain power indefinitely; instead there is a cycle of winning, enjoying, and then losing power.[37]

Pareto's work has been criticized for its ambiguity and untenable doctrines of biological and social elitism. Pareto thought of elites as the product of a meritocracy in which members achieve high status from outstanding capacity to perform—an efficient selection process among the unequally endowed. Later, however, he recognized that the relationships of capacity, performance, and status may differ among humans and therefore among elites.[38]

Both pluralism and elitism profess that the primary purpose of government is to safeguard and further the public interest. They differ as to what the public interest entails, and as to the proper role of government in securing it. All elite theories assume that the masses are incompetent, docile, and likely to undermine culture and liberty. However, the common beliefs that elitism is government by the few and democracy is government by the people, or that elitism is rule by selfish rulers and democracy is rule by the people, are oversimplifications. For example,

---

[36] Gaetano Mosca, *The Ruling Class* (Elementi di Scienza Politica), edited and revised by Arthur Livingston (New York: McGraw-Hill, 1939).

[37] Vilfredo Pareto, *The Mind and Society* (New York: Harcourt Brace, 1935), and *Treatise on General Sociology* (1916), reprinted in Giulio Farina (ed.), *Compendium of General Sociology* (Minneapolis: University of Minnesota Press, 1979).

[38] Zuckerman, *The Scientific Elite*, pp. 5–7.

Bachrach notes that Plato's guardians, Veblen's technocrats, and Mann-heim's intellectuals were types of elites capable of transcending selfish interests and ruling for the welfare of society. But Mosca and Pareto held that governing elites rule in their own interests.[39] Defenders of elite theory contend that the best interests of a free people depend on the ability of the talented to win the deference of the masses for the well-being of everyone, and that an open society, with its circulation of the elites, permits individuals of energy and merit to achieve positions of power through democratic processes.[40]

ELITE DOMINATION

Pareto's concept of the circulation of elites takes on new significance in the light of changes now going on in the structure of elites. Those who deny the existence of a governing elite view the United States as basically a middle-class society, with power dispersed among competing middle-class groups through a system of checks and balances. As we noted in Chapter 1, however, Bell, Kristol, Gouldner and others hold that in the postindustrial society a "new class" of managers, professionals, technicians, officials, and proprietors is emerging to join the rich and powerful. This new class is therefore reducing the influence of the old middle class. It is in effect an emerging elite.[41] How to control elites is thus a major question. Some believe that the common people have the wisdom to participate actively in running society, though this assumes effective communications and mechanisms of involvement. Others hold that only a trained and cultivated elite has a real feeling for the ethos of a society and should therefore dominate our social institutions. They assert that control by "mass man" is dangerous, because he can be misled by clever demagogues and shrewd manipulators.[42]

Although elites vary in their power and influence, the idea of one dominant governing elite cannot be supported either at the national or the community level. Hunter advanced a domination theory at the community level,[43] but Polsby argues that while power is frequently concentrated in the hands of a few, this does not mean that communities are run

---

[39] Peter Bachrach, *The Theory of Democratic Elitism: A Critique* (Boston: Little, Brown, 1967), pp. 1–3.

[40] E. Digby Baltzell, *The Protestant Establishment: Aristocracy and Caste in America* (New York: Random House, 1965).

[41] Richard Parker, *The Myth of the Middle Class* (New York: Harper & Row, 1972), pp. xi–xii. See also "Our New Elite: For Better or for Worse," *U.S. News and World Report*, February 25, 1980, pp. 65–68, and an interview with Michael Novak in the same issue, pp. 69–70.

[42] Robert Cooley Angell, *Free Society and Moral Crises* (Ann Arbor: University of Michigan Press, 1965), pp. 90–91.

[43] Floyd Hunter, *Community Power Structure* (Chapel Hill: University of North Carolina Press, 1953); Floyd Hunter, *Top Leadership U.S.A.* (Chapel Hill: University of North Carolina Press, 1959). Since research on a national scale is so costly, many studies are performed in communities. Their results are not capable of being generalized to the national level.

by a single all-purpose elite because (1) different small groups make decisions on various community problems, and the personnel of the groups changes; (2) decisions by small groups are considered routine or insignificant by community members; and (3) small groups have to work to achieve legitimacy before their decisions can become salient.[44]

The most forceful portrayal of elite domination at the national level is that of C. Wright Mills. Mills maintained that power is concentrated in a powerful, compact elite which dominates an interlocking system of economic, military, and government power structures, and that these structures shape religious, cultural, educational, and other spheres of life. Mills' views are similar to those of the English pluralists at the turn of the century; he believed that if pluralism existed, it could only be at the middle ranges of society where it would be unable to check the activities of the power elite.[45] Mills' assertions are controversial though provocative. Parsons thought his theories vague and impressionistic, and asserted that Mills did not clearly analyze prestigious groups such as the professions, which have penetrated the power structures of both business and government.[46]

Domhoff has argued that the upper class of American society constitutes a ruling class and is therefore a national institutional elite—an identifiable group that gets a disproportionate share of the country's wealth and places a disproportionate number of its members in our dominant organizations. He defines the ruling group according to one or more of the following criteria: (1) listing in the *Social Register*, (2) attendance at one

---

If it is true, as I believe, that the power elite consists of many thousands of people rather than several dozen; that they do not meet as a committee of the whole; that there are differences of opinion between them; that their motives are not well known to us beyond such obvious inferences as stability and power; and that they are not nearly so clever or powerful as the ultraconservatives think—it is nonetheless also true, I believe, that the power elite are more unified, more conscious, and more manipulative than the pluralists would have us believe, and certainly more so than any social group with the potential to contradict them.

G. WILLIAM DOMHOFF, *The Higher Circles* (New York: Random House, 1970), p. 299.

---

[44] Nelson W. Polsby, *Community Power and Political Theory* (New Haven, Conn.: Yale University Press, 1965).

[45] C. Wright Mills, *The Power Elite* (New York: Oxford University Press, 1959).

[46] Talcott Parsons, *Structure and Process in Modern Societies* (New York: Free Press, 1960), pp. 202, 218–219. For a critique of Parsons' critiques, see Alvin W. Gouldner, *The Coming Crisis of Western Sociology* (New York: Basic Books, 1970), pp. 313–320.

of a small number of prestigious prep schools, and (3) membership in exclusive clubs, and family wealth by inheritance or marriage. Instead of analyzing who actually makes key decisions in corporations and other organizations, Domhoff asserts that members of the upper class occupy key positions and therefore presumably hold the power to control these institutions.[47]

The meaning of *control* here comes into question. Domhoff found that major organizations in government, business, universities, the big foundations, the important media, the military, and political parties are run by members of the group he calls the ruling class. But he does not maintain that they thereby control public opinion as well; he asserts only that they have nearly unchallenged power to confer respectability on their preferred opinions and to downgrade or veto opposing opinions. There are limitations that prevent total or conspiratorial control. Organizations and social institutions are to an extent competitive and overlapping, and they may also be temporary. Interests diverge as well as converge. The upper class is not monolithic, with single, unified goals. The existence of an influential upper class is not in doubt, but the nature and extent of its control over major sectors of society has not been definitively established.

ELITISM AND INEQUALITY

The existence of a hierarchical social structure in the form of elites carries the implication of social inequality. Many are questioning the idea of social inequality for its inconsistency with democratic ideals. A major, unfinished task of elite theory is to explain the nature and extent of elitist influence in democracy. Conservatives accept elitism as the proper and necessary way of life in a democracy, whereas liberals deplore it as evidence of inequality and lack of justice. Underprivileged groups struggling for greater power take little comfort in the fact that elite groups fade as others rise, with the system open to entry into the power system.

We live in an increasingly egalitarian society that envisions equality of the common person, and views even the appearance of inequality as a failure of justice. The central issue is the nature of the equality being advocated. Equality of opportunity for every individual to participate in societal arrangements is seldom questioned. But equality of wealth, income, and power has been debated by philosophers and other thinkers for centuries. Social activists espouse equality of results rather than equality of opportunity. In general, however, economic inequality transmitted

---

[47] G. William Domhoff, *Who Rules America?* (Englewood Cliffs, N.J.: Prentice-Hall, 1967). For a more recent study, see Thomas R. Dye, *Who's Running America? The Carter Years*, 2nd ed. (Englewood Cliffs, N.J.: Prentice-Hall, 1979).

over generations in families is viewed unfavorably, while inequality arising from differences in individual effort or ability is accepted.[48]

The inequality of power and the ensuing struggle for power is a basic
force in society. Mulder believes that there will be a growing schism between elites with power and the powerless mass, resulting in threats to
the quality of work and life. This view discounts or ignores the fluidity of
elites portrayed by Pareto's circulation theory. Mulder argues that individuals can play the power game and take more responsibility for improving social groups and institutions.[49] Should individualism be carried to an
extreme, however, there might be a decline in the quality of the influential elites. There could be an egalitarian leveling that includes values,
persons, opinions, moral acts, and even art. There could be a "gutter
culture" in which the lower and less attractive aspects of human nature
become the norm.[50]

Elitism thus often becomes an epithet — a term of opprobrium to deplore the distinctions conferred by intellectual accomplishment, academic standards, and literary skills. The epithet often betrays a partisan
view, overlooking genuine accomplishments. Elites are natural targets
for suspicion and criticism, especially when things seem to go wrong in
society. Skepticism is a healthy form of curbing the unbridled power to
which elites often aspire. But reason suggests that critiques of the various
elites should be based on objective analysis and on the assumption that
elites will not go away. Instead, they will vie with each other for power.

Friedenberg notes that hostility toward elitism is so pervasive that
no social group can admit to an elitist position without losing both its
constituency and its self-esteem, and "any imputation of elitism automatically elicits the kind of embarrassed denial and insistence that one is
a regular guy. . . ." He says also that elites do not defend liberty frequently or vigorously enough to warrant the social costs they entail,
justifying the distrust that student movements have developed toward
the elites of their various countries. Though the despised elites are the
potential victims of the same forces that attack student movements, the
elites and members of the movement have remained mutually hostile.[51]

Unquestionably new concepts of justice, fairness, and equality are
contending for acceptance as a rational basis for morality. The new
equality "abandons equality of opportunity, equality before the law, and
other traditional concepts, for one whose exclusive concern is equality of

---

[48] John A. Brittain, *The Inheritance of Economic Status* (Washington, D.C.: The Brookings Institution, 1977).

[49] Mauk Mulder, *The Daily Power Game* (Boston: Martinus Nijhof, 1977).

[50] Donald Atwell Zoll, *The Twentieth Century Mind* (Baton Rouge, La.: Louisiana State University
Press, 1976), p. 13.

[51] Edgar Z. Friedenberg, *The Disposal of Liberty and Other Wastes* (Garden City, N.Y.: Doubleday,
1975), pp. 135–138.

condition or result."[52] As these changes become more apparent, managers will have to reassess their roles as leaders in society. According to Bell, structural position may define an elite, but in the United States the elite is defined more by outlook—a cosmopolitan, worldwide vision. Those who are at the top of organizations, or who possess economic or military power, do not automatically constitute an elite. Ultimately it is character and judgment rather than interests that generate an elite.[53]

MANAGEMENT AND PLURALISM

The absence of a viable alternative to pluralism, given the values of freedom and democracy, makes it imperative to manage the pluralistic system as best we can. The segmentation of society has been a structural feature of American society since the American Revolution. "What held Americans together was their capacity for living apart. Society depended on segmentation," writes Wiebe. Segments are the basic units of American life, but segmentation does not mean fragmentation. People identify with segments—ethnic, geographical, political, cultural, religious.[54]

Managers have considerable difficulty accepting segmentation, though management itself is highly segmented. Pluralism produces a competitiveness of ideas that implies criticism and change, thereby introducing uncertainties which affect decision making. Critics of pluralism focus primarily on one of the manager's most revered values—the market system. This can be explained by the fact that the traditional division of functions and responsibilities among households, firms, private organizations, and public authorities tends to break down not as a result of "evil forces," but from the unplanned side effects of ostensibly great improvements popular with the public. For example, services formerly performed by households, such as those for the sick, the elderly, or the handicapped, are being taken over by other social institutions. Resulting ideological and substantive conflicts generate government intervention to control economic and human life in order to combat market failures such as economic instability, inequality, and deficient supplies of goods, as well as fraud, harmful products, and other dangers. International forces make these problems global and matters of foreign as well as domestic policy. A circular process results as interventions cause market disturbances that require further interventions.[55]

---

[52] Edwin M. Epstein and Dow Votaw (eds.), *Rationality, Legitimacy, Responsibility: Search for New Directions in Business and Society* (Santa Monica, Calif.: Goodyear, 1978), p. 15.

[53] Daniel Bell, *The Cultural Contradictions of Capitalism* (New York: Basic Books, 1976), p. 201.

[54] Robert H. Wiebe, *The Segmented Society* (New York: Oxford University Press, 1975), pp. x, 46.

[55] Assar Lindbeck, *Can Pluralism Survive?* The Eleventh Annual William K. McInally Memorial Lecture, Graduate School of Business, University of Michigan, 1977, pp. 8–12.

The preservation of freedom and democracy under these conditions requires action on a number of fronts. Decentralized decision making can be fostered by reducing mergers, interlocking directorates where they exist, and encouraging competition. Limits can be placed on government intervention, overregulation, and dependence on subsidy and largess. The freedom and openness of the system can be improved to permit individuals and firms to take new initiatives for entering the various markets, facilitating a decentralized ownership and control of physical and financial capital.[56]

MANAGING CHANGE

In view of the pluralistic structure of society, conventional approaches to change need to be modified. Firefighting is sometimes necessary, but overall change strategies are needed in order to avoid continuous management by crisis. Coping and adaptation are often good tactics, but imaginative strategies are needed to focus decisions on comprehensive patterns of social problems rather than coping with them one at a time.

The aim of such strategies should be to minimize the number and severity of management-society conflicts. New change strategies envision what Post calls the "interactive" approach, in which the enterprise takes the lead in developing positions that are responsive to changing public goals.[57] Such leadership requires the monitoring of change, including a hearing for the various advocacies of interest groups, and even activists. It requires courage to be different from other firms in an industry, for example, and to enter into debate and face criticism when decisions that cannot please everyone have to be made.

An example of the interactive approach is that of Smith and Wesson, a firearm manufacturer, which in 1976 announced support for a federal system of *owner* (rather than gun) licensing. The firm was attacked by other firms in the industry and also by pro-gun groups. Boycotts and other punitive actions were threatened. Hard-core gun advocates called the company's view a sham; anti-gun advocates called it a sell-out. With both sides attacking, Post notes, the company gained by being an independent, responsive actor in the interactive mode.[58]

---

[56] Ibid., pp. 19–23.
[57] James E. Post, *Corporate Behavior and Social Change* (Reston, Va.: Reston, 1978), pp. 255–274.
[58] Ibid.

The case for managed pluralism is currently better than that for a total, centralized, superpower attempting to engineer Utopia. For some years now, our pluralistic institutions have been working to solve the problems of poverty, health care, equality of opportunity, and the abatement of pollution, urban decay, crime, racism, and the like. Politicians, businesspeople, labor leaders, pressure groups, and educators have espoused these goals, and progress has been made. But this progress whets the appetite for more, and accordingly our social institutions are changing. To meet changing needs, new organizational forms are appearing and new management precepts are evolving. It may be, however, that expectations for a perfect society go beyond the ability of the market system to fulfill. Therefore it may be necessary to modify expectations that require excessive bureaucratic, authoritarian intervention and control. Perfectionist, utopian aims are not only impossible, but are often used to justify violent means in support of ideological change.

The attainment of society's goals requires cooperation, and frequently collaboration, among the major sectors of action and interest. Conflict among them is to be expected, and while it can be counterproductive, it can also produce ideas, useful compromise, and even the improvement and refinement of actions. Conflict requires resolution processes and the reduction of the costs of excessive, unproductive conflict. The conflict is not entirely one of values or objectives, but also of the means for achieving them. The conflict over means arises from our lack of the knowledge needed for solving large, complex social problems.

Awareness of the interactive elements of the major groups in American society is increasing. For example, a report of the Committee for Economic Development states:

> . . . responsible management must have the vision and exert the leadership to develop a broader social role for the corporation if business is to continue to receive public confidence and support . . . there are limitations to what business can contribute to social progress, and the kind of society we want can be achieved only with the full participation of government through major contributions from all our institutions—in education, medicine, religion, labor, the arts, philanthropy, and many other fields.[59]

That business firms appreciate their role in a pluralistic society is exemplified in the following statement by the General Electric Company:

---

[59] Committee for Economic Development, *Social Responsibilities of Business Corporations* (New York, 1971), p. 61.

There is a developing consensus of legislative, administrative and public opinion that private enterprise has a part to play in the growing "public needs" sector — an area that, up till now, has been considered a government preserve. . . . If companies step up to this new opportunity, then they will have to develop new products and services, learn how to operate with new patterns of governmental and community relationships, and establish new organization structures and operating procedures. But they will have strengthened the trend to pluralism and arrested a top-heavy centralization of power and an excessive concentration of employment in government (with all that this would imply for employment and collective bargaining practices).[60]

Drucker writes that "the enterprise is an autonomous institution" which derives its power and function not from owners or from the political and legal organization of society; rather, it has a nature of its own. Although the enterprise is a legal fiction, a creature of the state, it follows the laws of its own being, and in nature and function is *sui generis*. Industrial society, argues Drucker, is a pluralist society in which the enterprise and government need to be organized according to the same beliefs and principles. Otherwise the society cannot survive. The problems of an industrial society are thus problems in pluralist organization. There is not one prime mover in society but at least two: state and enterprise. These two have to live in harmony, or they will not live at all. Drucker writes:

But society too must be organized so that the enterprise can function. Economic policy and political control must of course always focus on the common weal. But if the basic requirements of the enterprise have to be denied for the sake of the common welfare, society will become split against itself. We will not be able to maintain a free and functioning society if we fail in either task. We will, for the sake of function, have to sacrifice freedom and become totalitarian. Or we will, for the sake of freedom, sacrifice function and tumble into anarchy.[61]

Incident Case

Charlie Smith, plant manager of the Vortex Corporation, was a member of the local PTA, Boy Scout Council, a Protestant church, the Kiwanis Club, and eight other civic and professional organizations. He felt that demands on his time were overextended, but there were no memberships he felt able to drop. One day his boss, the president, told him he was sure

---

[60] *Our Future Business Environment: Developing Trends and Changing Institutions* (New York: General Electric Company, April 1968).

[61] Peter F. Drucker, *The New Society: The Anatomy of Industrial Order* (New York: Harper & Row, 1950), p. 37.

it would be good for the company if he were to run for election to the local school board. Charlie was very puzzled about what to do next.

What should Charlie do, and why?

Issues for Discussion and Analysis

1. Why does a society not self-destruct?

2. Why is "elitism" used as an epithet?

3. Is there or is there not a military-industrial complex that controls society in the United States?

4. What are the arguments for and against pluralism?

5. Why should business executives be on the boards of trustees of civic organizations?

6. In what ways does pluralism serve both public and private interests?

7. How have activist groups affected the management of business enterprises?

Class Project

Form teams among members, each team to be assigned the task of examining the following organizations from the point of view of the concepts explored in this chapter:

1. National Association of Manufacturers
2. U.S. Chamber of Commerce
3. American Medical Association
4. National Education Association
5. The American Enterprise Institute
6. The Committee for Economic Development

Each team should elect a spokesperson to present its findings to the class.

For Further Reading

BACHRACH, PETER. *The Theory of Democratic Elitism: A Critique* (Boston: Little, Brown, 1967).

BURCH, PHILIP H., JR. *Elites in American History: The New Deal to the Carter Administration* (New York: Holmes and Meier, 1980).

DAHL, ROBERT A. *Pluralist Democracy in the United States* (Chicago: Rand McNally, 1967).

DOUGLAS, JACK D. *The American Social Order: Social Rules in a Pluralistic Society* (New York: Free Press, 1971).

ETZIONI, AMITAI. *The Active Society* (New York: Free Press, 1968).

MCFARLAND, ANDREW S. *Power and Leadership in Pluralist Systems* (Stanford, Calif.: Stanford University Press, 1969).

NICHOLS, DAVID. *Three Varieties of Pluralism* (New York: St. Martin's Press, 1974).

NISBET, ROBERT. *Twilight of Authority* (New York: Oxford University Press, 1975).

O'BRIEN, DAVID J. *Neighborhood Organization and Interest-Group Processes* (Princeton, N.J.: Princeton University Press, 1975).

TUMIN, MELVIN M., and WALTER PLOTSCH. *Pluralism in a Democratic Society* (New York: Praeger, 1977).

ZUCKERMAN, HARRIET. *The Scientific Elite: Nobel Laureates in the United States* (New York: Free Press, 1977).

6

Management and Social Institutions

*[Phaedrus's thinking] was at a level at which everything
shifts and changes, at which institutional values and verities
are gone and there is nothing but one's own spirit to keep
one going. His early failure had released him from any felt
obligation to think along institutional lines and his thoughts
were already independent to a degree few people are familiar
with. He felt that institutions such as schools, churches,
governments and political organizations of every sort all
tended to direct thought for ends other than truth, for the
perpetuation of their own functions, and for the control of
individuals in the service of these functions.*

ROBERT M. PIRSIG,
Zen and the Art of Motorcycle Maintenance,
(New York: Morrow, 1974) pp. 113–114.

CONCEPTS DISCUSSED IN THIS CHAPTER

1. THE NATURE OF SOCIAL INSTITUTIONS
2. MUTUAL INTERACTIONS AMONG INSTITUTIONS
3. THE BASIC FUNCTIONS OF INSTITUTIONS
4. BUSINESS AS A SOCIAL INSTITUTION
5. MANAGEMENT STRATEGIES FOR SOCIAL RESPONSIBILITY

The concept of pluralism discussed in the previous chapter describes
the enormous variety of groups and organizations whose actions, interests, and beliefs are important influences in society. The concept of
social institutions is a form of pluralism that describes major structural

categories of related organizational and interest groups. The social institution called education, for example, includes state and national associations for teachers, parents, school administrators, and school boards, as well as a variety of schools, colleges, universities, textbook publishers, and others.

Social institutions are overlapping, amorphous, conceptual entities that are essentially unorganized, in that managers do not create or control them as such. Institutional influences on managers are subtle and indirect. Yet the behavior of constituent organizations and their managers, taken collectively, determines the way in which these institutions fulfill society's needs.

DEFINITIONAL PROBLEMS

For the purposes of this book, a *social institution* is defined as a collectivity of organizations in which there are recurring, continuous, or regularized activities that express common interests and aims which are normatively sanctioned. That is, society recognizes major classifications of interrelated organizations whose activities, roles, and functions are legitimate when performed according to appropriate social values, statuses, norms, and expectations.[1] Social institutions may be classified broadly according to their general functions and aims. *Political institutions* provide governance and regulate the distribution of power; *economic institutions* produce and distribute goods and services; *cultural institutions* deal with religious, artistic, or educational activities and traditions; and *kinship institutions* focus on marriage, the family, and child-rearing activities.

The term social institution has not been uniformly defined or consistently used. Smith, for example, analyzed 70 sociological definitions and found 8 common elements among them: (1) cultural norms, (2) interrelated structural parts, (3) persistence and stability, (4) functions, (5) sanctions, (6) cognitive elements, (7) regularized social interaction, and (8) material or physical culture traits.[2] These elements, in whole or in part, can be taken to characterize the general nature of social institutions. One caveat is required. The word *institution* itself is often used to designate particular organizations, such as a prison, a hospital, or even a large business firm. For example, Feibleman recognizes the use of the word *institution* at two levels of social organization — the level at which "education" is a social institution, and the level at which "Oxford Univer-

---

[1] Alan Wells, *Social Institutions* (New York: Basic Books, 1971), pp. 6-11.
[2] Harold E. Smith, "Toward a Clarification of the Concept of Social Institution," *Sociology and Social Research* 48 (1963-1964), pp. 202-204.

sity" is an institution.[3] We will avoid this latter usage, because it results in unnecessary conceptual confusion.

THE FUNCTIONS OF SOCIAL INSTITUTIONS

Social institutions provide a linkage system for the integration of complex processes needed to achieve a coherent, stable society. For example, the institutions of the family, religion, law, private property, economic activity, and political authority interact in such activities as raising children to adulthood or the governance of society.

Social institutions also symbolize, preserve, and legitimize the values, beliefs, norms, culture traits, and expectations that serve as standards against which to judge the behavior of organizations, groups, and individuals. Social institutions thus give direction and focus to the various units of society, resulting in the cohesion and continuity of the social order. They implement the application of common values, and provide for inculcating those values throughout the social system.[4]

A third major function of the social institution is to provide sanctions against those who trangress its rules, customs, and values to the detriment of the social welfare. Various forms of punishment, from ostracism to imprisonment or even death, are administered within the institutional framework. This does not rule out change, because some challenges to the system may eventually result in changing the norms, values, and beliefs espoused by an institution. A fourth function is therefore to manage the processes of change.

VALUE SHAPING

Value shaping as a major function of social institutions requires additional analysis at this point. Institutions espouse values that both reinforce their aims and identities, and also work for the welfare of society as a whole. The institutions of family, church, school, and state have special responsibilities for the nurture and transmission of basic values over successive generations.

Values are deep-seated judgments about the kinds of behavior that ought to prevail in society. They represent ideals rooted in tradition and the common experience of humans whose survival depends on complex, interdependent relationships. Values are basic ideas that guide people in striving, however imperfectly, to act in their own interests and in those

---

[3] James Feibleman, *The Institutions of Society* (New York: Humanities Press, 1968), pp. 20–21.

[4] Robert Cooley Angell, *Free Society and Moral Crisis* (Ann Arbor: University of Michigan Press, 1965), p. 30.

of society as a whole. Institutions thus are systems of social relationships people believe embody their common values. Institutions are not merely instruments of civilization, but are also a deeply ingrained facet of each individual's personality.

The interrelatedness of institutions is of central importance. The values fostered by each reinforce or conflict with the values of the others, and together they impinge on the behavior of both individuals and organizations. A significant feature of this interrelatedness is that several social institutions may share given functions, such as the responsibility for inculcating approved norms and values. A substitution process often occurs. What one institution does not do can be taken over by others. For example, when the family does not adequately socialize the child, the church or the school tends to assume a greater role. The leaders of social institutions thus share an interest in the performance of the others; this is one of the advantages of pluralism. (Specific examples of the functioning of value-shaping social institutions will be further analyzed in Chapter 8.)

MANAGERIAL ROLES

Because as individuals they belong to a variety of organizations, managers are in a position to help those organizations contribute to the work of their respective social institutions. The manager is a key factor in the interactions among organizations and institutions. The manager, in effect, provides linkages among social institutions by acting within their constituent organizations. For example, a manager serving on the city council can tie business precepts to local governmental problems; a government purchasing agent is linked to the business world through dealing with suppliers of goods and services.

> *All sectors of society face problems generated from previous success. All institutions are linked together in such a way that failure of any one drags others down with it, and causes still others to pick up its burden. At the least, leaders in one sector should have some understanding of the potential fallout they can expect from issues and crises now current in other sectors; at the most, their future decisions could take greater account of reverberations sent beyond the boundaries of a specific organization's domain.*
>
> HENRY M. BOETTINGER, "The Management Challenge," in The Conference Board, *Challenge to Leadership: Managing in a Changing World* (New York: Free Press, 1973), pp. 3–4.

By being aware of these linkages and the goals and values associated with the total system, managers can shape their roles in such a way as to help the organizational subsystems work toward the goals of the total system. Parsons, for example, presents a systems view of society based on values from which it is possible to develop a structural definition of roles in the system. Thus, since the American value system can be described in terms of universal achievement or performance patterns, the strategic subsystem is occupational — that is, the subsystem is organized around the adaptive problems of the total system.[5]

THE STRUCTURE OF SOCIAL INSTITUTIONS

The functioning of social institutions depends upon organizations as centers of action, which in turn depend upon managerial and professional capabilities. To study the managers, the organizations, or the social institutions in isolation is to overlook the need for an integrated focus that clarifies the linkages and interactions among them. A systems approach provides the necessary means of analyzing how social institutions mediate norms, values, and expectations in macro-level decision making.

The basic unit of a social institution is the individual organization. A complex organization, however, may contain groups that also fall in other institutional groupings. For example, the General Motors Institute, an accredited, degree-granting school, is in both the business and educational sectors. However, most organizations are readily classified by their primary institutional affiliation.

An integrated view of the structure of an institutional systems model is depicted in Figure 6.1. This is a feedback model showing the relations among three major components of public policy formation: society, governance mechanisms, and decision processes. Underlying this model are the eight institutional elements mentioned in the preceding section, and (not shown in the model) the other social institutions and their organizations, which have varying effects on the behavior portrayed by the model.

A number of integrating processes link organizations to their institutional affiliations and to one another. Among them are these:

1. Boundary spanners who provide formal linkages with other organizations in the institutional matrix.
2. Established communication networks.
3. Missions, objectives, or problems.
4. Individuals who assume a representation function for their organizations and institutions.
5. Informal or professional relationships among individuals in the constituent organizations.
6. The recognition of shared roles, statuses, values, and aims.

---

[5] Talcott Parsons, *Essays in Sociological Theory* (New York: Free Press, 1954), pp. 309–404.

Figure 6.1

An Institutional Systems Model of the Public Policy Process

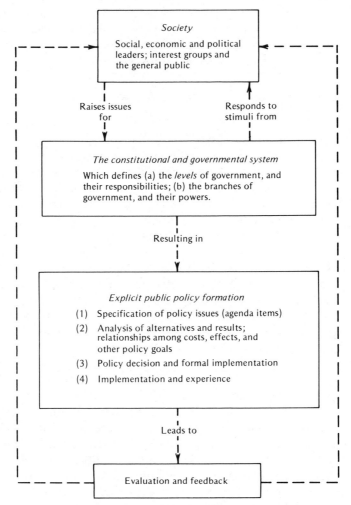

SOURCE: *Lee Preston and James E. Post*, Private Management and Public Policy: The Principle of Public Responsibility *(Englewood Cliffs, N.J.: Prentice-Hall, 1975), p. 72. Used by permission.*

Organizations provide social institutions with an important innovation function. Organization theory offers an alternative to revolution as an instrument of change, though it is difficult to achieve enough innovation to meet many crucial problems. According to Schulman:

The extent of the organizational crisis is indicated by the degree to which formal arrangements in both private and public sectors have come to support timidity, mediocrity, and encapsulated decision-making. The magnitude of the organizational crisis is best experienced in the enormous difficulty experienced in developing new organizational forms that are structurally geared to continuous innovation and thus capable of facilitating changes in the institutional life of society. The challenge upon us is whether we can respond to the imperative of institutional change through organizational innovation as well as through the ordeal of revolution.[6]

For at least three generations, the primary mode of organization has been bureaucracy. Capable of great efficiency, productivity, rational action, and virtually unlimited scales of operation, bureaucracy has an appealing, practical logic. But the bureaucratic values that have saturated organizations have tended to discourage innovative change.[7] Today bureaucracies are modifying their structures and management styles, designing open, adaptive structures that improve the organization's ability to perceive and cope with environmental forces. These changes bring organizations into closer relationship with one another and with social institutions, enhancing innovation and problem solving.

INSTITUTIONAL CHANGE AND THE POWER STRUCTURE

Social institutions are basically conservative and slow to change. Yet none remains unchanged. The changing needs of society foster both incremental and revolutionary changes in the relative power and influence of the major institutions. Religion was long the supreme institution; then business, economic and technical-scientific institutions became dominant as industrialization and large-scale corporate enterprise superseded feudal, cottage-industry, and handcraft societies. With the intensification of war, poverty, alienation, crime, and other social problems, government is now the dominant institution. And in Chapter 1 we noted that in the postindustrial society, higher education is contending for the center of power.

Alford classifies social institutions according to their structural interests, which can be dominant, challenging, or repressed. Dominant structural interests are those served by the institutional structures at any given time. The government, for example, is sufficiently dominant to assure that other institutions will serve its interests. Challenging structural interests arise from the changing structure and expectations of society, as the rise to power of education illustrates. Repressed structural interests are the opposite of the dominant ones; they will not gain power

---

[6] Jay Schulman, *Remaking an Organization* (Albany, N.Y.: SUNY Press, 1976), p. 229. Reprinted by permission of the State University of New York Press.

[7] See, for example, Dalton E. McFarland, *Managerial Innovation in the Metropolitan Hospital* (New York: Praeger, 1979).

unless they can mobilize unusual political energies. Here religion may be an example.[8]

Society exhibits a preference for a plurality of social institutions maintained in balance. Nevertheless, many people fear the possibility of one dominant institution. It is widely alleged that business (large and powerful corporate interests) is dominant, or that the military-industrial complex is in control. In an early book, Drucker called big business "the dominant institution of our time."[9] But later, in recognition of an emerging pluralism, he wrote that it is totally inadequate to see just one of the new institutions as *the* institution, with none superior or inferior to the others.[10] Still later, he wrote:

> The rhetoric of the New Left talks of our society as being a big-business society. But this is as outdated as the rhetoric of the New Left is altogether. Society in the West was a business society — seventy-five years ago. Then business was, indeed, the most powerful of all institutions — more powerful even than some governments. Since the turn of the century, however, the importance of business has gone down steadily — not because business has become smaller or weaker, but because the other institutions have grown so much faster. Society has become pluralist.[11]

Changes in the balance of forces result from inherent tendencies in the structures and functions of key groups in society. The interpenetration of the organizations in social institutions produces changes in their relative power positions. Organizations develop needs, interests, and orientations of their own that impinge on other groups, changing attitudes. Some religious groups, for example, develop universal orientations that may expand beyond the basic premises of a given institutional system.[12] The values of economic institutions invade other institutions that lack the socially rewarding meaning economic institutions have.[13]

To a large extent, the interpenetrating nature of organizations centers around exchange relationships in which resources play an important part.[14] Many organizations have as their main purpose the control and alteration of the activities of other organizations. One example is the

---

[8] Robert R. Alford, *Health Care Politics: Ideological and Interest Group Barriers to Reform* (Chicago: The University of Chicago Press, 1975), pp. 13–14.

[9] Peter F. Drucker, *Concept of the Corporation* (New York: John Day, 1946).

[10] Peter F. Drucker, *Age of Discontinuity: Guidelines to Our Changing Society* (New York: Harper & Row, 1969), p. 176.

[11] Peter F. Drucker, *Management: Tasks, Responsibilities, Practices* (New York: Harper & Row, 1973), p. 6.

[12] S. N. Eisenstadt, *Essays on Comparative Institutions* (New York: Wiley, 1965), p. 42.

[13] Melvin M. Tumin, "Some Dysfunctions of Institution Imbalance," *Behavioral Science* 1 (July 1956), pp. 218–223. See also Lee E. Preston and James E. Post, "Models of Management and Society," *Private Management and Public Policy* (Englewood Cliffs, N.J.: Prentice-Hall, 1975), chap. 2.

[14] Jeffrey Pfeffer and Gerald R. Salancik, *The External Control of Organizations: A Resource Dependence Perspective* (New York: Harper & Row, 1978), pp. 39–43; Howard Aldrich, *Organizations and Environments* (Englewood Cliffs, N.J.: Prentice-Hall, 1979), chap. 4.

academic or professional accrediting agency, which requires certain conditions to be met. All regulatory bodies are set up to control particular behaviors of organizations. Business firms influence the production processes of suppliers. This interdependence can bring strengths, but also problems. One problem, for example, is that when organization A is dependent on what organization B does, organization A is not entirely in control of the outcome of the relationship. Thus we distinguish between outcome interdependence and procedural or behavioral independence. Another distinction is whether the relationship is symbiotic or competitive. In competitive relations, the outcome of one organization is obtained when the outcome of the other is reduced. In symbiotic interdependence, the output of one is the input for another. And interdependence is no guarantee of desirable outcomes for either party to such relationships. Interdependencies are not necessarily balanced, or even fair.

The flexibility of social institutions and their ability to change is necessary to society's survival. Yet change is frequently thwarted by institutional interests centering on favored life styles and existing power centers. For example, efforts to change the institution of private property or to redistribute wealth are successfully resisted, for they would entail revolutionary adjustments in values and practices. Major changes that have occurred in social institutions in our society have required aggressive action by activists, protest movements, the counterculture, or the New Left.

The power struggles of the various social institutions lead some to hold that only the state, under a powerful government, can provide a balancing mechanism for preserving the social order. Others fear the dominance of the state. Sandoz affirms that the claims of institutions on the individual are not absolute, and that the political order of a society can pretend to no more than a limited and provisional function, since it is created by the people themselves. He writes:

> Political existence is not the whole of human existence; and for institutionalized order to arrogate plenary authority over the lives of men to itself is a totalitarian derailment whether committed by a church, a party, or a government. Moreover, there are in principle no permanent solutions to the problem of how satisfactorily to represent order. There is only the perennial task of modifying and adapting traditional patterns and contents of institutionalization to the needs of concrete men in particular societies with full attention to their essential humanity, the abiding truth of being, and the peculiar pragmatic exigencies of historical existence under changing conditions in the world.[15]

It is doubtful that any single institution can or should dominate the others. Pluralism requires multiple institutions, each with voice,

---

[15] Ellis Sandoz, *Political Apocalypse: A Study of Dostoevsky's Grand Inquisitor* (Baton Rouge: Louisiana State University Press, 1971).

autonomy, and influence. The problem of balance is worked out by each society according to its value systems. History reflects an ever-changing succession of institutional authorities: institutions wane or die when they lose their power to command respect and allegiance. Nisbet cites as examples the increasing mistrust of government reflected in the erosion of patriotism and its rituals, the decline of clear political beliefs, and the specter of lawlessness.[16] We will analyze the problem of declining confidence following a brief review of business as a focal institution.

BUSINESS AS A FOCAL INSTITUTION

In this book it is not possible to consider fully all the major social institutions and their relationships. To provide a central vantage point, we will treat business as a focal institution, based on the logic that business functions are pervasive in society. One could choose any institution as a focus, but business effectively reveals the management processes that provide linkages among the key institutions, and provides insights about the issues all social institutions now confront. Figure 6.2 illustrates this focal view, but for simplicity all possible interrelationships are not shown.

The pervasiveness of business and management functions throughout society reflects the existence of the universal objectives of obtaining

Figure 6.2

Interrelationships among Selected Social Institutions Based on Business as a Focal Institution

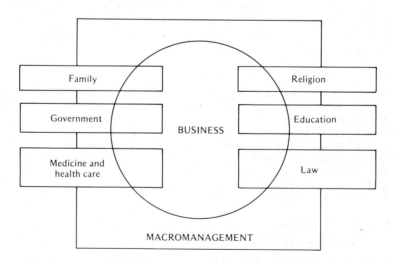

---

[16] Robert Nisbet, *The Twilight of Authority* (New York: Oxford University Press, 1975), pp. 13–14.

and allocating resources, and of the decision making that results in their use for the attainment of a variety of aims and results. Such a focus does not imply that business is the most significant or powerful institution, but only that it is a fruitful way to understand the institutional framework and its problem-solving capabilities.

Today's management transition to the postindustrial society depends upon bridging the gap between concepts of management and organization and the social institutions within which organizations operate. The tendency of academic disciplines to relate to only one of the major social institutions presents difficulties of integration. Some disciplines, such as philosophy, sociology, or management, can readily transcend institutional boundaries, so that managers today have a great opportunity to work on the difficult problems of integration and interaction among institutions.

Business organizations pose a difficult problem of analysis for a theory of institutions. The extent to which businesses embody and implement the common values of society is a serious issue. Protest movements, labor unions, and other groups are challenging the legitimacy of power and authority of business organizations; in effect, they question their fundamental values.

THE PROBLEM OF CONFIDENCE

Social institutions never function perfectly, and they have always been subject to criticism and attack. In the past two decades, however, dissatisfactions have increased in volume and intensity as the complexity and number of society's problems have increased. We place enormous burdens on social institutions, and serious disillusionment results when rising expectations are inadequately met. Our dreams and ideals contrast sharply with performance, leading to a reduction of confidence and trust in our institutions.[17]

Nisbet notes that disillusion is especially serious in the political order. We have turned to government for discipline and benefits, and debates over the merits of democracy, socialism, communism, or the planned economy center on humanity's intolerance for the imperfections of the state. In the fifteenth century, inflated expectations of the Church led to the remaking of Western Europe, and today's demands evoke similar pressures for reform in all our social institutions.[18] This disillusion with social institutions is worldwide and far-reaching. Coping in

---

[17] Morton Darrow, "Changing Values: Implications for Major Social Institutions," *Current Issues in Higher Education* (Washington, D.C.: American Council for Higher Education, 1979), pp. 11–21.

[18] Nisbet, *The Twilight of Authority*, pp. 15–16.

this global context is a new experience for the world's managers and leaders. The difficulties arise not only from rising expectations, but also from ambiguous or conflicting ones. Institutional purposes and responsibilities are hard to define, and the demands on any single institution often conflict with demands on the others.

Ideas, institutions, and techniques are intermingled in ways too complex to unravel. How one social institution affects others can be seen in the actions of government, a powerful force for change throughout society. The New Deal era of Franklin D. Roosevelt, the creation of the Tennessee Valley Authority, the social security system, the unleashing of nuclear power, and space programs produced sweeping changes in the socioeconomic perspectives of business, education, and government itself.[19] Some see these complex institutional interrelationships as a dangerous conspiracy. Others, such as Robert Penn Warren, see the overarching, interlocking, and mutually supportive structure of science, technology and big organizations as "the proudest moment of our society."[20] Doubtless the truth lies somewhere between these extremes.

The criticism of social institutions is necessarily indirect and based on inferences drawn from concrete experience. An institution, though it has a leadership elite, has no central core of individuals to blame for mismanagement. To judge the institution, we look at the actions of its organizations — the corporation, the school, the church, or the government. But as we examine performance failures we also question traditional values. The resulting loss of confidence is expressed in a variety of forms with emotional connotations: malaise, fear, anxiety, anomie (disintegration of normative codes), or alienation (feelings of powerlessness). Pessimism is rife, and the future looks more uncertain than we think it should.

Managers need to understand the distinction between criticism of performance and attack on values. In both cases, evidence is often partial, misleading, or self-serving. For example, critics who attack the corporation for its appetite for power, or for nurturing materialistic attitudes, are often generalizing from observations selected to support preconceived value judgments. Objectivity is difficult for both critics and defenders, but it is easier in the case of results or behavior than of values and beliefs. Some corporations do pay bribes, but one may question whether this argues that the capitalistic system should be discarded.

The criticism of social institutions and their organizations is healthy and necessary for progress and improvement. Nevertheless, ideological

---

[19] Robert A. Dahl, *Pluralist Democracy in the United States: Conflict and Consent* (Chicago: Rand McNally, 1967), p. 268.

[20] Robert Penn Warren, *Democracy and Poetry* (Cambridge, Mass.: Harvard University Press, 1975), p. 43.

issues arise when institutions come under attack.[21] Critics are not always above exaggerating the dangers of the future. Such phenomena as anomie or alienation cannot be ignored; they are disruptive and dysfunctional. Social unrest is born of change and the need for change. The conservative nature of institutions disappoints the impatient. Change is nevertheless unrelenting: we see growing populations, advancing industry and technology, the knowledge explosion, and the information technology revolution. Such changes are tests of the ability of social institutions to adapt and to cope with the frustrating gaps between institutional performance and our ideals.

Yet progress is hampered because our most serious problems cut across several institutions at once. Failure or reform in one depends on or leads to failure or reform in others. For example, problems like the maldistribution of wealth or of health care services cannot be solved by one institution alone, since forces from business, higher education, government, or even religion are involved in mutually interdependent ways. Yet the critics of particular social institutions often do not seem aware of this complexity. The interrelatedness of institutions is not an excuse for the failures of each to do what it can to reduce or eliminate problems within its purview. A factory can stop polluting the environment; schools can raise their level of effectiveness; government can reduce its overextended claims on business or education.

It is an exaggeration to call the loss of confidence and the raising of questions of legitimacy a crisis. Institutions continue to fulfill needs, to respond to criticism, and to change. But a revolution that would destroy or radically change our society is not imminent. Nevertheless, to manage society effectively requires that its problems be faced. We should not ignore or trivialize the unrest reflected in opinion polls, but at the same time we need not despairingly conclude that society is disintegrating or that our crises are unmanageable.

OPINION SURVEYS

Opinion polls, taken at given times, provide comparisons over time. Polls are meaningful only in a general way, and what they measure over time is change in the level of confidence. The expressions of opinion are highly volatile; they fluctuate depending on circumstances. For example, in comparing the attacks on two major institutions—government and business—Darrow found that the attacks focus not on institutional ends,

---

[21] For example, see Charles Perrow (ed.), *The Radical Attack on Business* (New York: Harcourt Brace Jovanovich, 1972); and the Editors of *Playboy*, *Voices of Concern* (New York: Harcourt Brace Jovanovich, 1971).

but rather on institutional means. Critics of government attack representative government, intrusions on privacy, the rule of law, majority rule, minority rights, and the party system. Attacks on corporate enterprise assail growth, materialism, environmental damage, the exploitation of nature, the application of science and technology, and the market mechanism. Darrow believes that attacks on social institutions should be analyzed in the broader context of societal development rather than of institutional failure.[22]

Some data from polls will show how opinions fluctuate. In 1976, loss of public confidence in higher education was reportedly "nothing short of a national tragedy," and "the damage already done is extensive and it will be catastrophic. . . ."[23] Again in 1976 Fred M. Hechinger, the former education editor of The New York Times, declared that "America is in a headlong retreat from its commitment to education," and "At stake is nothing less than the survival of American democracy." He also asserted that a slow-down in upward mobility constitutes a break with the most fundamental American ideals. The consequence will be a stratified, class-bound society ruled by a self-perpetuating power elite of economic and social privilege.[24] Hechinger has consistently conveyed a pessimistic view of education, for in 1979 he stated: "Public education in the United States is in mortal danger . . . and no signs of a determined rescue have appeared."[25] By 1977, however, various polls showed that public confidence increased in nearly all major social institutions except business. Attitudes toward business and industry are shown in Figure 6.3. The categories of "largely untrue" and "don't know" reflect serious confidence problems in business as an institution.

Public opinions about business show fluctuations similar to those in education. The drop in confidence in business since 1968 has been documented by various surveys. One, for example, found that the percentage of those who agree that "business tries to strike a fair balance between profits and the interest of the public" fell from 70 to 14 percent in this period. Another survey found a drop in the percentage of respondents who have "a great deal of confidence in the people in charge of running major companies," from 55 to 18 percent in this same period.[26] A 1979 survey found that 72 percent of the respondents charged business with "doing more harm than good." It also revealed that people have serious concerns about the way business handles specific problems, such as the

---

[22] Darrow, "Changing Values," pp. 13–14.

[23] Reported in Higher Education and National Affairs Newsletter 25 (March 21, 1976), p. 6. See also "Crisis in the Schools," U.S. News and World Report, September 1, 1975, pp. 42–59.

[24] Fred M. Hechinger, "Murder in Academe: The Demise of Education," Saturday Review, March 20, 1976, pp. 11–18.

[25] Fred M. Hechinger, "Schoolyard Blues: The Decline of Public Education," Saturday Review, January 20, 1979, pp. 20–22.

[26] Alan F. Westin, "Good Marks but Some Areas of Doubt," Business Week, May 14, 1979, pp. 14–16.

Figure 6.3

Attitudes toward Business and Industry

Question: American business and industry has been both credited and charged with many things. I'd like to know which of these statements you think are largely true, and which are largely untrue. The first one is "American business and industry has in most instances given good value for the money." Do you think that is largely true or largely untrue?

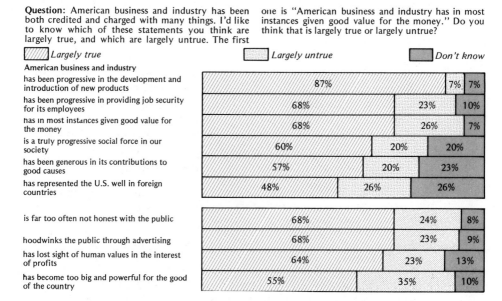

SOURCE: *Survey by the Roper Organization (Roper Report 78-7), July 8–15, 1978.*

privacy rights of employees or customers. They look to law and government for protection against violations of privacy and undue intrusion into their personal lives.[27]

The same fluctuating patterns were found in surveys of confidence in government. The Cadell polls concluded that in government and politics, the confidence problem approaches a crisis based on long-term rather than short-term outlooks.[28] By contrast, the findings from the Center for Political Studies at the University of Michigan contradict the Caddell assertion of crisis, holding that the decline of trust in government has leveled off.[29] There are methodological differences in the surveys done by the leading survey firms. One is the way in which questions are asked. Another is whether respondents are asked about the leaders of organizations, the institutions themselves, or confidence in general or in the system as a whole. Large numbers of people are pessimistic about the

[27] Ibid.; see also Paul N. Bloom and Louis W. Stern, "Emergence of Anti-Industrialism," *Business Horizons* 19 (October 1976), pp. 87–93.

[28] Patrick H. Caddell, "Crisis of Confidence I—Trapped in a Downward Spiral," *Public Opinion* 2 (October–November 1979), pp. 2–8.

[29] Warren E. Miller, "Crisis of Confidence II—Misreading the Public Pulse," *Public Opinion* 2 (October–November, 1979), pp. 9–15.

future of the economy or of the nation, but relatively optimistic about their personal fortunes. Public confidence is clearly a volatile phenomenon, but the persistence of inflation, energy problems, and other concerns continues to spur a critical examination of our social institutions.[30]

BUREAUCRACY BAITING

A popular form of attack on social institutions is directed at bureaucrats and bureaucracy. Symbolically, bureaucracy has come to stand for all that is wrong with modern society. The federal bureaucracy is alleged to be a monstrous growth that threatens democracy, undermines social justice, and fosters inefficiency, impersonality, alienation, and oppression. While there are reasons to question the growth of bureaucracy, it should not be saddled with all the evils of society. Miller writes:

> Such slipshod condemnations make it all the more difficult to combat effectively the expansion of bureaucracy, for they poison the intellectual atmosphere, creating a climate of nihilistic despair about the forces at work in modern societies. Moreover, bureaucracy baiters do not keep in mind that antibureaucratic movements often have been bent on undoing liberal democracy altogether. . . .[31]

The federal bureaucratic apparatus, though in need of critical attention, provides a strong, central administrative core essential to the government's function as a mediator of the public interest. At the same time, bureaucratic interests and powers cause social institutions to create rigidities and inequities of their own. Traditional institutions, endowed with symbolic significance, tend to defy innovation and reform even when social conditions have made them obsolete. So vigorous social action is required to produce changes in our institutionalized arrangements.[32]

MANAGEMENT STRATEGIES
FOR SOCIAL RESPONSIBILITY

While there is wisdom in the saying that "if a thing ain't broke, don't fix it," there is much to be fixed in our social institutions. Businesspeople, government officials, educators, and other leaders are not wisely or skill-

---

[30] "A Report from the Editors on the 'Crisis of Confidence'," *Public Opinion* 2 (August–September 1979), pp. 2–4 and 54.

[31] Stephen Miller, "Bureaucracy Baiting," *The American Scholar* 47 (spring 1978), p. 206. Reprinted by permission. See also Elliot Jaques, *A General Theory of Bureaucracy* (New York: Halsted Press, 1976), pp. 1–9.

[32] William M. Evan (ed.), *Inter-Organizational Relations* (Philadelphia: University of Pennsylvania Press, 1978), pp. 66–67.

fully meeting criticism, just or unjust. The reasons for this include: (1) the problems are exceedingly complex, perhaps insoluble; (2) leaders are on the defensive; (3) failures and problems tend to overshadow positive accomplishments; (4) the popular media stress failures, misconduct, and criticism; and (5) managers are pressed by day-to-day events, with little time for deep thought and long-run perspectives. Defenders seem to make excuses, find scapegoats, preserve myths and stereotypes, worship the past, or deny mistakes. There are very few frontal attacks on critics.

Business seems to have qualms about itself as a social institution, yielding by default much of the good will that supports its social legitimacy. As legitimacy totters, the public and politicians turn increasingly to government regulation. People see that they can influence bad government through the democratic process, but that they can work against bad things in business only through governmental institutions.[33]

Despite the array of strategies available to managers for coping with attacks and criticisms, business responses have been largely ineffective. The inadequacies of business responses reflect a fear of confrontation: business leaders do not want to appear out of step with the times, or to generate further criticism. Consequently, the responses are often tame, banal platitudes. Reliance on groups such as trade associations is also less effective than it could be, for they repeat many of the mistakes of individual firms and managers. They also separate the individual businessperson from close contacts with government officials.

It is, after all, a sound instinct which puts business below the professions, and burdens the business man with a social inferiority that he can never quite shake off, even in America. The business man, in fact, acquiesces in this assumption of his inferiority, even when he protests against it. He is the only man above the hangman and the scavenger who is forever apologizing for his occupation. He is the only one who always seeks to make it appear, when he attains the object of his labors, i.e., the making of a great deal of money, that it was not the object of his labors.

H. L. MENCKEN, "The Business Man," *A Mencken Chrestomathy* (New York: Knopf, 1949), p. 13.

One important result of the criticism of business has favorable connotations: the increased demand for disclosure and accountability. Critics see disclosure as a moral issue—the right thing to do—even though they understand the reasons for secrecy and privacy. Managers

---

[33] Roger M. D'Aprix, *The Believable Corporation* (New York: AMACOM, 1977). See also Wilson C. McWilliams and Henry A. Plotkin, "The Historic Reputation of American Business," *Journal of Contemporary Business* 5 (Autumn 1976), pp. 1–18.

keep problems inside to avoid outside pressure rather than out of sheer malice. Although public monitoring is widely resisted, many firms have improved their disclosure policies, and laws such as those for automobile recalls have aided this development. Accountability is a complex question that poses many administrative and regulatory issues.[34]

CHOOSING EFFECTIVE STRATEGIES

The reputation of business and business managers depends on developing better strategies for coping with criticism. The necessary strategies are both subtle and direct, and are designed to earn public acceptance and build an image of responsibility. The leadership elite in business fears, with good reason, the alternative to the free enterprise capitalistic system, which is the bureaucratic state run by military, administrative, and policy elites supported by scientific and technical cadres.

Business cannot afford strategies reflecting contempt for responsible conduct. It cannot rely on negative, submissive strategies, nor on warlike hostility to adversaries. Businesspeople have much to gain from viewing moralistic attacks in a historical perspective. Thorstein Veblen, Sinclair Lewis, Adolf Berle, and many others have recounted great confrontations between government and business in the past. Those who believe in a conspiracy between business and government should note the many tensions that have pervaded their interactions.[35]

Fundamental to all strategies is the need for businesspeople to be more accepting of the virtues of dissent and criticism in a free society, and for understanding the consequences if any institution should ever be effectively insulated from criticism. Managers do not forego their own rights to criticize government or labor. In a free and democratic society, criticism is to be encouraged and heeded. Another fundamental policy is to run a tight ship as free as possible from ethically and morally questionable behavior. By curtailing the actions that evoke public and legal sanctions, managers provide a strong base around which to build positive strategies.

The success of the chosen strategies varies according to the nature, sources, and targets of criticism, the skills of managers and critics, and the kinds of strategies selected. But there is no quick or certain fix; short-run, piecemeal responses are not effective; patient and continuous effort is required. Therefore, it is essential that managers develop a clearer

---

[34] Morton Mintz and Jerry S. Cohen, *Power Inc.* (New York: Viking Press, 1976); David Rockefeller, "The Role of Business in an Era of Growing Accountability," *Looking Ahead, National Planning Association Report,* 20 (April 1972), pp. 1–2 and 7.

[35] Arnold Rogow and Harold D. Lasswell, *Power, Corruption, and Rectitude* (Englewood Cliffs, N.J.: Prentice-Hall, 1963), pp. 98–99; Irving S. Michelman, *Business at Bay* (New York: Augustus M. Kelley, 1969).

understanding of their institutional and social roles.[36] We will now consider several specific strategies for business, our focal institution.

Planning: Better long-range planning is an important strategy for improving the social role of business enterprise. This aspect of planning encounters more difficulty than more specific forms such as marketing, financial, or product planning. It involves envisioning the probable social effects of every important decision, and incorporating the concept of social responsibility into all plans. Planning also implies change, and it is often difficult to admit that conditions reflect the need for change. On the other hand, business organizations often reflect adaptability and flexibility which, coupled with leadership and pragmatic optimism, can provide the impetus for planning.

Combating Hostility: Mistrust in institutions is one thing; hostility is another. Programs designed to alleviate the lack of confidence are unlikely to abate the antagonisms of the "new class," for example. The youth movement, the counterculture, and the New Left, the women's movement, environmentalists, minority groups, and consumer groups have posed difficult problems for business because their efforts are often colored by hostility. By pursuing redress in the political system, they have cast suspicion and doubt throughout society. Such groups have been vigorous and unrelenting in their attacks, both on specific corporations and at general levels such as "the corporation," "big business," "the military-industrial complex," or the market system of free enterprise capitalism. These groups are well organized, highly vocal, and charged with emotion that attracts public support. The public sees value in such things as consumerism, product safety, or environmental protection, even though they are often advocated by groups with radical or aggressive ideologies.[37]

Levitt notes that social activists and their confrontation tactics benefit society by helping to keep large bureaucracies honest and responsive to social needs. But they also are a divisive force, spreading discontent through virtually every sector of society. Our society can stand neither the one-sided accusatory rhetoric nor the over-idealization of what is right in America. Levitt's concern, probably an exaggerated one, is that the use of direct attacks instead of political action or persuasion can destroy the cohesiveness and stability of society. He argues that continual fault-finding, moral outrage, and exploitation of the media to portray society as corrupt and unjust could bring nihilism and chaos. To prevent these consequences, Levitt holds that society must cope better with

---

[36] Jeffrey Pfeffer, "Beyond Management and the Worker: The Institutional Function of Management," *The Academy of Management Review* 1 (April 1976), pp. 36–46.

[37] Irving Kristol, "Business and the New Class," *The Wall Street Journal*, May 19, 1975, p. 14.

the problems that give rise to the fulminations of "the third sector" by being responsive through the political system and through commitment to appropriate change.[38]

The strategy for combating this hostility is to reject the use of counterhostility. However, it should also include a greater use of confrontational tactics than has been apparent in business responses. To say or do nothing is a weak defense. The tactics of confrontation include vigorous defense, countercriticism, exposure of factual and other errors, and the rebuttal of faulty evidence in articles, speeches, and other media. Another group of positive tactics in this category is to defend or explain "the system" or some aspect of it through well-conceived educational programs, institutional advertising, and the like.

One example of a confrontation strategy occurred in the business response to a media event known as "Big Business Day." Ralph Nader and several activist groups designated April 17, 1980, for concerted actions in over 150 cities to highlight alleged corporate abuses. Eleven major forms were elected to a "Hall of Shame." The U.S. Chamber of Commerce spearheaded countervailing actions, recommending that business leaders distribute materials refuting the allegations. The Heritage Foundation organized a less well publicized "Growth Day" on the same date to promote big business.[39] Several firms ran ads blasting Big Business Day, but many ignored it. This turned out to be a sophomoric media event with little of substance happening for either side. But it signaled that business may be turning more and more toward a vigorous pursuit of its case.

Philanthropy: An example of how hostility can distort the business response to criticism is seen in recommendations to manipulate philanthropy to support only those universities and scholars who openly support and advocate the ideals of business and the free enterprise system. Leading industrialists, among them David Packard, William Simon, and Henry Ford II, have advocated the withholding of corporate and foundation grants from anyone showing hostility to business. Such tactics are misguided and are likely to suffer the disappointments of earlier economic education programs and the blitz campaigns of the seventies. They betray a misunderstanding of the university's need to pursue free and open research for truth, wherever it might lead. To deprive universities of financial support out of pique and frustration would in the long run be self-defeating.[40]

---

[38] Theodore Levitt, *The Third Sector* (New York: AMACOM, 1973).

[39] *Newsweek*, April 21, 1980, p. 78; *The Wall Street Journal*, April 9, 1980, p. 1.

[40] See James Kilpatrick, syndicated column of November 21, 1973; *The Wall Street Journal*, January 14, 1977, p. 18; *U.S. News and World Report*, January 24, 1977, p. 62; *The Chronicle of Higher Education*, March 15, 1976, p. 7; Robert H. Malott, "Corporate Support of Education: Some Strings Attached," and W. Cabot, "Corporate Support to Education: No Strings Attached," *Harvard Business Review* 56 (July–August 1978), pp. 133–138.

There is more pro-business, pro-free enterprise spirit in schools than many realize. In one survey, for example, more than 4 out of 5 professors of 4200 agreed with the statement that "the private business system in the U.S., for all its flaws, works better than any other system devised for advanced industrial society." More than two-thirds agreed that "the growth of government in the U.S. now poses a threat to the freedom and opportunity for individual initiative of the citizenry." More than half agreed that "economic growth, not redistribution, should be the primary objective of American economic policy."[41]

Cooptation: Businesspeople often seem overly suspicious and angry with professors, research, and universities. Yet paradoxically, they have spent millions trying to coopt them. Cooptation is the strategy of incorporating critics into the system under attack, to blunt the effects of the criticism through providing an inside, participative view. Examples include placing students, consumers, or public representatives on boards of directors or trustees, or electing students or businesspeople to university committees. Another illustration is the election of the president of the United Auto Workers to the board of directors of the Chrysler Corporation.

Cooptation carries certain risks. For example, the coopted individual may be better able to criticize after viewing things from inside. Concessions often must be made to persuade the critic to participate at all. Cooptation is a tradeoff strategy—both sides give up something to get other things in return. It is a slow and uncertain strategy, but it also reflects a healthy spirit of cooperation and compromise that can help to smooth over an adversary relationship.

Lobbying: Lobbying in political bodies is a legal and acceptable maneuver. This outreach into the environment provides a nexus between business and other social institutions. Although lobbying is a self-serving tactic, everyone recognizes business's right to influence political processes, and politicians welcome the information that helps them hear all sides of an issue. Lobbying takes place under legal and ethical strictures that attempt, not always successfully, to prevent abuses.

Lobbying has encountered government blocks, where firms have requests or job bids pending at the same time they are attempting to influence legislation. For example, in 1978 steel executives were told at a presidential breakfast that continued opposition to the government's energy legislation might cause the administration to put a low priority on its tariff negotiations with Japan.[42] Another observer noted that when politicians were attacking the oil industry, the chief executives of major

---

[41] *Chronicle of Higher Education*, January 16, 1978, p. 9.

[42] Clarence J. Brown, "The Servility of Business," *The Wall Street Journal*, November 29, 1978, p. 24.

companies did not come to their defense, but were conspicuous by their silence.[43]

Media Strategies: A unique historical development has occurred with respect to the media. The variety of media now makes it easier to check on the pronouncements and behavior of the managers of social institutions. In earlier times, published information was more consistent with the official views of the managers; now convincing accounts of social reality issue from different sources of varying degrees of independence. Those controlling social institutions can no longer monopolize authoritative accounts of their own management.[44] Nevertheless, it is also true that the media are selective. They edit, dramatize, and even favor some events and not others, according to their rules about what is worth reporting. Violence, scandals, conflict, and other discreditable events often overshadow the reporting of positive accomplishment. This is a problem for managers, as well as a delicate matter of responsibility and judgment for the media.

Media strategies require expertise and judgment in the use of communications techniques, but there must be a high-quality substantive base around which professional public and employee relations efforts can be more than a cosmetic or palliative strategy. Telling good things works better when there are genuinely valid accomplishments to report.[45]

Whereas firms have the benefit of professional staffs, managers as individuals often lack training in skills that make them effective in personal and interpersonal communications. Businesspeople often make vague or erroneous statements to journalists, or avoid them altogether. Their articles and speeches display a dull sameness, being generally written according to formulas by house writers. Afraid to say what they really think, they fall back on empty clichés and the standard patter of conventional wisdom. Their articles and speeches lack genuine feeling and the stamp of their own personalities. The remedy is for managers first to have something worth saying, and then to speak or write plainly and with the unique perspective of their own personalities. Business representatives need to project themselves more into arenas of controversy and debate their adversaries more effectively.

Another communications problem is the tendency of managers to present their companies in the most favorable light, with an eye on what competitors say and do. Annual reports and other communications are couched in the most general terms, although many readers would prefer more specific and accurate information. When businesspeople talk to

---

[43] Vermont Royster, "The Voice of Business," *The Wall Street Journal*, May 16, 1979, p. 16; see also David Vogel, *Lobbying the Corporation: Citizen Challenges to Business Authority* (New York: Basic Books, 1978).

[44] Alvin W. Gouldner, *The Dialectic of Ideology and Technology: The Origins, Grammar and Future of Ideology* (New York: Seabury Press, 1976), pp. 122–124.

[45] Roger M. D'Aprix, *The Believable Corporation*.

each other they deal with their real problems, but when they talk to consumers, shareholders, or activists, they talk down to them or resort to the commonplace.[46]

Companies use advertising campaigns to promote not only their products, but also the firm's image (institutional advertising) and their points of view toward social issues (advocacy advertising). These campaigns are not highly effective because people compare the generalities unfavorably with their own specific experiences, and because it is hard to change attitudes. Zoffer suggests a patient, more gradual approach. The credibility gap is not amenable to instant solutions, especially efforts that can be perceived as propaganda or brainwashing. He recommends: (1) a low-key, long-term educational effort, (2) a more direct, one-to-one communication strategy rather than a massive blitz, (3) a reassessment of each institution's role in society, with emphasis on how it serves society rather than how society serves it, and (4) a heavy and long-run but not heavy-handed investment in activities, including research, that will build confidence gradually.[47]

PLANNING FOR CHANGE

The dissatisfactions of so many Americans with the functioning of social institutions portend extensive changes in society. The desire for liberty, justice, and freedom remains strong, and it is likely that changes will attempt to preserve these ideals. Public sentiment is the most influential guardian of institutional patterns, and our institutions offer great opportunities for moral self-control. The critical issues are essentially moral ones, and leaders are needed who can solve problems and who are sensitive to change. Managers who are aware of moral nuances surrounding the need for change can contribute greatly to the improvement of our institutions. Angell writes:

> The good society, then, would be one in which leaders are working through many kinds of institutional groups to achieve the adjustments in the moral web that are both suitable to the conditions and consonant with common values. Thus could a dynamic and democratic society maintain a high level of moral integration even in this twentieth century.[48]

Incident Case

The following statement was made in early 1980 by a vice-president of marketing at a major supplier of graphite:

---

[46] Donald Winks, "Speaking Out – With a Forked Tongue," *Business Week*, July 2, 1979, p. 9.

[47] H. J. Zoffer, "Restoring Institutional Credibility," *MSU Business Topics* 25 (Autumn 1977), pp. 6–10.

[48] Angell, *Free Society*, p. 232.

I admit I'm prejudiced, but I wonder just who is my largest competitor—Union Carbide & Chemical, brokers, another graphite company? Or, my own government. The answer is, my own government, through its bureaucracies. It therefore follows: At what point does this competitor turn into an enemy? Now, the answer scares me. The Japanese beat us by using a triumvirate approach, complete cooperation between industry, labor, and government. It can work, but not here, where we are "free" to either cooperate or not cooperate. What irony!

Issues for Discussion and Analysis

1. Why are our major social institutions under attack? Who are the attackers? Will the attacks continue?

2. Assess the significance of the problem of lack of confidence and trust in social institutions. Is there a crisis of legitimacy? A crisis of power?

3. Why are business leaders finding it difficult to restore their tarnished image? What should they do to help restore public confidence in business?

4. What are the key roles of managers with respect to the problems of our social institutions?

5. What major changes in society are having an impact on business as a social institution?

Class Project

Divide the class members into groups of six or eight members. Assign each group a specific social institution, such as business, religion, education, government and so forth. Each team is to prepare a managerial defense of the public criticism levelled against the institution it is assigned. Select one team member to present an analysis to the class as a whole.

For Further Reading

THE CONFERENCE BOARD.   *Challenge to Leadership: Managing in a Changing World* (New York: Free Press, 1973).

DE GRE, GERARD L.   *Science as a Social Institution* (New York: Random House, 1965).

GALAMBOS, LOUIS.   *The Public Image of Big Business in America 1880–1940* (Baltimore: The Johns Hopkins University Press, 1976).

GRIMKÉ, FREDERICK.   *The Nature and Tendency of Free Institutions*, edited by John William Ward (Cambridge, Mass.: Harvard University Press, 1968).

HUDSON, KENNETH.   *The Businessman in Public* (New York: Wiley, 1976).

LAPHAM, LEWIS. *Fortune's Child* (Garden City, N.Y.: Doubleday, 1980).

MACPHERSON, C. B. (ED.). *Property: Mainstream and Critical Positions* (Toronto, Can.: University of Toronto Press, 1978).

MAYHEU, LEON. *Society: Institutions of Activity* (Glenview, Ill.: Scott, Foresman, 1971).

McCARTHY, EUGENE J. *The Hard Years: A Look at Contemporary America and American Institutions* (New York: Viking Press, 1975).

THOMPSON, CAREY C. *Institutional Adjustment: A Challenge to a Changing Economy* (Austin: University of Texas Press, 1967).

VOGEL, DAVID. *Lobbying the Corporation: Citizen Challenges to Business Authority* (New York: Basic Books, 1978).

WEIDENBAUM, MURRAY L. *Business, Government, and the Public* (Englewood Cliffs, N.J.: Prentice-Hall, 1977).

WELLS, ALAN. *Social Institutions* (New York: Basic Books, 1971).

7

Social Movements,
Issues, and Reform

. . . social movements alert us to unsatisfied or frustrated needs. They draw our attention to areas in which we can exercise the option of alleviating suffering and furnishing hope to our fellows. Social movements, in their capacity as gadflies, are indirect agents of change. They do their part by coming into being, and by pinpointing problems through their efforts to cope with them. Sympathetic observers (such as social scientists) must decipher these efforts and must deduce their implications for action. Society has to do the rest.

HANS TOCH,
The Social Psychology of Social Movements,
(Indianapolis: Bobbs-Merrill 1965), p. 247.

CONCEPTS DISCUSSED IN THIS CHAPTER

1. WHY SOCIAL MOVEMENTS ARISE, WHAT THEY DO, AND HOW THEY DO IT
2. COLLECTIVISM AND CONSTRUCTIVISM
3. THE NATURE OF SOCIAL PROBLEMS AND SOCIAL CHANGE
4. REFORM EFFORTS: SOCIAL PROBLEM SOLVING
5. SOCIAL PROGRESS

Much of the change in modern society results from social movements. As a form of collective action, movements mobilize those with social concerns to work for reform through political processes and influence on public opinion. Thus movements are more than temporary, illegitimate interruptions in the otherwise smooth functioning of society; they are vital forces in the struggle for progress in human affairs.

This chapter presents (1) some key definitions, (2) an analysis of the nature of social movements, including participation and leadership, and the functions of movements, and (3) a discussion of social change, reform, and protest in the framework of management and society.

WHAT IS A SOCIAL MOVEMENT?

A *social movement* represents a shared demand for change in some aspect of the social order. It carries an explicit, conscious indictment of all or part of the social order.[1] Toch defines a social movement as an effort by a large number of people to solve collectively a problem they feel they have in common.[2]

Movements are distinguished from other forms of collective behavior by being large, relatively long-lasting efforts with clear reform purposes. A social movement is not technically a group or an organization, although it thrives on their support and participation. Movements mobilize both individuals and action-oriented groups that form within it or become allies.

It is important to distinguish social movements from pressure or interest groups and political parties. A pressure group differs from a social movement chiefly by the limited goal it pursues. It does not aim primarily to change the social order. Movements are also less clearly organized than pressure groups. Political parties have programs or platforms focusing on political issues, and unlike movements, they have formal organizations.[3] Social movements should also be distinguished from general trends or tendencies. Movements may result from or even generate trends or tendencies, but not all social change arises from the concerted actions of social movements. Urbanization or industrialization are examples of trends or tendencies. They follow from an aggregation of individual decisions, and are social processes rather than movements.[4]

Some examples will help clarify these definitions. "Women's liberation" denotes a social movement which aims to restore, enlarge, or preserve women's rights and help them achieve more equality with men. Within the women's movement are various pressure groups such as the National Organization of Women and pressure groups advocating the Equal Rights Amendment to the Constitution. A number of interest groups support the precepts of women's liberation, along with other

---

[1] Joseph Gusfield, "The Study of Social Movements," in the *International Encyclopedia of the Social Sciences* (New York: Macmillan, 1968), p. 445.

[2] Hans Toch, *The Social Psychology of Social Movements* (Indianapolis: Bobbs-Merrill, 1965), p. 5.

[3] Rudolf Heberle, *Social Movements* (New York: Appleton-Century-Crofts, 1951), pp. 6–11.

[4] Ibid. See also Harry C. Boyte, *The Backyard Revolution: Understanding the New Citizen Movement* (Philadelphia: Temple University Press, 1980).

interests. An example here is the National Association of Media Women. Consumerism is another movement in which there are a number of pressure and interest groups, such as the American Council on Consumer Interests or the Consumers Union of the United States, Inc.

THE NATURE OF SOCIAL MOVEMENTS

Movements have little or no formal organization structures of operation and control. Instead, they have proponents, adherents, or believers, and leaders in the heroic or charismatic mode. They rely more on influence than on power. Influence is through persuasion, backed by the pressure of numbers and the ability to stay interesting to the media. As a result, their organizational features are unstable, short-lived, and dependent on the commitment and participation of advocates.[5]

Conflict and confrontation are key elements in the functioning of social movements. Movements may aim to preserve the status quo or to oppose change, but most seek major changes in values, institutions, activities, or the social system. Some movements stress protest; others aim to protect important interests. For example, consumerism, organized labor, or women's movement efforts actively identify and attack major concerns by uniting numbers of people with common interests, and their efforts therefore plunge these people into important social controversies.[6]

THE RISE AND FALL OF MOVEMENTS

Social movements arise spontaneously rather than by direct design. They have a life cycle of birth, maturation, and decline. Their origins are obscure, and maturation comes if dedicated adherents are won to the cause, especially if the movement gains acceptance in the wider reaches of society. Maturation, which involves adaptation and transformation, leads to increased bureaucratization, formalization, and self-preservation, and sometimes to the use of force or violence as the limits of persuasion are reached.

The decline of a movement may result from failure or success, as well as from forces that make it outmoded or obsolete. Social forces nearly always attempt to destroy or suppress movements that favor violence or extremism.[7] Failure and success are measured by goal achievement. If the goals cannot be attained, they must be changed or the move-

---

[5] Amitai Etzioni, *The Active Society* (New York: Free Press, 1968), p. 525.

[6] Michael Useem, *Protest Movements in America* (Indianapolis: Bobbs-Merrill, 1975); Lucy B. Creighton, *Pretenders to the Throne: The Consumer Movement in the United States* (Lexington, Mass: Lexington Books, 1976); Donald W. Hendon, "Toward A Theory of Consumerism," *Business Horizons* 18 (August 1975), pp. 16–24.

[7] Toch, *The Social Psychology of Social Movements*, pp. 203–228.

ment may cease. Success too brings problems. If goals are achieved, the movement grows not only in adherents but also in money, wealth, and power. Some movements, such as religious cults, acquire vast holdings of property, owning farms, stores, banks, and other business ventures. But this form of success may distort the original goals, turn the movement inward toward self-preservation or self-aggrandizement, or even corrupt its leaders.

Movements sometimes simply lose their vitality. Early enthusiasms wane as problems arise. Movements fall out of step with the times and die as stronger, more powerful or timely movements take over. For example, Bloom and Stern predict that by the year 2000 the consumerism movement will be dead, overpowered by a movement centered on anti-industrialism. Consumerism will become highly institutionalized and will lose its vitality. As problems associated with resource scarcity, pollution, communication, and system overload increase, people will become more interested in the anti-industrialism movement.[8]

PARTICIPATION IN SOCIAL MOVEMENTS

People join movements to work with others who share their concerns. Leaders persuade them to make moral, emotional, and intellectual commitments to achieve practical or idealistic aims, chiefly through political processes. Individuals also participate by belonging to organizations which work within movements that interest them.

Specific data on participation are difficult to obtain because movements are highly volatile; they change so rapidly that researchers have made few longitudinal or historical studies. Rothman reports a summary of research from which basic generalizations on the demography, psychological correlates, external social correlates, and other dynamic variables of participation were derived. The summary subjectively evaluated the quantity and quality of studies supporting each generalization, finding support for participation being associated with (1) youth, ages 15 to 25; (2) a higher level of education; (3) the individual's relative sense of deprivation; (4) a high level of status inconsistency; (5) awareness of social system or structural causes of social problems; and (6) attitudes and values of the individual's membership or reference group.[9]

The motivation to participate is a difficult problem of psychology, for a person's true motives are hard to discover. One may infer motives from observed behavior, but only at the risk of error. One may ask

---

[8] Paul N. Bloom and Louis W. Stern, "Emergence of Anti-Industrialism," *Business Horizons* 19 (October 1976), pp. 87–93. See also James Hitchcock, "The Dynamics of Popular Intellectual Change," *The American Scholar*, (Autumn 1976), pp. 522-535.

[9] Jack Rothman, *Planning and Organizing for Social Change* (New York: Columbia University Press, 1974), pp. 326–352.

individuals what motivates them, but their answers may be limited by the complexity or inaccessibility of needs, the inadequacy of language, or the desire to make an impression. People often say what they think the asker expects, or they may be unaware or ashamed of their reasons. The best way to assess motivation, according to Toch, is to ask individuals, but at the same time to check the responses by behavioral observations.[10]

Dissatisfaction that leads to joining movements often arises from a succession of disillusioning experiences. Some join from deep-seated, hidden impulses within the personality, such as the need for notoriety or companionship. Many see participation as a way of expressing the general beliefs, ideologies, or values that movements stand for. The motivation to join may differ from the motivation to become or remain active. Adherents who become disillusioned, or who want more progress, or whose needs change, may leave. A successful movement maintains the motivation of participants by stressing loyalty, commitment, camaraderie, brotherhood, emotional involvement, and the like. But results must eventually match expectations.[11]

Collectivism: The pluralist view is that organized groups seek positive goals through negotiated strategies. In contrast, social movements reflect the deep frustrations of the victims of social disorganization. Participants are the uprooted, who suffer from the stresses of society. Hoffer, for example, describes participation in mass movements as a fundamental irrationality. Individuals who participate out of discontent often have inflated visions of the future and are unaware of the difficulties that will arise.[12] Kornhauser sees mass behavior as focusing on objectives that are remote from daily life and personal experience.[13] Smelser describes a "short-circuiting" behavior in which the movement goes from a highly generalized, abstract view to direct action against a source of strain. The generalized belief becomes a myth by which to mobilize people.[14] None of these views eliminates the collective impulses in social movements.

Gamson, criticizing pluralist theory, attacks the collectivist tradition. The collective behavior concept can be used, he asserts, to discredit movements one dislikes, such as revolutions or the fascist movements of the 1930s, or the student rebellions of the 1960s and 1970s. He believes that the collectivism paradigm has inhibited the scientific study of social protest.[15]

---

[10] Toch, *The Social Psychology of Social Movements*, pp. 185–202. See also Heberle, *Social Movements*, pp. 93–117.

[11] John Wilson, *Introduction to Social Movements* (New York: Basic Books, 1979).

[12] Eric Hoffer, *The True Believer* (New York: Harper & Row, 1951), p. 7.

[13] William Kornhauser, *The Politics of Mass Society* (New York: Free Press, 1959).

[14] Neil Smelser, *Theory of Collective Behavior* (New York: Free Press, 1963).

[15] William A. Gamson, *The Strategy of Social Protest* (Homewood, Ill.: Dorsey Press, 1975), pp. 130–136. A reassessment of Gamson's book is contained in Jack A. Goldstone, *The Weakness of Organization: A New Look at Gamson's The Strategy of Social Protest* (Chicago: The University of Chicago Press, 1980).

Constructivism: Constructivism holds that since humans have created the institutions of society and civilization, humans can also alter them at will. Humans design their fate because they are endowed with reason. Hayek raises doubts, because humankind did not possess reason before civilization. Constructivism implies the ability to predict the future and shape society in purposive, rational ways. Such thinking assumes undue foresight and reliance on cause and effect. Humans act not only according to ends and means, but also by rules of conduct of which they are rarely aware and which they have not consciously invented.[16]

Constructivist thought sometimes takes the form of social engineering — the use of science and technology to better the human condition. The eighteenth-century Enlightenment emphasized a supreme rationality in the design of the social order which was reinforced by the Cartesian-Newtonian mechanical model of nature.[17] Although the roots of this idea go back to ancient civilizations, in the current age social engineering has gone out of favor. Bureaucratization, planning, big organization, fiscal control, and the like would increase under social engineering, which tends to ignore the qualitative aspects of human beings.

The lesson of constructivism for management is that social problems are solved not only according to rules for individuals, but also according to rules for society itself. Laws, morals, customs, and the values of society, whether explicitly stated or not, interact in the processes of social action.

LEADERSHIP IN SOCIAL MOVEMENTS

The decline of confidence in social institutions has brought an associated loss of confidence in their leaders. The leaders of social movements, at least before bureaucratization sets in, are freer of organizational and political constraints. Such leaders rely more on persuasion, commitment to objectives and ideals, and a host of personality attributes summed up in the concept of *charisma*.

Charisma: Weber defined charisma as ". . . a certain quality of an individual personality by virtue of which he is set apart from other men and treated as endowed with supernatural, superhuman, or at least specifically exceptional qualities."[18] Charisma is characteristic of the leaders of large social movements or revolutions. Two reasons can be suggested. First, situations calling for charismatic leadership involve antitraditional forces in which the character of desired change can become symbolically

---

[16] F. A. Hayek, *New Studies in Philosophy, Politics, Economics and the History of Ideas* (Chicago: The University of Chicago Press, 1978), excerpt reprinted in *Forbes*, December 10, 1979, pp. 109–114.

[17] Benjamin I. Schwartz, "The Rousseau Strain in the Contemporary World," *Daedalus* 197 (Summer 1978), pp. 193–194.

[18] Reinhardt Bendix, *Max Weber: An Intellectual Portrait* (Garden City, N.Y.: Doubleday, 1962), p. 88.

associated with a specific person.[19] Second, charismatic authority is sharply opposed both to rational and bureaucratic authority, thereby repudiating the past.[20]

No ordered change is possible without leadership. But recent social movements, such as the protest movements, rejected formal leaders or even the concept of leadership in organizations. Their view is that leadership is an alien activity of remote elites, or that it fosters sinister conspiracies and is dangerous for society. Burns notes that leadership can be directed toward creative and democratic ends only when it is open to a crucial role for intellectuals and generates popular participation through the system.[21] Intellectual leaders are caught between the tendency to be captives of the establishment and the temptation to retire into their ivory towers. Intellectuals need to provide expertise to the government and the public while at the same time being critical, and to maintain a commitment to important ends while remaining detached from traditional means.[22]

Leaders in political, educational, and business institutions are at the scenes of action and decision, and hence they are the ones whom the leaders of social movements need to influence. Yet the two types of leaders find it difficult to understand one another; conflict and distrust arise from the resistance to change by institutions that confronts the impatient, emotional, and aggressive pressures in social movements. Agreement on ends does not assure agreement as to means, or as to the timing of desirable change.

The leaders of a social movement are among its most active, committed adherents. Their personality traits accord with the special needs of movements—for example, in their willingness to accept risk. Leadership in movements is much riskier than in formal organizations; authority is earned, informal, and uncertain of duration. Such leaders usually serve without pay. Studies of social movements indicate that their leaders are above average in social background, intelligence, and skills. Leaders in social movements thus need the same qualities as leaders in conventional settings.[23]

Heroism: We often decry the absence of heroes in society. Beset by pressing issues, we yearn for courageous leaders of heroic stature. The need for honest, effective leaders is so intense that we look for heroes to

---

[19] Talcott Parsons, *Theories of Society*, vol. I. (New York: Free Press, 1961).

[20] S. N. Eisenstadt, *Selected Papers of Max Weber: On Charisma and Institution Building* (Chicago: The University of Chicago Press, 1968), p. 51.

[21] James McGregor Burns, *Uncommon Sense* (New York: Harper & Row, 1972), pp. 208–209.

[22] James McGregor Burns, *Leadership* (New York: Harper & Row, 1978).

[23] Armand L. Mauss, *Social Problems as Social Movements* (Philadelphia: Lippincott, 1975), pp. 52–55.

provide superhuman results. The leaders of social movements in part help to fulfill this need.

Heroes rise dramatically from special circumstances that identify them with their times. They take great risks and often give up their lives or reputations. They may go unrecognized until history honors them; as time passes, their prophetic voices are heard again. Heroes are more than celebrities, more than leaders, more than merely able. They exemplify sacrifice and boldness of action. Idealism and dreams are part of the heroic image. Two examples of heroic leadership are found in the black and women's movements. Martin Luther King, Jr., died amid his dream of racial equality. Muhummad Ali pursued his ideals and beliefs throughout the world. Betty Friedan, Barbara Jordan, and others in the women's movement were perhaps less heroic but nevertheless bold advocates of at first unpopular change. Lindbergh's heroic flight preserved his heroic image even after his political beliefs aroused anger, but society may withhold heroic ascriptions or allow them to fade. The astronauts are former heroes whom the public has largely forgotten, as are veterans of the Vietnam war. The phenomenon of the unsung hero is a common one. We cannot stand too many heroes at once; we often have a guilty conscience over needing them. And we select our heroes unpredictably.[24]

There is more than a touch of the heroic in all individuals, though few of them admit it or take the impulse seriously. Becker writes that if everyone honestly admitted the urge to be a hero, there would be a devastating release of truth.[25] Social movements provide a context in which our innate heroic impulses can be expressed.

We turn next to an examination of the ideas of social change, social progress, and social reform.

SOCIAL CHANGE

In the postindustrial society it is an arduous but vital task to define and cope with complex change, to assess priorities, and to carry out reforms. Decisions are forged out of controversy, since strategies arising from competing sources are conducted largely through the political processes in a free and open society. But the process of achieving a necessary consensus as to problems and priorities is embroiled in a maze of social, economic, and political interests.[26]

---

[24] Pete Axthelm, "Where Have All the Heroes Gone?" *Newsweek*, August 6, 1979, pp. 44–50. See also James McGregor Burns, *Leadership*, chap. 9.

[25] Ernest Becker, *Denial of Death* (New York: Free Press, 1973), pp. 5–6.

[26] Joseph A. Pechman (ed.), *Setting National Priorities* (Washington, D.C.: The Brookings Institution, 1978).

The requirements for identifying a social problem can be simply stated. There must be an awareness of the extent of pain or harm to society or to citizens. The problem must acquire a generic name, such as "corporate ethics," and it must be one around which those in power can rally public support. They will do so when they themselves have something to gain, such as a following or a political office. Finally, the communications media must inform the public about the issues and nourish the desire for action. The word *crisis* often lends a tone of urgency intended to galvanize leaders into action, and to focus the support of citizens.

But the matter is not as simple as it seems. One need only look at energy questions to see that consensus on the nature and extent of a problem and how it should be attacked is hard to achieve despite the pronouncements of experts and public figures. As shorthand labels for complex issues, the terms denoting problems are gross oversimplifications. For example, many people do not include alcohol and tobacco as part of our narcotics problem. Leaders may do what is easy, expedient, or self-serving, and may authenticate nonexistent or low-level problems they know how to deal with rather than those that are truly urgent.

The public does not perceive the interrelatedness of problems or the priorities among them. Individuals react more in short-run self-concern than long-run social concern. Moreover, millions of individuals have little direct experience with far-reaching problems such as drug abuse, crime, or even catastrophic illness. Distortions, doubtless unintended, result from the effects of media presentations. Gerbner and Gross found, for example, that heavy viewers of television estimated their chances of being victimized by a criminal at an astronomical rate bearing little relationship to actual crime rates.[27]

THE USES OF CONTENTION

Contention is pervasive in social discourse. Not even science can rid us of contention, which is rife within science itself. And while scientists are notably cautious about the use of their knowledge, the same cannot be said for politicians and administrators, or even for intellectuals. The outcomes of social contention are determined only in part by what is known, for knowledge keeps changing. The outcomes are also a consequence of who knows what, of how perceived or operational truths are

---

[27] George Gerbner and Larry Gross, "The Scary World of TV's Heavy Viewer," *Psychology Today*, April 1976, pp. 41–45, 89. The Gerbner studies have been partially refuted. Doob and McDonald found the Gerbner studies replicable in their finding that people who watch a lot of television are more likely to indicate fear of their environment. However, they found that this relationship disappears when studies are controlled for other variables, such as the actual incidence of crime in a neighborhood. See Anthony N. Doob and Glenn E. McDonald, "Television Viewing and Fear of Victimization: Is the Relationship Causal?" *Journal of Personality and Social Psychology* 37 (1979), pp. 170–179.

selected and disseminated and to what purpose, and of the skills of con-
tenders.

Contention produces tensions which, if unchecked, may tear the
fabric of society. But there are also benefits. Contention helps to develop
ideas for change; it mobilizes resources and guides their use; it provides
leaders with objectives and citizens with channels for voicing their concerns; it clarifies the power struggles within and among groups and
organizations.

The chief problem with contention is that it can lead to indecision
and delay, if not to violence. Debate must be followed by the actions of
power centers capable of resolving conflicts and evolving a consensus.

DISTORTION OF ISSUES

Many distortions pervade problem solving in society. Leaders may be
influential among citizens but not in politics. Elected political leaders are
often unable or unwilling to influence constituents in unpopular directions. To stay in office, they are reluctant to antagonize supporters.
Choosing sides involves risks, as revealed in the long and vigorous
debates over Vietnam war policies and tactics or in the handling of the
Panama Canal issue. Furthermore, the same divisiveness that plagues
politicians is also present in the general public.

Distortions also occur where scientific evidence contradicts the positions of vocal interest groups, such as environmentalists, futurists, labor
unions, or industrialists. Research that finds smoking less harmful than
many believe, pollution not dangerous to health, saccharin to be safe for
humans, or safety bag devices in automobiles not worth the cost is likely
to be rejected as counter to the common wisdom, or to unleash attacks on
the scientists. The media often favor the attackers. For example, scientists who reexamined the National Cancer Institute's statistics on the
incidence of cancer in New Jersey's industrial area concluded that the
cancer risk for the population as a whole from airborne chemicals is
largely hypothetical compared to the known risks of occupationally
caused cancer among workers. The press and the television media attacked this finding. A state senator charged that the scientists were
"spreading falsehoods" and were part of an "organized conspiracy." The
arguments clearly did not turn on scientific merits.[28]

Another source of distortion of social issues arises from the impulse
to blame someone for our troubles. If the cause can be assigned to an external source, we may claim that the problem is beyond our control.
Solution strategies are thus made to appear heroic in the face of intracti-
ble forces. We need scapegoats, such as giant corporations, international

---

[28] *The Wall Street Journal*, February 12, 1979, p. 12.

conspiracies, communism, or the gnomes of Zurich to explain our difficulties.

THE IDEA OF PROGRESS

The pluralistic society never reaches a stable equilibrium with regard to competing social philosophies. A persistent issue is whether there is "progress" for society or for humanity, and if so, what the nature of that progress is. Two views of progress emerged in the age of the Enlightenment. Locke, Voltaire, and Condorcet saw progress in the contrast between modernity and the medieval era, when bigotry, terror, and superstition reigned. Rousseau, by contrast, saw history as a process of decline, decay of morals, civic virtue, naturalness, and community.[29] Locke's positive views of progress held sway during the emergence and maturing of the Industrial Revolution, but doubts, disillusionment, and loss of faith in traditional values and social institutions have challenged the reality of progress and have led to calls for revising the philosophical foundations of management and social thought.[30]

Five major premises associated with progress are being challenged: belief in the value of the past; convictions about the nobility or even superiority of Western civilization; acceptance of the value of economic and technological growth; faith in reason and scholarly knowledge; and belief in the worth of life on earth. The challenges manifest themselves in revolt against rationalism and science, secular and religious irrationalism, anti-intellectualism, and narcissistic preoccupation with self. Religious faith, the underpinning of the idea of progress, has declined, with a resulting secularization of the idea of progress. Nisbet sees faint rays of hope in signs of religious renewal in Western societies;[31] Smith holds more pessimistically that placing hope on the sacred is an illusion.[32]

Progress remains an energizing force, and a reality of history despite setbacks and doubts. The kind and amount of progress depend on the focus selected for viewing it. For technical, scientific, and economic progress, there is at least a short-run case. For civilization viewed historically, there is a moderate case. The most difficult unresolved question is whether there is progress in overcoming the worst elements in human nature, which continues to exhibit a curious mixture of the evil and the sublime.

---

[29] Joseph Featherstone, "Rousseau and Modernity," *Daedalus* 107 (Summer 1978), p. 182.

[30] George C. Lodge, *The New American Ideology* (New York: Knopf, 1975).

[31] Robert Nisbet, *History of the Idea of Progress* (New York: Basic Books, 1980). See also Madison Pirie, *Trial and Error and the Idea of Progress* (La Salle, Ill.: Open Court, 1978); and Clarence C. Walton (ed.), *Business and Social Progress* (New York: Praeger, 1970).

[32] Morton Smith, *Hope and History, An Exploration* (New York: Harper & Row, 1980).

REFORM

The idea of reform brings together the concepts we have been discussing. Reform is a goal of social change implying progress and hope for a better society. Major social movements identify and pursue many of our expectations, though many reforms are pursued apart from movements.

Both progress and reform occur unevenly in history and at any given time, often with painful difficulty. There is no master coordinating scheme to prevent one sector of society from attempting gains at the expense of others. Proposed reforms are numerous and often too simple or naive. But even very logical reforms do not work if their proponents fail to consider the effects of the social and psychological factors that underlie the ways individuals and groups can react to the simplest forms of change.[33]

We are also naive about reform itself. The government pours money into problem areas without substantial results. This in turn produces calls for reform in politics and the government itself. In the field of education, for example, huge expenditures for buildings, teachers, equipment, and research have been accompanied by increased dissatisfaction with the educational system on the part of taxpayers, teachers, and students. In medicine, the nation spends increasing billions, yet the "health care crisis" endures. These examples reflect the piecemeal nature of our attacks on social issues; we do things without clearly assessing priorities or examining the basic values and beliefs that underlie our problems.

> *When I arise in the morning, I am torn by the twin desires to reform the world and enjoy the world. This makes it hard to plan the day.*
>
> E. B. WHITE

The role of government in large-scale social reform derives from the need for authority appropriate to each problem and acceptable to those whose lives are affected. Without authority, proposals, programs, or plans are merely promises or hopes. The distrust of leaders and of social institutions reflects the waning of the authoritative influence and the legitimacy that comes from within. Reform programs often start the other way around—that is, a bureaucrat or other reformer bestows on some locus of power the "authority" to institute a program planned in absentia and imposed paternalistically and without participation.[34]

---

[33] Jay W. Forrester, "Counterintuitive Behavior of Social Systems," *Technology Review*, January 1971, pp. 53–68.

[34] Iredell Jenkins, "Authority: Its Nature and Locus," in R. Baine Harris (ed.), *Authority: A Philosophical Analysis* (University, Ala.: University of Alabama Press, 1976), pp. 25–44.

Three criteria apply to use of authority in reform situations: the degree of choice permitted; the extent to which decisions are made by persons of knowledge, skill, and competence; and the principle of economy.[35] Obviously, many reform efforts do not meet these tests.

In a broad, overall assessment of the social welfare efforts of the 1960s, Levitan and Taggart suggest that government programs advanced under the Great Society concept had a massively beneficial effect in changing institutions and individuals, and hence for the improvement of society. They concluded that the goals were realistic and the programs were reasonably efficient.[36] These views are not widely accepted, especially with regard to the efficiency of methods, but also as to the quality of results. Many issues remain, and we have not yet found procedures and structures by which we can be confident of progress.

IDEALISM AND REFORM

Reform efforts are loaded with idealism. This is both favorable and unfavorable. Ideals have always moved humans to action, though they may be elusive, unattainable, or capable of generating evil as well as good. Ideals express aspirations rather than specific goals, and they are colored by emotional overtones and profound values. They generally appeal to the better side of human nature, and hence serve for many as motivators for change and progress. The principal difficulty with ideals is that they are remote from the practical realities of the present. Failure to progress toward ideals evokes frustration and discouragement. Furthermore, ideals take many forms, some of which are in conflict and hard to verbalize in ways that lead to action.

With respect to reform, let us consider the following as illustrative of idealism: (1) militancy, (2) prophetic influences, (3) muckraking, (4) utopianism, and (5) futurism.

Militancy: Whereas the early industrial society focused largely on economic institutions, today's society seeks improvement in all its social institutions, with a major role in politics and government. An improving society therefore requires the involvement of citizens who participate in the processes of governance.[37]

Reform efforts reflect degrees of militancy ranging from gradual persuasion to revolution. Reform movements accept the values of the existing order and attempt to correct institutional defects, whereas revolu-

---

[35] Robert A. Dahl, *After the Revolution: Authority in a Good Society* (New Haven, Conn.: Yale University Press, 1970), p. 115.

[36] Sar A. Levitan and Robert Taggart, *The Promise of Greatness* (Cambridge, Mass.: Harvard University Press, 1976).

[37] Ralf Dahrendorf, *The New Liberty: Survival and Justice in a Changing World* (Stanford, Calif.: Stanford University Press, 1975), pp. 69–82.

> The conscious recognition of grave national abuses casts a deep shadow across the traditional American patriotic vision. The sincere and candid reformer can no longer consider the national Promise as destined to automatic fulfillment. The reformers themselves are, no doubt, far from believing that whatever peril there is cannot be successfully averted. . . . They proclaim . . . their conviction of an indubitable and a beneficent national future. But they do not and cannot believe that this future will take care of itself. As reformers they are bound to assert that the national body requires for the time being a good deal of medical attendance, and many of them anticipate that even after the doctors have discontinued their daily visits the patient will still need the supervision of a sanitary specialist. He must be persuaded to behave so that he will not easily fall ill again. . . . Consequently, just in so far as reformers are reformers they are obliged to abandon the traditional American patriotic fatalism. The national Promise has been transformed into a closer equivalent of a national purpose, the fulfillment of which is a matter of conscious work.
>
> HERBERT CROLY, *The Promise of American Life* (New York, 1909), pp. 20–21.

tionary movements intend to overthrow the existing system and replace it with a new regime. Revolutionary movements challenge existing mores and propose new values, advocating immediate change. Reform movements seek gradual changes in morals, norms, values, and institutions through public dialogue and action.[38] Incrementalists favor gradual change, doing what is possible to direct change toward major goals. Revolutionaries find incrementalism too slow or believe it cannot work. They aim for the immediate and fundamental reorganization of society through drastic redistributions of power.

Activists are very militant, but most are not revolutionaries. They pose special problems for business and other social institutions. In the past, social activists wanted specific reforms. In early American history, the dominant groups were the mercantile and the aristocratic, landholding classes. During the Industrial Revolution, business became the ruling class, with industrialists joining the mercantile class. After the Civil War, many groups challenged business, agriculture, and government. The Granger movement and the antimonopoly movements expressed discontent with agriculture and business; the Populist and the Progressive movements sought political reform; the trade union movements fought for work reform.[39] Today's activists are demanding fundamental

---

[38] Robert Cooley Angell, *Free Society and Moral Crisis* (Ann Arbor: University of Michigan Press, 1965), p. 204.

[39] Andrew Hacker (ed.), *The Corporation Takeover* (New York: Harper & Row, 1964), pp. 136–137. See also Richard Hofstadter, *The Age of Reform* (New York: Random House, 1955).

reforms in large bureaucracies—corporate, judicial, governmental, professional, and educational. They express outrage against "the establishment," and demand the reordering of national priorities. They denounce the values of materialism, growth, and selfish interest. Activists create militant organizations with specific agendas, but these organizations tend to be ill-defined, loosely knit, and poorly managed. They struggle at great odds to keep their momentum, to keep followers committed, to project a heroic image in the pursuit of ideals, and to finance their efforts.

Anti-establishment activists have used abrasive, aggressive tactics often involving violence. Boorstin denounced the activists of the sixties as "the New Barbarians." Though few in number, they were disruptive, wild, disorganized, rude, and uncivilized. They had no substantive content, no ideology, no jargon. Hence their reliance upon violence.[40] By contrast, Burns interpreted the revolt of the young as acting in the interest of ideals. He did not regard revolutionaries, protesters, and rioters as terrorists or dangerous militants, but rather as akin to participants in the American Revolution.[41] Burns' analogy is weak, and Boorstin's views seem more plausible.

The dilemma posed by excessive militance is twofold: (1) how to get and keep the freedoms and material abundance we want without destroying an orderly society, and (2) how to restrain the violence of reformist forces that seek to undermine society.[42]

Reform, like pestilence, arrives with each generation. Not infrequently it arrives at the wrong time, for the wrong reasons, and leaves behind the wrong remedies.

RICHARD L. McANAW, "An Adventure in Policy Making: Ethics." Paper delivered at the 1976 annual meeting, Western Political Science Association, San Francisco, March 21–April 3, 1976, p. 2.

Prophets and Reform: The social function of the prophet is not to foretell the future but to alert us to impending dangers that need attention. The prophet is a special kind of expert, but unlike other experts prophets do not rely on scientific evidence, though they may find it useful. Instead they call on logic to convince and charisma to persuade. The task of prophets is partly to disturb us over our follies, and partly to encourage reform by indicating the dangers of the present. They try to persuade people that dire consequences will result from failure to change.

---

[40] Daniel J. Boorstin, *The Decline of Radicalism: Reflections on America Today* (New York: Random House, 1969).

[41] Burns, *Uncommon Sense.*

[42] Theodore Levitt, *The Third Sector* (New York: AMACOM, 1973), pp. 3–8.

Social crises have a way of bringing forth prophetic voices. Perceptive writers and critics have responded to our gravest problems with works that have become part of our literary heritage. Jonathan Edwards, Henry David Thoreau, and others were self-cast as prophets in response to social crises.[43] In modern times, the prophetic voices of Alexander Solzenhitsyn and W. Buckminster Fuller, and in management, Peter F. Drucker, are cases in point. Modern prophets are in the secular rather than the religious mode. They are not sustained by long historical tradition or the claim that they are speaking for God. The historical view of prophecy often gives rise to extreme pessimism. Since the Age of the Enlightenment, we observe in the social order a decline in the influence of authority and hence in the influence of prophets. Heilbroner writes:

> I believe that history reveals an unmistakable propensity for the degeneration of authority, which is indispensable to organized social life, and to structures of harsh domination. These are often, but by no means always, common structures of economic domination. The hegemony of males over females, priests over laities, military elites over society at large, is not always accompanied by acts of material exploitation. The exercise of, enjoyment of, and acquiescence in power for its own pleasures seems to be a widely diffused element in history.[44]

Prophets sometimes become the leaders of reform movements. Mosca provides insights about what it takes for them to be successful leaders: (1) a profound sense of their own importance, (2) a sincere belief in the efficacy of their own work, (3) a manifest destiny originating in God's desire for them to save humanity, (4) willingness to focus their entire life and effort on a single ideal aim, (5) a cultivated exaggeration or imbalance of their intellectual and moral faculties, (6) the capability of making their own personalities and examples a force for instilling enthusiasm and sacrifices in others (akin to Weber's concept of charisma).[45] All this at the risk of not being honored by more than a select few in their own time.

We treat prophets with a healthy skepticism. Faith in prophets is low because they are pessimistic, and because their pronouncements are unsettling. We find it hard to know whom to believe, so we await more evidence. Since the line between the true and the false prophet is very thin, we are skeptical of them all. Prophets are fond of declaring that we stand at a crossroad, between doom and salvation. This dramatizes

---

[43] Thomas A. Couser, *American Autobiography: The Prophetic Mode* (Amherst: University of Massachusetts Press, 1979).

[44] Robert Heilbroner, in reply to a letter from Hal Draper to the editor of *The New York Review of Books* (October 12, 1978), p. 83. Reprinted with permission from *The New York Review of Books*. Copyright © 1978 Nyrev, Inc. See also Nisbet, *Twilight of Authority*.

[45] Gaetano Mosca, *The Ruling Class* (New York: McGraw-Hill, 1939), pp. 166–170.

issues, and puts issues into blacks and whites. But prophets really do not know what lies ahead: in fact, we can go in many directions.

Muckrakers: Muckrakers are much maligned; like the prophets, we disregard them as alarmists. Muckrakers are mostly journalists whose task is the exposure of fraud, corruption, mistakes, or mismanagement. They write, often creatively, with great ardor. Reform demands that there must be both information and exhortation, with specific focus on things wrong. Muckrakers try to arouse public anger, though often with biased or incomplete evidence.

Hofstadter notes that the muckrakers of the Progressive era achieved a new nationwide character through media with huge circulations. They not only proclaimed the malpractices of businessmen and politicians, but also named the persons and their deeds. The muckrakers of this era were "limited by the disparity between the boldness of their means and the tameness of their ends." Their chief appeal was not to social change, but to indignation and guilt.[46] Except for writings on the Vietnam war, the universities, the CIA, and the Watergate scandals, muckraking lost its edge in the 1960s and 1970s. One could argue that there are not enough muckrakers in today's world of crises—or even better, that the ones we have are not good enough.

Muckraking is subject to the corrections of history. Only now are we getting a historical perspective on the turbulent decades of the 1960s and 1970s. And a new type of muckraker has joined the journalists and investigative reporters—the crusaders, activists, and polemicists who follow or generate social causes. In this group are activists in the women's movement, environmentalists, consumer advocates, and the like. Their muckraking functions are a necessary prelude to their advocacy of causes. In their common penchant for exposing the weaknesses of organizations and social institutions, the new muckrakers fulfill a useful function. However, advocacy often produces partisanship and prejudice that arouse controversy not only among the public, but also among the scientists, researchers, and intellectuals whom they attack. The new muckrakers, like prophets, accept martyrdom for the causes they affirm.

Among them are social scientists, who are now engaged in critical self-examination. Where they once believed in value-free science and in nonadvocacy, they now take positions on social issues and public policy, and devise action research to solve social problems. They are a new type of muckraker in their eagerness to disturb the common wisdom. Gary Marx identifies a type of muckraking sociological research which "at its best documents conditions that clash with basic values, fixes responsibility for them, and is capable of generating moral outrage." Such research, though more by consequences than intent, documents and

---

[46] Hofstadter, *The Age of Reform*, pp. 185–186.

publicizes incriminating evidence and scandalous affairs, and serves as a vehicle for social criticism and change.[47]

Muckrakers, both journalistic and academic, inform us of the questionable behavior of those in power and of the scandals of the mighty. They say little about programs for solving or preventing major problems, and their batting average as reformers tends to be low. Nevertheless, we need their help in tackling today's critical issues.[48]

Utopianism: In 1516 Sir Thomas More wrote of an imaginary, ideal country called Utopia. Since then the idea has come to mean a place of ideal perfection in social organization—laws, government, and social conditions. In the eighteenth and nineteenth centuries, utopian reformers such as Charles Owen and Charles Fourier designed experimental planned communities that combined cooperative philosophy with architectural planning to eliminate the evils of urban industrialization and establish social justice by rational effort. These experiments failed to achieve their idealistic aims, and the term *utopianism* thus came to imply the impractical or impossible ideal.

Utopia itself remains an impossible dream—yet the idea remains alive and is reflected in the writings of those who believe that humans are capable of transcending evil. For example, Erich Fromm writes that we need a humanistic science as the basis for applied science and the art of social reconstruction. He notes that we have achieved technical and scientific utopias, such as airborne flight or space exploration, and asserts that a similar level of effort will enable us to reach a human Utopia of peace, solidarity, and freedom from war and class struggle. He is pessimistic, however, about the chances for the necessary human and social changes. To propose reforms that do not change the system, he asserts, is futile because such proposals lack a sufficiently strong motivation.[49]

Futurism: Since the dawn of history humans have attempted to discern the future. Forecasting for businesses and for society has reached a new level of sophistication and technique, though prediction remains highly uncertain.

A new movement called futurism emerged in the early 1970s. Futurism addresses the need for societal change and hence for broad reforms in global social, political, and economic arrangements. Proposed changes center on three related areas: (1) a slowing of economic growth throughout the world, (2) cessation of environmental depletion and decay, and (3)

---

[47] Gary T. Marx (ed.), *Muckraking Sociology: Research as Social Criticism* (New Brunswick, N.J.: Transaction Books, 1972).

[48] Leonard Downie, Jr., *The New Muckrakers* (Washington, D.C.: New Republic, 1976); John M. Harrison and Harry H. Stein (eds.), *Muckraking: Past, Present and Future* (University Park: Pennsylvania State University Press, 1973).

[49] Erich Fromm, *To Have or To Be?* (New York: Harper & Row, 1976), pp. 174–175 and 201.

the formation of a world government that would supplant those of the nation-states.

Two Club of Rome reports provided one of the major thrusts of the futurists. These extensive studies attempted to show the consequences of continuing the status quo by extrapolating over the next few centuries the effects of insistence on economic growth.[50] A more balanced perspective using a 200-year time frame is that of Herman Kahn.[51] Alvin Toffler popularized futuristic thinking in his best-selling *Future Shock*.[52] Barry Commoner's work illustrates a popularized treatment of environmentalist-ecological views.[53] World society movements are advocated by Falk, Mendlovitz, and others.[54]

Futurism provides perspectives on a fundamental conflict in ideas about what society should be like. The conflict is between (1) forces making for a professionalized, technocratic, controlled society, and (2) forces making for a more self-reliant, people-oriented society. Management's inevitable role in resolving this issue is still unclear. Business resists the no-growth approach and government regulation and world government concepts. Futurists clearly have not made their case. They portray a dismal future unless revolutionary change occurs. Their assumptions and quantification techniques are questionable. Their pessimism holds little hope for humans through science, technology or the incremental improvement of society. We will consider further implications of futurism in chapter 17.

REFORM TARGETS

In contrast to the general persuasions of futurism, utopianism, or prophecy, social movements and other reform efforts ultimately focus on specific targets of improvement. Citizens generally see social reform as a matter of abolishing abuses. Patently abuses should be abolished—or better still, prevented. Abuses can be corrected by administrative actions or, if frequent and tolerated, they may become accepted and no longer seen as abuses. Abuses are generally dealt with individually, and often excused

---

[50] Donnella H. Meadows, Dennis L. Meadows, Jorgen Randers, and William Behrens III, *The Limits to Growth* (New York: Universe Press, 1972); and Mihajilo Mesarovic and Edward Pestel, *Mankind at the Turning Point* (New York: E. P. Dutton/Reader's Digest Press, 1974).

[51] Herman Kahn et al., *The Next 200 years: A Scenario for America and the World* (New York: William Morrow, 1976).

[52] Alvin Toffler, *Future Shock* (New York: Random House, 1970).

[53] Barry Commoner, *The Closing Circle: Nature, Man, and Technology* (New York: Knopf, 1971).

[54] Richard A. Falk, *A Study of Future Worlds* (New York: Free Press, 1974); Victor Ferkiss, *The Future of Technological Civilization* (New York: Braziller, 1974); Ragini Kophatarri, *Footsteps into the Future: Diagnosis for the Present World and a Design for an Alternative* (New York: Free Press, 1974); Saul H. Mendlovitz (ed.), *On the Creation of a Just World Order* (New York: Free Press, 1974); Ervin Laszlo, *A Strategy for the Future: The Systems Approach to World Order* (New York: Braziller, 1974).

as "rare" or "exceptional." Reform, by contrast, must deal with policy and its underlying fundamentals rather than the surface manifestations of particular abuses.

In a sense, social reform has become "professionalized." Reform requires the full-time efforts of many specialists, most of whom are members of the new professional and intellectual class of the emerging postindustrial society. Reform specialists are closely linked to government, as public employees or private consultants; they are in a powerful position to influence public policy in social problem solving. Decisions that were once forged out of protest and conflict can now be made by consensus, legislative acts, and administrative decisions within government. The difficult question is who will reform the reformers, the government itself, and how will they do it?[55]

Almost every major social issue has one or more reform movements associated with it. In addition to those already cited, there are major movements pushing for reform in women's rights, racial discrimination, minority rights, government regulation, corporations, ecological or environmental policies, work conditions, the economy, and Congress. These efforts will be analyzed in other chapters, where they can be treated in their appropriate contexts.

Incident Case

Professor Smith, teaching an undergraduate class in management, asked the students to cite a major reason why we do not make more progress in solving the worst problems in society. One student asserted that "we cannot trust statements made by leaders in society."

What arguments do you expect were generated by this statement?

Issues for Discussion and Analysis

1. What are the important factors that cause social movements to come into existence, and what factors lead to decline or loss of momentum?

2. Argue pro and con the contention that social movements are merely forums for agitators, troublemakers, radicals, and activists.

3. Explain the strengths and weaknesses of social movements as agents of reform, from the viewpoint of organization and management.

---

[55] William Schlesinger, *The New Reformers: Forces for Change in American Politics* (Boston: Houghton Mifflin, 1975).

4. Analyze the main improvements you believe have occurred as a result of reform movements.

Class Project

Invite a leader in an important social reform effort to appear before the class. Before the visit prepare some key questions for use in generating a discussion of the relevant issues.

For Further Reading

ALBIN, PETER S. *Progress without Poverty: Socially Responsible Economic Growth* (New York: Basic Books, 1979).

BERG, IVAR, MARCIA FREEDMAN, and MICHAEL FREEMAN. *Managers and Work Reform* (New York: Free Press, 1978).

CHRISTIANSON, PAUL KENNETH. *Reformers and Babylon* (Buffalo, N.Y.: University of Toronto Press, 1977).

DOUGLAS, JACK D. *The American Social Order* (New York: Free Press, 1971).

ELLIFF, JOHN T. *The Reform of F.B.I. Activities* (Princeton, N.J.: Princeton University Press, 1979).

GAMSON, WILLIAM A. *The Strategy of Social Protest* (Homewood, Ill.: Dorsey Press, 1975).

GILL, GERALD R. *Meanness Mania: The Changed Mood* (Washington, D.C.: Howard University Press, 1980).

GOLDSTONE, JACK A. *The Weakness of Organization: A New Look at Gamson's The Strategy of Social Protest* (Chicago: The University of Chicago Press, 1980).

GUENTHER, JOHN. *Moralists and Managers: Public Interest Movements in America* (Garden City, N.Y.: Anchor/Doubleday, 1976).

HOFSTADTER, RICHARD. *The Age of Reform* (New York: Knopf, 1968).

MAYO, ELTON. *The Social Problems of an Industrial Civilization* (Boston: Harvard University, Graduate School of Business Administration, 1945).

OBERSCHALL, ANTHONY. *Social Conflict and Social Movements* (Englewood Cliffs, N.J.: Prentice-Hall, 1973).

ROTHMAN, JACK. *Planning and Organizing for Social Change* (New York: Columbia University Press, 1974).

TOCH, HANS. *The Psychology of Social Movements* (Indianapolis: Bobbs-Merrill, 1965).

U.S. Government Printing Office. *Recapturing Confidence in Government — Public Personnel Management Reform* (Washington, D.C., 1979).

WALTON, CLARENCE C. (ed.). *Business and Social Progress* (New York: Praeger, 1970).

ZALTMAN, GERALD, et al. *Processes and Phenomena of Social Change* (New York: Wiley, 1973).

PART III

MANAGERIAL VALUES, ETHICS, AND MORALS

8

Managerial Values and Ideology

*Clarifying and internalizing values and goals is necessary for
any person as he or she grows to maturity. Especially in a
period of rapid change, these values provide a firm
foundation upon which to build a stable, challenging, and
satisfying life and career. These personal values are also the
building blocks out of which, together with society's
conditions and needs, can be fashioned the future goals and
policies of the business firm.*

GERALD F. CAVANAUGH,
American Business Values in Transition.
(Englewood Cliffs, N.J.: Prentice-Hall, 1976) p. 208.
Reprinted by permission.

CONCEPTS DISCUSSED IN THIS CHAPTER

1. IDEOLOGIES AND THEIR FUNCTIONS IN SOCIETY
2. IDEOLOGICAL ISSUES FOR MANAGERS
3. VALUES IN SOCIETY
4. VALUE PROBLEMS IN MANAGERIAL AND ORGANIZATIONAL BEHAVIOR

The social world in which managers must function confronts them
not only with facts and concrete situations calling for decisions, but also
with conflicting ideas and ideals that seek to guide and influence them.
Managers need a way of understanding this complexity to rationalize
their actions and inform their decisions. Ideologies and values help managers develop organized patterns of thought and analysis that give meaning to their work.

Philosophy and religion have long had deep concerns about values, but the study of ideologies is of comparatively recent origin. The social sciences have devoted considerable attention to them since the emergence of Mannheim's classic work, translated from the German in 1936.[1] Mannheim held that ideologies become utopian when groups begin to act on them and to challenge the existing order in the interest of their chosen ideas and ideals.

This chapter describes the nature of ideologies and values, and also includes an analysis of how they affect managers in their exercise of social responsibility.

IDEOLOGIES

An *ideology* is a coherent, systematic statement of basic values and purposes. It contains a cluster of values generally held by a group, whose members tend to support one another in their beliefs. An ideology seeks to provide systematic answers to such questions as "who are we?" "what are we doing?" and "why are we doing this?" It helps group members explain themselves and their actions to others.[2]

Ideologies are selective in the beliefs, attitudes, values, and ideals they espouse. They are also selective in the use of supporting evidence and arguments. Although the realities with which they deal are complex, ideologies provide a straightforward, uncomplicated view acceptable to adherents. An ideology has a high emotional content and thus serves to motivate adherents to ideals of steadfastness, dedication, and sacrifice.[3]

Dictionaries define ideology in broad terms: the doctrines, myths, and symbols of a social movement, institution, class, or group. More specifically, an ideology embodies values, beliefs, and ideals which tend to unite the members of a group, culture, or society. The term is often used disparagingly to denote visionary, abstract, impractical, or even fanatical ideas, but in this book we use the term neutrally to indicate the range of values and ideals that contend for general acceptance.

We often use adjectives to denote the nature of particular specific ideologies or the group under consideration; thus there may be a business, political, or managerial ideology. Examples of political ideology would be capitalism or socialism; business ideologies favor the tenets of capitalism, the corporation, or free enterprise; managerial ideologies reinforce the roles of managers as advocates of the market system that

---

[1] Karl Mannheim, *Ideology and Utopia*, trans. Louis Wirth and Edward Shils (New York: Harcourt Brace Jovanovich, 1936).

[2] Gerald F. Cavanaugh, *American Values in Transition* (Englewood Cliffs, N.J.: Prentice-Hall, 1976), pp. 14–16.

[3] Ibid.

capitalism provides. As broad concepts, the ideologies bearing specific labels tend to overlap or to be related to one another. The familiar "isms" — capitalism, socialism, liberalism, or conservatism — reflect political and economic controversies over how a society should be run.[4]

Ideologies are not coherent, systematic, precisely specified beliefs. They cannot be judged as true or false. They are a mixture of facts, values, myths, ethical concepts, and political ideas. The strength and nature of an ideology can only be estimated in terms of its capability for maintaining and extending effective influence over the conduct of significant numbers of people. So though it is possible to study ideologies objectively and scientifically, ideologies themselves are not congenial to scientific truth and objective evidence. Thought patterns in society are both convergent and divergent, a mixture of facts and ideas.[5]

An ideology should be distinguished from philosophy and religion. An ideology rises and declines; philosophy endures and flourishes even when ideologies decline. Philosophers are not bound by political party, group or faction; instead they examine humanity's problems logically to explain the individual's inner experience of the world. Unlike ideology, philosophy is devoid of slogans, catchwords, or orthodoxies. An ideology, by contrast, emerges from social pressures, becoming an "ism" independent of research and intellectual inquiry.[6] Ideologies are not religions, but they have been called a secular religion, or a substitute for religion. Ideologies provide intellectuals with the equivalent of the role of priests and prophets in traditional religions. In a highly secular society, they find ideology a validation of their messianic zeal to become the governing elite.[7]

THE FUNCTIONS OF IDEOLOGY

Ideologies bring into focus the preferred goals, priorities, and efforts essential to the life of the community. Important ideologies thus explain and legitimate the existing order, and its patterns of action, problem solving, and change. An ideology assists problem solving and issues of stability and governance by fostering the performance of five intellectual tasks: (1) the clarification of goals, (2) the description of trends and the degree to which goals are achieved, (3) the analysis of conditioning factors, (4) the projection of future developments, and (5) the evaluation of policy alternatives in relation to the system.[8]

---

[4] Ramon Sanchez, *Schooling American Society: A Democratic Ideology* (Syracuse, N.Y.: Syracuse University Press, 1976).

[5] Lewis S. Feuer, *Ideology and the Ideologists* (New York: Harper & Row, 1975), p. 181.

[6] Ibid., pp. 183–188.

[7] Ibid., pp. 166–173.

[8] Arnold A. Rogow and Harold D. Lasswell, *Power, Corruption, and Rectitude* (Englewood Cliffs, N.J.: Prentice-Hall, 1963), p. 121.

TABLE 8.1

Components and Conceptual Bases of Traditional Ideology

Basic Components	Great Ideas: The Conceptual Base of Traditional American Ideology
1. The individual Rights Place in society Fulfillment Self-respect	1. Individualism: equality; the idea of contract; interest group pluralism.
2. Means by which rights are guaranteed	2. Property rights: individual ownership of resources.
3. Mechanisms and criteria for controlling the exploitation of material resources	3. Competition: the open market; Adam Smith's concept that the uses of property are best controlled in an open market where individual proprietors compete to satisfy consumer desires.
4. Role of the state and function of government	4. The limited state: the least government is the best government.
5. Nature and organization of knowledge and science	5. Scientific specialization and fragmentation: if we attend to the parts, the whole will take care of itself.

SOURCE: *Abstracted from George C. Lodge,* The New American Ideology *(New York: Knopf, 1975), pp. 9–11.*

As a specific example, what has been called the American ideology is asserted to have five components, each with a corresponding conceptual base of traditional American ideas. These are shown in Table 8.1. The American ideology contains fundamental values that pertain to each of the components and their conceptual base. Table 8.1 also embodies some of the major concepts discussed in earlier chapters, such as pluralism, equality, knowledge, science, and the roles of experts.

Ideologies have both advantages and disadvantages. They serve as the public acknowledgment of aims and ideals, and provide coherence, norms, evaluative criteria, and motivation. They make the world more intelligible to those who espouse them. Another function of ideology is to mark off arenas of contention for power and influence. This function facilitates the analysis of conflict among social movements and groups. It may be examined in the context of four subfunctions: (1) interpretation of a problem and the identification of villains and heroes, (2) the provision of a blueprint of action for improvement, (3) the ascription of moral ideas or social philosophy to justify the program being advanced, and (4) the provision of a historical interpretation and moral evaluation of the groups concerned.[9]

---

[9] Anthony Oberschall, *Social Conflict and Social Movements* (Englewood Cliffs, N.J.: Prentice-Hall, 1973), p. 181.

Ideologies provide rallying points for people of similar views. They make the people's feelings toward value questions more consistent and explicit. The role of the ideology is to help relate the individual's conscience and value system to expected situations. For example, the person who regards himself as a political conservative is supported by conservative ideology when casting a vote. Ideologies also bring clarity and assurance and hence vigor to the individual's life and work.

The drawbacks to ideology include rigidity, through locking people and systems into classes, roles, and expectations. Fanaticism and unwillingness to compromise can cause anxieties, repel adherents, and impede progress and innovation. Defensiveness is a common characteristic of the proponents of ideologies. Ideologies can mask the true interests of specific groups, and there is no assurance that actual behavior will follow the expressed ideology.

In sum, ideologies exist to reflect commonalities of views, ideals, or values. They exert strong influences over society and hence on business and the corporation. Ideologies forge collectivities that can bring power and influence to a focus in dealing with social issues. Ideologies express the need for change and provide statements of how improvement might be achieved.[10]

APPLICATIONS

How an ideology affects practical problems is illustrated by the energy crisis. Polls show that Americans believe the energy crisis is basically economic, to be corrected by removing government constraints to increase supply. Yet administrators in the executive branch speak of the problem in abstractions and moralisms. When people do not understand an issue, they tend to moralize and to appeal to an ideology that provides beliefs which can be consulted when adjustments must be made. According to Mitchell, the 1976 congressional voting on a gas deregulation measure compared against the liberal-conservative ratings of the Americans for Democratic Action showed extraordinary correlations between the deregulation vote and the ratings. Even moderately liberal and moderately conservative representatives voted overwhelmingly in accord with their ideological leanings. Therefore, the deregulation vote was ideologically more polarizing than the average issue used to construct the ADA ideological ratings. Similar results would appear for other problems such as abortion, where facts are irrelevant, or capital punishment, where the facts are in dispute.[11]

The application of ideologies is further illustrated by their use in studies of power and social class. For example, Form and Rytina found

---

10 John Wilson, *Introduction to Social Movements* (New York: Basic Books, 1973), pp. 90–95.
11 Edward J. Mitchell, *Energy and Ideology* (Washington, D.C.: American Enterprise Institute, 1977), Reprint No. 77.

that people use dominant ideologies to interpret power arrangements in society, but that specific belief systems vary by social class. At the community level, the pluralistic model of power was selected most frequently as a description of the way the system works, but it was embraced most strongly by rich and middle-class income strata. The poor and the blacks perceived elitist and economic models of power. When queried about power in Congress, all strata selected "big business and the rich" as the most powerful groups. Yet the higher the income and education of the respondents, the less they believed that all groups should have equal political power. The poor and the blacks gave the most normative support to political pluralism. These findings cast doubt on the theory that the poor are able to exert a political authoritarianism, and suggest that all classes differentially select normative beliefs about the distribution of societal power.[12]

IDEOLOGICAL INSTABILITY

Ideological thought and influence fluctuate with the social and political currents of the time. In the 1950s a lessening of international tensions corresponded to a withering of ideology, causing observers such as Bell to proclaim its end as an adequate social or governing mechanism. Concepts of "Left" and "Right" had to many become less meaningful, and were being replaced by nonideological realities forced on leaders by the nature of political and social tasks. These tasks, Bell asserted, became narrowed by historical and technological developments that only a rational technocratic system could meet.[13]

SOURCE: Atlas, November 1975.

---

[12] William H. Form and Joan Rytina, "Ideological Beliefs on the Distribution of Power in the United States," *American Sociological Review* 34 (February 1969), pp. 19–31.

[13] Daniel Bell, *The End of Ideology* (New York: Free Press, 1960). See also Alvin W. Gouldner, *The Dialectic of Ideology and Technology: The Origins, Grammar and Future of Ideology* (New York: Seabury Press, 1976), chap. 12.

Nevertheless, decline does not mean disappearance. Loye points to the endurance of ideology in psychological man, whereas Bell's end of ideology is seen in sociological and political man. Although ideology is declining in the relations among organizations, states, and nations, it operates unabated in the psychology of the individual personality. Individualism remains a persistent value in the middle range between ideologies of the Left and Right.[14] Because political life is a mixture of action, contemplation, emotion, and philosophy, ideology will always be an inescapable component.[15]

Perhaps the most obvious evidence of the power of ideology arises in connection with the most trendy and fashionable of virtues, conservation. When an environmental group successfully sues to halt the leasing of an offshore petroleum deposit, that is conservation. When an oil company acquires an offshore lease and is believed to be withholding production, that is not conservation. That is monopoly, conspiracy, or a rip-off. The same act is noble when performed by one actor, nasty when performed by another. Clearly, the action, the consequences, the reality are not being assessed. If the oil company believes that petroleum is growing more scarce, withholding supplies for the future is not only in its own interest; it is also in the nation's interest. The company is performing an act of conservation that is socially desirable. It seems that when the priest performs the act, it is a sacrament; when the sinner performs it, it is a sacrilege.

EDWARD J. MITCHELL, *Energy and Ideology* (Washington, D.C.: American Enterprise Institute, 1977), Reprint No. 77, p. 6.

The instability of ideologies arises from their clash with each other and from their emphasis on differences among individuals and groups. Groups that are parts of larger movements with broad ideological goals are often forced to forego those objectives in their own self-interest. Another element in the decline of ideologies is their capacity to do great harm to society. Ideology exacerbates political fanaticism, exalts the ideologist as a hero, and defies criticism. Ideology has been the source of much violence, warfare, and oppression.[16]

IDEOLOGIES AND MANAGERS

The problems of conflict and change in ideologies are clearly apparent in the world of business, where national and international politics, management values, and concepts of economics meet. The capitalistic, free

---

[14] David Loye, *The Leadership Passion: A Psychology of Ideology* (San Francisco: Jossey-Bass, 1977), pp. 215–218.

[15] Robert J. Pranger, *Action, Symbolism, and Order* (Nashville, Tenn.: Vanderbilt University Press, 1965), p. 49.

[16] Feuer, *Ideology and the Ideologists*, pp. 191–210.

enterprise system and the market approach to the economy are opposed by socialism, communism, and other forms of the planned, controlled economy. The United States business and political ideology is somewhere between these extremes.[17]

The implications of these divergent ideologies will be examined in detail in Chapter 13, but here we will consider the ideological elements that impinge on managers. At issue is the conflict between the classical free enterprise creed and the social responsibility creed that appeared in the early 1960s:

The classical free enterprise creed holds that:

The aim of business is to maximize profits.

The pursuit of self-interest is the logical and efficient way to run a business.

Free enterprise is the only way to a free and economically progressive society.

Competition and the marketplace and not the government should be the primary regulator of business.

Free enterprise is in the democratic tradition.

The new social responsibility creed holds that:

The free-enterprise, maximum profit philosophy is an anachronism.

Times have changed; large companies stifle competition.

Large companies play not only an economic role, but social and political roles as well.

Business exists by the permission of society, and its aim should be to serve society rather than its own interests.

Business utilizes social capital and hence should pay the full social costs thereof.

The classical ideology, based on ideas presented over 300 years ago by John Locke and extended by Adam Smith, stresses individualism, whereas the ideology of social responsibility extols communitarianism — that is, it defines the individual as the citizen of a community whose needs dominate the rights and duties of individuals, and in which the government plays a strong role as planner and implementer of the common good. Labeling the two views Ideology I and Ideology II, the *Harvard Business Review* surveyed 1,844 readers to compare them. More than two-thirds preferred Ideology I and considered it the dominant ideology, but 78 percent anticipated that Ideology II would be dominant by 1985. A majority felt that the changes would bring social disaster, with burdensome government interference, loss of freedom, and the disintegration of

---

[17] See, for example, Milton J. Friedman, *Capitalism and Freedom* (Chicago: The University of Chicago Press, 1962); and John Kenneth Galbraith, *The New Industrial State*, 2nd ed. (Boston: Houghton Mifflin, 1971).

business. Most of the respondents who saw a change to Ideology II disliked or feared the prospect.[18]

There can be little doubt today that classical free enterprise ideology is undergoing modifications toward greater social responsibility.[19] Requirements for abating pollution, equal opportunity employment policy, energy controls, consumer rights, product and employee safety, and care in the use of resources all attest to this point. The debates continue because the generation of managers schooled in free enterprise values resists the challenges of the new generation of managers who accept the idea of social responsibility as the only hope for solving society's problems. But managers increasingly are becoming an insecure class as a result of the breakdown of "family capitalism" — owner-operated firms — and the rise of corporate capitalism. The new class of managers, recruited from the middle classes, lacks an assured sense of justification which the older system provided. They have no property stake in the system, nor can they bequeath their power to heirs. For them, achievement becomes the symbol of success and Ideology II becomes important as a means of justification — the social cement that binds the business class together.[20]

The central question is whether the basic values and concepts of free enterprise can be preserved while business adjusts to the new expectations for social responsibility. The word *communitarianism* is a euphemism for government intrusion and control over decisions that managers have in the past considered theirs to make. Communitarianism is a comfortable substitute for a much more controlled political and economic system. Lodge, for example, advocates federal and regional charters for corporations, and comprehensive central government planning. These views are based on the still questionable view that large corporations shape our society, that they are large and faceless collectives, controlling enormous wealth and power without legitimacy because ownership is by stockholders who do not function as owners.[21]

Managers are right to be skeptical of the dangers to freedom and democracy that Ideology II contains, so it is important for them to understand how ideologies develop and change. Inspection of the elements of the two ideologies discloses numerous points at which differences could be resolved, with business pursuing a middle ground consisting of both profit and social responsibility objectives. Proponents of social responsibility, for example, do not generally advocate abandoning profits, markets, freedom, or democracy. Proponents of free enterprise do not

[18] William F. Martin and George Cabot Lodge, "Our Society in 1985 — Business May Not Like It," *Harvard Business Review* 53 (November–December 1975), pp. 143–152.

[19] For an early focus on this issue, see Earl F. Cheit (ed.), *The Business Establishment* (New York: Wiley, 1964).

[20] Bell, *The End of Ideology*, p. 81.

[21] George C. Lodge, *The New American Ideology* (New York: Knopf, 1975).

deny the need for some degree of governmental regulation, more ethical behavior, better conservation efforts, equal employment opportunity, and other areas of social responsibility.

LEADERSHIP AND IDEOLOGY

Every organization needs its own ideology, and it is an obligation of its leaders to foster one. There can be unrecognized ideological issues that all members, but primarily leaders, should face. Where leaders fail to do this, other sources of ideology come to prevail.[22] For example, a "worker ideology" fostering unionism grew to have a powerful interest in part because managerial ideology recognized only its own.

George F. Will has written that leadership is the ability to inflict pain and get away with it. The ideological leader "gets away with it" because the personal needs of the leaders and the led are swallowed up in the purposes of an aim or a movement. At the very least, leaders focus on a transcending cause or quest. The leader's success is then judged by actual social change measured by ideological purposes, programs, and values.[23] Loye speaks of ideology as "the leadership passion," by which he means that ideology is deeply rooted in the human personality. Within individuals, it emerges in the form of Right vs. Left motivation and values. Within groups, it appears as leadership styles, tactics, and goals. Bridging the individual and the group is concern for power—how to get it and how to use it.[24]

BUREAUCRATIC IDEOLOGY

Closely akin to Ideology I is a kind of administrative ideology stemming from the theory and practices of bureaucracy. Bureaucratic ideology is rooted in the idea of technical rationality, which arranges means to the ends of efficiency and effectiveness. Rationality is attributed to organizations rather than to people. This leads to a contradiction in that what is efficient and effective for the organization may not be so for its managers. Bureaucratic ideology helps managers resolve the contradictions occurring in practice by explaining to managers how and why they should perform in the fact of inconsistencies in their role.[25] The belief system inherent in an ideology supplies a rhetoric and language that guide decision and action according to the bureaucracy's needs.[26]

---

[22] Barrows Dunham, *Heroes and Heretics: A Political History of Western Thought* (New York: Knopf, 1964), pp. 229–230.

[23] James MacGregor Burns, *Leadership*, pp. 248–251.

[24] Loye, *The Leadership Passion*, p. 3.

[25] Michael E. Urban, "Bureaucracy, Contradictions, and Ideology in Two Societies," *Administration and Society* 10 (May 1978), pp. 49–85.

[26] Dorothy Anderson Mariner, "Ideology and Rhetoric: Their Impact on an Organization and on Professional Aspirations," *Pacific Sociological Review* 14 (April 1971), pp. 197–243.

Another practical application of ideology can be seen in the way individual organizations develop it into a way of life. In the management of business firms, for example, leaders stress lofty, encompassing ideas that become an enduring theme or metaphor for the business.[27] For example, when Eddie Carlson took over ailing United Air Lines in 1970, he launched a "management visibility program"—requiring managers to stay in touch with field units—to instill a customer service theme. Alfred Sloan personified the theme of decentralization throughout General Motors, essentially by closely supervising the hiring of new employees to assure the preservation of his preferred values. Similarly, Thomas Watson, Sr., personified the service concept as a rallying ideology in IBM. The common denominator here is the coupling of the central motivating influences of key ideas with the energetic and persistent action of the leader.[28]

VALUES

We have seen that ideologies contain important values that contribute to the attainment of broad goals in society. Values also underlie other forms of individual and group behavior. Therefore we need to know what values are, where they come from, how they function, and what problems arise on their account.

VALUES DEFINED

A *value* is a combination of idea and attitude that reflects a scale of preference with respect to priorities, motives, or goals. Values high in the scale indicate what people want most in life, so important values are accompanied by strong emotional overtones. Values are a measure of the intensity of beliefs, attitudes, goals, and many other things.

It is important to distinguish between values and facts, though there are relations among them. Values themselves are facts of a special type, but other kinds of facts may or may not be valued. For example, the possession of a college degree would be a fact, but individuals vary in the extent to which they value such a possession. Values also exist at many levels. There are the values of individuals, values pertaining to groups, and values of the society or culture. Values in the various settings may be similar, overlapping, or unique to a given context. Therefore it is necessary to study values collectively and in relation to particular contexts.

Individual values are usually also social values in that they are widespread objects of regard. Attitudes such as love of money, hatred of

---

[27] Judith A. Merkle, *Management and Ideology: The Legacy of the International Scientific Management Movement* (Berkeley: University of California Press, 1980).

[28] "The Planning Fetish," Manager's Journal, *The Wall Street Journal*, July 7, 1980, p. 10.

foreigners, or respect for science reflect values with respect to money, foreigners, and science. There are many possible attitudes for every social value. There are also numerous possible values for any single attitude. Attitudes may reflect the individual's positive or negative position with respect to a given social value. For example, society may place a high value on wealth, but some individuals may reject wealth in favor of poverty.

There is an important relationship between norms and values. Both are ideas, but norms are standards by which value-related behavior is judged. A norm is a person's idea of what behavior ought to be in given circumstances; a value is a person's idea of what is desirable, what people *ought* to want, not necessarily what they actually want. Norms are often realized, but values are hardly ever fully attainable. If riches or a high score in bowling are values, it is hard to be too rich or to get too high a score. The line between norms and values is obviously not sharp. Because they are ideas in people's minds and thus under less direct pressure from external circumstances, they probably change more slowly than actual behavior. Note that norms and values of the members of a group are also assumed to be many and that there is no necessary logical consistency of norms among the members of a group. But there are universal or near universal values, as well as culturally distinctive values.

Value, the leading edge of reality, is no longer an irrelevant offshoot of structure. Value is the predecessor of structure. It's the preintellectual awareness that gives rise to it. Our structured reality is preselected on the basis of value, and really to understand structured reality requires an understanding of the value source from which it's derived.

ROBERT M. PERSIG, *Zen and the Art of Motorcycle Maintenance* (New York: William Morrow, 1974), p. 277.

VALUE SYSTEMS

Since values exist in conjunction with one another, they form patterns we call *value systems.* For the individual, the group, or the society, there are at any given time priorities of preference and interaction among the various values. Values are not considered in isolation: They relate to the culture, the array of social institutions, and the assumptions and concepts relevant in a particular society.

To be useful as guidance for decision and action there must be a degree of consistency and coordination among related values that viewing them as a system can provide. The value system thus sets a standard by which values can be compared, analyzed, and discussed. In each value field, such as science, business, or education, a logical examination of value choices is possible. Emerging changes can be examined according to their effects on the system, provided that there is general agreement on the basic features of the system itself. For example, business places a high value on profit and related values of marketing, the use of capital, and so on. A proposal to increase a corporation's philanthropy could then be tested against its effects on other values in the system. The same principle applies to the analysis of social institutions such as business in relation to other social institutions.[29] The basic elements of a value system are shown in Figure 8.1.

FIGURE 8.1

Schematic Model of a Value System for Managers

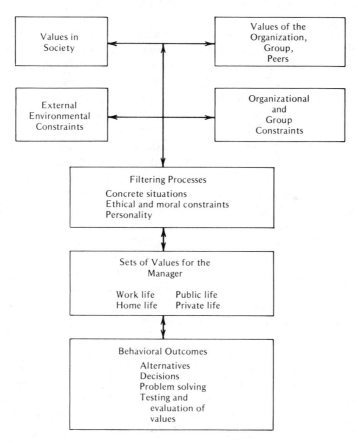

---

[29] S. Prakash Sethi, in his Foreword to Gerald F. Cavanaugh, *American Business Values in Transition* (Englewood Cliffs, N.J.: Prentice-Hall, 1976), p. xii.

> *Administration has no values of its own, except for the institutional ones just described. It has no ideas; it is just professional management. Theoretically it could accept any values.*
>
> CHARLES A. REICH, *The Greening of America* (New York: Random House, 1970), pg. 100.

SOURCES OF VALUES

Values may be observed from the perspective of the individual or the society. In either case, values are not derived scientifically, logically, or intellectually. They derive instead from complex social and psychological considerations.

Individuals do not choose their values in isolation, although they like to think that they do. As they mature, they acquire a value orientation whose function is to help them respond to their life experiences. The valuing process is effective to the degree that an individual is open to experiencing. A commonality or universality of value directions develops, making for the constructive enhancement of individuals and the community, and for the survival and evolution of the human species.

The maturation process is one of developing the self—the result of interaction with the environment and particularly from evaluational interactions with others. The self is an organized, fluid, but consistent conceptual pattern of perceptions of characteristics and relationships of the "I" or the "me" together with the values attached to these concepts. The individual also begins to build up a conception of self in relation to the environment. These experiences become invested with value that may be positive (I like it) or negative (I dislike it) in character.

Everybody is more or less interested in the values of others. This is essential to any kind of community life. We say a thing has value or is a value when people behave toward it so as to retain or increase their possession of it. When we first meet others, we try to find out what their values are. We listen to what they say, what others say about them, and notice how they spend their money, how they vote, whether they go to church, and many other things. Opinion polls are used to ascertain the values of various groups. Values are mainly inferred from observed behavior, but direct inquiries can also be made. Both sources of information pose difficulties. The inferences may be wrong, and people may not be willing or able to reveal their values accurately to the questioner. The character of a society is reflected in its institutionalized modes of meeting needs—holding property, raising children, running a business, and the like. Since this process commits the society to an integrated system of values, challenges to institutionalized behavior also challenge its underlying values. Social institutions are therefore repositories of values; they function as value maintainers, developers, and transmitters. Let us consider several examples of interrelatedness in our primary, value-shaping social institutions.

The family has a substantial stake in the business enterprise. It is a major consuming unit, and one or more of its members are often closely associated with a business enterprise as supplier, stockholder, or employee. Likewise, the business enterprise has a stake in the family, where it finds its markets and its employees. The family reinforces and reflects values being shaped by church, school, and state, and must be regarded as one of the primary sources of values held by managers.

Formal, organized religions and informal religious beliefs foster values in political, social, and economic affairs. In our society, the Judeo-Christian religious heritage predominates. The Christian side of this heritage has followed both Protestant and Catholic teachings, with basic similarities in some moral dilemmas and major differences in others. The Judaic tradition too can be seen at work in the values prevailing in society. The precise influence of religion on managerial and business policies, decisions, practices, aims, and philosophies is not clear; there are wide disagreements among both secular and religious scholars, and among practitioners, about the relevance of religion to business and about the practicality of such concepts as sharing, unselfishness, self-denial, and so on. Neither business nor organized religion have fully responded to these dilemmas, and such conflicts in values are hard to resolve.

Schools also play important roles in shaping values. Here, along with religious traditions and the family, democracy, human rights, equality of opportunity, and many other values are fostered. Free public education under local control has itself remained an important value, assuring the dissemination and transmission of other values throughout the culture and over succeeding generations.

In the world of governmental influences on values, we see constitutional and legal rights, such as private property, freedom of association, equality of opportunity, equality before the law, representative government, and so on. Moreover, it falls to the government to regulate organizations through licensing and other legal controls. For example, the government's control of business is reflected in laws prohibiting restraint of trade, price fixing, "unfair" trade practices, fair employment practices, and encouraging collective bargaining, consumer protection, and the like.[30]

---

[30] For a humanistic analysis of these matters, see Frank Goble, *Beyond Failure: How to Cure a Neurotic Society* (Ottawa, Ill.: Green Hill Publishers, 1977).

The existence of so many possible values makes choices difficult and conflicts among them inevitable. Value issues also pervade other areas of conflict, such as labor-management relations or the struggles between political parties.

There are no pat answers to value conflict. For the individual, the nature and extent of resolution of conflicts depends on psychological factors in the personality. Some face conflict by ignoring it, by doing what is expedient or necessary. Others see conflict as a challenge to the understanding of self and others. Since an ideal or permanent resolution of conflict is so elusive, the central question for the manager is not how material and spiritual values can be brought into agreement, but rather how to live with the stress of always falling short of one's ideals. The challenge is for the individual to find through consistent, creative effort the ideals that lead to a meaningful and purposeful life.

Reality has a habit of testing one's values. Successful coping with value issues results from the process of working back and forth from the general to the particular, refining the general and testing it against particular contexts. A deeper understanding rather than a right answer is the goal. Values are not really tested without confrontation.

Value differences may exist at a trivial or harmless level, such as a difference of opinion over which is the best restaurant in town. Major values pertain to fundamental orientations to the world we live in. Differences in fundamental values such as conservative versus liberal politics are more complex and harder to resolve. The most important values are the ultimate ones that guide individuals in their deepest concerns.

Contradictory or conflicting values pose problems not only for individuals, but also for social institutions. For example, the educational system finds its task of transmitting values complicated by existing value conceptions in students and changing value orientations in society. Differences between behavior according to a value and actual behavior intrude. Yet there are fundamental values that have stood the test of time and have pervaded cultures everywhere and in all ages. Fundamental values are embodied in the Constitution and Bill of Rights, the Ten Commandments and the Golden Rule, and these can be and have been preserved, even though technological society does not always facilitate total compliance with such beliefs.[31]

---

[31] Edward J. Nussel, "The American Value System: A Study in Contradiction," *The National Forum, Phi Kappa Phi Journal* 57 (Spring 1977), pp. 23–29.

Despite the acknowledgment of enduring human values, cries of alarm are often raised that values are declining. The prophets of doom portray a crisis of values that could lead to the decay or downfall of society.

All evidence points to the inevitability of changes in the normative structure of society. This normative structure consists of meaning, values, taboos, and norms. *Meanings and values* define the acceptable aspirations and goals for society's members; *taboos* prohibit undesirable or unsanctioned activities; *norms* specify the permissible means of achieving objectives. Etzioni states that there is an erosion of the normative structure, but that it is not in a crisis. New sets of beliefs and affirmations arise to replace the old. For example, a new vision of a society emphasizing "quality of life" has arisen.[32]

Much the same thing—the replacement of old values with the new—happens for individuals. The lowering or loss of one value inevitably means that energy can go into producing one or more new values. The individual who perceives and accepts that his or her self denies more of his or her experiences finds that he or she is replacing a value system in a continuing change process. The value system is dynamic. For healthy, integrated adjustment, one must constantly evaluate experiences to see whether they imply a change in the value structure.

The fact that people have the same basic needs and that values possess a high degree of commonality means that values change very slowly for large numbers of people. Continuity, not change, is the most striking characteristic of values today.[33] The idea of a crisis in values is misleading, for it implies a technological approach to a problem that is psychological or spiritual, not technological. We cannot manipulate values or society to forestall a crisis in values.[34] The frustrations and discontents of our time are less the products of the erosion of values than of our failure to fulfill our national values adequately. Inflation, poverty, unemployment, excessive regulation, hunger, overpopulation, and the like contradict our professed values, but the values remain as rallying points to which all citizens are called.

Changes in values, though gradual, also produce frustrations and many dangers. The extent of our changing values is illustrated in Table

---

[32] Amitai Etzioni, "Toward a New Affirmation," *The National Forum, Phi Kappa Phi Journal*, 58 (Fall 1978), pp. 37–42. See also Ronald Inglehart, *The Silent Revolution: Changing Values and Political Styles among Western Publics* (Princeton, N.J.: Princeton University Press, 1977).

[33] Everett C. Ladd, "Traditional Values Regnant," *Public Opinion*, March–April 1978, pp. 45–49.

[34] Comment by Irving Kristol in "Values in Contemporary Society," *Working Papers: The Rockefeller Foundation*, 1974, pp. 6–7.

TABLE 8.2

Value Trends in Work, Culture, Organization, and Ecology

Value Trends in the Work World	
Declining	*Emerging*
Status achievement	Self-expression achievement
Hard work a virtue	Rewarding work a virtue
Institutional leadership	Political and individual leadership
Group control	Individual control
Authoritarianism	Participation
Tradition	Experimentation
Value Trends in the Culture	
Belonging	Self-actualizing
Endurance of distress	Capacity for joy
Puritanism	Sensualism
Status quo-ism	Acceptance of change
Racism	Equality, shared power
Conformity	Individualism
Trends in Organizational Philosophies	
Mechanistic forms	Organic forms
Competitive relations	Collaborative relations
Separate objectives	Linked objectives
Own resources regarded as owned absolutely	Own resources regarded also as society's
Trends in Ecological Strategies	
Responsive to crisis	Anticipative of crisis
Specific measures	Comprehensive measures
Requiring consent	Requiring participation
Short planning horizon	Long planning horizon
Damping conflict	Confronting conflict
Detailed central control	Generalized central control
Standardized administration	Innovative administration
Separate services	Coordinated services

SOURCE: *Arnold Mitchell, "Changing Values," Associations Internationales (October 1971), pp. 220-221.*

8.2, which shows trends in work, culture, organizational philosophies, and ecological values. These are emerging changes that are arising not from single-minded contrivance or social engineering, but rather from other types of change in society.

VALUES AND TECHNOLOGY

Many value issues in an industrial society are associated with its technology. Advances in technology are relentless, requiring continuous adjustment to accompanying changes in values. Television and computers are examples. They show how the link between technology and science produces powerful social forces that rearrange our value structure. But the values are those of humans, not technology itself. Thus whether technology results in good or evil depends on human choices.

Technology poses serious problems because it can result in harmful effects, both direct and indirect. We have always feared the machine while reaping its advantages. Prophets of doom have provided us with eloquent statements of caution and critical thought. Ellul, for example, analyzes the awesome nature of a society that he feels has come to be dominated by technology.[35]

When technology entered the stage of rapid growth, it was soon seen that the price of progress was unemployment and a shift of jobs to new industries and occupations. More recently, we have become concerned with three additional dimensions of the problem: (1) that advanced technologies consume vast amounts of nonrenewable resources, (2) that technology produces undesirable side effects in the form of environmental damage, and (3) that technological advances induce high volumes of consumption which have generated undesirable values such as excessive materialism. These four problems are interrelated in complex ways, and solutions are elusive, uncertain, and sometimes unpopular.

Technology provides abundantly for human needs. Its most significant function is to increase productivity, thereby multiplying wealth, investment, and social and economic power. It also promises, along with science, to be the hope for survival of society and of people. Technology has in fact lessened our dependence—actual and psychological—on the materials of nature. It has extended our senses and our ability to see, think, and understand. Technology's challenge is that it be directed and controlled for the betterment of humankind.[36]

Social critics have increasingly attacked the materialism technology makes possible. If materialistic values are indeed rampant, the implication is that we prefer them over the dimensions of social costs. We have accepted the benefits of the technological system, but have hidden the social costs by allowing companies to shift their burden to society. Environmental protection laws seek to redistribute the costs so that companies directly pay more of the total costs of doing business.[37] (We will further analyze the problem of social costs and environmental issues in Chapter 17.)

There has been a noticeable shift from materialistic values in the 1960s and 1970s. Such values as self-expression and participation in the

---

[35] Jacques Ellul, *The Technological Society* (New York: Knopf, 1964). The evils of technology have also been denounced by such writers as Lewis Mumford, René Dubos, Charles A. Reich, and Barry Commoner.

[36] Richard Goodwin, *The American Condition* (Garden City, N.Y.: Doubleday, 1974), pp. 178–183.

[37] George C. Sawyer, *Business and Society* (Boston: Houghton Mifflin, 1979).

political system mark a new generation of "postmaterialists" — the highly educated, idealistic, cosmopolitan and nonauthoritarian people of Kristol's "new class." While relatively few in number, the postmaterialists are providing a glimpse of the higher goals humanity can perhaps achieve.[38] Their doctrinaire, uncompromising, and moralistic views, however, require us to make a careful assessment of our goals. It is doubtful if so-called materialism will be totally rejected. Foreigners often describe Americans as the least materialistic people who ever lived. Although there is an abundance of objects denoting tangible wealth, those objects also define the personality, liberate people for self-fulfillment, and reflect humanistic ideals and aspirations.[39] But we remain ambivalent in our attitudes toward technology. Humanity wants both to be saved from it and by it. Since resolving this paradox raises many issues of choice, values will continue to require our serious consideration.[40]

VALUES AND MANAGERS

Business and managerial values are pervasive influences on society's values, but business is also a reflection of fundamental values pervasive in society. The importance of relating business values to those of society has been described as follows:

> Much of the conflict, much of the apparent lack of unity and purpose in our national life, comes from our failure so far to reconcile business attitudes and aims — such as the pursuit of an ever higher standard of living — with the other fundamental values stemming from American religious and democratic traditions. If business could stand off and take a long look at itself, analyze its values, and try to realign them with those broader ideals of the good society, it could help more than any other force in the country to make stronger and more valid America's message to an uncertain world.[41]

Insofar as management and administration are viewed as science, only facts are relevant; facts and values should therefore be clearly separated.[42] But values are also facts, and management is more than a science. It is also full of choices and behavior predicated on values,

---

[38] Ronald Ingelhart, *The Silent Revolution.*

[39] E. F. Schumacher, "Toward an Appropriate Technology," *Atlantic*, April 1979, pp. 88–93; Daniel J. Boorstin, *The Republic of Technology* (New York: Harper & Row, 1978); Samuel C. Florman, *The Existential Pleasures of Engineering* (New York: St. Martin's Press, 1976).

[40] Carl H. Madden, *Clash of Culture: Management in an Age of Changing Values* (Washington, D.C.: National Planning Association, 1976).

[41] Thomas C. Cochran, "Business and the Democratic Tradition," *Harvard Business Review* 34 (March–April 1956), p. 48. Reprinted by permission of the *Harvard Business Review*. Copyright © 1956 by the President and Fellows of Harvard College; all rights reserved.

[42] Herbert A. Simon, *Administrative Behavior* (New York: Macmillan, 1957), p. 253.

ethical beliefs, and norms — what is good or preferable. Values need to be recognized because they function in the selection of goals and the means of achieving them.

Traditional business and managerial values are being challenged as out of harmony with newly emerging social values. Managers are urged to become social entrepreneurs whose organizations make constructive attacks on social problems. For example, Chamberlain advocates numerous corporate reforms, such as federal rather than state charters, a reduction of wasteful competition, and a reduced emphasis on profits. With work, consumption, and growth so widely questioned, traditional values are under great stress.[43] Chamberlain's description of our value problems is revealing, but his suggested remedies are unpersuasive.

The functions and influences of managerial values are clearly apparent in the techniques and philosophies of employee relations. The values of workers are not well understood, nor are they adequately integrated with policy. Employee values, with all their inconsistencies, conflicts, and unrealities, need to be considered. McMurry, for example, asserts that the arbitrary imposition of authoritarian "ultrarightist" management values leads to low morale. He recommends that managers also examine their own values for internal consistency, recognizing that most issues have two sides and that management does not have a monopoly on truth. Communications, for example, could be improved by emphasizing common values.[44]

Basic values learned early in the course of management careers tend to remain constant. A major study of key executives revealed that the more successful ones had less change in their values during the course of their careers than the less successful. The most successful leaders had a significantly greater social consciousness than the less successful.[45]

ORGANIZATIONALLY BASED VALUES

The design and operation of an organization or other social system is suffused with the values of its managers, but organizations also acquire values that become institutionalized as their own. The need for technical

[43] Neil Chamberlain, *Remaking American Values* (New York: Basic Books, 1976). See also Robert H. Bock, "Modern Values and Corporate Social Responsibility," *MSU Business Topics* 28 (Spring 1980), pp. 5–18.

[44] Robert N. McMurry, "Conflicts in Human Values," *Harvard Business Review* 41 (May–June 1963), pp. 131–145. See also Martha A. Brown, "Values — A Necessary but Neglected Ingredient of Motivation on the Job," *Academy of Management Review* 1 (October 1976), pp. 15–23; Vincent S. Flowers and Charles L. Hughes, "Choosing a Leadership Style," *Personnel* 55 (January–February 1978), pp. 48–59; H. J. Zoffer, "The Impact of Changing Values and Lifestyles in the Selection of Managers," *Personnel* 52 (January–February 1975), pp. 25–33; Richard H. Viola, *Organizations in a Changing Society: Administration and Human Values* (Philadelphia: W. B. Saunders, 1977).

[45] Henry A. Singer, "Human Values and Leadership: A Ten Year Study of Administrators in Large Organizations," *Human Organization* 35 (Spring 1976), pp. 83–87. See also George W. England, *The Manager and His Values: An International Perspective* (Cambridge, Mass.: Ballinger, 1975).

efficiency is the primary source of many of these values. Jacques suggests that bureaucratic values are being modified and that to remain viable, an organization must fulfill positive values such as openness and trust, and discourage hostility, suspicion, and mistrust. Positive values make it possible for individuals to engage in reciprocal social activity and collaborative work that enhances system survival.[46]

A more pessimistic view is that of Scott and Hart, who assert that the values of the modern organization are replacing the individualistic values of the traditional American system. Reminiscent of earlier "organization man" theory, Scott and Hart assert that society is gravely endangered by the "organizational imperative," which has transformed American values. Since so many have gained so much from organization (wealth, material benefit, jobs), a resulting mandate is that all behavior must enhance the health of organizations. This gives organizations a powerful hold over the values as well as the actions of their members.[47] Scott and Hart blame managers for not being concerned with value questions:

> It may well be that this new set of organizationally fostered values offends our deepest sense of humanity, and we know that the combination of management and technology holds both promise and danger. In our view the danger of this combination is out of proportion to its promise because of the unwillingness of those who should know better (e.g., management scholars) to reflect upon the values that underlie modern organizations and their implications. The fact that the discussion of values in management has not developed along with the development of our core technology creates pressing human problems that cannot be ignored, unless one believes that our present condition is acceptable.[48]

Scott and Hart also assert that the organizational imperative transcends other values:

> The organizational imperative is dominant because we made it so. We did this because we believed that the modern organization would provide us with material affluence, physical safety, and peace of mind. We were not aware, in the beginning, that we would have to buy a whole sack full of new values in the process. But something does not come for nothing; once the organizational imperative was set in motion, it became so powerful that we lost our sense of how to control it, let alone how to turn it off.[49]

While they would not do away with organizations (even if it were possible), they believe that the unanticipated effects of the overorganiza-

---

[46] Elliott Jacques, *A General Theory of Bureaucracy* (New York: Wiley, 1976), pp. 1–9.
[47] William G. Scott and David K. Hart, *Organizational America* (Boston: Houghton Mifflin, 1979). Reprinted by permission.
[48] Ibid., p. 79.
[49] Ibid., p. 78.

tion of contemporary society are seriously harmful, and that the long-range implications for the individual are negative.They state: "America is in the process of becoming something else, and there is real reason to believe that the something else may be quite unpleasant."[50] Thus Scott and Hart argue cogently that the needed reforms must come largely from professionals. Since these are trained in universities, it follows that education must come to stress the values of the individual in educating professionals, who are to lead us in creating a transcendent America freed from the tyranny of the organizational imperative. Scott and Hart conclude pessimistically that "This is more than a theoretical option, but not a very likely one. Unfortunately transcendent America is not our most probable future."[51]

To the extent that the organizational imperative exists, reform in society meets almost insurmountable obstacles. The governing elite could carry out reforms because it has power, but its members will not because they are conditioned to success-model careers that give them their livelihoods, plus status and prestige. The common masses could band together to demand reform, but they too are the beneficiaries of the system, and it takes an extreme force to bring them to concerted action. Therefore, reason Scott and Hart, the only chance for reform, and a slim one in their view, is in the hands of professionals, because modern organizations and their managerial elites cannot function without them. Professionals would have the technical knowledge and organizational expertise to galvanize mass support for change. Scott and Hart see little evidence, however, that professionals will rise to their responsibility. Professionals too are trained as followers, and generally do not attempt solutions to problems beyond their immediate tasks.[52]

Gouldner[53] and Bell[54] have described the emergence of a new class—the well-educated professionals, scientists, and technical specialists—rising to prominence and power in a knowledge-oriented society. It remains to be seen whether this new class will assume the awesome responsibility ascribed to it by Scott and Hart or whether instead its members will become a controlling elite with centralized power founded on the organizational imperative. The pessimist, of course, takes the latter view.

There is also much pessimism to be found in the behavior of managers themselves. Their espousal of individualism is subverted by their willingness to embrace the values of the organizational imperative. This

---

[50] Ibid., p. 9.

[51] Ibid., p. 229.

[52] Ibid., pp. 214–223.

[53] Alvin W. Gouldner, *The Future of Intellectuals and the Rise of the New Class* (New York: Seabury Press, 1979).

[54] Daniel Bell, *The Coming of the Post-Industrial Society* (New York: Basic Books, 1973).

is illustrated by the excuses offered for bribery and corruption, and by the willingness of so many to embrace the determinism of Skinner's operant conditioning. Those who fear the organizational imperative may take heart in Berg's analysis of the failure of management's work reform efforts. Personnel, human relations, and organizational behavior techniques have failed, he concludes, because they have not taken sufficient account of the underlying psychological and philosophical makeup of workers, and because managers have not understood the workers' real values.[55] Berg's thesis, if sound, calls for extensive changes in managerial philosophy and practice.

Incident Case

A high-level corporate executive, during an interview conducted by a researcher on managerial values, made the following statement: "Business requires competition. The tougher the competition, the better the service that business can perform. But competition means that someone gets hurt. If you really worry about moral and ethical values, you couldn't bring yourself to be truly competitive. If I stopped to worry about spiritual values, I couldn't be an effective executive."

Analyze the values and ideological basis of this statement.

Issues for Discussion and Analysis

1. Debate the assertion pro and con that fundamental values of the individual never change.

2. Analyze the differences that appear to exist between a managerial ideology and a political ideology.

3. How would one refute the thesis of George C. Lodge that managers should adjust to the "new ideology"?

4. Explain the difficulties and complications involved in the main approaches to identifying the values at work among a particular group of managers.

5. Are there universal values that underlie action in particular situations?

---

[55] Ivar Berg, Marcia Freedman, and Michael Freeman, *Managers and Work Reform: A Limited Engagement* (New York: Free Press, 1978).

6. How extensive is the problem of manipulating people in most organizations?

7. Why is the energy crisis more than a nuts-and-bolts economic issue?

8. Are the values of leaders in an organization likely to be different from or the same as those of their followers? Why or why not?

9. Are values probed in the search for the selection of new employees? Should they be?

10. What are some of the elements of management ideology? How do they compare to the ideology of a labor union?

11. Explain how you as a manager would take values and value conflicts into account in making decisions.

Class Project

1. Set up several investigatory teams to examine a number of research studies of values among such groups as youth, adults, unions, managers.

2. Ask each team to review its findings for the class as a whole.

For Further Reading

BROWN, HAROLD O. J.   *The Reconstruction of the Republic* (New Rochelle, N.Y.: Arlington House, 1977).

CAMPBELL, ANGUS, PHILIP E. CONVERSE, and WILLARD L. RODGERS.   *The Quality of American Life: Perceptions, Evaluations, and Satisfactions* (New York: Russell Sage Foundation, 1976).

CAVANAUGH, G. F.   *American Business Values in Transition* (Englewood Cliffs, N.J.: Prentice-Hall, 1976).

CHAMBERLAIN, NEIL.   *The Place of Business in America's Future: A Study in Social Values* (New York: Basic Books, 1973).

CHAMBERLAIN, NEIL.   *Remaking American Values* (New York: Basic Books, 1976).

CHURCHMAN, C. WEST.   *Prediction and Optimal Decision: Philosophical Issues of a Science of Values* (Englewood Cliffs, N.J.: Prentice-Hall, 1961).

CLOUGH, SHEPARD B.   *Basic Values of Western Civilization* (New York: Columbia University Press, 1960).

EDEL, ABRAHAM.   *Analyzing Concepts in Social Science: Science, Ideology and Value*, Vol. 1. *Exploring Fact and Value: Science, Ideology and Value*, Vol. 2. (New Brunswick, N.J.: Transaction Books, 1980).

FRIEDMAN, MILTON, LEONARD SILK, et al.   *The Business System: A Bicentennial View* (Hanover, N.H.: University Press of New England, 1977).

GOODWIN, RICHARD N.   *The American Condition* (Garden City, N.Y.: Double-day, 1974).

GOULDNER, ALVIN W.   *The Dialectic of Ideology and Technology* (New York: Seabury Press, 1976), chap. 12.

KLINEBERG, OTTO, et al.   *Students, Values, and Politics* (New York: Free Press, 1978).

LODGE, GEORGE C.   *The New American Ideology* (New York: Knopf, 1975).

NAVIA, LOUIS E., and EUGENE KELLY (eds.).   *Ethics and the Search for Values* (New York: Prometheus Books, 1980).

ROKEACH, MILTON.   *The Nature of Human Values* (New York: Free Press, 1973).

ROKEACH, MILTON (ed.).   *Understanding Human Values: Individual and Societal* (New York: Free Press, 1971).

SIKULA, ANDREW F.   (ed.). *Values, Motivation, and Management* (Champaign, Ill.: Stipes, 1972).

SLATER, PHILIP.   *Wealth Addiction* (New York: Dutton, 1980).

VICKERS, GEOFFREY.   *Value Systems and Social Process* (New York: Basic Books, 1968).

VOTAW, DOW, and S. PRAKASH SETHI.   *The Corporate Dilemma: Traditional Values vs. Contemporary Problems* (Englewood Cliffs, N.J.: Prentice-Hall, 1973).

9

Managerial Ethics and Morals

The only thing necessary for the triumph of evil is for good men to do nothing.

EDMUND BURKE

Diogenes would have been hard put to it to find an honest man in the Wall Street which I knew as a corporate attorney.

JAMES M. BECK, lawyer,
U.S. attorney, and congressman (1905–1917)

The dangers of America are not economics or from foreign foes; they are moral and spiritual.

HERBERT HOOVER, 1926

CONCEPTS DISCUSSED IN THIS CHAPTER

1. ETHICS AND MORALS IN SOCIETY
2. ETHICAL CONFLICT AND ETHICAL RELATIVITY
3. MORAL FOUNDATIONS OF POWER AND LEADERSHIP
4. ETHICAL ASPECTS OF THE DECISION-MAKING PROCESS

The purpose of this chapter is to analyze the problems of ethical and moral behavior on the part of managers and organizations, and in society as a whole. Ethical and moral issues are abundant in a society as complex as ours. New circumstances emerge to test traditional values, morals, and ethics. Our major social institutions are being critically examined on ethical and moral grounds. The postindustrial society will see even greater emphasis on doing what is right and preventing harm or evil.

But knowing what is right or what is wrong is not equivalent to doing right or wrong. Furthermore, what is acceptable to one person may be ethically wrong in the views of another. "Right" and "wrong" acts are frequently hard to judge in specific circumstances. Ethics and morals are in the nature of ideals toward which people strive in their daily conduct, even in the absence of fixed standards automatically governing their decisions.

Decision makers in business and other organizations face a paradox with respect to ethics and morals. On one hand, we extol virtues such as liberation, individual rights, or "doing one's own thing"; but on the other, we hold managers and their organizations to higher standards in society's interests. The liberated, perhaps narcissistic values of the youthful counterculture now pervade adulthood; drugs, alcohol, sexual license, and resistance to authority are widely accepted prerogatives for individuals, but rectitude by old-fashioned virtues is the standard to which officials and organizations are to conform. Both parties to the paradox — individuals and organizations — believe themselves to be acting under moral imperatives. War or draft resisters, for example, rightly hate war as immoral, though sometimes they condone violence to curb it. Organizations do something similar when they pay bribes or make illegal political campaign contributions in order to "stay profitable and keep our workers employed." In both cases, the ends are thought to justify the means.

ETHICS AND MORALS: AN OVERVIEW

SOME DEFINITIONS

In the preceding chapter we defined ideology as a composite belief system that embodies the most fundamental values of a group, a class, or a society. Values express what people want or desire relative to other things. Freedom is a value when it is preferred to nonfreedom; it and other values such as liberty, justice, or human rights make up the ideology of our capitalist system of economics and our democratic form of government. The concepts of ethics and morals introduce the notion of right and wrong into this framework. *Ethics* is the study or practice of what constitutes good or bad human conduct, including value-oriented behavior. *Morals* represent ultimate or absolute standards of the good and the true; they provide basic values and beliefs against which the ethics of conduct can be judged. Moral standards are a characteristic of society and of humanity deeply imbedded in culture and in tradition. Ethics are contemporary standards by which people evaluate their conduct or that of others.

Moral precepts are values of the highest order. They are affirmed in the human experience by religious tradition and extensive philosophical inquiry. In the United States and in much of Western society, it is the Judeo-Christian tradition which affirms the moral benchmarks that distinguish good from evil. For example, killing, stealing, or adultery are generally proscribed as immoral; honesty, obeying the law, and preserving life are considered moral. Moral as well as other precepts are imbedded in the law.

> The events of the past few years have amounted to a sort of trial by fire, a process of self-examination under pressure which, I submit, is characteristic of the American corporate system. In one way or another, just about every publicly held company in this country will have been through this process. And none will emerge unchanged, neither the relatively righteous — the overwhelming majority — nor the small number whose sins were uncovered and exposed to the public wrath.
>
> My point is that the system, in the time-honored phrase, has worked. Our sins were uncovered noisily, as they always are, and with so much gusto that it was easy for the impressionable to believe that we were going to hell in a handbasket. Well, maybe we were. But somehow we have not. And now that the dust has begun to settle we can survey the scene, estimate the damage, and get on with the job.
>
> WILLIAM M. AGEE, "The Moral and Ethical Climate in Today's Business World," p. 17, *MSU Business Topics*, Winter 1978. Reprinted by permission of the publisher, Division of Research, Graduate School of Business Administration, Michigan State University.

Behavior is ethical to the extent that it accords with moral beliefs about right and wrong. Moral standards are transcendant over all forms of human conduct, including the ethical. Morality is an elusive goal humans do not fully attain, and the difficulty of achieving moral absolutism makes ethical behavior judgmental, uncertain, and often imperfect.

Ethics is simultaneously an art (requiring judgment and practice), a branch of philosophy, and an object of scientific study. Ethics is not a science, but there is no reason to exclude ethical behavior from study by the methods of science. It is more difficult to study ethical questions scientifically and systematically, but the scientific model so successful in the physical sciences is equally applicable to the determination of true propositions about right conduct.[1]

In sum, managers as well as other humans are aware that actions may be judged right or wrong, and that there are gray areas in between

---

[1] John Sawhill, "A Question of Ethics," *Newsweek*, October 29, 1979, p. 27.

which depend upon human nature in many complex situations. Moral behavior represents the highest ideals of humanity, but rules and prescriptions for the ethical behavior that affirms an ultimate morality are often unclear.

ETHICAL AND MORAL RELATIVITY

The French philosopher Montaigne once noted that "what's right on this side of the Pyrenees (France) is wrong on the other side (Spain)." This assertion reveals that there are differences in morals and ethics among the various societies and cultures of the world. Cultural relativity is a fact that must be reckoned with. Accepting "bribes" may be common practice in a foreign culture, for example, but in ours it is an unethical, indeed illegal, practice.

Beyond cultural relativity is the question of the inherent relativity of values, ethics, and morals themselves. Cultural relativity implies the denial of or disagreement over the eternal verities that ought to apply to all human beings. Three philosophical approaches are identified with moral and ethical relativity: legalism, situation ethics, and existentialism.

Legalism takes the form of rules, codes, regulations, and law prescribed by religions. Judaism, Catholicism, and Protestantism have been highly legalistic. In this view, religious principles are not mere guidelines, but are directives with elaborate adjudication systems. *Existentialism* rejects all principles, rules, or directives, treating each situation as containing at a given time its own ethical solution. Universally valid moral, ethical, or valid precepts are denied, and there is seen to be no coherence, continuity, or social fabric with meaning — only the necessities of the here and now exist. *Situation ethics* holds that people enter into every decision situation with the ethical and moral maxims of their heritage and community, treating them with respect as illuminators of problems and guides to action. Its central concept is love, and if love seems better served by compromising or departing from affirmed moral precepts, they will be set aside. Situation ethics thus claims to make use of principles, but does not treat them as unyielding law.[2]

The issues separating the three approaches cannot easily be resolved. All have their limitations. Legalism results in an enormous body of laws and codes posing endless problems of application and judgment, conferring power on those who judge. Existentialism spawned the counterculture, with its rebellion against all authority and the absence of any constraints on behavior. Situation ethics simplistically equates love with justice, and has aroused a storm of controversy.[3]

---

[2] Joseph Fletcher, *Situation Ethics: The New Morality* (Philadelphia: Westminster Press, 1966), pp. 18–37.

[3] Harvey Cox (ed.), *The Situation Ethics Debate* (Philadelphia: Westminster Press, 1968).

But ethical and moral relativism is a pseudo-issue. It oversimplifies the complex nature of the quest for discerning morality in human conduct, and the problem of adapting ethical behavior to emerging understanding of moral precepts and values. Golembiewski writes that the moral order is unchanging and unchanged, and that the human drama unfolds in the form of adjusting ethical acts so as to approach more closely our knowledge of the moral order as it becomes increasingly precise.[4] This allows for a wide variation among people as to their ways of relating individually to the moral and ethical principles espoused by groups or societies. Telling right from wrong is often difficult, as is explaining why people do wrong when they know what is right.

> . . . what men have held to be moral or ethical or good since time immemorial are precisely those modes of behaviour which are best calculated to enhance the survival of one's own society: and at a deeper level and in more general terms, the survival of the human race. The reasonable man of the lawyers; the ethical or moral man of the philosophers; the good or godly man of the great religions; the normal man of the psychologists and psycho-analysts; the satisfied man of the utilitarians; all these men appear to conform to what might be called the sociological imperative that men must behave in such a way as to ensure that society can survive.
>
> ELLIOTT JACQUES, *A General Theory of Bureaucracy* (New York: Heinemann/Halsted Press, 1976), p. 5.

We will now examine moral and ethical issues at four levels of analysis: (1) society as a whole, (2) managerial ethics and morals, (3) organizational constraints, and (4) the ethics and morals of individuals.

THE ETHICAL AND MORAL FABRIC OF SOCIETY

Philosophers see the human predicament as one in which things often go badly for humanity. Our social institutions provide moral and ethical standards to counteract the tendency of things to go wrong for individuals or for society. There is thus a moral impulse in society which affirms such precepts as (1) don't do any harm, (2) do that which is good, (3) don't be unfair or unjust, and (4) avoid deception, dishonesty, and other acts which destroy trust.[5] Such moral guidelines are widely accepted in the abstract, and widely violated in practice. But they are significant as universal ideals to which imperfect humans aspire.

---

[4] Robert T. Golembiewski, *Men, Management, and Morality* (New York: McGraw-Hill, 1965), pp. 60–63.

[5] Geoffrey Warnock, *The Object of Morality* (New York: Methuen, 1971).

No one institution alone can protect society against moral decay. Interdependencies among business, education, religion, government, and the family, for example, reflect the interrelated roles the leaders of such institutions play in meeting the moral and ethical expectations of society. Our primary social institutions jointly nurture and preserve ethical and moral ideals, transmitting them to the young and providing sanctions against those who go too far or too quickly against societal norms. Social institutions form a powerful moral web, a structural base for attaching values to specific contexts.[6]

THE INFLUENCE OF RELIGION

Formal religions have, throughout history, greatly affected the conduct of business and economic activity. Slavery; exploitation of material resources and human beings; harsh, unsafe working conditions; child labor; and the insecurities of old age, for example, have improved through the pressures of social institutions. But these were problems of the preceding generation, and they have been followed by other dilemmas equally if not more difficult. Problems of segregation and discrimination in employment, mass unemployment, care for the aged and mentally ill — and, above all, problems stemming from concentrations of power in the hands of big corporations, big unions, and big government — have received more and more attention.

The Judeo-Christian tradition has always confronted the world with the dilemmas. It has called for the sharing of power and wealth rather than its accumulation, and advanced a basic ethic that recognizes the dignity of the person, the equality of all individuals in the eyes of God, and people's sense of brotherhood, community, and fellowship. Although businesspeople and many other Americans subscribe generally to the tenets of the Judeo-Christian heritage, they often undercut their faith in grappling with actual problems, such as productivity, inflation, market competition, labor unions, and government regulation. Religious institutions have not perfected human behavior nor eliminated the ongoing moral dilemmas of decision makers. The problems are far too complex. Moreover, religious institutions themselves have lacked unity and consistency of doctrine; the differences are not only among Judaism, Catholicism, and Protestantism, but also within each of these religious groups where there are wide ranges of practice and belief. The individual faces a bewildering array of possible acceptable responses to ethical and moral dilemmas.

The Protestant ethic, sometimes called the Puritan or work ethic, provided the values supporting the struggles of a frontier society in the process of industrialization. The Protestant ethic fostered such values as

---

[6] Robert Cooley Angell, *Free Society and Moral Crisis* (Ann Arbor: University of Michigan Press, 1965).

thrift, hard work, industriousness, responsibility, individualism, the phi-losophy of progress, a sense of mission, and respect for human dignity and worth. These values made possible new frontiers of growth, but the Protestant movement, particularly in its pietistic (Lutheran) and Calvinistic forms, also saw humans as sinful and guilty. Work was the road to salvation, but the human future was cast in the likelihood of destruction by triumphant evil.[7]

Religions emphasize the presence of sin and guilt as the conse-quences of immoral behavior. Sin, which is in effect an infraction of societal rules couched in religious significance, leads to guilt. Guilt is the pain humans feel when they transgress moral codes, and it is the dynamic feature of morality that causes most people to avoid creating harm or evil.[8] Guilt leads to remorse; the failure to feel guilt is the basic flaw in the psychopath or the antisocial person, who commits crimes without contrition.[9]

Menninger has recounted the psychological and social dangers of re-jecting the idea of sin. By ignoring or excusing sin or defining it out of ex-istence as the existentialists do, the personality is damaged and people are free to do great harm in the name of freedom, liberation, or the values of the narcissistic generation.[10] Lying provides a good example. A lie is a false statement made to others with intention to mislead or deceive. The excuse that this is done to avoid hurting someone, such as withholding from an individual a report that his illness is terminal, is inadequate; the person concerned may feel differently about the matter. Lying or decep-tion may be justified in a self-defense situation such as that of a hostage or a threat to life, where there are no good alternatives. But in general, ly-ing is a sin and trust remains a social necessity.[11]

THE INFLUENCE OF EDUCATION

Educational institutions play a vital role in the preservation and in-doctrination of ethical and social values in the young. Maturity, the ob-ject of learning, requires the capability of exercising ethical and moral judgment.

---

[7] For a concise analysis, see Richard Eells and Clarence Walton: *Conceptual Foundations of Business* (Homewood, Ill.: Irwin, 1961), pp. 491–498. For extended treatments, see Max Weber, *The Protes-tant Ethic and the Spirit of Capitalism* (New York: Scribner's, 1950); and R. H. Tawney, *Religion and the Rise of Capitalism* (New York: Harcourt Brace, 1926).

[8] Andrew Slaby and Laurence Tancredi, *Collusion for Conformity* (New York: Jason Aronson, 1975), p. 17.

[9] Willard Gaylin, "On Feeling Guilty," *Atlantic*, January 1979, pp. 78–82.

[10] Karl Menninger, *Whatever Became of Sin* (New York: Hawthorne Books, 1973). See also Edward Alsworth Ross, *Sin and Society: An Analysis of Latter-Day Iniquity* (Boston: Houghton Mifflin, 1970).

[11] Sissela Bok, *Lying: Moral Choice in Public and Private Life* (New York: Random House, 1978). For a review of how language and communications devices provide a "fake factor" that operates more subtly than outright lies, see Arthur Herzog, *The B.S. Factor* (New York: Simon and Schuster, 1973).

Schools are informal, indirect, and unsystematic in their approach to inculcating moral and ethical standards. Courses in ethics and related subjects are difficult to organize and teach effectively; few teachers feel well enough qualified or feel able to remain unbiased and objective. Also, other institutions, such as the family and the church, share the responsibilities for moral and ethical upbringing. Yet all subject matter contains ethical and moral implications, whether recognized or not. Therefore schools at all levels will always play a role in this process.

Schools themselves are a role model for coping with ethical and moral dilemmas. How they deal with cheating, lying, deception, plagiarism, fraudulent research, and the like conveys signals to students and to citizens. Professional schools of medicine, law, engineering, education, and business have special obligations to develop the ethical and moral understandings essential to good practice in their fields. But universities have not so far distinguished themselves for teaching high standards of ethical behavior. Fantastic deviations from time-tested ethical norms are tolerated under the belief that ends justify means. This is precisely the lesson pervading the Watergate scandals, where well-established, university-educated professionals with law degrees and master's degrees in business and economics ignored basic values to further the selfish interests of a coterie of public power grabbers. Clearly there is little necessary connection between being educated and being ethical.

Much of the worst behavior emanates from well-educated elites. In a random sampling of 328 United States executives on post-Watergate business morality, Carroll found that almost 60 percent, to prove their loyalty, would go along with their bosses even if it resulted in lies or other deceptions. Two out of three said that all managers are under pressure to compromise personal standards if necessary to achieve company goals. The only positive finding was that many managers believe that today's business ethics are far superior to those of earlier periods.[12]

LEADERSHIP, POWER, AND MORALITY

The world is critically short of leaders sensitive to morality. Though a leader may exercise great power, the exercise of power by brute force is not leadership. Tyranny is the opposite of leadership. Power wielders treat people as things; leaders do not. Moral leadership is complicated and subtle. Its ultimate test is its ability to transcend a myriad of claims based on everyday wants and needs to attain a higher level of moral development predicated on reasoned, explicit, conscious values. The best leaders in society are those who lead people upward toward higher values, purposes, or self-fulfillment.[13]

---

[12] Archie Carroll, "A Survey of Managerial Ethics: Is Business Morality Watergate Morality?" *Business and Society Review* 13 (Spring 1975), pp. 58–60.

[13] James Macgregor Burns, *Leadership* (New York: Harper & Row, 1978).

During the past decade, pollsters have found widespread pessimism in the form of declining confidence in government, business, and other institutions. One poll found that 68 percent of the respondents agreed with the statement that "over the past ten years America's leaders have consistently lied to the American people." The polls consistently reveal a lack of confidence in economic and political leadership, and doubt about the ability of government to meet the problems of the future. Although there are those who do not believe polls are valid, they show a remarkable consistency and reflect the fact that people have a better knowledge of economics and society than politicians think they have.[14]

The level of ethical and moral behavior in an organization is heavily influenced by its leaders, especially those at the top. A corporation's ethical attitude is ultimately the result of the chief executive's beliefs. It is the top leader who selects other key leaders, who tend to reflect the values they see their superiors favoring. But imitation is not the only process at work. Leaders must directly communicate ethical expectations, enforce them through the reward and punishment system, and follow up to see that ethical principles inform and influence everyday decisions.[15]

Society too attains its ethical ideals to the extent that its leaders exercise moral responsibilities. Prominent leaders play a strong role, but at the societal level middle-level leadership is also important. Mid-level leaders are in places of direct action and decision in all social institutions. Such leaders function in clarifying purposes, building coalitions, improving involvement and communication, and building morale. Ethical and moral behavior thrive best in environments where leaders lead ethically and morally in the public interest.

Moral, spiritual, and ethical leadership is lacking on the national scene, according to psychiatrist Robert Coles. He has studied upper-middle-class children, who hunger for honesty but see crooked leadership and phony behavior all around them. Family units, so important to social cohesion, are eroded by the anxieties of inflation, unemployment, high mobility of family heads, and the like. Leaders who grapple with these problems need to reject mechanistic, agnostic views to help people appreciate the full meaning of life.[16]

Appeals for better moral and ethical leadership should recognize the inherent conflict between ethical ideals and the demands of practical affairs. The Judeo-Christian tradition, for example, implicitly rejects

---

[14] Based on his own experience with the Gallup organization, Irving Crespi sees polls and survey research as valid and important for informing those in power. See "Modern Marketing Techniques: They Could Work in Washington Too," *Public Opinion* 2 (June–July 1979), pp. 16–19 and 55.

[15] John I. Reynolds, "Improving Business Ethics: The President's Lonely Task," *Business and Society* 19 (Fall 1978), pp. 10–16. See also K. Mark Weaver, "Top Management Impact on Ethical Behaviors," in Lyle R. Trueblood (ed.), *Annual Proceedings*, Southwest Division, Academy of Management, 1977, pp. 3–7.

[16] *Behavior Today*, May 3, 1976, p. 5.

secular interests such as profit, wealth, self-interest, and the use of power for empire-building. In such conflicts, if one side rejects power, the other side will use it to defeat the side that does not. For example, one cannot expect managers, whose prime task is to preserve the organization, to let ethics weaken their use of power. Managers are not depraved because they do this; they are doing what makes a manager a manager.[17] Resolutions of this dilemma are being acted out in the thousands of decisions managers make daily.

Another area of conflict in the moral dimensions of leadership is found in the political system. There are conflicts of national values and priorities which it is the task of politicians to mediate and resolve, and it is important for officials and politicians to be morally sensitive. Political campaigns often feature the need for moral leadership, even though few public policy issues concern morality itself. Issues are predominantly economic, political, or social. What political leaders often do is use morality to support their positions on the real issues. This is moralizing rather than working in the interests of morality. Thus one senator, for example, promised to provide "moral leadership" that would create jobs, close tax loopholes, break up monopolistic oil companies, and provide support for the old and the needy. War is another example in which the politician needs to sell conflict as a moral issue to rally public support.[18]

Morality was an important issue in President Carter's 1976 campaign. The Watergate scandals, bribery and corruption, lying politicians, padded expense accounts, enormous waste, and the manipulation of vast sums of money for special interests disillusioned the public about political and governmental morality. The resulting moral malaise is now changing to an intense moral concern in public life. Yet is it difficult for citizens to assess the nature and extent of moral laxity in politicians, so moral issues and conflicts will continue to occupy an important position in political discourse.[19]

THE ETHICS OF SOCIAL EXPERIMENTATION

One of society's major ethical quandaries centers on problems relating to the use of human subjects in research. The areas of concern in medical research include surgical or medical treatments, drug experiments, fetal research, genetic engineering, and behavior modification.[20] Concern is also increasing over the ethical dilemmas of social, psycho-

---

[17] Barrows Dunham, *Heroes and Heretics: A Political History of Western Thought* (New York: Knopf, 1964), p. 187.

[18] Stephen Hess, "When a Politician Preaches Morality," *The Wall Street Journal*, January 30, 1976, p. 17.

[19] George Melloan, "The Morality Issue," *The Wall Street Journal*, August 26, 1979, p. 14.

[20] Bernard Barber et al., *Research on Human Subjects: Problems of Social Control in Medical Experimentation* (New Brunswick, N.J.: Transaction Books, 1979).

logical, and public issue research involving humans, such as income maintenance projects, housing, insurance, educational, and a host of other experimental programs.[21]

Ethical questions abound. Should subjects be told the purpose of an experiment, and if so will this bias the results? Can researchers keep personal information confidential from support agencies such as the government? How can the subjects be safeguarded from harm or loss during or after an experiment?

Available standards are admittedly abstract and hard to apply in concrete cases. Government agencies carefully scrutinize the human impact of research projects, requiring the informing of subjects and the permission of appropriate authorities for research involving children, prisoners, or mental patients. A general principle is that the societal benefits must far outweigh the potential harm. But it is difficult to specify what constitutes full information to subjects and the degree of their understanding of risk when assenting to participation. Scattered decisions tend to indicate that courts will not allow researchers to withhold information from officials seeking access to files.

In the application of general guidelines, other ethical questions arise. What is the researcher's obligation to persons in a control group who do not get the same benefits as others in an experiment? Can poor people be offered financial inducements to participate? Who consents for minors or mental patients? Will people not in the experiment at all be harmed? What about people not in an experiment who assert the right to be in?

There are no easy answers to the ethical problems in research, so they will be a continuing problem. The ethical responsibility of the researcher, apart from legal requirements, is to try to make sure that the benefits heavily outweigh the risks to subjects, that everything has been done to minimize the risks, and that subjects have the information necessary for deciding whether or not to participate.

MANAGERIAL ETHICS AND MORALS

Every decision a manager makes has an ethical dimension. In some decisions ethics plays only a trivial role, but the important ones affect large numbers of people for good or ill. The potential for doing good or evil is present in the way every manager defines and approaches the responsibility of managing.

Society provides moral guidelines, but ethical behavior is learned by experience in applying them. One manager who thought deeply about

---

[21] Alice M. Rivlin and P. Michael Timpane, *Ethical and Legal Issues of Social Experimentation* (Washington, D.C.: The Brookings Institution, 1975).

ethics raised the following questions: (1) Who formed my sense of ethics? (2) Whose ethics do I help form? (3) What should be the balance? This insight reveals that doing things ethically is the product of common experiences among people living and working together.

Many managers show a concern for ethics, and many organizations directly stress ethical means of attaining objectives. Many also object to giving ethics a role in decisions on the grounds that ethical standards are too personal, vague, general, variable, subjective, and situation-bound. Some see no need for ethics other than obeying the law. Thus, for example, affirmative action programs often seem excessively legalistic.

People of good will disagree over what is ethical, and it is hard to know who is right. Doing things ethically often requires courage because an ethical act may run counter to current opinion, clash with other values such as profit, or be a threat to insecure managers. The successful combination of prudence and courage is hard to achieve.

ETHICS AND MORALS IN BUSINESS

Polls consistently show that nearly half the nation's young persons and adults believe that corporations are interested only in profits and care little about the idea of quality of life or the well-being of society. This is more than an image problem, yet business responses have relied heavily on image-building techniques. Despite what has been done, business has not shaken its amoral image, and firms have been confused and misguided in their handling of ethical issues.[22]

Yet most companies and managers care about the moral principles that underlie ethics. However, they seldom publicly defend their actions from a moral point of view, and the absence of moral discourse feeds suspicion and distrust. It is rare for companies or managers or even professionals to criticize the questionable behavior of their colleagues. This ethical silence is not a conspiracy or a coverup, but continuing the tacit acceptance of immoral behavior and the avoidance of moral language will intensify the already growing public anger. Public dissatisfaction over the ethics of business performance is deeper than many believe.

Generalized allegations of corruption are unfair because the preponderant share of business activity is ethically and morally acceptable. Scandals involving major breaches of the law taint all business with suspicion and distrust. In areas beyond the reach of the law there are also questions of ethics and morals. Both lawbreaking and dubious but legal behaviors need the serious attention of managers. What is needed is to overcome an older notion of business ethics — that business is inherently

---

[22] Joseph A. Pichler and Richard T. De George, "Ethics: Principles and Disclosures," *World* (Peat, Marwick Mitchell & Company), Spring 1979, pp. 28–32.

immoral and hence *beneath* serious attention. Also needed is to reject the opposite notion — that business is solely concerned with producing and marketing, and therefore is *above* moral considerations. Between these extremes is the need for clarification of standards of behavior and a concept of what ethical and moral improvement means in everyday affairs.[23]

We will now consider several examples of ethical conflicts that cut across organizational and even national boundaries. In later sections we will analyze internal and individual ethical conflicts.

BRIBERY, PAYOFFS, AND KICKBACKS

Bribery and related corruptions stem from the inadequate moral approach of some managers, from the forces generated by demands for profit, and from international business relations that encounter cultural differences in ethical and moral beliefs. An example of the problem of managerial attitudes and philosophies is a study that found executives about equally divided as to their attitudes toward bribery or payoffs in doing business abroad. Fifty-two percent of the respondents said that companies should follow American standards, and 48 percent said they should follow the standards of the countries in which they operate. Only one out of four reported that their companies had written policies. Most payoff demands come from governments, so the problem is more likely in firms that sell to governments rather than to consumers or through middlemen.[24]

Rationalizations for bribery and payoffs include the drive for profits, which leads to corner-cutting, fudging of agreements, or padding of expense accounts. Also ethical tenets slow things down, get in the way, or seem outmoded and inconvenient. Business becomes a rough and tumble world that encourages the use of "angles" and loopholes, favoring "operators" and "wheeler-dealers."[25]

Bribery and other corruptions involve costs that can be passed along in the price structure and are hence looked at simply as a cost of doing business. The "when in Rome do as the Romans do" philosophy is frequently followed out of fear that profits will be lost if one does not do what competitors are willing to do. Corruption has its uses in "greasing the skids," and in the case of governments, bureaucrats are spending other people's money. Also, bribery and other wrongful acts can be defined out of existence by ignoring them — it's the other person's

---

[23] Max Ways, "Business Faces Growing Pressures to Behave Better," *Fortune*, May 1974, pp. 193–195, 310–320.

[24] *The Wall Street Journal*, February 13, 1976, p. 12.

[25] Kirkpatrick Sale, *Power Shift: The Rise of the Southern Rim and Its Challenge to the Eastern Establishment* (New York: Random House, 1975), p. 72.

problem.[26] Corrupt practices are also couched in euphemisms such as expediting, service fees, bidding tactics, gift-giving, priority rearrangement, and the like.

Reisman notes three forms of bribery: (1) transaction bribes, sometimes called "grease" or facilitating payments; (2) variance bribes, to get a variance from a law or to change a law to benefit the briber; and (3) outright purchase—such as "buying" a judge or a legislator. All three types demonstrate the discrepancy between belief or myth and the operational code. We have myths that clearly express the rules and prohibitions we believe in, but those who know the operational code know when, by whom, and how the "wrong" things necessary for power, influence, and success are done.[27]

Some of the worst business scandals have occurred in the largest, most prominent, and powerful firms. One of the worst of over 200 cases investigated by the Securities and Exchange Commission and by congressional committees was that of the Lockheed Aviation Corporation, which between 1970 and 1975 paid over $202 million to foreign governments, political parties, and sales agents, of which $30 million were actual bribes known to management. Northrop Corporation, Gulf Oil Company, United Brands Company, Exxon Corporation, Mobil Oil Corporation, and many others were found in the 1970s to have been involved in bribery, illegal political contributions, and other corruptions. Actions taken in such cases involve long and costly investigations, and plowing through murky accounting practices. Sanctions have been relatively light—modest fines, few imprisonments, with virtually no condemnation or ostracism by the business community, not even the National Manufacturers Association, the U.S. Chamber of Commerce, or other respected associations.[28]

Corruption leads to the excessive controls and regulations which managers deplore. But laws cannot stamp out all wrongful behavior, nor can they be effective unless ethical and moral standards are developed and enforced by managers and their organizations. For example, in a series of laboratory experiments where subjects were presented with decision opportunities involving kickbacks, it was found that when unethical behavior was rewarded, it increased. It also increased under competitive pressures. The overall findings were that unethical decision making

---

[26] Milton Friedman, "The Uses of Corruption," *Newsweek*, March 22, 1976, p. 73; "The Global Costs of Bribery," *Business Week*, March 15, 1976, pp. 22–24; Joseph M. Waldman, "A Primer on Corruption," *Business Studies* 12 (Fall 1972), pp. 27–34.

[27] W. Michael Reisman, *Folded Lies: Bribery, Crusades, and Reforms* (New York: Macmillan, 1979).

[28] "How Clean Is Business?" *Newsweek*, September 1, 1975; Arthur Schlesinger, Jr., "Government, Business, and Morality," *The Wall Street Journal*, June 1, 1976, p. 14; for the Lockheed story, see David Boulton, *The Grease Machine* (New York: Harper & Row, 1979). See also Irving Kristol, "Business Ethics and Economic Man," *The Wall Street Journal*, March 20, 1979, p. 17; David N. Aicchirite, "Illegal Payments, Deception of Auditors, and Reports on Internal Control," *MSU Business Topics* 28 (Spring 1980), pp. 57–62.

results from a combination of personality, cultural and value orientation, and environmental rewards and punishments. An organizational ethics policy was found to reduce unethical behavior.[29]

MORAL ISSUES IN INVESTMENT POLICY

Portfolio managers have been forced by public outcry and activist movements to reassess their attitudes to investment in morally questionable situations. The issue is whether funds should be deployed so as to enhance social, political, and moral objectives. The important questions are these: (1) Are there companies whose securities should not be held for social, political, or moral reasons? (2) Should the portfolio manager vote the stock by such considerations? (3) Should investments be used positively to attain social, political, or moral aims? There are no pat answers to such questions, which are often debated on ideological as well as moral grounds. The attempt to use noneconomic criteria for investment decisions is fraught with difficulty. It is hard, for example, to appraise the possible consequences and to determine their effects. Harms and benefits are hard to measure. It is even more difficult to choose the social ends being sought.

Despite the difficulties, healthy questions are being raised and many companies and universities are reviewing the moral implications of their investment policies, so that they can develop better policies and devise minimum safeguards against undue reliance on purely economic criteria.[30]

PROFITS AND THE MARKET

"Free enterprise" concepts incorporating both economic and political ideals stress the role of profits and the market system. Surveys often show that citizens do not readily understand the role of profits, and that they consistently see profits as far greater than business firms calculate them to be. Statistics can be advanced by both sides. Returns on sales usually look larger than returns on investment, so the definition of the measure of profit is important. Many executives are concerned that they have not effectively communicated the role of profit, and they react negatively to the frequently encountered view that profits are evil. They see the media as an agent of distortion in the public's understanding of profit.

---

[29] Harvey Hegarty and Henry P. Sims, Jr., "Some Determinants of Unethical Decision Behavior: An Experiment," *Journal of Applied Psychology* 63 (1978), pp. 451–457; and "Organizational Philosophy, Policies and Objectives Related to Unethical Decision Behavior: A Laboratory Experiment," *Journal of Applied Psychology* 64 (1979), pp. 331–338.

[30] Burton G. Malkiel and Richard E. Quandt, "Moral Issues in Investment Policy," *Harvard Business Review* 49 (March–April 1971), pp. 37–47; Charles W. Powers (ed.), *People/Profits: The Ethics of Investment* (New York: Council on Religion and International Affairs, 1972).

"As far as the seven deadly sins go, I can't get very excited over 'sloth'."

SOURCE: The Wall Street Journal, *June 5, 1980, p. 24.*

Silk and Vogel conclude that basically Americans have no quarrel with profit, and that they accord it a more important role than many business-people think.[31]

ETHICS IN THE ORGANIZATION

We noted earlier that the ethical and moral aspects of decision and action collide with certain features of organization, such as the hierarchy of status and authority and the tendency to value unfailing loyalty. Internal conflicts over matters of ethics and morals also arise out of the complexity of situations, the difficulty of general or ambiguous standards, and the problems of interpersonal relations.

The act of organizing has chiefly been considered a technical problem. That is, relating the parts of an operating system focuses on processes and techniques that empirical study can resolve. Engineers do this every day. Moral and ethical issues arise in determining what values are to guide the ways of achieving desired relationships, especially among

---

[31] Leonard Silk and David Vogel, *Ethics and Profits* (New York: Simon and Schuster, 1976). See also Benjamin M. Friedman, *New Challenges to the Role of Profit* (Lexington, Mass.: Lexington Books, 1978); and Robert K. Mueller, *Metadevelopment: Beyond the Bottom Line* (Lexington, Mass.: Lexington Books, 1977).

people. There are substantial limits on the degree to which work can violate the values derived from the Judeo-Christian tradition.

Many managers feel that most of the blame for unethical behavior is due to individual failure and not to lack of organizational controls. Yet they feel there should be an absolute standard of social conduct, enforced not by peers, but by the immediate organizational framework to which they can turn for guidance.[32] Thus the hierarchy plays a key role in ethical performance. Carroll's studies found that 64 percent of the executives he surveyed agreed with the proposition that managers today feel under pressure to compromise personal standards to achieve company goals, and 59 percent agreed that managers should have gone along with their bosses on ethical issues to show their loyalty.[33] Newstrom and Ruch found in a sample of 121 managers that (1) the ethical beliefs of employees are similar to those of top management, (2) managers have a propensity to capitalize on being unethical if conditions remove or lessen the barriers against such behavior, and (3) managers believe their peers to be more unethical than they themselves claim to be.[34]

Systems views of organizations show effects on morals and ethics similar to those of hierarchies. System welfare becomes an overriding goal which at times transcends individual or group standards. Pleas for loyalty, team play, and the like may squelch dissent. Concern for ethics is influenced by the system and hierarchical contexts. For many individuals, a situation ethics point of view is necessary. Lying can even seem heroic when the individual sacrifices his or her integrity for the common good.[35]

One of earliest assessments of morality in organizations was that of Chester I. Barnard, who held that personal morality based on the Judeo-Christian tradition must be supplemented and extended by clearly setting forth the organization's ethical norms of executive conduct. Simon advanced an organization ethic recognizing that individuals decide by personal standards, but also that the organization has its standards of decision making. Conflicts between individual and organizational ethics mean that moral and ethical actions are a matter of cooperative social relations.[36]

---

[32] Steven N. Brenner and Earl A. Molendar, "Is the Ethics of Business Changing?" *Harvard Business Review* 55 (January–February 1977), pp. 57–71.

[33] Carroll, "A Survey of Managerial Ethics." See also Archie B. Carroll, "Business Ethics and the Management Hierarchy," *National Forum, Phi Kappa Phi Journal* 58 (Summer 1978), pp. 37–40.

[34] John N. Newstrom and William A. Ruch, "The Ethics of Management and the Management of Ethics," *MSU Business Topics* 23 (Winter 1975), pp. 29–37.

[35] Barrows Dunham, *Heroes and Heretics*, pp. 303–304. See also William G. Scott, "Organicism: The Moral Anesthetic of Management," *Academy of Management Review* 46 (January 1979), pp. 21–28.

[36] Chester I. Barnard, *Organization and Management* (Cambridge, Mass.: Harvard University Press, 1938); Herbert A. Simon, *Administrative Behavior* (New York: Macmillan, 1976); T. Edwin Boling, "The Management Ethics 'Crisis': An Organizational Perspective," *Academy of Management Review* 3 (April 1978), pp. 360–365.

Organizations have moral rights and resonsibilities, but practical matters pose many difficulties. Balancing the competing interests of shareholders, customers, employees, and the general public is a task for corporation executives, for example, but in practice the organization's structure and ideology work against this balance. Executives are not accountable to the people in the same ways elected government officials are.[37] Ethical issues pervade the communications process. Public relations efforts and the firm's advertising image often do not match the organization's behavior. Accounting and legal units encounter pressures that challenge the firm's moral and ethical beliefs.[38]

Ethical issues of enormous import are involved in the organization's treatment of employees. Behavioral management techniques designed to influence employee behavior in meeting organizational needs are highly successful, but they raise the specter of brainwashing, manipulation, and control, which are typically thought undesirable in society. Positive reinforcement could be a form of bribery; techniques can be misused, or directed at unsuspecting individuals; control methods can be deceptive. Guarding against these negative elements is a management problem, but it should also be recognized that socialization of members into the organizational setting is a natural and inevitable process, that individual values change slowly, and that people have defenses against intrusion into their freedom and conscience.[39]

INDIVIDUAL ETHICS

Organizational needs for conformity, homogeneity, and bureaucratic predictability clash with the needs of individuals for freedom, variety, conscience, self-fulfillment, and the like. The organization and its ideology exert powerful pressure on individuals to place organizational imperatives over their own. Whyte saw this long ago as an insidious loss of individuality.[40] More recently, Scott and Hart have resurrected the "organization man" concept in a different light—that of homogenizing and transcending individual values.[41]

Individual managers are aware that business is a rough and tumble game for themselves as well as organizations that compete with one

---

[37] Silk and Vogel, *Ethics and Profits*, p. 215.

[38] Clarence Walton (ed.), *The Ethics of Corporate Conduct* (Englewood Cliffs, N.J.: Prentice-Hall, 1977); Roger D'Aprix, *The Believable Corporation* (New York: AMACOM, 1977); "The Image Makers," *The Wall Street Journal*, August 1, 1978, p. 1.

[39] Charles C. Manz and Henry P. Sims, Jr., "The Ethics of Behavioral Management," in Edwin A. Gerloff (ed.), *1980 Proceedings of the Annual Meeting*, Southwest Division, Academy of Management, March 19–22, 1980, pp. 96–100.

[40] William H. Whyte, *The Organization Man* (New York: Simon and Schuster, 1956).

[41] William G. Scott and David K. Hart, *The Organizational Imperative* (Boston: Houghton Mifflin, 1979), p. 63.

another. Management is not only a game, but also a drama in which the manager plays a heroic role. Managers must handle crises, allocate resources, accept risk and blame, and deal with conflicts among stake-holders — consumers, shareholders, suppliers, and employees. The aspects of drama in managerial roles serve to camouflage gaps in managerial knowledge and expertise, and to enable managers to perform decently — to take action — even when expectations and common understandings are not present.

Dramatic and gamesmanship roles are played out in a context that contains constraining factors. Once a job is accepted, the individual finds that it is defined by the organization. Therefore it becomes a matter of conscience to what extent the individual accepts or rejects the constraints, and what one owes to himself or herself and to society versus what is owed to the organization. Specialists, professionals, and experts have special problems in this regard, which we examined in Part One of this book. There is a conflict between the specialized job and the unspecialized conscience.[42]

The Judeo-Christian ethic informs the conscience of most people, businesspeople as well as others. Managers are not usually eloquent in philosophy or theology, nor are they experts on morality, but they frequently acknowledge basic beliefs in such precepts as the Ten Commandments, the Golden Rule, or "the greatest good for the greatest number." Only a few believe that values are culturally determined, but a growing number believe that what is right or wrong depends on the situation.[43]

In grappling with the ethical aspects of decisions, the element of conscience comes into play in the gray areas beyond what is illegal or immoral according to basic religious tenets. Some will capitalize on the shades of gray, coming close to illegal or unethical behavior without violating actual standards. Some will make mistakes, later perhaps trying to make amends for the harm that is done. This balancing act must occur wherever laws are unclear, codes are vague, or the ground rules are soft. Departures from strict standards are often excused by the existence of crises or emergencies, such as inflation or wartime demands.

There is disagreement among philosophers and other scholars as to whether individual morality is increasing or decreasing in society. Cahn, for example, doubts that industrialization has brought any moral improvement, and asserts that business honesty relates to the trivial aspects of moral life. Honesty is rooted in economic necessity rather than higher ideals of political order, religious commitment, or artistic pursuits.[44] Zoll

---

[42] Charles Frankel, *The Democratic Prospect* (New York: Harper & Row, 1962), pp. 148–156.

[43] Joseph W. McGuire, "The Business of Business Ethics," *National Forum, Phi Kappa Phi Journal* 58 (Summer 1978), pp. 32–36. See also Harold L. Johnson, "Can the Businessman Apply Christianity?" *Harvard Business Review* 35 (September–October 1957), pp. 68–71.

[44] Edmond Cahn, *The Moral Decision* (Bloomington: Indiana University Press, 1955), pp. 124–130.

notes the widespread abrogation of moral responsibility prevalent today.[45] On the other hand, Aiken declares that the so-called new morality, which many consider so challenging to traditional values, in actuality portrays a growing sense of moral responsibility.[46] Ideas about what is moral are clearly changing as people discern new needs and new problems.

ETHICS AND SELF-INTEREST

Socrates said that morality is the controlled gratification of impulse. Society provides rewards for approved behavior and sanctions for the unapproved. This idea reflects a powerful motive for individual ethics and morals. The group spirit is a powerful influence. Managers are more likely to follow rules respected by their peers rather than those of moralists, economists, or politicians. But one should also be aware of opposite tendencies in the impact of the group on the individual. Niebuhr writes: "In every human group there is less reason to guide and check impulse, less capacity for self-transcendance, less ability to comprehend the needs of others and therefore more unrestrained egoism than the individuals, who compose the group, reveal in their personal relationships."[47]

The fact that self-interest is a generally recognized norm of business conduct means that managers are likely to be guided by it rather than their real feelings or nonbusiness norms. To the extent that self-interest prevails, managers are tempted to do things that in other circumstances they would not do. Consequently self-interest is translated into euphemistic terms, such as "enlightened self-interest." Frequent appeals to enlightened self-interest reflect the difficulty of relating certain behaviors to self-interest at all.[48]

CONFLICTS OF INTEREST

Even more important than self-interest issues are conflicts of interest. Conflict of interest is a clash between one's self-interest and the interests of the organization or the public interest. Obviously such conflicts are hard to define in concrete cases. Laws are increasingly used to prohibit many forms of such conflict, and courts, regulatory agencies, and business firms deal continuously with such issues. Many state ethics laws focus primarily on conflicts of interest.

---

[45] Donald Otwell Zoll, *The Twentieth Century Mind* (Baton Rouge: Louisiana State University Press, 1967), p. 19.

[46] Henry David Aiken, "The New Morals," *Harper's*, February 1968, pp. 58–72.

[47] Reinhold Niebuhr, *Moral Man and Immoral Society* (New York: Scribner's, 1932), pp. xi–xii.

[48] James C. Worthy, *Big Business and Free Men* (New York: Harper & Row, 1959), pp. 28–29.

Examples of conflicts of interest include these:

1. The insider who can profit personally from privileged information — such as selling one's stock before the public learns the company is in trouble.
2. Taking a kickback to turn a company decision in someone's favor.
3. The public accountant who does what the company wants even though it harms stockholders or the public.
4. Bank officials whose loan information can make or lose millions for the bank.
5. Stockbrokers who are also investment advisors or investors for their own account.
6. Favoring one's former company or industry after leaving to take a government position.
7. Leaving the government to write "insider, muckraking books," or to take a position in an industry one has regulated or has been close to.

Such conflicts are infinitely hard for the individual to resolve and for government to regulate. The principal reforms widely advocated, other than restrictions of law, include (1) avoiding membership or participation in groups where a conflict of interest might be involved, (2) strict disclosure rules, (3) higher accountability standards, and (4) providing specific codes of conduct wherever possible. It is unrealistic, perhaps even undesirable, to eliminate all interest conflicts. Not all conflict is undesirable, and efforts to abolish conflicts of interest have led to other problems, such as the unwillingness of talented, independent, outside professionals to serve on boards of directors, and the loss of freedom and spontaneity that organizations need in working out their problems. Laws stressing the avoidance of conflict of interest have led businesspeople, scientists, and many others to decline government service, and many already in government have hastened to get out before rules for limiting their postgovernment careers become applicable.[49]

ETHICAL REINFORCEMENT AND IMPROVEMENT

Businesses and other large organizations are a jungle of ethical conflict and moral temptations that offer no black or white alternatives, but rather murky areas where pressures find fertile ground. For example, is bluffing in negotiations merely a game tactic, or is it a form of lying or deceit? How far should advertising go to describe a product as better than it really is? When do "commonly accepted accounting principles" get modified to show a better profit? Is industrial espionage a legitimate part of the business game? Why should a manager not take advantage of those

---

[49] Joseph M. McGuire, "Conflict of Interest: Whose Interest? And What Conflict?" in Richard T. Pichler and Richard T. DeGeorge (eds.), *Free Enterprise and Public Policy: Original Essays on Moral Issues in Business* (New York: Oxford University Press, 1978), pp. 214–231; and Edmund Beard, "Conflict of Interest and Public Service," pp. 232–247.

who are weaker? It is ethical to withhold information that others may need? Why do some managers steal and cheat? The common denominator of such questions is the difference between social or religious ethical standards and the ethics of everyday business decisions.

The answers to such questions can be obtained only when managers and their organizations confront them by evolving a moral and ethical climate that gives order and meaning to concrete cases. It could be expected that the integrity of ethical and moral beliefs would be a factor in the selection and placement of employees. However, this is an exception rather than the rule. More frequent are such devices as (1) formal codes of conduct, (2) ethical advisors, (3) watchdog groups, and (4) whistle blowing.

CODES AND CREEDS

Professional groups have long utilized codes of ethics. Now businesses and industries are making increased use of them. *Codes* contain specific "shalts" and "shalt nots"; *creeds* describe the general beliefs of an organization or a group.

The advantages of written guidelines are that all persons may consult the same document and the same set of expectations. Writing demands clarity, explicitness, and careful thought, which in itself is an important process. Codes rely on self-enforcement rather than external regulation. The drawbacks are that the writing process takes time; the contents need continuous review and evaluation with respect to applicability, relevance, and usefulness; they can serve only as guidelines, not formulas or unfailing rules; they can be filed and forgotten or treated as a mere public relations effort; they can oversimplify the complicated nature of human conduct; it is hard to get agreement on what the codes should say and how they should say it; and to be acceptable to those involved, they are often watered down or oversimplified.

The advantages outweigh the disadvantages. More and more companies are coordinating their ethical codes with management creeds, philosophies, policies, and objectives. Some include sanctions and enforcement provisions. Even so, the level of generality and subjectivity remains high. But codes are useful in the training and orientation of new employees, in the establishment of an ethical climate, and in evaluating the performance of managers.

Codes and creeds are based on conscience as expressed in the organizational and managerial philosophy. Ethical codes help to engender the evolution of managerial philosophy and to generate attention to the emotional qualities that convert codes to a philosophy and a conscience. Even though individuals often have high ethical and moral standards, codes are needed to clarify the ambiguities that are always present in the ethical-moral dimension of decision making.[50]

Leys describes three classes of discretionary power which a code should cover: discretion to choose (1) the means to achieve a predetermined end, (2) end results, and (3) actions as they are influenced by competing criteria.[51] These possible dimensions of a code cover the complete array of settings in which ethical problems exist.

Codes of ethics are also formulated on a group basis, such as industry or trade groups, or the professions. These codes are designed not only to guide personal decisions, but to preserve professional values, and to develop uniform standards of conduct which are part of the group identity and mission. Such codes regulate the behavior of individuals in their mutual interests and in the group's performance of its technical and social responsibilities.[52] Enforcement is a problem because only limited sanctions are likely to be invoked against violators.

One of the unwritten codes of professionals is that they will criticize other professionals only in rare and extreme situations. Yet professionals also maintain that they alone are qualified to judge their colleagues. This paradox accounts for some of the dissatisfactions of the public over the performance of professionals. The problem arises from the fact that the learning and teaching of ethical concepts is not done within a primary group, such as a family, which can have a deep influence on practitioners. Professionals are already adults when they acquire their training, and that training does not adequately reinforce the ethical implications of professional conduct.

Professional ethics is "an admirable alternative to legalistic regulation in areas of change or of unsettled principle," writes Haberstroh. He also notes that the absence of ethical codes does not mean that ethics are inconsequential in management, and that very strong ethical systems nevertheless exist informally within firms.[53] It was the ethical component of professional behavior that led some of our great thinkers to declare that business, if not management, should be a profession. Durkheim, for example, recommended the corporate organization of professions in business as a way of raising standards of morality and of

---

[50] John Carrell, "Ethics and the Emerging Philosophy of Business," *Business Studies* (North Texas State University), Spring 1964, pp. 5–12. See also James Owens, "Business Ethics: Age-old Ideal, Now Real," *Business Horizons* 21 (February 1978), pp. 26–30.

[51] Wayne A. R. Leys, "Ethics and Administrative Discretion," *Public Administration Review* 3 (January 1973), pp. 10–23.

[52] Ivan Hill, *The Ethical Basis of Economic Freedom* (Chapel Hill, N.C.: American Viewpoint, 1976); see also William J. Byron, "The Meaning of Ethics in Business," *Business Horizons* 20 (December 1977), pp. 31–34.

[53] Chadwick J. Haberstroh, "The Legitimacy of Management Authority," *Industrial Management Review* 5 (Spring 1964), pp. 19–24.

Ten Commandments for Bureaucrats

   I. *Put loyalty to the highest moral principles and to country above loyalty to persons, party, or Government department.*

  II. *Uphold the Constitution, laws, and regulations of the United States and of all governments therein and never be a party to their evasion.*

 III. *Give a full day's labor for a full day's pay, giving earnest effort and best thought to the performance of duties.*

  IV. *Seek to find and employ more efficient and economical ways of getting tasks accomplished.*

   V. *Never discriminate unfairly by the dispensing of special favors or privileges to anyone, whether for remuneration or not; and never accept, for himself or herself or for family members, favors or benefits under circumstances which might be construed by reasonable persons as influencing the performance of governmental duties.*

  VI. *Make no private promises of any kind binding upon the duties of office, since a Government employee has no private word which can be binding on public duty.*

 VII. *Engage in no business with the Government, either directly or indirectly, which is inconsistent with the conscientious performance of governmental duties.*

VIII. *Never use any information gained confidentially in the performance of governmental duties as a means of making private profits.*

  IX. *Expose corruption wherever discovered.*

   X. *Uphold these principles, ever conscious that public office is a public trust.*

---

subordinating individual interest to the public interest.[54] Tawney wrote that although to idealize the professional spirit would be absurd, professionalism should be enlarged because it is necessary to a properly functioning society.[55] And in 1912 Brandeis said, "As the profession of business develops the great industrial and social problems expressed in the present social unrest will one by one find solution," and "business should be, and to some extent already is, one of the professions."[56]

The professionally oriented manager will find ethical attitudes increasingly demanded. The task is tougher, however, where meaningful codes of ethics are absent. Managers are indeed fortunate to work for an organization whose top leaders place a high priority on ethics and whose

---

[54] Emile Durkheim, *Professional Ethics and Civic Morals* (New York: Free Press, 1958).

[55] R. H. Tawney, *The Acquisitive Society* (New York: Harcourt Brace Jovanovich, 1921).

[56] Louis Brandeis, in an address delivered at Brown University, 1912. Republished in *Business—A Profession*, by Augustus M. Kelley, Publishers, 1971, pp. 1–15. For an analysis of codes and creeds in political life, see Dunham, *Heroes and Heretics*, pp. 12–24.

example merits following. Unethical demands or behavior of colleagues, subordinates, or even superiors, need not be condoned.

ETHICAL ADVISORS

We have previously noted our society's extreme dependence on experts, advisors, and analysts. Ethics is no exception. Many companies today are employing advisors on issues of ethics, morals, and social responsibility. The areas from which they are drawn are varied. Some are ministers or theologians; some are from academic specialties. Others include attorneys, consumers or other public advocates, and counselors in special areas such as psychology or sociology. In most cases, the advisor is associated with the board of directors or the chief executive; in a few cases, the advisors operate at the upper-middle levels. The use of advisors for ethics and morals demonstrates the company concern and intent, and offers an additional outside perspective. The major pitfall is undue reliance on the advisor at the sacrifice of the manager's direct assumption of responsibility.[57]

WATCHDOG AGENCIES

On principle, many people do not wish to rely unduly on self-regulated behavior. Business firms are increasingly urged to elect independent outsiders to their boards of directors to represent various interests, such as consumer groups, labor unions, or the public. For the same reasons, students may be appointed to university committees and boards. Corporate boards of directors are criticized for consisting predominantly of members from management. These kinds of reforms will be analyzed more fully in Chapter 14.

Watchdog agencies are proliferating in federal and state governments. Oversight committees, ethics commissions, and various types of coordinating boards are numerous. Their influence is hard to measure, and their effectiveness remains in question. They are subject to the same limitations as other kinds of efforts to improve ethics. Most such agencies have few real powers to levy meaningful sanctions. The ethics committees in the Congress, for example, require complicated, time-consuming investigations; they are not free of political considerations; and findings of guilt are quite rare and penalties mild. Regulatory agencies have in part a watchdog function. They operate through the legal system, and the costs in time and money are high and the results often disappointing. This problem will be examined more extensively in Chapters 14 and 15.

---

[57] John F. Steiner, "The Prospect of Ethical Advisors for Business Corporations," *Business and Society* 16 (Spring 1976), pp. 5–10.

The federal Ethics in Government Act of 1978 illustrates the difficulties of attempting to legislate ethical behavior. This law requires anyone accepting a government position to complete a lengthy, comprehensive questionnaire, some of the provisions of which are dubious in their triviality or generality. One question asks, "Have you ever been fined more than $25 for a traffic violation?" Another asks, "Have you ever been publicly identified with a particularly controversial national or local issue?"[58] Well-intentioned restrictions have had the effect, clearly unintended, of discouraging able people from entering government service.

WHISTLE BLOWING

Whistle blowing is disclosing the misdeeds of superiors or colleagues to preserve ethical behavior and to prevent or eliminate wasteful, harmful or illegal acts. Whistle blowers take great risks, and frequently their fate is ostracism, loss of job, or even threats to life or safety. The opprobrium accorded to them reflects a higher value on loyalty than on conscience; the team spirit code is often placed above the ethical code.

As a result of Watergate and other scandals, and the resulting demand for better ethics, people are increasingly willing to take the risks of whistle blowing. Some do it for reasons of conscience, others for self-preservation — the avoidance of complicity and penalties for participating in frauds, for example.[59] The attitudes of managers show a reduced emphasis on the value of loyalty at all costs. People have learned to limit their sense of obligation and gratitude to the company that employs them. The threat of severance is not taken lightly, but blind deference to authority is becoming rarer.[60] Many now settle for mid-level, respectable success rather than maximizing their way to the top. Ambition for status and pay is no longer the motivation for loyalty that it once was.

Whistle blowing is a last-resort tactic. It is understandable that a person concerned with an ethical issue would approach whistle blowing with prudence and good judgment. It is a test of character to realize that doing right according to one's conscience cannot usually be without economic or other costs.[61] Because illegal and unethical acts are often the result of corporate structure or policy rather than the whims of individuals, firms could consider using workshops and training programs, and

---

[58] William F. Buckley, syndicated column dated December 11, 1980.

[59] *The Wall Street Journal*, May 22, 1976, p. 1.

[60] Edward Wersband and Thomas M. Franck, *Resignation in Protest: Political and Ethical Choices between Loyalty to Team and Loyalty to Conscience in American Public Life* (New York: Grossman, 1975).

[61] Andrew Hacker, "Loyalty — And the Whistle Blower," *Across the Board*, November 1978, pp. 4–9 and 67.

taking concrete steps so that whistle blowers as well as others can communicate their reservations without penalties.[62]

Incident Case

You are the head of a large corporation shipping perishable goods to a foreign country. At one foreign port, a harbormaster is holding up the unloading and demanding a $5000 payment, failing which the shipment, worth twenty times the bribe, will be lost. The harbormaster is the prime minister's brother-in-law. Your country representative cables you for instructions.

What happens next?

Issues for Analysis and Discussion

1. What should a businessman do if, in deciding to relocate his firm to another city, he knows that the departure will seriously hurt the community? Is there a difference if the businessman is an owner risking his own money, or a hired manager risking other people's money?

2. How do students in business or public administration learn the ethics relevant to decision making in their fields?

3. Why do some students cheat on examinations, and what can be done about it?

4. Is lying in performing one's duties justifiable when (1) it is to the individual's advantage, (2) it is for the good of the organization?

5. Should college administrators take a strong stand on the moral behavior of students?

6. Should the present generation give up its values and morals to have peace and harmony?

7. Is it lack of leadership that has lowered moral standards?

---

[62] James A. Waters, "Catch 20.5: Corporate Morality as an Organization Phenomenon," *Organizational Dynamics* 6 (Spring 1978), pp. 3–19. See also Alan F. Westin (ed.), *Whistle Blowing* (New York: McGraw-Hill, 1980).

8. Does good staff work include a responsibility to raise social, ethical, and moral issues for top management?

9. Under what conditions is it legitimate to harm an individual for the good of the whole group?

10. What are the advantages and difficulties in the development and use of codes of conduct?

Class Projects

1. Collect a number of product advertisements by major companies, and analyze them according to the moral and ethical issues discussed in this chapter.

2. Invite a partner from a local advertising agency to a class session and interview her or him concerning his or her views about the ethics of advertising.

For Further Reading

BAIER, KURT. *The Moral Point of View* (Ithaca, N.Y.: Cornell University Press, 1958).

BLUM, LAWRENCE A. *Friendship, Altruism, and Morality* (Boston: Routledge and Kegan Paul, 1980).

BOYD, K. (ed.). *The Ethics of Resource Allocation* (New York: Columbia University Press, 1979).

ENGLEBOURG, SAUL. *Power and Morality* (Westport, Conn.: Greenwood Press, 1980).

FRANKENA, WILLIAM K. *Thinking about Morality* (Ann Arbor: University of Michigan Press, 1980).

FRIED, CHARLES. *Right and Wrong* (Cambridge, Mass.: Harvard University Press, 1978).

GOODPASTER, K. E. (ed.). *Perspectives on Morality: Essays by William K. Frankena* (Notre Dame, Ind.: University of Notre Dame Press, 1976).

GOODPASTER, KENNETH, and KENNETH SAYERS (eds.). *Ethics and Problems of the Twenty-first Century* (Notre Dame, Ind.: University of Notre Dame Press, 1979).

HAMMAKER, PAUL M., ALEXANDER B. HORNIMAN, and LOUIS T. RADER. *Standards of Conduct in Business* (Charlottesville: University Press of Virginia, 1977).

HANCOCK, ROGER N. *Twentieth Century Ethics* (New York: Columbia University Press, 1974).

HARMAN, GILBERT. *The Nature of Morality: An Introduction to Ethics* (New York: Oxford University Press, 1978).

HILL, IVAN (ed.). *The Ethical Basis of Economic Freedom* (Chapel Hill, N.C.: American Viewpoint, 1976).

HOROWITZ, ROBERT H. (ed.).   *The Moral Foundations of the American Republic* (Charlottesville: University Press of Virginia, 1977).

KUGEL, YARACHMIEL, and GLADYS W. GRUENBERG.   *Ethical Perspectives on Business and Society* (Lexington, Mass.: D.C. Heath, 1977).

MACKIE, J. L.   *Ethics: Inventing Right and Wrong* (London: Penguin Books, 1978).

REISMAN, W. MICHAEL.   *Folded Lies: Bribery, Crusades, and Reform* (New York: Free Press, 1978).

SINGER, PETER.   *Practical Ethics* (New York: Cambridge University Press, 1980).

SOUTHARD, SAMUEL.   *Ethics for Executives* (New York: Cornerstone, 1977).

SUFRIN, SYDNEY C.   *The Management of Business Ethics* (Port Washington, N.Y.: Kennikat Press, 1980).

10

The Ethics of Work and Success

There is a passage from the Gita *that comes to mind: "Work done with anxiety about results is far inferior to work done in the calm of self-surrender." Anxiety about getting the approval of friends or the community, or about whether it will be patentable, always leads to inferior work.*

CHARLES EAMES

Blessed be he who has found his work; let him ask no other blessedness.

THOMAS CARLYLE

Without work all life goes rotten. But when work is soulless, life stifles and dies.

ALBERT CAMUS

CONCEPTS DISCUSSED IN THIS CHAPTER

    1. THE NATURE AND MEANING OF WORK

    2. THE "WORK ETHIC"

    3. WORK REFORM AND THE EMPLOYEE RELATIONS FUNCTION

    4. ETHICAL, MORAL, AND VALUE ISSUES IN WORK

    5. WORK IN THE FUTURE

The work required to sustain a modern society is highly differentiated, ranging from the simple and trivial to the highly complex. Work is not only invested with social, economic, and cultural significance, but also with intense meaning for individuals. Ethical and moral issues therefore abound in work at all levels.

In the processes of industrialization and technological change, society went through a major transition resulting not only in an increasingly complex work system, but also in changes in the values, attitudes, and moral precepts associated with work. Preindustrial society was agricultural, and the production of goods was rooted in individual craftspeople, manual labor, small family enterprises, and ethnic traditions.[1] Industrialization brought an increased specialization of labor, the factory system, and new needs for skilled, semi-skilled and technical labor. The emerging system also required more clerical workers, more managers, new organizational structures, and better concepts of personnel management. Thus the transition consisted of shifting from a physical to a mental orientation in work. Educational institutions flourished to prepare the new types of workers, and Frederick Taylor's concept of scientific management found fertile ground in rationalizing the emerging industrial system.[2]

Today we are experiencing a large increase in the relatively autonomous work of professionals, independent practitioners, knowledge workers, and experts. In the 1960s the numbers of people engaged in providing services came to exceed those in manufacturing occupations. These changes have had an enormous impact on the ethical and moral orientations associated with work.

Classification of the various types of work is complicated by the variety of work and its many contexts. The broadest classification is by occupational criteria, chiefly those provided by the government agencies to facilitate statistical comparisons. Occupational categories have also come to reflect the relative status and prestige rankings conferred by society as a whole.

Another common classification is according to industrial and non-industrial criteria, but Vickers prefers instead a classification comprised of three dimensions: (1) the degree of physical involvement, (2) the degree of mental involvement, and (3) the degree of career involvement. He also classifies work situations by levels of complexity: (1) solitary versus team or group jobs, (2) the extent to which workers identify with the

[1] Herbert C. Gutman, *Work, Culture and Society in Industrializing America* (New York: Knopf, 1976); Walter S. Neff, *Work and Human Behavior* (New York: Atherton Press, 1968), chaps. 3, 4.

[2] Sudhir Kahar, *Frederick Taylor: A Study in Personality and Innovation* (Cambridge, Mass.: MIT Press, 1970).

success of the operation, and (3) the quality of attitudes toward work transmitted by society.[3]

THE NATURE AND MEANING OF WORK

Work can be viewed culturally, technologically, managerially, and individually. All definitions are attempts to interpret work as a universally observable phenomenon. Therefore, information about work may at times appear inconsistent. The manager's task is to effect a synthesis of conflicting views about work as performed by members of the organization.

WORK VIEWED CULTURALLY

Work is a fundamental part of the social fabric of a society. It is a universal activity by which humans benefit from nature's resources. Indeed, it accounts for the growth and development of culture itself beyond the needs for mere physical survival. Work is surrounded by an array of institutionalized attitudes, beliefs, norms, values, forms, customs, and activities, so that work is rich in forms and meanings, both to the individual and to society. It occupies a large share of the time of most people, and is part of the meaning individuals attach to life itself.

Human needs, both inborn and socially determined, are a constant inducement to exertion. When this exertion is goal-directed and sustained by personal or social discipline, we call it work. Work thus has its beginning in the poverty or intransigence of the environment, the scarcity of resources, and the necessity of altering or processing resources for adequate satisfaction of human needs. But work becomes imbued with personal and social values. Accordingly, philosophers and theologians have contributed to our ideas about work, noting its two-sided, paradoxical character. On one hand, work is painful, difficult, annoying—a hardship to be avoided or minimized. On the other hand, it is essential to need fulfillment, the development of culture, and the meaning and enjoyment of life. Many persons experience a joy in work and its achievement, and most cultures endow work with the best rewards. There is, therefore, a mix of positive and negative feelings about work. Figure 10.1 shows how feelings and attitudes about work have changed over time along with evolving views of human nature.

Work has always been an important public issue. Government agencies exist to explain it, measure it, improve it, facilitate it, and to abate unemployment, promote safety, and mediate labor disputes. A cabinet officer, the secretary of labor, focuses on the interests of workers and

---

[3] Sir Geoffrey Vickers, *Towards a Sociology of Management* (New York: Basic Books, 1967), pp. 122–126.

Figure 10.1

Major Themes Surrounding the Meaning of Work

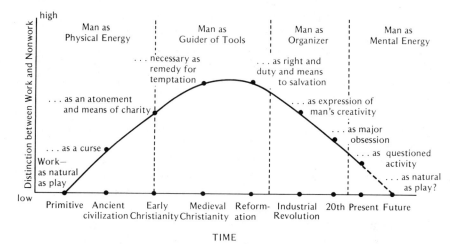

SOURCE: *Barry Z. Posner, W. Alan Randolph, and Max S. Wortman, Jr., "A New Ethic for Work: The Worth Ethic,"* Human Resource Management *14 (Fall 1975), p. 16. Used by permission.*

their problems. Politicians, economists, religious leaders, educators, and many others share these concens.

WORK VIEWED TECHNOLOGICALLY

In the technological concept of work, economic goals are reached through the institutionalized mechanisms of production and distribution in the economic and social systems. Work is broadly defined to be synonymous with labor, technological expertise, and specialization.

Changes in technology, and hence changes in the basic character of work, are continuous and for the most part evolutionary. However, from time to time, revolutionary technological changes bring rapid and extensive changes in work. As technology changes, humans must adapt by learning new methods, skills, and processes, giving up old habits, knowledge, and skills, and coping with unemployment. Computers, for example, have spawned new occupations and new technological capabilities that affect not only work itself, but also its values.

WORK VIEWED MANAGERIALLY

To view work managerially is to place it in the context of the organization where decisions and policies are made. The work to be done necessitates personnel techniques—recruiting, selecting, placing, training and paying employees, whether blue- or white-collar, managerial or rank and file. Labor is a valuable resource; highly talented, skilled employees are often difficult to find, and the administrative problems of recruiting, developing, and rewarding good employees are complex.

Work in organizations is highly disciplined, formally directed, and carefully controlled according to intended purposes. Managerially speaking, we are not interested in work done for work's sake, or work done primarily for the benefit or private satisfaction of the individual. The management problem in painting one's own house, for example, is slight. Work as a collective effort of many requires skills of management and leadership.

Work in the management context is a mixture of prescribed and discretionary content. Prescribed content includes all the things a role occupant must do to avoid a charge of negligence or insubordination. Role occupants know when they have completed prescribed work, which has definite points of completion in time, a relatively observable and measurable accountability. Discretionary work consists of all decisions a role occupant is authorized to make and is held responsible for making. In general, the higher the level of the employee, the wider the areas of discretion. For every employee, the balance between prescribed and discretionary work is a function of delegation from superior to subordinate, and in addition, the processes of negotiation and collaboration between the two.

Just as individuals exhibit a wide range of attitudes and beliefs concerning work, so companies express various philosophies and values about work and people. In an industrialized society, values favoring work tend to prevail. Companies are to a large extent carriers and exponents of these values, since they are the chief beneficiaries of positive attitudes toward work, occupations, and careers. The components of company value systems are both expressed and implied, with companies varying in the depth and scope with which they include them in formal documents, such as codes or policy statements.[4]

WORK AND THE INDIVIDUAL

The individual's views about work reflect the general values of the culture. Of course, particular individuals at particular times may show variations from the cultural norms. But society prescribes the overall tenor of one's beliefs, fosters life styles available to individuals, and con-

---

[4] Eli Ginzberg, "Man and His Work," in Dale S. Beach (ed.), *Managing People at Work*, 3rd ed. (New York: Macmillan, 1980), pp. 3–10.

ditions the habits and attitudes people develop about work. Although these cultural norms change gradually, they exert a relatively persistent, stable influence over most persons.

The importance of work to the individual is twofold: (1) it provides a livelihood, and (2) it defines the individual's role within the organization and within the community. Work for most people in our culture means employment in an organization—a company or a corporation. But "the company" or "the corporation" are abstractions. The heart of the employment relationship is the fact that in reality people work for and with others.

In our society, individuals are free to choose their occupations, develop careers, and pursue educational efforts so as to be able to do their chosen work. It is assumed that matters of competence and ability will sort out the confusions of mistaken aspirations and wrong choices.

WORK AND PERSONALITY

The individual's work is one of the important elements of social identity and of the individual's selfhood or personality. People hold jobs whose occupational classifications denote approximate income levels, social and economic status, and a personal identity that provides important information to others.

People need to rationalize what they do, to make sense of it to themselves and others. Rules of conduct, only in part formalized and only in part in the nature of a code of ethics, facilitate the bonds of colleagueship in jobs and occupations. Such rules cover the handling of mistakes, the definition of role expectations with respect to colleagueship, and the determination of who is to be regarded as a colleague.[5] Work is a kind of social drama enacted before the eyes of others. The script consists of cues from habit, experience, tradition, defined roles, and occupational tasks.[6]

The interrelationships between personality and work have been investigated chiefly from the theoretical perspectives of psychoanalysis, psychiatry, psychology, and social psychology. Freud had little to say about work except incidentally to his views of child maturation and adult functioning. He saw work as fulfilling external necessity, manifesting the power of love, but also as a painful burden. He saw work as binding people closely to reality and into a spirit of community, and as having a balancing effect on the contests within the personality.[7] Neo-Freudians have given more attention to work, exploring instincts and motives for mastery, achievement, the relation of work to love, and differences between work and play.

---

[5] Everett Hughes, *Men and Their Work* (New York: Free Press, 1958), pp. 46–47.

[6] Ibid., pp. 53–55.

[7] Sigmund Freud, *Civilization and Its Discontents* (New York: Hogarth Press, 1980), p. 34.

FIGURE 10.2

Values in the Workplace

EXISTENTIAL. This employee likes a job where the goals and problems are more important than the money or the prestige associated with the position. He prefers work of his own choosing that offers continuing challenge and requires imagination and initiative. To him, a good boss is one who gives him access to the information he needs and lets him do the job in his own way.

⑦

SOCIOCENTRIC. A job which allows the development of friendly relationships with people in his work group appeals to this employee. Working with people toward a common goal is more important than getting caught up in a materialistic rat race. He likes a boss who fosters close harmony by being more a friendly person than a boss.

⑥

MANIPULATIVE. The preferred job for this employee is varied, allows free wheeling and dealing, and offers pay and bonuses on the basis of results. He feels responsible for his own success and is constantly on the lookout for new opportunities. A good boss for this employee understands the politics of getting the job done, knows how to bargain, and is firm but fair.

⑤

CONFORMIST. This employee likes job security, well-defined rules, and equal treatment. He feels entitled to some good breaks in exchange for his loyalty. His mode of dress and subservience to protocol cause him to blend with the masses and lack individuality.

④

EGOCENTRIC. The two major requirements of a job for this employee are that it pay well and that it keep people off his back. He shuns work that ties him down, but will do it if he must to get the money he wants. Because of his raw, rugged value system, he needs a boss who is tough but allows him to be tough too.

③

TRIBALISTIC. This employee is best suited to routine work, friendly people, fair play, and above all a good boss. He likes a boss who tells him exactly what to do and how to do it, and who encourages him by doing it with him. An employee at this level may realize he doesn't have the best job in the world, but feels he does as well as others with jobs like his.

②

REACTIVE. This level of psychological development is restricted primarily to infants, people with serious brain deterioration, and certain psychopathic conditions. For practical purposes, employees are not ordinarily found at Level 1.

①

SOURCE: *V. S. Flowers, C. L. Hughes, M. S. Myers, and S. S. Myers,* Managerial Values for Working *(New York: AMACOM, 1975).*

There is a large literature on the psychology of work and a special branch of knowledge called industrial psychology. These have focused primarily on the detection, measurement, and description of individual differences in work behavior, especially the assessment of capabilities for doing work, the motivation problems of work, and technical systems for selecting, training, or rewarding employees.

As part of the total personality, psychologists distinguish a work personality that gradually makes its appearance as the child is socialized into adulthood in a long process of development and differentiation. The *work personality* is a concrete set of interrelated motives, coping styles, and defensive maneuvers with which individuals confront the demand to work. It reflects the manner in which the individual assumes the role of a productive person. People vary in the ease and efficiency with which they assume this role, and some cannot do it at all. The expectation that an individual will be productive is related to important prevailing cultural values.[8] The range of value-related personality patterns found in work settings is shown in Figure 10.2.

ETHICS AND SELF-RESPECT

Self-respect is an important aspect of personality in relation to work. It requires that one's own values and the company's values be made explicit in terms of context, method, and purpose. People who stay at jobs that violate their values may become demoralized and suffer depression and physical ailments. One of the best rewards for doing work well is self-respect.

In a study that examined self-respect among managers, a substantial majority of the 2259 respondents placed ethics and values high on the list of factors affecting self-respect. They emphasized moral or religious values and attitudes, both on a personal and a corporate level, stressing fair dealing with others, especially subordinates. Such values as honesty, and playing it straight in an unethical or moderately ethical environment, were also important. The integrity and credibility of a firm's management philosophy and attitude toward people were also deemed basic to self-respect. The study concluded that there are four types of good conduct at work: (1) moral, (2) ethical, (3) saintly-heroic, and (4) deontological. Moral conduct ensures the survival of the system and of interpersonal relationships; the omission of moral behavior is damaging to all.

Ethical conduct maintains and promotes values in situations where survival and security are not at stake. Ethical actions go beyond what is necessary in particular situations. Saintly-heroic conduct occurs when a situation invites it. It involves a form of martyrdom. An example would be a department head who forgoes a salary raise so he can give his subordinates more. Deontological conduct has to be done because of the nature of existence. It is occasional and rarely repetitive, and usually involves actions toward people a person knows only slightly. For example, if

---

[8] Walter S. Neff, *Work and Human Behavior*, pp. 151–164.

someone needs a dollar and you think that person is all right, you give her what she needs if you have it.

There is a counterfeit to each of the four types of good conduct. Counterfeit actions appear to be moral, but in fact have one or more unethical elements. An example would be calling a conference to let subordinates help solve a problem, without any intention of using the advice obtained.[9]

THE WORK ETHIC

What we call today the "work ethic" developed historically as the "Protestant ethic," sometimes called the "Puritan ethic." The work ethic emerged out of evolving religious beliefs about work. Work was seen as a "calling"—a vocation, the proof of the individual's goodness and worth.

In the West, two hundred years of moral and religious education preceded the rise of modern, large-scale industry in which technical and administrative organization make heavy demands on the discipline of individual workers. The early Greeks and Romans thought work a curse, a punishment of angry gods. Agriculture was somewhat acceptable because it provided sustenance, but mechanical arts brutalized the mind. Manual labor was for slaves. The Hebrews, who also thought of work as punishment and painful drudgery, considered it the necessary expiation of sin originally committed by the forefathers of the human race. Thus work acquired meaning as a means to atone for the sins of ancestors and gain spiritual dignity.

Early Christianity followed the Hebrew beliefs, but in addition to expiation, it developed the thought that work was not only necessary to earn one's living, but also made it possible to share one's fortunes with those more needy. This made wealth more respectable and permissible, for it was no longer equated with wickedness. Through the centuries of growth in the medieval and modern Catholic Church, additional dignity and meaning was ascribed to physical labor. Again, work was permissible for the welfare of humans; wealth was justified as a means of charity. Property rights emerged as a cornerstone of society. Usury was frowned on, but gradually there emerged a sort of respectability for commerce and trade. But work could not be tolerated as an end in itself; it was merely a means toward an end—the life hereafter.[10]

It was Protestantism, however, which established work in modern society as the basis of life and living. Luther proclaimed that work is a way of serving God. Whatever one's field of endeavor, it was to be viewed

---

[9] Preston G. McLean and Katherine Jillson, *The Manager and Self-Respect* (New York: AMACOM, 1975), pp. 16–29.

[10] Adriano Tilgher, "Work through the Ages," in Sigmund Nosow and William H. Form (eds.), *Man, Work, and Society* (New York: Basic Books, 1962), pp. 11–17.

©*Field Newspaper Syndicate, 1978. Used by permission.*

as a vocation or calling. All endeavors contributing to human welfare were equally worthy in God's sight. It was a duty to labor faithfully in the calling to which God assigned one. Calvinism added the thought that work is the will of God and all humans should do it, but that the fruits of a person's labor were for the good of society and not for the individual. The benefits of work were to be returned to the system through investment and reinvestment.

In his pioneering work on the Protestant ethic, Weber attempted to show that religious beliefs had a direct influence on the economic activities of social groups. As concern for salvation waned, the Puritan creed became secularized. And a secular ideology of individual striving and success paralleled the growing demand of industry on the efforts and self-discipline of employees. There was a need for an ethic of work performance that affected both employers and employees. In contrast to the discretion possible for craft workers working alone or in small groups, the factory system required that work be performed with regularity and intensity, and according to standardized methods. Workers had to learn to follow general rules and specific orders, emphasize accuracy, and use carefully the tools and machinery owned by others. Whereas the principal means of controlling workers under serfdom or slavery was the use of coercion, fear, indoctrination or submissiveness, and punishment, management ideology came to stress motivation, leadership, and employee welfare as inducements to the acceptance of legitimate organizational authority.[11]

THE CHANGING WORK ETHIC

The Protestant ethic in its classical form no longer exists, though many still believe in it or act as if they do. So many changes have occurred in society that the Protestant ethic no longer suffices to explain

---

[11] Max Weber, *The Protestant Ethic and the Spirit of Capitalism*, trans. Talcott Parsons (New York: Scribner's 1958), first published in Germany in 1904–1905. See also Reinhard Bendix, *Work and Authority in Industry* (New York: Wiley, 1956), pp. 202–211; Herbert G. Gutman, *Work, Culture, and Society, and Industrializing America: Essays in American Working-Class and Social History* (New York: Knopf, 1976); Daniel T. Rodgers, *The Work Ethic in Industrial America 1850–1920* (Chicago: The University of Chicago Press, 1978).

why people work. This does not mean that the work ethic derived from ideas of the Protestant Reformation has disappeared, but rather that it is changing in character. Those who deplore these changes are the ones who allege that the work ethic no longer exists.

Many studies show that people of all ages, races, and classes claim to believe in the inherent moral value of hard work. The meaning of this morality, however, is changing. Hard work is coming to be seen by many workers as a means to "self-enrichment," rather than as morally worthwhile in itself. When work fails to meet workers' expectations, they lose interest. The preoccupation with self that is the hallmark of newer values places the burden of providing incentives for hard work more squarely on the employer than under the old value system.[12]

More people are working today than ever before — not only in terms of absolute numbers, but also proportionately in the growth of the workforce. Levitan, who disagrees that the work ethic is dead, notes that while rates of productivity are slowing, it still is increasing. We are a "fat" society, enabling us to employ wives, children, and others not formerly in the workforce; we create many jobs not clearly for the purpose of increasing productivity. As we convert to a service economy, it becomes clear that in some kinds of work, like teaching or surgery, increased productivity might even lower the quality of service.[13] The not for profit sectors of the economy now generate one in every three jobs.[14]

The affluence of society partly accounts for the problems of the work ethic, for it has changed the attitudes and values of those who work. Carrot and stick management no longer functions to secure the unquestioned obedience and conformity of workers, nor are threats of firing or wage penalties viable as methods of management control. Psychological tools for motivation have not lived up to their promise, and are questioned as unfair manipulation. People today are better educated, more independent, and more critical of management. They not only value the system's freeing them from much drudgery through better working conditions and more leisure, but the system with its relative affluence paradoxically makes it possible for them to question the system and demand more from it in the form of meaningful, fulfilling work.

Bell sees this paradox as one of the cultural contradictions of capitalism. He asserts that the Protestant ethic was eroded long before the rise of the counterculture, lingering only ideologically in the minds of moralists intent on admonishing others with the Puritan methology. The result is, he feels, to leave capitalism with no basic or transcendent

---

[12] Daniel Yankelovich, "Work, Values, and the New Breed," in Clark Kerr and Jerome Rostow (eds.), *Work in America: The Decade Ahead* (New York: Van Nostrand-Reinhold, 1979). See also Richard Sennett, *Authority* (New York: Knopf, 1980), pp. 104–116.

[13] Sar A. Levitan, "The Work Ethic Lives," *Across the Board*, August 1979, pp. 82–84.

[14] Eli Ginzberg, *Good Jobs, Bad Jobs, No Jobs* (Cambridge, Mass.: Harvard University Press, 1979).

moral structure. By trying to get workers to work hard, pursue careers, and save for delayed gratification, while at the same time using advertising to encourage consumption, instant joy, unlimited pleasure, relaxation, and "letting go," business only confuses the issue.[15]

Patterns and habits do exist that modify the effects of the work ethic. For example, such phenomena as early retirement, keeping people in school longer, or requiring military service can reduce the numbers available to the workforce. Much of this activity is wasteful, for it is difficult to show that such things are necessary or that they contribute to individual or social welfare. There is also a small but perhaps growing number of individuals who are dropouts by design. Rejecting employment, they turn to a simple, self-sufficient, modest existence.[16]

Most people today are unwilling to engage in menial work or sheer drudgery, but they are constantly enlarging their notions of what drudgery is. As society has buffered the vast majority of people from destitution and starvation, they have begun to value more than monetary income from their work; they want self-fulfillment, personal satisfaction, and personal growth.[17] Making work in modern settings more amenable to these new outlooks is a monumental task for managers.

THE SUCCESS ETHIC

The growth of industrialized society also brought a "Horatio Alger" success ethic that became part of the American Dream. With freedom to pursue one's chosen occupation as a calling, the individual had only to obey the tenets of the Protestant ethic to succeed. Success became the measure of one's worth, and success in turn was measured in terms of wealth and climbing the hierarchies of the organization, the organizational structure, and the social status system.[18]

The Horatio Alger novels depicted businessmen as people who, because of high moral character, made profits. Today, Kristol suggests, businesspeople believe they are honorable because they make profits:

> Withoug realizing it, they are standing Horatio Alger on his head. It won't work. That inverted moral ethos makes no moral sense, as our culture keeps telling us. . . .[19]

---

[15] Daniel Bell, *The Cultural Contradictions of Capitalism* (New York: Basic Books, 1976), pp. 55 and 71-72.

[16] "The Great Male Copout from the Work Ethic," *Business Week*, November 14, 1977, pp. 156-166.

[17] Jerome M. Rosow, "Changing Attitudes to Work and Life Styles," *Journal of Contemporary Business* 8 (Fourth Quarter 1979), pp. 5-18.

[18] Richard M. Huber, *The American Idea of Success* (New York: McGraw-Hill, 1972); Thomas C. Hunter, *Beginnings* (New York: Crowell, 1978). Moses Rischin, *The American Gospel of Success* (Chicago: Quadrangle Books, 1965).

[19] Irving Kristol, "Horatio Alger and Profits," *The Wall Street Journal*, July 11, 1974, p. 14.

"And now—a few words about work ethics."

SOURCE: The Wall Street Journal, *January 25, 1980.*

The success ethic implies a sense of individualism and competitiveness in the possibilities for upward mobility. It accepts that those who lose in these struggles may get hurt, and those who do not struggle are destined to be "average." The success ethic, like its counterpart the Protestant ethic, is under increasing challenge. Many managers question the sacrifices they and their families must make for success. The increasing number of dropouts from industry, the increasing acceptance of leveling off in one's career, and the desire to start one's own business is partial evidence of the challenge. The rise of the two-paycheck family blunts the financial impact of reducing the success drive.[20]

Although success remains an important idea, the definition of success is changing. The success ethic has been more diverse and its expression more varied than previously thought.[21] One survey of nearly 3000 businessmen found that the shift in success-related values is from the tangibles of money and wealth to less tangible ones such as richness of experience, the pleasures of achievement, or the rewards of self-expres-

[20] "Why 'Success' Isn't What It Used To Be," *U.S. News and World Report,* July 30, 1979, p. 48; Frederick C. Thayer, *An End to Hierarchy! An End to Competition!* (New York: New Viewpoints, 1973).

[21] John G. Cawelti, *Apostles of the Self-Made Man* (Chicago: The University of Chicago Press, 1965).

sion. More than half the respondents intended to change occupations and pursue second careers to enhance their personal satisfactions.[22]

There can be little question that new ideas about success will greatly affect the management of organizations. How managers meet this challenge involves such issues as (1) the quality of work life, (2) the alienation of workers, and (3) work reform efforts.

THE QUALITY OF WORK LIFE

Literally no aspect of work in modern society is free of moral and ethical challenges. The most important of these relate to the concept of the quality of work life not only for rank and file workers, but also for managers. The need to maintain an organizational climate conducive to effective, efficient, and satisfying work has long been recognized in all types of organizations. Two separate, interrelated, but sometimes conflicting efforts reflect this aim: personnel management programs, and research in human relations and organizational behavior. Such issues as privacy on the job, unfair or inequitable treatment, excessive conflict, the safety and health of employees, counseling troubled employees, and the participation of employees in management decisions reflect ethical and moral judgments as well as economic criteria.

The main elements in the quality of work life include the tasks performed, the physical environment, the social or interpersonal environment, the administrative system and its leaders, and the relationships of people to life on and off the job. The relative importance of these elements varies according to demographic variables, socioeconomic status, culture, personality, and political or ideological factors. These elements must be addressed in any effort to enhance the quality of working life.[23]

JOB AND WORK SATISFACTION

The quality of work life is an abstract concept, but it is usually measured statistically by surveys or opinion polls. It is also measured qualitatively through interviews. Job and work satisfaction are not the same, though they may be related. Job satisfaction relates to how one feels about a specific job or position within an organization. Work satisfaction

---

[22] Dale Tarnowieski, *The Changing Success Ethic, An AMA Survey Report* (New York: American Management Associations, 1973). See also Benjamin DeMott, "Beyond the Dream of Success," *Change*, August 1976, pp. 32–37; and Rosabeth Moss Kanter, *Men and Women of the Corporation* (New York: Basic Books, 1977).

[23] Louis E. Davis and Albert B. Cherns (eds.), *Quality of Working Life*, vol. 1 (New York: Free Press, 1975). See also J. Richard Hackman and J. Lloyd Suttle, *Improving Life at Work* (Santa Monica, Calif.: Goodyear, 1977).

consists of attitudes toward one's vocation, calling, or occupation. Satisfaction in both cases is an elusive, ideal goal that is not perfectly attained. But a great deal of time, money, and energy is spent in efforts to improve the degree of satisfaction wherever possible. There is no guarantee that, once attained, a high level of job satisfaction will last, since the conditions from which it results may change. Therefore, periodic surveys and continuous maintenance processes are required.

Nationwide or cross-sectional surveys of job and work attitudes are inconsistent in their results, and firm conclusions are not possible. This is due only in part to technical limitations in survey techniques; it is due also to the complexity of the topics investigated and the problems of converting language to quantitative data.

Interview approaches frequently result in negative findings. Terkel, a journalist, presents a discouraging view of work among 133 workers in as many different jobs. He found them highly dissatisfied, with high fear and anxiety resulting in effort and risk avoidance, the desire for immediate gratification, and doubts about the fairness or existence of proper rewards and good supervision. A limitation of such surveys is the absence of interviews with successful, satisfied, and fulfilled workers, preventing comparison with dissatisfied attitudes. The workers in Terkel's sample, interestingly, showed a common desire to work and to gain satisfaction from their jobs. They were not considering not working, and many expressed a fear of retirement. One derives from this book an indication of some of the qualitative shortcomings of management.[24]

The literature of worker discontent is often produced by writers having little real experience with the work settings in which most people struggle. An exception is Schrank's report based on his own participant observation. He provides excellent insights showing how socializing, work autonomy, participation, opportunities for creativity, and the like relate to job satisfaction.[25]

Formal polls and surveys permit comparisons over time and the segmenting of dissatisfaction and other problems by age, sex, occupation, and other factors. The general tendency of these surveys is to indicate that job dissatisfaction is not as rampant as many suppose, but also that there is much room for improvement. A Conference Board survey, for example, disclosed that 87 percent of the respondents were happy with their work; only 13 percent were dissatisfied or very dissatisfied. Such matters as pay, standard of living, working conditions, and psychic rewards were satisfactory. Satisfaction was found to be higher among older and higher paid workers.[26] A *Saturday Review* survey of 3382

---

[24] Studs Terkel, *Working* (New York: Pantheon, 1974).

[25] Robert Schrank, *Ten Thousand Working Days* (Cambridge, Mass.: MIT Press, 1978).

[26] *Special Consumer Survey Report* (New York: The Conference Board, July 1978).

readers found that half of them were pleased or excited about their work. Only 16 percent were anxious or depressed, while 34 percent were ambivalent. The respondents dissatisfied with their current jobs cited the difficulties of changing careers, monetary limitations, lack of alternative opportunities, and the dearth of jobs in their preferred field as holding them back from improvement. Sixty one percent regarded making a contribution to society as very important, but only 39 percent could do so in their present job.[27]

An early article by Morse and Weiss concluded that even if workers had an independent means of support, they would still want to work. People who inherit money or win huge sweepstakes usually continue on their jobs, but this was found to depend on age (younger workers preferred to continue) and amount of education (professionals preferred to continue more than unskilled laborers).[28] In a replication study, however, Vecchio concluded that a leisure ethic may have replaced the traditional work ethic in the twenty years since the Morse and Weiss research. He found a 39 percent increase in the number of male workers who would stop working if given the opportunity. These findings support the cultural change theorists who point to a decline in the value and meaning of work, and to the growing tendency to value early retirement, self-indulgence, and other narcissistic factors.[29]

Pressures for improving the quality of work life are imbedded in pressures for improving the quality of life in society. The recognition of this problem as a concern for society brings government into the scene of action.[30] Management has long been concerned, primarily because of the implications for efficiency and productivity. Unions too, having progressed in economic dimensions, are increasingly turning their attention to quality of work considerations. It is inevitable that unions will take a strong interest in any programs devised by management to enhance the quality of work life.[31]

ALIENATION

Alienation is the term behavioral scientists and intellectuals use to depict the condition wherein humans are dissociated from intimate connection with work, organizations, society, or each other. Alienation

---

27 "On the Job," *Saturday Review*, May 1980, p. 16.
28 N. C. Morse and R. S. Weiss, "The Function and Meaning of Work and the Job," *American Sociological Review* 20 (1955), pp. 191–198.
29 Robert P. Vecchio, "The Function and Meaning of Work on the Job: Morse and Weiss Revisited," *Academy of Management Journal* 23 (June 1980), pp. 361–367.
30 *Work in America, Report of a Special Task Force to the Secretary of Health, Education and Welfare* (Cambridge, Mass.: MIT Press, undated).
31 "Hot UAW Issue: Quality of Work Life," *Business Week*, September 17, 1979, pp. 120–122.

results from feelings of powerlessness, meaninglessness, isolation, and self-estrangement. Alienation occurs with respect to the individual's relationship to society and to work. The typical response of the alienated person is withdrawal from work, political activity, or community concerns. Those who do not withdraw often turn to radical political movements as a defense against the frustrations caused by the forces of alienation.[32]

Behavioral science theories attribute alienation to hierarchical, bureaucratic norms such as those implied by the scientific management movement of the 1920s, or to the impact of technology. Aiken and Hage, for example, found that alienation from work and alienation from expressive (interpersonal) relations were more pronounced in highly centralized and highly formalized organizations.[33] Ellul speaks of the dissociation produced by technologies that subjugate the human personality to the norms of specialized tasks and conformity to the norms of efficiency. If work is a profound expression of life, it is unnatural to compartmentalize the personality into separate work and leisure components.[34]

Dissatisfying physical and social environments may produce alienation from work when people are unable to control immediate work processes, develop a sense of meaning and purpose, be integrated into the organization or the community, or find self-expression and creativity in work. Alienation from society or community is likely to be transmitted to the world of work. This shows up in the employment of younger workers who have grown up with the changing values of an emergent society. It is not true, as is often alleged, that the young won't work. They do have different values and attitudes which require work that enhances their personalities and leads to personal fulfillment. To avoid alienating them, managers must accept the challenge of making work more meaningful, as measured by the newly emerging values.[35]

Alienation exists, but it ebbs and flows according to conditions at work and in society. It need not be taken for granted, unduly feared, or accepted as inevitable. Blauner recommended that efforts to reduce the factory worker's sense of alienation take into account the conditions in each factory, rather than assuming all situations to be the same. His empirical study showed that alienation can be examined by systematic concepts and propositions without discarding humane values. The moral power inherent in the alienation concept is in its view of human potentiality.[36]

---

32 *Work in America*, pp. 22 and 30–32.
33 Michael Aiken and Jerald Hage, "Organizational Alienation: A Comparative Analysis," *American Sociological Review* 31 (August 1966), pp. 497–507.
34 Jacques Ellul, *The Technological Society* (New York: Random House, 1964), pp. 398–402. See also James B. Gilbert, *Work Without Salvation: America's Intellectuals and Industrial Alienation* (Baltimore: Johns Hopkins University Press, 1978).
35 Ronald N. Taylor and Mark Thompson, "Work Value Systems of Young Workers," *Academy of Management Journal* 19 (December 1976), pp. 522–527.
36 Robert Blauner, *Alienation and Freedom* (Chicago: The University of Chicago Press, 1964), p. 187.

WORK REFORM

Work reform is a goal of many components of society.[37] Society's concerns for the quality of work life, for example, are reflected in laws and governmental policies with respect to working conditions, employee rights, collective bargaining, the problems of equal opportunity, and fair employment practices. In recent years, however, employee expectations have gone far beyond the tangibles of working conditions, giving new meaning to the idea of quality of work life. Increasing attention is being paid to intrinsic satisfactions such as challenge, self-fulfillment, and psychic rewards.

Unions are increasingly including quality of work life issues in their collective bargaining efforts.[38] Managers too have espoused innumerable practices and programs which, though designed primarily for increasing worker productivity, can be said to envision quality of work life goals as well. Individuals do not have to be persuaded that such goals can lead to good outcomes for them.

Work reform efforts in business organizations, our primary focus here, have affected millions of people, and they reflect enormous expenditures of time, energy, and money (see Figure 10.3). The scientific management movement of the 1920s developed precepts about managing employees that became the foundation of standard personnel practices. These precepts were modified in the 1940s and the 1950s by human relations concepts touting better interpersonal relations, leadership, high morale, and employee participation. Vestiges of the fading human relations approach remain today, but they have been transformed into a new and more rigorous discipline called organizational behavior.

These movements substantially advanced older management philosophy and techniques. However, lasting solutions elude even the most progressive managements. Quality of work life programs face the difficulty of persuading managers to accept meaningful participation of employees as a fundamental, underlying philosophy. Such programs as flextime, job enrichment, management by objectives, systems approaches, job rotation, and job enlargement have some value, but they tend to appear as cosmetic touches designed to get more performance from workers rather than to confront their intrinsic psychological needs.[39] Such programs often start out as "experiments," with workers responding favorably to the increased attention given them. Later the

---

[37] James O'Toole, *Work, Learning, and the American Future* (San Francisco: Jossey-Bass, 1977).

[38] "Beyond Bargaining: Unions and Bosses Try Trust," *Business Week*, May 5, 1980, pp. 43–44; Paul D. Greenberg and Edward M. Glaser (eds.), *Some Issues in Joint Union-Management Quality of Life Improvement Efforts* (Kalamazoo: The W. E. Upjohn Institute for Employment Research, 1980).

[39] George W. Bolander, "Implementing Quality of Work Programs: Recognizing the Barriers," *MSU Business Topics*, Spring 1979, pp. 33–40.

Figure 10.3

Changes in Work Pattern. Reprinted from U.S. News Washington Letter.

Some astonishing changes are foreseen in the way we Americans work.

Work ''decentralization'' is occurring even now, will pick up momentum. At least one U.S. firm already equips its salespeople with small computers which can be carried like a suitcase on trips out of town. By hooking up the units to phone lines and TV sets they retrieve data and file reports.

More and more people will toil at home -- AWAY from downtown offices. There'll be less need to go to the city, since computers, video terminals, other electronic tools will let white collar workers operate from any site.

Demand for at-home ''office space'' in future houses and apartments. Watch how architects, builders, developers latch onto that concept pronto. Working couples may want his/her computers, special nooks for video gear.

Potentially staggering implications in this work-at-home trend:

Downtown office space may be less essential and its value could fall.
Commercial and municipal parking lots will find they have empty slots.
Rush-hour traffic could become a memory -- fewer commuters on the road.
In-town restaurants, movies, stores face potential losses in trade.
Suburban burglaries should dip, what with owners around more hours.

Granted, such effects aren't imminent. Not next year or year after. But taking shape now and sure to spread as the '80's pass and '90's arrive.

Corporations will probably never eliminate the headquarters location. Yet with growing numbers of people doing information-manipulating chores, it won't be as necessary to ''warehouse'' large cadres of workers in town.

Work week of future? A bare 4 to 5 hours a day for some, it's estimated. Productivity? To leap -- new job methods, machines, robots and education. However, some fear that a decreasing ''work ethic'' may offset these gains.

You'll see more citizens handling governmental duties as a sideline -- using some of their spare hours to work without pay for hometown government. There will also be a quantum jump in adult education and multiple careers. And, greater voluntary participation in work of church and charity groups.

Women will make big strides in U.S. workforce, attain more equality.

Says who? Say those who have studied female gains of recent times. In the past 20 years, women banking and financial officers have increased in number from 2,100 to 122,000. In sales management? From 200 to 12,000. One futurist predicts that within 20 years females will hold the top spots in 10% of the nation's 500 largest companies. It's also widely predicted that women will fill more mayoral chairs, run police and fire departments. And before this century ends, reach the White House or the vice-presidency.

One obstacle: ''Too many female organizations fussing with menfolk.'' That's not our view but the assessment of Eileen Galley, head of the IOWE--the Intl. Organization of Women Executives. She says 1,400 groups sprouted in the past three years alone and she feels that too many are preoccupied with ''hardening'' the attitudes of women toward men. ''Counterproductive.''

Women on Supreme Court before long. ''Fresh ideas are needed there.''

Labor unions? Some say tougher, others say weaker. Mixed forecast.
Two incomes? By year 2000, almost 75% of married couples both working.
Stay-at-home husbands? Also to increase -- a domestic role-reversal.
Working couples with jobs in different cities? Much of that as well.
Family incomes? Women will contribute 40% of total by end of 1980's.
How does that compare with the present? A big gain. Only 26.1% today.

SOURCE: U.S. News and World Report, *December 1, 1980, p. 55. Copyright 1980 U.S. News & World Report, Inc.*

rosy glow fades. Also, they are often static, one-time "quick fixes" that lead to disappointing long-term results.[40]

Work reform programs have done best in smaller firms where total, organizationwide programs become a way of life that emphasizes team-work, cooperation, trust, responsibility, and participation. Paradoxically, work reforms reflecting these democratic values are more likely to suc-ceed under a despotic top management that can combat the resistance of threatened middle managers or union officials.[41]

That problems of morale, leadership, motivation, productivity, labor relations, and the like persist despite large sums spent on training and research raises questions about the fundamental assumptions underlying managerial thinking about work and employees. There has been little incisive criticism of the philosophies and beliefs underlying the pursuit of work reform; although the counterculture and the exponents of social reforms such as consumerists or environmentalists have grappled peri-pherally with work reform, their influence remains diffused and indeed may be declining.

Work reform efforts must be regarded as only moderately successful. Many improvements have occurred, but the search for a better quality of work life continues. Berg and associates have provided the only existing incisive critique of managerial work reform efforts. They conclude that the inadequacies of work reform are due to failure to understand the needs and psychology of employees, and to directing work reform pro-grams more to the needs of the organization than to those of workers. Part of the problem has been that the work reform movement attracted allies who oversimplified its problems, acted on incomplete information, and therefore made the movement vulnerable to skepticism. Also, the popular media generalized freely from the work of less scrupulous ex-perts, who raised hopes to unrealistic heights. Berg writes:

> While many experts have sought to fathom employee reactions to work, the relation of these reactions to performance, and the usefulness of a variety of tactics for improving morale, only one segment of this body of investigators and theoreticians has gained much popular attention. It is also the case, perhaps understandably, that the work of the most zealous but least radically threatening representatives of this contingent of experts has gained the lion's share of attention. It is unfortunately also the case that a number of the experts to whom attention is most readily paid have been inclined to market their expertise without guarding against com-promising their scientific obligations to be cautious. Finally, it is the case that the movement to reform work includes among its more articulate spokesmen a number of persons whose aims are less to serve discontented

---

[40] James O'Toole, "Thank God It's Monday," *The Wilson Quarterly* 4 (Winter 1980), pp. 126–137.
[41] Ibid., p. 132.

workers as such than to design arrangements that may suffice to dampen worker's interests in alternative arrangements.[42]

We will now examine quality of work life issues further by analyzing the impact of personnel administration programs, efforts to "humanize" work and the workplace, and its organizational aspects.

THE LIMITATIONS OF PERSONNEL PROGRAMS

Two parallel but contradictory ethical assumptions run threadlike through all organizational systems of personnel administration. The first is that it is good, and right, to recognize the selfhood and the psychological needs of employees, and to establish conditions that maximize the work satisfactions of individuals. The second is that it is good, and right, for managers to set aside such matters as selfhood, psychological needs, and work satisfaction if company welfare is thereby perceived to be in jeopardy. Both assumptions have been apparent in personnel programs since the early 1900s.

The first ethical assumption was the impulse behind the human relations movement, which attempted with only moderate success to patch up the defects of the bureaucratic model of organization that emerged with the scientific management movement. The second ethical assumption, that "circumstances alter cases," and that when the chips are down, profit or company welfare comes first, is more difficult to trace. It appears, for example, in the characteristic patterns of labor-management relations — in bargaining, negotiating, and settling grievances — where attention focuses on economic results. Negotiations are described in "cents per hour we gave the workers," not in terms of changing the style of management. This second assumption also underlies the frequent recurrence of so-called hard-line company policies that follow from periods of increased labor supply.[43]

The fact that these two contradictory ethical assumptions coexist is startling. How can this be explained? The answer seems to be that *managers do not actually perceive the two assumptions as contradictory*. The discrepancy is characterized as one of theory and not of practice. Managers often act one way and profess another; they accept the first assumption and thereby dignify the individual, while at the same time acting according to the second. They can readily do this if they believe that the second assumption is the best, or more fundamental, of the two. In other words, they have in mind the primacy of company welfare, which they

---

[42] Ivar Berg, Marcia Freedman, and Michael Freeman, *Managers and Work Reform: A Limited Engagement* (New York: Free Press, 1978), p. 246. See also Joaleel Ahmad, *The Expert and the Administrator* (Pittsburgh: Pittsburgh University Press, 1959).

[43] Charles R. Milton, *Ethics and Expediency in Personnel Management: A Critical History of Personnel Philosophy* (Columbia, S.C.: University of South Carolina Press, 1970).

feel will also be compatible with the first assumption. But if it is not, then the first assumption gives way.

Personnel techniques and programs are characterized more by the propensity to adapt than to innovate. They are designed more to cope with legal requirements than to solve the problems that originated control by law. More behavioral science knowledge about humans at work is ignored than is utilized. Traditional structures, policies, and techniques of personnel administration have become moribund. Designed primarily for rank and file workers, they have not dealt imaginatively with managers or professional employees. Companies with sophisticated programs for managers and professionals have assigned such functions to separate departments of equal or higher status, under such rubrics as organizational behavior or development. Personnel managers now constitute an embattled profession with uncertain aims and many confusions.[44]

THE HUMANIZATION OF WORK

What does it mean to humanize work? Why should work be humanized? If humanizing work is more than a slogan or catchy phrase, it expresses the intent to stimulate the development of mature, human, and humanely productive individuals who are not alienated from work, the organization, or the community. Work has both negative and positive attributes; humanization accentuates the positive and attempts to minimize the negative features. Research shows that workers wish to avoid jobs that are monotonous, boring, repetitive, or isolated from others. They dislike oversupervision, excessive controls, and forced dependence on the whims of the boss. They like jobs that permit activeness, planning, judgment, opportunity, variety, and challenge. They wish to be treated with dignity and respect and not as machines.

Humanization invokes processes of activation, enlarged consciousness, and the expressions of hope and confidence. But humanization concepts also challenge traditional forms of management, leadership styles, and bureaucratic attitudes. This is to say that new values and new concepts of what is moral in the workplace are replacing the old.[45] This transformation is occurring because society and its workers are demanding it. They are well educated, and have experienced the munificence and abundance of capitalistic enterprise.[46]

---

[44] Charles J. Coleman, "The Personnel Director: A Cautious Hero Indeed," *Human Resource Management* 18 (Winter 1979), pp. 14–20; John Ingalls, "Speaking from Experience: The Decline and Fall of Personnel," *Training and Development Journal* 34 (January 1980), pp. 30–32; Jack L. Rettig and Robert F. McCain, "Job Satisfactions of Personnel Managers," *The Personnel Administrator* 23 (September 1978), pp. 23–26.

[45] David W. Ewing, *Freedom inside the Organization* (New York: Dutton, 1977).

[46] Paul Dickson, *The Future of the Work Place* (New York: Weybright and Talley, 1975); Clark Kerr and Jerome Rostow (eds.), *Work in America: The Decade Ahead* (New York: Van Nostrand-Reinhold, 1979).

Humanizing work and the workplace is not merely a matter of re-arranging tasks or the organization structure, although changes in these areas often help. The main problem is to engender a humanistic philosophy without undermining or unduly threatening good managers. If fully operationalized, the humanization of work adds up to a new vision of industrial democracy that applies ethical and moral attitudes to decision making.[47]

ORGANIZATIONAL ASPECTS

Work, in both its technological and human aspects, lies at the core of managerial responsibility. Technological processes define the limits within which the organization operates in producing goods and services. It also limits the efforts to humanize work. Ambivalent views of technology influence task structure in relation to jobholders. On one hand, we need and favor technology for its individual and social benefits; on the other, we fear and distrust its possible distortions of the human personality and its massive impact on society.

Every organization is an approximation of an ideal image. There is no perfect structural arrangement of tasks or people, so work reforms proceed fitfully and haltingly. But organizations are increasingly being evaluated not only by traditional accounting or financial criteria, but also by qualitative effects on people. Organizations now try to achieve their economic objectives with minimal human costs. These human costs are physical, social, and psychological. Physical labor has become easier, and work is less burdensome than ever, largely as a result of improved technologies. Minimizing the social and psychological pressures on individuals is exceedingly difficult. Job design and organizational structuring are accomplished more by the dictates of the work or of the organization than by their effect on people. But even where jobs and organizations are well designed, their potentials are blunted by archaic habits and obsolete management and leadership styles.

The imperatives of the organization pose even more dangers to freedom, justice, human rights, and society generally than technology. Scott and Hart see little but the oppressive tendencies in organizations.[48] Suppression of the individuality of humans remains widespread, but there is ample evidence that countervailing forces are at work among individuals and throughout society that open new horizons and form the basis of

---

[47] "Workers' Participation," symposium issue of *Industrial Relations* 18 (Fall 1979). See also W. J. Heisler and John W. Houck (eds.), *A Matter of Dignity: Inquiries into the Humanization of Work* (Notre Dame, Ind.: Notre Dame University Press, 1977).

[48] William G. Scott and David K. Hart, *Organizational America* (Boston: Houghton Mifflin, 1979); Rosemary J. Erickson, "The Changing Workplace and Work Force," *Training and Development Journal* 34 (January 1980), pp. 62–65.

hope for a better quality of work life in which ethical and moral behavior may reach a new plane.

Incident Case

Managerial tactics are as a rule not very nice. One case is of a sandbagging manager who disapproved of a plan put forward by one of his men but didn't want to openly veto it. A veto, the manager felt, would solidify opposition to his position. So he seemingly encouraged the subordinate in his endeavor but killed it at budget time by failing to find funds for it, saying: "Sorry, Charlie, just couldn't get the money for you."

What are the ethical implications?

Issues for Discussion and Analysis

1. What are the moral and ethical implications of the statement, "equal pay for equal work"? What are the practical implications?

2. What is meant by the phrase "quality of working life"? What is the organization's responsibility in this area?

3. What kind of supervision or leadership style is needed for each of the value categories described in Figure 10.1?

4. How can it be argued that the work reform movement in business enterprise has been a failure?

5. Are companies doing more or less than they ought to be doing to improve the employment situation of minorities and disadvantaged persons?

6. Outline the case for and against the view that the work ethic has declined.

7. Should personnel managers be concerned with ethical problems in developing personnel programs? Are they concerned?

Class Project

Form several subcommittees among class members. Assign each to investigate a main aspect of the problem of developing a philosophy and strategy by which a company can meet its social responsibilities with respect to the ethical issues of work.

For Further Reading

ANDRISANI, PAUL J., EILEEN APPELBAUM, ROSS KOPPEL, and ROBERT C. MILJUS. *Work Attitudes and Work Experience: Evidence from the National Longitudinal Surveys* (New York: Praeger, 1978).

ANTHONY, P. D. *Ideology of Work* (New York, Methuen, 1979).

BERG, IVAR, MARCIA FREEDMAN, and MICHAEL FREEMAN. *Managers and Work Reform: A Limited Engagement* (New York: Free Press, 1978).

BERNSTEIN, PAUL. *Workplace Democratization* (New Brunswick, N.J.: Transaction Books, 1980).

CHERRINGTON, DAVID J. *The Work Ethic: Working Values and Values That Work* (New York: AMACOM, 1980).

CLAYRE, ALISDAIR. *Work and Play: Ideas and Experience of Work and Leisure* (New York: Harper & Row, 1975).

DERR, C. BROOKLYN (ed.). *Work, Family and the Career: New Frontiers in Theory and Research* (New York: Praeger, 1980).

FLOWERS, V. S., and OTHERS. *Managerial Values for Working* (New York: AMACOM, 1975).

HEISLER, J. J., and JOHN W. HOUCK (eds.). *A Matter of Dignity: Inquiries into the Humanization of Work* (Notre Dame, Ind.: The University of Notre Dame Press, 1977).

KRANTZ, DAVID L. *Radical Career Change: Life Beyond Work* (New York: Free Press, 1978).

O'TOOLE, JAMES. *Work, Learning, and the American Future* (San Francisco: Jossey-Bass, 1977).

PALM, GORAN. *The Flight from Work* (New York: Cambridge University Press, 1978).

RATNER, RONNIE STEINBERG (ed.). *Equal Employment Policy for Women: Strategies for Implementation in the United States, Canada, and Western Europe* (Philadelphia: Temple University Press, 1980).

ROSOW, JEROME M. (ed.). *The Worker and the Job: Coping with Change* (Englewood Cliffs, N.J.: Prentice-Hall, 1974).

SCHRANK, ROBERT. *Ten Thousand Working Days* (Cambridge, Mass.: Mitt Press, 1978).

SHEPPARD, C. S., and D. C. CARROLL (eds.). *Working in the Twenty-First Century* (New York: Wiley, 1980).

SUSMAN, GERALD I. *Autonomy at Work: A Sociotechnical Analysis of Participative Management* (New York: Praeger, 1976).

TAYLOR, BLAINE. *The Success Ethic in a Shattered American Dream* (Washington, D.C.: Acropolis Books, 1976).

TERKEL, STUDS. *Working* (New York: Pantheon, 1974).

VEBLEN, THORSTEIN. *The Instinct of Workmanship* (New York: Norton, 1964).

The Social Role of the Manager

A great society is a society in which its men of business think greatly of their functions.

Alfred North Whitehead

For there is nothing important except people. A person is defined solely by the extent of his influence over other people, by the sphere of his interrelationships; and morality is an utterly meaningless term unless defined as the good one does to others, the fulfilling of one's function in the sociopolitical whole.

from Ursula K. LeGuin,
The Lathe of Heaven. Copyright © 1971 by
Ursula K. LeGuin. (New York: Charles Scribner's Sons, 1971).
Reprinted with the permission of Charles Scribner's Sons.

Concepts Discussed in This Chapter

1. ROLE BEHAVIOR

2. SOCIAL ROLES

3. THE INFLUENCE OF SOCIAL ROLES ON RESPONSIBLE DECISION MAKING

4. POWER, AUTHORITY, AND CONFLICT IN SOCIAL ROLES

5. HUMANISM AND SOCIAL ROLES

Our discussions of ethics, morals, values, and social responsibility can be summed up in the idea of the social role of the manager. This of course is not the manager's only role, but it is one of the most important. All other managerial roles, such as husbanding resources, functioning efficiently, supervising people, or producing goods or services, reflect the combined power of decisions made not only for economic and technical aims, but also for human and social ends.

As one of our most pervasive social institutions, business is intimately connected with the other structural elements of society. Managerial decisions therefore cannot be made in isolation from the community or society as a whole. Managers individually and collectively are responsible for relating business to the relevant parts of the external environment. Such efforts involve managers in the performance of a social role.

ROLE BEHAVIOR AND ORGANIZATIONAL ROLES

It is useful to categorize social behavior into various patterns called *roles*. The process of socialization indoctrinates individuals from birth with the codes and norms of expectations embodied in roles, which in turn become rooted in habit, custom, and routine in the individual's life. The purpose of roles is to equip the person with sets of ready responses to recurring or repetitive situations. The individual can then act so that others understand and accept the actions. Being able to perform expected roles yields a sense of satisfaction and feelings of being accepted by and integrated into one's group. A pattern of complementary roles distributes responsibility for action, making it possible for large numbers of people to combine their efforts in complex, continuing activities, without knowing everything that is going on.

Although prescribed or assumed roles form the basis of much of the useful actions in organizations and society, they do not account for all behavior. Some behavior is random, perhaps indulged in unconsciously or for the sheer pleasure it affords. Also, unique situations may occur for which little or no role behavior has been learned or seems adequate.

Collaboration and cooperation are two important forms of behavior necessary to organizational life and purpose. Roles help govern these two processes. Every firm has a social as well as economic or technical structure. Each individual has a social place as well as a physical station and a job and occupational status. Failure to understand the organization's social structure (and therefore to rely only on the technical aspects of organization) leads to mistaking logical coordination for social integration, thereby causing lack of communication and other problems.

An understanding of the manager's social role requires an understanding of the general nature of roles in organizations. A role is a behavior pattern guided by expectations directed to an organization member as a holder of a position. These expectations derive largely from others, but position holders are usually not passive performers. Therefore we may distinguish two types of role content: prescribed and discretionary. *Prescribed content* includes the activities and responsibilities defined by the formal organizational system. These reflect the task expectations of one's boss, the general requirements of the technology, and the expectations of other parts of the system to which the tasks are related. Prescribed content is reflected, though not generally made explicit, in job descriptions, organization manuals or organization charts.

Discretionary content arises from the creative, individualistic way individuals perceive their tasks and their role requirements. The skills, experiences, insights, and personality of the individual are brought to bear in shaping the roles being performed. Every role has some discretionary content, but the degree of flexibility in discretionary behavior is relatively large in managerial tasks and responsibilities. There is also an advisory element in discretionary role behavior. Role behavior is constrained and directed when deviations from expected norms are questioned, evaluations are made, and justifications are called for.[1]

> . . . it is fundamental that there be a power of conforming to routine, of supervising routine, of constructing routine, and of understanding routine both as to its internal structure and as to its external purposes. Such a power is the bedrock of all practical efficiency. But for the production of the requisite Foresight, something more is wanted. This extra endowment can only be described as a philosophic power of understanding the complex flux of the varieties of human societies: for instance, the habit of noting varieties of demands on life, of serious purposes, of frivolous amusements.
>
> ALFRED NORTH WHITEHEAD, *Adventures of Ideas* (New York: Macmillan, 1933; Mentor edition, New American Library, 1955), p. 103.

Creative, ambitious, and energetic managers play a large part in defining their particular roles. Their experiences and personalities temper and adjust the expectations of others within limits that are determined by the situation, by personality, and by unfolding events. No roles can specify what the unknown situations of the future will require. Change provides opportunities for discretionary role content, and it explains why, for example, when one executive succeeds another, their ways of doing things are often very different. Some perform their roles so well that successors cannot match it.

It is implied that position holders will play their formal, positional role in the best way possible, meeting the demands and accepting the limitations. Supporting roles geared to a main role also exist to facilitate the stability or predictability of actions. There is give and take among all

---

[1] Sir Geoffrey Vickers, *The Art of Judgment* (New York: Basic Books, 1965), pp. 229–230.

related roles as individuals make continuous adjustments and refinements. Where a manager changes or exceeds the limits others expect, sanctions and restraining pressures may occur, but the imprecision of roles leaves ample scope for individual initiatives.[2] Organizations and societies consist structurally and psychologically of networks of roles, built from self as well as mutual expectations and operating in a changing but ongoing situation.

DECISIONS AND THE MANAGER'S SOCIAL ROLE

Social motives exist when decision makers attend to a decision's potential influences on other individuals or groups, or on society itself. The individual selects a situation-specific combination of social and other motives such as self-interest, self-sacrifice, altruism, aggression, cooperation, and competition among those affected by or carrying out the decision.[3] Decisions that harm others may often be attributable to ill-formed managerial roles. One study found, for example, that when the manager's role was deliberately expanded to include the concept of social responsibility as interpreted by the board of directors, irresponsible decisions fell from 79 percent to 23 percent.[4]

Circumlocution helps to make decisions more palatable to those who benefit from them. Workers, for example, might be suspicious if a generous act were presented as anything other than self-interest. Any departure from the classical role of "boss" may make managers feel uncomfortable or even resentful of their own classical role as workers, which calls for them to dislike being indebted to management for favors.[5] To make such decisions in the expectation of getting credit reflects pitfalls which, for example, were evident in the paternalism of early industrialization. Acts done to benefit others often encounter the critical response, "Why are they doing this?"

It is sound practice for decision makers to consider the social impact of decisions. Social uncertainties make this difficult, but an organization's legitimacy depends on managerial awareness of the values and directions of a changing society. Failing to think imaginatively about managing, despite social uncertainty, is a failure to take one's responsibilities seriously, and to respond to one of management's great chal-

---

[2] Sir Geoffrey Vickers, *Towards a Sociology of Management* (New York: Basic Books, 1967), pp. 96–100.

[3] K. R. MacCrimmon and D. M. Messnick, "A Framework for Social Motives," *Behavioral Science* 21 (March 1976), pp. 86–100.

[4] J. Scott Armstrong, "Social Responsibility in Management," *Journal of Business Research* 5 (September 1977), pp. 185–213.

[5] James C. Worthy, *Big Business and Free Men* (New York: Harper & Row, 1959), p. 1.

lenges.[6] Ewing notes that due process of law, privacy, and freedom of speech are guaranteed rights for all Americans, yet these rights are widely denied in workplace settings. Pressures from the hierarchial nature of the organization structure invite the subordinate's fear of job loss in the exercise of these rights. Even in organizations that incorporate these rights into their ideologies, such as unions or government agencies, they are often violated.[7] Here again is an opportunity for decision makers to analyze the social aspects of role performance.

Roles concentrate attention of the interrelatedness and interdependence of human beings in various systems of action by creating mutual expectations about the attitudes or behaviors of significant others in the course of social relations, and by regularizing human action.[8] Thus a role is a social prescription of some but not all the premises that enter into an individual's choice of behavior. In the analysis of particular roles, one should consider three major problems: the degree of consensus that exists in any given policy-making process on the definition of particular roles; the conformity of the role incumbent to the expectations of others; and methods of resolving conflict that call social issues into consideration.[9]

The manager's awareness of the problems of social responsibility has been heightened by innumerable pressures in society. Traditionally, managers have always thought of themselves as having a fiduciary responsibility or trusteeship as the guardian of resources and the security of the organization and its properties. Many have also recognized the concept of stewardship. Today's emphasis, however, focuses on actions and concrete behaviors measured against more demanding social and human expectations. In discerning how managers view their social role it is difficult, but desirable, to distinguish between propaganda, public relations puffery, pious declarations, and rationalizations on the one hand, and serious managerial actions on the other.

Responsibilities to owners, stockholders, employees, consumers, and suppliers are not necessarily born of altruism, but the concept is nevertheless relevant. That economic concerns indicate a social responsibility rooted in self-interest need not deprive managers of credit for desiring to fulfill these responsibilities. Now, however, the meaning of social responsibility extends beyond effective economic performance, and profits are no longer the sole criterion by which managers are measured. Therefore managers are in effect being asked, and even

---

6 James E. Post, "The Challenge of Managing under Social Uncertainty," *Business Horizons* 20 (August 1977), pp. 51–60.

7 David E. Ewing, *Freedom Inside the Organization* (New York: Dutton, 1977).

8 Heinz Eulau, *Journeys and Politics* (Indianapolis: Bobbs-Merrill, 1964), p. 256.

9 Neal Gross, W. S. Mason, and A. McEachern, *Explorations in Role Analysis* (New York: Wiley, 1958).

required, to enrich their views of responsibility by acknowledging its social dimensions.

POWER, AUTHORITY, AND CONFLICT IN THE SOCIAL ROLE

The manager's social role entails responsibilities for the appropriate use of power and authority, and for the resolution of role conflicts that are inherent in the increasing number of roles managers must play. The social role implies that human, group, community, and societal expectations will be considered in the enactment of the other roles expected of managers.

There are times in the work of every manager when special needs demand conscious, deliberate attention to the behavior of people around him or her. Dealing with other people, either higher up, lower down, or at the peer level involves the manager in the social context of ongoing relationships. An instinctive grasp of social currents is also important. The manager needs reflective power, a philosophic habit, to help judge every situation. This requires a continuous review of society's general tendencies. This habit of general thought, undaunted by novelty, is the gift of philosophy. An unspecialized aptitude for eliciting generalizations from particulars and for seeing the divergency of generalities in varying circumstances is required.[10]

POWER

Executives and managers exert a tremendous power over the lives of the people with whom they work every day, and through their organizations, on society. That power is by no means unlimited; constraining forces encourage discretion in its use. The social role is one of the most important of such constraining forces.

Power has many sources and takes a variety of forms. Power may be derived from expertise, the control of information needed by others, the forces of personality or driving ambition, or the right to reward or punish others. One of the most important sources of power, however, is the administrative power inherent in organizational positions. Thus power is defined as any form of influence that produces obedience or conformity in others.[11]

Administrative power is that delegated along with authority to posi-

---

[10] Alfred North Whitehead, *Adventures in Ideas* (New York: New American Library, 1955), pp. 103–104.

[11] Paul G. Swingle, *The Management of Power* (Hillsdale, N.J.: Lawrence Erlbaum Associates, 1976).

tion holders or to positions in such a way as to organize tasks and responsibilities horizontally and vertically in the organizational structure. When a hierarchy is defined and functional operating areas are established, narrow concepts of power and authority suffice to achieve the organization's primary objectives. However, when tasks and responsibilities also include their social aspects or the enlargement of social roles, the net effect is to dilute power because its more qualitative and emotional characteristics come to be important, and these are hard to measure or appraise. A power-hungry or power-obsessed individual cares little for any social role because of its dilution of power. Exploitative, manipulative forms of power are inconsistent with the social ethic.[12]

That power is socially conferred is an important inducement to performing the managerial role under the guidance of social responsibility considerations. Power exists only when those subject to it acquiesce in its use: the politician must heed constituents; the manager knows that subordinates must accept power over them, and that they have many strategies to blunt their superior's power. A major requirement is that power be legitimate, and legitimacy results from acceptance, which cannot be abused without causing power to fade.[13]

AUTHORITY

Authority is a form of power, and what has been said about power is also true of authority. Authority is largely positional power legitimized by delegation, but managers have considerable discretion in its use, and its application therefore varies in accordance with each manager's leadership style. The manager's social role requires that abuses and distortions be avoided. Authority has limits that derive from the social system which confers it. It is legitimized not only by delegation, but also by the acceptance of those subject to it. The social role of the manager with respect to the internal administration of an organization must include continuous attention to the impact of authority on human values and the quality of work life offered to its members.

Society too has problems of power and authority which managers face as part of their social role. According to Nisbet, we live in a twilight age of political and cultural crisis: erosion of patriotism, decline of political ideology and political parties, decay of social institutions, and the increasing militarization of power. By burdening government with the responsibility for curing all social ills we are in danger of politicizing the other social institutions — education, business, and the church. Thus

---

[12] Bertrand Russell, *Power* (London: Allen and Unwin, 1938).

[13] R. G. Siu, *The Craft of Power* (New York: Wiley, 1979), p. 84. For an essay on power and morality, see pp. 195–211.

traditional authority is lost in the transfer of power to government, and even government is increasingly distrusted along with the rest.[14]

Nisbet's views paint a discouraging picture, but he sees possibilities for reversing the erosion of authority in the restoration of pluralism and the rediscovery of the social components of action in society. Social initiatives that spring from groups, neighborhoods, localities, and voluntary associations provide a healthy diversity of social membership and separation of the social from the political, the public from the private.[15] Nisbet's views are controversial, for they are very conservative. Yet they argue a persuasive case for restoring authority to a more vital role in democratic society. His suggestions contain many opportunities for managers to develop the social aspects of their roles.

CONFLICT

The manager's social role has been greatly influenced by two conflicting ethical imperatives. The first, the individual ethic, holds that individuals should strive for individual gain, and that unlimited competition should exist among them. This led by analogy to Social Darwinism, which espouses the "survival of the fittest." Social benefits, in this view, result automatically as each individual seeks his or her own interest. One readily recognizes here the Adam Smith philosophy, which coincided with the religious orientation of the Protestant ethic: the fittest would not only be the richest, but also morally the best.[16]

Managers still stress economic or profit motivations. Business firms have supported programs for economic education in high schools and universities, and endowed "free enterprise" professorial chairs. Free enterprise ideology defines social responsibility primarily as economic performance measured by material outcomes. Milton Friedman went so far as to declare that the only social responsibility of a business is to make a profit:

> When the businessman learns to give up the personal quest for standards of moral action in his role as businessman and permits society its proper role in this area he may then be freed to go about the task which justifies his control of society's resources — the creation of wealth.[17]

The social ethic is at the opposite pole of the conflicting ethical philosophies. The social ethic holds that people are dominated by the social influences of the group or organization, and that managers of today's

---

[14] Robert Nisbet, *Twilight of Authority* (New York: Oxford University Press, 1975).

[15] Ibid., chap. 5. See also Richard Sennett, *Authority* (New York: Knopf, 1980).

[16] Robert T. Golembiewski, *Men, Management and Morality: Toward a New Organization Ethic* (New York: McGraw-Hill, 1965), pp. 38–49.

[17] Milton Friedman, *Capitalism and Freedom* (Chicago: The University of Chicago Press, 1963), p. 2.

organizations are victims of pressures to conform, to be docile and sub-missive and to put the organization's interests ahead of their own. The social ethic was attacked by William H. Whyte, who saw the social or group ethic as making pressures against individuality morally legitimate. Whyte's popularization of this concept influenced many who tended to exaggerate and distort his observations, but even so his book itself, while containing many insights, was rightly attacked for its overstatements, caricatures, and faulty use of evidence.[18]

Argyris has made a research-based case showing that authoritarian management styles encouraged by traditional, bureaucratic theories pro-duce subservience, passive dependence, and conformity in employees, interfering with their psychological maturity and reducing innovative-ness and personal competence.[19] Running counter to Whyte's concept of the organization man, Warner's research concluded that managers are much more autonomous than Whyte believed. He provides a definition of autonomy based on the work of Piaget:

> Essentially, by an autonomous person I refer to that man or woman who has internalized his experiences in the society in such a way that he is able to make his own decisions from within, rather than being completely dependent upon the influences and instructions coming from without. This means that he is morally autonomous, in the sense that he can apply the rules of the society himself, by his own decisions, that he knows and can act on what is right and wrong, and intellectually he is capable of mak-ing the discriminations that are necessary in a fluid society to operate in positions that are often ambiguous.[20]

The trenchant analysis of Scott and Hart has revived the organization man issue, but they treat it in a more scholarly way than Whyte. They draw upon sociology, economics, and political science perspectives that go beyond the psychological approach of Argyris. Their analysis portrays the encroachment of subtle demands by the organization on the individ-ual. They believe that people are indoctrinated by cultural influences and social institutions, as well as by their organizational experiences, into uncritical and unthinking acceptance of the organization's imperatives.[21]

We do not have to choose between the two conflicting ethics, for there is no empirical research that places one above the other. In design-ing their social role, managers should understand the conflict and strive

---

[18] William H. Whyte, *The Organization Man* (New York: Simon and Schuster, 1956).

[19] Chris Argyris, *Integrating the Individual and the Organization* (New York: Wiley, 1964); *Inter-personal Competence and Organizational Effectiveness* (Homewood, Ill.: Dorsey Press, 1962).

[20] W. Lloyd Warner, *The Corporation in the Emergent American Society*. Distinguished Ford Founda-tion Lecture, New York University, (New York: Harper & Row, 1962), pp. 48–49. See also W. Lloyd Warner and James Abegglen, *Big Business Leaders in America* (New York: Harper & Row, 1955).

[21] William G. Scott and David G. Hart, *Organizational America* (Boston: Houghton Mifflin, 1979). See also Kenneth Boulding, *The Organizational Revolution* (New York: Harper & Row, 1953).

for a balanced consideration of both sets of pressures. Clearly the trend has been to see the individualist ethic as a caricature of self-interest, and to modify it in the direction of social values.

The element of trust pervades role networks, but role conflict is common as position holders interpret situations and the effects of their own and other roles in the system. For example, institutional roles may conflict with personal roles, or one role player may expand into the role territory of another. Such conflicts do not frustrate roles or make them unplayable. The resolution of role conflict and the integration of multiple roles are a normal part of the managerial task.[22]

DEVELOPING THE MANAGER'S SOCIAL ROLE

Compared to managerial roles, social roles are ill-defined. Behavior and its appraisal are even more subjective. Whether social roles produce profits, or should be undertaken at what costs, or whether they should operate without consideration of costs at all are imponderables. Some criteria for social action are quantifiable; others are not. Philanthropy, for example, can be measured in dollars, though its results cannot be. The monetary costs of plant abandonment or relocation can be measured, but the human costs are beyond assessment. To acknowledge social responsibility, therefore, requires thinking beyond dollars and accepting risks that are justifiable mainly through qualitative judgments.

Commitment to the social role and the capability of performing it are two essential managerial characteristics. We will discuss these characteristics by considering the manager's personality, and the matter of conscience.

PERSONALITY AND THE SOCIAL ROLE

Being accepted as a responsible member of management is very important to the manager. From the viewpoint of the manager's personal life, membership in a management group implies a loyalty to the group and to the organization. These loyalties are not necessarily compatible or consistent across all situations the manager confronts.

The core concept of personality is the self, or in psychoanalytical terms, the ego. The self has an individual and a social aspect. The personal self is what individuals believe they are and want to be. The social self is the way we appear to others and the way we think we appear to others.[23] There is tension between the two sources of self-image because

---

[22] Sir Geoffrey Vickers, *Making Institutions Work* (New York: Wiley, 1963), pp. 28–31 and 107–108.

[23] Henry P. Knowles and Borje O. Saxberg, *Personality and Leadership Behavior* (Reading, Mass.: Addison-Wesley, 1971), pp. 71–86.

they consist of impressions and perceptions that are often imprecise. Therefore the manager's social role develops in the context of an organization in which forces that require adjustments of the personal self to the expectations of the social role are constantly at work. When the social self creates burdens the personal self finds difficult, the personal self turns to defensive tactics to protect it.

There is a sharp distinction between person and role. One advantage that a role confers is that the individual can be detached from the role behavior, rendering the performance impersonal and thereby protecting the personality. If A discharges B, it can be ascribed to the boss's official role rather than to his or her own makeup. In this way, organizations protect the self-esteem of managers, and role relations come to the support of ego defenses. Self-esteem comes from rewarding career satisfactions, but too much reliance on impersonality will eventually undermine the mutual support of the individual and the organization.

Organizational training and development — manifest forms of socialization — tend to reinforce the isolation of the self because they are geared to the needs of the organization rather than of the individual. The organization aims to integrate the various roles it needs rather than to organize the roles to fit the persons. Most training emphasizes occupational rather than social roles.[24] But effective performance of the social role requires that it be integrated into the personality, so that managers see that it meets their ego and self-fulfillment needs. Otherwise the manager will communicate one set of attitudes in words, but a quite different set by the way he or she thinks or acts.[25]

As categories of moral action, the individual and individuality lie at the center of Western civilization. This is more than a problem of philosophy: it is also a problem of great concern to psychologists and social psychologists. The historical and cultural roots of individuality are the concern of anthropologists and other behavioral scientists, who study how social processes become imbedded within the self.[26]

Individuals often ascribe success and failure to personal deficiencies, even though the actual causes may be in the organization or even outside it. It is easy to be suspicious that one's failure is within oneself rather than in the system or the breaks of the game. Envy, jealousy, hostility, and frustration are likely when an individual sees others achieving the things he or she would like to achieve.

Organizational pressures on the manager's personality that interfere with the elaboration of social roles have been vividly portrayed by

---

[24] Abraham Zaleznik and Manfred F. R. Kets De Vries, *Power and the Corporate Mind* (Boston: Houghton Mifflin, 1975), pp. 264–265.

[25] Gordon L. Lippitt, *Organization Renewal* (New York: Appleton-Century-Crofts, 1969), pp. 61–68.

[26] Kenelm Burridge, *Someone, No One: An Essay on Individuality* (Princeton, N.J.: Princeton University Press, 1980).

novelists. They reveal much about the psychological assumptions of organizational life. The protagonists in Heller's *Something Happened* and in Wilson's *The Man in the Grey Flannel Suit*, for example, are seen to wrestle with the impact of conflicts between the drive for success and the needs of the self.[27]

THE MANAGER'S CONSCIENCE

When asked what the most important motive for acting ethically in business is, many businesspeople say it is a matter of conscience. They make statements like "I have to live with myself," or "I need peace of mind," or "I can sleep better at night if I do the ethical thing."

Conscience represents the internalization of the values and norms of society so that the individual behaves in ways society regards as normal, ethical, and appropriate. As children mature they learn the difference between approved and unapproved behavior, so that conscience develops as a monitoring device. The individual feels rewarded for behaving ethically, or punished for behaving unethically. Some managers stress natural sanctions—those which become available in the present life. Others emphasize supernatural sanctions, which bring reward or punishment in the life hereafter. Thus a religious influence bears upon the individual's conscience.

Roles are normatively regulated. Social roles are regulated by social norms, which in turn are components of culture. Norms express the way people ought to behave in carrying out important social functions. Therefore, all managerial work has moral aspects. In facing the moral aspects of decision, the manager seeks guidance which is found not only in the normative expectations of others, and in the normative prescriptions of social institutions such as the church and state, but also in moral codes that are self-enforced through the individual's conscience.

To speak of conscience is to raise the problem of moralism and moralizing. Responding to one's conscience as a motivating force must be placed alongside the more popularly acceptable motivation of profit or economic gain. Baumhart writes: "Though the economic outcome may be identical in the two cases, the man who makes decisions according to his conscience gives us more hope that he will act ethically in the face of pressure and temptation."[28]

The idea of partially implicit codes (personal) that exert a significant influence on conduct in an organized and predictable manner is per-

---

[27] James M. Glass, "Organization and Action: The Executive's Personality Type as a Pathological Formation," *Journal of Contemporary Business* 5 (Autumn 1976), pp. 91–111. See also H. R. Smith, "Novelists and Businessmen: Schizophrenia in the Complex Society," *Journal of Contemporary Business* 5 (Autumn 1976), pp. 19–45.

[28] Raymond Baumhart, S.J., *Ethics in Business* (New York: Holt, Rinehart and Winston, 1968), p. 55.

suasive. Barnard holds that several sets of these codes may exist in the same individual. A given code held by an individual may vary along two dimensions. The first is quality of the code — whether it is simple or complex, whether it reflects a high or low sense of values, whether it is comprehensive or narrow. The second dimension is the responsibility of the individual to this code, which Barnard defines as "the power of a particular private code . . . to control the conduct of an individual."[29]

Problems arise not only when there is a conflict between codes, but also when the quality of the code may not meet the requirements of a complex situation, or when the individual is irresponsible and therefore inconsistent and unpredictable with respect to the codes he or she holds. The higher the level of executive, and the greater the number and complexity of codes, the greater the likelihood of conflict between or among the codes. When such conflict occurs, there may be paralysis of action, conformity to one code and violation of another, or a search for substitute action.[30]

FULFILLING THE SOCIAL ROLE OF THE MANAGER

We saw in earlier chapters that managers, especially those in business, are widely criticized not for technical or economic deficiencies, but for social ones. Despite increasing attention to social responsibility, unfavorable attitudes among intellectuals, activist groups, and citizens generally continue. Anger, fear, distrust, and other negative emotions follow, for example, from the quarterly profit announcements of the major oil companies. High profits during the energy crisis arouses suspicions that they are obtained by means contrary to the public interest. Explanations for high profits, even when logically valid, are unpersuasive because more subtle social pressures generate an emotional public outcry. The time for social responsibility has clearly arrived, but the verbalization of platitudes and good will is not sufficient to restore our lost confidence in business, education, government, health care, or the professions. Increasingly the emphasis will be on action and performance, and on responsibilities logically ascribed to the social role.

What can managers do to design and maintain an effective social role? Since there is no fixed, precise concept of this role that is equally applicable to all managers, it is possible only to suggest some general guidelines that seem likely to enhance the manager's social performance. Four sets of guidelines will be discussed: (1) the effectiveness of management

---

[29] Chester Barnard, *Organization and Management* (Cambridge, Mass.: Harvard University Press, 1962), p. 263.

[30] George Strother, "The Moral Codes of Executives: A Watergate-Inspired Look at Barnard's Theory of Executive Responsibility," *Academy of Management Review* 1 (Spring 1976), pp. 13–20.

itself; (2) personal values, ethics, and moral standards, (3) the influence of humanism and the humanities; and (4) social decision frameworks.

EFFECTIVE MANAGEMENT

The social role is not divorced from or above and beyond technical and economic performance roles. They are in practice intertwined, which indicates that the manager's social responsibility begins with the obligation to manage well. Mismanagement in whatever form it appears ill serves organization members as well as the community, the public, and other stakeholders. In the enterprise, confusion, service delays, structural chaos, poor interpersonal relations, deciding by expediency, and reliance on authoritarian management practices are examples of patterns of behavior that add up to mismanagement. Hostility, anger, fear, distrust, and the like reflect a disturbed morale that runs counter to goals of efficiency, effectiveness, and productivity because they stifle creativity and destroy the sense of fulfillment people hope for in their jobs.

Mismanagement tends to induce cynicism among the critics of management. For example, Armstrong writes:

> Managers are omnipresent — the hidden part of any goods or service. They have taken over hospitals, universities, foundations, and restaurants. Managers are interested in management, and management is a non-good. One cannot do a blessed thing with it — he cannot ride it, eat it, or endure it. He can, if he is sufficiently masochistic, read it (for it thrives on memoranda and, now and again, a business history). The product or service to whose provision management is attached seems to be the manager's remotest concern. A manager is dedicated not to the quality of goods but only to the processes of decision-making that affect them. Managers are rather like the products of some schools of education, wherein novices learn that it matters less *what* one teaches than *how* one teaches.[31]

Lack of concern for substance rather than management processes themselves leads to mediocrity. Armstrong writes further:

> Management seems a kind of canker on our time. It is practically ineradicable, diminishing before the urgencies of no power known to man. Even President Carter seems unable to extirpate it from that over which, nominally at least, he is in charge. Still the public does not protest. A people, I suppose, gets the management it fails to resist. . . . Whether they commit or approve, people whose values are invested in the processes rather than in the virtues of their decisions are spearheading our evolution into a new form of society, one which might very well be called a mediocracy.[32]

---

[31] Robert Plant Armstrong, "Rapport," *Book Forum* 4 (July 1979), p. 364.
[32] Ibid.

The impact of mismanagement on societies should not be underestimated. When mismanagement occurs in government or the political system, it is particularly dangerous to society. Vacca writes:

> I have pointed to the problems of mismanagement as a remote cause of the dark age that is imminent, but we must not forget that this is also a continuously active cause accompanying and aggravating the process of breakdown. Mismanagement is found everywhere: in the third world, where it maintains extremely low levels of life; in the Soviet Union, where it represents, perhaps, an inheritance from the Tsarist administration . . . and in the developed nations of the West, where it protects inefficiency and infects their growing congestion like a deadly germ. Anyone proposing and actively fostering large plans for the healing and improving of modern society ought not to minimize the virulence of this plague, this rottenness. . . .[33]

PERSONAL ETHICS AND MORALS

Ethical and moral behavior, we have shown, is learned through socialization, and it reflects the extent to which the individual internalizes the codes and norms of society, and how he or she interprets the conditions under which they are applied. It follows that ethical and moral behavior cannot be precisely identified, described, or measured; rather, it is a dynamic, uncertain process. But the individual may devote thought, analysis, introspection, and self-examination to these dimensions of behavior. And concrete situations are constant tests of their application.

Managers can place ethics high on their agendas at home, in the office, and in the company and trade association. Management meetings can include regular discussions of the moral dimensions of decisions. Managers can seek expert counsel on ethics. To put moral health on the same level as mental and physical health, or indeed above them, they can read widely but selectively in the vast literature of ethics and philosophy. Devoting time to the study of ethics along with colleagues and other resource persons enables managers to critically examine the value orientations reflected in work and management issues.[34]

In every organization there is a great variation in the range of ethical and moral standards of its members. Some will profess very high standards; others are satisfied with less. In either case, it does little good to profess high standards unless one is willing to act on them. The individual who acts on moderate standards but sticks to them may be more moral than one with high standards who is never able to carry them out.

---

[33] Excerpt from *The Coming Dark Age* by Robert Vacca, translated by Dr. J. S. Whale. Copyright © 1973 by Doubleday & Company, Inc. Reprinted by permission of the publisher.

[34] Louis Finkelstein, "The Businessman's Moral Failure," *Fortune*, September 1958. Reprinted in John A. Larson (ed.), *The Responsibile Businessman: Readings from Fortune* (New York: Holt, Rinehart and Winston, 1966). See also Alvar O. Elbing, "The Value Issue of Business: The Responsibility of the Businessman," *Academy of Management Journal* 13 (March 1970), pp. 79–89.

Moral compromise sometimes occurs from "anticipatory socialization," in which managers adopt the values and orientations of higher-status groups whose ranks they hope to enter by promotion. Moral compromise also occurs when managers are overly influenced by the standards of reference groups which they value. According to Kirk, American businesspeople are inhumane. This does not mean inhuman, or insufficiently humanitarian. Businesspeople, however, like most Americans, are deficient in the disciplines that nurture the spirit. They are largely ignorant of the great body of literature that records the wisdom of the ages and instructs us in human nature. It is not easy to humanize oneself. At the age of 60, not many businesspeople do.[35]

The importance of the human disciplines to the functioning of industry and commerce transcends the simple though important skills of literacy. Even if the humanities are chiefly important to a person's soul and the higher purposes of life, they are good for profits too. One of the ends of a liberal education is to fit people for whatever lot may be theirs; and some of the accomplishments of the humanities are remarkably important to the management of the modern economy.[36] Humanistic knowledge is a largely untapped source of enrichment for management theory, practice, and philosophy. Humanistic thought and deeper inquiries into human nature yield insights into how management enhances or impedes human progress. But it is not enough merely to apply humanistic knowledge to traditional management thinking or practice. Managerial practices themselves need to be reformulated in humanistic and societal terms. Personnel and human relations programs, for example, do not come to grips with humanistic influences. Management instead has drawn selectively from the social and behavioral sciences to extract conformity and effort from employees, with relatively little attention to the deeper impulses of human nature.

The role of humanism is to inform the conscience of today's managers, and thereby to become an integral part of management philosophy. The problems of society are also problems for managers whose power and control of resources entails social responsibilities. Managers need the rights and privileges which society confers. Therefore managerial thought needs a macrolevel view that incorporates the insights of humanistic discourse.[37] Humanism embraces several humanistic concerns, including (1) the study of the humanities, (2) any system of thought or ethics concerned with the interests and ideals of people, (3)

---

[35] Russell Kirk, "The Inhumane Businessman," *Fortune*, May 1957. Reprinted in John A. Larson (ed.), *The Responsible Businessman: Readings from Fortune* (New York: Holt, Rinehart and Winston, 1966).

[36] Ibid.

[37] Dalton E. McFarland, "Management, Humanism, and Society: The Case for Macromanagement Theory," *The Academy of Management Review* 2 (October 1977), pp. 613–623.

the view that the welfare and happiness of humankind in the present life are of primary importance, and (4) a philosophy that rejects belief in the supernatural and prefers the methods of reason, science, and democracy in human affairs.[38] These precepts have many implications for the manager's social role.

The kind of management needed in social institutions and in society at large is far different from that suitable for internal organizational effectiveness or efficiency. What we know and act upon in society depends on a sense of collective purpose and the capacity for managing cohesion and interdependence. What the managers of an organization know and do depends on their sense of personal responsibility and the perception of values in action. Humanistic knowledge can thus be important for managers.

We have never taken seriously the cliché that management is an art; it is more fashionable to advocate precision and science in management. Actually management is only partly an art, but the literal significance of the phrase depends on the definition of both art and management. Boettinger defines art as "the imposition of a pattern, the vision of a whole, on many disparate parts so as to create a representation of that vision; art is an imposition of order on chaos."[39] This implies that management consists of organizing human talent for the attainment of great human purposes.

To ascribe an element of art to management is to recognize the presence of loosely coupled arrangements, the unmechanistic nature of the forces at work, and the interplay of human imagination with problems arising from both the material and the human aspects of the manager's task. Management as an art implies awareness of human emotions, untapped human talents, and a spiritual dimension in every person. The sculptor or painter has a personal responsibility for her art and for her own development. Managers develop in the social context of the organization. They need no sense of art to solve problems one at a time. Art enters in for those who sense in every problem its relatedness to the whole—to society and to human beings as well as to the organization itself. Science as well as art enters into the equation. Churchman, in examining the relationships among humanity, science, and management, informs those who despair of human beings as evil, deceptive causes of instability in the world system that neither management nor science alone can stave off disaster. But reason and rational decision making may combine management and science to give some promise of accomplishment through seeing all the parts of each problem in relation to the

---

[38] Richard W. Coan, *Hero, Artist, Sage, or Saint* (New York: Columbia University Press, 1977), pp. 275–276.

[39] Henry M. Boettinger, "Is Management Really an Art?" *Harvard Business Review* 53 (January–February 1975), pp. 54–64.

whole. Science becomes successful when viewed as a type of management; management is successful when allied with science.[40]

Management has been attacked for its dehumanizing tendencies, but in the past management responded primarily to expectations for efficiency; only recently have humanizing expectations appeared. Baill notes that one of the dehumanizing aspects of management is that certain skills and behaviors are defined as essential, but everything else is eliminated. He adds: "If management is truly a performing art and the management job is varied, then a manager must feel comfortable exhibiting the full range of human characteristics."[41]

The organization, because of its structure and the management styles it evokes, can be both a constraint and a liberation for humanistic tendencies. The human relations movement and the more recent organizational behavior approaches have found only moderate success in eliminating the built-in dehumanizing tendencies of modern organizations. Human relations and industrial relations techniques have been designed more to get workers to behave in accordance with company needs than with their own real needs and interests. People "process" other people who must work according to other people's needs, regulations, and instructions. Officialdom can manipulate people while escaping accountability and squelching feedback. The hierarchy structures a bureaucracy that sustains itself apart from particular persons.[42] These dehumanizing factors are not inevitable, but minimizing them is a difficult and so far uncompleted task.

There is a tension between humanism that meets the needs of individuals for meaning in work and fulfillment in their lives, and materialism which demands productivity that yields personal income. Morrow and Thayer have argued, not persuasively, that the dominant paradigm of materialism should be separated from humanism, because they are inherently incompatible.[43] More realistically, there is a need to design jobs and organizations more adequately with humans in mind. Ackoff writes: "A central problem of the Systems Age is how to humanize organizations and institutions; how to design them so that they better serve the purposes of their members and still effectively pursue their own purposes. To do so usually requires a change in both their form and function."[44]

Schulman alludes to the need for humanistic reform in organiza-

---

[40] C. West Churchman, *Challenge to Reason* (New York: McGraw-Hill, 1968), p. 104.

[41] Peter B. Baill, "Management as a Performing Art," *Personnel* 53 (July–August 1974), pp. 12–21.

[42] H. Roy Kaplan and Curt Tausky, "Humanism and Organizations," *Public Administration Review* 37 (March–April 1977), pp. 171–180; Ivar Berg, Marcia Freedman, and Michael Freeman, *Managers and Work Reform: A Limited Engagement* (New York: Free Press, 1978); Frederick C. Thayer, *An End to Hierarchy! An End to Competition!* (New York: New Viewpoints, 1973).

[43] Allyn A. Morrow and Frederick C. Thayer, "Materialism and Humanism: Organization Theory's Odd Couple," *Administration and Society* 10 (May 1978), pp. 88–106.

[44] Russel L. Ackoff, *Redesigning the Future: A Systems Approach to Societal Problems* (New York: Wiley, 1974), pp. 37–38.

tional life. He says: "The contemporary crisis in the United States and the world . . . is a crisis of organizational life. Modern complex organization, man's collective means for survival and development, is increasingly unable to cope with the tempo of current events and current aspirations."[45] Dahrendorf, too, centers human problems in the context of the organization: "If we seem unable to solve our problems — those of survival and justice — it is not our abilities which are at fault, but the ossified structures of society in which progress so often turns to bureaucracy."[46]

In performing a social role, the manager confronts a number of constraints inherent in the particular organization. Priorities are constantly established and reviewed for the allocation of resources and the commitment of goals. Large volumes of proposals and requests from external claimants require evaluation and decision. The fundamental decisions are those of top managers and the board of directors as to the general level of social performance. Rule-of-thumb goals may be set in the budgetary process. For example, a firm may decide that responses to philanthropic opportunities should approximate 5 percent of the previous year's net income. Within such limits, a host of individual decisions can follow.

Relevant criteria are both quantitative and qualitative. Quantitative criteria include size of the organization, profitability, cost-benefit analyses, and data concerning the impact of the organization on the community or society, as in the case of discharging chemical wastes into streams, or of air or noise pollution. Among the qualitative criteria are the moral and ethical aspects, public sentiment, future trends, assessment of consequences of granting or not granting requests, impact on the organizational image, and the feelings and attitudes of employees, customers, and suppliers.

In the enactment of their social role, managers should be aware of the organizational criteria that are likely to be applied. Ultimately the social responsibility of the organization is a composite result of the social roles of all its managers. The meshing of social roles into this composite result requires planning and care in the decision process. Although the decision maker's conscience is an individual matter, that individual need not be cut off from information and guidance obtained through collaborating with others.

SOCIAL DECISION FRAMEWORKS

The social role of the manager is a function not only of personal inclinations, habits, and beliefs, but also of organizational elements such as structure, climate of morals, policies, management styles, and the like.

---

[45] Jay Schulman, *Remaking an Organization* (Albany, N.Y.: SUNY Press, 1969), p. 229.

[46] Rolf Dahrendorf, *The New Liberty: Survival and Justice in a Changing World* (Stanford, Calif.: Stanford University Press, 1975), p. 3; O. B. Hardison, Jr., *Toward Freedom and Dignity: The Humanities and the Idea of Humanity* (Baltimore: Johns Hopkins University Press, 1972), pp. 124–147.

Figure 11.1

Decision-Making Flow Chart

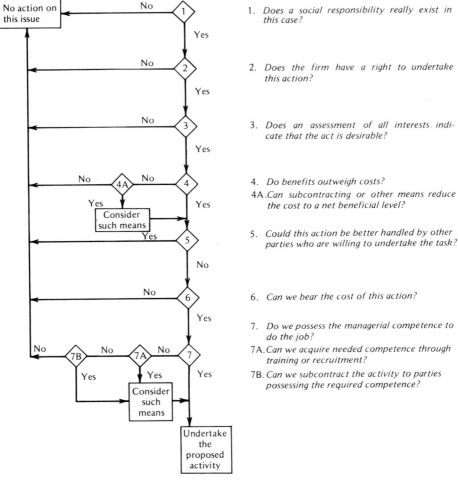

1. *Does a social responsibility really exist in this case?*

2. *Does the firm have a right to undertake this action?*

3. *Does an assessment of all interests indicate that the act is desirable?*

4. *Do benefits outweigh costs?*
4A. *Can subcontracting or other means reduce the cost to a net beneficial level?*

5. *Could this action be better handled by other parties who are willing to undertake the task?*

6. *Can we bear the cost of this action?*

7. *Do we possess the managerial competence to do the job?*
7A. *Can we acquire needed competence through training or recruitment?*
7B. *Can we subcontract the activity to parties possessing the required competence?*

SOURCE: *Ramon J. Aldag and Donald W. Jackson, Jr., "A Managerial Framework for Social Decision Making," p. 34, MSU Business Topics, Spring 1975. Reprinted by permission of the publisher, Division of Research, Graduate School of Business Administration, Michigan State University.*

To facilitate the performance of social roles by individuals, the organization needs to design an appropriate framework in which the means of resolving social responsibility issues are clear. A systematic way of determining the inevitable tradeoffs consists of decision criteria for weighing the relevant elements of the issues. Figure 11.1 shows a decision-making flow chart that can help managers carry out this process. This chart does not remove all subjectivity, but it summarizes the major questions that arise in social responsibility decisions. This process model is useful not only for examining organizational constraints, such as financial limits to philanthropic decisions, but also for clarifying many aspects of the manager's social role.

CIVIC DUTIES

How the manager's social role fits into the organizational context is illustrated by the problems of involvement in civic duties. The key characteristic is that such activities are largely external: participating in local government, political activities, or national and community groups espousing social concerns.

A difficult problem is the distinction between what managers do on their own time versus what they are permitted to do on company time and at company expense. Another is whether managers participating in civic affairs represent only themselves of their companies. Many companies, for example, regard a certain amount of civic effort as a contribution to society in the form of company time or other resources. It is natural that this form of philanthropy must be guarded against excesses, and that the costs are related in certain ways to company interests. For example, a pharmaceutical company may encourage its managers to work on fund-raising for multiple sclerosis research, but not for a garden club. Most firms are not strict about this, however, giving moderate support to the widespread interests of their managers.

Serving the government at company expense is often approved for brief periods. A notable case is the J. C. Penney Company, which loaned one of its top executives to New York City during its financial crisis in 1978. But when managers run for political office or otherwise are active in partisan politics, companies usually follow a policy of no support, and individuals participate on their private time.

Stretching the work day to include civic duties often results in fatigue and health problems that in turn arouse the frustration and hostility of family members, and lower the effectiveness of the manager's company performance. One solution to these problems is to establish departments of external affairs that can mediate the decisions and administer the outside activities of managers. Federated Stores, for example, broke external affairs out of the CEO's job at Rich's, one of its subsidiaries, and established a new position for this function.[47]

---

[47] *The Wall Street Journal*, June 11, 1980, p. 1.

Incident Case

In the XYZ Corporation, a major computer and business machine manufacturer, the vice-president of external affairs proposed to the chief executive officer and the board of directors that two specific programs be adopted to give evidence of the company's sense of social responsibility:

1. The company would pay the salaries of 20 employees who volunteer to work for one year on a social project of their choosing. Rationale: The company wants to put something back into society.
2. The company will detach 18 of its top professional people who have volunteered to teach for one year in colleges with predominantly minority enrollments. The company will pay their salaries and expenses.

What considerations enter into the appraisal of these proposals? What different points of view may come up?

Issues for Discussion and Analysis

1. One authority on social responsibility declares that "the day of plunder, human exploitation, financial chicanery and the robber barons has largely passed." Is this statement valid?

2. Should the job descriptions of first-line supervisors and middle-level managers include the expectations of top management concerning the performance of the manager's social role? Why or why not?

3. Evaluate the potentialities for incorporating social role concepts into the company's managerial training and development programs.

4. Since managers are heavily career-oriented and so fully indoctrinated in profits, productivity, and other economic objectives, how can the company go about adding social responsibility expectations into their jobs?

5. What special skills and talents do you think managers can bring to the problems of civic groups or government agencies that request their help?

6. What should a manager do when some action or plan of the company involves him or her in decisions that run counter to his or her conscience?

7. Argue for or against the statement that good ethics is good business.

8. If your business is about to go bankrupt, and it becomes apparent that a few desperate unethical decisions would help to avoid bankruptcy, what would you do, and why?

Class Project

Invite a chief executive officer or other top manager to a class session. Ask him or her to provide a list of outside activities, and to discuss the problems and benefits he or she has experienced in these activities.

For Further Reading

ANTHONY, P. D.   *Ideology of Work* (New York: Methuen, 1979).

THE CONFERENCE BOARD.   *Challenge to Leadership* (New York: Free Press, 1973).

EPSTEIN, EDWIN M., and DOW VOTAW (eds.).   *Legitimacy, Responsibility, and Rationality* (Santa Monica, Calif.: Goodyear, 1978).

GOLEMBIEWSKI, ROBERT T.   *Men, Management and Morality* (New York: McGraw-Hill, 1965).

HARRIS, R. BLAIN (ed.).   *Authority: A Philosophical Analysis* (University: University of Alabama Press, 1976).

LEONARD, GEORGE B.   *The Transformation* (New York: Delacorte Press, 1972).

LEVISON, ANDREW.   *The Working Class Majority* (New York: Coward, McCann and Geoghegan, 19).

MACCOBY, MICHAEL.   *The Gamesman* (New York: Simon and Schuster, 1976).

NISBET, ROBERT. *Twilight of Authority* (New York: Oxford University Press, 1975).

NOSSITER, BERNARD D.   *The Myth Makers* (Boston: Houghton Mifflin, 1964).

SENNETT, RICHARD.   *Authority* (New York: Knopf, 1980).

SENNETT, RICHARD.   *The Fall of Public Man* (New York: Random House, 1978).

PART IV

SOCIAL ISSUES
AND
MANAGERIAL STRATEGIES

12

Government, Business, and Public Policy

Democracy is a charming form of government, full of variety and disorder, dispensing a sort of equality to equals and unequals alike.

PLATO, *The Republic*, Book VIII

For forms of government let fools contest;
Whate'er is best administer'd is best.

ALEXANDER POPE

CONCEPTS DISCUSSED IN THIS CHAPTER

1. GOVERNMENT IN A REPRESENTATIVE DEMOCRACY
2. GOVERNMENT AS A SOCIAL INSTITUTION UNDER CAPITALISM
3. ISSUES IN PUBLIC POLICY
4. THE PUBLIC VERSUS PRIVATE INTERESTS
5. GOVERNMENT REFORM EFFORTS AND MANAGERIAL COMPETENCE

The effectiveness and success of the capitalistic, free enterprise system are closely linked to the system of government not only with respect to its form, but also to its ideals and the actions that influence business and political activity. Government, especially at the federal level, is in theory supposed to encourage and protect the business and economic system, and to restrain activities, such as monopoly, that are thought contrary to the public interest.

The Founding Fathers developed a remarkable Constitution for the United States which, though amended from time to time, has provided a lasting basic framework of checks and balances among the legislative, judicial, and executive branches of government. These mechanisms were designed to guard against tryanny, to preserve human rights, and to place government under the control of its citizens. This framework, now over 200 years old, has endured despite enormous growth in the population and change in the activities in which people engage. It has remained viable despite demands and conditions that could not have been anticipated in the beginning, and despite its faults, difficulties, and conflicts with rival systems.

In form our government is democratic republic. It is under popular rule through Congress, a system of representative, elective offices for legislative functions. It is augmented by an elaborate system of appointive offices for the executive functions, and a judicial system for interpreting and applying law in accordance with the Constitution. State and local units of government have unique jurisdictions, but are subject in numerous respects to the federal government.

In a direct democracy, rule is by the majority of citizens. In a representative democracy, a republic such as ours, rule is by majority in Congress, who are in turn elected by a majority or a plurality of the eligible voters who go to the polls. Since the majority could tyrannize the minority, the republic places constitutional limits on the powers of the majority to prevent it from doing things like violating the rights of the minority. Such a system requires an enlightened, educated citizenry with long-run sensitivity to the rights of minority groups. Democracy can fail and can suppress freedom, but constitutional safeguards can be preserved through vigilance and care.[1]

Democracy, with its espousal of freedom, carries inevitable risks. Freedom of thought welcomes criticism and the publicizing of mistakes, even those threatening to the established order. But this same freedom also makes it possible for a democracy to survive its mistakes by calling for the courage to admit them and to meet the challenges that bad news brings. As a result, there is a constant change process at work to enhance the system's vitality.

GOVERNMENT AS A SOCIAL INSTITUTION

An existing society reflects a balancing of the influences of its major social institutions. The driving forces within them are the values and ideals professed but imperfectly attained by society's members. Government becomes a primary social institution because of its pivotal place in the distribution of fundamental rights and duties and of the benefits of social cooperation. Government is thus at the center of human efforts to pursue values such as justice and equality.

---

[1] John Hospers, "The Course of Democracy," *The National Forum, Phi Kappa Phi Journal* 69 (Winter 1979), pp. 35–40.

> *Democracy is neither easy, quiet, orderly, nor safe. It assumes con-*
> *flict not only as the normal but also as the necessary condition of*
> *existence, and it defines itself as the continuing process of change.*
> *Change implies movement, which implies friction, which implies*
> *unhappiness. The structure of the idea resembles a suspension bridge*
> *rather than an Egyptian tomb. Its strength, which is the strength of*
> *life itself, depends upon stress and the balance struck between coun-*
> *tervailing forces. The idea collapses unless the stresses oppose one*
> *another with equal weight — unless enough people have enough cour-*
> *age to sustain the argument between government and the governed,*
> *between city and town, capital and labor, men and women, matter*
> *and mind.*
>
> LEWIS H. LAPHAM, "The Retreat from Democracy," *Harper's*,
> December 1977, pp. 11–16. ©1977 by Harper's Magazine. All rights
> reserved. Reprinted by special permission.

The institutional structure consists of established social positions; hierarchies of power, opportunity, and wealth persist. People born into different positions have different expectations of life as determined by political, economic, and social circumstance. Inequality, according to Rawls, persists because society's institutions favor certain starting places over others, and inequality is unjust. He argues that institutions are not only pervasive but affect people's initial chances in life; yet they cannot possibly be justified by appeal to merit. The justice of the social structure depends heavily on how fundamental rights and duties are assigned and on the economic opportunities and social conditions in the various sectors of society.[2]

Rawls' position is controversial, for it would seem to demand a forced equality of result, as opposed to equality of opportunity with rewards based on merit. Not even in totalitarian states has literal equality been achieved. Moreover, freedom suffers when property and justice are at the direct disposition of the state, which can withhold them from doubters and critics. Freedom of expression and opposition requires both resources and a system of law at some protective distance from the state, so that a healthy opposition has an economic and legal base.[3]

Government, as with other social institutions, has grown large and hard to understand, thereby creating fear and anxiety because values seem threatened. Geekie reasons that public schools do not provide most citizens with the structural mechanics necessary for a practical understanding of the interdependence of institutions. Hence we need better explanations of how such institutions actually work. The purpose of

---

[2] John Rawls, *A Theory of Justice* (Cambridge, Mass.: Harvard University Press, 1971), p. 7.

[3] Arthur Schlesinger, "The Future of Democracy," *The Wall Street Journal*, October 31, 1977, p. 14.

government, according to Geekie, is that of keeping the other institutions of society working—a residual responsibility not needed or brought into existence unless others fail. Therefore it is not surprising that government grows; it is a natural occurrence and not a sinister plot. Institutional failures are more abundant in a large, complex society, so government assumes the responsibility of propping them up.[4]

One sees examples of this popping up everywhere. In education, government tries to make the schools work better. In business, government rescues bankrupt companies. Transport services, urban problems, small business, crime, and health all illustrate problem-solving attempts in the form of enormous bureaucracies. Almost all our public agencies reflect the linking of government to the failures of other institutions, and indeed of citizens themselves.

In a democratic republic, the questions of how much government should there be, and what is the proper role of government are continuously debated.[5] Libertarians and right-wing groups assert that the least government is the best government.[6] Conservatives allow for a moderate role of government in a limited range of public interest issues.[7] They agree, for example, that monopolies must be curbed by governmental controls. Liberals, the Left, and radicals urge government remedies for social problems almost without restraint.[8]

Safeguarding liberty, justice, property, and the freedom of individuals is basic to good government, though it is difficult to perform since these abstractions are hard to apply in practice. This role, on the surface at least, is in conflict with the need to intervene in the activities of other institutions to keep them functioning properly. Is not such intervention an encroachment on the freedoms of the failing institutions? Geekie suggests that the need to intervene often follows from the encroachment of one institution on the rights of others that is harmful to the public in-

---

[4] William J. Geekie, "Letter from a Bureaucrat," *Across the Board* 15 (January 1978), pp. 40–46; see also Thomas E. Borcherding (ed.), *Budgets and Bureaucrats: The Sources of Government Growth* (Durham, N.C.: Duke University Press, 1977).

[5] Jethro K. Lieberman, "How Much Government?" *The Center magazine* 10 (May–June 1977), pp. 63–77; Roger A. Freedman, *The Growth of the American Government: The Morphology of the Welfare State* (Stanford, Calif.: Stanford University Press, 1975); David Fromkin, *The Question of Government: An Inquiry into the Breakdown of Modern Political Systems* (New York: Scribner's, 1975).

[6] Robert Nozick, *Anarchy, State, and Utopia* (New York: Basic Books, 1974). Hilaire Belloc, *The Servile State* (Indianapolis: Liberty Press/Liberty Classics, 1978, reprint of 1913 edition); Alan Crawford, *Thunder on the Right: The "New Right" and the Politics of Resentment* (New York: Pantheon, 1980; Harold O. J. Brown, *The Reconstruction of the Republic* (New York: Arlington House, 1977).

[7] Auberon E. W. Herbert, *The Right and Wrong of Compulsion by the State, and Other Essays* (Indianapolis: Liberty Press/Liberty Classics, 1978, reprint of an earlier edition); Herman Goldstein, *Policing a Free Society* (Cambridge, Mass.: Ballinger, 1977); James M. Buchanan, *The Limits of Liberty* (Chicago: The University of Chicago Press, 1975); W. Allen Wallis, *The Overgoverned Society* (New York: Free Press, 1976).

[8] John Kenneth Galbraith, *The New Industrial State*, 3rd ed. (Boston: Houghton Mifflin, 1978); Henry Fairlie, "In Defense of Big Government," *The New Republic* 174 (March 13, 1976), pp. 24–27.

terest. When, for example, a manufacturing firm pollutes the environment, government intervenes for the health and survival of all citizens. This changes the firm's behavior by stopping it from harming others, which is not the same as curtailing the legitimate freedom of those involved.[9]

The sections that follow will further analyze the role of government with respect to (1) public policy issues, and (2) government organization, management, and reform.

PUBLIC POLICY ISSUES

Our pluralistic society, coupled with freedom of thought and expression, and valuing the pursuit of self-interest as long as it does not harm others, means that government faces the many demands of special interest groups. Ideally actions and decisions in response to these pressures are preceded by a logical analysis of goals and priorities, followed by a rational assessment of resources and costs. Following these steps, methods and programs can be worked out. The realities are otherwise: ends and means are not always clearly distinguished, problems are not clearly defined and in any case the major ones are ill-structured by nature; political considerations are inevitable in governmental planning and action; and pressures spell urgencies that preclude the adequate analysis of relevant information.

The determination of goals and priorities is a difficult process that defies our ability to understand it. One major study attempting to do so reported that the cause of ineffective government is a lack of competence rather than a matter of policies or of ends and purposes.[10] Others, who see fundamental disagreements over the relationship of the public and private sectors, and even over the meaning of justice, equality, or liberty, and conflicting views of problems such as energy or environmental issues, are probably closer to the root causes of our difficulties.

This raises doubts that better management in the technical sense would suffice to restore the public's confidence in government. Questions of competence, even when legitimate, make scapegoating possible. Bureaucrats are blamed for our ailments, even though they may administer programs and policies quite well. Bureaucrats and politicians in turn blame "the people" or "the public," ascribing failures to greed, selfishness, or disinterest.[11]

Public policy today has been expanded to include new functions and

---

[9] Geekie, "Letter from a Bureaucrat," p. 44.

[10] Joseph A. Pechman (ed.), *Setting National Priorities: Agenda for the 1980s* (Washington, D.C.: The Brookings Institution, 1980).

[11] Irving Kristol, "Blame It on the People," *The Wall Street Journal,* July 19, 1974, p. 14.

aims. This expansion of government activity Bell calls the "revolution of rising entitlements." Governmental functions were formerly confined to those which individuals could not do themselves or which were common necessities: military defense, highways, postal services, and the like. In the 1930s government began to assume a direct responsibility for the health of the economy, which led to the social security program, revenue sharing, controls over monetary supply, pricing policies, and transfer payments effecting the redistribution of incomes. The 1940s brought World War II and government participation in the reconstruction of Germany and Japan. In the 1950s a government effort emerged to influence science and technology, at first for military reasons but later more broadly. In the 1960s a host of social policy commitments developed to redress problems such as civil rights, poverty, health care, environmental problems, and many other features of the system.[12]

A new public philosophy is effecting changes in public policy: materialism and hedonism are declining in the emerging postindustrial society. Working with survey data collected from the United States and ten Western European countries between 1968 and 1976, Inglehart predicts a new postmaterialistic outlook, combined with new political skills among the masses that enable them to intervene successfully in political processes. The postmaterialistic outlook is more concerned with self-expression and the quality of life than with acquisition and physical security. Education, a product of affluence, is the strongest predictor of postmaterialism, whose values are twice as common among university graduates as among primary school graduates. Nevertheless, he feels that postmaterialistic values are percolating down to the blue-collar workers. Increasingly, the young are demanding participation in making decisions, not merely in selecting the decision makers. Their participation is likely to be intense, unconventional, and activist, but not so radical as modern conscious-raising techniques would imply.[13]

Figure 12.1 shows the administrative structure by which the federal government carries out its special programs for assistance to various program beneficiaries.

PRESSURE GROUP INFLUENCES

The era of rising entitlements, the demands for equality and other "rights," instant communications, the spirit of activism, the presence of real needs due to a variety of conditions, and the eagerness of politicians to please constituents, and the eagerness of politicians to please constituents all work together to foster movements and interest groups. These

---

12 Daniel Bell, "The Revolution of Rising Entitlements," *Fortune*, April 1975, pp. 99–103 and 185–187.
13 Ronald Inglehart, *The Silent Revolution: Changing Values and Political Styles among Western Publics* (Princeton, N.J.: Princeton University Press, 1977).

FIGURE 12.1

Administrative Levels Used in Providing Assistance to Program Beneficiaries

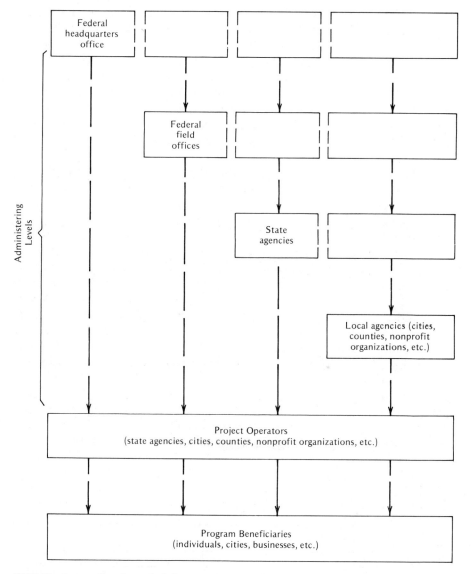

SOURCE: *Comptroller General of the United States.* The Federal Government Should But Doesn't Know the Cost of Administering Its Assistance Programs, *GGD-77-87 (Washington, D.C.: U.S. General Accounting Office, 1978), p. 3*

groups are well organized and provided with capable leadership, and attain considerable power to influence government. This abets the piecemeal nature of public policy, for the groups are often in contention over conflicting aims and demands. For example, the demands of environmentalists for bans on toxic substances may be opposed by farmers who need to kill crop insects for better harvests.

The conflicts among pressure groups and between the groups and the administrative-legislative branches of government are basic. A central issue is how to balance the demands of special interests for preferential treatment against the need to act impartially in the public interest. In the balancing effort, questions of the legitimacy of demands arise, along with considerations of the scope, influence, styles, and impact of the interactions between the state and pressure groups.

Table 12.1 presents a classification of these factors according to four types of interactions with varying impacts. *Legitimate* interactions reflect acceptance of pressure groups, which are legally and officially involved in making and implementing policy. This kind of involvement is found principally in West Germany, the Low Countries, and Scandinavia. *Clientela* relationships exist when an interest group is accepted by an agency as the natural expression and representative of a given social sector, as when the U.S. Chamber of Commerce speaks for business interests. A *parantela* relationship describes a situation in which an interest group and the government have a close fraternal tie (kinship) with each other. It is found in countries, such as France, Italy, or Latin American nations, which have a single dominant political party. *Illegitimate* group processes exist where interactions are outside normal political relationships but occur anyway. They are often the result of efforts to suppress pluralism, or occur when a group does not represent the constituency it claims.

According to Peters, the extent of conflict between the state and its interest groups varies widely among cultures, but most societies have

TABLE 12.1

Types of Interaction between Pressure Groups and Bureaucracy

Types	*Scope*	*Influence*	*Style*	*Impact*
Legitimate	Broad	Great	Bargaining	Redistribution/self-regulation
Clientela	Narrow	Moderate	Symbiosis	Self-regulation/distribution
Parantela	Narrow	Moderate	Kinship	Regulation/distribution
Illegitimate	Variable	None/great	Confrontation	None/redistribution

SOURCE: *This table drawn from "Insiders and Outsiders: The Politics of Pressure Group Influence on Bureaucracy" by B. Guy Peters is reprinted from* Administration and Society *Vol. 9, No. 2 (August 1977) pp. 191-218 by permission of the Publisher, Sage Publications, Inc.*

found ways to ameliorate the conflict, achieving extensive group coexistence and collaboration.[14] It is a tribute to our pluralistic system in the United States that there is substantial accommodation in these types of conflict.

Nevertheless, there can be considerable knocking about in the pursuit of rights and benefits. Rousseau contributed the idea of the *social contract*, a philosophy of containment of pressures so as to minimize harm. The social contract is an unspoken agreement that in order to live together in society, we must forego things that we might otherwise want or claim the right to do. Humans lose by the social contract a degree of natural liberty, in return acquiring a civil liberty limited by the general will of the people. The social contract is a dynamic process, evolving in accordance with basic changes in society.

Laws are created to restrain or punish those who do not accept the social contract. Civil laws codify prohibited behaviors such as murder or theft, but they depend on their prior acceptance of restrictions by society as a whole. The social contract is a very subtle idea, but it is necessary if society is to hold together. It makes it possible to assume that physicians will treat the sick, lawyers defend the accused, the old will rear the young, and the like. The social contract thus covers many of the assumptions we make about how life's problems are met in society.

The clash of interests often leads to events that appear to violate the social contract, and even the laws that support it. Interest groups crusade on moral as well as technical or other grounds, in the effort to secure rights or entitlements. Public sector strikes, such as those among police, firefighters, or groups in a position to disrupt large sectors of the economic or political system, fall into this category.[15]

PUBLIC VS. PRIVATE INTERESTS

The private sector includes the people generally, and their representative interest groups. The public sector, with its professionals, bureaucrats, and politicians, includes an array of government agencies and a vast number of officials and workers at federal, state, and local levels. These may be grouped by interests such as military, health, educational, welfare, highways.

The concepts of private and public interests are hard to come to grips with in practical situations. In fact, the two sets of interests are heavily intertwined, and it is hard to differentiate mere slogans from the real interests at issue. Proposals for even further intertwining come even from

---

[14] B. Guy Peters, "Insiders and Outsiders: The Politics of Pressure Group Influence on Bureaucracy," *Administration and Society*, August 1977, pp. 191–218.

[15] John Guinther, *Moralists and Managers: Public Interest Movements in America* (Garden City, N.Y.: Doubleday, 1976).

business executives who, for example, need the government's help in meeting foreign competition. The urgency of social problem solving intensifies the linkages between the public and private sectors, with conflicts reflected in a host of budgetary and cost problems. The processes of public choice amid such conflicts are extremely complex.[16]

It is in the American tradition that many individuals and private groups choose to serve the public interest; the furtherance of public purpose is not a government monopoly. There is an enormous number of organizations in the nonprofit sector that pump money philanthropically into the pursuit of public aims. Many of these are oriented toward the local community — a healthy opposition to the inordinate dependence on the federal government that has emerged. Gardner argues that we need to restore our battered sense of community and to involve people in coherent social groupings, such as families, neighborhoods, and communities. Not every problem requires large-scale, costly organization.[17]

The distinction between public and private interests has become less clear as government has assumed increasing responsibilities for meeting social problems. Two sets of phenomena are at work: (1) the government has called increasingly for the assistance and involvement of nonprofit organizations, and (2) new forms of organization, quasi-public in character, are a blend of public and private efforts.

The nonprofit organizations to which the government turns are numerous, but they can be considered in terms of three main categories: private, quasi-public, and public. *Private purpose* organizations helpful to government include a variety of types such as social, fraternal, civic, literary, patriotic, athletic, and agricultural. Farmer or consumer cooperatives, chambers of commerce, trade associations, labor unions, and scientific or professional societies are examples. *Quasi-public organizations* are organized for purposes generally recognized as relating to the public interest. These include foundations, universities, voluntary hospitals, "think tanks," museums, libraries, and the like. *Public organizations* are created by the government to fulfill special purposes outside the regular government establishment. They take the form of "authorities" such as the Tennessee Valley Authority, government corporations, public benefit agencies, research units, and the like. The U.S. Postal Service, Amtrak, and the Federal Deposit Insurance Corporation are familiar examples.[18] Linkages between the private and the public sector are also provided in the form of presidential commissions, which are usually relatively temporary and used to investigate problems, study alternatives, or authenticate a government interest.

---

[16] Clifford S. Russell, *Collective Decision Making: Applications from Public Choice Theory* (Baltimore: Resources for the Future, Inc., 1980).

[17] John W. Gardner, "The Private Pursuit of Public Purpose," *The Chronicle of Higher Education,* January 8, 1979, p. 96; Andrew S. McFarland, *Public Interest Lobbies: Decision Making on Energy* (Washington, D.C.: American Enterprise Institute, 1976).

[18] John J. Corson, *Business in a Humane Society* (New York: McGraw-Hill, 1971).

> *Few young men of high gifts and fine tastes look forward to enter-*
> *ing public life, for the probability of disappointments and vexations of*
> *a life in Congress so far outweigh its attractions that nothing but*
> *exceptional ambition or a strong sense of public duty suffices to draw*
> *such men into it. Law, education, literature, the higher walks of*
> *commerce, finance, or railway work offer a better prospect of enjoy-*
> *ment or distinction.*
>
> LORD JAMES BRYCE, *The American Commonwealth*, 1893.

There has thus been substantial innovation in the design of combinations of private and public elements of organization design. Although the extent of these arrangements is often confusing and very costly, the advantage is that specialized talents, outside views and experiences, and citizen participation can be brought together. Such frameworks allow for considerable managerial independence, and also for essential public controls or influences over work on public issues.

But turning to consultants, commissions, and nonprofit organizations is only a partial answer for social problems. What is also required is to elect and appoint the most capable persons to public positions, for it is they who must take formal action. It is difficult even for the most able members of Congress to judge the long-term effects of policy alternatives, and easy to vote politically for constituent interests, real or imagined. The life and work styles of congressional members is not conducive to reflective, general policy analysis. Faced with an enormous work burden, they have specialized in narrow segments of interest. In an analysis of how House members spend their time, for example, it was found that each has only an average of 11 minutes a day to think about public policy. To deal with increased legislative, mail, and casework chores, congressional staffs have tripled since 1957. In 1976, for example, the Senate employed more than 1500 staff members and 3200 staff aides. The House had 1548 committee-staff persons and 7000 aides on personal staffs.[19]

SOCIAL PROGRAMS

Since the 1960s there has been a proliferation of social programs requiring many new bureaucratic agencies. In their efforts to ameliorate society's problems, legislators translate issues into public policy, and then to programs and newly created agencies. Older units seldom quit, so that overlapping occurs and the costs of programming remain high. The fortunes

---

[19] Michael A. Scully, "Well-Meaning Government," *Harper's*, August 1980, p. 14; Michael J. Malbin, *Unelected Representatives: Congressional Staff and the Future of Representative Government* (New York: Basic Books, 1980); Harrison W. Fox, Jr., and Susan Webb Hammond, *Congressional Staffs: The Invisible Force in American Lawmaking* (New York: Free Press, 1977).

of interest groups become identified with them; and emotional, philosophical, and other normative ties help to preserve programs indefinitely.

Programs have the advantage of incorporating various incentives for the implementation of public policy. Schultze notes that incentives are necessary because the attainment of national objectives increasingly depends on the joint action of many independent decision makers, private as well as public, and because the growing complexity and geographical diversity of public programs requires decentralized decision making within the public sector itself. Management in the form of a structure of incentives, rules, organizational structures, performance measures, and penalties and rewards is necessary to ensure that the results of public programs coincide with their original objectives.[20]

Efforts to build incentives into social programs have been widely questioned. Contrary to Schultze's integrative, managerial orientation, Lindblom and Hirschman suggest that an unbalanced economy may be more productive and quicker to develop than a balanced one, that a carefully thought out plan of research may be a hindrance rather than a help in achieving the desired goal, and that sometimes it may be easier to solve a problem if it is not fully understood. They cite other research to show that development is both less costly and more speedy when marked by duplication, confusion, and lack of communication among people working along parallel lines. They argue against too strenuous attempts at integrating various subsystems into a well-articulated, harmonious, general system, and advocate the full exploitation of fruitful ideas regardless of their fit to some preconceived pattern of specifications.[21]

Earlier, Lindblom suggested that there is no intrinsic merit to methodical, systematic, or scientific decision making. In examining the decision behavior of public administrators, he found that actual decision making departs considerably from the traditional model of rational, step-by-step choice procedures with clear objectives, policy formulation through means-end analysis, and every important relevant factor taken into account. Instead, he found that the selection of value goals and empirical analysis is often inappropriate or limited, that the test of a good policy is that various analysts can agree on it even though they cannot agree that it is the most appropriate means to an accepted objective, and that important possible outcomes, potential policies, and values are neglected.[22]

For deep-seated social and economic problems, it tends to be political

[20] Charles L. Schultze, "The Role of Incentives, Penalties, and Rewards in Attaining Effective Policy," in *The Analysis and Evaluation of Public Expenditures: The PPB System*, Joint Economic Committee, Congress of the United States, vol. 1, 1976, pp. 87–98.

[21] Albert O. Hirschman and Charles E. Lindblom, "Economic Development, Research and Development, Policy Making: Some Converging Views," *Behavioral Science*, April 1961, pp. 211–222.

[22] Charles E. Lindblom, "The Science of 'Muddling Through'," *Public Administration Review* 19 (Spring 1959), pp. 79–88.

leaders in government, acting in behalf of the public or segments of it, who authenticate the problems to which resources will be devoted in search of solutions or improvements. But these leaders are as much political beings as they are managers; managers on the scene of action are hired or appointed. And in programming, the contest for votes arouses political conflicts between would-be reformers in politics and the functioning of the governmental system. Tax revolts are a reflection of voter frustration with complex programs of political origin. But reformers, if elected, fail to achieve many of their reform goals, as the weight of bureaucracy makes itself felt. And the price of problem-solving programs is very high. In the absence of consistent policy and adequate planning, we have been unable to buy our way into a better society.[23] Program evaluation presents major difficulties and uncertainties.[24] Another problem is finding able administrators who know how to balance humane considerations with the bureaucratic structure of new programs.

Administrators or managers are not necessarily the prime movers in defining problems or choosing the methods by which they will be solved. They come into the picture later, after resources have been allocated and policies formed by legislators. Actions are then taken according to administrative interpretations of legislative intent. Although the latitudes of discretion within this framework are very broad, programs nevertheless reflect some degree of problem definition, accompanied by funding or budgets, and a time span. There are start-up and operating costs measured in both time and money. A program's existence implies organized, coordinated effort, with progress measured by the time span and the expenditure of money, as well as by results. Some programs, it is true, are indefinite, but here progress is measured in periods such as fiscal years, and the fortunes of the program swing with changing fiscal events.

Programs tend to proliferate and overlap. For example, one investigator located 44 publicly financed manpower programs in New York City, but he was not certain even after diligent search that all of them had been found. There are overlapping levels and jurisdictions, bringing into play the conflict of political factors at state, local, national, or regional levels. A further problem in programming is the high degree of normative, emotional involvement. Program directors and staff specialists are not selected primarily for their administrative or managerial abilities, but more for their commitment to the ideals and values the programs are

[23] John E. Tropman et al. (eds.), *Strategic Perspectives on Social Policy* (New York: Pergamon Press, 1976); "After 15 Years of 'Great Society' Spending," *U.S. News and World Report,* June 30, 1980, pp. 36–38; George W. Downs, Jr., *Bureaucracy, Innovation, and Public Policy* (Lexington, Mass.: Lexington Books, 1976).

[24] Marvin Weisinger, Isabel P. Robinault, and Eleanor Carol Bennett (eds.), *Program Evaluation: Selected Readings* (New York: Research Utilization Laboratory, 1975); Daniel Katz, Barbara A. Crutek, Robert L. Kahn, and Eugenia Barton, *Bureaucratic Encounters: A Pilot Study in the Evaluation of Government Services* (Ann Arbor: Institute for Social Research, University of Michigan, 1975).

taken to represent. There is a difference in the affective or emotional content of what is being done in the public sector compared to what is done in the private sector. In a business firm, involvement and commitment are often verbalized and may be present in some individuals to varying degrees and at varying times, but the mantle is lightly worn.

From the premise of a high degree of emotionality and idealism, we may logically hypothesize a concept of *mission intensity*. The greater the intensity of the mission of the unit, the greater the propensity to dispense with formal organizational and administrative arrangements. As emotional values and commitment increase, we move from the style of management advocated by Schultze toward that recommended by Lindblom. A serious consequence of mission intensity is the desire to dispense with formal arrangements, to short-circuit administrative procedures, to get on with the job, and to cut out the "red tape."

To the other problems of program management in the public sector we must add the constraint of citizen participation, for it intensifies the emotional components and adds to the pressures to short-circuit management technique in favor of mission-oriented, quick results. The Economic Opportunity Act of 1964, for example, provided that community action programs must be "developed, conducted, and administered with the maximum feasible participation of residents in the area and members of groups served." The impact of such a provision depends, of course, on its interpretation and application, and the purpose and nature of citizen participation is not always clear. It can mean (1) that there should be a grassroots democracy in which all citizens take an active role in collaborative relationship, so that those being helped can, through active roles in decision making, get the kind of help they need and improve their sense of social worth, or (2) involvement in the actual delivery of services, serving as day-care workers and the like, thereby raising their economic status and self-respect.

PATERNALISM

It would be wrong to suppose that the government's social programming stems only from the need to respond to the increasing demands of an era of rising entitlements. Once the machinery is set in motion, it begins to acquire a momentum that encourages origination by government rather than according to grass-roots needs. Government programs now go far beyond the traditional ones — schools, police and fire protection, highways, military defense. They have come to include a host of programs that impose some people's values, often those of bureaucrats, on others. Paternalism is deciding what is good for other people whether they agree or not. To the extent that paternalism is present, it is an insidious intrusion into the private lives of people. It is also wasteful and inefficient, and its costs preclude devoting funds to other, perhaps more important, uses.[25]

  There are also moral issues in the excessive invasion of human lives.

FIGURE 12.2

Factors in Federal Influence

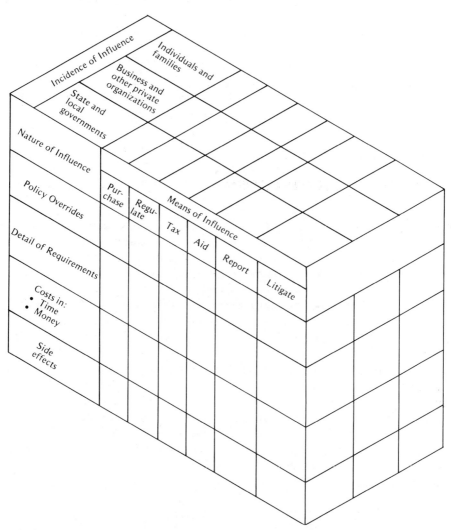

SOURCE: *Report of Advisory Commission on Intergovernmental Relations,* The Federal Role in the Federal System: The Dynamics of Growth *(Washington, D.C.: U.S. Government Printing Office, 1980), p. 81.*

[25] Milton Friedman, "The Paternal State," *Newsweek,* January 22, 1979, p. 56.

George Will writes of the "therapeutic ethic" that has invaded public policy. This ethic is the idea that the morally correct way to cope with problem people, nations, or pressure groups is to provide social services that remove the causes of antisocial behavior. Religious groups, particularly the evangelical movements, are increasingly injecting moralism into politics in their opposition to social programs.[26]

Offsetting the paternalistic drawbacks one may argue persuasively that the humane considerations underlying social programs are compelling. No one advocates poverty, ill health, neglect, and uncontrolled inflation. But disagreements arise over means, not ends. Some do not wish to solve social problems by constructing a welfare state or at the expense of waste and inefficiency. The dependence on government for protection against any and all risk by groups and individuals can reflect serious flaws of character in those who succumb to it.[27] The scope of the federal government's influence in society is illustrated in Figure 12.2.

MANAGEMENT, REORGANIZATION, AND GOVERNMENT REFORM

A great deal of invective and moral outrage is being directed against the activities as well as the form of government. Muckrakers have a field day excoriating the enormous waste, mismanagement, inefficiency, fraud, and corruption. But government remains a behemoth, impenetrable to reform or reorganization efforts. Muckrakers, investigative reporters, and researchers come up with many cases arousing anger and outrage, but they are short on explanations of causes and the direction remedies might take. Their cases are shortly thereafter forgotten in a flood of new accusations.

Efforts to abate the flood of proliferating services and regulations are engulfed in misapprehensions about the causes of problems. The recipients of services and benefits are not to blame. They are behaving rationally. The real users are at a secondary level—those who provide services to the primary recipients, thereby gaining jobs or business advantages, and people generally who willingly or by default turn problems over to the government that might be handled better in other ways. We are a nation of "government service addicts."[28]

---

[26] George F. Will, "Who Put Morality into Politics?" *Newsweek*, September 15, 1980, p. 108. See also J. Dudley McClain, Jr., "Political Morality, Governmental Responsiveness, and Citizen Support," *National Forum, Phi Kappa Phi Journal* 56 (Summer 1976), pp. 3–8.

[27] For a broad analysis of social planning and control, see Morris Janowitz, *The Last Half-Century: Societal Change in Politics in America* (Chicago: The University of Chicago Press, 1978); Committee for Economic Development, *Redefining the Government's Role in the Market System* (New York: Committee for Economic Development, July 1979).

[28] Gerald J. Thompson, "Government Services—A Dangerous Addiction," *U.S. News and World Report*, June 23, 1980, pp. 75–76.

Another misapprehension is that it is often believed that better management or government reform somehow is the answer to failing or questionable programs. Desirable as these may be, they evade the deeper conceptual issues underlying programs and activities. It is difficult to question the rationale or purpose of programs with helping missions, since the critic would be seen as opposing the grand purpose itself rather than the means by which the purpose is being achieved. Questioning the millions of dollars spent on preventing child abuse easily translates to favoring the neglect of child abuse problems.

Another serious flaw in social problem solving by government is that more money is the answer. A bureaucrat whose agency is unsuccessful is not likely to criticize its concept or to recommend its abolition. Instead, pressures are directed to obtain even more funds to rescue a faltering situation. It is doubtful that better management or reform of governmental structures or procedures will go to the heart of the major issues facing the nation. Nevertheless, there is intrinsic merit in making government as efficient and cost-effective as possible. Successful reforms would go far toward restoring confidence in government and in reducing the burdens of taxation and government intervention. We noted in Chapter 6, however, that reforms are extremely difficult to achieve, and that they often raise problems greater than those they attempt to solve. It is not generally believed that constitutional changes are necessary in order to achieve political or government reform, or to solve our major social problems. Our political system adapts to changing needs by gradual, often unnoticed changes in habits and procedures.[29]

POLITICAL AND GOVERNMENT REFORM

All reform efforts sooner or later involve governmental and political processes and issues. Therefore, efforts to reform government itself are particularly important, since reforms in other areas depend heavily on how well our government functions.

Political and government reforms are related but separate targets of attention. Political reforms focus on the behavior of politicians, the problems of election campaigns, the representation of citizen interests, the functions and behavior of political parties, and the like. Government reforms focus on problems of administration, organization, budgeting, finance, programs, public policy, the nature of bureaucracy, and the behavior of government officials. Reform efforts in both sectors have great political appeal, but enormous obstacles to genuine reform are numerous.

Political and government reform efforts are fragmented and piecemeal in nature, whereas a comprehensive reform agenda projected over a

---

[29] Henry Fairlie, "Constitutional Complaints," *Harper's*, June 1980, pp. 27–36; Bob Eckhardt and Charles Black, *The Tides of Power* (New Haven, Conn.: Yale University Press, 1980).

decade would make sense. Long-range planning needs to be directed at complicated interrelated federal, state, and local activities to realign and clarify their missions and procedures. The difficulty lies not only in the effort required, but also in the fact that it does not fit election cycles. Politicians promise reforms, only to discover in office how hard it is to accomplish them.

Reforms advocated in recent years are aimed at reducing waste, duplication, the cost of government, unnecessary paperwork, overregulation, and "bureaucratese." Moderate progress has been made. At a broader level, efforts are being made toward tax reform, welfare reform, finance and budgetary reform, social security reform, and the like.

> *The best political community is formed by citizens of the middle class. Those states are likely to be well administered in which the middle class is large, and larger if possible than both the other classes, or at any rate than either singly; for the addition of the middle class turns the scale and prevents either of the extremes from being dominant.*
>
> ARISTOTLE, *Politics*, Book IV.

Political reforms, such as the Campaign Reform Law of 1974, often make matters worse instead of better. This law limited the amounts individuals can contribute to campaigns and also permitted corporations to set up political action committees (PACs) which can contribute to campaigns. These "reforms" strengthened single-issue, ideological, special interest groups of the Left and Right by drying up individual campaign contributions that could counterbalance them. These groups can now spend their money to influence policy in ways congressional reformers cannot get at. Such groups find their strength not in financial resources, but in skillful use of the media and their ability to mobilize grassroots support.[30]

The cumulative impact of a large number of reforms tending to professionalize our politicians is also interesting as an unintended consequence. A number of laws now tend to isolate and protect the politicians, much as bureaucrats are shielded in the civil service system. Ethics laws, disclosure and divestment practices, rules about what individuals can and cannot do after leaving office, and restrictions on writing, speaking, and advising all lead to divorcing the elected or the appointed official from his or her past and future. The aim of keeping politicians from undesirable temptations and influences is understandable, but one may still question whether insulating them from the world is wise. There is

---

[30] *The Wall Street Journal*, August 7, 1979, p. 20.

evidence that these "reforms" have caused a substantial number of members of Congress to leave political life, and have made government jobs unattractive to high-caliber managerial talent.[31]

GOVERNMENT REORGANIZATION

Reform efforts directed at government reorganization are popular with politicians because of their appeal to the public demands for efficiency and for restraining "big government." The growth of governmental services and other activities has resulted in a huge structural apparatus with agencies, boards, councils, programs, commissions, and bureaus overlapping, competing, and compounding the costs of government.

The result of big government is that almost everyone can get something, and almost everyone can find something to be offended about. Efforts to curb government, if taken seriously, mean that services would be reduced, programs would be canceled, and other ways of meeting needs would have to be found. Powerful lobbies therefore come to the rescue of their own interests, while advocating that it is others which must be cut. It is a paradox that while government grows in response to "needs" and demands, people become less satisfied with it, as evidenced by voter turnouts and surveys that show people do not understand the government as they once did.

This paradox explains why some observers refer to "the decline of the national government," or to the "retreat from democracy."[32] Anxieties arise over waste, inefficiency, corruption, and the intrusion of government into private lives and business activities on a scale never experienced in this country before. Organizational as well as legislative and other reforms are increasingly demanded.

Organizational reform is thus only a partial response to these anxieties. But better organization would go far to restore the confidence of people in the workings of the government. The trouble is that any substantial proposal for reorganization must be coordinated with Congress, with political factors thus affecting the decisions. In sum, a powerful assortment of resistance forces combat change: legislators, lobbies and interest groups, and government employees whose jobs or empires are threatened. The overlapping of interests within government itself is illustrated in Figure 12.3, which shows congressional relationships with what was then the cabinet department called Health, Education and Welfare (HEW).

---

[31] Meg Greenfield, *Newsweek*, June 18, 1979, p. 96; *The Wall Street Journal*, April 3, 1978, p. 20; Otis G. Pike, "Goodbye to Congress and All That," *Harper's*, June 1978, pp. 94–96.

[32] Lewis H. Lapham, "The Retreat from Democracy," *Harper's*, December 1977; Robert J. Pranger, *The Decline of the National Government* Reprint No. 40 (Washington, D.C.: American Enterprise Institute, 1976)

FIGURE 12.3

Charts of Multiple Jurisdictions

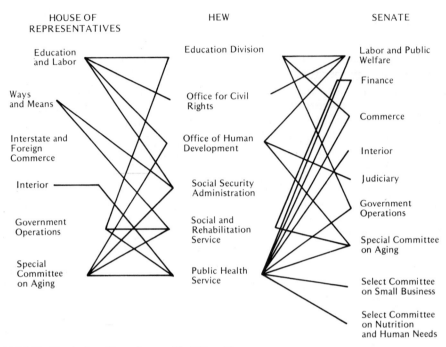

SOURCE: Birmingham News, *January 23, 1977, p. F1.*

It is virtually impossible to attach reliable cost-savings figures to cut-backs that are made. Often those cut from one agency are merely transferred to other agencies. After the cuts, agancies may again grow to their former size. Claims for net savings to taxpayers have to be regarded cautiously. In 1977, the OMB itself took a cut of 139 persons from its staff of 709, but 83 of these were placed elsewhere in government.[33] Reorganization efforts succeed better when directed at the less important agencies such as Civil Defense, the Immigration and Naturalization Service, or data processing units. Many changes do not represent cutting at all, but rather recombinations or relocations of agencies, or changes in titles. This kind of shuffling tends to lower morale as well as to confine reorganization to process functions rather than basic structural implementations of major goals.[34]

---

[33] "Reorganization Loses Out to Politics," *Business Week*, August 1, 1977, p. 22.

[34] Stephen Hess, "Reorganization Revisited," *The Wall Street Journal*, September 25, 1978, p. 28; and Peter F. Drucker, "Meaningful Reorganization," *The Wall Street Journal*, February 4, 1977, p. 12.

The Reorganization Act of 1977 was passed to facilitate presidential reorganization of the federal government, as President Carter had promised in his campaign for office. Despite the power of the president's office, reorganization efforts proceeded slowly and met firm roadblocks. Major reorganizations involve many competing interests that can bring pressure against change. Reorganization by consolidation and merger threatens empires and jobs, as well as interests in Congress, the U.S. Civil Service Commission, the Office of Management and Budget, and the units that stand to gain or lose by proposed changes. Congressional Oversight Committees are created to protect constituents, recipients, or beneficiaries of services. Unions, employees, and activist groups threaten strikes, picketing, and other opposition tactics. While attrition policies have been somewhat successful during staffing cutbacks, inequalities of treatment and unfairness do occur. Civil service regulations interfere in various ways with the retention, transfer, pay, and dismissal problems associated with reorganization.[35]

Reorganization is so difficult and complex that even small successes come only with great cost in terms of working time, and the costs of research, planning, and gaining support for proposals. The psychic costs of anxiety and dislocations reveal an enormous but unmeasurable human cost. The main alternatives are to operate with less than perfect structures which accept some drawbacks such as duplication, and head off organizational problems by better attention to structural problems when new agencies come into being.

BETTER MANAGEMENT

The two alternatives just cited both indicate the role of managerial skills, theories, and techniques in government administration. Government activity is a special monopoly involving the public trust. The public, too, has a responsibility for active, informed participation in government affairs.

The application of management expertise in running the government and solving social problems is a worthy aim that should receive continuous attention. However, we should be aware of the special problems that pertain to management in government. Running the government is not the same as running a business or directing a voluntary association. One of the main problems is therefore to recognize that this special context has unique characteristics, especially those related to the values surrounding each problem or activity, and to the political ramifications of

---

[35] For an excellent discussion of these and related problems, see Michael P. Balzano, *Reorganizing the Federal Bureaucracy: The Rhetoric and the Reality, Studies in Political and Social Process* (Washington, D.C.: American Enterprise Institute, 1977).

every government plan or decision. Administrative modes of behavior must often give way to these other considerations.

It is difficult for managers to act in the private or the public contexts with respect to overall systems influences and requirements. Actual, probable, and intended consequences are hard to discern, and unintended consequences follow from the failure to think beyond the confines of a single unit. One agency's solution often impinges on other agencies for which that solution poses new problems. In large-scale government activities, there are bound to be serious mistakes. Computers, operations research, and econometric techniques often compound errors in a costly way. For example, a 1974 study concluded, based on a computer programming error, that Social Security had seriously depressed personal savings. Policies were adopted based on the findings. Another research team discovered the error, throwing grave doubt on the policies.[36]

Gulick goes so far as to assert that "the present challenge is not primarily managerial; it is first of all ethical and political, and it is aimed at the core of our democratic faith." Government cannot rely solely on doing its work, delivering services, allocating resources, increasing productivity or improving management in general. It is also necessary to define goals, set ethical standards, develop the undeveloped, educate voters, apply new technologies, and evaluate results.[37] Only a very broad definition of management would encompass all this. Malek, a former high-level government official, agrees that management reform alone will not solve the ills of government, but he is optimistic about the possibilities of improvement. He believes that management in government lacks discipline. There are bad appointments, wrong dismissals, training failures, coverups of mistakes, crisis orientations, self-protective bureaucracies, and failures to fix accountability.[38] These problems are amenable to modern management techniques.

Evaluation of managerial practice in government is difficult because program, agency, or the administrator's results are hard to evaluate. Goals are broad, unclear, varied, and even contradictory. For example, is the U.S. Employment Service trying to help poor people get jobs, or to help employers find low-cost labor? Methods of calculating costs, benefits, productivity, efficiency, and the like are primitive or nonexistent.

In addition to congressional investigations, reviews, and other forms of oversight, entire agencies are created as "watchdog units" to spotlight difficulties, uncover bad management, or check deviations from policy.

---

[36] *Business Week*, September 22, 1980, p. 25.

[37] Luther Gulick, "Democracy and Administration Face the Future," *Public Administration Review* 37 (November–December 1977), pp. 706–707.

[38] Frederic V. Malek, *Washington's Hidden Tragedy: The Failure to Make Government Work* (New York: Free Press, 1978).

One such agency is the Advisory Commission on Intergovernmental Relations, created in 1959. Its mandate is to observe and report on allocations of governmental functions. It has recognized serious allocation problems and advanced far-reaching solutions. For example, it has suggested that some functions, such as welfare, be taken over completely by the federal government while others, such as educational grants, police support, and the like be handed over to the state and local levels.[39] The General Accounting Office (GAO) is another such watchdog agency. Its activities have aroused storms of controversy, especially among those who see it as encroaching on areas in which it has no expertise and where intrusion is unwarranted. The size of the task is a problem for the GAO; in 1979 it had 4200 investigators, and over 1500 investigations going on simultaneously, over 400 of them at the Pentagon. Congress has greatly expanded the GAO function beyond simple voucher auditing to include assessment of executive branch policy decisions as well as management itself. So conflicts between Congress, the GAO, and those it watches are certain to continue in the future.[40]

Every president struggles with the problem of efficient government. President Johnson attempted to implement a Planning Programming and Budget System (PPBS). This is a management technique oriented toward programs rather than the organization itself. It examines long-run needs and evaluates programs having similar objectives. It worked with partial success in the Defense Department in the 1960s, but did not survive efforts to extend it to the rest of government, and it was eventually abandoned. President Carter implemented a zero base budgeting system in which individual units build their budgets from zero. Rather than assume a continuation of the agency or its various activities, everything has to be justified for each budget cycle. Its aim is to provoke more intensive evaluation of policies and programs. Proposals for sunset laws that would automatically terminate programs according to a firm schedule, unless rescued by Congress, are frequently considered, as are many other attempts to put management expertise to work in the government. These plans and proposals are difficult to pass in Congress; and when they do, they encounter a great difficulty.

The General Accounting Office and the Office of Management and Budget are making valiant efforts to improve the operations of government, but the task is so large that their efforts have been piecemeal and their success modest in the absence of an overall, total approach with teeth. Proposals for a Government Accountability Act were submitted to the 95th Congress and then to the 96th, but the proposals were not enacted.

---

[39] *The Wall Street Journal*, September 3, 1980, p. 26.
[40] *Business Week*, July 9, 1979, pp. 62–63.

ETHICS IN GOVERNMENT

Ethical scandals and issues have pervaded government at all levels. In view of the heavy intrusion of government into the lives of people and their organizations, it is imperative that government units institute ethical reforms. This is widely happening, but only with considerable difficulty. Many states, for example, have passed ethics laws dealing with conflicts of interest and disclosures of financial interests. These laws are hard to enforce, and the burden of cases demanding decisions as to what behavior is unethical is very large.

Self-reform is difficult for legislators. In Congress, for example, there are gentlemanly, kid-glove traditions that hide all but the worst cases. Censure and removal decisions are few and very difficult; they entail enormous wrangling and a great deal of litigation in the courts. Misconduct by members of Congress is extensive, but voters repeatedly return offenders to office.[41] Campaign laws, ethical codes, and other means have been devised to curb the problem, with only mixed success.[42]

Incident Case

In 1958, Congress adopted a "Code of Ethics for Government Service." (See pg. 212 of text). This document remained filed and forgotten until 1980, when a Washington, D.C., organization called the Ethics Resource Center got Congress to pass a bill requiring the code to be posted publicly in all post offices and U.S. government offices employing 20 or more persons. The center provided, at no cost to the government, 200,000 plastic-laminated copies of the code.

The code has 10 "commandments." The first exhorts government employees to "put loyalty to the highest moral principles and to country above loyalty to persons, party or government department."

Others ban the accepting or dispensing of special privileges or favors and urge a full day's labor for a full day's pay and efforts to find more efficient ways to accomplish tasks.

Whistle blowers would seem to be encouraged by the commandment to "expose corruption wherever discovered."

What do you think will be the outcome of these efforts?

Issues for Discussion and Analysis

1. How can a company best encourage its employees to participate in public affairs? What difficulties might a company experience in taking the steps you suggest?

2. Recommend some ways in which the business point of view could be better conveyed (a) to the general public, and (b) to politicians and government administrators.

3. Why do presidents and other officials find it so difficult to improve the organization structure of the federal government?

---

[41] *U.S. News and World Report*, June 23, 1980, p. 61.

[42] Congressional Quarterly, *Congressional Ethics*, 2nd ed. (Washington, D.C.: Congressional Quarterly, Inc., 1980).

4. What are the key elements in the formation of public policy? How does the process differ at federal, state, and local levels?

5. How do you assess the current state of our national goals? What are the difficulties that characterize social goal formation?

6. How do you account for the proliferation of "social" programs and the emergence of the "era of rising entitlements"?

7. Can basic management techniques and skills used in the business world work in government? Why or why not? What problems do civil service managers in government face that business managers do not?

Class Project

Divide the class into three task forces, each to investigate one of the following agencies whose mission is to improve federal government operations:

1. The Government Services Administration
2. The Government Accounting Office
3. The Office of Management and Budget

Each task force should (1) investigate the agency's mission, (2) explore the evaluations of its performance, and (3) report the findings to the class.

For Further Reading

BRAGAW, LOUIS K. *Managing a Federal Agency: The Hidden Stimulus* (Baltimore: Johns Hopkins University Press, 1980).

DUNLOP, JOHN T. (ed.). *Business and Public Policy* (Cambridge, Mass.: Harvard University Press, 1980).

DYE, THOMAS, R. *Policy Analysis: What Governments Do, Why They Do It, and What Difference It Makes* (Alabama: University of Alabama Press, 1976).

ECKHARDT, BOB, and CHARLES BLACK. *The Tides of Power* (New Haven, Conn.: Yale University Press, 1976).

FLATHMAN, RICHARD E. *The Practice of Political Authority: Authority and the Authoritative* (Chicago: The University of Chicago Press, 1980).

FRANKEL, CHARLES (ed). *Controversies and Decisions: The Social Sciences and Public Policy* (New York: Russell Sage Foundation, 1976).

FREEDMAN, ROGER A. *The Growth of American Government: The Morphology of the Welfare State* (Stanford, Calif.: Stanford University Press, 1975).

FROMKIN, DAVID *The Question of Government: An Inquiry into the Breakdown of Political Systems* (New York: Scribner's, 1975).

GEEKIE, WILLIAM J. *Why Government Fails* (Roslyn Heights, N.Y.: Libra Publishers, 1976).

GOHAGAN, JOHN K. *Quantitative Analyses for Public Policy* (New York: McGraw-Hill, 1980).

GOLDWIN, ROBERT A. (ed.). *Bureaucrats, Policy Analysis, Statesmen: Who Leads?* (Washington, D.C.: American Enterprise Institute, 1980).

HAMILTON, JAMES. *The Power to Probe: A Study of Congressional Investigations* (New York: Random House, 1976).

HELCO, HUGH. *A Government of Strangers: Executive Politics in Washington* (Washington, D.C.: The Brookings Institution, 1977).

HOOK, SYDNEY. *Philosophy and Public Policy* (Carbondale: Southern Illinois University Press, 1980).

HOROWITZ, IRVING LOUIS, and JAMES EVERETT KATZ. *Social Science and Public Policy in the United States* (New York: Praeger, 1975).

KAPLAN, ABRAHAM. *American Ethics and Public Policy* (New York: Oxford University Press, 1963).

KAUFMAN, HERBERT. *Are Government Organizations Immortal?* (New York: The Brookings Institution, 1976).

LEVITAN, SAR A. *Programs in Aid to the Poor for the 1980s*, 4th ed. (Baltimore: Johns Hopkins University Press, 1980).

LEVITAN, SAR A., and ROBERT TAGGART. *The Promise of Greatness* (Cambridge, Mass.: Harvard University Press, 1978).

LEVITAN, SAR A., and GREGORY WURZBURG. *Evaluating Federal Social Programs: An Uncertain Art* (Kalamazoo, Mich.: W. E. Upjohn Institute for Employment Research, 1979).

LYNCH, THOMAS D. *Policy Analysis in Public Policymaking* (Lexington, Mass.: Lexington Books, 1975).

LYNN, LAURENCE. *Managing the Public's Business: The Job of the Government Executive* (New York: Basic Books, 1981).

MAINZER, LOUIS. *Political Bureaucracy* (Glenview, Ill.: Scott, Foresman, 1973).

MALEK, FREDERICK V. *Washington's Hidden Tragedy: The Failure to Make Government Work* (New York: Free Press, 1978).

MELTSNER, ARNOLD J. *Policy Analysts in the Bureaucracy* (Berkeley: University of California Press, 1976).

MEYER, MARSHALL W. *Change in Public Bureaucracies* (New York: Cambridge University Press, 1979).

OGUL, MORRIS S. *Congress Oversees the Bureaucracy: Studies in Legislative Supervision* (Pittsburgh: University of Pittsburgh Press, 1978).

ROCKEFELLER FOUNDATION. *Philosophy and Public Policy: Working Papers* (New York: The Rockefeller Foundation, October 1980).

ROSE, RICHARD, and GUY PETERS. *Can Government Go Bankrupt?* (New York: Basic Books, 1978).

SLAYTON, PHILIP, and MICHAEL TREBILCOCK (eds.). *The Professions and Public Policy* (Toronto: University of Toronto Press, 1978).

SNEED, JOSEPH D., and STEVEN A. WALDHORN. *Restructuring the Federal System* (New York: Crane, Russak, 1975).

13

Business
and Government Relations

The businessman dealing with a large political question is really a painful sight.

the first HENRY CABOT LODGE

What the nation needs from business and government is an understanding that neither one of those institutions has a monopoly on intelligence or probity, or the wisdom to prescribe all by itself for the public welfare.

IRVING S. SHAPIRO,
Chairman and Chief Executive Officer,
E. I. du Pont de Nemours and Company

CONCEPTS DISCUSSED IN THIS CHAPTER

1. HOW BUSINESS AND GOVERNMENT NEED EACH OTHER
2. ADVERSARY RELATIONSHIPS
3. COOPERATIVE RELATIONSHIPS
4. BUSINESS AND MANAGEMENT IN GOVERNMENT AND POLITICS
5. EXECUTIVE AND MANAGERIAL PARTICIPATION IN GOVERNMENT AND POLITICS

The relations between government and business have never been simple or easy, but in recent years their difficulties have increased as each has grown in power and complexity. Government and business are more extensively interrelated than ever before. Some interactions reflect severe conflict and tension; othere exhibit forms of collaboration and cooperation.

The delicate balance between the two social institutions is continuously undergoing adjustment as each accommodates to influences the other. Both have needs the other must fulfill, so that a continuous state of mutual interdependence exists. Some of these needs are illustrated in Table 13.1. Government both promotes and regulates the monetary system, which influences the money supply, interest rates, and price levels. It provides rules of the game, a stable legal, social, and political environment, security of person and property, order and justice, and a reliable system of coinage and currency. From business the government, for itself and for the people, needs efficient enterprise that generates taxes, goods and services, and capital.

Two sets of values thus come into potential conflict: those of capitalism, which emphasize productivity, efficiency, and other economic values, as opposed to social values such as cooperation, fraternity, altruism, community, compassion. People attach varying weights to these sets of values; hence there are tensions and conflicts. These tensions are healthy when they result in debate and analysis. Otherwise an ideological polarization around each set of values would occur, resulting in focusing only on the defects in society.[1]

Managers are ambivalent in their attitudes toward the relations of business and government. They want to be free of government when they are doing well, and helped by government when they are doing poorly. There is both an adversary relationship deriving from mutual needs and

TABLE 13.1

Illustrative Needs of Mutual Interdependence of the Public and Private Sectors

What Government Needs from the Market	What the Market Needs from the Government
1. A marketplace and market system	1. The exercise of legal powers to make and enforce the rules of economic activity
2. Material resources, services, and finished goods	2. Security of property rights
3. Financial support of government activities and programs (through taxation)	3. Stability of governmental processes
4. Reliability and efficiency of productive effort	4. Reliable monetary system
5. Decentralized economic activity and power to limit monopoly and unfair competition	5. Stable physical and social infrastructure
	6. Decentralized power centers to limit government in a democracy

[1] Arthur M. Okun, "Our Blend of Democracy and Capitalism: It Works But It Is in Danger," *Across the Board*, March 1979, pp. 69–70.

interdependencies. Conflict and cooperation are never static conditions; they continuously adapt as circumstances change. For example, many firms in the 1960s and 1970s advocated free trade policies among the countries of the world. They sought the government's encouragement. In the recession years of the early 1980s, many of the same firms advocated tariff barriers to keep foreign goods from displacing theirs.

This switch of attitudes did not arise out of meanness or conspiracy, but from reactions to new world conditions. The realms of business and of government are both separate and intertwined as to objectives, policies, and activities. Business positions on controversial issues reflect the need for profitable operations. Government's responsibility is for an orderly society designed to protect the public interest beyond the confines of any single social institution.

ADVERSARY RELATIONSHIPS

Adversary relationships exist when business opposes certain government activities, or when government seeks to restrain or require business activity in the public interest. The words *intervention*, *intrusion*, or *domination* reflect the emotional overtones with which business often regards the government when restraints are applied. The enormous expansion of government intervention in business has intensified this adversary relationship, raising doubts about the nature of the public interest and the ways it can be met.

The extent of governmental intervention cannot be measured precisely, but it is possible to cite some indicators. Government itself has grown enormously since the 1920s. Government expenditures at all levels in 1929 represented 11 percent of the nation's entire production of goods and services. By 1950, it had climbed to 23 percent, by 1960 to 30 percent, by 1970 to 35 percent, and by 1977 to 37 percent. Government regulations are carried in a document called the *Federal Register*, first published in 1936. That year, it comprised 2,400 pages; by 1970 it was 20,036 pages, by 1975 it was 60,00 pages, and by 1978 it was 68,000 pages.[2]

Feelings of interference have increased as public pressures have extended the government beyond its traditional roles, such as protecting an orderly, competitive market system, or protecting territorial boundaries, into areas such as environmental protection, energy con-

---

[2] William J. Baroody, Sr., "Education: More Than Mere Knowledge" (Washington, D.C.: American Enterprise Institute, 1980), Reprint No. 114, p. 4. See also Report of the Advisory Commission on Intergovernmental Relations, *The Federal Role in the Federal System: The Dynamics of Growth* (Washington, D.C.: U.S. Government Printing Office, 1980).

trols, or health and safety problems. The business point of view holds that the government has no investment in business and no accountability to stockholders or the electorate, so agencies can issue mandates and render legal interpretations that can determine the success or failure of many businesses. These views are not wholly accurate in all cases, but they reflect the fact that government mandates add enormous costs which companies must pay to achieve compliance. They lead to threats that employment, payrolls, prices, and taxes will suffer.

Johnson argues that the "monster state," with its intrusions into business and private life, suffers impairment of its basic functions. Inflation gets out of control so that the currency is no longer stable. Capital dries up so that the economy is no longer burgeoning. The search for justice becomes more elusive as bureaucratic and legalistic squabbles among government units cause them to investigate and even sue one another. Unlawful activities increase, and the protection of national interests on the world scene becomes more precarious as war and terrorism become rampant. Financing the increased activities increases the burden of taxation, and budgets go out of control.[3]

These arguments summarize conservative views of the role government should play in our society. They reflect the causes of public unrest and loss of confidence in both business and government. More liberal views hold that business and government should learn how together they can take better account of the undeniable persistence of poverty, injustice, and other human sufferings without giving way completely to the totalitarian administrative state. The adversarial issues between business and government are thus over means rather than ends.

Business indicts government as the cause of the slowing down of capital investment and productivity. It blames the government for building inflation into the economy, for shortsighted tax policies, for petty regulations, for enormous paperwork, and for imposing arbitrary standards in such matters as pollution control. General Motors, for example, claims expenditures of $1.9 billion annually to comply with government safety, environmental controls, and paperwork requirements. On the other hand, even industry representatives agree that without government action, very little improvement is safety, health, pollution and other problems would have occurred.[4]

Adversary relations center largely on governmental policies and actions in the market system. Business representatives generally accept the need for minimum regulation of market processes, but they want them

---

[3] Paul Johnson, "The Things That Are Caesar's," A Frances Boyer lecture on public policy (Washington, D.C.: American Enterprise Institute, 1980), pp. 10–14.

[4] James Fallows, "American Industry: What Ails It, How to Save It," *Atlantic*, September 1980, pp. 40–41.

kept as free as possible beyond the minimum. They suggest that as a positive approach to social problems, the market system should be used instead of government intervention. They are critical of government policies and decision processes, and the failures of cost-benefit analysis.[5] We will return to these topics in Chapter 14.

ADVOCACY PROBLEMS

Advocacy efforts are an interesting aspect of the adversary relationship in coping with social problems. Business firms are now running paid advertisements taking sides on many public issues. Such "advocacy advertising" is highly controversial: critics demand that it be regulated to prevent it from becoming deceptive propaganda; proponents regard it as an indispensable form of communication under the rights of free speech.

Business has found in advocacy advertising an aggressive technique to combat criticism, in contrast to the traditional ways of ignoring criticism or reacting defensively to attacks one at a time. The effectiveness of such techniques is hard to measure; at best, we have only opinion polls on both sides of the issue. Advocacy advertising reflects the business view that the media do not adequately portray accurate or balanced views. Critics hold that such means are not readily available to opponents, who may not have the resources to engage in advertising efforts. Sethi holds that advocacy advertising as carried on by many large firms in recent years is of questionable value and of doubtful effectiveness on economic, sociopolitical, and ideological grounds, but that it can serve to enlarge public debate on issues normally dealt with only in academic journals or in legislative halls.[6]

Another problem of advocacy is found in the work of public interest attorneys. In 1977 California passed a law allowing a lawyer to serve as a "private attorney general" in cases that protect citizen's rights. The law permits judges to order the state to pay legal fees as compensation for improving the social welfare. The problem is that state legislators have refused to pay the legal fees in several cases. In one case, for example, the state refused to pay a $600,000 fee to a firm of public advocates that won a judgment in its favor. There are movements in such cases to force the corporate defendants to pay the fees, and several court decisions have so ruled. These issues will remain in controversy for some time in the future.[7]

---

[5] Committee for Economic Development, *Redefining Government's Role in the Market System, Statement on National Policy* (New York, July 1979).

[6] Prakash Sethi, *Advocacy Advertisng and Large Corporations* (Lexington, Mass.: Lexington Books, 1977); see also "Industry Fights Back," *Saturday Review*, January 21, 1978, pp. 20–21.

[7] "Paying Public Interest Law Fees," *Business Week*, August 4, 1980, p. 53.

COOPERATIVE RELATIONSHIPS

So much attention has been given to adversary relationships that they overshadow the many ways in which government and business work together. Government is more than a regulatory institution. It is also a customer of business, though often a hard one to satisfy. Government is also a source of information, services, research and development support, and even subsidies, for business activities.

Good working relations between business and government are facilitated through innumerable points of contact, a reflection of the fact that both groups try hard to work together. Communication and joint efforts occur through business and trade associations, advisory commissions, planning councils, voluntary exchanges, and lobbying efforts, as well as business firms. Another illustration is the government practice of drawing upon businesspeople to fill a variety of appointed or informal positions. Senior executives, as well as labor leaders and academicians, often accept government posts at less pay than their previous positions; many do so as public service without pay. Executives frequently run for political office.

Now that social ills are becoming accepted responsibilities of both business and government, a new level of cooperation and joint effort may be reached; indeed, it will be necessary since such problems cut across these and other social institutions. Problems of funding or cost sharing and problems of role — who does what — will doubtless remain, as will adversary interests and pressures for special advantages. Government decisions are based on politics, whereas those of business are geared to the profit and loss statement.

I once regarded the state as a means whereby the less fortunate among us could be enabled to achieve the self-expression and moral fulfillment which is their aspiration as creatures made in God's image. While continuing to desire the end, I no longer have any confidence in the state as the means. On the contrary, I have come to see it as the biggest single obstacle to the individual self-expression and moral maturity of all of us, and not least the poor, the weak, the humble, and the passive.

PAUL JOHNSON, *The Things That Are Not Caesar's* (Washington, D.C.: American Enterprise Institute, 1980), p. 15.

It is important to liberty and freedom that controversy, dissent, and conflict are permitted. If government and business should engage in collusion or conspiracy to dominate the whole of society, our basic values would be endangered. Nazi Germany and Fascist Italy were examples. To preserve political and civil liberties, it is essential to preserve economic liberties as well. Neither government nor business should degenerate into a mere appendage of the other.[8]

The participation of business and its representatives in government and political affairs promises to develop new relationships in areas heretofore regarded exclusively as those of government, and which neither could accomplish alone. Problems such as training the disadvantaged, rebuilding slums and ghettoes, or helping blacks and other minorities establish their own enterprises, could not be done by government alone. Business, with its profit-and-loss discipline and its managerial knowhow, brings special capabilities to the joint efforts. Government's role, at federal, state, and local levels, includes planning, problem assessment, creating markets, and the contracting out of social tasks.

New patterns of organization better fitted for business-government collaboration take the form of hybrid corporations such as the U.S. Postal Service, Comsat (Communications Satellite Corporation) or Amtrak (National Railroad Passenger Corporation). Set up as quasi-public corporations, such structures provide a degree of "privatization" of services and activities formerly performed by government alone. This strategy places greater stress on the market system, but maintains some form of government surveillance. For example, the Postal Reorganization Act of 1970 removed the service from political control, creating a public corporation under a nine-member governing board. Although key decisions are overseen by Congress, the board has considerable management independence; it selects the Postmaster General. An independent expert Postal Rate Commission recommends rates and fees to Congress.[9]

Despite the many variations being developed for combined government-business ventures, the costs to the consumer are not necessarily reduced. This is because costs to both taxpayers and consumers are involved, and in any case costs are hard to figure. Costs are only in part a function of organization and management; they are driven up also by uncontrollable forces in society itself. Finally, costs and efficiency matters are often overshadowed by political controversies.

Cooperation between business and government has met with only limited success. In Cleveland, for example, local businessmen pitched in to help restore effective management. They formed a committee called the Operations Improvement Task Force, consisting of 89 local businessmen. In three months they came up with over 750 recommendations for

---

[8] Gurney Breckenfeld, "Government's Hammerlock on Business," *Saturday Review*, July 10, 1976, pp. 24–28.

[9] Transcript of AEI Forum 24, "The U.S. Postal System: Can It Deliver?" (Washington, D.C.: American Enterprise Institute, 1978).

solving Cleveland's financial problems.[10] Similarly, over 90 private businessmen worked with New York City's Management Advisory Board. Eight of the nine board members were businessmen, as were three members of the Emergency Financial Control Board, and ten members of the Temporary Commission on City Finances. The time of executives on loan was valued at $2.6 million. The results were mixed; savings of $78 million were realized, but potential savings could have reached $676 million. Civil Service laws, political pork barrels, outmoded organization structures, and lack of good accounting and of computerization frustrated the executives.[11]

PARTICIPATION IN GOVERNMENT AND POLITICS

Businesspersons may become involved in government and politics as citizens or as representatives of their firms or of industry and business generally. The dividing line between personal and business interests is often unclear. What is generally clear is the dividing line between career officials—appointed and elected persons who devote their working lives to government—and business executives who move in and out of government in relatively temporary assignments. Both exhibit substantial commitment and devotion to their assigned tasks; both experience frustrations and difficulties in meeting the challenges of public responsibility.

We will next analyze the various forms of individual and company involvement in politics and government. An analysis of regulation is, however, so extensive that it will be presented separately in Chapter 14.

BUSINESS INVOLVEMENT

There is a notable discrepancy between recognition of the importance of the company's role in political affairs and the ability to carry out specific, well-conceived programs of political action. Among the reasons for this are the following:

Time, money and effort are required for successful programs.

Nonpartisan company positions seem to have little influence, and partisan efforts involve conflict and controversy, thus encouraging divisiveness internally and endangering public relations.

Many managers are unfamiliar with political and governmental processes,

---

[10] "Running a City Like a Business," *Business Week*, June 2, 1980, p. 100.

[11] "New York Falls Back on a Rich Resource," *Business Week*, November 10, 1975, pp. 83–88. See also David Rogers, *Can Business Management Save the Cities? The Case of New York* (New York: Free Press, 1978).

thus they are not confident or skillful in knowing what to do and how to do it.

Legal and ethical complications present risks and uncertainties that are difficult to handle.

Serious problems have arisen in companies that have undertaken such problems.

At the national level, direct company contributions to political parties or campaigns are illegal. Scandals have occurred in which companies gave illegal contributions and politicians accepted them. The Campaign Act of 1974 provided a legitimate channel for political contributions by the establishment of company Political Action Committees (PACs). Their main purpose is to raise and allocate political campaign funds. Company PACs are also permitted to make pitches to top officials and stockholders in behalf of favored candidates.

Early PACs were inexperienced and relatively ineffective. The quality of PAC actions and the amounts of the contributions are the key elements. David Keene, a key strategist of the 1976 Reagan-for-President drive, has severely criticized PACs for their lack of sophistication, knowledge, and political courage, and for being far less effective in politics than labor unions. In 1976, only 40 of 400 PACs contributed most of the funds, and over one-third raised less than $1000. Only four mailed information to company stockholders. Much of the money was used to support or gain access to incumbents, whether or not they were pro-business. Some played it safe by giving equally to Democrats and Republicans.[12] By 1980, the situation had improved. PACs became more aggressive and more numerous. Over 1750 such PACs existed in 1980, and in an 18 month period they raised over $48 million compared to the $18 million raised by unions.[13]

Despite the increased activity of PACs, many problems remain for company political efforts. Many companies are secretive and coy about their political views, and hesitant to take strong positions, at least publicly. Companies have difficulty dealing with the wide ranges of opinion found among managers and workers. It is difficult to avoid feelings of pressure tactics, so they lean toward nonpartisan positions. Some companies have used the reward system, such as promotions, to increase the political activity of their managers, but at the risk of resistance from those who prefer to keep their political views private. It is difficult for employees to feel free to express opinions adverse to the company's espoused beliefs.[14]

---

[12] Alan L. Otten, "Business in Politics," *The Wall Street Journal*, April 28, 1977, p. 14.

[13] Dennis Farney, "Business Invests Time, Money, to Shape a Pro-Industry Congress," *The Wall Street Journal*, September 17, 1980, p. 33.

[14] "Browbeating Employees into Lobbyists," *Business Week*, March 10, 1980, pp. 132–133.

Some firms meet these problems by stressing general involvement, good citizenship, and "political awareness." They have also set up task forces, seminars, and workshops to teach practical political skills. These are usually "voluntary," but are conducted on company time. Companies vigorously deny that they coerce employees into political views or activities, and especially into making financial contributions to PACs. Whether coerced or not, company PACs collected $17.7 million from their executives and managers in 1978.[15] PACs are forbidden by law to use physical force, job discrimination, financial reprisals, or threats thereof, in obtaining contributions. Most company PACs do not solicit from rank and file workers, many of whom contribute to union PACs.

It is too early to make definitive judgments about the wisdom or influence of company PACs. It would appear that they can be as successful as union or other PACs, provided that care is used to avoid their pitfalls.

SUBSIDIES, BAILOUTS, AND FINANCIAL ASSISTANCE

Another form of business-government relations is that of government financial assistance to firms and industries. These involvements include subsidies, bailouts, and many types of services, benefits, loans, and payments to ailing or fledgling firms.

These activities display the ambivalence of companies and businesspeople toward government. They want government to reduce its involvement in business, but also to be supported and rescued by government. Beneath their antipathy toward government and their criticisms of it lies a not too well disguised reliance on government. It is in part borne of a natural desire for an orderly, predictable system, and in part of the recognition that freedom is a relative term and that world conditions are changing.

Even in the pursuit of urgent needs, dealing with the government is not easy. Rules, regulations, bureaucratic red tape, inflexibility and waste are some of the drawbacks. And in recent years, government largess has been used in a threatening, coercive way to get business to behave as the government wants it to. Financial entanglements are so close that separation of business and government is virtually impossible.

Subsidies are a form of government support to keep firms or industries in business under adverse conditions. Farm subsidies are a notable example, and they illustrate how difficult it is to remove a subsidy program once it is in place. Subsidies are widespread in the transportation system, where airlines, railroads, and buses are supported. Some subsidies are direct, such as mail-carrying subsidies for airlines or crop-support payments for tobacco farmers. The Federal Aviation Act of 1958,

---

[15] *The Wall Street Journal*, July 24, 1980, p. 1.

for example, requires the Civil Aeronautics Board to subsidize an air car-
rier in trouble so long as its management is "honest, efficient, and
economical." Others are indirect or hidden, such as building highways for
use by truckers.

Bailouts take the form of federal loan guarantee for companies close
to failure. The Lockheed Aviation Corporation and the Chrysler Corporation were extended such government assistance, but not without enormous controversy and extensive congressional debate. The rationale for
such guarantees consists of the fear that unemployment, welfare payments, loss of tax revenues, and other economic traumas would be more
costly that the costs of rescue. Difficult questions arise. What is the
proper role of government in these areas? Does the assistance involve the
use of tax monies to help private firms survive? Do competitors suffer
when the rescued firms gains an unfair edge? What precedents are set for
future requests? Do rescues reward bad management, or are there extenu-
ating circumstances?

About 6000 to 7000 firms go bankrupt and out of existence every
year. They are mainly small firms unable to muster the support of powerful unions, banks, or lobbyists. Companies needing a bailout argue that it
is the government which causes problems of the type experienced by
Chrysler, by refusing to levy import restrictions, by requiring expensive
fuel economy and safety standards, and so on. Opponents of bailouts such
as Chrysler's hold that poor management was the true cause—failure to
anticipate the demand for smaller, safer, more fuel-efficient cars, and
allowing plant facilities to become outmoded and unprofitable.[16]

In the case of Chrysler, Congress placed certain safeguards and controls over the company along with the loan guarantees. Such controls
represent interference in the management of the company. In the case of
small business, controversies also rage. Tired of government waste and
inefficiency, many small firms reject government assistance. The Small
Business Administration, the Commerce Department's Economic Development Administration, and the Business Services Centers of the General Services Administration have been strongly criticized for falling
short of their goals. Government agencies have been criticized for unnecessary duplication of services and other failings.[17]

Business has been quite successful in its involvements with the local
level of government. The acute problems of cities and other localities
have drawn a large segment of the business community into local economic and social problems. Businesses have a stake in their communities. They need strong, efficient local governments and a hospitable
climate for business. The extent of business involvement in local affairs

16 AEI Forums, "U.S. Industry in Trouble: What Is the Government's Responsibility?" (Washington,
    D.C.: American Enterprise Institute, 1979).
17 "Business Gives Federal Aid Low Marks," U.S. News and World Report, September 15, 1980, p. 84.

is more beneath the surface than direct. In a 1977 survey of 1100 firms, 400 indicated no direct local involvement. Four hundred other firms said their involvement ranged from providing executives for particular projects to long-term participation, such as employees holding policy-making positions in local government. The forms of assistance, especially in urban areas, included the loan of executives, providing management advice, economic development, community goal setting, financial management, and the loan of facilities. Most business assistance programs to local government were rated as successful.[18]

Still other controversies rage over the government's efforts to stimulate the economy. Some argue that the government should use its resources to help the winners rather than to bail out the losers. Others say it is impossible to forecast which firms and industries have the potential for success, and in any case the nation does not want the government to be the determinant of who succeeds and who fails.[19]

INDIVIDUAL INVOLVEMENT

Theorists of the eighteenth and nineteenth centuries considered as political behavior only that involving government and public policies. This was logical, since government was the only organized institution with sufficient decision-making power to affect large groups or society as a whole. Today most political scientists also recognize the political nature of "private governments," such as the large corporations, universities, and labor unions. The corporation is political in its internal bureaucratic apparatus and in its impact on government and other institutions.[20]

The relationship between government and the various social classes, such as managers, contains many ambiguities. It is these ambiguities which limit the likelihood that managerialism or managers will come to dominate the state. First, managers do not constitute a homogeneous class, or even a true social class as such. Second, the managerial functions do not include several of the most important roles of the state. Third, the state, since it is independent of a single institution, is likely to follow the interests of all other social groups as well as the pursuit of its own political and administrative interests.[21]

---

[18] The Conference Board, *Business Involvement with Local Government*, Information Bulletin No. 30, October 1977.

[19] "U.S. Aid for Promising Industries?" *U.S. News and World Report*, September 22, 1980, pp. 61–62. See also Phyllis S. McGrath, *Redefining Corporate-Federal Relations* (New York: The Conference Board, 1979).

[20] Peter Bachrach, *The Theory of Democratic Elitism* (Boston: Little, Brown, 1967).

[21] Colin Crouch, "The Ideology of a Managerial Elite: The National Board for Prices and Incomes 1965–1970," in Ivor Crew (ed.), *British Political Sociology Yearbook*, vol. 1 (New York: Wiley, 1974), p. 78.

Those who urge the involvement of managers in government and politics often do so by viewing such activity as a function of leadership. This implies that it is particularly important for the top echelons of managers to make their influence felt. Lundborg believes that leaders have been ineffective in dealing with legislative issues for three reasons: (1) They usually oppose something they don't like; (2) they enter into the discussion too late; and (3) they are often on the "wrong" side—as in resisting the rights movements of women and minorities. By defaulting on early discussions of the problems, they must later fight a rearguard, defensive action on methods.[22]

The activities of businesspersons in political arenas is necessarily colored by a degree of self-interest and partisan defenses of their own companies' welfare. This is normal, but today self or company interests cannot be the sole motivation. Global issues and the interplay of social institutions within societies everywhere preclude this narrow view. The particular attribute businesspersons bring to government is their orientation toward decision, action, and risktaking—precisely the elements often missing among goverment officials. Business executives have constituents to satisfy, but these are not the counterparts of those with which Congress, politicians, and government administrators must deal. Also, accountability in government is more diffused, and progress harder to measure.

Executives and managers have much to gain by personal participation in government service, whether by appointment or by elective office. Rewards come from having an impact on important problems, learning about power relations in government, and discovering the psychic satisfactions of working on broad, major problems. For many, government service can be a strategic factor in career development. Financial rewards are less likely, however, since pay scales in government are usually lower than those of business at comparable levels.

In addition to serving in an elected or appointive full-time government post, business executives have opportunities for participation in other ways, both formal and informal. They can serve on boards, commissions, and other groups, or run for state, county, or local offices. Many of these posts, such as serving on a local school board or university board of trustees, permit retaining one's full-time position in the company. Executives can also participate as citizens—in voting, registration drives, or supporting a political party.

At whatever level or location of participation, the impact of the company and its many policies and attitudes toward the individual's "outside" life are important considerations. For example, there are usually policies on leaves of absence. Policies may also include official views as

---

[22] Louis B. Lundborg, "Making Profits Is Not Enough," *Across the Board*, February 1977, pp. 54–58.

to what degree the individual's beliefs or actions should be conveyed as a reflection of company interest. Policies also reflect the extent to which any type of political activity is favored or not within the company.

The average businessman has gotten where he is because he has more than average ability. He has the mental capacity for factual analysis that leads to sound conclusions and right actions. Obviously, his batting average has to be pretty good to keep him moving up—or at least keep him where he is. These talents are exactly the ones that must be applied to political activity if the tremendous power now contained in it is not to become an actual danger to the welfare of the people of this country.

ERNEST T. WEIR (1951)

Several factors influence the willingness of individuals in business to engage in political or governmental activities. First, there are distinctions in what individuals do and what the company does officially throught its legal or public affairs departments. Second, an absence of policy may be interpreted as disapproval of such activities. Third, written policies may not actually be carried out in practice, raising doubts about what activities are "safe." Fourth, individuals can be encouraged if potential rewards can be derived or undue sanctions will not be invoked. Fifth, individuals may prefer nongovernmental forms of public service in civic, religious or charitable agencies, thus fulfilling community obligations rather than posing political dilemmas. Sixth, many executives have negative attitudes toward politics, politicians, and government; they are regarded as adversaries, and joining them may be seen as desertion or disloyalty by peers, subordinates, or superiors.

The company that wants its managers to be politically involved either as individuals or in behalf of the company needs to guard against restraining influences. Under a policy of encouragement, companies must keep the reward system attuned to it. Encouragement comes also to those who see that colleagues participate to good purpose and at minimal risk from internal repercussions. In positive policies and programs directed at individual participation in public sector activities, the role of top management, especially the chief executive officer, is crucial. The CEO serves as a role model for others in the company. Most of them agree that they should play a role in the development of public policy, but there is wide disagreement on how best to direct their participation. One survey of 300 CEOs found that eight out of ten who spoke out publicly on policy matters during the previous year made their views known to senior government officials. Nine out of ten reported that they believed that they should inform employees and stockholders of their public policy positions, and that they should accept part-time appointments in government. Variations occur among CEOs as to their role perceptions. In large firms, the external features of the CEO role play a larger part in the process than in smaller firms; the company's size also accounts for some variations. Since large firms have more at stake, more resources, and more interactions with government, they are likely to be more active. Some industries, such as public utilities, are more involved with government than others.[23]

Local and state governments have made increasing use of ad hoc task forces of executives selected for their specific skills for solving problems. Often they are faster and more effective, and certainly less costly, than consultants. Although task forces are usually temporary, an increasing number are being instutionalized as formal, permanent units within the governmental structure, but with financial support from business firms.

Another form of business and government collaboration at the individual level is job swapping. The 1970 President Nixon established the President's Executive Exchange Program, but it did not flourish. In 1980 President Carter revived the idea, placing it under a presidential commission headed by a businessman. In its first ten years, the program utilized 375 middle managers from more than 200 corporations who spent more than a year in government agencies, and 175 middle-echelon civil servants spent similar periods with business firms. The aim is to make each side more knowledgeable and sophisticated in the political, social, and economic realities of the other side.[24]

Conditions for the success of such programs are hard to meet. Selection of qualified persons is imperative. The early programs were not well administered, and many participants reported frustration and disappointment rather than a successful experience. Follow-up procedures to keep participants in touch with their former situations after they returned to their home bases were not carried out. Some found their negative stereotypes confirmed rather than dispelled; others found their receptions cool upon returning to their original employer. The logistics of moving temporarily to a new place of work are costly and difficult, and the problem of salary differences must be met. If such difficulties can be minimized, it is possible for such programs to be useful. Much depends on how well they are administered.

BUSINESS AND GOVERNMENT ELITES

The interconnection between business and government occur at three main levels: federal, state, and local. Within each level, there is a leadership elite that spearheads the identification and assessment of problems

---

[23] David G. Moore, *Politics and the Corporate Chief Executive*, Research Report No. 777 (New York: The Conference Board, 1980).

[24] "When Bureaucrats and Executives Swap Jobs," *Business Week*, February 18, 1980, pp. 99–103.

and influences the changes necessary to solve or prevent them.

Business or managerial elites are not only a force within business and economic institutions, but also in society as a whole through interaction with political elites. Empirically, the heads of giant corporations belong to the political elite. Both decisions and nondecisions of corporation managers influence public policy. The size, power, ubiquity, and public acceptance of huge corporations inevitably involve them in important public issues. By deciding to act or not to act in support of public policy, a company could be instrumental in the success or failure of major programs such as those for racial integration.

Epstein notes that the leaders of corporate organizations form a hierarchical, bureaucratic structure, with the resulting concentration of power at the top lessening the influence of organization members. The top leadership controls the major resources, the members come to have little interest in directing the organization. The elite thus develops concerns and interests of its own, including the maintenance of its own power.[25]

It is not surprising that, given the nature of industrial society, elite figures rise to the top in both business and government. In both structures, the elites consist of professional executives and managers, rather than property owners or persons of wealth. The extent and nature of the power of the business elite and its participation in the national political elite is a continuing uncertainty. Parsons holds that the business elite can no longer lead the American community as it has in the past, because its influence has been eroded by the rising autonomy of the government and its efforts to control business. Thus the national elite is in a state of transition involving the decline in the prominence of business. Parsons' theory of the mutual interaction of social institutions implies that the active participation of business is required for effective political leadership, and that business has at least some veto power over what is done in society. The result is a negotiated order of shifting alliances, with interlocking memberships of power figures in the various social elites. There is general agreement that a business elite plays a strong role in the national elite, but authorities disagree widely over the legitimacy of this elite.[26]

The extent of interlocking of business and other elites is also in doubt, but there appears to be much less interlocking than many suppose. A high degree of interlocking would argue in favor of a convergence theory of elites, in which business, government, cultural, and military elites combine as a national power elite. A low degree of interlocking implies a pluralistic model in which elites maintain substantial autonomy and must work together to achieve effective power. There is no doubt

[25] Edwin M. Epstein, *The Corporation in American Politics* (Englewood Cliffs, N.J.: Prentice-Hall, 1969), p. 264.

[26] Talcott Parsons, *Structure and Process in Modern Societies* (New York: Free Press, 1960), pp. 211–233.

that the society's institutional structure concentrates a great deal of authority in elites.

Dye et al. found considerable specialization among elites, with little or no overlap among corporate, government, and military sectors. To the extent that there is an apparent convergence, it is due not to interlocking positions, but rather to interactions among the various elites. Government authority does not overlap with corporate authority, nor is high position in a corporation a requisite of high public office. Thus there is neither a significant horizontal nor vertical overlap.[27]

Despite the case for a business elite based on political influence and power, it is possible that mounting criticism of business will tend to erode that power and hence its elite status. Much depends on how well business leaders combat the public's loss of esteem and respect for business and its managers. Their progress is slow because their aims are misdirected. They address only surface issues, wrongfully blaming "socialist" academics and assuming that "sound economics" will lead to a changed ideology in schools and colleges. They also place too much reliance on efficient performance as the route to regaining lost prestige.[28]

PROBLEMS IN BUSINESS-GOVERNMENT RELATIONSHIPS

In recent decades the magnitude of governmental subsidy, contract, grant, and regulatory processes has greatly increased. Much of this activity brings government into interaction with business. The first three types represent positive forms of assistance or the exchange of services or goods; the fourth represents patterns of restraint, guidance, and control aimed at assuring that desired activities will be performed and activities not in the public interest will be prevented, restrained, or if necessary, punished.

This system of business-government relations often falls short of its ideals and goals. Neither institution is homogeneous, so that across-the-board problems are hard to manage. For example, there are differences in the needs and perspectives of small business and big business, service and manufacturing industries, and modern and outmoded firms. There are differences also in federal, state, and local levels of government, and

---

[27] Thomas R. Dye, Eugene R. DeClercq, and John Q. Pickering, "Concentration, Specialization, and Interlocking among Institutional Elites," *Social Science Quarterly* 54 (June 1973), pp. 8–28. For a historical treatment of this theme, see Philip H. Burch, Jr., *Elites in American History: The New Deal to the Carter Administration* (New York: Holmes & Meier, 1980).

[28] Paul A. Samuelson, "Businessman Blues," *Newsweek*, August 8, 1977, p. 70; William G. Scott and David K. Hart, "Administrative Crises: The Neglect of Metaphysical Speculation," *Public Administration Review* 33 (September 1973), pp. 415–416.

interrelations among these must be considered as government relates to business activities.[29]

> *"It seems to me," Mr. Dooley once commented, that th' on'y thing to do is to keep polyticians an' businessmen apart. They seem to have a bad infloonce on each other. Whiniver I see an aldherman an' a banker walkin' down th' sthreet together I know th' Recordin' Angel will have to ordher another bottle iv ink."*
>
> PETER DUNNE FINLEY, *Dissertations by Mr. Dooley* (New York: Harper & Row, 1906), p. 275.

The result of an action in one sector, even though it is successful, may do harm to other sectors. Public or special interest groups attack or support activities in both business and government, thus complicating the interactions between them. Thus government bears a responsibility for balancing many contending pressures, a major one being to manage as fairly as possible those issues which arouse differential interests. Clearly judgmental assessments predominate over measurable ones in deciding what is "fair" or what is in the public interest.

Let us now consider a number of difficulties widely apparent in business-government relationships. The following problems are typically found: (1) institutional roles and expectations, (2) boundary spanning, and (3) resistance to change.

INSTITUTIONAL ROLES AND EXPECTATIONS

As society has called on government and business to meet a growing array of needs and to respond to social change, each has come into an expanded role with respect to the other. Roles and expectations once familiar are giving way to new ones, increasing the difficulty of defining or understanding the emerging roles.

Caught up in the pressures to alleviate problems on many fronts, there is too little time for discussions of fundamental issues that would help them see the evolution of the overall institutional framework. Values, philosophies, and theories are secondary to making progress or achieving the illusion of it. An illustration is found in the vastly increased use by government of contracting out public work. The problem is to develop institutional arrangements and understanding that will enable the administrative and legislative branches of government to

---

[29] M. A. Murray, "Comparing Public and Private Management: An Exploratory Essay," *Public Administration Review* 35 (July 1975), pp. 364–371; J. L. Bower, "Effective Public Management: It Isn't the Same as Effective Business Management," *Harvard Business Review* 55 (March–April 1977), pp. 131–140.

maintain a strong control and policy-level direction over contract matters, while at the same time giving contractors the freedom and independence that maximizes their incentives for effective, creative efforts.

The elements of partnership between government and business have not yet matched the extent of adversary relationships. For this to happen will require adjustments to complicated shifts in power and the abandoning of outmoded dogmas. Business representatives often feel that the government listens more to unions, minorities, or even scientists than to them. But if the partnership is to evolve into a more decisive, satisfying role, managers in both business and government will need to work out their estrangements. Many areas of joint interest have come to be identified, along with the recognition that neither side can achieve social goals alone. Progress is reflected in the growing recognition of mutual goals and the possibilities for combined efforts in housing, health care, education, and the like.[30]

In the institutional interactions of business and government, it is government that often takes the initiative. This is because constituents and interest groups are vocal and direct the government's attention to their needs. These processes generate enormous planning efforts on the part of government, which attaches them to broad social goals such as prosperity, economic growth, or the improved quality of life. Eventually a degree of government intervention in business (as well as other social institutions) occurs. Business is therefore extensively affected by the resulting programs, regulations, contracts, or subsidies designed to influence products, distribution, financing, employment, or pricing. Such influences are often viewed as intrusions on free enterprise, which they often are. But they may also be viewed as opportunities for new and exciting variations in the institutional role of business.[31]

When intervention is excessive or misdirected, it intensifies business-government conflict. The same is true of other mistakes of government. These include such things as overemphasizing problems, short-run, expedient tactics, blindness to economic realities such as prices, profits, or even technological requirements, and the tendency to discount elements of risk. Also, government frequently overestimates its own abilities and underestimates those of business.[32]

The enormity of our economic problems alone poses staggering needs for the 1980s. For solving the problems of technology, competitive-

---

[30] An early analysis of these themes can be found in John J. Corson, *Business in a Humane Society* (New York: McGraw-Hill, 1971).

[31] Ira S. Ruein and Raymond Hunt, "Approaches to Managerial Control in Interpenetrating Systems: The Case of Government-Industry Relations," *Academy of Management Journal* 16 (April 1973), pp. 296–311; Brian E. Owen, "Business Manager's Influence (or Lack of Influence) on Government," *The Business Quarterly* 41 (Autumn 1976), pp. 58–69.

[32] D. H. Thain, "Mistakes of Government in Dealing with Business," *The Business Quarterly* 44 (Winter 1979), pp. 20–29.

ness, investment, exports, growth, and capital, national leaders have proposed a gigantic "reindustrialization effort." Such a goal would cost trillions, and involve the need for business, bureaucratic, and political elites to work together on a scale heretofore unknown. The scale of such a goal indicates that resources would have to go into industries with potential for adaptation and growth, rather than shielding declining sectors against change. Mobilizing the necessary support would entail the involvement of all social groups. [33]

BOUNDARY SPANNING

Business and government units are continuously engaged in various forms of interorganizational exchange. The management of these exchanges is called *boundary spanning.*

Exchange transactions involve material resources, personnel, money, ideas, information, services, finished goods, and the like. The transactions involve special managerial and organizational techniques and processes, especially planning, communicating, negotiating, and logistics. Organizations are structured with boundary-spanning roles, enabling them to deal with each other. [34]

The role of a boundary spanner, sometimes called a gatekeeper, is to mediate the assigned responsibilities for particular exchange transactions. The net result of such transactions is to enable the organization to interact with relevant others, and thus to obtain what it needs from the environment or to provide what the environment needs from it. To varying degrees, organizations have options about whether to adapt to environmental change or to influence that change. Interorganizational transactions thus have elements of self-interest and altruism as motivating forces.

Organizations establish territorial and jurisdictional boundaries. When rigidly followed, the organization is said to be relatively closed, firmly controlling exchange transactions. Organizations that treat their boundaries as more permeable are considered relatively open, receptive to exchanges with the environment. Open organizations are better prepared for adaptation and change, since ideas, new information, and outside activities more readily find their way in.

Boundary spanning may be formal or informal. In a sense, all organization members are boundary spanners since they have outside contacts of many kinds. Formal boundary spanning occurs when transactional tasks are assigned to specific positions. Examples are the tasks of sales-

---

[33] "The Reindustrialization of America," special issue, *Business Week*, June 30, 1980.

[34] Andrew H. Van De Ven, "On the Nature, Formation, and Maintenance of Relations among Organizations," *Academy of Management Review* 1 (October 1976), pp. 24–36.

people, personnel recruiters, or public relations officers. In government and business organizations, relatively little systematic attention has been given to problems of management at the boundaries. Job exchanges, mentioned earlier, are an illustration of the effort to improve understandings and skills across boundaries. Provincial attitudes sometimes result in boundary guarding rather than boundary spanning. Another problem is that the academic counterparts of the two institutions — schools of business and schools of public administration — are usually separated within universities, and commonalities of skills and interests are overlooked. Training and education for managers in both sectors has neglected boundary spanning.[35]

RESISTANCE TO CHANGE

To varying degrees and with varying strategies, those with whom the government works attempt to restrain or modify changes which they see as too restrictive or against their beliefs. These processes begin as legislation and programs come forth in planning, where the best opportunities for influence lie. If the end result is judged to be a problem, one or a combination of strategies will be used.

One strategy is to pursue crippling amendments in the legislative process. This happened with the Highway Beautification Act of 1965, which attempted to abolish billboards along America's highways. By 1980 there were still 14 billboards for every 10 miles of highway. Billboard owners sought changes in the statute "in the effort to clarify Congress's original intent." The result, critics contend, was that the law was transformed into little more than a costly subsidy for the outdoor advertising industry; environmentalists want the law repealed, whereas the industry wants it retained.[36]

Another set of strategies involves pursuing dissent in the courts. The result is costly litigation, with some successes and failures. For example, the struggle of Sears, Roebuck and Company promises to continue for years. In 1979 Sears sued 10 agencies of the federal government for creating a "racially and sexually imbalanced civilian work force" and for making it hard for companies to set things right. The attack was against contradictory rulings and requirements within government, and against loading all the blame on corporations.[37] Many similar battles have been fought against the Occupational Health and Safety Act of 1970, and progress was made administratively in getting OSHA (Office of Safety and

---

[35] Mitchell C. Lynch, "The Public Sector," Manager's Journal, *The Wall Street Journal*, September 10, 1979, p. 30; James S. Gillies, "Business and Government Relations: An Academic Politician's Viewpoint," *AACSB Bulletin* 13 (March 1978), pp. 26–31.

[36] *U.S. News and World Report*, September 22, 1980, p. 64.

[37] *Business Week*, April 7, 1980, pp. 112–121.

Health Administration) to reduce a vast number of ridiculous and impractical requirements that resulted from the law.

Resistance continues to plague affirmative action programs, antipollution laws, and many other restrictive government efforts. We will return to these problems in the following chapter.

Incident Case

In the June 1979 issue of the *FDA Consumer*, an official magazine of the Food and Drug Administration, a feature article entitled "Letter to a Young Saccharin User" raised a storm of controversy from soft drink producers. The letter asked for information on what would happen if its writer, aged 12, drank two cans of diet soda per day. The rest of the article was a personal response from the FDA commissioner saying the FDA believed saccharin might cause cancer.

Soft drink producers seeking to find out more about the situation used the Freedom of Information Act to inspect the documents. They discovered that the author of the letter did not exist. They labeled the article a "sham" and a piece of propaganda. They wrote their protest to members of Congress. The FDA defended the article on the grounds that the industry objectors were overreacting, and that there was a real author who had written a similar letter which they had altered for the purposes of the article.

Are there ethical issues in this case?

Discuss the nature of the adversary relations exhibited here.

Should anything further be done? If so, by whom?

What other factors are at work here?

Issues for Discussion and Analysis

1. What factors may serve to prevent or minimize collusion between business and government to the detriment of the public interest?

2. What are the main justifications for setting up government corporations, hybrid organizations, and the various "Authorities"?

3. How can government best meet the various forms of resistance to change when new programs are introduced?

4. How can the training of private and public sector managers for social responsibilities be improved?

5. What are the pros and cons of the idea that business managers and executives should be active in (a) politics, and (b) government?

6. What has caused the increasing amount of government intervention in the activities of business firms?

7. Explain the principal forms of dependency that characterize business and government relations. In view of these dependencies, how is it that so many adversary relationships also arise?

8. In terms of macromanagement theory, analyze the significance of business-government relations.

Class Project

1. Divide the class into two groups.

2. Have the individuals in group I search for case examples illustrating cooperative relationships between business firms and government units.

3. Have the individuals in group II search for illustrations of adversary relationships between business firms and government units.

4. Each group should then analyze the significant factors in the cases found, and select several to be presented for discussion by the entire class.

For Further Reading

BRUYN, SEVERYN T. *The Social Economy: People Transforming Modern Business* (New York: Halsted Press, 1977).

EDMUNDS, STAHRL W. *Basics of Private and Public Management* (Lexington, Mass.: Lexington Books, 1978).

GUINTHER, JOHN. *Moralists and Managers: Public Interest Movements in America* (Garden City, N.Y.: Anchor Books, 1976).

JACOBY, NEIL H. (ed.). *The Business-Government Relationship: A Reassessment* (Pacific Palisades, Calif: Goodyear, 1976).

KLEIN, THOMAS A. *Social Costs and Benefits of Business* (Englewood Cliffs, N.J.: Prentice-Hall, 1977).

MAZZOLINI, RENATO. *Government Controlled Enterprises* (New York: Wiley, 1979).

PFEFFER, JEFFREY, and GERALD R. SALANCIK. *The External Control of Organizations* (New York: Harper & Row, 1978).

SUMMER, CHARLES E. *Strategic Behavior in Government and Business* (Boston: Little, Brown, 1980).

WALLACE, PHYLLIS A. *Equal Employment Opportunity and the AT & T Case* (Cambridge, Mass.: MIT Press, 1976).

WALSH, ANNMARIE HAUCK. *The Public's Business: The Politics and Practices of Government Corporations* (Cambridge, Mass.: MIT Press, 1978).

WEIDENBAUM, MURRAY L. *Business, Government, and the Public* (Englewood Cliffs, N.J.: Prentice-Hall, 1977).

14

Government Regulation: Problems and Issues

You don't suppose you can run a railway in accordance with the statutes, do you?

CORNELIUS VANDERBILT,
mid-nineteenth century.

Experience should teach us to be most on our guard to protect liberty when government's purposes are beneficent . . . . The greatest dangers to liberty lurk in insidious encroachment by men of zeal, well-meaning but without understanding.

LOUIS BRANDEIS

CONCEPTS DISCUSSED IN THIS CHAPTER

1. THE INCREASING SCOPE AND COST OF GOVERNMENT REGULATION
2. COST-BENEFIT ANALYSIS
3. SOCIAL COSTS AND SOCIAL BALANCE
4. MANAGING UNDER REGULATED ENVIRONMENTS
5. ECONOMIC VERSUS SOCIAL REGULATION
6. REGULATORY REFORM EFFORTS

Government regulation is one of our most stubborn social, economic, and political issues. Everyone agrees that there must be some degree of societal control over business and other institutions, but virtually everyone disagrees as to how many and what kind of controls are desirable. A large segment of our working organizations—schools, universities, and business firms—feel we are the victims of regulatory overkill. Taxpayers and consumers are revolting against the costs induced by regulation. But interest groups and many other organizations such as business firms plead for regulation in the interests of their causes or their special needs. These paradoxical pressures are difficult to resolve.

The pros and cons of regulation generate strong emotions, political conflicts, and ideological controversies that often tend to override the statistical data produced by each side. Regulation and its related philosophies of governance pervade the political and economic system, and their fortunes ebb and flow in accordance with the general political climate. Regulation is also spurred by special events such as war, depression, or recession, and by changing public sentiment with respect to the issues of the day. Heavy regulation eventually leads to resistance and other forms of opposition, followed by curtailment, but the successive cycles of sentiment toward regulation leave it at a new high compared to previous periods.

This chapter examines the nature and extent of government regulation and its important problems. The analysis will proceed in four parts: (1) the increasing scope and cost of government regulation, (2) managing under regulated environments, (3) major problems in regulation, and (4) regulatory reform efforts.

THE GROWTH OF GOVERNMENT REGULATION

Government has penetrated deeply into the private lives of citizens and into the activities of organizations in business, education, health care, and other sectors. Though these interventions are well-intentioned, there are many questions about the scope, extent, consequences, and management of regulatory processes.

Regulation has increased enormously since the late 1960s. The aims of regulation have changed significantly during this expansion. Whereas regulation was traditionally economic in character and mainly directed toward controlling the activities of entire industries, a new wave of legislation has focused on broad social issues, thereby affecting day-to-day management within every organizational unit, not only in business but in other social institutions as well.

The distinction between economic and social regulation is not clear-cut, since in a sense economic regulation serves both economic and social purposes. But the differences in their missions and their jurisdic-tional domains are striking and they account, as we will see later, for many regulatory issues and controversies. Economic regulation attempts chiefly to promote the welfare of an industry by establishing a com-mission or other agency focusing on its particular problems—pricing, competition, and the like. Examples include the Interstate Commerce

Commission, the Civil Aeronautics Board, the Federal Power Commission, or the Federal Communications Commission.

Social regulation uses similar structural devices—commissions or other agencies—but they are charged with regulating specific problems rather than industries. They attack such problems as coping with pollution, conserving energy, eliminating job discrimination, or reducing product hazards, which cut across all organizational units. Examples of this type of regulation include the Environmental Protection Agency, the Equal Employment Opportunity Commission, and the Federal Energy Administration.[1]

The growth of regulation is reflected in the rising number of officials and agencies, and in the dollars allocated in the federal budget. Government regulators now number more than 150,000 officials in over 100 agencies, representing about 800 million man-hours of work. Today's steel industry, for example, comes under 27 regulatory agencies, 20 of which did not exist in 1970. The proliferation of regulatory legislation is illustrated in Table 14.1, which shows the growing number of regulatory laws focused on both economic and social issues.

The costs of regulation have increased along with the number of agencies and laws. Clearly the major increases are found in the area of social rather than economic regulation.

THE COSTS OF REGULATION

The costs of regulation include not only those of establishing and managing government agencies, but also of enforcement. In addition, there are the costs of compliance incurred by regulated organizations. These are known as incremental costs—the direct costs of managerial and paperwork to comply with a regulation that would not have been needed in the absence of regulation. Almost no studies attempt to discover total costs, which would include secondary costs such as opportunity costs, the costs of new or changed equipment, changes in productivity, or delays involved in administrative or judicial processes relating to regulation. Like other costs, incremental and secondary costs are hard to measure.

The costs shown in Table 14.2 are those of the federal budget for operating regulatory agencies. True costs are hard to determine, but additional cost burdens fall heavily on various groups in society. Table 14.3, for example, shows estimated annual costs of federal paperwork to

---

[1] Murray L. Weidenbaum, "The New Wave of Government Regulation of Business," *Business and Society Review*, Fall 1975, pp. 1–9; William Lilley III and James C. Miller III, "The New 'Social Regulation'," *The Public Interest*, Spring 1977, pp. 49–61.

TABLE 14.1

Selected List of Federal Regulatory Laws, 1972–1980

Year Enacted	Title of Statute
1972	Consumer Product Safety Act
	Equal Employment Opportunity Act
	Federal Election Campaign Act
	Federal Environmental Pesticide Control Act
	Federal Water Pollution Control Act Amendments
	Noise Control Act
	Ports and Waterways Safety Act
1973	Agriculture and Consumer Protection Act
	Economic Stabilization Act Amendments
	Emergency Petroleum Allocation Act
	Flood Disaster Protection Act
	Comprehensive Employment and Training Act
1974	Atomic Energy Act
	Commodity Futures Trading Commission Act
	Council on Wage and Price Stability Act
	Employee Retirement Income Security Act
	Federal Energy Administration Act
	Hazardous Materials Transportation Act
	Housing and Community Development Act
	Magnuson-Moss Warranty—Federal Trade Commission Improvement Act
	Pension Reform Act
	Privacy Act
	Safe Drinking Water Act
1975	Energy Policy and Conservation Act
	Consumer Goods Pricing Act
1976	Hart-Scott-Rodino Antitrust Amendments Act
	Federal Election Campaign Act Amendments
	Government in the Sunshine Act
	Federal Coal Leasing Amendments Act
	Fishery Conservation and Management Act
	Tax Reform Act
1977	House Ethics Code
	Senate Ethics Code
	Fair Debt Collection Practices Act
	Department of Energy Organization Act
	Surface Mining and Control Act
	Export Administration Amendments
	Securities and Exchange Act Amendments
	Saccharin Study and Labelling Act
1978	Civil Service Reform Act
	Ethics in Government Act
1979	Department of Education Organization Act
	Trade Reorganization Plan
	Emergency Energy Conservation Act
	Trade Agreements Act
	Export Administration Act
	Shipping Act Amendments
1980	Paperwork Reduction Act
	Regulatory Flexibility Act

TABLE 14.2

Growth of 57 Federal Regulatory Agencies. Selected Fiscal Years, 1971–1981

Area	1971	1977	1978	1979	1980 (est.)	1981 (est.)
			Expenditures ($ billions)			
Social regulation						
Consumer safety and health	$0.6	1.8	2.3	2.5	2.6	2.9
Job safety and other working conditions	$0.1	0.5	0.5	0.6	0.7	0.8
Energy and the environment	$0.1	1.0	1.3	1.5	1.7	2.2
	$0.8	3.3	4.1	4.6	5.0	5.9
Economic regulation						
Finance and banking	$0.1	0.2	0.3	0.3	0.3	0.3
Other industry-specific	$0.2	0.3	0.3	0.3	0.4	0.4
General business	$0.1	0.2	0.2	0.3	0.3	0.3
	$0.4	0.7	0.8	0.9	1.0	1.0
Total	$1.2	4.0	4.9	5.5	6.0	6.9
Total in 1970 Dollars*	$1.2	2.6	3.0	3.0	3.1	3.2
			Permanent full-time positions (thousands)			
Social regulation	10.8	58.4	61.9	63.6	65.4	66.2
Economic regulation	18.3	23.6	24.3	23.9	24.5	24.6
Total	29.1	82.0	86.2	87.5	89.9	90.8

*Adjusted by GNP deflator (actual and, for 1980–81, estimated in 1981 budget).
SOURCE: Center for the Study of American Business, Washington University. From Regulation 4 (March/April 1980) p. 8, Copyright American Enterprise Institute.

TABLE 14.3

Estimated Costs of Federal Paperwork to Various Social Sectors, 1977

Sector	Amounts
The federal government	$43 billion
Private industry	$25–32 billion
State and local governments	$5–9 billion
Individuals	$8.7 billion
Farmers	$300 million
Labor organizations	$75 million

SOURCE: Final Report, Commission on Federal Paperwork (Washington, D.C.: U.S. Government Printing Office, 1977).

selected segments of society. Regulation accounts for a large share of such costs.[2]

Several examples will illustrate the extent of the enormous paperwork burden for private industry:

[2] These estimates were included in the final report of the Commission on Federal Paperwork, which was phased out at the end of 1977.

> When the Federal Trade Commission required 345 firms to report detailed information on each line of business, it cost over $500,000 per company, with a total cost of $190 million.
>
> The Dow Chemical Company paid out $147 million on regulatory compliance in one year, estimating that it spent $5 million on salaries and expenses for executives who testified on federal regulations.
>
> A pharmaceutical company found that it spent more on government paperwork each year than on research for drugs to combat cancer and heart disease.
>
> One oil company produced 636 miles of computer tape in one year's reports to a federal energy agency.[3]

Large companies find it easier to meet reporting and compliance costs than small ones, so treating all companies alike results in a heavier burden for the smaller firms. President Carter achieved about a 14 percent drop in the paperwork burden in 1978–1979 by pushing recommendations of the Commission on Federal Paperwork which had been formed in 1975. The efforts to reduce federal paperwork have been the responsibility of the Office of Management and Budget, which changed from measuring the burden of paperwork by the number of reports to the number of hours required. Following the 1979 progress, however, improvement came to a halt as the system ran out of easy targets. The rigidities of government bureaucracy make the reduction of paperwork an almost insurmountable task.[4]

One study of 48 firms in 20 industries measured incremental costs resulting from the regulations of six federal agencies (EPA, EEOC, OSHA, DOE, ERISA, and FTC). The 48 firms incurred $2.6 billion in incremental costs in 1977, for these six programs. This was equivalent to a price level impact of more than 1 percent.[5] So regulation is clearly very costly, raising the possibility that it contributes to inflation since the costs are passed along to consumers. Poor management makes the cost burdens worse. Regulation machinery is ponderous and inefficient. Regulators often decide on inadequate or insufficient information; they often ignore available information. They give insufficient attention to alternatives and innovative, lower-cost ways of solving problems. Another source of higher costs is that standards are high, with regulators pushing them even higher. Costs rise at a geometric rather than an arithmetic rates at the higher ranges of performance. For example, 90 percent of an ideal standard may be realistically expected, but the costs of pushing for

---

[3] Keith Davis, William C. Frederick, and Robert L. Blomstrom, *Business and Society*, 4th ed. (New York: McGraw-Hill, 1980), pp. 278–280.

[4] Richard M. Neustadt, "Taming the Paperwork Tiger," *Regulation*, January–February 1981, pp. 28–32.

[5] "Government and Business—Too Much? Not Enough?" A dialogue at the Ohio State University (Columbus: College of Administrative Science, The Ohio State University, 1978).

another 2 or 3 percent are extraordinarily high, and attaining the maximum would add impossibly to costs.

A central feature of the cost problem is the failure to use cost-benefit analysis. This is not a foolproof technique, but it has been successful in other areas. It requires that the benefits of a regulation be assessed against the costs. Benefits, of course, are hard to measure because subjective estimates of value must be made for alleviating dangers or human suffering. Some regulations, however, are so trivial or ridiculous that only the most extreme and unrealistic assumptions could find them beneficial.

Regulators have wide discretion over "tight" or "loose" control, but they seldom make this judgment on a cost-benefit basis. Controls go tight or slack more according to political circumstances that influence the pressures on agency heads. Agency heads also change frequently; and some are more zealous than others. Regulatory zeal is particularly characteristic of mission-oriented social regulators, who are often appointed out of the experience with interest groups that fought for the regulations as they were developed. Regulatory zeal accounts in part for the overkill phenomenon in regulation—diligent attention to trivial, even ridiculous rulings and guidelines.

SOCIAL COSTS

Economists and government officials widely view regulation as a powerful engine for the redistribution of wealth. Regulation is not a "free good"; it is subject to the laws of supply and demand. It is also interlocked with political processes that inject power relations into the equation. Where regulation arises out of market inadequacies, traditional economic theory holds that it is the way to cope with resulting misallocations and maldistributions of wealth and resources. However, a revisionist economic theory is now emerging which holds that regulation does not work this way, and indeed may have generated resource misallocation.[6]

The increased amount and costs of social interest regulation reflects society's intent to establish in public policy the idea that business should bear a fairer share of the social costs involved in its activities. The using up of nonrenewable resources, the pollution of air, water, and land, or other alterations in the environment produce social costs which the government wants the firms incurring them to bear. To protect the public interest, the government fosters laws and policies designed to restrain the harmful results of economic effort.

---

[6] Sam Peltzman, "Toward a More General Theory of Regulation," *Journal of Law and Economics* 19 (August 1976), pp. 211–240.

Regulation now focuses more on what people or businesses must do, rather than on what they must not do, as was the case in early regulatory history. Since the firms must increase their prices to pass costs along to consumers, regulation can have a strong inflationary impact on the economy.[7] Public policy holds that only by forcing business to recognize and pay a greater share of the social costs can those costs be brought under managerial control, made visible, and judged by consumers. The payment of social costs is thus done by pricing rather than taxation.

> *I believe the root of the regulatory impulse is often arrogance. If you scratch an advocate of regulation, you are likely to find, very close to the surface, an arrogant impulse to substitute some personal vision of order for the apparent disorder of the marketplace.*
>
> *Practically all of us are arrogant. Most businessmen are arrogant, particularly if, as in my case, they are chief executives. But happily, there are checks against arrogance in business. The free market and the free consumer usually dictate to business.*
>
> *But when arrogance is embodied in public policy — whether by legislation or administrative fiat — there are no effective checks on it. It becomes institutionalized — immortalized.*
>
> ROBERT T. QUITTMEYER, president and chief executive officer of Amstar Corporation, in a speech to the Swiss-American Chamber of Commerce in Geneva, Switzerland, 1977.

Although regulation is now centered more on social goals than economic ones, it should be noted that the impact of social regulation falls heavily on business. The government perceives business not only as the cause of many social issues, but also as part of the cure. Moreover, business is so pervasive in all other social institutions that regulating business activity is an important influence on them also. Social concerns now dominate economic decisions in business, education, health care, and other social institutions. The idea that identifiable social costs can result from the actions of business is not new, although it has only recently come to be dealt with by regulatory means. J. M. Clark noted in 1926 that social costs occur wherever there are interests which the general system of legal rights does not cover — interests which could be hidden or evaded without consent or compensation. He also noted that the evils of business activity are diffused, falling on innocent parties. Therefore, the state should minimize those evils, and require the business responsible for them to bear a fairer share of their costs.[8]

---

[7] John H. Perkins, "Inflation by Regulation: The Consumer Is the Victim," *Across the Board*, July 1979, pp. 78–82.

[8] J. M. Clark, *The Social Control of Business* (Chicago: The University of Chicago Press, 1926), p. 178.

MANAGING IN REGULATED ENVIRONMENTS

For managers and their organizations, regulation is an explicit demand for meeting certain types of social responsibility. Therefore managers need to review the problems of social programs, the use of social capital, and the balance of social costs and benefits.[9]

MANAGERIAL STRATEGIES IN REGULATION

The growth in the number, size, and scope of regulatory agencies, the spiraling costs of regulation, and the outpouring of trivial, difficult, intrusive, or conflicting standards are realities that call for managerial analysis and the formation of strategies for coping with regulatory issues. Without planned strategies, managers can only attack issues ideologically or politically — methods that are slow and expensive. Complaining, without action, is ineffective.

An important step in dealing with a regulatory issue is to develop a sharper perception of its purposes, its strengths and weaknesses, its failures and successes. This enables managers to avoid myths, stereotyped thinking, shallow or shortsighted views, misconceived strategies of attack and resistance, or succumbing helplessly to the excessive intrusions of government. Take, for example, the issue of how much and what kind of regulation there should be. Positions range from assertions of overkill, and dire consequences such as inflation, unemployment, bankruptcy, and the loss of freedoms and rights on the one hand, to assertions that regulation results in improved social welfare, changes behavior for the better, and fulfills the public interest. Advocates of both polar extremes are busy and vocal, but managers have to act in concrete situations where more balanced perspectives are more useful.

To forge a strategy, managers need to analyze concretely the effects of regulation on the economics of the firm and the industry, and on competition within and between industries. Another strategic element is the effects of changing regulations on product, marketing, and financial plans, both present and contemplated. Finally, managers should consider the impacts of regulation on the organizational structure of the firm. Regulation is more extensive and has a longer history in some industries than in others. Transportation, gas and electric utilities, telecommunications, and finance have significant experiences with regulation that can serve in modeling the strategies of less-regulated industries. In the former, one may see how regulation affects the nature and degree of com-

---

[9] George C. Sawyer, *Business and Society: Managing Corporate Social Impact* (Boston: Houghton Mifflin, 1979).

petition, has differential effects on members of the industry, and evokes organization designs tailored to the regulatory environment.[10]

Executives pay increasing lip service to the need to restore the vitality of the third sector—private nonprofit institutions and organizations—but an examination of their concrete proposals to roll back government regulation shows the profit sector preoccupied with its own immediate interests. The regulations that are likely to be reduced over the next few years are those that are particularly obnoxious to particular segments of the business community—particularly small business or financially pressed industries such as steel or autos—not those that affect both profit and nonprofit sectors alike. Moreover, instead of a more rational, responsible weighing of economic costs and social benefits, business is as likely to prove as insensitive to legitimate social concerns as the public interest movement has been to economic costs. Particular industries are likely to use the public's current antiregulatory movement simply to get rid of regulations that offend them, not merely those that are indeed superfluous or counterproductive.

DAVID VOGEL, "The Inadequacy of Contemporary Opposition to Business," *Daedalus* 109 (Summer 1980), p. 56.

The general strategic options available to managers include (1) adapting the firm's operating strategies to fit regulation-induced changes in products or markets; (2) changing the organization to fit the new regulatory environment; (3) influencing regulatory policies, procedures, and laws; (4) ignoring legislation and paying the fines; and (5) tying up enforcement in legal appeals. The need for adaptive strategy is illustrated by efforts to deregulate certain industries. Organizational strategies are illustrated by structural changes required in production planning to meet EPA antipollution requirement schedules and deadlines. Organizational changes, such as withdrawal from regulated activity, diversification into nonregulated activities as a hedge against the impact of regulation, or mergers with other firms, help reduce the firm's dependence on, or vulnerability to regulation. The third option, to change the regulatory environment, can be pursued through lobbying, political action committees, trade associations, and the like.[11]

The managerial skills required for pursuing these strategies are extensive and unfamiliar to many managers. There are technical, economic, legal, and political questions involved, so managers need the help

---

[10] M. Porter, "How Competitive Forces Shape Strategy," *Harvard Business Review* 57 (March–April 1979), pp. 137–146; R. Leone, "The Real Cost of Regulation," *Harvard Business Review* 55 (November–December 1977), pp. 57–67.

[11] Daniel M. Kasper, "Managing in the Regulated Environment," Unpublished Working Paper HBS 79-26, Graduate School of Business, Harvard University, 1979.

of a variety of experts. But managers cannot substitute experts for their own intensive study of regulation.[12]

PROBLEMS OF REGULATION

Battle lines between the regulators and the regulated are sharply drawn. On each side are managers trying to do their job as they see it. They have both personal motivations and official responsibilities. Under such conditions, problems are inevitable. In this section we will briefly review the major problems of the regulators, and then analyze the problems of the regulated with respect to economic and social regulation.

THE PROBLEMS OF REGULATORS

Regulators must perform difficult tasks under a number of limitations. Their work begins with legislation, which is often ambiguous as to intent, poorly drawn, and embroils them in continuous court and administrative procedures. Built-in contradictions have to be resolved in the unfolding of the regulatory efforts.

Agencies and commissions are often understaffed and underfinanced; they meet legal roadblocks thrown up by organizations able to pay high-priced legal specialists. Enforcement is difficult because precise information is hard to get and analyze well enough to convict violators, many of whom find the light penalties scarcely a deterrent. Huge case burdens slow the work and strain resources. The Federal Trade Commission, for example, has about 700 professional specialists to monitor the business practices of 14 million firms and review over 12,000 cease-and-desist orders annually.[13]

Regulators incur criticism both for what they do and what they do not do. The agency that does its job may be attacked by those it regulates, but if it goes too easy, the supporting interest groups will be affronted. For example, the federal Consumer Product Safety Commission, which can ban, recall, and set safety standards for more than 10,000 consumer items, has not had to bear much of the antiregulation attack. Proponents say this is because the commission is politically astute; others say it is because it isn't doing its job. The commission has avoided some criticism by acting against individual firms rather than attempting to achieve in-

---

[12] Raymond M. Momboisse, "How to Survive in the Regulatory Jungle," *Management Review* 66 (September 1977), pp. 43–47; James E. Post and John F. Mahon, "Articulated Turbulence: The Effect of Regulatory Agencies on Corporate Responses to Social Change," *Academy of Management Review* 5 (July 1980), pp. 399–408; Peter H. Schuck, "Regulation: Asking the Right Questions," *National Journal* 11 (April 28, 1979), pp. 1–20.

[13] "Too Much Regulation? Not as Regulators Tell It," *U.S. News and World Report*, October 8, 1979, pp. 74–75.

dustrywide standards. It has also encouraged the development of voluntary standards by industry groups, thereby arousing the antagonism of public interest groups.[14]

Regulators have been accused of allowing the regulated to "capture" them—a form of cooptation. The "capture theory" holds that regulatory agencies have come under the control or influence of the interests they are to regulate. This could happen if an agency hires industry representatives as officials or consultants, or is influenced by lobbying, by pressures for administrative change, or by the erosion resulting from negotiated settlements. Popular opinion readily believes in the capture theory, but research holds that it fails to explain the behavior of regulatory agencies in too many cases to warrant wide acceptance.[15]

Though capture theories are rejected, regulators and the regulated do come to have a mutual interdependence in their relationships. Regulatory bodies develop a bureaucratic trustworthiness on which the regulated come to depend, minimizing a dangerous, competitive politics. Stigler writes: "The regulation agency must eventually become the agency of the regulated industry if it has a well-defined area of responsibility. This is not to say that it will be bribed into corruption or even that relationships between agency and industry are always cordial. Yet each needs the other."[16]

The extent of the dependency of those regulated on the regulators is shown in the fact that the former give strong political support to regulators. Both trucking firms and the Teamsters' union opposed deregulation of their industry, for regulation helps the industry by restricting competition and keeping prices higher. Certain states have attempted to eliminate the licensing of cosmetologists, barbers, psychologists, pest controllers, library examiners, and many other trades and professions, only to discover that practitioners want to keep the regulations.[17]

Staffing of regulatory agencies, especially the agency head, is a critical factor in their success. Appointments must avoid violent industry opposition and preferably have industry support. Often the commissioners come from the industry rather than from the political sphere. This provides both technical knowledge and liaison with the industry. This is more frequent for economic than for social regulation, which cuts across industries and therefore is less likely to be bureaucratized or form links between career employees and those regulated.

---

[14] "Safety Commission Has Avoided War on Regulation," *The Wall Street Journal*, February 6, 1980, p. 20.

[15] Douglas D. Anderson, "The Politics of Regulation," Working Paper 79-37, Graduate School of Business Administration, Harvard University, 1979.

[16] George J. Stigler, *The Citizen and the State: Essays on Regulation* (Chicago: The University of Chicago Press, 1975), pp. 162–163.

[17] Richard Reeves, "All That 'Over-Regulation' Not Always so Unpopular," syndicated column dated December 12, 1979.

We turn now to a consideration of the problems of the regulated. Since these problems are different, we will first analyze economic regulation, and then social regulation.

ECONOMIC REGULATION

Economic regulation is directed at problems of competition the market system does not or cannot regulate. It attempts to keep the marketplace organized and to protect the business environment. This realm includes licensing procedures, antimonopoly or antitrust efforts, incorporation procedures, certain financial reporting requirements, money and money supply management, enforcement of private contracts, and protecting private property. Economic regulation benefits most businesses, so that business widely initiates and supports it as long as the system applies fairly to all firms in an industry.

A major problem is to assess correctly the nature of market inadequacies. Schultze notes that regulatory responses to market problems lack sufficient analysis:

> Usually, when a specific problem has been singled out for public action, little attempt has been made to isolate the causes of market failure and deal with them in a way which preserves as many as possible of the elements of voluntary choice and private incentives. Rather, intervention typically substitutes a centralized command-and-control approach to decision-making over a far broader area then is necessary to deal with the specific market failure in question.[18]

Schultze further asserts that one broad class of market failures stems from the inability of the unaided private market to put a price on important side effects of economic transactions, so that they can be incorporated into the system, balancing costs against gains. Public policy regulates first, then considers pricing alternatives. This is illustrated by pollution control requirements that call for expensive technological responses, without flexibility for assessing wide variations in the costs of alternatives.[19]

Economic regulation is little noticed by the public except when end-result problems such as shortages of power, natural gas, or gasoline occur. Then public opinion swings toward rationing and price controls. People are concerned about the fairness of allocation itself, rather than the distributional effects in the usual sense.[20]

---

[18] Charles L. Schultze, *The Public Use of Private Interest*, (Wash. D.C.: The Brookings Institution, 1977), p. 46.

[19] Ibid., p. 55. See also Almarin Phillips, "Regulation and Its Alternatives," in *Regulating Business: The Search for an Optimum* (San Francisco: Institute for Contemporary Studies, 1978), pp. 157–172.

[20] Bruce M. Owen and Ronald Braeutigam, *The Regulation Game: Strategic Use of the Administrative Process* (Cambridge, Mass.: Ballinger, 1975), pp. 32–35.

Economic regulation is a continuous problem, rife with legal maneuvers, litigation, and long-drawn-out agency investigations. Major economic regulatory agencies have existed for a long time. The Interstate Commerce Commission was established in 1887, the Federal Trade Commission in 1914, and the Securities and Exchange Commission in 1933. Many economists believe that the older agencies have become tired and shopworn, outlasting the original problems that generated them. Stigler asserts that they weaken the defenses of consumers in the market system, and even impose new burdens on them without corresponding protections.[21] The economic regulatory agencies have been widely attacked for years, and increasingly so in recent years. So many expectations exist that virtually no one is satisfied with their performance. Let us consider two examples: The Federal Trade Commission and the Securities and Exchange Commission.

The Federal Trade Commission. Stone found in a lengthy study of the FTC that its lack of success was not due entirely to inactivity, bad personnel, or bad judgment, though these were involved at times. Rather, it has been largely due to problems of resource shortages, litigation and delays, ineffective sanctions, and a host of other procedural, policy, and legislative flaws.[22]

Antitrust legislation, directed at regulating unfair competition, began with the Sherman Antitrust Act of 1890. It contains two broad goals: the prohibition of restraint of trade through conspiracy, collusion, or combination, and the prevention of monopoly through individual or joint activity. The Sherman Act was modified by the Clayton Act of 1914 and the Robinson-Patman Act of 1936. These acts were not aimed at the restraint of trade, as is the Sherman Act, but at certain practices that could result in market restraints. The Federal Trade Commission Act, passed in 1914 and amended in 1938, 1973, and 1975, supplements and extends the Sherman and Clayton Acts in prohibiting unfair business methods, acts, or practices.

The prohibitions of the antitrust laws are general, leaving specifics to be interpreted case by case by the commission, the courts, and the Antitrust Division of the Department of Justice. As a result, antitrust agencies have considerable power, but enforcement involves long, difficult litigations and administrative proceedings.[23]

An example of an FTC case is that of its proceedings against the "big three" breakfast cereal makers. After four years, over 130 witnesses, and 40,872 pages of testimony, the hearings ended in June of 1980. But the

---

[21] Stigler, *The Citizen and the State*, pp. 178–188.

[22] Alan Stone, *Economic Regulation and the Public Interest: The Federal Trade Commission in Theory and Practice* (Ithaca, N.Y.: Cornell University Press, 1977), pp. 257–270.

[23] Jerrold G. Van Cise, *The Federal Antitrust Laws*, 3rd rev. ed. (Washington, D.C.: American Enterprise Institute, 1975), pp. 1–22.

decision was not expected until the fall of 1981. The cereal makers also raised technicalities that could cause the whole effort to start over. The FTC did not charge the companies with overt conspiracy to maintain their 80 percent market share, but rather of acting with "tacit understanding" to limit competiton and keep prices up. This "shared monopoly" concept is controversial; it indicates the sweeping changes that the commission rather than Congress decides. The remedies sought by the FTC are to require each firm to spin off a separate new company, and to license at no cost any of its existing brands to other companies.[24]

> *It will be of little avail to the people that the laws are made by men of their own choice, if the laws be so voluminous that they cannot be read, or so incoherent that they cannot be understood; if they be repealed or revised before they are promulgated, or undergo such incessant changes that no man who knows what the law is today can guess what it will be tomorrow.*
>
> *Federalist* No. 62.

Several efforts have been made to improve the ability of antitrust agencies to curb monopolies, but mergers and the formation of conglomerates have continued despite regulatory constraints. These do not necessarily result in monopoly control of markets, though they do constitute power centers of great influence.[25] But while the growth of conglomerates is permitted, antitrust efforts are directed at breaking up huge firms such as IBM, General Motors, or the cereal makers.

The IBM case is instructive. By 1979, the government's case, which began in 1969, was still in the courts with little hope of settlement. IBM's share of the computer market was around 70 percent during this time, well above the usual standard for pursuing monopoly charges. Yet both the industry and IBM performed well on pricing, innovation, production, and efficiency. To antitrust regulators, however, performance is irrelevant; all that matters is market share. The protracted proceedings themselves have had a regulatory impact on IBM; it has behaved very well in relation to competitors.[26]

The success of the FTC, both in its antitrust and consumer protection duties, fluctuates widely with jousting between it and Congress as each adopts changing strategies. In 1975, the FTC adopted a get-tough

---

[24] *The Wall Street Journal*, June 25, 1980, p. 25. See also Brian F. Harris, *Shared Monopoly and the Cereal Industry* (East Lansing: Division of Research, Graduate School of Business Administration, Michigan State University, 1979).

[25] George J. Benston, *Conglomerate Mergers: Causes, Consequences, and Remedies* (Washington, D.C.: American Enterprise Institute, 1980).

[26] Hendrik S. Southakker, "Uncle Sam vs. IBM: Why?" *The Wall Street Journal*, February 5, 1979, p. 28.

policy, shifting from a case-by-case policy of pursuing complaints to the establishment of broad industry rules and then punishment of violators.[27] But such activism has met with counterattack strategies by business, such as resisting FTC orders, filing suits against it, and political pressures against the broadening of the agency's intrusions into "social" regulation.[28] By 1980 the attacks and criticisms brought on substantial efforts in Congress to curb the FTC's new approach. The government had never been a staunch advocate of the FTC, giving it little independence and encouragement, and reducing its efforts to trivial matters.[29]

The Securities and Exchange Commission. The problems of the SEC have been similar to those of the FTC, except that for most of its history it had a reputation as one of the government's most admired and respected agencies, vigilant, productive, with freedom from both politics and industry domination.

The SEC was created in 1934 to protect shareholders from stock frauds and misleading financial reports. Yet by the early 1980s the agency had brought down the wrath of the securities industry by its vigorous attempts to "right many wrongs." It had become overzealous to the point where adversaries claim that it is now trying to run corporations. Opponents allege that the SEC is attempting to restructure securities markets, though its mandate from Congress was only to facilitate the exchanges; that it subjectively attacks corporate bribery yet lets offenders off with light penalties; that it enters directly into corporate affairs beyond its traditional scope; that it has interfered with the accounting profession by unrealistic interpretations of its professional rules.[30] Between 1975 and 1980, the U.S. Supreme Court began to restrict the SEC by curtailing opportunities for private citizens to bring suits under SEC rulings and by imposing stiffer standards of proof on the SEC and private individuals. In this period, the SEC lost 12 of the 18 cases it took to court.[31]

SOCIAL REGULATION

Economic regulators sometimes use their powers to seek social goals. Some have proposed the opposite—using social goals to enforce antitrust regulations. For example, one proposal would outlaw all

---

[27] *Business Week*, May 19, 1975, pp. 64–65.

[28] "The Escalating Struggle between the FTC and Business," *Business Week*, December 13, 1976, pp. 52–60.

[29] Robert Sherrill, "Jousting on the Hill: Skewering the Consumer's Defender," *Saturday Review*, March 29, 1980, pp. 18–22; Norman Kangun and R. Charles Moyer, "The Failings of Regulation," *MSU Business Topics* 24 (Spring 1976), pp. 6–14.

[30] "Why the SEC's Enforcer Is in Over His Head," *Business Week*, October 11, 1976, pp. 70–75; "The SEC: Going Too Far Too Fast," *Business Week*, November 27, 1978, pp. 86–92.

[31] "High Court Rulings Are Putting the SEC on a Short Leash," *The Wall Street Journal*, October 2, 1980, p. 30.

mergers between companies with more than $2 billion in sales or assets and force others, with sales or assets over $350 million, to prove that there would be a *significant social advantage* to acquiring any company with similar market position.[32] Such proposals, however, have not received much support in Congress.

Direct social regulation establishes major federal agencies, such as the Equal Employment Opportunity Commission, the Occupational Safety and Health Administration, or the Environmental Protection Agency. They are charged with meeting broad social goals and society-wide concerns. The volume of social regulation is overwhelming; detailed regulations are not in the legislation, but in the broad discretionary powers of regulatory agencies and officials. A relatively brief law often results in thousands of pages of administrative guidelines, directives, and orders. Each year 60,000 to 80,000 pages of regulations, often contradictory, ambiguous, or confusing, are published. That such regulations sometimes transcend or overlook the original intent of the law is not surprising. Guidelines and rulings are made by officials at the lower, operating levels who are not publicly identified or accountable, and with limited perspective. They become more concerned with uniformity and enforceability than with the impact of regulation on those forced to comply.

Social legislation leaves wide discretion to the regulators for setting standards, investigating cases, and enforcing compliance through negotiated settlements and court actions to achieve remedies. The tendency has been for such agencies to set standards that are too high, too numerous, too trivial, technically impossible, or devoid of cost-benefit analysis. Business sees inspections and investigations as undue "fishing expeditions" undertaken without prior complaints, search warrants, or evidence of wrongdoing. The result is burdensome paperwork, lengthy court cases, excessive costs, and continuous adversary relationships. Regulators encounter resistance that throws them into power plays and political controversies. Regulators become prosecutors, and the regulated become litigious. Both attacks and defenses display the righteous zeal of causes. The more trivial or inappropriate the regulation, the more intense the adversary relations become.

Regulators have enormous powers that can be brought to bear on those who defy or resist regulation. By denying federal grants and contracts to firms, schools, cities, or states, regulators can compel compliance. For example, the New York City's Metropolitan Transportation Board risked losing $400 million in federal transit aid by voting to defy Department of Transportation rules requiring that public buses, subways, and commuter railways be accessible to wheelchair users. The goal

---

[32] "Social Goals Become an Antitrust Weapon," *Business Week*, April 9, 1979.

was noble, but the equipment is costly and usage is low. The MTA esti-mated the compliance costs of capital investment to be $1.5 billion, with maintenance an additional $100 million a year. Door to door taxi services would cost about $7 per ride, whereas the DOT requirements would cost $38 per ride.[33]

Another criticism of social regulation is that of conflicting or over-lapping requirements of the several agencies of government. The EPA has ordered plants to convert from coal to oil to reduce air pollution, and at the same time the DOE has ordered the same plants to convert from oil to coal to save energy. Antipollution requirements drive marginal plants out of business, which contradicts federal goals of reducing unemployment. The result is that companies find it hard to obey some laws without breaking others. The EPA wants steel mills to put hoods over their coke ovens to reduce air pollution, but OSHA opposes this because they in-crease emissions breathed by workers. One survey found over 50 federal programs providing services to handicapped youths. These agencies were totally without coordination.[34]

Problems of conflicts and overlap are a reflection not only of red tape and administrative ineptitude, but also of the difficulties of setting at-tainable, realistic, and effective standards. Technological difficulties abound. Everyone wants clean air, clean water, less noise, and protection from carcinogens, but the standards are hard to specify. No one really knows what harms result from given substances, but regulations are often put into effect anyway, causing the disruption of industries and dif-ficult problems of compliance. For example, the Delaney amendment to the Food, Drug and Cosmetic Act of 1938 requires the FDA to ban the use in any food of substances known to produce cancer in any species, in any dosage, in any circumstances. Yet in the case of cyclamates, a person would have to drink several cases of diet drinks every day for a normal life span to get results equivalent to those for laboratory rats.

To illustrate the administrative problems of social regulation, let us briefly consider what has happened in the regulation of water pollution, employee health and safety, and equal opportunity employment.

The Environmental Protection Agency deals with water and other forms of pollution and damage. An overwhelming technical knowledge is demanded of the EPA, which has to set effluent limitations for each firm. There are 62,000 point sources of water pollution, each with a cost-benefit calculation as to control methods. By mid-1976 the EPA has issued or developed 492 different effluent guidelines and 45,000 in-dividual plant permits. The scope of such efforts gives ample opportunity

---

[33] *The Wall Street Journal*, September 29, 1980, p. 30.

[34] "Federal Regulations: Catch-22 for Business," *U.S. News and World Report*, January 22, 1979, pp. 60–61.

for contesting the regulations. Technological and economic factors often change midstream, so the process starts over. The result is an over-burdened agency, slow to act and unable to enforce its many directives.[35] (In Chapter 15 we will analyze such problems in more detail.)

In the name of education, welfare, taxation, safety, health, and environment, to mention but a few of the laudable ends involved, the new despotism confronts us at every turn. Its effectiveness lies, as I say, in part through liaison with humanitarian rather than nakedly exploitative objectives but also, and perhaps most significantly, in its capacity to deal with the human will rather than with mere human actions. By the very existence of one or other of the regulatory offices of the invisible government that now occupies foremost place, the wills of educators, researchers, artists, philanthropists, and enterprisers in all areas, as well as in business, are bound to be affected: to be shaped, bent, driven, even extinguished.

From *Twilight of Authority* by ROBERT NISBET. Copyright © 1975 by ROBERT NISBET. Reprinted by permission of Oxford University Press, Inc., New York.

The Occupational Health and Safety Act of 1970 was passed to assure the health and safety of working conditions for employees. OSHA is a complicated piece of legislation that has proved difficult to enforce. It functions by standards put forth in administrative rulings, followed by inspections, with cease and desist orders and fines as the means of enforcement. Employers may appeal citations to the Occupational Health and Safety Administration, but many of these issues end up in the courts. Vehement objections center on the number and triviality of OSHA safety standards, the impossible and contradictory nature of many standards, its inspection programs, and the light penalties assessed (averaging $25 per violation). Critics also hold that it overemphasizes safety over health problems.

OSHA has issued over 4000 standards. Both the Department of Labor and OSHA can set standards and conduct inspections; there is often confusion and conflict between their edicts, and also with standards of the several states. Inspections are scheduled in response to employee complaints or in the course of regular inspection programs. No prior notice is permitted, but employers and employees may have their representatives accompany the inspectors.

Fundamental disagreements are also raised over the broad mandate of the act. The difficult questions include these: To what degree should government attempt to require safety and health provisions? Is there a

---

[35] Schultze, "The Public Use of Private Interest," p. 46.   See also "Is the EPA Saddled with More Than It Can Handle?" *Business Week*, May 26, 1980, p. 148.

real need for the act? How can standards be better set? What impact has the act had on safety and health? Are there alternatives? One major study argues that the act's mandate is inconsistent with the goal of promoting the social welfare, and that the government should not force more safety and health on society than the workers would choose for themselves if they had to pay the costs directly.[36] OSHA has made progress in reducing the number of standards, improving their quality, and in meeting the problems of inspection and enforcement. Continuous studies are being made by the government to improve the defects of the system.[37]

The EEOC too has faced enormous problems. In 1977, for example, it had a backlog of 130,000 cases. By 1980, however, a new administrator had reduced the case load to about 44,000 using a voluntary settlement system of negotiations between employers and complainants. Critics nevertheless contend that the EEOC has become "an imperial bureaucracy," with vague and sweeping guidelines that go far beyond the intent of Congress and the courts. Although these guidelines lack the force of law, they indicate the agency's position in possible litigations, so many employers feel obligated to comply.[38]

Equal opportunity regulation is also carried out by the Department of Labor, which has used the power to cancel company contracts with the federal government to gain compliance. Executive Order 11246 prohibits race and sex discrimination by federal contractors. In the case of the Prudential Insurance Company, the Secretary of Labor barred the company from doing business with the federal government for not supplying requested personnel information. The company was not even charged with employment discrimination. The action was to obtain records needed to determine whether there was any race or sex discrimination. Over $100 million in insurance premiums would have been denied the company, but a federal judge intervened to stop the proceedings. The company had offered the information as a printout from the computer tapes, or if forced to turn over the tapes, asked that the tapes and any materials they generated be returned. The Labor Department rejected this offer, insisting on the original tapes without conditions.[39]

Social regulation, despite worthy aims and intentions, characteristically becomes enmeshed in detailed facets of operations. Its interventions also threaten democratic processes by concentrating enormous powers in the presidency and on zealous bureaucrats. Another danger is

---

[36] Robert Stewart Smith, *The Occupational Safety and Health Act: Its Goals and Achievements* (Washington, D.C.: American Enterprise Institute, 1976).

[37] Paul W. MacAvoy (ed.), *OSHA Safety Regulations: Report of the Presidential Task Force* (Washington, D.C.: American Enterprise Institute, 1977); see also "Restraining OSHA: It's Just a Matter of Time," *Business Week*, May 5, 1980, p. 110.

[38] "Guideline—Happy at the EEOC?" *The Wall Street Journal*, August 28, 1980, p. 18.

[39] *The Wall Street Journal*, July 29, 1980, p. 4, and August 26, 1980, p. 32.

that the overkill and oppressive nature of social regulation could under-mine the public's faith in government and generate a backlash that will hinder reasonable and prudent regulation. The belief that people must be protected from themselves provides society with a powerful weapon for restricting free expression.[40]

Companies, however, have found powerful protections in the form of constitutional provisions against invasion of property or unreasonable search and seizures. Companies are increasingly aggressive in attacking agency demands when they are unfair, burdensome, or trivial. They also use advertising and public relations tactics to inform the public, but their main battles are in the courts. Sears, Roebuck and Company, for exam-ple, sued the federal government for "creating a society from which an employer cannot draw a balanced, integrated labor force." Although the company lost, it was admired by many for opposing the negative effects of regulation. In another case, a company showed that ear protectors could quiet noise for far less than OSHA's $30 million demand to alter the machinery, and it succeeded in obtaining a court injunction against this demand. The higher penalties beginning to be levied by regulatory agen-cies often make resistance tactics pay off.[41]

In fairness to the government, it can be said that American business has grown and prospered even while government has become gigantic and intrusive. The growth and success of business was not caused by govern-ment, but neither did government prevent it. This idea leads David T. Kearns, president and chief operating officer of Xerox Corporation, to assert that business has been hiding behind government regulations as an excuse for lackluster management, poor technology, and declining pro-ductivity. Blame, he notes, should be placed instead on the decline of research and development, innovation, and risk taking by managers.[42] Similar criticism holds that business, despite its claims for social respon-sibility, has lacked genuine social concern, and that it has to be prodded by social legislation if progress in human welfare is to be made.

REGULATORY REFORM

Regulatory reform means different things to different people. The regulated want less or better managed regulation; regulators often prefer more regulation; interest groups and citizens want more protections. Everyone agrees that reforms are needed, but they differ on precisely what the reforms should be or how they should be carried out.

---

[40] Andrew Slaby and Laurence Tancrede, *Collusion for Conformity* (New York: Jason Aronson, 1975), p. 12.

[41] "Business Comes Out Swinging against Regulators," *Business Week*, April 7, 1980, pp. 112–121.

[42] *Newsweek*, May 5, 1980, p. 13.

Regulatory reform has followed three main strategies: (1) managerial—reducing administrative delays and making the agencies more efficient and responsive to the executive branch; (2) political—changing the political environment and agency procedures to improve the balance of relationships between regulated interests and those of consumers; and (3) controlling the social costs of regulatory agencies through improved analytical procedures and reviews by outside groups.

The history of regulatory reform, beginning in the mid-1930s, is dismal. Despite the fact that every U.S. president since Harry S. Truman has attempted it through executive orders, advisory commissions, review boards, and the like, the regulatory Leviathan has grown steadily.[43] Reforms have seldom addressed major policy issues, or the overall philosophy of regulation. Separating real reforms from political rhetoric is difficult.[44] Most reforms have been procedural and piecemeal—that is, on an agency basis—or have consisted of structural realignments or cosmetic improvements.

REFORM PROCEDURES

Regulatory reform procedures were greatly strengthened during the Carter administration, and significant reforms were achieved in the economic sector of regulation. Executive Order 12044 (1978) revised the procedures for developing regulations by requiring (1) the establishment of the need for regulation, (2) effective oversight of their agencies by agency heads, (3) timely participation from the private sector, (4) the consideration of meaningful alternatives, and (5) the minimization of compliance costs and paperwork.

Congress has proposed congressional and presidential veto powers over proposed regulations, as well as automatic termination of federal programs after a stipulated time unless Congress reauthorizes them (sunset laws). The Carter administration vigorously opposed vetoes, and sunset laws have been enacted by several states, but not by the federal government. The Carter administration also implemented three procedural reforms. The first was a requirement that regulatory impact analysis be done by each agency proposing new regulations, including the impact on inflation. This policy is monitored by the Office of Management and the Budget. A second reform established the Regulatory Analysis Review Group, consisting of close advisers to the president. The group makes studies of specific regulations to see if they can be eliminated or

---

[43] *Government Regulation: Proposals for Procedural Reform, AEI Legislative Analyses* (Washington, D.C.: American Enterprise Institute, 1979), pp. 3–6.

[44] James P. McCarty, "The Politics of Regulation," *Personnel Administration* 25 (June 1980), pp. 25–30. See also Bruce E. Bobbitt, "The 'State' of Regulatory Reform," *Regulation* (September–October 1980), pp. 38–42.

improved. A third device is the Regulatory Council, which is charged with coordinating regulatory activities among agencies, and with informing the public on the status of regulatory reforms. The Regulatory Council consists of 36 major agencies and departments with major regulatory responsibilities. All three reform procedures were incorporated into Executive Order 12044, and in the proposed Regulatory Reform Act of 1980.[45]

REFORM ISSUES

A number of difficult issues have surrounded the reform efforts of the government. Once instituted, a particular reform still generates controversy and resistance. Evaluating the effectiveness of reform is a slow and difficult process. Another reform problem pertains to the power to discipline, since intervention and compliance problems exist on a large scale, and regulatory agencies are frequently accused of curtailing freedom and going beyond their mandates to enforce regulations.[46]

> *Ill-conceived regulatory reform will itself create obstacles to good government. I believe that real regulatory reform requires the reassessment of the objectives and continuing relevance of specific areas of government regulation, and a determination of whether particular regulations do more harm than good. This is a process which must be undertaken with a rational, measured approach which recognizes that there was, and probably still is, a valid reason for the law in question, and its regulatory implementation. Nevertheless, we should review whether that reason still supports the expense and effort necessary to comply with the law.*
>
> *In order to put regulatory reform into its proper context, we must recognize that our present condition of government overregulation is a political phenomenon. The regulatory agencies are not the product of some hostile power. They were created and have been shaped by duly elected governments. If the agencies have gone out of control, they must ultimately be made accountable by the electorate.*
>
> ROBERTA S. KARMEL, commissioner of the Securities and Exchange Commission, *The Wall Street Journal*, August 24, 1978, p. 12.

Deciding how far regulators can go in expressing their views on matters that are or are likely to be before their agencies is another issue. The courts have sometimes prohibited the expression of favorable or unfavorable opinions on pending proposals. For example, the courts

---

[45] U.S. Regulatory Council, *Regulatory Reform Highlights: An Inventory of Initiatives 1978–1980* (Washington, D.C.: U.S. Government Printing Office, 1980).

[46] Paul W. MacAvoy (ed.), *Unsettled Questions on Regulation Reform*, Studies in Government Regulation (Washington, D.C.: American Enterprise Institute, 1978).

prevented the chairman of the FTC from voting on proposals for regulating advertising aimed at children, because he had publicly favored the proposals. Such restrictions could have the adverse effect of discouraging regulators from saying anything. Yet the expression of agency head opinions could tend to bias the results. Some feel that regulators should be silent about specific cases under review, but not with respect to setting rules and guidelines, which is in effect a quasi-legislative process.[47] The expression of opinion is in part a function of the personality of agency heads. Some are more vocal, dynamic, and aggressive than others, raising the problem of criteria for the selection of agency personnel.

While great attention is given to regulatory reform, one can also argue that those currently regulated could accept more responsibility for their own behavior. Business could improve many kinds of conduct that would lessen or avoid the need for regulation. Business could make concrete suggestions that address the goals and problems regulations seek to meet. Consumers, too, could accept more discretion and responsibility. Providing adequate information to them works in this direction, but the trend is to ban dangerous products or substances and to set standards requiring expensive alterations in products or production processes. Thus the government assumes a parental role — as, for example, in regulating advertising directed at children, and tries to provide an almost risk-free life for all. The costs of informational approaches are far less than those of direct intervention. Economic incentives are not as widely used as they could be. They are an alternative to more coercive enforcement techniques. With few exceptions, senior executives of American industry oppose major overhauls of the regulations governing their business. They prefer certainty to the pitfalls of change. The minority that does favor a total overhaul are those who have had disappointing experiences with "social regulation" groups, such as the DOE, EEOC, or the FDA.[48]

Better laws and better management in regulatory agencies are urgent needs, though it can be said for regulators that their tasks are monumental. They are caught in the middle between impatient proponents and disturbed opponents. The difficulties of regulators are often imbedded in restrictions or inadequacies in the legislation that prevent rational decisions. Objective reports, however, indicate widespread dissatisfaction with all forms of regulation.

A review of the criteria for establishing regulatory machinery would assist the reform process by preventive action. For example, regulation is doubtful if it causes real or probable social damage, misjudges the public interest, or attempts to deal with occasional social misbehavior or

---

[47] Stan Crock, "Should Regulators Have Opinions?" *The Wall Street Journal*, January 8, 1979, p. 14.

[48] James Greene, *Regulatory Problems and Regulatory Reform: The Perceptions of Business* (New York: The Conference Board, 1980).

lawbreaking which law enforcement could correct. Reforms should make matters better, not worse. For example, adding more procedural regulations for regulators increases the bureaucratic burden without substantive improvements.

Finding innovative responses to regulatory problems is another issue. It is difficult to define what is actually an innovation. Seventy of the 376 reform initiatives reported for 1978–1980 were classified by the Regulatory Council as innovations.[49] An example of the innovative approach is the effort in Congress to shorten lawsuits by reducing the burden of proof on the Justice Department. In late 1977 President Carter established a National Commission for the Review of Antitrust Laws and Procedures, which completed its work in January 1979. It made two recommendations which, if instituted by Congress, would change the ground rules of antitrust regulation to: (1) eliminate the need for the plaintiff (government) to show that specific company activities have a dangerous probability of successful monopolizing, and merely demonstrate that the defendant has significantly threatened competition, and (2) establish as a presumption that persistent monopoly power can continue only through deliberate conduct that violates Sherman Act standards. The latter approach would shorten trials by not requiring the government to prove the defendant's anticompetitive conduct, and by not allowing defendants to introduce justifications for their conduct. The focus on trials could therefore be limited to adjudicating remedies.[50]

SUBSTANTIVE REFORMS: DEREGULATION

Reforms have gone forward mainly in economic regulation such as the transportation, communication, finance, banking, and drug industries, but also in social regulation such as environment and natural resources, health and safety, trade practices, human resources, and energy. Deregulation is the principal reform in the economic sector, and administrative reforms have characterized the other sectors.

A variety of other responses to the groundswell of complaints about regulation include cost-benefit analysis, sunset laws, self-regulation, paperwork reduction, and language simplification.[51] The most far-reaching of substantive reforms is that of deregulation, which moved forward

---

[49] U.S. Regulatory Council, *Regulatory Reform Highlights*. See also Alfred E. Kahn, "Using the Market in Regulation," *Business Week*, December 15, 1980, p. 14.

[50] "No Fault Monopoly," *Across the Board*, November 1979, pp. 54–64.

[51] See, for example, James C. Miller III and Bruce Yandie, "Benefit/Cost Analysis: New Thermostat for the Regulatory Caldron," *Business* 30 (March–April 1980), pp. 15–18; James Greene, "Regulatory Problems and Regulatory Reform: The Perceptions of Business," *Business* 30 (March–April 1980), pp. 23–30; AEI Legislative Analysis, *Zero-Base Budgeting and Sunset Legislation* (Washington, D.C.: American Enterprise Institute, 1978).

extensively in the Carter administration in airlines, trucking, railroads, petroleum, and natural gas.

Battling with regulators is often so costly that some firms pay their fines even when they seem unjustified. The cost of fighting is often more than the fine. However, the Equal Access to Justice Act of 1980 requires federal agencies to pay the legal expenses of those who successfully fight agency actions that are not proper, and the agency must show that its actions were "substantially justified."

Deregulation is a reduction of governmental influence, intrusion, and control which results in substantial curtailment of regualtion over major industrial segments. In some cases, regulations are reduced in scope or eliminated; in others, entire agencies are phased out of existence.

Industries and executives have been ambivalent about deregulation, and many have fought against it. By opening up rate structures, removing route restrictions, and making competition freer, firms in the transportation fields experienced major disruptions of long-standing practices. Many fear competition, for it can drive customers from the regulated to the unregulated sectors. Prices tend to rise at first after deregulation, but are predicted to settle back again as the forces of competition work out. Unions have joined with industry in opposing deregulation, for example in trucking and the airlines. The impetus for deregulation comes from the government itself, and from some regulatory officials. The courts have also shown a disposition toward deregulation. The Regulatory Reform Act proposed to Congress in 1980 contained the innovative idea of allowing agencies to deregulate on an experimental basis to test the results before permanently changing laws and regulations.[52]

Is deregulation working? This question must be answered differently for each industry and for each company, but the general indications are that deregulation works well after painful adjustments to the new system are made. Deregulation proceedings are generally stretched out to minimize adverse effects. For example, airline deregulation began with the Airline Deregulation Act of 1978, but deregulation will not be complete until the Civil Aeronautics Board is phased out in 1984. The airlines and their unions generally opposed deregulation. An exception was United Airlines, which strongly supported it, and following passage of the legislation radically restructured its routes, abandoning service between 123 pairs of cities and adding 80 other pairs. These risky decisions reflect the company's strategy of going according to the opportunities

---

[52] A. Lee Fritschler and Bernard H. Ross, *Business Regulation and Government Decision Making* (Cambridge, Mass.: Winthrop, 1980), pp. 62–64, and 193–197; Barry M. Mitnick, "Deregulation as a Process of Organizational Reduction," *Public Administration Review* 38 (July–August 1978), pp. 350–357.

made possible by deregulation, rather than avoiding its dangers.[53] Airline deregulation has worked out well, according to most observers. No change in regulations will please everyone, but the dangers of deregulation can be exaggerated. The evidence indicates that airline deregulation has been good for both the industry and its customers.[54]

Deregulation of railroad freight rate controls, passed in 1980, has been favored by the carriers. Prices were expected to rise at first, but to settle back in a free competitive market. But most of the nation's 17,000 trucking firms opposed the repeal of controls governing the entry of new firms into the market and shielding collective rate-setting agreements from the antitrust laws.[55]

Incident Case

Bowers Foundry, Inc., is a 50-year-old, family-owned metal foundry and plating company supplying parts to the auto industry; it has 25 employees, one of whom works full time on government records and reports.

A. H. Conwell, president, tries to keep track of federal safety programs by reading the *Federal Register*. He hasn't seen any Labor Department safety literature. Mr. Conwell reads business and trade publications rather than wading through "the detailed, and to him, often uninterpretable materials prepared by the government itself," the interviewers report.

Mr. Conwell declares that "there is no way you can keep up with all the regulations and run a business at the same time." He concedes there are "bound to be some laws that we're not following because they may not have filtered down to this level."

The firm has been cited for a health violation because of an excessive concentration of zinc at its plant. Bowers received a $120,000 Small Business Administration loan to help correct the problem, but Mr. Conwell figures he needs to spend another $200,000 for pollution control related to this problem. "He laments the need to make capital investments of this kind," the study reports, "much preferring to have spent such money in ways that might have improved productivity and the firm's competitive position."

---

[53] *Business Week*, August 18, 1980, pp. 78–82.

[54] James C. Miller III, "Is Airline Deregulation Working?" *The Wall Street Journal*, March 26, 1980, p. 22.

[55] *U.S. News and World Report*, June 30, 1980, pp. 39–40; *Business Week*, May 19, 1980, pp. 144–146; MacAvoy, *Unsettled Questions*, pp. 7–13.

Evaluate the prospects for compliance of the company with government standards.

Assess the difficulties expressed by Mr. Conwell.

Issues for Discussion and Analysis

1. Why are cyclamates banned, but not saccharin? On what basis should the FDA be allowed to ban "toxic" substances?

2. The federal program providing basic financial aid to college students uses application procedures, needs criteria, and processing schedules completely at odds with those used by three other federal student aid programs which supplement the basic plan. Why does this happen? What could be done about it?

3. Should a Consumer Protection Agency be established?

4. Debate the "pro" and "con" arguments for the statement that "social regulation has not proved to be in the best interests of the public."

5. Why has deregulation become an important public policy issue for the 1980s?

6. Evaluate the benefits and drawbacks of current deregulation efforts.

Class Project

In a class session, discuss the issue of the federal government's desire to have automobiles equipped with air-bag safety systems. Analyze the concepts of regulation that apply to this problem, and establish sub-problems associated with the general problem. Set up investigatory groups to study each part of the problem, and ask them to report back to the class.

For Further Reading

BJORK, ROBERT H.   *The Antitrust Paradox* (New York: Basic Books, 1978).

BLAIR, ROGER D., and STEPHEN RUBIN (eds.).   *Regulating the Professions: A Public Policy Symposium* (Lexington, Mass.: Lexington Books, 1980).

CARRON, ANDREW S., and PAUL W. MACAVOY.   *The Decline of Service in the Regulated Industries* (Washington, D.C.: American Enterprise Institute, 1981).

CLARK, TIMOTHY B., MARVIN H. KOSTERS, and JAMES C. MILLER III (eds.).   *Reforming Regulation* (Washington, D.C.: American Enterprise Institute, 1980).

FRITSCHLER, A. LEE, and BERNARD H. ROSS. *Business Regulation and Government Decision Making* (Cambridge, Mass.: Winthrop, 1980).

GREER, SCOTT, RONALD HEDLUND, and JAMES E. GIBSON. *Accountability in Urban Society* (Beverly Hills, Calif.: Sage, 1978).

INSTITUTE FOR CONTEMPORARY STUDIES. *Regulating Business: The Search for an Optimum* (San Francisco: Institute for Contemporary Studies, 1978).

KATZMANN, ROBERT A. *Regulatory Bureaucracy: The Federal Trade Commission and Antitrust Policy* (Cambridge, Mass.: MIT Press, 1980).

LEVIN, HARVEY J. *Fact and Fancy in Television Regulation: An Economic Study of Policy Alternatives* (New York: Russell Sage Foundation, 1980).

MENDELOFF, JOHN. *Regulating Safety: An Economic and Political Analysis of Occupational Safety and Health Policy* (Cambridge, Mass.: MIT Press, 1979).

MITNICK, BARRY M. *The Political Economy of Regulation: Creating, Designing and Removing Regulatory Forms* (New York: Columbia University Press, 1980).

OWEN, BRUCE M., and RONALD BRAEUTIGAM. *The Regulation Game* (Cambridge, Mass.: Ballinger, 1978).

SEABURY, PAUL (ed.). *Bureaucrats and Brainpower: Government Regulation of Universities* (San Francisco: Institute for Contemporary Studies, 1979).

SOLO, ROBERT A. *The Political Authority and the Market System* (Cincinnati: South-Western, 1976).

STIGLER, GEORGE J. *The Citizen and the State: Essays on Regulation* (Chicago: The University of Chicago Press, 1975).

STONE, ALAN. *Economic Regulation and the Public Interest: The Federal Trade Commission in Theory and Practice* (Ithaca, N.Y.: Cornell University Press, 1977).

WAX, MURRAY L. (ed.). *Federal Regulations: Ethical Issues and Social Research* (Boulder, Col.: Westview Press, 1979).

WEIDENBAUM, MURRAY L. *The Future of Business Regulation* (New York: AMACOM, 1979).

WELBORN, DAVID M. *Governance of Federal Regulatory Agencies* (Knoxville: University of Tennessee Press, 1977).

WHITE, LAWRENCE J. *Reforming Regulation: Processes & Problems* (Englewood Cliffs, N.J.: Prentice-Hall, 1981).

WILSON, JAMES Q.(ed.). *The Politics of Regulation* (New York: Basic Books, 1980).

YOUNG, ORAN R. *Compliance and Public Authority: A Theory with International Applications* (Baltimore: Johns Hopkins University Press, 1979).

15

The Corporation
and Social Responsibility

The business of America is business.

CALVIN COOLIDGE

*No other institution in American history—not even
slavery—has ever been so consistently unpopular as has the
large corporation with the American public.*

IRVING KRISTOL

CONCEPTS DISCUSSED IN THIS CHAPTER

1. THE LEGAL AND SOCIAL NATURE OF THE CORPORATION
2. CORPORATE SOCIAL ISSUES AND RESPONSIBILITIES
3. CRITIQUES OF THE CORPORATION
4. CORPORATE RESPONSES TO CRITICISM
5. CORPORATE RESPONSIVENESS TO SOCIETY

Today's corporations are a large and vital part of the capitalistic system of enterprise in the framework of a democratic society. In the previous chapter we examined the processes by which government regulates business activity to achieve both economic and social objectives. The corporation faces challenges not only from regulation, but from deep controversies regarding its role and responsibilities in relation to society. Therefore a study of the corporation will serve to illustrate and apply the fundamentals covered in the preceding three chapters.

THE CONCEPT OF THE CORPORATION

Business firms are organized as proprietorships, partnerships, or corporations. *Proprietorships*, the most numerous and the oldest form of enterprise, are owner-managed or single-owner firms. Proprietors invest their own capital, and their firms are relatively small in terms of business volume and number of employees. *Partnerships* consist of two or more combined owners, allowing for growth through greater talents and capital than an individual alone can provide. Partnerships are legally dissolved upon the death or withdrawal of any partner, and the partners are liable to the extent of their personal wealth for the firm's debts. Since any one partner's decisions are binding upon the others, harmony among the partners is important, and partnerships have relatively short lives.

Corporations appeared shortly after the American Revolution. Legally, a *corporation* is an artificial person capable of perpetual existence, and acting as a single person. Selling shares of stock raises capital from large numbers of people who may be of modest means, and they are protected by a limited liability consisting of the value of their shares. This permits firms to continue as owners change, to raise very large amounts of capital, and to achieve enormous growth.

Corporations exist by government assent in the form of broad state charters. In the eighteenth century the charter granted special privileges to accomplish a specific public function. Until the latter half of the nineteenth century, the corporate form was not widely used, nor did it include the principle of limited liability. From then on, limited liablity became very important as the nation entered a period of rapid industrial growth requiring large amounts of capital. This period also saw the end of corporate charters as devices to control particular areas of trade and commerce. Another change was that instead of legislative enactments for each corporation, states began to permit them to be formed under general laws or constitutional provisions.

The corporation is clearly a remarkable and successful social invention. It will remain an important business form in the future, but will also continue to change along with the evolving needs and expectations of society. Though chartered by states, today's corporations are inextricably linked to interaction with and influence by the federal government. The problems of the modern corporation lie chiefly in the growing areas of social as well as economic performance as mediated by the federal government acting in the public interest. This puts the corporation directly into issues of a political nature.[1]

---

[1] Edwin M. Epstein, *The Corporation in American Politics* (Englewood Cliffs, N.J.: Prentice-Hall, 1969).

That the corporation is legally a person does not mean that it can be treated in society as though it were an actual person; there are important differences between human and artificial beings. Incentives that influence individuals in socially desirable directions are not necessarily effective with respect to corporations.[2]

Among the many studies of the corporation are several that were turning points in its history. They have focused on such questions as legitimacy, power, economic concentration, size, and corporate governance. One classic study is that of Berle and Means in 1933. They analyzed the power system and legitimacy of corporations and its relationship to private property. They definitively established that the corporate system separates owners from control, which has come into the hands of self-perpetuating managers over whom stockholders have little direct control or influence.[3]

The Berle and Means study pointed to the need for more control over corporate enterprise. A few later studies were critical of Berle and Means, but its implications have not been refuted.[4] Indeed, later studies have confirmed their findings. Edward S. Mason, for example, contended that corporations are run by managers with too much power and authority and whose responsibilities are vague. Corporate empires built by the self-selection of managers are to him a problem of legitimacy.[5] Robert A. Gordon also has suggested that the freedom of management from meaningful control by both stockholders and boards of directors requires a much greater degree of social control over corporate management.[6]

Another group of studies analyzes the political and sociological consequences of corporate behavior. Drucker used intensive observational methods in General Motors to examine the management and organizational precepts which made it so successful and which were widely imitated.[7] Epstein investigated the political behavior of business corporations — questions of power, legitimacy, and public policies toward their

---

[2] Christopher D. Stone, *Where the Law Ends: The Social Control of Corporate Behavior* (New York: Harper & Row, 1975).

[3] Adolph A Berle, Jr., and Gardiner C. Means, *The Modern Corporation and Private Property* (New York: Macmillan, 1933). This book was revised in 1968.

[4] For example, see Cleve S. Beed, "The Separation of Ownership from Control," *Journal of Economic Studies* 1 (Summer 1966), pp. 3–29; and David McCord Wright, "The Modern Corporation — Twenty Years After," *University of Chicago Law Review* 19 (Summer 1952), pp. 662–667.

[5] Edward S. Mason (ed.), *The Corporation in Modern Society* (Cambridge, Mass.: Harvard University Press, 1959); "The Apologetics of Managerialism," *Journal of Business* 31 (January 1958), pp. 26–38. See also Robert J. Larner, "Ownership and Control in the 200 Largest Corporations, 1929 and 1963," *American Economic Review* 56 (September 1966), pp. 777–787.

[6] Robert Aaron Gordon, *Business Leadership in the Large Corporation* (Berkeley: University of California Press, 1961).

[7] Peter F. Drucker, *The Concept of the Corporation* (New York: John Day, 1946). Reissued with an Epilogue as a Mentor Executive Library Book, New American Library of World Literature, 1964).

political activities.[8] Bell examined the shift from treating corporations solely as economic institutions to viewing them also as social institutions entering the postindustrial era.[9]

We will turn now to an examination of the problems corporations face in meeting their social responsibilities.

SOCIAL RESPONSIBILITY ISSUES

The term *social responsibility* does not have a universal definition, but each corporation directly or indirectly manifests its unique interpretation. For our purposes, a general definition is as follows:

> Social responsibility is the recognition of mutual interdependencies among individuals, organizations, and social institutions, and behavior that reflects that awareness within a framework of moral, ethical and economic values.

This is a systems theory definition. A range of activities reflects the degree to which a corporation recognizes these social interdependencies. Minimum recognition is among those firms that adopt Milton Friedman's view that the only social responsibility is to make a profit through economic performance. At a moderate level are the firms that concentrate on economic results, but engage in traditional philanthropy or community service. Maximum recognition is found in corporations that actively identify with major social goals, such as helping humankind or "involved citizen" roles. Corporations tend to give primary consideration to economic responsibilities. One survey of 220 firms found that social responsibility was not a dominant consideration.[10] Whatever the level of response a firm may choose, a mix of social and economic responsibility is a pervasive element in all that it does.

Social responsibility itself is not an option. The corporation's problem is how best to meet social expectations along with its economic ones. Thus there are limits to the corporation's social responsibility. For example, public opinion does not accept the corporation as the institution through which it functions in other spheres, such as education, foreign affairs, or other areas of public policy. Corporations have their own unique role, which begins with economic performance but now embraces a social component.

Public attitudes toward corporate social responsibility are varied. A study of attitudes toward eleven social issues showed three clusters of at-

---

[8] Epstein, *The Corporation in American Politics.*

[9] Daniel Bell, *The Coming of the Post-Industrial Society* (New York: Basic Books, 1973), chap. 4.

[10] Kamol M. Abouzeid and Charles N. Weaver, "Social Responsibility in the Corporate Goal Hierarchy," *Business Horizons* 21 (June 1978), pp. 29–35.

titudes: (1) a large public showing interest in all social issues but emphasizing the firm's economic functions, (2) an active public concerned about all issues except philanthropy, and (3) a public which identifies only with issues that concern it directly.[11] The corporate response to the demands of social responsibility therefore indicates the need for a broad, well-planned, proactive external affairs effort based on concrete objectives set with varied publics in mind.[12]

It is unfair to saddle corporations with the blame or responsibility for all the ills and evils in society, since accountability implies authority. For example, one may feel that the maldistribution of wealth is a social problem, but it would be unfair to blame corporations, since such a problem goes beyond their authority. There are also limits to the ability of corporations to take direct action to cure social ills that they themselves do not cause. Most social problems require action by all segments of society, and what needs to be considered are the areas where the interest of corporations coincide with or are antagonistic to those of the public.[13]

In coping with social issues, there are things only the government can do, such as directing the welfare system. Some problems, such as health care, require a shared responsibility in which government may take the initiative. But many actions fall to corporations, through even here government has used both persuasion and coercion to speed progress. Pollution abatement is an example.

SOCIAL PROBLEMS OF THE CORPORATION

The corporation's problems are in large part due to its successes, which include excellent economic performance, technological progress, economic growth, and providing for military needs. Yet public demands for more and better products are virtually insatiable, so economic success demonstrates that expectations for more are reasonable, and managers feel comfortable about their ability to meet these kinds of needs.

Since the early 1960s, the corporation has confronted a growing number of social demands reaching beyond economic performance. There are two aspects of these social demands: (1) that the corporation's economic activities be carried out without harm to people, society, or the environment; and (2) that corporations, being powerful, should serve the public welfare and help solve society's ills. The first aspect is preventive, and the second is corrective.

Accordingly, a new corporate ideology is developing. It embraces

---

[11] James E. Grunig, "A New Measure of Public Opinions on Corporate Social Responsibility," *Academy of Management Journal* 22 (December 1979), pp. 738–764.

[12] W. Harvey Hegarty, John C. Alpin, and Richard A. Coser, "Achieving Corporate Success in External Affairs," *Business Horizons* 21 (October 1978), pp. 65–74.

[13] Neil W. Chamberlain, *The Limits of Corporate Responsibility* (New York: Basic Books, 1973).

three aspects of social responsibility: (1) corporate leadership will succeed in proportion to its ability to achieve goals related to the human needs of workers, consumers, and society at large; (2) corporate actions and policies must be planned and implemented with regard for their impact on the society in which the corporation functions; and (3) those who move the corporation closer to the achievement of both economic and social goals should be singled out for the greatest rewards.[14]

The corporation has proved to be highly adaptive to economic and social change. It has adapted to the evolving concept of managed capitalism that has supplanted the classical philosophy of pure free enterprise capitalism. The corporation has also adapted to these changes by accepting a great deal of social regulation, such as equal opportunity employment, and by recognizing that social concerns pervade its economic decisions. These adaptations have not come easily or without resistance and antagonism. There are honest differences of opinion about how social issues can best be met. Adaptability alone, however, is not enough; corporations are also expected to take the initiative in performing their social role.

CRITICISM OF CORPORATIONS

Though corporations are changing, the volume of criticism, both justified and unjustified, remains high. Dissatisfaction with business, described in previous chapters, also applies to the corporation. Here we will review those that are particularly crucial to the corporation.

To start with, corporations are highly visible, making them ready targets for attack. They have resources and strategies for meeting demands or refuting attacks. The size and scope of their activities have impacts on segments of society that are increasingly vocal and well organized, with the media attuned to issues and technologically equipped to keep the public informed.

The corporation serves many constituencies, which can produce contradictory criticisms. The corporation is responsible in different ways to stockholders, consumers, employees, suppliers, and the community, as well as to society at large. Special interest groups and federal, state, and local governments add complex dimensions. An example of conflicting pressures is the objection of some stockholders to corporate philanthropy. Another is the demand that products be made safer and at the same time at lower cost. Although corporations try to resolve such conflicts, they are a source of continuing hostility.

The portrayal of corporate behavior in novels, movies, and television

---

[14] Roger M. D'Aprix, *In Search of a Corporate Soul* (New York: AMACOM, 1976), pp. 199–200.

stresses the seamier side. Journalistic portrayals often exaggerate corporate cruelty to people or the resentments of managers who tell "the inside story." Margolis, for example, gives a grotesque picture of managers as downtrodden, inhibited, docile, and dependent.[15] De Mare's case studies of ten corporate executives reveals much about their personal problems, but does little to clarify the moral dilemmas and ambiguities pervading management.[16] A book depicting life inside General Motors yields interesting insights from the experiences of John DeLorean, a vice-president who resigned in frustration, but its indictment of the General Motors management system is unconvincing.[17]

Criticism has been so extensive that some observers forecast the decline or even the disappearance of the corporation. Bell sees the forces of government and education as leading to a relative decline for corporations.[18] Jensen and Meckling deem the corporation unable to survive.[19] Such views are too extreme, and they are born of exaggerated fear of the changes that are taking place in the corporate sector.

Hostility toward corporations arises also from the decline in the respect and legitimacy of all our social institutions. There is a congruence of anticorporation beliefs among socialists, populists, politicians, and intellectuals. The intellectual class seems the crucial element, providing a theoretical apparatus indispensable for attacking the institutions of capitalism.[20] This intellectual class provides substantial ammunition for those who hold that economic and social processes work so inadequately as to require government intervention.

Criticism may be justified or unjustified, but there are no definite standards for judging which is the case. Clearly corporations merit criticism for harmful actions such as unsafe or defective products, false or misleading advertising, or corrupt practices. Although violations of criminal law are subject to prosecution, legal remedies are often slow and uncertain; convictions are hard to obtain and penalties are often light. Preventive actions can minimize these problems. It is even harder to judge complaints that fall under civil law or are simply thought to be wrong or harmful. Individuals or groups may use civil suits to redress specific wrongs. When behavior affects a larger number, class action suits may be brought. For righting wrongs beyond this level, we have the

---

[15] Diane R. Margolis, *The Managers* (New York: William Morrow, 1979).

[16] George de Mare, *Corporate Lives* (New York: Van Nostrand-Reinhold, 1976).

[17] J. Patrick Wright, *On a Clear Day You Can See General Motors* (New York: Wright Enterprises, 1980).

[18] Bell, *The Coming of the Post-Industrial Society.*

[19] Michael C. Jensen and William H. Meckling, "Can the Corporation be Saved?" *MBA*, March 1977, pp. 15–24. See also Robert L. Heilbroner, *Business Civilization and Decline* (New York: Norton, 1976).

[20] Robert H. Bork, "Assault on the Corporation," *Across the Board*, February 1978, pp. 50–54.

regulatory processes described in the preceding chapter, and beyond that the social initiatives of the responsible corporation.[21]

Political ideology colors the criticism of the corporation, which comes both from the Left and the Right. The Left attacks the corporation's size, power, greed, selfishness, corruption, exploitation of labor, and fostering of materialism. Specifically, critics in this group berate large national and international combines, high executive salaries, corporate relocations that cause unemployment and hurt communities, the elitism of top management, and the ability of corporations to function as an interest group in controversies with government and the public. The Left, along with a host of professional corporation haters among intellectuals, environmentalists, church groups, so-called liberation movements, consumerists, and other special interest groups, sees more government control as the logical answer.[22] Members of the Right attack corporations on ethical and moral grounds, and on their departures from traditional capitalism. They criticize excessive profits, materialism, and crime and corruption. Ideologically, the conservative Right includes many businesspersons, but the Right has been less vocal and incisive in its criticism than the Left.

We are by long habit accustomed to supposing that whatever subserves the public interest belongs, by implication, to government. But that way of thinking obscures the singularity of the function which the corporation performs in American society. The corporation is not part of government; nevertheless, it has a public character.It is a trustee of the public interest. But the public whose interest it is charged with conducting is society at large — not the segment of society which claims its profits, but the moral community which requires its services.

Reprinted by permission of the Harvard Business Review. Excerpt from "Is the Corporation Above the Law?" by John F. A. Taylor (March–April 1965). Copyright © 1965 by the President and Fellows of Harvard College; all rights reserved.

THE CORPORATE RESPONSE

The consequence of continuing criticism has been to confront corporations with an enduring sense of crisis, to engender feelings of public dissatisfaction and distrust, and to arouse hostility, guilt, and defensiveness

---

[21] For a legal-historical analysis, see James Willard Hurst, *The Legitimacy of the Corporation* (Charlottesville: The University Press of Virginia, 1970).

[22] Robert Lekachman, "A Cure for the Corporate Neurosis," *Saturday Review*, January 21, 1978, pp. 30–34; Charles Perrow, *The Radical Attack on Business* (New York: Harcourt Brace Jovanovich, 1972); Herman Nickel, "The Corporation Haters," *Fortune*, June 16, 1980, pp. 122–136.

among corporation executives.[23] These conditions have also aroused philosophical, strategic, and practical responses variously expressed as "enlightened self-interest," the enlarged social conscience of the corporation, and action programs to relate the corporation to the mainstream of social purpose.

Corporation executives, in meeting criticism, encounter a problem of identity that may influence the corporate response to social issues. The heads of major corporations have in recent years lost the functions that once conferred moral authority and personal confidence. They are no longer owners and risk takers, but instead are hired managers. The change from owners to salaried managers has been accompanied by a changed public opinion that reflects and reinforces decreased respect. Moreover, the executives of major corporations have advanced by almost total absorption in the operations of their companies. They have not learned to debate with their more vocal critics, and they do not have the time or the inclination to do so. Even if they had the training and taste for public discord, however, many think it dangerous to their companies to oppose the political trends that surround public issues. Though it seems paradoxical, executives defend the corporation inadequately because they have a less personal stake in its survival. Owners no longer pass their businesses on to their children, and managerial employees have a less direct economic interest in the survival of the system beyond their own lifetimes.

DEFENSES OF THE CORPORATION

Corporations are not without defenders. They themselves devise defensive strategies to combat criticisms. In addition, a few scholarly efforts have attempted to present defenses of the corporation.

Corporations and executives react both emotionally and rationally to criticism. Emotional responses express fears and anxieties, such as seeing criticism as implying the end of free enterprise, the advent of socialism, or the misguided conspiracies of intellectuals, politicians, academics, liberals, or socialists. Unfair or distorted criticism clashes with the values of managers, understandably arousing the emotions of those committed to personal and corporate success. Rational responses reflect logical beliefs that facts, economic education, better public relations, and efficient production will refute or blunt the criticism. Both emotional and rational responses such as these are defensive ones. In this respect, Barber concludes that liberals should put aside their prejudices, and managers should stop panicking at every sign of national planning.[24]

---

[23] David P. Ewing, "The Corporation as Public Enemy No. 1," *Saturday Review*, January 21, 1978, pp. 12–16.

[24] Richard J. Barber, *The American Corporation* (New York: Dutton, 1970).

Before strategies and plans can be adopted, it is important to assess the validity of the criticisms. The corporation is an inviting target for those who are trying to reorganize society. What may start out as objective criticism accumulates distortions and myths as it grows. On close analysis, many of the criticisms are myths or factual distortions that can be refuted or debated as issues.[25]

THE CORPORATE IMAGE

Neither what business people say nor carefully crafted public relations and image building have been effective in responding to the criticism of corporations. Both corporations and their managers are more likely to be judged on what they do than on what they say. But better communication about what is done would be helpful.

Image building is too often relegated solely to the public relations and advertising functions. Public relations techniques, while not in themselves a sufficient response, can be helpful if well done. But there must be a reality behind the rhetoric. The increasing criticism has been a revitalizing force in the advertising and public relations industry.[26]

An example of how distorted images occur can be seen in opinion surveys on company profits. When asked how much profit corporations make on the dollar, consumers name an amount about three times as great as the average profit of manufacturing corporations. But if they are also asked what corporations *should* make, they give the same responses. Consumers do have an inflated notion of how much corporations make and also what they should make. Without the follow-up question it would be very easy for the corporation to become defensive about consumer antipathy, or to view people as economic illiterates. People know that businesses need and are entitled to profits; they are more interested in safe, useful products and fair prices. Instead of reporting only dollar amounts of profits, companies could report profits as a percentage of revenues or as return on investment. Companies hesitate to do this because they fear unfair comparisons if they are not near the national norm. But it would help to educate the public about economic issues.

The corporation's tarnished image degrades managers' self-esteem, and erodes their faith in the business system. Like other groups subjected to criticism, they develop feelings of impotence, frustration, and a belief that outside forces determine their future. Public relations efforts go part way to restore this loss of self-esteem and hence to build faith in their ability to do what society needs.

---

[25] Arie Y. Lewin and J. G. Wiles, "The End of Corporate Enterprise?" *Dun's Review*, October 1977, pp. 129–134.

[26] "The Corporate Image: PR to the Rescue," *Business Week*, Special Report, January 27, 1979, pp. 47–61. See also D'Aprix, *In Search of a Corporate Soul.*

Advocacy advertising is intended to inform and educate the public and to present the corporation's side of the case on issues of concern. The effects of such advertising are hard to measure. They often appear to be self-serving, or watered down, simplistic explanations. Unless accompanied by real changes in behavior, such efforts will be of uncertain value.

SCHOLARLY DEFENSES

Defenses of corporate enterprise or attempts to refute criticisms tend to appear narrow, self-serving, and inadequate compared to the vigor and righteousness of critical advocates of social responsibility. Nevertheless, research-based defenses are increasing. Four of these will now be briefly described.

Jacoby draws on his personal experiences as an economist, corporate director, and business school dean to argue that (1) industrial concentration has not increased over the postwar period, (2) that government regulatory agencies have not been "captured" by big business, (3) that manufacturers of military equipment have little influence over military outlays, (4) that multinational firms benefit their host countries, and (5) that the political power of corporations is both exaggerated and declining.[27] This book was severely criticized by a business executive as shallow, naive, and full of errors, jargon, and unsupported allegations.[28] Despite its weaknesses, however, the book represents a beginning in the effort to formulate favorable corporate perspectives.

In a high-quality study of the legal aspects of corporate behavior, Hessen astutely refutes criticisms and misconceptions of the corporate form of business organization and the responsibilities that flow from corporate chartering. He argues that the prevailing view of the corporation as a "concession" awarded by state charters is wrong. He advances instead of concession theory an "inherence theory" in which corporations are created and sustained by an exercise of individual rights, especially freedom of association and freedom of contract.[29] In advancing this theory, Hessen refutes many of the commonly held myths and distortions that activists have leveled against the corporation. The book devotes considerable attention to countering the attacks and suggested reforms of Ralph Nader.

Another type of effort is to refute specific criticisms issue by issue. This has been done by the Law and Economics Center of the University

27 Neil H. Jacoby, *Corporate Power and Social Responsibility* (New York: McGraw-Hill, 1973).

28 Eli Goldston, "Recycling the Gospel of Adam Smith," *Business Week*, July 21, 1973, pp. 10–13.

29 Robert Hessen, *In Defense of the Corporation* (Stanford, Calif.: Hoover Institution Press, 1979). See also reviews of this book by Albert T. Sommers in *Across the Board*, November 1979, pp. 3–7, and by Edwin A. Locke in *Academy of Management Review* 4 (October 1979), pp. 475–477.

of Miami, which compiled answers to 61 questions raised by critics, and answering essays by 37 scholars.[30] Like the Jacoby book, this work at least implies that the corporation is worth defending, but it does not escape the charge of being self-serving and oversimplified.

Still another way of meeting criticism is to present evidence of the success record of specific corporations in social performance areas. Bradshaw and Vogel asked noted critics to select the corporations they admire or think have made significant social contributions. Their examples indicate that a wide range of activities have been pursued. They show that the leaders of the social responsibility movement are not out to destroy the corporation or to eliminate the profit motive. Corporate adversaries recognize along with businesspeople that profitability is a necessary condition of responsible social performance, although the critics also believe that corporations must improve their effects on people and society in ways that are not necessarily reflected in profit and loss statements.[31]

A major question is whether corporations can address themselves effectively to society's concerns while at the same time advocating free market capitalism. Advocacy must come from the leaders of corporations, not merely from a few dissident intellectuals who have defended the system. Few will respect corporations whose leaders must be convinced that legitimacy is not gained by giving in to excessive demands for reform. Their worsened performance will be blamed on them, not on the reforms. Moral authority is not necessarily conferred; often it can be earned by asserting it.[32]

Corporate responsiveness must reach beyond defensiveness and advocacy, however. We will now consider the positive responses of corporations to social responsibility issues.

POSITIVE RESPONSES

Defensive approaches lead to firefighting against public pressure, resistance, and adversary techniques with respect to interest groups, social movements, and the government. A different approach, one requiring a different philosophy and management technique, is a proactive one in which corporations undertake planning and analysis designed to guide the social responsibility aspects of decisions. Thinking about public policy issues before they move too far along on their life cycles shifts the

---

[30] M. Bruce Johnson (ed.), *The Attack on Corporate America: The Corporate Issues Sourcebook* (New York: McGraw-Hill, 1978).

[31] Thornton Bradshaw and David Vogel, *Corporations and Their Critics* (New York: McGraw-Hill, 1980).

[32] Robert A. Bork, "Assault on the Corporation."

focus from responding under pressure to responding by management initiative.[33]

The corporate response process includes four stages. First there arises an awareness of or an interest in an issue. This requires that mangement scan the environment for external signals, such as those from government or from interest groups. Certain managers can be officially assigned as boundary spanners for this function. Second, an organizational commitment develops from "bottom up" pressures or from policies and decisions from top management. At this stage priorities among key issues can be determined. Third, the organization determines what actions or programs are needed, and assigns these responsiblities to appropriate units. Fourth, evaluative techniques are applied to assess the consequences of social performance.

Of all our institutions, it is the corporation, virtually alone, which has undergone the most successful change. That change has succeeded because when the corporation was confronted with the demands of a changing society, the corporation undertook to change itself — to change from within rather than forcing change to be imposed from without. On much reflection, I am not certain institutions can be changed in any other way. If institutions are changed from without, by laws or decrees, or by the influence of physical demonstrations and confrontations, they cease to be the same institution; in fact, they cease even to be institutions, becoming, instead, captives and creatures of other forces.

JOHN D. HARPER, *A View of the Corporate Role in Society* (Pittsburgh: Carnegie-Mellon University Press, 1977), pp. 34–35.

Positive strategies of corporate response recognize that business needs to set its house in order, develop a more definite theory of governance, become more visible, and become more in tune with society's larger goals. Beyond defensive strategies, there are four others that are not mutually exclusive but can be followed in varying combinations. These are as follows:

1. *Adaptive Strategy.* Involves a passive adjustment to changes the corporation must accept. It represents accommodating to inevitable change, and adjusting to issues as they arise from government or pressure groups. It is a reactive strategy in which the firm does only what is required.
2. *Interactive Strategy.* Recognizes that issues are complex and that other

---

[33] James E. Post, *Corporate Behavior and Social Change* (Englewood Cliffs, N.J.: Prentice-Hall, 1978), pp. 27–40.

      social institutions are involved in major problem-solving efforts. Issues
      are met through collaboration, bargaining and negotiation, debate,
      compromise, cooperation, and other interactive processes. This is an
      effort to be reasonably progressive.
3. *Proactive.* Sees the corporation as making plans, setting goals, and ini-
      tiating actions under a "lead the industry" philosophy. Attention is
      paid to forecasting and preparing for change.

Adaptive strategies have been followed in coping with such problems
as energy shortages or equal opportunity employment. An element of
resistance is sometimes involved in which the corporation maintains
counterpressures against overregulation and public policies it considers
adverse to its interests. For example, the Equal Employment Advisory
Council (EEAC) has been a low-profile champion of the employers' position on equal opportunity. It emerged into prominence to lobby against
pressures from liberals and women's rights groups to establish a wage
policy known as "comparable worth." This doctrine holds that traditionally female jobs automatically receive less pay than traditionally
male jobs of comparable worth, and that this is as discriminatory as paying a man and a woman differently for the same job. For example, a male
store clerk may get $14,000 in salary, while a beginning librarian may get
only $11,000.[34]

An example of an area in which interactive strategies apply is the
problem of urban transportation. Here the corporation may be requested
to adjust work schedules and plant locations or develop car pooling as
community leaders attempt to remedy transportation problems. An example of an interactive strategy is a 1976 program of General Motors to
make a massive effort to redevelop the housing and decayed neighborhoods adjacent to its facilities in Detroit.[35]

An example of a proactive strategy is the way in which corporations
are devising new organization structures to place social responsibility efforts at the top management level. The following position titles are illustrative:

Executive vice-president of legal and government affairs (INA Corporation)
Senior vice-president for public and government affairs (Allied Chemical
    Company)
Vice-president for national affairs (Anheuser-Busch, Inc.)
Senior vice-president for public affairs (LTV Corporation)

---

[34] *Business Week*, November 10, 1980, pp. 100–105.

[35] For further perspectives on strategic issues, see Gerald D. Keim, "Corporate Social Responsibility:
An Assessment of the Enlightened Self-Interest Model," *The Academy of Management Review* 3
(January 1978), pp. 32–39; Gerald D. Keim, "Managerial Behavior and the Social Responsibility
Debate: Goals versus Restraints," *Academy of Management Journal* 21 (March 1978), pp. 57–68;
James E. Grunig, "A New Measure of Public Opinions on Corporate Social Responsibility," *Academy
of Management Journal* 22 (December 1979), pp. 738–764; and Gordon H. Fitch, "Achieving Cor-
porate Responsibility," *The Academy of Management Review* 1 (January 1976), pp. 38–46.

Vice-president for public affairs (Bethlehem Steel Company)
Director of public affairs (Borg-Warner Corporation)

Many companies today are improving the management of social responsibilities through comprehensive, integrated, and organizationwide
strategies and techniques. For example, the Mead Corporation utilizes a
plan for integrating public affairs issues with all sectors of its business.
The plan consists of a Washington, D.C., office, the governmental affairs
unit in corporate headquarters, governmental affairs representatives in
major states, and a network of involved managers throughout the company. The structure is illustrated in Figure 15.1. The Mead Corporation
also launched an issues management program in which the govenmental
affairs structure works with specific units to identify major issues, to
keep managers informed, and to prepare corporate spokespersons. The
first unit selected for this step was the human resources staff and the
roles and interactions of the two groups are shown in Figure 15.2.

A major problem of corporate responsibility units is to avoid undue
centralization. Social responsibility must be a pervasive concern
throughout the organization. The central group needs to develop procedures to train all managers in handling social issues, and help them
understand the social consequences of their decisions. The Mead program accomplishes these aims.

Major problems of strategy are involved in two additional areas (1)

FIGURE 15.1

Corporate Organization for Government Affairs, Mead Corporation

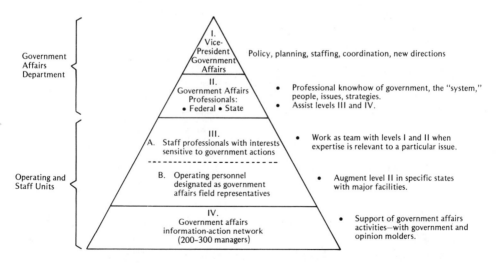

SOURCE: *Redefining Corporate-Federal Relations (New York: The Conference Board, 1979), p. 30.*

FIGURE 15.2

Issues in Management Program in the Mead Corporation

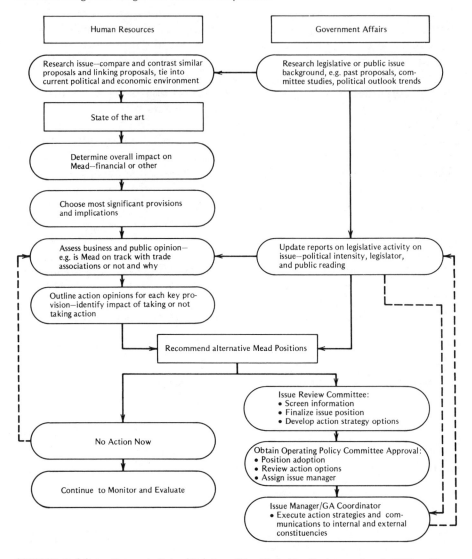

SOURCE: Redefining Corporate-Federal Relations (New York: The Conference Board, 1979), p. 31.

corporate social reporting, and (2) corporate change and reform of governance. We will next discuss corporate social reporting, and take up the questions of reform and governance in the following chapter.

SOCIAL AUDITS

General legislation, regulations, and contract procedures, and the pressures of interest groups, have worked toward an increasing concern for social costs, the budgeting of social responsibility efforts, and the trend toward corporate accountability through more adequate reporting and disclosure. Some requirements, such as those for the disclosure of certain information in the sale of securities, are mandated by law and enforced by the Securities and Exchange Commission. In many areas, however, the nature and degree of reporting and disclosure are discretionary. It is the latter with which we are concerned here.

One of the earliest suggestions for the idea of the social audit came in 1953.[36] In 1958 Blum endorsed this idea, and indicated its applicability to problems of human relations among employees.[37] By the 1979s, techniques began to develop. Bauer and Fenn described a low-risk four-step model consisting of (1) an inventory of corporate activities having a social impact, (2) analysis of the circumstances surrounding these activities, (3) an informal evaluation of the most relevant programs, perhaps with the assistance of an outside expert, and (4) an assessment of how the programs mesh with social and corporation objectives. They saw those procedures as a way to communicate and to enhance public trust in the company.[38]

Social reporting is broader than the social audit, which is primarily for internal use. Both techniques involve two dimensions: measurement and reporting. Seven approaches have been most prominent:

1. *The Cost or Outlay Approach.* The company identifies the dollar costs of activities designed to meet social objectives. This method encounters difficulties in allocating costs to social programs versus those for day to day operations.
2. *Human Asset Accounting.* This is an attempt to measure the dollar value of the productive capabilities of the firm's human talent, and employee-related factors such as loyalty, morale, or company reputation.
3. *Cost-Benefit Approach.* Sometimes called the balance sheet approach, it attempts to assess the benefits to society (stated as assets) compared to the costs (stated as liabilities). This method was initiated by the Abt Associates consulting firm, and has been used by General Motors. It uses both a social balance sheet and a social income statement. The Abt model is so complex and subjective that many variations have appeared to simplify it and apply it on a more practical level.[39]

[36] Howard R. Bowen, *Social Responsibilities of the Businessman* (New York: Harper & Row, 1953).
[37] Fred H. Blum, "Social Audit of the Enterprise," *Harvard Business Review* 36 (March–April 1958), pp. 77–86.
[38] Raymond A. Bauer and Dan H. Fenn, Jr., *The Corporate Social Audit* (New York: Praeger, 1972).
[39] Clark C. Abt, *The Social Audit for Management* (New York: AMACOM, 1977).

4. *The Inventory Approach.* This is a listing and description of programs and activities intended to help solve social problems or have benefits to society. Its main defect is the avoidance of dealing with cost problems.
5. *Program Management Approach.* This approach focuses on special programs such as philanthropy and other voluntary activities. These items can be costed, and it accords with traditional views of corporate responsibility. However, it does not examine the costs of the social impacts of normal business operations.
6. *Social Indicator Approach.* This approach uses the development of measures (indicators) of community well-being, and measures of corporate activities related to the indicators. It utilizes statistical and other data that are available or can be obtained for the purpose.[40]
7. *The Process Audit.* This approach is essentially that of the Bauer and Fenn four-step model.

Audit techniques have the advantage of systematizing corporate planning and programming for social responsibility. When they focus on costs, they force managers to do some careful thinking about their activities in this area. They enable comparisons over time, which can help set priorities and allocate funds. They identify issues and priorities.

These techniques have many difficulties in common. They tend to reflect a spurious accuracy when in the form of dollars assigned to essentially subjective elements. Conventional accounting practices are not really useful, but they may at times provide perspectives.[41] It is possible to measure how clean water or air is, but the impact of pollution on society or the community is hard to measure. There are limits to the kinds of corporate social impact it is feasible to attempt to measure. For example, how does the corporation affect the family or the divorce rate? Audit and reporting procedures are therefore selective, and they do not address every demand that is voiced.

Social audits may be for internal use, external use, or both. Corporate reporting on social issues is sporadic. Many companies report on a few aspects of social performance, but few provide comprehensive information in annual reports or in separate documents. General Motors has published an annual Public Interest Report since 1971. Aetna Life and Casualty Company issues periodic reports; the First National Bank of Minneapolis issues periodic reports using social indicators.[42]

Voluntary disclosures in annual or other reports are highly selective

---

[40] Raymond A. Bauer (ed.), *Social Indicators* (Cambridge, Mass.: MIT Press, 1966).

[41] U.S. Department of Commerce, *Corporate Social Reporting in the United States and Western Europe, Report of the Task Force on Corporate Social Performance* (Washington, D.C.: U.S. Department of Commerce, 1979), pp. 5–9. See also Neil C. Churchill and Arthur B. Toan, Jr., "Reporting on Corporate Social Responsibility: A Progress Report," *Journal of Contemporary Business* 7 (Winter 1978), pp. 5–17; Barry N. Spicer, "Accounting for Corporate Social Performance: Some Problems and Issues," *Journal of Contemporary Business* 7 (Winter 1978), pp. 151–170; Jeffrey Gale, "Social Decision-Oriented Measurement: Some Considerations," *Journal of Contemporary Business* 7 (Winter 1978), pp. 55–74; Harold L. Johnson, *Disclosure of Social Performance: Survey, Evaluation, and Prospects* (New York: Praeger, 1979).

and invariably express positive rather than negative matters. Many of the statements of a social responsibility nature are purposefully vague. Buried in the notes to a financial statement of one company was the following:

> The Corporation is involved in several proceedings related to environmental matters. The corporation has and will continue to take all practicable measures to comply with applicable environmental laws and regulations or to seek relief from such requirements when appropriate. As

TABLE 15.1

A Model for Social Auditing (Reporting)

1. An Enumeration of social expectations and the corporation's response	A summary and candid enumeration by program areas (e.g., consumer affairs, employee relations, physical environment, local community development) of what is expected, and the corporation's reasoning as to why it has undertaken certain activities and not undertaken others.
2. A statement of the corporation's social objectives and the priorities attached to specific activities	For each program area the corporation would report what it will strive to accomplish and what priority it places on the activities it will undertake.
3. A description of the corporation's goals in each program area and of the activities it will conduct	For each priority activity, the corporation will state a specific goal (in quantitative terms when possible) and describe how it is striving to reach that goal (e.g., to improve educational facilities in the community it will make available qualified teachers from among members of its staff).
4. A statement indicating the resources committed to achieve objectives and goals	A summary report, in quantitative terms, by program area and activity, of the costs— direct and indirect—assumed by the corporation.
5. A statement of the accomplishments and/or progress made in achieving each objective and each goal	A summary, describing in quantitative measures when feasible and through objective, narrative statement when quantification is impracticable, the extent of achievement of each objective and each goal.

SOURCE: John J. Corson and George A. Steiner, "Measuring Business's Social Performance: The Corporate Social Audit" (New York: Committee for Economic Development, 1974), p. 34.

---

[42] U.S. Department of Commerce, *Corporate Social Reporting in the United States and Western Europe*, pp. 12–29. See also James E. Post and John F. Mahon, "Articulated Turbulence: The Effect of Regulatory Agencies on Corporate Responses to Social Change," *Academy of Management Review* 1 (July 1980), pop. 399–408; Lee E. Preston, "Analyzing Corporate Social Performance: Methods and Results," *Journal of Contemporary Business* 7 (Winter 1978), pp. 135–150; Sandra L. Holmes, "Executive Perceptions of Corporate Social Responsibility," *Business Horizons* 19 (June 1976), pp. 34–40; Sandra L. Holmes, "Corporate Social Performance: Past and Present Areas of Commitment," *Academy of Mangement Journal* 20 (September 1977), pp. 433–438; and James M. Higgins, "A Proposed Social Performance Evaluation System," *Atlanta Economic Review* 27 (May–June 1977), pp. 4–9.

TABLE 15.2

American Institute of Certified Public Accountants Guidelines for
Internal Social Measurement Systems

1. Not all social phenomena will be measured; instead, emphasis will be given to significant actions and impacts affecting areas of primary social concern.
2. Within each area of emphasis, measurements will be made of selected attributes, chosen because they indicate the essence of actions taken and impacts made by the company.
3. A variety of units of measure will be employed, and narrative descriptions will be used where quantitative measurements are not practical.
4. Although occasionally there will be attempts to assess impacts on the quality of human life directly, the measurements will usually relate to impacts on social conditions thought to affect the quality of human life to a significant extent.
5. Where the measurement of impacts on social conditions is not practical, an attempt will be made to measure actions and their immediate results. (These may often be measured, in any event, because of the intrinsic value of that information.)
6. The distinction between and economic information will often be obscure.
7. The system will not possess complete neutrality.

SOURCE: *U.S. Department of Commerce, Corporate Social Reporting in the United States and Western Europe, Report of the Task Force on Corporate Social Performance (Washington, D.C., 1979), p. 35.*

in the past, expenditures for installation and operation of environmental related facilities will continue to be significant.

Table 15.1 shows one suggested model for social auditing and reporting procedures. The American Institute of Certified Public Accountants Guidelines are shown in Table 15.2. An important issue in social reporting is whether corporations should be free to choose the subject matter and the manner of its dissemination. Dilley suggests that some authoritative body should decide, and require standards which would assure comparability over time, completeness, and objectivity. He notes also that the disclosing corporations should not be expected to measure the social impact of their actions. Due to indirect consequences, these effects are often not measurable. Instead, corporations should disclose sufficient information about their actions so that interested parties have data for comparisons. Determining the implications of the socially relevant actions should be left to these interested parties.[43]

Incident Case

The country's largest greeting card manufacturer, Hallmark Cards, is the sponsor of one of the major urban redevelopments in the nation, called

---

[43] Steven C. Dilley, "External Reporting of Social Responsibility," *MSU Business Topics*, Autumn 1975, p. 25. See also Lee E. Preston and James E. Post, *Private Management and Public Policy* (Englewood Cliffs, N.J.: Prentice-Hall, 1975), chap. 9.

Crown Center. This $200 million project is an attempt to reclaim blighted land in downtown Kansas City. A 100-acre sore spot is being transformed into an attractive business and residential community. When it is completed in 1983, Crown Center will have 1 million square feet of office space, 2200 apartments, a 730-room hotel, and an entertainment complex of restaurants, theaters, a skating rink, and a planetarium. This "city within a city" is being financed entirely by private capital. The idea came from Joyce C. Hall, the 80-year-old founder and chairman of Hallmark, a family-owned business that has also made its mark as a sponsor for 20 years of outstanding dramatic shows on television.

Rationalize the case for and against developments of this type.

What problems do developments of this type cause?

Issues for Discussion and Analysis

1. Of the many allegations made in criticism of today's corporations, which in your opinion are the most valid? Which are the least valid?

2. It is sometimes argued that giant corporations should be broken up into smaller units. What are the implications of such proposals? What would be the likely effects of doing so?

3. What particular problems do you feel that macromanagement theory should address with respect to the social responsibility of multinational firms?

4. What internal problems or conflicts arise when managers attempt to consider the social responsibility aspects of decisions? How can such matters be resolved?

5. Evaluate the various response strategies managers use to counter the criticism they experience in social responsibility issues.

6. What has been the impact of social responsibility issues on organizational structures, and why?

7. Why are public relations efforts a necessary but insufficient means of responding to enlarged social expectations?

8. What entrepreneurial opportunities are contained in the ideas associated with the acceptance of greater social responsibility by companies?

9. What are the primary functions of the social audit? What are its limitations?

Class Project

Set up three-person task forces to investigate each of the following aspects of corporations and their behavior. Each task force is to report back to the class as a whole.

1. Planned obsolescence
2. Product safety
3. Corporate size and power
4. Truth in lending, packaging, and advertising
5. Regulation of corporations
6. Legal basis of the corporation
7. The leadership of major corporations
8. The basic concept of the corporation

For Further Reading

ABT, CLARK C. *The Social Audit for Management* (New York: AMACOM, 1977).

ACKERMAN, ROBERT, and RAYMOND BAUER. *Corporate Social Responses: The Modern Dilemma* (Reston, Va.: Reston, 1976).

APTER, DAVID E., and LOUIS WOLF GOODMAN (eds.). *The Multinational Corporation and Social Change* (New York: Praeger, 1976).

BEAUCHAMP, TOM L., and NORMAN E. BOWER. *Ethical Theory and Business* (Englewood Cliffs, N.J.: Prentice-Hall, 1979).

BLUMBERG, PHILLIP I. *The Megacorporation in American Society* (Englewood Cliffs, N.J.: Prentice-Hall, 1975).

BOARMAN, PATRICK M., and HANS SCHOLLHAMMER (eds.). *Multinational Corporations and Governments* (New York: Praeger, 1975).

BROWN, COURTNEY C. *Toward the Next Corporation* (New York: Free Press, 1979).

CHANDLER, ALFRED D., JR. *The Visible Hand: The Managerial Revolution in American Business* (Cambridge, Mass.: Harvard University Press, 1977).

CHANDLER, ALFRED D., JR., and HERMAN DAEMS (eds.). *Managerial Hierarchies: Comparative Perspectives on the Rise of the Modern Industrial Enterprise* (Cambridge, Mass.: Harvard University Press 1980).

DEVANNA, MARY ANNE, and NOEL M. TICHY (eds.). *Organization Design for Multinational Corporations* (New York: Praeger, 1980).

ESTES, RALPH W. *Corporate Social Accounting* (New York: Wiley, 1976).

GLADWIN, THOMAS N., and MAURICE F. STRONG. *Environment, Planning and the Multinational Corporation* (Greenwich, Conn.: JAI Press, 1977).

HELLMAN, RAINER. *Transnational Control of Multinational Corporations* (New York: Praeger, 1977).

HESSEN, ROBERT. *In Defense of the Corporation* (Stanford, Calif.: Stanford University, Hoover Institution Press, 1979).

JOHNSON, HAROLD L. *Disclosure of Corporate Social Performance: Survey, Evaluation, and Prospects* (New York: Praeger, 1979).

KUHNE, ROBERT J. *Co-Determination in Business: Workers' Representatives in the Boardroom* (New York: Praeger, 1980).

MUELLER, ROBERT K. *Metadevelopment: Beyond the Bottom Line* (Lexington, Mass.: Lexington Books, 1977).

PRESTON, LEE E. (ed.). *Research in Corporate Social Performance and Policy: An Annual Compilation of Research*, Vol. 1 (Greenwich, Conn.: JAI Press, 1978).

SPAGHT, MONROE E. *The Multinational Corporation: Its Manners, Methods, and Myths* (New York: Columbia University Press, 1978).

U.S. DEPARTMENT OF COMMERCE. *Corporate Social Reporting in the United States and Western Europe, Report of the Task Force on Corporate Social Performance* (Washington, D.C.: U.S. Department of Commerce, July 1979).

VERNON, RAYMOND. *Storm over the Multinationals: The Real Issues* (Cambridge, Mass.: Harvard University Press, 1977).

WATTENBERG, BEN J., and RICHARD J. WHALEN. *The Wealth Weapon: U.S. Foreign Policy and Multinational Corporations* (New Brunswick, N.J.: Transaction Books, 1980).

16

Corporate Change and Reform

A large organization does not become bureaucratic solely as a result of structure or size. Business becomes leaden when it loses sight of its purpose — when the fear of making an error overwhelms the fear of missing an opportunity.

DAVID ROCKEFELLER

I think the corporation today is the basic source of generic power and has the greatest ability either for ill or for good to turn this country around.

RALPH NADER

CONCEPTS DISCUSSED IN THIS CHAPTER

1. THE CORPORATION'S ROLE IN SOCIETY

2. CORPORATE LEGITIMACY

3. CORPORATE GOVERNANCE AND ITS REFORM

4. MORALITY AND ETHICS OF CORPORATIONS

By the time of the 1980 national elections, it became clear that business had become more successful politically. That is, there was progress in regulatory improvement and in deregulation. According to Vogel, these gains were by default, not due mainly to the appeal of conservative economic and social policies, but rather to the inadequacy of Left-liberal thought. The use of public funds to satisfy social needs and the use of regulation to increase accountability in the public sector could be seen as declining, and as having made problems worse rather than solving them.[1]

---

[1] David Vogel, "The Inadequacy of Contemporary Opposition to Business," *Daedalus*, Summer 1980, pp. 47–58.

Nevertheless, pressures for reform can be expected to continue to influence the corporation significantly. Whereas regulatory methods attempt to control what corporations *do*, reforms in governance attempt to control what corporations *are*, in order to influence how they do what they do.

Problems of reform focus on three distinct but interrelated questions: (1) how should corporations be governed? (2) what is the appropriate role of the corporation in society? and (3) what are the ethical and moral dimensions in corporate behavior? All the confusions and conflicts of critics and defenders are embodied in these three questions.

CORPORATE GOVERNANCE

Problems of governance pertain to the establishment, maintenance, and operation of the corporation as it functions in the interests of the public and of its various constituent groups. Critics of the corporation believe its malfunctions are due to built-in defects that imply a need for governance reforms which center on financial controls, economic impacts, corporate charters, boards of directors, and other fundamentals of the legal and managerial structure. Critics see a need to correct deficiencies they believe allow corporations to become too powerful or too inconsiderate of their responsibilities to society.

Whereas activist critics prefer reforms in the legal bases by which corporations operate — reforms requiring the passage of far-reaching legislation — corporations advocate gradual improvement through traditional market mechanisms and voluntary reforms. Critics seek to convert the traditional theories and myths of corporate governance into realities. For example, consumers are supposed to "vote with their dollars"; stockholders are supposed to control the corporation by voting their shares. But consumers, stockholders, and employees feel they do not have adequate influence on the corporation, and dissatisfaction has risen to new highs. To overcome such feelings, reform proposals seek to alter the relationships between the corporation and its constituent groups to give them more power and control over decisions that affect them.

It is easy to exaggerate the extent to which most reform proposals would meet the allegations of activist critics. Changes in governance, however advisable on other grounds, would have little impact on the public perception of the corporation and its role in society. Anticorporate sentiment is directed to the entire role of business and free enterprise in our lives. Change in the details of, say, stockholder voting, will not placate the hostile. Tinkering with corporate governance for no better reason than to diffuse hostility and to avoid genuine reforms is futile.

Many reform suggestions seek to alter the structure, composition, and functions of the board of directors. The aim of these reforms is to increase the independence and responsibility of boards, which have been criticized for their failure to monitor managerial performance and to have the corporation address controversial social issues. The collapse of firms such as the Equity Funding Life Insurance Company or the Penn Central Railroad brings sharply into focus the weaknesses of the control and direction of many boards. Corrupt practices and bad management often go unnoticed. Stone raises an important query about such debacles: If eminent and successful directors cannot attend to the critical factors in such collapses, how can they be effective in dealing with the more subtle issues of social responsibility?[2] It would be wrong to see board reforms as a cure for all the ills of which corporations are accused. Nevertheless, fundamental changes in the board, if linked with other changes in the corporate system, could lead to significant improvements.

Stone divides corporate behavior into two segments. Class A behavior is relatively feasible to deal with through moderate changes in the character of the board. Class B behavior is hard to change through board or other internal structural reforms. Class A behavior shows substantial overlapping of public and private interests, and there is likely to be a congruence of beliefs about what corporations should not do—violate law, produce unsafe products, and the like. Class B behavior shows less overlap in public and private interests: A board might not curtail even clearly harmful acts that the public opposes. An example is pollution or other environmental harms which are not unlawful, but in which correction conflicts with the need for profit. Another is the "citizenship" problem, such as moving a plant out of a community, or overseas labor and investment policies. Reforms clearly will differ between class A and class B problems. The latter would require more extreme, more intrusive solutions; the former imply relatively modest changes. In practice, the distinctions between class A and class B behavior are not always clear.[3]

We will now turn to an analysis of the major current proposals for board reform. These have to do with (1) the composition of the board, (2) the public responsibility committee, and (3) procedural and operating problems.

The key issue in board composition is the balance between insiders, who are elected from the top management group, and outsiders. Critics question the use of board members whose own work is of concern to the board. In small, closely held family or owner-operated corporations, little

---

[2] Christopher D. Stone, *Where the Law Ends: The Social Control of Corporate Behavior* (New York: Harper & Row, 1975), pp. 128–130.

[3] Ibid., pp. 135–138.

harm may result. In large, high-impact firms, insiders are likely to be less critical and demanding, and there are other ways for insiders to influence actions without voting on board issues.

Outside directors have advantages and disadvantages. The advantages include independence of thought and action, attachment to related aspects of the firm's environment, and the ability to bring broad knowledge and experience to the board's deliberations. However, a totally outside board would deprive it of the expertise and technical knowledge which only insiders close to operations possess. It is hard for outsiders to understand fully the needs, problems, and operations of the company.[4] Most boards therefore appoint a majority of outsiders but retain the use of insiders who can relate to internal problems.

Boards with outsider majorities have increased rapidly. In 1971 only 64 percent of the corporations had such majorities; this increased to 70 percent in 1978 and 88 percent in 1980. The New York Stock Exchange policy now requires listed companies to have a majority of outside directors. Outside directors' pay has been increasing, and now averages more than $20,000 per year. Boards are also attempting to increase the number of women and minority group members.[5] Another reform move is to get nominating committees to be more objective in nominating new board members. Boards need a diversity of talents and kinds of experience, so selection should be guided by this need.

The widespread use of outside directors appears to have curtailed "rubber stamp" boards; boards are becoming increasingly assertive and willing to take risks. Other factors contributing to this development are the requirement that audit committees be composed of outsiders, pressures from government agencies such as the SEC, and the increasing number of stockholder suits. Through the widespread use of working committees, boards no longer appear satisfied with what management tells them. The power of outsiders is clearly seen in the increasing number of cases in which the outsider-dominated board has ousted chief executive officers. For example, in 1979 the board of General Automation replaced Lawrence A. Goshorn, who was chairman of the board, president, and chief executive officer. He was also the largest stockholder, the only CEO the company had ever had, and the company's founder.[6]

[4] Stanley C. Vance, *Managers in the Conglomerate Era* (New York: Wiley, 1971). See also Stanley C. Vance, "The SEC and Corporate Cloning," *Director's Monthly* 2 (September–October 1978), pp. 34–35; Robert M. Estes, "Corporate Governance in the Courts," *Harvard Business Review* 58 (July–August 1980), pp. 50–58.

[5] *The Wall Street Journal*, November 3, 1980, p. 33. See also Paul B Firstenberg and Burton G. Malkiel, "Why Corporate Boards Need Independent Directors," *Management Review*, 69 (April 1980), pp. 26–28, 37.

[6] *Business Week*, September 10, 1979, pp. 73–83. For a scorecard system of evaluating chief executive officers, see Edward McSweeney, "A Score Card for Rating Management," *Business Week*, June 8, 1974, pp. 12–15. See also Stanley C. Vance, "Corporate Governance: Assessing Corporate Performance By Boardroom Attributes," *Journal of Business Research* 6 (1978) pp. 203–220.

One reform consistently rejected by corporations and by Congress is to appoint board members as general representatives of the public, or to represent special constituencies, such as labor, consumers, or even regulatory agencies. This would redefine the corporation as a quasi-public agency, and it is intended to force boards to a greater consideration of corporate goals balanced against social and political objectives. It would politicize the corporation and divorce it from primary concern with long-run profitability. It is a drastic reform that would hamper corporate performance. If outside directors represent special interests, the economic flexibility of the company might suffer and board effectiveness might be undermined by creating conflicts in policy that corporate management would try to dodge.[7]

Another way to benefit from outsiders is the use of director-caliber experts appointed to an advisory council. For example, Hercules, Inc., appointed such a council of four prestigious experts to evaluate company plans and advise on potential new markets for the company's products. The panel was deemed better than an inside committee, which might not be objective toward change, and better than consultants, who are oriented toward one-shot assignments. Advisory councils are helpful in evaluating technical trends, and in steering companies into new enterprises.[8]

Stone believes both general and special public directorships are worth trying. They address themselves to the class B behaviors that lie beyond the traditional province of boards. The difficulties of the general public directorship are numerous. Identifying just what a public member represents and what constitutes the public interest is difficult. Appointing only one or two such members means that others could outvote them. Finally, it is unclear how such members would resolve the contention between corporate and public needs. Special interest public members could be appointed to cover identified critical areas of social concern that are most amenable to their influence — such as foreign relations, technological innovation, product safety, and the like. Such directors might be especially helpful in cases where market forces and ordinary legal mechanisms alone seem inadequate to keep the corporation within socially desirable bounds.[9]

Constituency representative board composition is only one of the reforms included in the Corporate Democracy Act proposed in Congress in 1980. The proposal also contained provisions for encouraging shareholder proxy resolutions (which shareholders show little interest in), and a ban on interlocking directorates (which have not been proved harmful

---

[7] S. Prakash Sethi, Bernard Cunningham, and Carl Swanson, "The Catch-22 in Reform Proposals for Restructuring Corporate Boards," *Management Review* 68 (January 1979), pp. 27–28, 38–41.

[8] *Business Week*, November 12, 1979, pp. 131–137.

[9] Stone, *Where the Law Ends*, pp. 152–183.

and no longer worry trustbusters). Proposals of this type have not been well received in Congress.

Another reform proposal is to set up public responsibility committees of the board of directors. This is a voluntary organizational innovation rather than legally required action. It consists of a standing committee of five to seven board members initiated by a board resolution that details the committee's purposes, duties, and procedures. A typical example is as follows:

1. Identify the major constituencies—both internal and external—who normally judge the behavior and performance of the corporation; examine what they expect of the corporation's performance socially and environmentally.
2. Recommend specific issues for board and management consideration, and determine their relative priorities.
3. Recommend corporate policy to respond to the priority issues.
4. Consider and recommend potential new areas of social responsibility and involvement.
5. Examine the report to the full board on corporate attitudes toward the needs and concerns of the major constituencies of the corporation.
6. Recommend where duties and responsibilities lie throughout the company with respect to the priority issues.

On May 13, 1980, Douglas A. Fraser, president of the United Auto Workers Union, was elected to the board of directors of the Chrysler Corporation. This carries bargaining and legal risks for Mr. Fraser.

In a proxy statement recently mailed to all Chrysler shareholders, Fraser defines his role in a way obviously meant to allay criticism: "I believe my activities as a director will advance the interests of the broad Chrysler community—shareholders, workers, suppliers, dealers, consumers, and the public." The statement was drafted after UAW lawyers analyzed court decisions on fiduciary responsibility. John A. Fillion, the union's general counsel, cites court rulings that say a corporation has a threefold duty: to its shareholders, its employees, and the public. A director, therefore, Fillion says, is similarly obligated. "Under the evolving law of the responsibility of directors, Doug stands no greater danger of a conflict of interest than any other board member with a traditional background," the lawyer adds. "If there is a conflict, we'll back off."

Business Week, May 19, 1980, p. 149.

The value of a public responsibility committee is that it assigns to a working group responsibilities to which the full board otherwise cannot devote enough time and attention. It deals with sensitive issues in which the expertise of chosen committee members can be very helpful. It can monitor both the internal and exteral environments for social responsibility trends and issues. Opponents, however, feel that only the full board should work on matters so important. Some view it as a fad, or say that directors do not have any feel for or knowledge of such issues. Small firms have little need for such committees. Boards consisting mainly of insiders would have few who could serve capably on such committees. On balance, the arguments for are superior to those against.[10]

The third category of board reforms consists of a miscellany of suggestions considered or mandated in rulings by regulatory and other government agencies. The SEC, for example, became interested in greater accountability in corporations as a result of disclosures of widespread payoffs and bribes. It considered adopting a rule that all publicly held corporations must have financial audit committees consisting of independent, outside directors. Since it found that 85 percent already have such committees, it decided to forego the ruling, hoping that the rest would set them up on their own. It also found that only 29 percent of the corporations require nominating committees to foster director independence and increased accountabilty, but delayed any ruling to see if the practice would increase.[11]

The Federal Corrupt Practices Act of 1977, focusing on antibribery provisions, also contained a reform provision that requires all SEC-regulated companies to devise and maintain effective systems of internal accounting control, providing reasonable assurances that (1) access to the firm's assets and the execution of transactions are in accordance with management's authorization, (2) accountability for assets is maintained, and (3) transactions are recorded so as to permit preparation of certified financial statements. However, one study showed that these requirements produced new control procedures in only 10 percent of the 50 companies studied. A new procedure has to be adopted only if the benefits exceed the costs. What companies do instead is establish documentation to prove compliance if they are challenged in court. The FCPA appears to have encouraged greater use of company codes of conduct, and the strengthening of financial audit staffs.[12]

Other suggestions for board improvement include (1) clarification of the roles, duties, and responsibilities of directors, (2) increasing the compensation of directors, (3) providing small staffs to assist board members and their committees, (4) developing better reporting systems to stockholders, (5) improving the information upon which board members act,

---

[10] Michael L. Loudal, Raymond A. Bauer, and Nancy H. Treverton, "Public Responsibility Committees of the Board," *Harvard Business Review* 55 (May–June 1977), pp. 40–60 and 64. See also Phyllis S. McGrath, *Corporate Directorship Practices: The Public Policy Committee* (New York: The Conference Board, 1980).

[11] *The Wall Street Journal*, September 5, 1980, p. 3.

[12] Michael W. Maker and Bernard J. White, "Corruption Control," *The Wall Street Journal*, August 25, 1980, p. 14.

and (6) changing the standards of legal liabilities of directors.[13]

This latter problem needs further clarification. Even if the duties of directors are specified, the problem of getting directors to do what they are supposed to do remains. It is a problem of incentives, rewards, and penalties. Positive rewards for directors who perform well are scarce: there are limits to rewarding them through pay: there is no promotion ladder to climb; performance according to social needs may draw the disapproval of peers and the managers who bring them onto the board. Therefore negative approaches, principally the threat of legal liability also other penalties, are used, but they are not as effective as positive rewards. Even if sued, directors receive light penalties or have them paid by their companies or by liability insurance.

Stone suggests, therefore, that liability for ordinary, traditional standards of negligence should be withdrawn, establishing instead a three-point program of legal responsibility involving (1) making directors liable for *gross* negligence, self-dealing, or losses from civil or criminal liability; (2) attaching liability to failure to perform mandated, vital director functions; and (3) reconsidering the sanctions applied to improper acts or nonperformance of duty. In general, he recommends relaxing director liabilities and eliminating indemnification of directors by the company or by insurance, on the grounds that the present system prevents directors from taking risks or becoming involved in issues, and causes managers to hide shortcomings and failures from the directors.[14] Drucker holds that the only way for directors to protect themselves against liability actions is to think through their responsibilities and to organize themselves for discharging them.[15]

FEDERAL CHARTERING

Another widely suggested reform is federal rather than state chartering. Centralization and uniformity of chartering procedures would result. The aim would be to permit the federal government greater control over corporations. However, this is a poor reform because revocation of a charter, although unlikely, would nevertheless be a constant threat to stability.[16] This would create uncertainties about cancellation, lead to short-run planning and distortions in investment decisions, and unnecessary fluctuations in stock market prices.[17] Ralph Nader has been a

---

[13] W. Stanton Halverson, "How to Manage the Management Bureaucracy," *Management Review* 67 (July 1978), pp. 26–40.

[14] Stone, *Where the Law Ends*, pp. 144–149.

[15] *The Wall Street Journal*, June 1, 1978, p. 21.

[16] Ralph K. Winter, *Government and the Corporation* (Washington, D.C.: American Enterprise Institute, 1978), p. 56; see also pp. 47–67.

[17] M. Bruce Johnson (ed.), *The Attack on Corporate America: The Corporate Issues Sourcebook* (New York: McGraw-Hill, 1978), pp. 135–170.

persistent advocate of federal chartering designed to prevent executives from making decisions that have led to what he considers irresponsible technology, product dangers, pollution, and monopoly practices.[18] His proposals aim at making corporations responsible to consumers through laws enforceable by federal chartering. Any such proposal that would have a chance in Congress would almost certainly be less restrictive than the Nader proposals.[19]

Federal chartering represents a return to the old system under which government confers monopoly privileges and entry control to the favored few. This sytem prevailed until a few years after the Revolutionary war, but was rejected in favor of modern state charters without special privilege. State incorporation laws do not lead to the problems of monopoly and harm to stockholder rights alleged by Nader and others, because state chartering is more consistent with open entry into the business system.

THE CORPORATION'S ROLE IN SOCIETY

Powerful forces have cast the corporation into the limelight, where its behavior is thoroughly examined. Discontent with corporate performance and lack of social responsiveness have generated group and public pressures that have brought about many changes in the traditional role of the corporation. Despite these pressures, the process of change remains gradual and evolutionary. But it is occurring.

The interrelated nature of the corporation and society is reflected in the way in which changing social expectations affect not only the corporation as an entity, but also operating problems such as product design, marketing policy, and employment procedures. Almost everything a corporation now does must be examined for its impact on public interest groups or on the general public. Managers are highly skilled in making operating decisions and in solving conventional, well-defined problems having mainly internal significance. Most of them are less skilled in relating to new sets of external configurations that now affect the internal system.[20]

Figure 16.1 shows a schematic model of the corporation in its social context. The key elements are public values, governmental processes, and the corporation's influences over them. The model suggests that the principle of enlightened self-interest can be reconciled with corporate

---

[18] Ralph Nader, Mark Green, and Joel Seligman, *Taming the Giant Corporation* (New York: Norton, 1976).

[19] The American Assembly, *Running the American Corporation* (Englewood Cliffs, N.J.: Prentice-Hall, 1978), pp. 41, 50.

[20] S. Prakash Sethi, *The Unstable Ground: Corporate Social Policy in a Dynamic Society* (Los Angeles: Melville, 1974), pp. 215–221. See also Alvin Toffler, "The Third Wave: The Corporate Identity Crisis," *Management Review*, 69 (May 1980), pp. 8–17.

FIGURE 16.1

Model Showing Dynamic Relationships between the Corporation and the Social Context

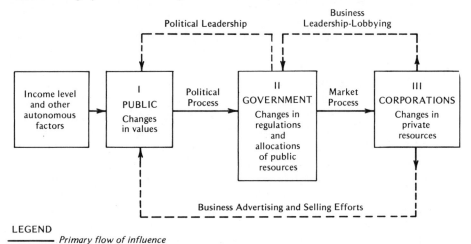

LEGEND
——————— *Primary flow of influence*

— — — — *Secondary flow of influence*

SOURCE: Neil H. Jacoby, Corporate Power and Social Responsibility (New York: Macmillan, 1973), p. 189.

concern for social responsibility, and that no firm can afford to ignore public attitudes and expectations. Therefore, the potential conflict between profit maximization and corporate social activity is also reconciled. Jacoby writes: "The popular notion that a company that pursues profit must eschew a social role or that social involvement means a sacrifice of profit are unfounded."[21]

Two points follow from this analysis. First, two areas of performance must be satisfied in meeting social expectations: one is economic performance, and the other is social performance. One without the other is not enough.[22] Second, the strategic planning process in most corporations needs to be extended and strengthened to include in performance the concept of social responsiveness and initiatives. Such planning leads to proactive strategies and to careful balancing of social and economic priorities. Strategic planning includes (1) long-term environmental forecasts, (2) identifying alternative futures, and (3) determining action scenarios in accordance with evolving priorities.[23]

Corporations are one of the most effective instruments by which

---

[21] Neil H. Jacoby, *Corporate Power and Social Responsibility* (New York: Macmillan, 1973), p. 237.

[22] George P. Hinckley and James E. Post, "The Performance Context of Corporate Responsibility," in Sethi, *The Unstable Ground*, pp. 293–302.

[23] Ian H. Wilson, "Reforming the Strategic Planning Process: Integration of Social Responsibility and Business Needs," in Sethi, *The Unstable Ground*, pp. 245–255. See also Melvin Anshen, *Corporate Strategies for Social Performance* (New York: Macmillan, 1980), chap. 4; and Robert W. Ackerman, *The Social Challenge to Business* (Cambridge, Mass.: Harvard University Press, 1975), pp. 1–41.

society obtains many of its needs. They are primary actors in society — producers, distributors, taxpayers, investors, service providers, and the like. One may see in the functions the corporation performs a number of social roles: the corporation as citizen, producer, employer, resource manager, investor, competitor, innovator. The problem of social control of corporations is how to get them to accept social roles as an integral part of their performance.

The two main approaches society may use toward this end are law and moral suasion, and incentives to change perceptions and attitudes, and thus behavior. Stone argues that traditional legal sanctions have had only limited success in bringing about internal changes leading to improved social performance. Such changes are now up to the corporations themselves. Moreover, many corporate social problems are not susceptible to traditional legal restraints. Stone believes that the law should be brought to bear directly on internal decision processes, instead of waiting to deal with corporate acts after they have occurred.[24] This degree of intrusion by government would not, of course, be acceptable to the corporation. However, Stone makes an additional plea for analyzing the culture of the corporation, and through education, communication, and persuasion, changing attitudes toward the assumption of positive social roles.[25]

The corporation's social role differs depending on the context or system within which it is considered. At the most compact level, community relationships are important; at the other extreme is the global outreach of the multinational corporations.

THE CORPORATION'S ROLE IN THE COMMUNITY

Corporations have major impacts on their communities. Traditionally these have taken the form of the holding and use of property, the employment of citizens, relations with banks, suppliers, local customers, and school systems, and some degree of philanthropy to local institutions and groups. But increased emphases on broader social responsibilities have added new dimensions — the problems of pollution, safety, environmental damage, and the like. The traditional views are susceptible to measurement and can be reported statistically. The latter types of responsibility are more complex, harder to measure, and have therefore not been intensively studied.

The fact that the corporation and the community are parts of an interpenetrating system permits a systematic analysis of community relations in the context of its involvements with society. Post notes that the nature of this interpenetration between a form and society varies

---

[24] Stone, *Where the Law Ends*, pp. 119–121.
[25] Ibid., pp. 229–248.

with the scope of the relationship, the salience of specific issues, and the continuity of the corporation's dealings with relevant publics.[26]

The system is most apparent in urban settings, where the problems of cities have a major impact on corporations and where corporations can influence the kinds of actions taken to abate them. Post, for example, provides a detailed case study of the Aetna Life and Casualty Company that shows the dimensions of interpenetration over a period reflecting considerable evolutionary change in corporate practice. Prior to the 1960s civic involvement was high in areas affecting employment, but low on matters such as community development. Management's perception of community involvement was narrow and not guided by specific policies. By the mid-1960s, corporate and community "statesmen" began to work together in an *ad hoc* phase of supporting more community efforts. A second stage was the evolution of programmatic responses to problems such as housing and the redevelopment of blighted areas. In the early 1970s, Aetna's involvement became characterized by an urban affairs perspective requiring new structural units in the organization. The final stage saw the evolution of a planning and strategy approach to urban affairs that represented a full-scale commitment to this level of involvement.[27]

Corporations have great power and resources, and a high potential for harming or helping their communities. Communities are increasingly placing local controls over corporations, but at the same time seeking their involvement and assistance. This assistance is not confined to monetary considerations, but extends to supplying managerial expertise and institutional support for a wide assortment of community problems.[28]

MULTINATIONAL CORPORATIONS

The multinational corporation extends beyond a single society or even a single culture to the entire world, at a time when world conditions of uncertainty, the danger of war and political disturbance, and issues of population, hunger, and poverty pose enormous problems. Attacks on the corporation have been especially hostile with respect to multinational firms. They are often viewed as sinister conspiracies, corrupt and selfish pursuers of profit, and exploiters of the peoples of the world. By contrast, it can be noted that United States corporations expanding internationally have responded to economic needs expressed by developing

---

[26] James E. Post, *Corporate Behavior and Social Change* (Englewood Cliffs, N.J.: Prentice-Hall, pp. 236–237.

[27] Ibid., pp. 237–253.

[28] Manuel F. Cohen, "The Corporation within the Community," in Edward J. Bander (ed.), *The Corporation in a Democratic Society* (New York: Wilson, 1975), pp. 28–38.

and industrializing countries, and have taken huge risks in investing in countries where political and economic stability is uncertain.

Fears of multinational corporations center on their vast size, their power over resources, their lack of accountability, doubts that competitive market practices work, and their role in resource allocations, tax avoidance, currency manipulation, bribery, and environmental problems.[29] The evidence for these malfunctions is anecdotal rather than conclusive. The charges have been refuted as being possible but not necessary outcomes, since many factors countering the alleged dangers are also at work.[30]

In an increasingly interdependent world, strategic planning and the adoption of appropriate strategies are vital management responsibilities. Among the trends that require thoughtful analysis are the following:

1. The internationalizing of political and economic institutions is increasing among the less developed nations, especially so-called Third World countries.
2. Less developed countries have resources needed by more developed nations.
3. New and emerging patterns of government and business relationships create uncertainties that must be understood and faced.
4. New nations are arising and reforming amid drives against colonialism and demands for independence. New leaders are coming into prominence all over the world.
5. Value systems are changing to reinforce egalitarianism, human rights, and a sense of identity in all nations.
6. Relative stages of maturity of institutional interrelationships require clarification.
7. World turbulence is a continuing cause for concern as technology influences industries, socioeconomic maturity, and the balance of forces between cooperating and competing systems.[31]

Since the American enterprise system and its corporations operate on a global scale, they have created an intricate network of economic and political ties. The impacts of this activity on other nations and cultures have generated feelings of both acceptance and hostility. The American corporation is an inviting target for attack on both economic and political fronts. Corporations thus take great risks—takeovers of their property, guerrilla warfare, kidnapping and killing or maiming executives, cartelization of trade such as OPEC, and extreme forms of government regula-

---

[29] Bander, *The Corporation in a Democratic Society*, pp. 148–170.

[30] Dennis E. Logue, "Do Multinational Corporations Escape Political Oversight?" in Johnson (ed.), *The Attack on Corporate America*, pp. 48–53. See also Neil H. Jacoby, *Corporate Power and Social Responsibility*, chap. 5.

[31] Reprinted by permission of the publisher, from *Corporate Responsibilities and Opportunities to 1990* edited by Ellen T. Curtiss, Phillip A. Untersee (Lexington, Mass.: Lexington Books, D.C. Heath and Company, Copyright 1979, D.C. Heath and Company). See also Grover Starling, *The Changing Environment of Business* (Boston: Kent, 1980), chap. 4.

tion. Under many of these conditions it is difficult to persuade executives to accept overseas duties, and for their families to accompany them. Many nations require that certain percentages of their own nationals be hired. In both cases there is a problem of training and developing the managers and the workforce. At present, roughly three-fourths of all American investment overseas is in Europe, where there is greater stability and better communications, transportation, and distribution systems.[32]

LEGITIMACY OF THE CORPORATION

The corporation's survival is dependent on its ability to continue to merit its status as a legtimate socioeconomic institution. Basically this means that corporations must be accountable to society for their use of power. Legitimacy is won or lost by the consistency with which the corporation is able to perform in accordance with society's expectations. Legitimacy cannot be defined or measured precisely, nor can it be automatically or permanently conferred. It is a consequence of what the corporation does or does not do. Legitimacy is earned and maintained according to the corporation's benefits to society.

Legitimacy in a legal sense is conditioned by the corporate governance system, which concludes four elements: (1) the electoral processes for boards of directors and stockholder influence, (2) the stock market, (3) the legal system of state corporate law, and (4) disclosure requirements under federal regulation.[33] Corporate legitimacy, however, is not strictly a matter of legalities. The core problem of corporate legitimacy is the way it uses power and authority, manages resources, and relates to the other institutions of society.

In addition to providing goods, services, and employment, the corporation has evolved as a social and political organization, in itself a basic social institution, and a center of power that resembles a private government. Questions of legitimacy stay in the forefront because society is changing the rules of the game from those allied solely with profit to those which ensure that social needs reflected in the climate of public opinion will be considered along with profit. The corporation can no longer conduct its operations on a purely economic basis; therefore, political considerations cannot be ignored.

Thus the corporation is not a power center untouched by others. Various interest groups now contest the corporation's power. Unions, consumers, agricultural groups, ethnic and racial organizations, and many others also have power, resources, and energy to confront what

---

[32] Richard Eells, *The Political Crisis of the Enterprise System* (New York: Macmillan, 1980), pp. 1–5.

[33] Elliott J. Weiss, "Governance, Disclosure, and Corporate Legitimacy," in the American Assembly, *Running the American Corporation* (Englewood Cliffs, N.J.: Prentice-Hall, 1978), pp. 58–85.

they consider to be the corporation's deficiencies. Since these groups tend to view corporate political power with suspicion, an important constraint on corporate power has developed. Democracy and pluralism still have great strength in the social order, so that threats to the corporation from the Left and the Right are seen also as threats to the democratic system, and hence guarded against by the electorate.[34] Fears that giant corporations will take over the whole of society or conquer all competing groups are thus without support. Kristol writes: "A democracy is not likely to permit huge and powerful institutions, with multiple 'spillover' effects on large sectors of the population, to define their interests in a limited way or to go about pursuing them in a single-minded way. It insists that such institutions show a proper attentiveness to what is conceived to be, at any moment, 'the public interest.'"[35]

Legitimacy is defined as the belief in and acceptance of the rightness, propriety, moral goodness, or appropriateness of persons, institutions, or modes of behavior. Legitimacy may be both internal and external. Internal legitimacy views the corporation as a political participant, as determined by its organizational purpose, constituencies, sources of managerial authority, and system of governance. External legitimacy is perceived in terms of theories of political democracy, the implications of corporate activity for other social interests, and the maintenance of an open political order in society.[36]

Over the years the public has conferred both external and internal legitimacy on the corporation by a general acceptance of its authority rather than its power, though some degree of power is always associated with authority. This public acceptance behind legitimacy is enhanced by the acknowledgment of corporate leaders of greater responsibility to a broader constituency, and a progressive decline in the arbitrariness of managerial decision making. The public has confirmed external legitimacy by its acceptance of corporate political involvement.[37]

Legitimacy of the corporation requires the presence of a relevant business ideology. Berle has suggested that legitimacy is tied to accountability and responsibility in the use of power:

> Whenever there is a question of power there is a question of legitimacy. As things stand now, these instrumentalities of tremendous power have the slenderest claim of legitimacy. This is probably a transitory period.

---

[34] Edwin M. Epstein, *The Corporation in American Politics* (Englewood Cliffs, N.J.: Prentice-Hall, 1969), p. 225.

[35] Irving Kristol, *Two Cheers for Capitalism* (New York: Basic Books, 1978), p. 75. See also Edwin M. Epstein and Dow Votaw (eds.), *Rationality, Legitimacy, and Responsibility: The Search for New Directions in Business and Society* (Santa Monica, Calif.: Goodyear, 1978), pp. 69–97.

[36] Edwin M. Epstein, *The Corporation in American Politics* (Englewood Cliffs, N.J.: Prentice-Hall, 1969), pp. 254–255.

[37] Ibid., pp. 256–286.

They must find some claim of legitimacy, which also means finding a field of responsibility and a field of accountability. Legitimacy, responsibility and accountability are essential to any power system if it is to endure.[38]

The often-evident lack of confidence in the corporation reflects the new expectations without which legitimacy will be further eroded. In the search for legitimacy, therefore, moral and ethical issues must be faced along with political and economic ones.

MORALITY AND ETHICS IN CORPORATIONS

Corporate reforms, as we have seen, take the form of legal restrictions intended to prevent or punish wrongful behavior. This results in *ad hoc* cases against particular corporations governed by specific laws. Many firms thus conclude that corporate social responsibility means to obey the laws and to follow regulations. In this view, if corporations act irresponsibly or governance goes against the public interest, laws should be passed to control them. Otherwise they are free to do as they choose.

The law, however, is limited in what it can accomplish. Stone argues that this approach puts the problem backwards; law does not work, so we need corporate social responsibility beyond the law. Laws generally prohibit things, as a "morality of duty"; what is needed is a "morality of aspirations" reaching beyond the law into personal and institutional behavior.[39]

In addition to reforms in governance and assessment of the corporate role in society, moral and ethical issues must be faced if we are to restore public trust, which is the fundamental basis of legitimacy. Moral and ethical issues are difficult for corporations, since they are controversial and pose problems of vagueness and uncertainty. Traditionally, corporate defenders rely on the concept of "enlightened self-interest" to protect profit as the basic element of corporate performance, thus limiting actions taken in the public interest. Drucker rejects the enlightened self-interest model as automatically benefiting society, asserting that the rhetoric of profit maximization and profit motive are not only antisocial but also amoral.[40]

The perspective of amorality has also been raised by Scott and Hart, who reason that (1) the manager's task is to preserve organizational health by making decisions that do the corporation the most good, (2)

---

[38] Adolf A. Berle, Jr., "Economic Power and the Free Society," a pamphlet published by the Robert Maynard Hutchins Center for Democratic Institutions, Santa Barbara, Calif. (New York: Fund for the Republic, 1958), p. 16.

[39] Stone, *Where the Law Ends*, p. 101.

[40] Peter F. Drucker, *Management* (New York: Harper & Row, 1974), pp. 807–811. See also Reginald H. Jones, "The Legitimacy of the Business Corporation," *Business Horizons* 20 (August 1977), pp. 5–9.

managers thus act from expediency, which is to say, amorally, and (3) managers are protected in their expedient behavior by a "shield of elitist invisibility"—the cover of anonymity and the difficulty of blaming individuals for wrongful acts or mistakes. This shield, which protects managers from congressional inquiry, legal actions, or control by the board of directors, takes three forms. First, the corporation is personified—anthropomorphized—so that it is the company and not the individual that acts. Second, performance is measured by operational rather than ethical or moral criteria. Third, corporate value systems are developed internally and are thus hidden from public scrutiny.[41]

The unethical or wrongful acts of corporations are actually those of individuals acting in the corporation's behalf. When such acts occur, punishment of the corporation also punishes innocent people, such as stockholders or consumers (through pricing to recover the costs of fines and damages). Where a wrongful act could result in suits by hundreds of plaintiffs, courts are sometimes reluctant to award punitive damages on so large a scale. Corporations thus get off lightly because of the reluctance to blame them for what goes wrong. Stone cites the Richardson-Merrill case, in which the company released into the marketplace $7 million worth of a new drug called MER/29, designed to reduce cholesterol levels. The drug caused the side effects of cataracts and blindness. FDA approval was obtained after laboratory employees knowingly and upon instruction from their bosses falsified the research data to hide the side effects. In such cases it is hard to blame the officers and directors. The law holds no one directly liable, and the corporation inflicts harm but is not accountable. The corporation can lose only what damages for injuries are proved against it in civil suits, a far less significant deterrent than punitive awards.[42]

THE INSTITUTIONALIZATION OF ETHICAL POLICY

Any significant improvement of the corporation's ethical and moral deficiencies requires a special effort to clarify issues and guide the behavior of individuals.

There has been an increase in the corporation's effort to institutionalize ethical standards of behavior not only by adopting ethical codes but also by establishing ethics committees. In 1977, for example, a survey showed that 5.6 percent of 501 boards of directors had an ethics committee. While this figure is small, none of the companies had such committees in the previous year. Forty-six percent of the board chairmen reported that ethics and morality was an area of growing concern to

---

[41] William G. Scott and David K. Hart, *Organizational America* (Boston: Houghton Mifflin, 1979), pp. 36–43.

[42] Stone, *Where the Law Ends*, pp. 54–57.

them. Another study in 1979 found that 54 percent of the boards surveyed felt greater concern for corporate ethics than in the previous year, surpassing their interest in financial results, stockholder relations and the like.[43]

The institutionalization of ethics means that the corporation puts ethics formally, systematically, and clearly into the policy formation process. Institutionalization represents applied, practical ethics, which though grounded in the philosophical and religious teachings of all beliefs, expresses the "right and wrong" dimensions of corporate and managerial behavior. Institutionalization does not happen suddenly; it evolves through critical stages of planning and analysis. In the Norton Company, for example, researchers found a mix of motivations, and a three-stage evolution that included (1) a company policy or code of ethics, (2) a formal ethics committee on the board of directors, and (3) management development programs incorporating ethical considerations. Of the three stages, codes are the most frequent among major companies, followed by the use of board comittees. Incorporating ethics into management development programs is still rare, and is done only by the larger firms, such as IBM, Allied Chemical Company, and the General Electric Company.[44]

Positive procedures for promoting ethical and moral behavior need to consider the organizational blocks that inhibit the uncovering of the unethical impulses and actions. These blocks are the unintended consequences of normal, acceptable management practice. Waters notes seven major blocks:

1. *Strong role models* by which employees are integrated into the organization but which can indoctrinate them into performing illegally or unethically.
2. *Strict lines of command*, by which individuals blindly accept higher authority.
3. *Group cohesiveness*, by which people do not wish to risk losing group support by rejecting unethical behavior.
4. *Ambiguity about priorities*, which creates uncertainty about what is important.
5. *Compartmentalization of decisions*, which produces different ethical standards in different parts of the organization.
6. *The division of work*, which prevents holistic or complete views of what is going on.
7. *Protection from outside scrutiny* through control of linkages with the external social system.[45]

[43] Theodore V. Purcell, S.J., and James Weber, S.J., *Institutionalizing Corporate Ethics: A Case History* (New York: The President's Association, 1979), p. 5.

[44] Ibid., pp. 9–32.

[45] James A. Waters, "Catch 20.5: Corporate Morality as an Organizational Phenomenon," *Organizational Dynamics*, Spring 1978 (New York: AMACOM, a Division of American Management Associations), pp. 3–19.

The problems of corporate ethics and morality are fundamentally those of individuals, but individuals are subject to the context in which they work. The corporation sets the moral and ethical climate of performance, and putting its house in order will go far to generate behavior that will restore legitimacy and public confidence.[46]

THE SOCIAL CONSCIENCE OF THE CORPORATION

Although the corporation is legally a fictional "person" but in reality does not behave as a real person, it can be said to have a social conscience that is reflected in its social performance and responsiveness. Like the organization's climate or morale, the social conscience is hard to measure and hard to manage. But it can be perceived by insiders and outsiders as an ethical or moral element that guides its behavior.

An example of the influence of the social conscience is provided by the way corporations deal with the problems of urban crisis. Should corporations locate facilities in ghettos? Should they finance the redevelopment of urban slums? Should they help to combat crime and drug problems, and unemployment? Do these activities go beyond traditional philanthropy? Cohn suggests the following criteria for coping with such issues: (1) the need to arrive at realistic objectives, (2) the need to review the range of program possibilities before selecting a strategy, (3) the importance of estimating resources required to achieve program objectives, (4) the need to choose an affordable program, (5) the need to understand the political and social dimensions of urban problems, and (6) the need to adopt suitable organizational arrangements.[47]

The operation of the social conscience of the corporation is reflected in stockholder-originated resolutions that are often directed at social issues, such as prohibiting the manufacture of dangerous chemicals, curbing a company's operations in South Africa because of Apartheid, and various other reforms of interest to them. Such proposals also try to get companies to refuse grants to colleges that work in or invest in South Africa, or that employ "avowed Communists" or refuse to cooperate with the CIA. It is true that such resolutions are seldom passed by a majority of stockholders, typically getting only 3 percent of the vote or less. But that level of favorable votes is often viewed as a success because it makes the resolution a public declaration, which activist stockholders deem important.[48]

---

[46] Gerald Prout, "On Expecting Corporate Ethical Reform," *Public Administration Review* 4 (Summer 1978), pp. 13–21; Kenneth R. Andrews, "Can the Best Corporations Be Made Moral?" *Harvard Business Review* 51 (May–June 1973), pp. 57–64; Leonard Silk and David Vogel, *Ethics and Profit: The Crises of Confidence in American Business* (New York: Simon and Schuster, 1976); Vincent Barry, *Moral Issues in Business* (Belmont, Calif.: Wadsworth, 1979).

[47] Jules Cohn, *The Conscience of the Corporations: Business and Urban Affairs 1967–1970* (Baltimore: Johns Hopkins University Press, 1971).

[48] *Chronicle of Higher Education*, March 27, 1980, p. 6.

Corporations holding large blocks of the stock of other corporations, and other institutional investors such as bank and university trust funds, increasingly vote their stock in favor of activist positions. Among the corporations that have voted their proxies against management's position on social issues in companies in which they hold stock are the Aetna Life and Casualty Company, the Bank of America, Phillips-Van Heusen, and Morgan Guarantee Trust.[49]

Stone raises the important question, "Why aren't corporations more moral?" The answers are subtle. First, corporations need to be profitable at some satisfactory level. Firms close to the margin will tend to cut corners everywhere they can—on worker safety, product quality, or wherever else they can. Second, companies with enough profits to put something extra into social problems, such as environmental protection, risk stockholder uprisings. Third, there is a reluctance to be heroic when rewards come primarily from profit making. Long habit keeps profit objectives ahead of others. Fourth, bureaucracy encourages depersonalization and the rigidity of employee roles. Fifth, in an institutional framework, people do things they ordinarily wouldn't and are shielded from personal responsibility. These factors appear to stem from profit orientations, but in reality they go deeply into the manager's psyche, where the rules of the game hold sway. The culture of the corporation works against its social conscience. This means that the improvement of moral and ethical behavior lies in the difficult process of changing attitudes which are endemic in the corporate structure.[50]

An example of how the corporation's social conscience can be tested by external events is the case of the Dow Chemical Company, the maker of napalm used in the Vietnam war. Dow recruiters were confronted in the 1960s by student activists protesting the manufacture of napalm. Dow continued to make the product and to recruit from campuses during this period. Executives interpreted the student position as opposition to the war rather than to the company itself, and took the position that Dow had to fulfill its obligations to the government. During this period, its government contracts amounted to less than 5 percent of its total business. The company saw its obligation as one of maintaining a strong, innovative organization of hiring the best people it could, without passing judgment on the government. It felt morally obligated to be open to anyone who sought employment with the firm.[51]

Another example of the corporate conscience is provided by the issue of free speech. This problem has been and will continue to be a complex issue in the courts. Free speech problems arise when employees criticize the company or its executives and are disciplined for "disloyalty," or

---

[49] *Business Week*, January 19, 1974, pp. 66–67.

[50] Stone, *Where the Law Ends*, pp. 233–243.

[51] *Business Week*, February 10, 1968, pp. 118–124; "The Corporate Conscience," *Business Roundtable*, Graduate School of Business Administration, Michigan State University, undated.

when a corporation takes a position on political matters that differs from the views of its stockholders. Recent court decisions have held that discharge was too severe a penalty for employees who publicly denounced their firm as bigoted and racist,[52] and that a state prohibition on the corporation's spending to influence votes on questions not materially affecting its business interests was unconstitutional.[53]

Incident Case

The XYZ Company, a nationally known chemical manufacturing and processing firm, became aware that in its forecasting and planning there was virtually a total preoccupation with finance, the economy, and product problems. Thereupon the board of directors requested that the president take steps to incorporate social forecasting and analysis into the company's planning functions.

What sorts of things does social forecasting try to do and why?

What steps could the president take?

Issues for Discussion and Analysis

1. Economist Henry Wallach stated that "In an age when the corporate income tax rate is 48 percent, it should be obvious that society can make corporations do anything it wants." Why then do we have so many problems of corporate behavior?

2. In the corporate context, how much can we rely on self-reform? Have not most of our major corporations made significant changes without regulation or coercion?

3. Why is the legitimacy of the corporation so widely challenged today? What should corporations do or not do about the problem of legitimacy?

4. Debate the statement that "the major proposals for board reform would do little to restore faith in corporations, but instead would destroy important facets of the free enterprise system."

5. Is there such thing as the corporate conscience? If so, what are its manifestations?

---

52 *The Wall Street Journal*, November 10, 1980, p. 28.

53 *The Wall Street Journal*, January 1, 1979, p. 23.

6. How can corporations improve and maintain a sound ethical position in modern society? How can ethical conflicts be resolved? How much ethical reform may we expect from corporations?

7. Analyze the issues of social change that surround corporate efforts to improve social responsibility performance. Relate your discussion to the evolution of macromanagement theory.

Class Project

Form panels of class members to make presentations to the entire class on the problems associated with:

1. Truth in lending
2. Truth in advertising
3. Planned obsolescence
4. Product liability
5. Self-regulation
6. Class action suits
7. Public interest advocates
8. Interlocking directorates

For Further Reading

ACKERMAN, ROBERT W. *The Social Challenge to Business* (Cambridge, Mass.: Harvard University Press, 1975).

ANSHEN, MELVIN. *Corporate Strategies for Social Performance* (New York: Macmillan, 1980), chap. 6.

ANSHEN, MELVIN (ed.). *Managing the Socially Responsible Corporation* (New York: Macmillan, 1974).

BLUMBERG, PHILLIP I. *The Megacorporation in American Society: The Scope of Corporate Power* (Englewood Cliffs, N.J.: Prentice-Hall, 1975).

BROWN, COURTNEY. *Putting the Corporate Board to Work* (New York: Macmillan, 1976).

HARPER, JOHN D. *A View of the Corporate Role in Society* (Pittsburgh: Carnegie-Mellon University Press, 1977).

NADER, RALPH, MARK GREEN, and JOEL SELIGMAN. *Taming the Corporate Giant* (New York: Norton, 1977).

PALUSZEK, JOHN L. *Will the Corporation Survive?* (Reston, Va.: Reston, 1977).

SETHI, S. PRAKASH. *The Unstable Ground: Corporate Social Policy in a Dynamic Society* (Los Angeles: Melville, 1974).

STEVENSON, RUSSELL B., JR. *Corporations and Information: Secrecy, Access, and Disclosure* (Baltimore: Johns Hopkins University Press, 1980).

STONE, CHRISTOPHER D. *Where the Law Ends: The Social Control of Corporate Behavior* (New York: Harper & Row, 1975).

WALTON, CLARENCE (ed.). *The Ethics of Corporate Conduct* (New York: American Assembly, Columbia University Press, 1977).

17

Coping with Environmental Issues

All that we have to do to make the world physically successful for all humanity is to raise the overall efficiency of world mechanisms from 4% to 12%. This obviously means a design revolution.

R. BUCKMINSTER FULLER

. . . for knowing afar off (which is only given a prudent man to do) the evils that are brewing, they are easily cured. But when, for want of such knowledge, they are allowed to grow until everyone can recognize them, there is no longer any remedy that can be found.

NICCOLO MACHIAVELLI

CONCEPTS DISCUSSED IN THIS CHAPTER

1. HOW COMPANIES RELATE TO ENVIRONMENTAL ISSUES
2. NATURE AND SOURCES OF ENVIRONMENTAL PROBLEMS
3. ECOLOGY AND THE ECOSYSTEM
4. THE ENVIRONMENTALIST MOVEMENT
5. MAJOR ENVIRONMENTAL ISSUES: DEPLETION, DAMAGE, AND POLLUTION
6. HOW GOVERNMENT AND BUSINESS STRIVE TO PRESERVE THE QUALITY OF LIFE

The interaction of private and public sector decision making and the continuous negotiations between government and business are strikingly exemplified in problems of environmental quality. Each sector perceives the public interest differently, and public and special interest groups taking assertive actions to influence both sectors make the issues even more complex.

Business firms differ in the extent of the environmental decisions they face. State and local units as well as the federal government attempt to control environmental problems, but their standards, objectives, and rulings are often in conflict. Legal and economic conflicts thus pervade environmental issues, along with many subjective questions about goals and methods.

Pragmatism rather than ideology or public relations characterizes the interactive policy making on issues of environmental quality. Democratic pluralism assures that all voices will be heard, but results depend on the integration of the combined business and political power structure. Since decision making occurs within several different hierarchical structures, and since costs are a basic issue for all, attaining the objective of environmental quality is a difficult and time-consuming process. The worst offenders are often the most difficult to entice into the game. It is also difficult to maintain the interest and commitment of the public, whose members tend to be apathetic or ill-informed, except when disasters such as Three Mile Island strike.

The costs of planning, information gathering, and negotiations are large, and to them we must add those of implementation and enforcement. The balance and distribution of costs depend heavily on the information analysis, negotiating skills, and decision making of the participants. Decisions often involve complex technological factors that can change after decisions are made. In all these decision problems, some level of government is involved, but firms possess the ultimate legal and economic control and responsibilities.[1]

We will now examine environmental problems with respect to (1) the nature and sources of the issues, (2) a comparative analysis of the major types of problems, and (3) how management copes strategically with environmental imperatives.

NATURE AND SOURCES OF ENVIRONMENTAL ISSUES

The term *environment* is used in two ways in the literature of management. The first is an administrative view consisting of perceived external factors that affect the organization's internal operations. We are primarily concerned in this chapter with a second use of the term, which refers to the earth's natural and physical resources, along with the habits, values, philosophies, and practices that accompany their use in providing for

---

[1] James S. Russell and Warren J. Samuels, "Corporate and Public Responsibility in Environmental Policy: A Case Study," *MSU Business Topics*, (Autumn 1979), pp. 23–32. See also Harold and Margaret Sprout, *Contexts of Environmental Politics* (Lexington: University Press of Kentucky, 1979); Gerald O. Barney (ed.), *The Unfinished Agenda: The Citizen's Policy Guide to Environmental Issues* (New York: Crowell, 1977).

human wants and needs. Both concepts of the environment are important, and they are also interrelated in complex ways.

ECOLOGY

The science of *ecology* deals with the survival of living organisms or a population of organisms in their natural habitats. By analogy we use the concept to describe many different aspects of the problem of protecting the environment for the welfare and survival of humans. Ecology takes a holistic approach to interacting elements or problems, and we speak in this context of the *ecosystem*.

The ecological focus thus brings together a number of elements that were formerly considered separately. Among these elements are population pressures, scientific and technological developments, large-scale production, and a host of political, economic, and social problems built around them. The impact of human activity on the environment has given rise to serious problems of air, water, noise, and land pollution, waste of resources, dangerous effects on the health of humans and animals, and damage to the environment itself. Often these considerations are lumped together under the idea of a "quality of life" that we seek to enhance and protect.

We have become acutely aware of ecological problems since the 1960s. Every human produces environmental harm just by living, but in a sense every human can be an ecologist, concerned with conservation of resources and doing the least harm to the environment. Concerned citizens are an ally of the politicians who guide the government in minimizing or regulating environmental impacts. The ecological imperative says "minimize waste and harm, and maximize the use of resources." All this leads to greater interaction among government, business, and the public. Ecosystem planning, including cost-benefit analysis, is needed for better decisions on ends, means, and incentives to govern the multifaceted efforts involved.

ENVIRONMENTALISM AS A SOCIAL MOVEMENT

The thrust of environmental pressures is provided by a highly complex social movement consisting of many groups that perceive common interests but also have divergent interests. Conservation has been a steady social movement since the emphasis it received during the administration of Theodore Roosevelt. This group consists of nature lovers and professionals in various sciences such as forestry, agriculture, the mineral industries, and the animal sciences. New levels of sophistication, however, have resulted from the activities of journalists, researchers, consumer advocates, economists, and politicians who are now also concerned about environmental issues.

Social movements wax and wane. Environmentalists have had strong public support since the 1960s, but there is evidence that their influence is declining. Among the reasons are the following:

1. The public loses interest and tires of repeated emphasis on problems.
2. The public has a short attention span, since there are so many critical public issues.
3. People become overconfident, believing that technology will inevitably cure the problems.
4. Opposition movements and interest groups arise to put forth offsetting evidence and counterpropositions.
5. Cost factors are continuously interfering and working against ameliorative solutions.
6. People dislike the changes that by implication will ensue from environmental controls, which raise fears of unemployment, inflation, and other problems.
7. The movement contains so much diversity that it is difficult to find unity and cooperation among the differing interests.
8. Changes in the political climate, such as a change in the party in power, may dampen the enthusiasm for causes in which the federal government's assistance is needed.

Despite these difficulties, environmentalism will continue to influence management and government decision making for some time to come. Business and government are locked into policies, programs, regulatory legislation, and administrative dicta that cannot easily be erased. The emphasis on safety, health, human rights, and risk avoidance will remain high. In fact, these problems will remain even if environmentalism declines as a social movement.

The environmentalist movement has encountered a number of difficulties that may reduce its influence. One is the surge of tax reduction efforts in several states, which could impair environmentalist legislation, reduce enforcement, and lower government support for conservation and environmental protection. Another problem is that, as inflation and unemployment grow worse, there are pressures to ease standards and controls that seem to interfere with economic improvement. Environmentalists have also been accused of lack of balanced perspective, such as showing more interest in preserving wildlife than in controlling health problems in cities. Environmentalists are criticized for resisting government programs and proposals such as the Energy Mobilization Board, synthetic fuels production, and building nuclear power plants.

Environmentalists refute these criticisms by noting the successful record of laws passed in the 1970s, growth to over 2 million supporters and a high level of public approval, the creation of a new pollution control industry, reductions in the plundering of natural resources, the savings resulting from conservation, and improvements in the health and welfare of people. No doubt these contentious issues will continue, but perhaps we will also find some degree of resolution in the decade of the 1980s.

THE ROLE OF GOVERNMENT

To meet environmental issues, government must play a major role. Self-regulation should not be discounted, but persuasion, incentives, jawboning, and law enter in to assure that ecological problems are attacked. Government may use grants, subsidies, proscriptive and regulatory laws.

Some environmentalists see government as the only force for environmental protection. They demand a politically controlled and directed society, reflecting the weaknesses of voluntarism and the difficulty of changing consumption habits, production techniques, and reducing the influence of greed and materialism. Hence complex value issues and conflicts surround environmental goals. The impact on management is clear: Environmental issues must be considered in all decision making, especially in adapting to new technologies, forging new values in business, and in response to new demands for a better quality of life.

The presence of government in coping with environmental issues is inevitable, as are the political problems that accompany the formation and execution of public policy. Environmental issues are a special case within the broad category of government regulation. Despite the abundance of governmental regulation of environmental problems, however, there are some who deem the government's role as insufficient, and in fact blame the government for tolerating or exacerbating environmental problems. Their reasoning holds that a pluralistic society and its adherence to democratic principles leads to unprincipled compromise, and politics is swayed by monetary considerations to the point where the government does not act against the selfish corporations.[2] These arguments are faulty because they erroneously assume that (1) corporations should get most of the blame and that they have no sense of social responsibility with respect to environmental problems, (2) that the profit motive explains all corporate behavior, (3) that environmental problems are so bad the political and government system needs radical change, and (4) that the government is the tool of exploitive corporations.

Many writers believe that environmental problems are global and that we must therefore find worldwide solutions.[3] This leads to notions

---

[2] Robert Rienow, "Business Corporations and Environmental Protection," *National Forum*, *Phi Kappa Phi Journal*, Summer 1978, pp. 20–22.

[3] Ervin Laszlo (ed.), *The World System: Models, Norms, Variations* (New York: Braziller, 1973); Ervin Laszlo, *The Systems View of the World* (New York: Braziller, 1972).

of a total world social order that would transcend traditional nation-states. While it is conceivable that in the distant future such a development might be required by environmental disasters of as yet uncertain character, it is more feasible at present to adopt the premise that the nation-state is the basic unit of policy formation. This indicates a need for comparative studies such as that of Kelley, which examined a wide array of environmental issues in the United States, Japan, and the Soviet Union. This study concluded that despite the different cultures and value systems, they converge in dealing with environmental problems in that (1) each displays a marked discrepancy between what is said and what is done, and (2) each has a virtual absence of a public interest frame of reference.[4] These findings cast doubt on the hypothesis that government and corporate willful conspiracies prevent progress toward the solution of environmental issues.

ENVIRONMENTAL ISSUES

Environmental problems are varied, extensive, costly, and controversial. The threats they pose to the security, welfare, and happiness of humans range from immediate concerns to long-range probabilities. More than other kinds of threats, environmental problems challenge to the fullest the ability of the societies of the world to manage natural resources more carefully. The overall problem is threefold, involving technology, politics, and management in issues of great complexity.

The problems with which we must cope can be analyzed in three broad categories: (1) the scarcity and depletion of resources, (2) damage to the environment, and (3) harm to the safety and quality of life of humans.

SCARCITY OF RESOURCES

Resources are classified as renewable and unrenewable. Trees used in pulp and paper manufacturing are renewable through the careful management of forests. Metals such as lead, iron ore, bauxite, zinc, or copper are nonrenewable, and the earth's supplies are limited. Although substitute materials are being discovered and experiments in their use are numerous, deeper but more costly extraction limits the value of this solution.

Growing scarcities threaten our way of life because they alter the technologies of production, the costs of goods and services, and the growth foundation of industrialized society. The dimensions of this

---

[4] Donald R. Kelley, Kenneth R. Stunkel, and Richard R. Wescott, *The Economic Superpowers and the Environment* (San Francisco: Freeman, 1976). See also Sprout and Sprout, *Contexts of Environmental Politics*, and Walt Anderson (ed.), *Politics and Environment: A Reader in Ecological Crisis* (Pacific Palisades, Calif.: Goodyear, 1975).

problem are not clear, but what is clear is that public policy is increasingly and appropriately concerned with resource protection and utilization. Opinions as to the severity of the problem range from complacence and blind faith in technology to predictions of ultimate disaster for the human race.

Among the disaster theories are those that borrow the concept of entropy from the science of physics. The second law of thermodynamics holds that when energy is produced or converted from one form to another, some of it is inevitably lost. This loss is a waste, called *entropy*. It represents an inevitable progression from order to disorder, as when coal that is burned becomes ash. The ultimate inference is that the world is running downhill and will not support life in the far distant future. Rifkin and Howard assert that, since energy and all other resources are giving out, it is illogical to struggle for industrialized systems in the effort to raise our standard of living. They dismiss conservation approaches such as recycling and switching to different forms of energy as ineffective because ultimately such methods result in even more demands on resources. They propose instead a low-entropy society that would radically minimize energy use — reversion to a rural society where families become self-sustaining units.[5] The Rifkin solution is unrealistic because it overlooks the enormous resilience of humans, who are demonstrably unwilling to surrender the benefits of technological progress. Unpredictable technological developments could render disaster predictions absurd. Pricing mechanisms have already produced many adaptations in energy use.

A more balanced view than that of the environmental pessimists is that of René Dubos, who points out the ambivalent attitudes of even the most dedicated environmentalists, who advocate a "land ethic" that implies that nature knows best and should not be interfered with. In advocating biotic communities living close to nature, they misconstrue humankind's relationship with the earth and fail to recognize the extent to which humans have improved the natural environment. It is not true, asserts Dubos, that humans damage the earth whenever they intervene in the natural order. Nature has extreme restorative capacities, and it is not true that natural processes always produce the most viable ecosystems. He notes, for example, that 200 years ago 70 percent of the land in Rhode Island had been cleared of forest, but with the abandonment of poor farmland, the trees returned so rapidly that only 30 percent of the land remains cleared today. Ecological recoveries are evident. Lake Erie, the Thames River, and the Willamette River in Oregon are examples of natural recovery assisted by human intervention. Dubos believes that

---

[5] Jeremy Rifkin, with Ted Howard, *Entropy* (New York: Viking Press, 1980).

ecology is not so much dependent on esoteric technologies as on good management and social will.[6]

While there is reason to be concerned with environmental problems, a balanced view requires a better information base and a rational approach that tames the emotional and crisis pressures which point to radical or impractical solutions.[7] Interdisciplinary research offers hope for developing better quality of life measurements, though this requires public recognition of criteria and definitions of society's desired condition.[8]

The conflict between scarcity and growth is one of our most serious dilemmas. The conflict is even incorporated into regulatory laws that affirm both an intention to control pollution and an intention to foster employment and industrial development. A Missouri law is typical; it states that the purpose and intent of its antipollution law is to "maintain purity of the air resources of the state, to protect the health, general welfare and physical property of the people, maximum employment and full industrial development of the state." These ambivalences reflect the desire of people to have their cake and eat it too. Perhaps the twin goals are not entirely inconsistent.

In advocating no-growth philosophies, environmentalists have ignored the general context of economic development within which environmental problems have been generated. Appealing to a middle-class constituency, the environmental movement operates by a kind of Protestant ethic of cleanliness. But the public worries more about crime, war, or unemployment than about ecology. Both Right and Left proponents of ecology advance equally plausible points of view with equal ferocity, but Horowitz writes that the environmentalist movement "can be viewed as a coalition of economic conservatism and scientific narrowness that is often masked by radical slogans and a secular vision of the religious life."[9] He writes also that Americans prefer industrialism to cleanliness, and points to the industrial apparatus spawned by the movement, allowing society to capitalize on its fears.[10]

There is evidence that growth has become less of a secular religion than it was a decade ago. The Woodlands Conference, a group conducting

[6] René Dubos, "The Despairing Optimist," *American Scholar,* Summer 1977, p. 280, and the *Resilience of Ecosystems* (Boulder, Colo.: Colorado Associated University Press, 1978).

[7] Bernard Frieden, *The Environmental Protection Hustle* (Cambridge, Mass.: MIT Press, 1979); Donald C. King and Robert L. Thornton, "Ecology—The Fear Appeal in the Public Sector," *MSU Business Topics* 20 (Winter 1972), pp. 35–38.

[8] Donald R. Hudson, "Measuring the Quality of Life," *Atlanta Economic Review* 27 (May–June 1977), pp. 15–21.

[9] Irving Horowitz, *Ideology and Utopia in the United States 1956–1976* (New York: Oxford University Press, 1977), pp. 419–426.

[10] Ibid., p. 423.

a ten-year study of growth that began in 1974, concluded in 1979 that a new growth ethic is emerging. Polls reflect prevalent attitudes such as "small is beautiful," doing without, living with basic essentials, and enjoying nonmaterialistic experiences. The pursuit of economic stability even at the cost of reduced consumption, with more modest expectations from science and technology and stress on the need for people to control their destinies, are important elements of the new ethic. Along with these attitudes is a growing recognition that there are limits to government as the instrument for doing things in the public interest.[11] These trends indicate a moderated but continuing growth policy that will change in direction and offer hope without succumbing to a no-growth ideal.

ENERGY

The most basic scarcity is found in energy. Industrial civilization is founded on technologies built around abundant energy that create life styles and consumption habits which may not be sustainable in the post-industrial society. Energy has become more costly and less available. Since it is a key factor in coping with other environmental problems and in any technological solutions that might be possible, the energy issue contains moral, economic, technical, and political issues that impinge on one another. Oil and gas, for example, are essential in the manufacture of plastics and other synthetic materials. World production of synthetics increased from 10 million tons in 1960 to 80 million tons in 1979, and the increase promises to continue as adjustments are made to industrial problems relating to environmental conditions. In 1980, synthetic materials consumed 3 percent of the world's oil and gas annually, and the amount could rise to 6 percent by the 1990s.[12] The use of these energy sources in manufactured products requires foregoing their use as sources of power in homes, automobiles, or factories.

The environmental movement contains many public interest groups, most of which are vocal on energy and have taken active roles in lobbying for energy and other legislation. Energy appears to have become the major environmental issue of the 1980s, and ecologically oriented organizations are shifting their emphasis on pollution to questions of energy. These groups have tended to emphasize renewable resources such as solar energy and fuel from agricultural products, while resisting nuclear power and the use of coal, oil, and gas because of their negative

[11] Harlan Cleveland, "The Management of Sustainable Growth," opening and closing remarks at the Third Biennial Woodlands Conference as Growth Policy, October 28–31, 1979. See also Richard Lecomber, *Economic Growth versus the Environment* (New York: Halsted Press, 1975).

[12] *American Business*, July 1980, p. 3.

impacts. These groups have also opposed the waiving of environmental standards as a means of expediting energy projects.

> *There is a huge, perhaps unreconcilable struggle between those who are interested in a model of zero growth and those who are interested in a model of economic equity. The zero-growth model is an effort to freeze the relationships that obtain at present levels of income and opportunity. The equity model involves the redistribution of what wealth does exist by generating new forms of production if required. This is not so much a struggle between zero growth and full growth as between balances to be maintained and equities to be established. The suspicion that the environment movement in America is concerned with keeping in place the advantages of some, rather than extending the benefits of democracy to all, is what this study is about. This too indicates a note of consensus politics, and the tragedy here is between perfectly decent people lining up on two sides of a metaphysical fence that cannot be bridged without a real loss, either environmental or economic. Who is to make that decision?*
>
> From *Ideology and Utopia in the United States 1956–1976* by IRVING LOUIS HOROWITZ. Copyright © 1977 by IRVING LOUIS HOROWITZ. Reprinted by permission of Oxford University Press, Inc.

One major study concluded that the influence of seven public interest groups on energy policy is significant, and will continue to be. It also found that such groups believe that many policies are controlled by special interest groups and that the function of public interest groups is to counteract their power. Coalitions are continuously forming and reforming around specific issues. Public interest groups have become increasingly critical of nuclear power, have opposed deregulation of gas and oil prices, and have emphasized conservation. Since public interest lobbies make their decisions by member consensus, there are minority groups within that can block or alter their positions.[13]

The rise of public interest lobbies is a reflection of the increasing role of government in energy matters. There has been no consistent, comprehensive national energy policy; instead, there have been piecemeal efforts directed at specific parts of the total problem. The government acts according to political considerations as well as economic or social criteria. The extensive role of government implies the abandonment of reliance on market mechanisms to regulate the allocation of energy resources. Government must operate through congressional legislation, which is more responsive to interest groups than to the vague concept of

---

[13] Andrew S. McFarland, *Public Interest Lobbies: Decision Making on Energy* (Washington, D.C.: American Enterprise Institute, 1976).

the public welfare. Beyond legislation lies the administrative powers that fall to government officials, who can then wield enormous power over the business and economic system.

Government approaches under the Carter administration included (1) the use of subsidies to direct resource use, (2) intervention in behalf of environmental protection, (3) new antitrust legislation as a reaction to the energy crisis, (4) the use of price controls, (5) proposals to treat the energy industry as a public utility, (6) the maintenance of a strategic petroleum reserve, and (7) financing energy research, including that on synthetic fuels. But these areas of action were not welded into a coherent, comprehensive strategy. Instead, various overlapping agencies worked at cross purposes and produced confusion, uncertainty, and frustration. Past energy policy is widely regarded as a failure and an indication that future energy policies are not likely to be effective.[14]

In 1977 under the Carter administration Congress established the Department of Energy (DOE) as a cabinet-level unit. At issue during the debates was the question of whether the department should be weak or strong. Initially the DOE was not assigned the responsibility for many energy problems, which remained under the purview of other agencies. Offshore oil leases remained under the Department of the Interior; standards for automobile fuel efficiency remained under the Department of Transportation.[15] In 1981, the new Reagan administration considered dismantling the DOE.

The formation of the DOE followed long and tempestous wrangling over how to organize the government for energy policies and programs during the Nixon and Ford administrations. In this period there was a succession of nine "energy czars," each struggling to bring order out of the jungle of agencies concerned with energy issues.[16] The DOE had a bigger impact than previous efforts under the strong but controversial leadership of James P. Schlesinger, who was undaunted by the political battles that raged around his edicts. Subsequently, President Carter replaced Schlesinger with a calmer and less contentious official, but neither succeeded in fully coordinating and synthesizing a truly coherent national energy policy. Getting proposals through Congress was the major difficulty.

One of the most troublesome energy issues is that of nuclear power. Political battles rage between proponents and opponents. Mayors, businesspersons, trade associations, and many citizens favor the develop-

---

[14] Walter J. Mead. *Energy and the Environment: Conflict in Public Policy* (Washington, D.C.: American Enterprise Institute, 1978).

[15] A. Lee Fritschler and Bernard H. Ross, *Business Regulation and Government Decision Making* (Cambridge, Mass.: Winthrop, 1980), pp. 154–155.

[16] John C. Whitaker, *Striking a Balance: Environment and Natural Resources Policy in the Nixon-Ford Years* (Washington, D.C.: American Enterprise Institute, 1976), pp. 66–71.

ment of nuclear power as one part of an energy strategy. A large number of public interest groups, environmentalists, and many citizens reject nuclear power because of the dangers they feel will accompany the construction and operation of such facilities. The Atomic Energy Commission, now called the Nuclear Regulatory Commission, is the federal government unit that regulates the nuclear power industry. Weingast notes that during the 1960s the AEC gradually changed from an agency largely influenced by producers (a capture theory) to one influenced primarily by pressure groups—chiefly environmentalists. As a result, regulation became far more complex and stringent. Construction delays became longer, driving up costs, and the number of applications for plants dropped off. Many protest marches have contributed to the delays and increased costs, but the delay and cost problems are also the result of technical requirements.[17]

States and local communities also react strongly to nuclear plant proposals, and have laws and ordinances affecting them. In one small southern town of 18,000 people, for example, the Westinghouse Electric Company proposed a large nuclear fuel fabrication plant to employ 400 people with a payroll of $6.5 million a year. Strong environmentalist resistance came from the town and its surrounding areas; opponents entered nearly 100 specific objections which must be considered in hearings held by the NRC. The allegations include hazards to both people and the natural environment. City officials and the Chamber of Commerce favored the plan because of its impact on the local economy. The demands of opponents are for 100 percent safety, whereas proponents can promise only that the plant will be as safe as the possibilities for human error permit. The issues are complex and obviously must be dealt with as particular cases. Proponents of such plants argue that the risks are no greater, and probably less than, the possible hazards of other types of plants.[18]

ENVIRONMENTAL HAZARDS

A growing awareness of the dangers of environmental consequences has emerged in our society. These dangers include (1) the pollution of land, water, and air, with resulting effects on human health and on wildlife, through the discharge of wastes; (2) harms to workers due to toxic substances associated with production processes and the work environment; and (3) dangers to consumers from products containing harmful substances.

---

[17] Barry R. Weingast, "Congress, Regulation, and the Decline of Nuclear Power," *Public Policy* 28 (Spring 1980), pp. 231–255.

[18] Desaix B. Myers III, *The Nuclear Power Debate: Moral, Economic, Technical and Political Issues* (New York: Praeger, 1977).

In all three areas, there have been long time lags until the harmful effects have appeared. Scientific evidence as to actual or potential harm is costly to obtain, uncertain or controversial in nature, and difficult to translate into control standards. Therefore, both prevention and remediation are difficult problems. The surrounding controversies are the subject of an increasing amount of litigation. Examples of environmental degradation and resulting conflicts with environmentalists are found in the Appalachian region, the Far West, and in Alaska. Corporations are increasingly being required to bear the responsibility for their impact on land and natural resources. Environmentalists base their case not only on the welfare and survival of humanity, but on esthetic values and on recreational uses of huge land areas that must be foregone for production purposes.

In Appalachia, environmentalists assert that the southern and central regions have been turned into a gullied desert despite abundant rain. Strip mining for coal in 2 million acres of land in eastern Kentucky and portions of West Virginia and Alabama has changed the land so that millions of tons of mud have washed down into creek and river channels. As the long-wall machines and continuous miners advance, wells go dry because the water drains into the voids. Nonresident corporations own and exploit more than 5 million acres of Appalachian land. Their operations have affected the lives of mountaineers, and endangered the health and safety of miners. The Appalachian area lacks recreation facilities, good access roads, water supplies, and sewage disposal facilities. Schools need modernizing; flood control and programs for restoring the land to its original contours and conditions are key objectives.[19]

The federal Surface Mine Reclamation Act of 1977 taxes the mining concerns to raise money for such projects. Corporations, too, are voluntarily responding to these needs. The Harbert Corporation, for example, is conducting a reclamation program in its Appalachian mines to create a master plan for restoring over 10,000 acres of land that would restructure it for the best possible use after the coal is gone. Wildlife in this area has again become abundant, but the plan is directed toward the economic life of the region and the long-run welfare of the people.[20]

In the land- and space-conscious West, a range war, known as the Sagebrush Rebellion, pits ranchers, loggers, miners, and others against Washington officials in a fight over the land and mineral and water resources. The trouble began as a fight over the federal government's vast landholdings, but it now includes many other environmental issues. The

---

[19] Harry M. Caudill, "Appalachian Life and Corporate Responsibility," National Forum, *Phi Kappa Phi Journal* 58 (Summer 1978), pp. 15–19.

[20] John M. Harbert III, "Appalachia: Its Coal, Its People, Its Future," speech delivered on March 18, 1980, to the leaders of Bell County, Kentucky.

argument is between those who would preserve the environment, its scenic and recreational characteristics and its resources, and those who demand that exploration for oil, minerals, and other resources be increased. The Federal Land Policy and Management Act of 1976 says that the government must hold these lands in protected trust. Washington therefore resists turning public lands over to local governments, whose residents argue they could do a better job than Washington bureaucrats. Environmentalists oppose giving free rein to local governments on the ground that real estate developers, mining firms, and lumber companies will ravish the environment. More disturbing than federal land ownership in the eyes of many westerners is increasing government restriction on private uses of public lands, such as for grazing livestock. Tightened enforcement of federal environmental rules and laws protecting endangered wildlife is further shrinking the amount of land available for farming, ranching, mining, and lumbering. In Idaho, a business group has fought a proposal to expand the Snake River birds of prey national conservation area. The refuge, one of the largest nesting grounds for eagles, hawks, and falcons in the United States, grew from 26,000 acres in 1971 to 539,000 in 1977. The government is continuing to add more acreage, even through it idles irrigated cropland.[21]

No company should be expected to let itself be forced out of business by the costs of pollution control. It should resist by seeking to have the cost borne, or at least shared, by the public. It is not illegal, immoral or even anti-ecology to accept the goals of ecology but argue over who is going to pay the bill; and, of course, nothing in the antitrust laws prohibits an entire industry from joining together to seek legislative or other governmental relief where costs of pollution control threaten to make it noncompetitive with foreign concerns.

American Bar Association official, speaking at a conference on the Clayton Act.

In 1980 Congress passed legislation protecting over 1 million acres of Alaskan land from use for obtaining oil, gas, timber, and minerals. The bill, signed by President Carter, doubled Alaska's national park system and doubled its wildlife refuges. Of the total, 56.7 million acres were designated as wilderness, to be untouched by development. The entire acreage is bigger than the state of California but less than one-third of Alaska's land mass. This kind of bill indicates the government's intention not to let economic development take precedence over conservation.[22]

---

[21] *U.S. News and World Report*, December 1, 1980, pp. 29–30.
[22] Associated Press news release dated December 3, 1980.

Pollution results from toxic or disagreeable substances that escape or are discarded from human activities. Pollutants contaminate air, water, and land, thus endangering natural resources and human health and welfare. Some forms of pollution threaten permanent damage to the environment; others cause harms that can be minimized by reclamation processes. Some harms are known, but continuous research is needed to check on as yet unknown consequences of our productive efforts.

Pollution is not new. Noisy, filthy, and dangerous living conditions have always affected humankind. There were instances of water pollution in Rome before 100 B.C., and of air pollution in England as early as the fourteenth century. Environmental damage is more important today. It is considerably worse, and affects more people. We now notice it more and are less tolerant of it. Environmental harm is roughly proportional to the scale and variety of production and consumption. The huge increase in the earth's population, the expansion of production and consumption, and the impact of advanced technologies have increased the scale, pervasiveness, and variety of environmental degradation throughout the world.

Environmentalists are concerned about a future in which pollution goes uncontrolled. Their attacks on business firms, technology, growth, and the main tenets of the capitalistic system are emotional and ideological as well as rational. They believe that traditional incentives and market forces cause rather than prevent environmental problems. In an age when technology produces so many wonders, they feel that the problems of noise, air, and water pollution are solvable. However, it is not only business firms that pollute; government agencies, nonprofit institutions, households, and individuals are also polluters. Therefore it is difficult to sort out the responsibilities of business from those of other sectors. Ultimately, environmental improvement reflects a new philosophy on the quality of life, and requires a variety of solutions that entail dramatic changes in our life styles. Every person is a party to these efforts.

The government's antipollution efforts are under the jurisdiction of the Environmental Protection Agency (EPA), created by the Nixon administration in 1970. This agency employs approximately 10,000 people. A 1979 Business Roundtable study found that in the companies surveyed, EPA regulations accounted for 77 percent of their total costs of regulation.[23] The costs of pollution control are social costs that in former years companies did not pay. It is clearly the nation's policy to require companies to pay a greater share of these social costs, even though they are

---

[23] Fritschler and Ross, *Business Regulation*, pp. 65–66.

ultimately passed on to consumers. Companies also pay punitive damages when lawsuits are won by various claimants.

The task of the EPA is to set and enforce standards for clean air and water, and to regulate environmental problems under a number of separate laws bearing on specific areas. Setting standards is difficult because technology changes, necessitating changes in standards. Also, the scientific evidence for harm and its correctives is often uncertain.

The EPA has in general set up time schedules by which the "best available technology" (BAT) is to be in place at later dates, with lower standards in the intervening years. This BAT, however, applies across whole industries, affecting companies differently according to their cost and profit structures. The Clean Water Act, for example, requires that the "best available technology that is economically feasible," the best practical technology (BPT), be in place by 1987. But that part of the law, which set intermediate standards for 1977, did not allow for variances for economic reasons, and the right of the EPA to enforce BAT rather than BPT standards for 1977 requirements was upheld by a 1980 Supreme Court decision. Also, the EPA has wide latitude in deciding what is available and what is practical.

Antipollution efforts are characterized by frequent negotiations and court cases in developing and applying standards. The government has been under pressure to ease standards where economic hardships are evident, but reducing standards is resisted by environmentalists and has occurred only minimally. The Business Roundtable, for example, made a $600,000 study of the Clean Air Act of 1970, which concluded that in passing the act Congress had relied on medical studies that were not scientifically supportable, and that the regulations could be loosened so as to cut compliance costs by half without jeopardizing public health. The study attacked the administration of the act as ignoring other socioeconomic goals such as productivity and unemployment. It objected to requirements so strict that an unrealistic, totally risk-free environment would result, yet a cost-benefit analysis does not support such a goal. Compliance with the 1977 standards set by Congress were estimated to cost the utility industry $6.6 billion by 1990, which would produce only $5.8 billion in benefits. Scaling back to save ratepayers $3.1 billion would result in little loss in air quality. The 1977 standards would cost all industries $415 billion by 1987.[24]

Rothenberg notes that there are many kinds and degrees of pollution. The assimilative capacity of the environment varies with the nature of the wastes, the medium into which wastes are discharged, and actions taken to augment the assimilative capacity. Also, waste products can be

---

[24] Associated Press report dated November 23, 1980.

altered by varying the rate and composition of primary consumption and production, by changing inputs or technologies, or by adopting measures to recycle, modify, reduce, or denature the residual discharges. He notes also that (1) every method of decreasing pollution incurs some social cost, (2) disposal of wastes in the common environment is not a rare phenomenon, and (3) pollution is not the intended goal of polluters. It is a by-product of consumption and production. Thus the popular stereotype of the polluter as a corporate or executive villain is unfair. The villainy is predominantly in the breakdown of market signals which results in systematically distorted choices. Though some pollution is inevitable, genuine social problems lie in its character and magnitude—the wrong amount, the wrong sort, and in the wrong places.[25] The goal of anti-pollution efforts therefore is to reduce, not eliminate, pollution.

Waste disposal is a critical part of the pollution problem. If all wastes were solids that accumulated where they were generated, each waste producer could be required to incur the costs of disposing them. However, it has been necessary to reserve land specifically for the disposal of some wastes, such as those of nuclear plants. Other wastes are controlled by decontamination processes before discharging them into the air, water, or land.

In addition to regulating and, where possible, prohibiting pollution, the government's approach includes public subsidies, environmental research, and variety of policies designed to assist companies in adhering to regulations and improving pollution control. However, because many different federal units are involved, as are state and local governments, there is often conflict and inconsistency among their standards and enforcement. Some states and local units have adopted even stronger standards than those of the federal government.

An interesting compromise on standards, known as the "bubble policy," has been evolved by the EPA. The policy treats an industrial plant as if it were an imaginary bubble that has a single stack emitting all pollutants. Companies can submit proposals for limiting emissions on a plantwide basis rather than meeting separate limits for each source of pollutants. Over 100 companies had submitted proposals by the end of 1980, but few had yet been accepted by EPA. In Armco Steel company, for example, the director of environmental engineering for Armco stated that the company could control six times as much pollution for one-third the cost in half the time, at a fraction of the energy required. Business firms believe the policies will reduce compliance costs, but environmentalists protest they are too easy on companies.

Some companies found that waiting for EPA approval of their bubble

---

25 Jerome Rothenberg, "The Physical Environment," in James W. McKie (ed.), *Social Responsibility in the Business Predicament* (Washington, D.C.: The Brookings Institution, 1974), pp. 191–215.

proposal would delay expenditures for expensive treatment equipment which, if it had to be installed later, would prevent them from meeting standards for 1982 on time. They could receive stiff fines for this. Others object that the rules for bubble policy are so strict that options for offsetting one polluting source against another are limited. It remains hard to determine the measured standards for the various sources. The bubble idea has logic and common sense on its side, but immense difficulties in implementation.[26]

Another idea for helping firms comply with antipollution regulation is to allow them to pay charges for the privilege, until compliance becomes possible. This is more feasible at state and local levels. In Pennsylvania, for example, a motor inn was allowed to continue dumping 400,000 gallons of sewage a month into an underground stream, paying $29,000 over two years while a new sewage treatment plant was constructed.[27] In 1980 Maryland proposed a whole system for banking and marketing rights to pollute. The proposal would allow a company with low pollution levels to store "air quality credits" which it could later sell to another company or apply to its own increased pollution due to expansion. The object is to encourage new plant development and to reduce the costs of pollution control. Also, under the Clean Air Act, companies wishing to build a new plant in a high pollution location can do so if the new plant offsets pollution reduction in another existing facility.[28]

There has been a shortage of acceptable dumping grounds for chemical wastes. There has also been a great deal of illegal dumping by firms that contract out the dumping to firms specializing in this service. However, stiff enforcement was instituted in 1980, and several firms were heavily fined.[29]

In December of 1980, a federal toxic waste bill was signed into law. It was directed at problems such as the Love Canal disaster, where it was discovered that toxic wastes disposed of years earlier had poisoned land on which many people were living, causing them to develop severe illness. The bill (1) created a "superfund" for use in cleaning up active or inactive chemical dump sites and spills into land or water, and (2) provided that the government can suc firms known to be responsible to cover the cost. The superfund was planned at a $1.6 billion level, although earlier bills envisioned $4.2 billion. The fund accumulates through fees levied on chemical firms for 87.5 percent of the total, with the other 12.5 percent coming from general tax revenues.

The Resource Conservation and Recovery Act of 1976 represented a clampdown by Congress on dumping hazardous wastes. In 1980 the EPA

---

[26] *The Wall Street Journal*, October 1, 1980, p. 1.

[27] *The Wall Street Journal*, April 16, 1980, p. 1.

[28] *Business Week*, August 18, 1980, pp. 29–30.

[29] *The Wall Street Journal*, September 2, 1980, p. 48.

announced 2000 pages of rules and regulations designed to discover who generates wastes, who transports them, and how they are disposed of. The new system makes companies liable for what happens to their hazardous wastes after they leave the plant. The regulations were estimated to cost these firms $1 billion and 5.2 million man-hours of labor to comply. The EPA estimates that 57 million tons of hazardous wastes are produced annually, with only 10 percent disposed of properly. The EPA crackdown should thus result in substantial improvement.

The problem of regulating pollution is clearly a matter of several interrelated complex issues with elusive solutions. Toxic studies are often not rigorous, but even so they arouse fears and anxieties that can only lead to costly remedies. In the case of Love Canal, scientists debate whether the evidence of an abnormal incidence of cancer and birth defects was sufficient to justify relocating hundreds of people.[30] Even greater fears and anxieties emerge when the wastes are of nuclear origin. Scientists, moreover, cannot quickly find specific answers. For example, federal investigators found an unusually high incidence of brain tumors among petrochemical workers at plants of the Dow Chemical Company and the Union Carbide Company, but one year later had not found what chemicals had caused the problem. Employees who work for many years close to potent chemical substances, however, may be exposing themselves to a cancer risk of from two to three times the norm for the nation as a whole.

MANAGEMENT ISSUES

Management is becoming increasingly aware that economic development, technological change, and even the survival of their firms depend on actions that are compatible with protecting the environment. Payoffs to management for ecologically appropriate decisions include the increases in profit that can be achieved through waste avoidance and efficient operations, the opportunity to investigate new areas in which to develop products and services, and avoiding the costs of conflict and mistakes. A 1978 estimate of the impact of environmental policies in the United States showed that the annual benefits of improvements in air quality since 1970 were $21.4 billion, and that the total annual benefits in 1985 due to improved water quality will be $12.3 billion. By the end of 1980, it was further estimated that environmental regulation would have added only 0.1 percent to the consumer price index, reduced unemployment by 0.4 percent, and increased the gross national product by $9.3 billion.[31]

---

[30] *The Wall Street Journal*, October 20, 1980, p. 26.

[31] *Tenth Annual Report of the Council on Environmental Quality* (Washington, D.C.: U.S. Government Printing Office, 1980), pp. 655–662.

Companies today are placing environmental problems high on their agendas. Increasingly they are appointing new environmental managers, and upgrading their status and responsibilities. Staffs and budgets are being enlarged. Top managements are pursuing environmental concerns as well, and they give direct access to their environmental affairs managers. Few management officials are environmental activists, but they are concerned with bringing about a balance between environmental issues and corporate concerns for profit, stability, and survival. A great deal of expertise is required for handling company responses to environmental concerns. Specialists are also helpful in steering companies through the maze of regulations. Reducing pollution at the source in a preventive way costs less than detoxification or other forms of reclamation. Doing what is right environmentally can also reduce the number of lawsuits and damage payments. So environmental specialists are beginning to earn the respect of officials inside and outside the company.[32]

The principal remedies for environmental problems are in the hands of the affected parties. Companies can act for improvement through voluntary means such as market agreements. The concept of social responsibility through corporate initiatives is paramount in areas where market incentives and legal remedies are insufficient. Such social responsibility includes self-policing by firms of their own waste removal activities. Second, the firm can apply pressure on other firms to police their emissions by manipulating transactions with other firms in the market. Third, firms can take initiatives in social nonmarket programs in the community, such as organizing community clean-up campaigns and compensation plans for victims harmed by various activities. Companies need to incorporate environmental concerns into the total planning system.[33] Social audit and social accounting techniques can provide analysis, information, and other aids to decision making.[34]

Some mutual investment companies have established special funds for equity investments in companies which, in the opinion of the fund's management, not only meet traditional investment standards, but also show evidence in the conduct of their business, relative to other companies in the same industry, of contributing to the enhancement of the quality of life in America. For example, the Dreyfus Third Century Fund, Inc., says it will consider a company's record in the areas of (1) protection

---

[32] "The New Corporate Environmentalists," *Business Week*, May 28, 1979, pp. 154–162; Robert Cahn, "A Place for Environment in the Corporate Structure," *Management Review* 68 (April 1979), pp. 15–20.

[33] D. J. Davidson, *The Environmental Factor: An Approach for Managers* (New York: Halsted Press, 1978); Peter C. Ball, Jr., and Peter Lorange, "Managing Your Strategic Responsiveness to the Environment," *Managerial Planning* 28 (November–December 1979), pp. 3–9, 27.

[34] Meinholf Dirks and Lee E. Preston, "Corporate Social Accounting Reporting for the Physical Environment: A Critical Review and Implementation Proposal," *Accounting, Organizations and Society* 2 (January 1977), pp. 3–32; L. R. Caldwell, "Management of Resources and the Environment: A Problem of Administrative Coordination," *International Review of Administrative Sciences* 38 (1972), pp. 115–127.

and improvement of the environment and the proper use of our natural resources, (2) occupational health and safety, (3) consumer protection and product purity, and (4) equal employment opportunity. In addition, consideration is given to companies that have developed, or are actively engaged in developing, technology, products, or services which will contribute to the enhancement of the quality of life in America. The prospectus lists a number of companies enhancing the quality of life by the conduct of their business.

THE IMPACT OF ECOLOGY EFFECTS ON MANAGEMENT

Environmental preservation and improvements call for a redirection of technological efforts as well as a restructuring of life styles and consumption habits. In both areas, management plays a significant role. The environmentalist movement has also brought to the fore many issues that greatly affect the management of business firms. These include (1) impacts on profitability through cost considerations, (2) the passage of regulatory legislation, (3) the nature of products desired by consumers, (4) the nature of the processes by which products and services are made available to consumers, and (5) changes in marketing techniques, practices, and philosophies.[35]

In the early days of the environmentalist movement, fears arose concerning the impact of costs which, though increasingly acknowledged as covering important actions, could reduce profits and mean a decline in the Gross National Product. Quinn argued, however, that environmental improvement could become a dynamic, vital force by creating new markets, and indeed a new industry.[36] The chemical waste disposal problem, for example, has led to the establishment of many firms that specialize in this field.

Early in the environmentalist movement, great faith was placed on cost-benefit analysis. This was a logical strategy in view of the many cost uncertainties involved. With the passage of time, however, a more restrained view of cost-benefit techniques emerged. Ashby, for example, notes that enthusiasm for cost-benefit analysis as an instrument of environmental policy has cooled because economists have tried to convert social values to monetary values. The assumption that this can be done has proved wrong, and unquantified, subjective values have often compelled politicians to overturn the sophisticated cost-benefit studies using quantitative data. He writes further:

---

[35] Etienne Cracco and Jacques Rostenne, "The Socio-Ecological Product," *MSU Business Topics*, Summer 1971, pp. 27–34; Bernard M. Bass and R. Bass, "Concern for the Environment: Implications for Industrial and Organizational Psychology," *American Psychologist* 31 (February 1976), pp. 158–166.

[36] James Brian Quinn, "Next Big Industry: Environmental Improvement," *Harvard Business Review* 49 (September–October 1971), pp. 29–40.

This is not because cost-benefit analysis is an unreliable technique but because it embodies an unacceptable premise, namely that the question to be answered is "What is efficient for society?" rather than "What is good for society?" For some enterprises—industry, for instance, where the aim is to maximize efficiency—this premise may be acceptable. For the protection of the environment this premise is not acceptable because it warps the perspective of the policymaker. By all means use the most cost-effective way to achieve the end, once the end has been determined; but do not use cost-benefit analysis to determine the end.[37]

ENVIRONMENTAL SCANNING

Environmental problems should be addressed by every firm in developing strategic conceptualization of long-term objectives. For such strategy to be effective, there must be a proper match between environmental opportunities and organization resources.[38]

Environmental scanning techniques are now widely used for systematic information searches to improve forecasting and planning. The object is to provide a holistic view of factors in the environment affecting the organization's future. Scanning goes beyond economic and technical issues to include social and political trends.[39] Scanning procedures review and keep track of many sources of information: appropriate literature, contacts with outsiders, relationships with external organizations, special consultants, and the like. The resulting inputs are then analyzed and prepared for dissemination to internal units for discussion and planning purposes.

Scanning provides information on which to base all types of plans and decisions. It is especially important for developing guidelines, policies, and goals for the specific purpose of coping with the problems discussed in this chapter. For example, Figure 17.1 shows the Shell Oil Company's corporate position on environmental conservation. Figure 17.2 shows Shell's Environmental Affairs Charter. Such documents declare what a company believes and what it intends to do. By taking a stand, by developing policies and establishing systematic procedures, companies can be better prepared for the uncertain future.[40]

---

[37] Eric Ashby, *Reconciling Man with the Environment* (Stanford, Calif.: Stanford University Press, 1978), p. 56.

[38] Richard F. Vancil, "Strategy Formation in Complex Organizations," *Sloan Management Review* 17 (Winter 1976), pp. 1–18.

[39] John F. Preble, "Corporate Use of Environmental Scanning," *University of Michigan Business Review* 30 (September 1978), pp. 12–17; Philip S. Thomas, "Environmental Scanning: The State of the Art," *Long Range Planning* 13 (February 1980), pp. 20–28; Lee E. Preston and James E. Post, *Private Management and Public Policy* (Englewood Cliffs, N.J.: Prentice-Hall, 1978), chap. 10.

[40] James K. Brown, *This Business of Issues: Coping with the Company's Environments* (New York: The Conference Board, 1979).

FIGURE 17.1

Shell Oil Company's Corporate Statement

CORPORATE POSITION
ON ENVIRONMENTAL CONSERVATION

Shell Oil Company and its subsidiaries, as responsible members of society, share a nationwide concern for the protection of this country's environmntal resources. With this in mind, our company's policy is:

- To treat with appropriate concern all materials and operations which contribute to the degradation of the environment;
- To comply with all regulations affecting water or air emissions, solid wastes, and light or sound intensities established by legislation for improving the environment;
- To provide such additional protection for the environment as is responsible, feasible, and practical;
- To encourage, support and conduct research for the purposes of achieving realistic environmental standards and to improve methods of environmental management;
- To make available to others new conservation methods or techniques we may develop which will contribute to better environmental management;
- To cooperate with government, industry and associations in the establishment of pollution criteria and standards which relate either to our own operations or use of our products;
- To support and encourage programs aimed at street and highway cleanup and to conduct programs for the renewal and beautification of our service stations, plant sites and manufacturing facilities;
- To keep employees, regulatory authorities and the public informed about our environmental conservation activities;
- To anticipate future environmental requirements, and to provide for them in long-range planning.

Accordingly, we will strive for the best environmental conditions in all our operations and shall consider the protection of air, marine and fresh waters, and land, and the control of light and noise as a normal part of our business.

SOURCE: Shell Position Paper, 1977.

FIGURE 17.2

Shell's Charter

ENVIRONMENTAL AFFAIRS
CHARTER FOR THE SHELL COMPANIES

Environmental Affairs serves as the focal point for coordination on all matters concerning environmental conservation for Shell Oil Company, its operating divisions, subsidiaries and affiliates. It is concerned with pollution problems that originate from the use of Shell products and from the operation of Shell plants and facilities.

Environmental Affairs is mainly concerned with the development of Shell policies and position on environmental protection matters with representation of Shell at governmental, industry and other meetings or hearings. It is involved in the collection, evaluation and dissemination of pertinent conservation information, both internally and to governmental agencies, industry associations and public groups.

Assigned Tasks

- Develop and recommend company policy with respect to environmental conservation.
- Implement approved policies and maintain coordination throughout the company.
- Provide a continuing and professional overview of the company's environmental effort.
- Keep abreast of technical and legal developments, and legislative trends in the field of environmental protection. Evaluate this information and advise appropriate managerial personnel of the probable long- and short-term effects, together with recommended courses of action.
- Maintain awareness of existing environmental law and regulation, and advise and assist in achieving its compliance.
- Engage in proposed environmental law and regulation proceedings by coordinating appropriate corporate positions and arranging that they be advanced in an appropriate and timely manner.
- Participate in various types of environmental hearings of federal, state and local bodies as Shell's representative or coordinate arrangements of other Shell personnel.

- Consult and maintain liaison with all departments of the company to ensure effective coordination of environmental conservation activities, on both the national and local levels. Liaison is also maintained with associated companies of the Royal Dutch/Shell Group concerning related developments that may have international significance.
- Participate on industry environmental committees at the policy-making level and coordinate membership of company personnel on society and local industry committees or groups.
- Review conservation problems referred by various company departments and assist in the development of recommended courses of action.

Incident Case

A high-level government adviser publicly stated: "Our environmental problems could be solved if those in charge really wanted to solve them." The press gave wide circulation to this view. A business executive wrote to the president of the United States and to the adviser, objecting to the statement and presenting a refutation of it.

What could the business executive say? What factors would affect his rejoinder?

Issues for Discussion and Analysis

1. Protection of the environment is addressed by federal, state, and local laws. How can conflicts among these jurisdictions best the resolved?

2. Do companies have any obligation to go beyond legal requirements in protecting and maintaining a safe and sound environment?

3. What weight should be given to the argument that environmental programs cost more than anticipated revenues or benefits?

4. Do environmental requirements have different impacts on small and large firms? Why or why not?

5. Are the antipollution requirements of society as a whole excessive for companies as compared to those for auto owners, homeowners, and power consumers?

6. What new organizational arrangements have been necessary in order for companies to respond effectively to environmental problems? Why should an organization try to adapt its organization structure to such problems?

7. Do environmentalists go to extremes in what they advocate? If so, what problems does this cause? If not, what role can they best play in future planning for the quality of life?

8. What have been the federal government's main problems in devising an effective national energy policy?

9. The nine volume, 1,900-page environmental impact statement on the MX missile, released in 1981, cost $16 million to produce. Argue for or against such a requirement.

Class Project

Form several groups, each of which is to make a formal analytical presentation to the class on topics chosen from the following:

1. Environmental regulations: federal, state, and local
2. Problems common to air, water, and noise pollution
3. Issues of solid and liquid waste disposal
4. Special issues pertaining to energy problems
5. The impact of technology, population, and economic growth on the environment
6. The role of science in environmental affairs
7. How companies organize to cope with environmental issues
8. What is meant by the phrase "Quality of life."

For Further Reading

ANDERSON, WALT (ed.).   *Politics and Environment: A Reader in Ecological Crisis* (Pacific Palisades, Calif.: Goodyear, 1975).

ASHBY, ERIC.   *Reconciling Man with the Environment* (Stanford, Calif.: Stanford University Press, 1978).

BAUGHMAN, JAMES P., GEORGE C. LODGE, and HOWARD PIFER.   *Environmental Analysis for Management* (Homewood, Ill.: Irwin, 1974).

COMMONER, BARRY.   *The Poverty of Power* (New York: Knopf, 1976).

DARMSTADTER, JOEL, et al.   *How Industrial Societies Use Energy: A Comparative Analysis* (Baltimore: The Johns Hopkins University Press, 1977).

DAVISON, D. J.   *The Environmental Factor: An Approach for Managers* (New York: Wiley, 1978).

ELKINS, ARTHUR, and DENNIS W. CALLAGHAN.   *A Managerial Odyssey: Problems in Business and Its Environment* (Reading, Mass.: Addison-Wesley, 1978).

FRIEDEN, BERNARD.   *The Environmental Protection Hustle* (Cambridge, Mass.: MIT Press, 1979).

HAYES, DENIS.   *Rays of Hope: The Transition to a Post-Petroleum World* (New York: Norton, 1977).

KELLEY, DONALD R., KENNETH R. STUNKEL, and CHARLES R. WESCOTT.   *The Economic Superpowers and the Environment* (San Francisco: Freeman, 1976).

MYERS, DESAIX B. III.   *The Nuclear Power Debate: Moral, Economic, Technical and Political Issues* (New York: Praeger, 1977).

RHILICH, GEORGE (ed.).   *Environmental Management: An Approach for Managers* (Cambridge, Mass.: MIT Press, 1976).

RIDKER, RONALD G., and WILLIAM D. WATSON.   *To Choose a Future: Resource and Environmental Consequences of Alternative Growth Paths* (Washington, D.C.: Resources for the Future, 1980).

RIFKIN, JEREMY, with TED HOWARD.   *Entropy* (New York: Viking Press, 1980).

SPROUT, HAROLD, and MARGARET SPROUT.   *Contexts of Environmental Politics* (Lexington: University Press of Kentucky, 1979).

COMPREHENSIVE CASES

I. The Fair Labor Standards Act of 1938

The Fair Labor Standards Act of 1938 forbids a company from employing people in their homes to produce its products. Its intent was to eradicate sweatshop abuses in big cities, especially in New York, where thousands of laborers were being exploited. Many of these workers made clothing in tenements and were paid by the piece so their unscrupulous employers could claim them as independent contractors exempt from employment laws.

Zealous enforcement can often work a hardship on individuals. For example, Ellen Welsh earned $72 a week at her kitchen table in Bennington, Vermont, knitting ski hats to sell to sport clothes firms. The 23-year-old mother of two small girls, Mrs. Welsh regards herself as a self-employed person. But the Department of Labor contended that Mrs. Welsh is an employee and therefore has to work in a factory. Hundreds of women working in Vermont could be hurt enforcing the Fair Labor Standards Act. It could kill a healthy cottage industry by compelling owners of small clothing companies to open factories or seek supplies overseas.

The Labor Department is suing the firm to which Mrs. Welsh supplies ski hats, alleging violations of sweatshop laws. The department wants to require that all the work be done in factories, where the environment can be regulated. It alleges a history of exploitation in the knitwear industry, but knitters in Bennington say they don't feel exploited and they don't want the government butting in.

An administrator in the department's wage and hour division said that it doesn't matter if knitters are content, and that it doesn't work to let workers decide if they need protecting.

The women contend that they need the money, and need to stay home to care for small children. They enjoy working at their own pace and having the option of not working at all. Some are totally dependent on the income.

The government became involved in these cases when a seamstress in one of the knitwear factories complained that she wasn't making the minimum wage. A compliance officer discovered she was actually making more than the minimum wage, but in auditing the company's payroll records he noted entries for payment to home knitters, which led to the lawsuit.

Another firm that was threatened with a government suit found that the bank had learned about the threat and had withdrawn a commitment for a working capital loan, fearing that the loss of the home knitters could kill the business. The owner said he could not afford to set up a factory. A labor department official said that such cases are routine and that these matters don't have the highest priority.

A lawyer for the knitwear company where Mrs. Welsh works said he saw little chance of beating the government on the point of law involved, but he hoped to convince the court that the practical realities of home knitting don't justify stopping it.

Analyze this case with respect to the social responsibility of business and government.

3. Hooker Electrochemical Company

From 1942 to 1953, the Hooker Electrochemical Company had used excavations from the abandoned Love Canal in Niagara Falls, New York, as a chemical dump site. In 1953, under threat of seizure by eminent domain, it sold the canal and surrounding property to the Niagara Falls School Board for $1. Shortly afterward, the school board built an elementary school on the central portion of the property, with part of the building and playground over the dump site itself. Later the school board announced plans to sell part of the property to a construction firm for subdividing into residential sites. Hooker accepted the use of the property as a school and playground because the buildings would remain on the surface and the chemicals were lying at a depth that would not be dangerous. But the school board's sale for purposes that would lead to subsoil construction and disturbance of the dangerous chemicals was vigorously protested. November 1957 school board minutes and news accounts revealed that a lawyer for Hooker twice issued strong public warnings about potential health hazards with the new developments at Love Canal. Subsequently the school board's sale was completed and private homes were built. While the company's warnings do not necessarily absolve it of all responsibility for the misfortunes of the families, the company appears to have made a strong effort to avoid the catastrophes that resulted.

It may still bear some responsibility for the seepage of toxic chemicals into the basements of nearby homes; this will be determined in a court case in which the Environmental Protection Agency is suing Hooker for the costs of cleanup and relocation of families. It charged that Hooker failed to place an adequate clay cap or other appropriate seal over the dump site when it gave the land to the school board. Hooker argues that its clay cap was sufficient but was disturbed by the construction. Although houses were not built over the canal itself, two city streets and a state expressway were built across the dump site, and Hooker contends that the property was also dug into as a source of landfill.

The EPA lawsuit charges that Hooker did not warn anybody living in the canal vicinity that contact with material at the canal could be injurious. There were known cases in which as early as 1958 children playing above the dump site had to be treated for chemical burns. In 1968 the company failed to warn the State Department of Transportation of possible hazards in the construction of the expressway across the dump site. It will be up to the courts to decide how often and how long a company that no longer owns a dump site property should be legally responsible for monitoring and protesting its misuse.

Activists have vigorously denounced the Hooker Chemical Company (its new name) for its past actions, ignoring the two instances in which the company went out of its way to alert the pubic to possible dangers. Contrary to the half-truths and innuendoes of professional corporate haters, the story does not appear to provide an object lesson in unbridled corporate callousness or villainy.

Could Hooker have taken other actions to prevent the sale of the property for home construction purposes?

How could these kinds of problems best be prevented?

4. Engineering Specifications

A student in a class in business ethics made the following comments:

> This will be my first course in how business practices relate to ethical and social responsibilities. I feel that legal responsibilities and social responsibilities are two entirely different things. Several business practices that my company uses seem to be well within the boundaries of our legal system but socially irresponsible. For example, one practice is to influence your friends in the engineering field to design and specify jobs so that for practical purposes they use only the product we manufacture. Although the specifications are usually written allowing alternate materials so that the owner will be satisfied with them, alternatives are usually specified so that they are more costly and will not be competitive with our materials. Since many of our materials are actually superior to those of our competitors', there are justifications for writing a specification around our materials. I see no conflict here between social and legal responsibilities. However, during the design stage we furnish the customer's design engineer with estimates of our materials and their costs. Based on this estimate, he determines whether or not to design his job around our materials. Then, after the design is put up for bids, we often forget the original estimate that we gave the engineer. When we see the job advertised for bids and the specifications locked around our material, we often quote prices well above that given to the engineer during the design estimate period. I believe that this is a socially irresponsible attitude and look forward to seeing what this course has to say about it.

Explain why you agree or disagree with this statement.

What can be done about this problem?

5. The Wagner Company

The Wagner Company is a general contracting firm that has been expanding its capabilities into the area of waste water treatment plants. Such construction frequently involves federal, state, or local government funding and the restrictions associated with it. Recent jobs have specified that the general contractor include a minimum percentage of minority business enterprises as subcontractors.

The treatment plants involve competitive bidding by general contractors for the lowest acceptable contractor price. In each bidding situation, the Wagner Company has made an effort to comply with the regulations on minority business enterprise, and although many in the company view the rules as shortsighted and hard to follow, the company has opened up subcontracting bid requests to local minority business enterprises, and followed up each letter with telephone contacts. The company has even bought advertising space in local newspapers and radio spots in order to inform interested minority business enterprises that they are bidding on a job and requesting their participation as subcontract bidders.

In several cases the company found that the lowest bids from subcontractors were not from minority business enterprises. In fact, very few of the bids were from minority business enterprises. Thus the Wagner Company people feel that they face a dilemma. Should the company use the lowest subcontract bid in the overall bid to sharpen its competitive edge, or should it include the higher price resulting from the minority business enterprise bids?

In some cases, the company was unsure of the ability of the minority business enterprise or the experience of the nonminority contractor. Since the lowest possible bidder receives the general contract, the general contractor is interested in the lowest fair price and also wants to ensure that the construction will reflect quality work.

If the contractor does not use the lowest bid, then the scales of justice are tipped against the subcontractor who bid in good faith and offered the lowest price. Also, the purchasers of the project, usually a community, will be forced to bear costs of construction higher than if the minority business enterprise regulations are not involved. Company policies are to hire minority subcontractors regularly, but only when the quality of their work is assured and only when their bid is the lowest. There is no apparent effort to discourage minority involvement on the subcontractor level. The company feels that the most people are served best when the contractors are allowed to perform quality construction at the lowest price, as long as that contractor proceeds with a policy of hiring on the basis of the best work at the lowest price.

How do you evaluate the company's policies and practices?

What causes the company to feel there is a problem?

6. Copycat Products

Alex T. Hanford is the new products director of the Clean-All Products Company, a division of a large conglomerate in the household cleanser industry. In a speech at an American Marketing Association conference on new products, Mr. Hanford expounded on a theme called "Replicate, Don't Innovate." He said that trying to innovate as the only way to success is one of the greatest myths ever created. Instead, he suggested, be a copycat. His reasoning was that someone else has done your homework for you, and they have taken the risk, the time, and spent the dollars.

Clean-All Products had successfully imitated a copy of a competitor's rug and room deodorant. Hanford said that Clean-All management was at first skeptical about the competitor's product, which was test marketed in mid-1977 and introduced nationally a year later. According to Hanford, "we found it pretty hard to believe that Carpet Fresh had any potential at all." However, when his company monitored the competitor's test markets, it found that the idea was terrific. In December 1978, Clean-All began a crash project to duplicate the product. A copy was on the supermarket shelves within six months — far sooner than the two years or more it usually takes to develop a new product.

Advertising Age, a trade publication, reported Mr. Hanford's remarks. Many marketing executives privately criticized his approach as one that does little to promote economic growth; some were surprised that such a well-known firm as Clean-All would stoop to imitation. An *Advertising Age* editorial said: "Where would the replicators be without the innovators? They wouldn't even have material on which to base their speeches." Weeks after the *Advertising Age* story, the competitor brought suit in federal district court in New Jersey, charging Clean-All with patent infringement and asking for damages totaling triple the profits from Clean-All's copy. The suit quoted Hanford's remarks extensively.

Imitation is not unusual in consumer product marketing. A 1965 *Harvard Business Review* article entitled "Innovative Imitation" urged companies to search for products they would copy through "reverse R&D — working backwards from what others had done and trying to do the same thing for oneself." Imitations have occurred in computers, television sets, many food items, and in the razor blade industry. Even Clean-All's competitor says it sometimes follows other company's ideas. "When we see something successful, we try to put a unique twist on it," said the president of its Consumer Products Division. Its new room freshener, for example, is strikingly similar except for its package, shape, and scent to the Clorox Company's Twice as Fresh. Nevertheless, the competitor's executives were surprised by Clean-All's imitation because they came in with an exact copy. One executive said: "If they had gone us one better in technology, we would have said 'C'est la guerre'."

Sales of carpet deodorant amounted to about $60 million in 1979; with other firms jumping into the market, Clean-All's competitor had roughly about 60 percent of the market.

Some marketing executives in the industry commented on this case that the affair was mostly a case of indiscretion. One said, "If you can imitate and get away with it, you should hide what you are doing. You don't win anything by shooting your mouth off in the marketplace."

Were these incidents more than merely a public relations blunder?

How does the idea of fair competition apply?

Is product imitation ethical or unethical?

7. The Ugly Side of Business

"Talk to any reporter about Lester Brink and he will tell you that Les is one of the frankest corporate executives around. He'll meet with anybody and talk about anything."

The above statement was made by the vice-president of public relations of one of the nation's largest chemical firms, to one of the nation's well-known national business news reporters. Acting on these impressive words, the reporter asked to see Mr. Brink, to talk with him about Hans Klein.

Klein is a well-known figure to the prosecutors of Nazi war criminals at the Nuremberg trials. A brilliant scientist, he was the overall head of poison gas activity at Auschwitz. He was also a director of a nearby I. G. Farben plant in which inmates of the concentration camp, used as slave labor, were dying by the hundreds of exhaustion. For his participation in the Nazi war effort, Klein received a sentence of eight years. That sentence was later commuted to three years by John J. McCloy, who at the time was the U.S. High Commissioner of Germany.

Subsequently Brink made a strong personal pitch to bring Klein into the United States, expressing "deep admiration" for the convicted war criminal in a private letter to the U.S. ambassador to Germany. He made two visits to the United States in 1968 and 1969, but adverse publicity blocked later entries. Apparently trying to capitalize on Klein's scientific expertise in synthetic rubber and other chemicals, Brink hired him as a company consultant, stationed at his firm's Mannheim location.

The reporter intended to ask Brink this question: At what point, if ever, does corporate morality supersede the profit motive? However, he was unable to get an interview with Brink, who stated that he was unavailable for comment.

Lester Brink also refused to talk to television reporters about his ties to people or companies with former Nazi connections. The alleged ties included his firm's biggest stockholder, a West Germany industrial giant whose growth was greatly accelerated during the Hitler era by gobbling up Jewish-owned businesses through coercion.

Are there justifications for Mr. Brink's side of the case?

What questions of professional ethics are involved?

8. Language and the Government

The separatist election in Quebec in 1980 resulted in part over conflicts arising from two languages competing in one nation. A similar issue has emerged in the United States with the rapid influx of Cubans seeking refuge here, and the enormous number of illegal aliens from Mexico. There has been a trend in the United States away from foreign language instruction in public schools, despite the obvious benefits of bilingualism.

The Elementary and Secondary Education Act of 1965 was amended by a $7.5 million pilot program allowing Spanish-speaking students to be taught basic subjects in Spanish. As their English improved, the students were to switch into it, but they would not be handicapped so as to lag behind in their achievements.

The courts then entered the picture. In the 1974 case of *Lau* v. *Nichols*, the U.S. Supreme Court ruled that Chinese students were discriminated against in San Francisco by being taught in English. It ordered relief but did not specify what form the relief should take. The Office of Civil Rights of the Department of Health, Education and Welfare could have opted to increase special English instruction for the Chinese, or to impose a requirement that instruction would be in Chinese. It chose the latter option.

As a result, students now have the right to be taught in any one of 60-odd languages. Costs were predicted to reach $192 million by 1981, and by 1980 had already cost a total of $942 million since 1974. School districts that do not comply face a cutoff of federal funds. A bilingual, bicultural program is mandatory if there are 20 or more students of similar linguistic background in a district. This is by administrative ruling rather than a matter of specific law.

The bilingual system has been aggressively fought for by relevant defending groups, who see it as a cause, and as the source of thousands of teaching jobs. In one state, a teachers' lobby went to court to overturn a requirement that teachers in bilingual programs should be able to speak English, which the state educational association held was racist and inconvenient. But the court upheld the state's ruling.

What basic public policy issues are evident in this case?

In addition to costs, what other problems do you see?

What sociological and political factors are at work here?

What are the management problems of public school systems in this area?

9. Superior Construction Company, Inc.

The construction industry has one of the highest accident rates in the United States, and consequently it attracts a great deal of attention from the Occupational Safety and Health Administration (OSHA).

A manager in the Superior Construction Company related the following case:

> My employer, a person truly committed to his employees' welfare, one day decided to invite an OSHA inspector to visit a pair of construction sites so that the company might better acquaint itself with potentially dangerous practices. He also requested that surprise visits be made so that the job superintendent and workmen would not be expecting an inspection and true construction practice could be observed.
>
> The OSHA inspector refused to visit the sites since no complaint from workmen had been filed. Also, the inspector would not participate in any visit in which the job superintendent had no time to prepare for it. Considering OSHA's reputation, the refusal was probably best for the company, since my employer is apparently more concerned with safety than OSHA. Also, had OSHA made the inspection, all infractions would probably have to have been corrected or a penalty would have been assessed, and OSHA would not have made recommendations as to how to remedy the infractions.
>
> It would seem that attempts by OSHA to protect workmen would be more successful and the goals of OSHA better realized if the administration would attempt better cooperation with industry. Social responsibility of the government agency could be better realized through positive but nonbinding recommendations requested by industry. Such a cooperative and positive attitude would better allow the goals of OSHA and industry to be realized, and the greatest beneficiary would be society as a whole.

On the basis of this case, what problems of governmental social responsibility can you suggest?

10. Union Carbide Corporation

Stung by hostility toward the company and a "Bad-guy" image in the press, and plagued by class action lawsuits in the early 1970s, the Union Carbide Corporation decided to turn the situation around with a vigorously proactive strategy.

It established its own Environmental Impact Analysis program, a formal, quantified approach to avoid relying on subjective or vague information. Under the EIA program, each plant provides the environmental protection manager with details on every aspect of its products and processes. The corporate office then plots these data against various environmental areas (air, water, noise) and rates each operation from 0 (no impact) to 4 (major impact with immediate shutdown for correction). The resulting visual matrix pinpoints trouble spots. Any rating above 1.5 calls for the plant to come up with a corrective action plan.

The plan also called for ratings of public opinion on the company's environmental performance. A rating of 0 means that even if a pollution problem exists, neither the public nor environmentalists have expressed concern. A rating of 4 means that painful publicity may be imminent. A rating of 1.5 or higher calls for the same immediate action as an imminent health hazard.

The first EIA operations were done manually, but later the program switched to computerization. The computer bank contains detailed information on 600 processes and 450 products, along with environmental rules and research study results. The system resulted not only in the ability to meet environmental problems in their early stages, but also in three additional payoffs: (1) measures of materials balances are available, and can be balanced against output measures to pinpoint waste; (2) the data show where raw materials can be recovered from the wastes; and (3) engineers found they could use the data base as a source of information about manufacturing processes they were working on. The data were also used in planning new plants to make them as environmentally sound as possible.

Demands on personnel for supplying data were heavy, but objections to the work were offset by demonstrated cost savings and by an improvement in the corporate image.

Appraise the benefits and difficulties of the EIA approach.

How could one be sure that the ratings used are fair and accurate?

II. Haney Corporation

The Haney Corporation is a leading manufacturer of builders' supplies widely used by residential and commercial construction firms. It has eight plants located in strategic marketing areas of the United States, and employs over 11,000 workers.

In 1980 the company's board decided to join the increasing number of companies that take steps to help employees participate in grassroots politics. The objective of such concepts is to organize employees and shareholders into a concerted voice powerful enough to have more influence in getting Congress to listen to the views of business. The efforts were called the Civic Action Program.

In addition to launching a corporate political action committee, legal since 1975, the company organized a series of brown-bag luncheon sessions in each plant for the purpose of discussing political issues and various types of political action. Economic education programs had already been widely conducted, so this area was not included in the session agendas. In the sessions, a management representative gives the company's views on political issues and urges employees to study the issues further, in groups of twelve.

Employees who voluntarily sign up for the Civic Action Program regularly receive company mailings of political information and the company's position on legislative issues. Haney's program also sponsors regular political action courses designed to help individuals learn and apply political skills, and encourages financial contributions to the company PAC. A staff of six, with a budget of $800,000 annually, was established.

To get the training groups going, the executive in charge of the Civic Action Program visited all the plants and other installations and offices to recruit local committee chairs. These were selected from middle management in an effort to avoid the appearance of propagandizing the groups. He insisted that the group sessions emphasize the need to hear all sides of the issues discussed. Speakers with opposing views were often invited to the sessions.

After the Civic Action Program was launched, its director received 53 letters from employees and shareholders complaining that politicking is an improper use of corporate funds.

How do you evaluate Haney's approach to political action and influence?

What problems might result from the program?

How would you improve the program?

12. Illegal Aliens

Estimates of the numbers of illegal aliens in the United States range from 1 million to more than 8 million. Although there are few hard data, it appears that California has the most, followed by Texas. Chicago has attracted a large number of illegal aliens from Mexico for decades, and natives of Caribbean countries are flocking to Miami, New York, and Washington, D.C.

Asked about the burden of illegal aliens on his state's economy, California's Governor Jerry Brown replied that a number of industries there couldn't function without them. The garment industry, hotels and restaurants, agriculture, health care, and assembly operations in California rely heavily on the cheap, often exploited, labor of the "undocumented" worker, the euphemism used to identify the illegal alien. Many claim that these people will ease the shortage of unskilled labor in the future, that they will be the blue-collar workers of tomorrow. According to an official of the California Manufacturers Association, they are a positive force because they take jobs that go begging.

A case in point: Edgar, an undocumented worker from Nicaragua, paid what is known as a "coyote" $400 to take him across the Mexican border to California. He stayed with relatives in Los Angeles until he found work as a bundler in a garment shop. He was paid $60 a week in cash for 55 hours' work. He received no overtime or social security benefits.

In California, the head of an agency that enforces labor standards has investigated how unscrupulous businesses have prospered at the expense of people like Edgar. He has collected $4.5 million in back wages for undocumented workers and others since he began the enforcement drive in 1978. He found minimum wage and overtime violations in 79 percent of the 2100 garment shops and 63 percent of the 2500 restaurants he checked in Los Angeles County. Mexican undocumented workers fill the overwhelming majority of menial jobs in both industries.

Another study found that 82 percent of the 500 Hispanic garment workers were undocumented, as were more than 70 percent of 326 restaurant and hotel workers. The study also found that few of the nearly 1200 black and Hispanic unemployed whom they interviewed in Los Angeles said they would accept the kinds of minimum wage jobs held by undocumented workers. Although 60 percent said they were willing to do the work, hardly any would do it at the $3.10 minimum wage.

One expert saw in all this the institutionalizing of dual labor markets. An official of the Manufacturers' Association said that this is the only way many labor-intensive industries can stay in California: "Either they come up with something like the undocumented or they go somewhere else and find a cheap labor supply." Others claim that assuming that illegal aliens are the means to keep industry from fleeing may be a strategic mistake. Undocumented workers may be giving a small entrepreneur another ten years before he has to leave, but in the long run they could hurt business.

Businesspeople may become less enthusiastic about such employees if unions organize them in substantial numbers. Most unions still view illegal aliens as threats to American jobs, but the ILGWU has made a concerted effort to unionize the undocumented workers, with mixed results.

Some assert that undocumented workers rarely take advantage of welfare and other social services for fear of being caught and deported. For the same reason, they cannot get social security benefits. Thus they give more than they get. But it all depends on how one looks at the process. Some form of amnesty may be granted to the undocumented workers already in the country. Then they will not fear to apply for public services and the burden will increase.

What values are reflected in this case?

Appraise the ethical issues involved.

What actions could managers and government officials take in response to these problems?

13. Pollution Control

According to a midlevel manager in a manufacturing plant, we should not only examine the responsibility of business to society, but also recognize that society has a strong responsibility to business. The point is demonstrated by the pollution problem that the company had generated in its mill in Houston, Texas. This mill was a major polluter of the Houston Shipping Channel. Both the federal and the state governments insisted that this pollution be stopped. Both governments gave the company a specific date by which the pollution must cease. The company had just completed an antipollution system in a mill in another part of the country that handled the same type of pollution problem as that in Houston. In this system, the company would pump toxic acid pollutants into a well approximately 4000 feet deep, containing them below ground until they disintegrated into harmless materials. The actual system analysis indicated that they would be retained below ground forever. But if they were able to find a way back to the surface, the time it would take as well as the contact with the earth's minerals would reduce the pollutants to harmless materials.

The company proposed this system to both the federal and state governments as a solution for the Houston problem. The federal government accepted this method of disposal. The state government, pressured by local and environmental groups, rejected it. The state insisted that acid waste be treated and rendered harmless in conventional above-ground treatment facilities. So the company began to design a more conventional type of chemical treatment plant for its Houston works. It submitted this proposal to the state government, and the state found it acceptable. The federal government refused to accept this type of waste treatment. It believed the deep well pump storage system was a much better solution and insisted that the company use it. The company also preferred the deep well method because it did not cost as much.

But, in any case, the two governments could not agree, each refusing to allow the company to move in either direction. Meantime, the deadline for cleaning up the pollution expired. One would think that because the company was trying very hard to comply with society's requirements, the date of compliance would have been extended, at least until the two governments could agree. The date was not extended, and a $5000 per day fine was levied against the mill. The fine continued to be levied even though the company was eager to cooperate and the delay was caused by failure of the federal and state governments to reach a joint solution. The company had to take the case to court to force the two governing agencies to work together. Finally, a pollution treatment facility was agreed upon. It was installed and has been functioning for some years. However, the $5000 per day fine was collected.

Was there an injustice in this case?

How can such problems as these be avoided?

14. Systogenic Corporation

The Systogenic Corporation manufactures and markets nationally a product called Disappear for use in cleaning plumbing fixtures. The product is in the form of a cannister that releases minute amounts of a chemical into the water when it is flushed from the tank.

In late 1980, the Systogenic Corporation decided to launch a multi-million-dollar advertising campaign specifically directed against its major competitors. The company charged that competitors' products did more than clean—they contained calcium hypochlorite as the main cleaning agent, and could destroy plastic, rubber, and even the metal parts if fixtures were not used regularly so that the water containing the chemical stands for a period of time.

Several parts and fixture manufacturers changed their warranties so that they do not apply if hypochlorite cleaners are used. They alleged that cleaner-damaged parts could cause flooding and create liability for damages.

The Systogenic Corporation claimed that the advertising campaign was needed so that its product could be distinguished from hypochlorite cleaners. Spending on the program was planned for a total of $1 million to $5 million. Competing firms denied that their products would harm plumbing and threatened court action to halt the advertising compaign. The competitors alleged that the Systogenic Corporation was running scared due to loss of sales. They also launched laboratory tests of their products. Systogenic had had a 30 percent reduction in sales in the previous year.

What are the ethical and moral issues of Systogenic's planned advertising compaign?

Is Systogenics being socially responsible by raising issues about the use of hypochlorite cleaners?

15. Problems of the Board of Directors

The Allstar Computer Company, a $100 million-a-year computer manufacturer, experienced a major upheaval as a result of action by independent (outside) directors. In October of 1980, the Board ousted Nelson P. Grimm as chairman, president, and chief executive officer. Grimm, a 44 year old executive, was the company's founder and largest stockholder, and the only CEO the 15 year old company had ever had. Until the ouster, the independent members of the board had rarely opposed him.

The boardroom battle began when Grimm announced in a meeting of San Diego businessmen that Allstar would move its headquarters from Sacramento to San Diego's most elegant district. The announcement upset the four outside directors who constituted a majority of the board. L. T. Harwood, the leader in the ouster move, differed with Grimm on the facts of the case. He stated that the company had just spent $2 million renovating its Sacramento headquarters, and questioned Grimm's sudden and unexpected decision. Grimm replied that the move had been under discussion for some time prior to his announcement, and that the board had supported the idea.

Harwood said that Grimm had not only refused to give the board the cost estimates for the move, but had also suggested that the company acquire a $3.5 million ranch near the new site, for his own residence. This the board refused to do, and it vetoed the proposed move by a four to two vote. Grimm accused the outside directors of lacking vision, and said there was no vote against the move until after he was fired.

Grimm told Harwood he was no longer wanted as a director of Allstar. Grimm and Harwood differ on their response, each contending that the other had suggested a consulting position as an alternative. Later Harwood wrote Grimm offering to resign as director for a consulting fee of $100,000, which Grimm refused to pay.

Harwood then took an active role in a director's probe of Allstar's administrative affairs, uncovering what he called excessive staffing. Grimm cancelled a plan to fly all directors to Hawaii for a week-long meeting. The probes allegedly found that Grimm used company funds without board approval for private plane trips and leasing a $30,000 Mercedes for himself instead of the authorized Lincoln.

When the board later repeated its opposition to the move, it discovered that Grimm had already signed a $35,000 contract for design work on the new headquarters. Grimm said that this work was required to get the cost estimates the board had said it wanted.

At the time Grimm's ouster was being discussed, Allstar's earnings for the first nine months of that fiscal year fell by 54 percent on a 26 percent increase in revenues. The company fell from fourth place in the market to seventh.

The board brought in a general management consultant to replace Grimm, appointing him president and CEO. At the same time Harwood was elected Chairman of the Board, pending the election of a new slate of directors. Grimm remained a member of the board of directors. Meanwhile Grimm organized a $35 million shareholders suit against the outside directors, charging them with breach of fiduciary duties, internal mismanagement, and conspiracy to defraud. The board filed a countersuit against Grimm seeking $375,000 damages for misuse of corporate funds.

How would proposed board reforms affect the events depicted in this case?

Analyze the ethical questions involved.

As an inside director, what would be your actions and opinions?

16. Slush Fund Controversies

In the mid-1970s a number of leading firms were found to have broken the law by contributing corporate funds to Richard Nixon's political campaign. These included the Gulf Oil Corporation, Goodyear Tire and Rubber Company, American Airlines, Inc., and Minnesota Mining and Manufacturing Company. In the Northrop Corporation, Ashland Oil, Inc., and Phillips Petroleum Company, top executives were found guilty, or admitted they were guilty, of the unlawful use of company money by establishing slush funds for political purposes.

Boards of directors have frequently supported the guilty executives, few of whom received jail sentences. Many of the executives were allowed to keep their positions, including those at Northrop, Ashland, and Phillips. Self-serving justifications by boards and by executives were numerous; criticism within the business community was virtually nonexistent.

Prosecutors, in order to uncover the slush funds, announced that they would charge the "primarily responsible official" with a misdemeanor rather than a felony. As first offenders, judges tended to assess light penalties, such as modest fines.

The known offenders were involved in complex schemes for kickbacks and laundering funds through Swiss banks, cooperating subordinates, subsidiaries, or consultants. Coverups and lying, including backdated promissory notes, accompanied the wrongful acts. The offending executives argued that "the laws weren't being enforced" at the time of their acts, or that they were merely continuing what former executives had begun.

In the Gulf Oil case, tough action was taken against the chairman of the board and three other top executives. The Mellon family interests on the board demanded their resignation, refusing to bargain or pardon the executives throughout a grueling two-day board meeting. Various proposals were advanced by the ousted officials' lawyers and supporters on the board which would have allowed them to remain corporate officers.

In reaching its decision, the Gulf Oil Corporation's directors set up an independent fact-finding committee headed by an outside lawyer. The report suggested that the board chairman had "perhaps closed his eyes to what was going on." The committee's report commended the corporation for its part in a "classic ethics case" which would "set a new standard of corporate social responsibility."

Following these problems, Gulf Oil and a number of other companies began requiring signed letters from officials stating that they had complied with corporate policies against illegal political contributions.

What factors seem to determine what a corporation might do when its key officers are found guilty of breaking the law?

How can incidents of this type be prevented?

17. Whistle Blowing

Following the Watergate scandals and the discovery of high-level wrong-doing by some executives of large corporations, there was an increase in the number of "whistle blowers"—individuals willing to reveal fraudulent, harmful, or wasteful activities on the part of their employers.

The risks of whistle blowing are high. In many such cases, the individuals experienced highly unfavorable consequences. One, for example, was forced to give up a promising insurance career; another's marriage broke up over the strain; a third was the target of death threats.

A teacher of ethics courses stated that loyalty is valued more than conscience. The team spirit mentality prevails. A company president said that "management tends to look askance at whistle blowing, and the culture has negative attitudes toward informers." Another executive condoned informing "about criminal acts," but not against unsubstantiated allegations.

Little legal protection exists for whistle blowers, and they generally get little support from colleagues. Reprisals appear to be frequent. Some resign in protest, but in so doing they risk blacklisting by their industry or career group. A midlevel executive who exposed $2 billion worth of bogus policies in the Equity Funding Insurance scandal resigned and then blew the whistle, but was criticized for not reporting the frauds sooner. He had known of the fraudulent policies for two years. He countered that he was trying to protect his family by lining up another job first, and also that he was afraid of reprisals. In the same case another resigning manager stated that an equity funding officer threatened him with a Mafia contract on his life.

If you were going to blow the whistle on some illegal behavior in your company, how would you do it?

How can the problem of reprisals be dealt with?

Can whistle blowing be useful in cases where the behavior in question is legal but doubtful on ethical grounds?

18. Monsanto Company

The following stockholder resolution was submitted to the annual meeting of the board of directors of Monsanto on April 25, 1980:

Resolution
"WHEREAS the continued production of nuclear weapons increases both the likelihood of a global nuclear confrontation and a resultant increased threat to the communities in which manufacturing facilities are located;

"WHEREAS the Monsanto Company manages for the Department of Energy the Mound facility at Miamisburg, Ohio;

"WHEREAS the Mount Facility produces detonators for nuclear weapons and radioactive heat sources for powering space missions;

"WHEREAS in recent years, a serious national movement of concern about and opposition to nuclear weapons facilities has developed; and

"WHEREAS increasing attention is being paid to nuclear disarmament and our Company has made disclosure in its 1979 First-Quarter and Annual Meeting Report of the extent of its involvement in nuclear weapons production;

"THEREFORE BE IT RESOLVED that the shareholders request the Board of Directors to appoint a special committee to evaluate the Company's operations at the Mound Facility.

The committee would:

1. give special emphasis to the moral, social and economic implications of continued nuclear weapons production especially as it relates to a shift in U.S. military strategy and the health and safety of the workforce and surrounding community;
2. hold at least one open session during which input from concerned shareholders, church leaders, labor and disarmament experts would be solicited;
3. report its recommendations to the Board of Directors within six months of the 1980 annual meeting; and
4. provide all shareholders with a copy of its report."

The statement submitted by these several stockholders in support of their above proposal is as follows:

"The threat of nuclear war is too grave, the problem is too large and the responsibility is too widespread for anyone, including the Company that operates the facilities, to avoid facing the issue at this moment.

"The social cost and moral ambiguity of operating nuclear facilities has become clearer in the last year. The Mound facility has been the object of significant public interest. We believe that Monsanto's management owes us a serious assessment of its work and the advisability of renewing our DOE contracts. We also believe that it is in the best interests of the 1700 workers and shareholders alike.

"Now that a national debate over nuclear energy is in progress, the time seems right for a full assessment of Monsanto's role in the nuclear economy. An open session during which testimony is presented by the community at large and those most concerned about escalating arms production is crucial to such a process. This is the time for management and shareholders alike to declare their concern about Mound's part in nuclear weapons and radioactive heat source production, not after hundreds of workers have been laid off or a major nuclear accident/incident has occurred."

The Board of Directors recommends a vote AGAINST the above proposal.

As summarized in the company's 1979 first-quarter and annual meeting reports, Monsanto's operation of the government's Mound facility, under contract with the U.S. Department of Energy, is consistent with its proper role as a responsible corporate citizen. The primary purpose of the Mound facility operations is to produce and evaluate non-nuclear conponents for nuclear defense weapons. Management continues to believe that it is appropriate for responsible companies such as Monsanto to participate in efforts to ensure this country's defensive capabilities. Recent world developments underscore the significance of this effort. Another thrust of the Mound operations is in energy-related work. Again, this effort is clearly related to our national interests, especially in light of the worldwide energy crisis. Further, while pursuing these valid and vitally important objectives, the company continuously monitors operations at Mound to protect the health and safety of both its employees and the local community.

Accordingly, the company is of the opinion that it is not necessary for the board of directors to appoint a special committee to evaluate its operations at the Mound facility. These activities have been and will continue to be conducted in a responsible fashion, with appropriate attention being given to the various attendant implications. Monsanto continues to believe that its operation of the Mound facility serves the interests of the company, its stockholders, and the country.

The affirmative vote of a majority of the combined votes of the common and preferred stock of the company that are cast at the annual meeting on this stockholder proposal is required for approval.

How do you evaluate the significance of stockholder resolutions?

Is the company procedure a desirable one? Why or why not?

19. Issues of Nuclear Power

The power shortages that developed in the 1970s have aroused extreme controversy which contains both political and technical elements. The chief executive officer of one of the nation's largest manufacturing firms has stated: "The vote in Maine to keep a controversial nuclear installation is a hopeful sign for a more intelligent response to energy problems." His company's technical experts believe that nuclear power is necessary for energy independence, but that the "no nukes" campaign has caused a serious lag in development. In arguing for nuclear power, the chief executive stated: "There's not been a single fatality at any nuclear plant. No other energy source can say this. While most people have a fear of the invisible, it is technically impossible to blow up a nuclear installation, so such fears are unfounded. Also unfounded are fears of radioactive leaks. There hasn't been a significant leak, and nuclear plants have achieved increasing reliability."

When challenged on his position, the chief executive acknowledged that waste disposal is a problem for nuclear plants, but stated that "the Germans have found it practical to deposit nuclear wastes in deep salt caverns which will keep them stable for eons, and that we have similar caverns in the U.S. Waste disposal is more of a political problem than a technical one, so the government becomes deeply involved in the controversies."

How do you evaluate the arguments of the chief executive?

What machinery does the federal government use in controlling nuclear power development and hazardous waste?

If you were debating the chief executive officer, what arguments would you use to refute him?

20. The Manager's Leadership Style

In 1963 Eddie Rickenbacker was forced out of Eastern Airlines after 23 years as its chief executive. Serling reports in *From the Captain to the Colonel* (Dial Press 1980) that Rickenbacker relied on an authoritarian management style. At a typical management meeting, events such as the following would occur:

1. One by one each member of the audience — 250 city sales managers and 250 airport operations managers — mounts the dais and reads a report on his performance during the previous six months: how many tickets sold, how many phone calls answered, how many reservations made, how many passengers enplaned, how many meals and bags handled, and all at what cost. If the performance does not live up to the forecast made six months earlier, an explanation is demanded — and it had better be good.

2. Rickenbacker is playing with a loaded deck. He has had an advance copy of each man's report to study for weeks. Consequently, he interrupts continually with a barrage of questions. One man argues back. Although events later prove the man right, no one tells the captain he is wrong anymore. The man is off the payroll the next morning. At the meeting another man nervously pleads for money to help him reach more prospective customers. The brutal public humiliation continues.

3. "Son," inquires Rickenbacker, "do you know how much profit we make on every passenger in your city?"

    "No, but I guess it isn't very much."

    "Well, you damn well ought to know we lose money on every one of your passengers. The fact that you want Eastern to pour money we don't have into your operation so it can lose still more money tells me you're not very good at your job."

    Crestfallen and beet red, the man resumes reading his report.

What are the ethical implications of this leadership style?

21. The Synfuels Project

In the fall of 1980, the federal government created the U.S. Synthetic Fuels Corporation, headed on an interim appointment by Deputy Energy Secretary John C. Sawhill. In the following decade this corporation was to supervise the granting of approximately $88 billion in seed money to help develop alternative energy sources to reduce dependence on foreign oil, and boost the economy. The idea is to reduce the risk of synfuel ventures, enticing private industry to do the work. The corporation makes direct loans, loan guarantees, and guarantees prices for some new fuels, and envisions contracts to buy fixed amounts of other fuels. The new corporation can also fund as many as three projects to be government owned.

Six board members, none from the oil industry, were appointed. Sawhill's appointment was well received by politicians and industry officials. Sawhill lobbied for the job, although others were considered.

Sawhill faced many difficulties, including getting the Senate's confirmation, problems of staffing, environmental issues, and the admittedly fuzzy economics of energy. Doubts about the future of the Synfuels Corporation and its chairman arose after the election of Ronald Reagan as president. Following the election, a large number of energy experts left Washington for lucrative posts in the private sector with firms standing to benefit from synfuels projects.

In December 1980 the Department of Energy allocated $270 million for 79 synfuels projects. It had earlier allocated $200 million in grants. The projects are for synthetic fuel feasibility studies, design work, and research. The monies were appropriated by Congress for the 1980–81 fiscal year. Monies from the windfall profits tax on oil firms was expected to be allocated to synfuels projects.

How has the Synfuels Corporation been performing since these events occurred?

Discuss the problems associated with evaluating the corporation's performance.

What public policy issues are raised by this case?

INCIDENT CASES

1. A student in the job market indicated that he saw nothing wrong with accepting travel expense reimbursements for three different company interviews which he made all in one trip. The companies that paid his travel expenses knew that the other companies were also paying, and encouraged the student to accept this largess freely.

What are the ethics apparent in this case?

2. A young executive who had been moving rapidly up the financial ladder in a large bank organization unequivocally stated in a private conversation: "It is impossible to conduct business in the United States today without breaking the law."

Comment on this statement.

3. According to the president of a large metropolitan bank, "Our bank lending officers must learn the moral criteria for the decisions they are going to make. We lend money only for what we think are moral purposes, good purposes. Those judgments aren't easy to make, but we require it."

Analyze the implications of the above statement.

4. Ray Boswell sought the advice of a successful manager about the following problem:

My company is in an industry characterized by cutthroat competition. It uses certain practices for getting business which I consider unethical, but if I don't do things that way I'll be out. What can I do to cope with this?"

What would you reply if you were the one Mr. Boswell consulted?

5. In 1980 Quaker Oats introduced a learning program for young children on its Life cereal boxes. The back and side panels of 12 million packages will be used to print a series of six lessons designed to increase the learning power of children. The company also has pressed for high-quality programming on television. In addition, a few years ago, when confronted with a decision on where to place a new plant, Quaker settled on Danville, Illinois, but refused to give the final okay on the site until the city passed a fair housing ordinance.

Comment on the extent and nature of the company's social responsibility as evidenced in this case.

6. Standard Oil of Indiana used its muscle to accomplish what the federal government could not — integration in the ranks of the Chicago construction trades. In putting up its new skyscraper headquarters building on the city's lakefront, Indiana Standard insisted that minority employment goals be used in the selection of the construction workforce. This resulted in construction crews with a minority representation of about one-third.

What problems and benefits are likely for the company?

8. Senator William Proxmire monthly makes Golden Fleece Awards, in recognition of ridiculous waste of taxpayer monies. One of these was bestowed upon an Office of Education Grant of $219,592 to develop a "curriculum package" intended to teach college students how to watch television, and to understand the differences between soap operas and situation comedies. This grant was included as part of an $823,000 grant to a major eastern university's School of Public Communication for developing critical television viewing skills.

Evaluate the important dimensions of this problem.

9. The newly appointed executive vice-president and chief financial officer of a leading cereal and milling corporation stated that his chief worry was inflation. Known to be critical of his other businesspeople, he stated: "One of the distressing things is that a lot of businessmen are in favor of a tax cut. Business is the one sector that ought to rise up and say we have serious inflation and ought to combat it. We should forego a tax cut now for the long-term health of the economy. Federal spending won't be cut, so a tax cut can only increase the deficit. A budget deficit is like monetary policy; issuing Treasury Bonds is the same as printing money. So we would be coming out of the recession heading for more inflation."

What implications can you draw from this case that illuminate the problems of capitalism?

Acronyms

EXECUTIVE AGENCIES

ACUS–Administrative Conference of the United States

USDA–United States Department of Agriculture
AMS–Agriculture Marketing Service
FmHA–Farmers Home Administration
FSQS–Food Safety and Quality Service
SCS–Soil Conservation Service

DOC–Department of Commerce
EDA–Economic Development Administration
MARAD–Maritime Administration
NOAA–National Oceanic and Atmospheric Administration
NTIA–National Telecommunications and Information Administration

DOE–Department of Energy
ERA–Economic Regulatory Administration

HHS–Department of Health and Human Services
FDA–Food and Drug Administration
HCFA–Health Care Financing Administration
NIMH–National Institute of Mental Health
OSMA–Office of Small Manufacturers Assistance
PHS–Public Health Service
SSA–Social Security Administration

HUD–Department of Housing and Urban Development
FHA–Federal Housing Administration

DOI–Department of the Interior
BLM–Bureau of Land Management
HCRS–Heritage Conservation and Recreation Service
OSM–Office of Surface Mining Reclamation and Enforcement

DOJ–Department of Justice
INS–Immigration and Naturalization Service
LEAA–Law Enforcement Assistance Administration

DOI–Department of the Interior
BLM–Bureau of Land Management
HCRS–Heritage Conservation and Recreation Service
OSM–Office of Surface Mining Reclamation and Enforcement

DOL–Department of Labor
ESA–Employment Standards Administration
ETA–Employment and Training Administration
LMSA–Labor Management Service Administration
MSHA–Mine Safety and Health Administration
OFCCP–Office of Federal Contract Compliance Programs
OSHA–Occupational Safety and Health Administration

DOT–Department of Transportation
FAA–Federal Aviation Administration
FHWA–Federal Highway Administration
FRA–Federal Railroad Administration
NHTSA–National Highway Traffic Safety Administration

459

USCG—*United States Coast Guard*
UMTA—*Urban Mass Transportation
Administration*

TREAS—*Department of the Treasury*
ATF—*Bureau of Alcohol, Tobacco, and
Firearms*
IRS—*Internal Revenue Service*
OCC—*Office of the Comptroller of the
Currency*

EPA—*Environmental Protection
Agency*

EEOC—*Equal Employment
Opportunity Commission*

GSA—*General Services Administration*
NARS—*National Archives and Records
Service*

NCUA—*National Credit Union
Administration*
SBA—*Small Business Administration*
USITC—*United States International
Trade Commission*
VA—*Veterans Administration*

INDEPENDENT REGULATORY AGENCIES

CAB—*Civil Aeronautics Board*
CFTC—*Commodity Futures Trading
Commission*
CPSC—*Consumer Product Safety
Commission*

FCC—*Federal Communications
Commission*
FDIC—*Federal Deposit Insurance
Corporation*
FEC—*Federal Election Commission*
FERC—*Federal Energy Regulatory
Commission*
FHLBB—*Federal Home Loan Bank
Board*
FMC—*Federal Maritime Commission*
FMSHRC—*Federal Mine Safety and
Health Review Commission*
FRS—*Federal Reserve System*
FTC—*Federal Trade Commission*
ICC—*Interstate Commerce
Commission*
NLRB—*National Labor Relations Board*
NRC—*Nuclear Regulatory Commission*
OSHRC—*Occupational Safety and
Health Review Commission*
PRC—*Postal Rate Commission*
SEC—*Securities and Exchange
Commission*

FORMAL COORDINATION BODIES

FFIEC—*Federal Financial Institutions
Examination Council*
IRLG—*Interagency Regulatory Liaison
Group*
RPC—*Radiation Policy Council*
USRC—*United States Regulatory
Council*

SOURCE: U.S. Regulatory Council, *Regulatory Reform Highlights: An Inventory of Initiatives,
1978–1980* (Washington, D.C., April 1980).

Name Index

Subject Index

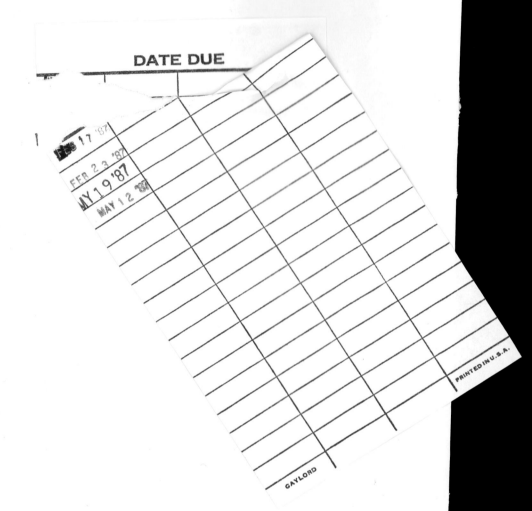